Practitioner's Guide to Assessing Intelligence and Achievement

Edited by

Jack A. Naglieri
Sam Goldstein

JOHN WILEY & SONS, INC

Library of Congress Cataloging-in-Publication Data:

Practitioner's guide to assessing intelligence and achievement / edited by Jack A. Naglieri, Sam Goldstein.
    p. cm.
  Includes index.
  ISBN 978-0-470-13538-9 (cloth)
  1. Intelligence tests. 2. Achievement tests. I. Naglieri, Jack A. II. Goldstein, Sam, 1952-

BF431.P675 2009
  153.9'3–dc22

                          2008052154

For Andrea, Antonia, and Jack Jr.

JN

For Allyson, Ryan, and Janet.

SG

We dedicate this book to the extraordinary leadership of Alan and Nadeen Kaufman, whose vision for change stimulated the development of the many new tests included in this book and resulted in a significant evolutionary step in the field of assessment. Thanks for your vision of change.

CONTENTS

The field of assessment psychology (see Graham & Naglieri, 2003) has changed dramatically since the late 1970s, when we began our careers as psychologists. At that time, there were two well-established options to measure intelligence, the Wechsler (WISC-R) and Binet LM, and a newcomer, the McCarthy Scales of Children's Abilities. The dominant achievement test was the Wide Range Achievement Test. Matarazzo and Wechsler's measurement and appraisal of adult intelligence and Sattler's assessment texts were the main books available. Evolution in the field began with the extraordinary insight of Alan and Nadeen Kaufman and the publication of the Kaufman Assessment Battery for Children (K-ABC). Suddenly, it became apparent that there was great room for improvement in the IQ and achievement tests that we were using to make important decisions about children and adults.

The mid-1980s through the 1990s was a time of change in the field of assessment. Intelligence tests were revised and modified. For example, the Wechsler went from a two-, to three-, to four-dimensional instrument. Theory became increasingly important and efforts were made to apply theory to existing tests. Achievement tests were developed that provided greater coverage of content. IQ tests were challenged by measures of basic psychological processes such as the K-ABC and the Cognitive Assessment System (CAS).

The past 20 years have seen substantial improvements in the quality of psychological and educational tests. Standardization samples that previously had been modest approximations of the U.S. population were now developed with the utmost care and accuracy. Today, estimates of the U.S. population can be made with a level of precision that was not achieved in the 1980s. Not only have we been able to improve the quality of standardization samples, but we have greatly improved the psychometric quality of these tests and developed new approaches to assessment.

The assessment of IQ has expanded to include measures that approach intelligence from a theory-driven perspective. For example, tests that reflect the author's intention to change from the verbal/nonverbal test content perspective to an organization based on underlying cognitive processes (e.g., K-ABC and CAS) have dramatically expanded the variety of instruments in this area. Additionally, we now have nonverbal measures of general ability specifically designed to better assess culturally and linguistically diverse populations, such as the CTONI, UNIT, and WNV. Similarly, we have more achievement test options, including those that are designed to measure a wide variety of academic skills (e.g., WIAT-II) and those that are more specific (e.g., CTOPP and DIBELS).

As the number of test options in the field has increased, so, too, has the complexity of assessing the utility of these tests, especially for those entering the field. The number of questions about these instruments is wide ranging, with potentially significant consequences. How can a psychologist or educator make informed decisions about which ones meet varying needs in the field? Can we assume that all tests have excellent psychometric qualities? What evidence is there that these various measures are effective for the purposes for which they were developed and used? These and many other questions formed the impetus for this book.

The goal of this book is to provide readers with a single source from which to examine ability and achievement tests along the same general criteria. Chapters are presented in alphabetical order by test name in three groups: (1) intelligence tests with diverse test content, (2) nonverbal intelligence tests, and (3) achievement tests.

Each chapter was written from the same outline, typically, by the test's author(s). The chapters provide the authors an opportunity to illustrate the qualities of their test and the extent to which their particular approach to test development and their test's characteristics meet the demands practitioners face today and will likely face in the future. We hope this book will allow readers to make informed decisions about the best use of each of these tests.

ACKNOWLEDGMENTS

Thanks to Kathleen Gardner for her editorial assistance and to Isabel Pratt and Lisa Gebo of Wiley for sharing our vision for this volume.

J.A.N. & S.G.

FOREWORD

The clinical assessment of intelligence and achievement is at a crossroads for two reasons. First, there is a marked change in the types of ability and achievement tests that have been published in the past 10 years. Traditional intelligence tests are being challenged by theory-based measures of cognitive processing, and achievement tests that have explicit implications for instruction are being stressed. Second, within the educational arena, the passage of the Individuals with Disabilities Educational Improvement Act (IDEA 2004) in the United States has led many states to determine how to best implement the ambiguous legal guidelines for identifying children with specific learning disabilities (SLD), sometimes passing that decision on to the local districts. Given IDEA, there is considerable controversy about how assessment should change, but it seems clear that the outcomes of these decisions will greatly determine how standardized instruments may be used for SLD diagnosis. To some, standardized assessment of cognitive ability and academic skills is an essential component of a comprehensive assessment; for others, the response-to-intervention method alone is sufficient.

To some professionals in education, standardized assessment of cognitive ability and academic skills served the primary purpose of entering numbers into a discrepancy formula to diagnose SLD. Now that IDEA 2004 no longer mandates identifying an ability–achievement discrepancy to diagnose SLD, some of these professionals are content to rely only on response-to-intervention (RTI) to identify children with SLD. They are happy to kick standardized tests, especially measures of mental processing and cognitive abilities, out the door, without ceremony or fanfare. They would like to see a quick cremation of the diverse instruments that have been developed to measure intelligence, by any definition; and while the door is open, why not get rid of standardized achievement tests as well, because (they argue), what more does anyone need to know about a child's achievement that hasn't already been learned during the RTI phase of the evaluation?

Jack Naglieri and Sam Goldstein's *A Practitioner's Guide to Assessment of Intelligence and Achievement* is not targeted for those professionals whose minds are closed to the benefits of standardized tests and who are caught up in the "RTI-only" mantra. Most of the chapters in this book, with all their riches and insights, will do them little good. But *A Practitioner's Guide* is a goldmine for professionals who want to understand the individual child or adolescent referred for evaluation and who realize that each student's unique pattern of strengths and weaknesses provides a dynamic resource for identifying disorders of basic psychological processes and for informing and personalizing interventions. And even the RTI-only people will enjoy Chapter 14, on phonological processing; Chapter 15, on the DIBELS; error analysis on the KTEA-II (Chapter 17); the use of the relative proficiency index (RPI) on the WJ-III Achievement Scale to create appropriate instructional recommendations (Chapter 19); and the systematic treatment of progress monitoring and evaluation of interventions on the BASI (Chapter 13), the Gray Oral (Chapter 16), and the WRAT4 (Chapter 20).

Naglieri and Goldstein are both superstars in the field of assessment who each possess enormous expertise in test development, test research, and clinical practice. My ties to my close friend and colleague, Jack Naglieri, stretch back more than 30 years, to a time when he was my brilliant doctoral student and leader of the graduate-student team that helped Nadeen and me develop the original K-ABC. He subsequently moved the field of assessment forward in a dramatic way when he collaborated with J. P. Das to develop the Luria-inspired PASS theory and the innovative Cognitive Assessment System (CAS). His considerable inspiration and perspiration, sprinkled with an abundance of creativity, reflect a direct translation of the principles that, as a mentor, I have always tried to instill in my graduate students: (1) Scientifically supported practice needs to be rooted in good science; (2) intelligence tests should be based on sound theory, without constraints from the past; (3) new approaches must embrace new technologies while maintaining a healthy respect for the contributions of old technologies; and (4) cognitive and academic assessment, to be truly meaningful, must translate directly to interventions and be fair to ethnic minorities. Sam Goldstein's considerable contributions via research, writing, test development, and international speaking engagements also reflect these principles, as does *A Practitioner's Guide to Assessment of Intelligence and Achievement*.

In the introductory chapter of this book, Naglieri and Goldstein confront the relevance of theory to practice by posing two questions: "But readers may wonder what relevance the underlying conceptualization of a test has? How important is a theory for application in the real world?" These questions are answered briefly in Chapter 1 and extensively in Chapters 3 through 8, which deal with the major cognitive and processing batteries (except for the DAS-II). These chapters are typically coauthored by at least one of the test authors, and they all emphasize the role that theory plays in providing a scientific foundation for the test and in promoting sound theory-based interpretation and application of the profile of scores.

In addition to top-notch coverage of virtually all major comprehensive measures of processes and abilities, *A Practitioner's Guide* has many other special features that make it stand out:

- It includes thorough coverage of the major *nonverbal* measures of cognitive abilities and processing, a topic that frequently does not receive complete coverage despite the key roles played by nonverbal tests for the fair assessment of ELL students, those with hearing impairments, and those who otherwise cannot be tested validly on verbal measures (Chapters 9 through 12, plus the KABC-II Nonverbal Scale in Chapter 4).

- It has the most thorough coverage of the crucial area of achievement assessment that exists anywhere. The achievement test—often the kid brother of the cognitive test that receives little respect or breadth of coverage—is elevated to the forefront of *A Practitioner's Guide*. Eight important tests are covered in Chapters 13 through 20, and they are treated in a way that enables readers to understand the integral role that they play for truly understanding the intricacies of a child's pattern of strengths and weaknesses and the key linkup between processing deficit and specific academic failure. As mentioned earlier, achievement tests that hold great promise for implementing progress monitoring and evaluating scientifically based intervention strategies are covered with the same depth as the more traditional approaches to standardized assessment of academic achievement.

- Chapter 2 deals directly with the IDEA 2004 guidelines, and offers systematic, scientific methods for diagnosing children with SLD that are far more sensible and practical than the crude ability–achievement formula that has dominated the SLD assessment scene since the passage of the Education of All Handicapped Children Act of 1975.

- The chapters are practitioner focused, straightforward, explicit in their instruction to the student, and relevant to new IDEA 2004 requirements, and include pertinent diagrams and figures as well as "tips to remember." At the same time, each chapter allows for enough instruction to allow students to learn how to use the test, usually from the direct perspective of a test author. Moreover, because the chapters were faithful to the specific topical outline proposed by Naglieri and Goldstein, the chapters contain similar content and organization, facilitating comparisons across tests.

- The topics covered are timely (e.g., IDEA 2004 issues), the chapters are quite readable, and, overall, the book is structured to deal with issues that are most relevant to practitioners, while deemphasizing complex statistical issues.

These features make Naglieri and Goldstein's *A Practitioner's Guide to Assessment of Intelligence and Achievement* an ideal text for the basic course in intelligence testing that is invariably included in the curriculum of graduate training programs for school psychologists, neuropsychologists, and clinical psychologists, especially those courses that include achievement testing alongside cognitive assessment. The book is also well suited to serve as the main source of instruction for graduate (or advanced undergraduate) students' first course in assessment. These students need to learn the basics of the tests and how to use them. Naglieri and Goldstein's book does just that, and it does it well. Finally, this volume will serve as a valuable desk reference for new and experienced clinicians.

ALAN S. KAUFMAN
Clinical Professor of Psychology
Yale Child Study Center
Yale University School of Medicine
New Haven, CT
December 1, 2008

Introduction

Understanding the Strengths and Weaknesses of Intelligence and Achievement Tests

Jack Naglieri, Sam Goldstein

It is essential that any study and measurement of human intelligence and academic achievement recognize the importance of the brain. The human brain is an amazing organ—a product of an ongoing, six-billion-year construction project. In its physical form and function, the human brain represents millions upon millions of trial-and-error adaptive adjustments. Comprised of an estimated 100 billion neurons and many more glial cells, it is organized into thousands of regions. The human brain, in a seamlessly integrated manner, governs body functions and movement, but more important, it is the seat of intelligence and regulates cognition and achievement. Not surprisingly, although the brains of different animals may not look exactly alike, they all work according to the same principles and mechanisms. These neurons and glial cells communicate using a nearly infinite number of synaptic connections, yet the entire organ in humans weighs only about three pounds. Consider also that an infant is born with a brain of 300 to 400 cm, tripling in size by the adult years. Yet, between birth and the conclusion of the first two decades of life, a nearly infinite acquisition of knowledge and behaviors characterizes human development. Gram for gram, the human brain delivers an almost-dazzling array of motoric, behavioral, cognitive, and emotional capacities nearly impossible to fathom in light of its size.

In her extremely cogent and interesting book, *Brain Dance* (2004), Dean Falk, a professor of anthropology at Florida State University, describes the conditions and circumstances that allowed a group of ape-like individuals to evolve over a period of at least five million years into *Homo sapiens*. During this process, the brain became increasingly more specialized, evolving a broad range of abilities as well as right-brain/left-brain and male/female differences. As Falk notes, in less than two million years, brain size doubled in the *Homo* species, from around 650 cm to 1350 cm. Only a small portion of this newly evolved, larger brain was tied to increasing body size. As Falk points out, this process was unprecedented in the evolutionary histories of other mammals. As brain size increased, neurons enlarged and became more widely spaced and the cerebral cortex became more convoluted. No new structures were found in these larger human brains.

3

However, these larger brains set the foundation for an accelerated evolutionary process never before witnessed in any earthbound, mammalian species. In this process, the prefrontal cortex and the posterior areas of the brain associated with sensory processing in particular became especially convoluted. The shift in neurochemicals, anatomy of neurons, and brain function provided the underlying mechanics of our rapid evolutionary progression, a pattern that was most certainly driven by natural selection.

It is a fascinating historical phenomenon that although scientists and philosophers have written about the intellectual and academic capabilities of the human brain over the last 2,000 years, it is just within the past 100 years, but especially the past 50 years, that we have witnessed an explosion of theories and tests to measure these qualities. This growth has created an often-confusing menu of clinical and educational tools from which to choose. The goal of this book is to help the reader contextualize the strengths and weaknesses of the tests presented and to apply a balanced perspective on their critique. To do so, we asked authors to cover the following 15 essential aspects:

Theory Underlying the Test

1. Historical information, definition of the constructs, and development of the subtests

Description of the Test

2. Subtest background
3. Scales the test yields
4. Structure of the test

Administration and Scoring

5. Tips on administration
6. How to score the test

Standardization, Norms, and Reliability

7. Characteristics of the standardization sample
8. Reliability of the scales

Use of the Test (Including Validity Research on Each Topic)

9. Interpretation methods
10. Identification of special populations
11. Interventions based on test results

Validity

12. Relationships between ability and achievement
13. Fairness, sex, race, and ethnic differences
14. Profiles of abilities and their relationship to diagnosis and treatment planning
15. Factor structure

In this chapter, we review critical points and issues the reader should consider when evaluating the various instruments within the context of the field today and in consideration of what can be reasonably expected for the future. We further urge the reader to carefully examine each author's contribution with attention to the specific details presented and the extent to which each test addresses the issues that were covered.

ASSESSING STRENGTHS AND LIMITATIONS OF ABILITY TESTS

Traditional tests of intelligence were initiated in 1905 with the publication of the Stanford-Binet and further solidified in 1939 with the publication of the Wechsler-Bellevue Scales. These tests made a substantial contribution to our society, shaped how we define intelligence, and influenced the lives of countless children and adults in the United States and around the world (Anastasi & Urbina, 1997). Even though high-quality intelligence and achievement tests are among the most influential contributions made by psychology to society in general, they have also been the subject of considerable criticism. The value of these tests has been demonstrated by a substantial literature (see Graham & Naglieri, 2002; Jensen, 1998; and Ramsey & Reynolds, 2004) even though there are criticisms that range from emotionally to scientifically based. The strengths and weaknesses of the tests presented in this book should be apparent by the content of each chapter, and especially what information was and was not provided.

In order to best determine the utility of each test, readers should consider the strengths and limitations as reported by the authors or their representatives. One point that needs to be stressed is that sometimes a "limitation" of a test may not be evidenced by lack of empirical evidence or poor quality, but rather by misapplication or misinterpretation of scores. For example, sometimes tests are criticized when they are used for a reason for which they were not developed or intended (e.g., using verbal and performance IQ scores for determining which instructional method to employ). Similarly, some tests are criticized when used in ways for which research suggests the test is ill-suited (e.g., subtest profile analysis). Readers should also consider the source of the criticisms, and the extent to which charges are valid and supported by research findings and not based solely on a critic's opinion or straw-man arguments.

The information provided in these chapters helps us understand the authors' position on the most appropriate use of their test. For example, a test such as the Wechsler Nonverbal Scale of Ability (Wechsler & Naglieri, 2006) will not be able to inform us about the examinee's level of verbal expression and verbal comprehension; it was not developed for that purpose. That is not a limitation of the test itself, but rather an indication of how it should and should not be used. Similarly, using the WISC-IV with an examinee who has limited English-language skills will yield an estimate of ability that, according to Yoakum and Yerkes (1920), will likely be inaccurate because it has been known for nearly 100 years that a person could do poorly on verbal and quantitative tests because of limited skills in English. To avoid "injustice by reason of relative unfamiliarity with English" (p. 19), these persons should be tested with

nonverbal measures of general ability (see the tests included in the nonverbal test section of this book). It is important to understand that using a verbal test to measure general ability for someone who does not have an adequate knowledge of English does not mean that the test is invalid. Instead, the score should be interpreted differently (as a measure of English-language comprehension and expression) because of the context within which it was used. The point is, however, that a test of general ability that contains verbal examinations is not inherently faulty, but rather its application to a person who does not speak English undermines the effort to estimate intelligence accurately. Criticisms of the test, therefore, must be viewed within the context of the test's use.

The limitations of traditional IQ tests containing verbal, quantitative, and performance scales have been recognized by practitioners and test developers in the field. This has led to an effort to provide so-called *nonverbal tests of ability*, which comprise a substantial portion of this book. These nonverbal tests of general ability represent an effort on the part of test developers to meet the need for a way to measure ability for diverse populations. By measuring ability using tests of general ability that do not involve verbal or quantitative content, the tests offer a specific methodology designed explicitly for assessing diverse populations. That is, nonverbal tests of ability meet a particular need in the field that traditional multicontent tests like the Wechsler and Binet could not adequately address. Just as nonverbal tests of general ability have changed the field, the availability of cognitive processing–based measures of ability has also altered the landscape considerably.

Tests built to measure cognitive processes meet the need for a new approach to assessment that reconceptualizes ability within the context of basic psychological processes. The KABC-II and the CAS stand out as methods of conceptualizing and measuring ability very differently from the verbal/quantitative/nonverbal test content perspective utilized since the early 1900s.

These tests are also distinguished from more traditional tests because they were explicitly developed to measure basic psychological processes while avoiding achievement-laden test content. The availability of these tests has also raised the awareness of users and test developers of the need for theoretically–based measures of ability that are appropriate for assessment of culturally and linguistically diverse populations, strongly correlated with achievement, and are linked to intervention. The KABC-II and CAS chapters should be viewed within this larger context and with recognition that theory-based instruments offer considerable advantages.

INTELLIGENCE TESTS AND THEORIES

The field of intelligence testing has evolved considerably over the past 20 years and, most important, the value of having a test that is based in a theory has become much more salient. Although we may discuss the theory behind a test, we often do not reflect carefully upon precisely what this means. According to the United States National Academy of Sciences, in the general population the word *theory* means a hunch or speculation and is often used as an antonym for a hypothesis or opinion. In contrast, a scientific definition of the word *theory* "refers to a comprehensive explanation of an important feature of nature that is supported by many facts gathered over time. Theories also allow scientists to make predictions about as yet unobserved phenomena" (Wikipedia, 2008). In the science of assessment psychology, we should use the word *theory* only to describe a model of a construct that has been tested using scientific experimentation, has demonstrated validity, and can be used to predict future behavior. It is quite important to ask the question, "What theory underlies each of the various ability tests included in this book?"

There is considerable variability in the answers to the question, "What theory was used to describe this test of ability?" For example, the term *general intelligence* is used to describe tests like the WISC-IV as well as the UNIT, CTONI, and WNV. Some authors merge different views to describe their approach to explaining what the test measures (e.g., KABC-II) and the theory behind the test. Other authors take a much more liberal approach and apply a model to a previously developed test, and still others take a strict approach of building a test explicitly according to one theory (e.g., CAS). Ultimately, it is the responsibility of the test authors to precisely define the idea, model, or theory behind the test, demonstrate the extent to which the test represents their view, and provide evidence for both the approach and its operationalization in that particular test.

Readers may wonder about the relevance of the underlying conceptualization of a test. How important is a theory for application in the real world? Does a test built on a theory offer advantages over one built on an atheoretical basis? Does this really matter? These are the kinds of questions that must be understood in order to effectively use tests of intelligence, ability, or cognitive processing. In our view, understanding the authors' definition of what their intelligence, ability, or cognitive processing test measures is critical to understanding what the test measures, the relevance that information has for diagnosis and treatment, and how the test will be applied in practice, and especially, explained to teachers and parents.

Readers may wonder what importance a test's theory holds for the practicing psychologist or the educator. The answer is that theory holds considerable importance to understanding and interpreting the scores from a test. We suggest that (1) the user must understand where each test falls on the continuum between an idea and a theory; (2) if the test was built on a theory, then that theory must be clearly articulated and well understood so that it can be used for interpretation of the test; (3) the validity for the organization of the test must be carefully scrutinized by each and every user; and

(4) communication of the findings to consumers must be based on the theory. Why? Because in order to interpret the results from any test, the user must know what the test was designed to measure, whether it does so adequately, and what validity evidence there is for the utility of the constructs. Readers should carefully consider the extent to which this information is provided in each of the chapters.

STANDARDIZATION, NORMS, AND PSYCHOMETRICS

The field of assessment, and especially intelligence and achievement testing, has advanced considerably in the past 25 years to a point where we assume that any test sold by the major companies is well developed, standardized, and normed. The quality of all intelligence and achievement tests is amply described in the chapters contained in this book. Readers should not, however, assume that every test was normed with the same level of sophistication and adequately documented. For example, whereas some of the tests are exemplifiers of excellence, some are less well developed; for example, documentation of the representative nature of the standardization group is inadequate (e.g., DIBELS). Readers should also carefully examine the types of test scores obtained and be cautious of tests that yield only raw scores, which can be misleading (Naglieri & Crocket, 2005). For a review of important psychometric issues, the value of a representative sample, and the statistical characteristics of a test with which the practitioner should be provided, see Naglieri and Chambers (2008) and Urbina (2004).

DIAGNOSIS AND INTERVENTION

Educational diagnosis and eligibility determination are being substantially influenced by the Individuals with Disabilities Education Improvement Act (IDEA) of 2004. This law is having considerable influence on the way school psychologists use intelligence and achievement tests. This law has also influenced community-based decision making in mental health and clinical settings. One of the most important changes particularly relevant to the tests included in this book involves the identification of children with specific learning disabilities (SLD) (see Hale, Flanagan, & Naglieri, 2008; and Hale, Kaufman, Naglieri, & Kavale, 2006), but other issues, such as bias in testing, relevance to intervention, and ongoing treatment monitoring, are also implicated. The issues emphasized in IDEA are included in the chapters contained in this book. For authors of ability tests, this includes evidence of test bias, assessment of basic psychological processes, relevance to identification of SLD, and instructional implications (see KABC-II and CAS). For authors of achievement tests, this also includes relevance to ongoing progress monitoring (see DIBELS and WRAT-PM).

The IDEA and federal regulations have created an opportunity for change in the way school psychologists use ability and achievement tests that will be clear throughout the chapters in this book. Readers should pay particular attention to the similarities and differences among the authors' methods for applying their tests to the question of SLD diagnosis. For example, the deemphasis of the IQ-Ability test difference (e.g., WISC-IV versus WIAT-II) as a criterion for SLD has led to greater emphasis on tests of basic psychological processes (e.g., K-ABC and CAS) and the need for screening of academic skills (e.g., BASI) and ongoing progress monitoring (WRAT-PM). Test authors are developing methods of assessment that can address the demands of today's practitioners. For example, the presence of a processing disorder along with learning failure represents the essence of SLD (Kavale, Kaufman, Naglieri, & Hale, 2005). The cognitive processing measures included in this book enable practitioners to document the essential operational marker for SLD—consistency between cognitive deficits and academic deficits coupled with a significant discrepancy between cognitive assets and cognitive deficits (e.g., Hale & Fiorello, 2004; Kavale et al., 2005; Naglieri, 1999, 2000, 2008). One of the most important advantages of this approach is that it unites an identification method with the definition included in IDEA as suggested by Hale, Kaufman, Naglieri, and Kavale (2006). The next step, of course, is the determination of appropriate interventions.

There is considerable controversy about the connection between tests of intelligence and cognitive processing with instruction, perhaps best illustrated by the view proposed by Vellutino, Scanlon, Small, and Fanuele (2003) that tests of ability are irrelevant because they do not predict response to treatment. Some of the chapters in this book provide a view of how instruction can be linked to assessment of cognitive processes and how instruction can be guided by monitoring the academic progress of students on a frequent basis (e.g., DIBELS and WRAT-PM). The extension of assessment information to instruction will likely remain a contentious issue for some time.

INTELLIGENCE TEST BIAS

The characteristics of the U.S. population continue to change and the need for fair assessment of culturally and linguistically diverse populations, especially the Hispanic population, has become increasingly important. IDEA 2004 clearly states that assessments must be selected and administered so as to be nondiscriminatory on a racial or cultural basis. It is critical, therefore, that any measure of ability that is used should have been evaluated for test bias (see Reynolds & Ramsay, 2003, for a summary of test bias issues).

The ability tests presented in the book differ considerably in their conceptualizations and operationalizations of the construct. The two types of tests of general ability (those that

include verbal, quantitative, and nonverbal content and those that use only nonverbal test questions) are distinct from the cognitive processing–based measures. Readers should consider the psychometric and impact-related issues related to the scores that these three types of tests yield for various race and ethnic groups. What will become apparent is that while researchers have recognized the value of general intelligence tests with diverse content, these tests yield the largest mean-score race and ethnic differences. When ability is measured using nonverbal tests or conceptualized according to basic psychological processes, both of which avoid the knowledge required to answer verbal and quantitative questions, race and ethnic differences are reduced (Fagan, 2000; Suzuki & Valencia, 1997). Nonverbal and cognitive processing–based tests that do not rely on questions that contain language and quantitative content are, therefore, deemed more appropriate for assessment of culturally and linguistically diverse populations (Fagan, 2000; Suzuki & Valencia, 1997). Importantly, the chapters on nonverbal and cognitive processing tests provide two important approaches that measure ability without the loss of predictive validity and at the same time result in a more equitable system for evaluating culturally and linguistically diverse populations.

THE CHANGING FACE OF ACHIEVEMENT TESTING

The chapters included in this book that cover evaluation of achievement illustrate important changes in the way academic skills are conceptualized and measured. The tests vary in their scope. For example, tests such as the K-TEA and WIAT-II offer measurement of a broad spectrum of skills that are standardized on large samples that represent the U.S. population. These achievement tests also vary in scope. For example, the WJ-III offers a large number of subtests, whereas the WRAT-4 measures relatively fewer areas. The WRAT-4 also provides a way to measure progress over time, as does the BASI, but the BASI provides for both individual as well as group testing options. Tests like the CTOPP and GORT provide specialized measures of achievement. These tests differ in their psychometric characteristics and normative samples, which have important implications for usefulness and defensibility.

SUMMARY

We anticipate that this book will greatly aid users' understanding of the strengths and weaknesses of the various tests presented. Ultimately, it is the responsibility of the test authors to provide evidence of the quality of their tests and the contexts within which they are most defensibly used. It is the responsibility of the test user to be informed of the various quality issues associated with each test and the interpretive methods the authors recommend. Our goal is, of course, to provide the very best information to the consumers of this information for the benefit of the client.

REFERENCES

Anastasi, A., & Urbina, S. (1997). *Psychological testing* (7th ed.). Upper Saddle River, NJ: Prentice Hall.

Fagan, J. R. (2000). A theory of intelligence as processing: Implications for society. *Psychology, Public Policy, and Law, 6,* 168–179.

Falk, D. (2004). *Brain dance—revised and expanded edition.* Gainesville, FL: University Press.

Graham, J. R., & Naglieri, J. A. (Eds.) (2002). *Handbook of assessment psychology.* New York: Wiley.

Hale, J. B., & Fiorello, C. A. (2004). *School neuropsychology: A practitioner's handbook.* New York: Guilford Press.

Hale, J. N., Flanagan, D. P., & Naglieri, J. A. (2008). Alternative research-based methods for IDEA 2004 identification of children with specific learning disabilities. *Communiqué, 36,* 14–15.

Hale, J. B., Kaufman, A., Naglieri, J. A., & Kavale, K. A. (2006). Implementation of IDEA: Integrating response to intervention and cognitive assessment methods. *Psychology in the Schools, 43,* 753–770.

Jensen, A. R. (1998). *The g factor: The science of mental ability.* Westport, CT: Praeger.

Kavale, K. A., Kaufman, A. S., Naglieri, J. A., & Hale, J. B. (2005). Changing procedures for identifying learning disabilities: The danger of poorly supported ideas. *The School Psychologist, 59,* 16–25.

Naglieri, J. A. (1999). *Essentials of CAS assessment.* New York: Wiley.

Naglieri, J. A. (2000). Can profile analysis of ability test scores work? An illustration using the PASS theory and CAS with an unselected cohort. *School Psychology Quarterly, 15,* 419–433.

Naglieri, J. A. (2008). Best practices in linking cognitive assessment of students with learning disabilities to interventions. In A. Thomas and J. Grimes (Eds.), *Best practices in school psychology* (5th ed., pp. 679–696). Bethesda, MD: NASP.

Naglieri, J. A., & Chambers, K. (2008). Psychometric issues and current scales for assessing autism spectrum disorders. In S. Goldstein, J. A. Naglieri, & S. Ozonoff (Eds.), *Assessment of autism spectrum disorders* (pp. 55–90). New York: Springer.

Naglieri, J. A., & Crockett, D. (2005) Response to Intervention (RTI): Is it a scientifically proven method? *NASP Communiqué, 34,* 38–39.

Ramsay, M. C., & Reynolds, C. R. (2004). Relations between intelligence and achievement tests. In G. Goldstein and S. Beers (Eds.), *Comprehensive handbook of psychological assessment* (pp. 25–50). New York: Wiley.

Reynolds, C. R., & Ramsay, M. C. (2003). Bias in psychological assessment: An empirical review and recommendations. In J. Graham and J. A. Naglieri (Eds.), *Assessment psychology* (pp. 67–93). New York: Wiley.

Suzuki, L. A., & Valencia, R. R. (1997). Race-ethnicity and measured intelligence. *American Psychologist, 52,* 1103–1114.

Urbina, S. (2004). *Essentials of psychological testing.* New York: Wiley.

Vellutino, F. R., Scanlon, D. M., Small, S., & Fanuele, D. (2003, December). Response to intervention as a vehicle for distinguishing between reading disabled and non-reading disabled children: Evidence for the role of kindergarten and first grade intervention. Paper presented at the *National Research Center on Learning Disabilities Responsiveness-to-Intervention Symposium*, Kansas City, MO.

Wechsler, D., & Naglieri, J. A. (2006). *Wechsler Nonverbal Scale of Ability*. San Antonio, TX: Pearson.

Yoakum, C. S., & Yerkes, R. M. (1920). *Army Mental Tests*. New York: Henry Holt & Company.

Current Issues in the Assessment of Intelligence, Specific Learning Disability, and Attention Deficit Hyperactivity Disorder

Sam Goldstein, Sean Cunningham

In this chapter, we first offer a brief discussion of a number of critical issues concerning the nexus between measures of intelligence and achievement. We then address these tests as they relate to the two most common conditions—attention deficit hyperactivity and specific learning disability—for which they are used to make diagnostic, placement, and treatment decisions.

INTELLIGENCE AND ACHIEVEMENT

Tests of intelligence have traditionally consisted of verbal, quantitative, and nonverbal components. This division was primarily based on practical reasons as opposed to theoretical or scientifically guided principles. Perhaps the first to utilize this model was the Stanford-Binet (Binet & Simon, 1905). The traditional model of intelligence was developed out of the use of the Army Alpha (verbal) and Army Beta (nonverbal) tests during World War I. The Army Alpha and Beta tests were developed, not necessarily to measure different aspects of intelligence, as is the case today with verbal and nonverbal components of intelligence tests, but to be equitable to individuals who did not possess a good understanding of the English language. Individuals who did not have a firm understanding of English were able to take the Army Beta tests and avoid risk of failure that taking the Army Alpha test would provide. The establishment of Army Alpha and Army Beta tests theoretically allowed those giving and taking the tests to be better able to establish an accurate intelligence score. The first comprehensive intelligence test, the Wechsler-Bellevue Scales (Wechsler, 1939), contained a format similar to the Army Alpha and Army Beta tests, combining these divided parts of verbal and nonverbal domains into an overall score of intelligence. Jensen (1998) has demonstrated experimental support for the conceptualization of intelligence as measured by the Binet and Wechsler tests; however, it has been proposed that because these contemporary divisions of intelligence (i.e., verbal, nonverbal) are based on practical circumstances, "the result has been that our [intelligence] tests have been used to define the theory of intelligence the test is intended to measure" (Naglieri, 2008, p. 68).

Contemporary ways to assess intelligence have come under scrutiny, as they have been found to overlap considerably with measures of achievement. Recently, Naglieri and Bornstein (2003) have shown that items used on current measures of intelligence share properties with items from tests of achievement, suggesting a good deal of relatedness between the assessments of the two constructs. In fact, high correlations have been found between measures of intelligence and achievement. In contrast, Rindermann (2007) has suggested that the similarities on scores between the two tests result from one common, latent ability. In examining correlations between different types of intelligence and achievement tests, Rindermann (2007) concluded from a large-scale cross-cultural study that a single latent factor, "general innate cognitive ability," appears to be responsible for high associations between measures of achievement and cognitive abilities. In addition to this claim, however, Rindermann also noted considerable overlap between the contents of cognitive and achievement measures. This finding appears to offer some explanation for the findings of Naglieri and Bornstein (2003) about the relatedness between scores on intelligence and achievement tests when content overlap is or is not present. It appears, then, that in addition to content overlap, a general underlying ability or dominant latent factor may be responsible for related performance on intelligence and achievement tests as well. Rindermann concludes, "it may not be unreasonable to hypothesize that the cognitive demands and processes involved in solving student achievement test tasks are similar to the ones involved in solving classical intelligence test tasks" (Rindermann, 2007, p. 689).

As a result of the overlap between intelligence and achievement tests, the endorsement of nonverbal tests has gathered recent attention as a unique and fair way to measure intelligence. Nonverbal tests have demonstrated validity in measuring intelligence as exemplified by high correlations with traditional measures of intelligence (Wechsler & Naglieri, 2006). Examples of nonverbal tests include the Naglieri Nonverbal Ability Test (NNAT; Naglieri, 1997, 2003), Wechsler Nonverbal Scale of Ability (WNV; Wechsler & Naglieri, 2006), and the Universal Nonverbal Intelligence Test (UNIT; Bracken & McCallum, 1998). The items that comprise nonverbal intelligence tests are unique in that they do not share the overlap in content with achievement measures. Because nonverbal measures do not share the content overlap with achievement measures, the variance they capture may be more unique to an individual's intellectual ability. It can be reasonably concluded, then, that nonverbal measures of intelligence provide a more accurate measure of cognitive ability or intelligence when compared to intelligence tests based on a more traditional framework (e.g., division into verbal and nonverbal domains).

Beyond lacking the overlap in content with achievement tests, nonverbal tests of intelligence share additional benefits beyond what more traditional measures of intelligence have to offer. First, nonverbal measures can be administered in group format. Additionally, nonverbal measures of cognitive ability have been demonstrated to be culturally fair, providing similar scores among minorities and individuals with limited English-language skills (Naglieri, 2008; Wechsler & Naglieri, 2006). As a result, nonverbal measures of cognitive ability can work to eliminate the underrepresentation of minorities in gifted and talented programs. Nonverbal measures for gifted minority children have been shown to identify similar percentages of minority children as having the range of scores that would be essential to be identified for gifted programs (Naglieri & Ford, 2003). Furthermore, score discrepancies exist between males and females on traditional measures of intelligence (Lynn, Fergusson, & Horwood, 2005; Lynn, Raine, Venables, Mednick, & Irwing, 2005; Slate, 1998). However, studies have demonstrated that score discrepancies between sexes become less salient as males and females earn the same scores when nonverbal measures are used (Rojahn & Naglieri, 2006).

Because of the previously mentioned benefits of nonverbal measures of ability, researchers have recently proposed that these tests of cognitive ability that stray from the traditional framework (e.g., CAS, K-ABC) offer a better assessment of intellect and demonstrate better clinical utility (Das, Naglieri, & Kirby, 1994; Fagan, 2000; Kaufman, & Kaufman, 2004; Naglieri, 2002, 2003; Naglieri, Goldstein, DeLauder, & Schwebach, 2006). Naglieri (1999) assessed the correlations between several types of intelligence tests and achievement data, finding that tests of intelligence based more on a general intelligence model (e.g., Wechsler scales) correlated less with measures of achievement than cognitively based instruments assessing intellect (e.g., K-ABC, CAS). Similar results have been echoed in other studies (Naglieri & Bornstein, 2003; Naglieri, Goldstein, DeLauder, & Schwebach, 2006; Ramsey & Reynolds, 2003). These results indicate that the cognitively based measures of intelligence may be a more beneficial clinical tool in examining and predicting scores between intellect and achievement. Therefore, they may demonstrate better use in clinical decision-making contexts (e.g., determination of specific learning disability).

A final area to consider when examining traditional models of measuring intelligence with more contemporary measures of ability has to do with testing minority students and students with English as their second language. Individuals possessing a limited understanding of English and/or lack of proper education and subsequent deficiencies in academic skills are likely to have compromised verbal scores on tests of intelligence. Naglieri and Yazzie (1983) demonstrated this phenomenon in a study

examining Native American Navajo children living on a reservation. These students spoke English as a second language and performed low on Verbal, but average on Performance Scales of the Wechsler Intelligence Test. As a result, and as previously discussed, the use of nonverbal tests of ability has been proposed as more culturally fair in assessing intelligence in children, suggesting that nonverbal tests are advantages in that they provide a "more equitable evaluation from culturally and linguistically diverse populations" (Naglieri & Ford, 2005, p. 30). Thus, in some ways, concepts of intelligence testing have come full circle over the past 100 years, beginning with the Army Alpha and Beta tests.

ATTENTION DEFICIT HYPERACTIVITY DISORDER

The childhood cognitive and behavioral problems categorized as disorders of attention, impulsivity, and hyperactivity have over the past 50 years presented a clinical challenge for neuropsychologists. The symptom constellation referred to as *attention deficit disorder* or *attention deficit hyperactivity disorder (ADHD)* (APA, 2000) has become one of the most widely researched areas in childhood and adolescence with an increasing interest throughout the adult lifespan. Problems arising from this constellation of symptoms have constituted the most chronic childhood behavior disorder (Wender, 1975) and the largest single source of referrals to mental health centers (Barkley, 1990; Gadow, Sprafkin, & Nolan, 2001). In clinic-referred settings, males outnumber females 6 to 1. In epidemiological studies of community-based settings, the ratio is 3 to 1 (Barkley, 2008). The incidence of diagnosis continues to increase with a 70% increase in the diagnosis of children and nearly a 100% increase in the diagnosis of adults between 2000 and 2003 (CDC, 2005). It is now estimated that between 4% and 8% of the population has received a diagnosis of ADHD (CDC, 2005; Cuffe, Moore,

& McKeown, 2005). Females are the fastest growing group (Medco, 2005). Broad-based definitions of ADHD find epidemiology of nearly 16% in adults while more narrow definitions report an incidence of 3% to 4% (Faraone & Biederman, 2005). Additionally, incidence has been reported to be higher in populations of individuals with other impairments (Altfas, 2002).

The development of a norm-referenced, psychometric assessment battery specifically designed for ADHD has been an elusive goal for researchers and clinicians. Thus, it is not surprising when reviewing the extensive literature attempting to hypothetically and objectively define specific neuropsychological impairments occurring consistently in children with ADHD that no tried-and-true battery or pattern of impairment comes to light. As Levine (1992) has noted, ADHD symptoms appear to reflect "elusive entities and . . . mistaken identities." The comorbidity issue and the lack of specificity that many tests hold in discriminating ADHD from other disorders further complicates this endeavor. Compromised scores may be due to a variety of causes, leading some researchers to suggest that a profile of test scores be utilized in defining and explaining neuropsychological impairments in children with ADHD (Aylward, Verhulst, & Bell, 1993; Naglieri, 2000). Clinical or laboratory tests alone or in combination have been found to result in classification decisions that frequently disagree with the diagnosis of ADHD when it is based on parent interview, history, and behavior rating scales (Doyle, Biederman, & Seidman, 2000; DuPaul, Anastopoulos, Shelton, Guevremont, & Metevia, 1992). Further, Szatmari, Offord, Siegel, and Finlayson (1990) report that neuropsychological tests appear to distinguish children with ADHD from those with pure anxiety or affective disorders. However, they may not as efficiently distinguish ADHD from other disruptive disorders. These authors concluded that neuropsychological tests were more strongly associated with externalizing than internalizing diagnoses. They appear to correlate with psychiatric symptoms at school but

not at home. Additionally, traditional neuropsychological instruments used to infer attention and impulse problems often do not correlate with each other (Naglieri, Goldstein, DeLauder, & Schwebach, 2005). Thus, it is not surprising that Barkley (1991) suggests that when results of the standardized behavior ratings, observations, and history conflict with laboratory measures, the latter should be disregarded in favor of the former as these are considered more ecologically valid sources of data.

Perhaps no other single instrument secondary to continuous performance tests has been touted to be as effective in facilitating the diagnosis ADHD as the Wechsler Intelligence Scale for Children. Researchers have suggested that children with ADHD demonstrate a very different profile from that of normals as well as different profiles across the various subtypes of ADHD (Carlson, Lahey, & Neeper, 1986). Subtests of the Wechsler Intelligence Scale for Children over four editions have been suggested as measures of vigilance and concentration (Gardner, 1979), efficient mental tracking (Lezak, 1983), and divided attention (van Zomeren, 1981). In 1979, Alan Kaufman suggested that the second edition of the Wechsler Scale, Coding, Arithmetic, and Digit Span subtests, factored into an index he referred to as Freedom from Distractibility. Kaufman suggested that the Freedom from Distractibility factor should be at least three points below the verbal and performance factors and that factor scores should not be excessively different from each other as it would be suspected that such a pattern might reflect learning disability.

In 1988, Jerome Sattler suggested that the Arithmetic, Coding, Information, and Digit Span (ACID) subtests on a second edition of the Wechsler provided a profile that could identify attention problems and learning disability. It should be noted that this ACID profile was found in only 11% of a sample of children with ADHD (Wechsler, 1989). The Freedom from Distractibility factor has also not been found to correlate well with observation or parent or teacher reports of ADHD symptoms (Cowen, 1991). Yet children with ADHD demonstrated lower Freedom from Distractibility and Processing Speed indices on the third edition of the Wechsler Intelligence Scale for Children in comparison to Verbal Comprehension and Perceptual Organization index scores, a pattern that differed from the standardization sample (Mealer, Morgan, & Luscomb, 1996; Prifitera & Dersh, 1993). The Freedom from Distractibility factor, however, in the current edition of the Wechsler Intelligence Scale for Children (4th edition), no longer emerges as a single factor. Digit Span and Coding load on separate factors and Arithmetic is an optional test (Wechsler, 2003). Despite these data, Molter (1995) suggested that the differences between the Verbal, Comprehension, and Freedom from Distractibility indices may actually reflect problems related to auditory process or memory rather than ADHD. It is reasonable for the evaluator to heed the advice offered by Anastopoulos, Spisto, and Maher (1993) that evaluators not rely heavily on factors of the Wechsler Intelligence Scale for Children in ruling in or out the diagnosis of ADHD.

It has also been suggested that children with ADHD experience greater problems with sequential rather than simultaneous tasks on the Kaufman Assessment Battery for Children (Carter, Zelko, Oas, & Waltonen, 1990). However, this finding has not been consistently reported. Harvey and Chernouskas (1995) provided preliminary evidence that children with ADHD may present a distinctive pattern of scores on the Woodcock Johnson Psychoeducational Battery. In particular, it was suggested these youth demonstrate problems with basic writing skills, writing fluency, and processing speed. Finally, a number of studies have suggested that measurement of specific intellectual processes may differentiate youth with various subtypes of ADHD (Paolito, 1999; Naglieri, 1999). However, data generated by instruments such as the Cognitive Assessment System (Naglieri & Das, 1997a) are not necessary in

making the diagnosis of ADHD but can provide useful information concerning differences in cognitive processes among diagnosed youth.

Although a number of paper-and-pencil tasks have been used over the years in research settings to identify symptoms of ADHD, most have not lent themselves easily to clinical use. In research studies, some of these tests, such as the Matching Familiar Figures Test (Kagan, 1964), appear to have strong positive and negative predictive power for identifying impulsive children. However, in clinical practice such instruments have not proven reliable for confirming the diagnosis of ADHD. Computerized instruments designed to measure sustained attention and the ability to inhibit impulsive responding (Conners, 2008; Gordon, 1993; Greenberg, 1991) have become increasingly popular among neuropsychologists. However, it is important to remember that although these instruments may demonstrate strong positive predictive power (e.g., if the child fails the task, it strongly confirms the presence of symptoms related to ADHD), they possess poor negative predictive power (e.g., if the child passes the task, conclusions cannot be drawn one way or the other concerning the diagnosis) (McGee, Clark, & Symons, 2000). Nonetheless, many evaluators rely on such instruments to provide additional data as part of the diagnostic process rather than a specific data point to confirm or disconfirm the diagnosis of ADHD (Riccio, Reynolds, & Lowe, 2001). The interested reader is referred to Conners (1994) or Homack and Reynolds (2005) for a thorough review of the literature concerning computerized assessment of ADHD.

Due to the pervasive, multisetting nature of problems related to ADHD and the high comorbidity with other childhood disorders, assessment for ADHD must be accompanied by a thorough emotional, developmental, and behavioral evaluation. It should be noted, however, that the diagnosis of ADHD should be firmly based on the accepted standard, in this case the DSM-IV-TR diagnostic criteria. Evaluators should be aware that efforts to include additional data to prove/disprove the diagnosis run the risk of introducing increasing variance (Naglieri, Goldstein, & Schwebach, 2004). The comprehensive evaluation should collect data concerning the child's behavior at home as well as with friends and at school, academic and intellectual functioning, medical status, and emotional/development. It is suggested that evaluators consider the following multistep process in the evaluation of ADHD:

1. A complete history must be obtained. This is not a cursory process. Sufficient time (approximately one-and-a-half to two hours) should be set aside to obtain a narrative of the child's development, behavior, extended family history, family relations, and current functioning. Within the context of the interview, efforts should be made to trace a developmental course that appears to fit ADHD as well as to identify core symptoms and those related to other childhood disorders. Possessing a thorough knowledge of the diagnostic criteria for common and uncommon (e.g., high functioning autism) childhood internalizing and externalizing disorders should be a paramount concern for the evaluator to facilitate the identification of high- as well as low-incidence disorders.

2. Data obtained from the history should be supplemented by the completion of a number of standardized, factor-analyzed questionnaires concerning children's problems. At least two adults who interact with the child on a regular basis, ideally a parent and a teacher, should be requested to complete questionnaires. For general child assessment, a valuable questionnaire is the recently published Conners Behavior Rating Scales—Parent and Teacher Form (Conners, 2008). The Conners Parent and Teacher Rating Scales—Revised (Conners, 2008); the Child Behavior Checklist (Achenbach, 1996); the Comprehensive Teacher's Rating Scale (Ullmann, Sleator, & Sprague, 1988); Childhood Attention Problems Scale (Edelbrock, 1990); and Academic Performance and ADHD Rating Scales (DuPaul, 1990) are also helpful. However, these questionnaires alone do not provide sufficient information for diagnosis. They simply provide an organized report of behavior. They describe what the observer sees, but not why it is being seen.

3. Based on the history and questionnaires, the evaluator should be able to generate a consistent set of data and a series of hypotheses to explain the child's behavior across a variety of settings.

4. Requests should be made to review school records, including report cards and results of group achievement testing. If weak performance or learning disabilities are suspected, or if the child is already receiving special education services, the neuropsychologist should review all assessment data as well as the child's Individualized Education Plan. Then it is proper to decide which tests and what amount of time should be used to arrive at the most accurate evaluation of the child. Neuropsychologists should be cautioned, as just reviewed, that there are no specific laboratory tests to evaluate ADHD that have demonstrated sufficient positive and negative predictive power to be relied on. The primary purpose of face-to-face assessment with a child should involve addressing issues related to the child's emotional status, self-esteem, cognitive development, and learning disabilities. Observation of the child's behavior during assessment may also yield clues regarding his or her interpersonal style and temperament.

SPECIFIC LEARNING DISABILITY

Specific learning disabilities, including reading disabilities, are the most prevalent group of neurobehavioral disorders affecting children and adults. There is a strong genetic component to these disabilities (for review, see Goldstein &

Reynolds, 1999, and Goldstein & Schwebach, 2009). Unlike most other neuropsychological disorders, learning disabilities are not a single, relatively well-defined entity or syndrome. Rather, learning disabilities encompass an extremely heterogeneous group of problems with diverse characteristics resulting from a variety of biological influences, including genetic factors, environmental insults to the brain, and possibly, as recent research on brain development suggests, extreme lack of early environmental stimulation. As a result, the multifaceted field of learning disabilities is complex and often contentious, with many competing theories, definitions, diagnostic procedures, and suggested avenues of intervention.

Diagnosing a learning disability primarily based on any type of a discrepancy between ability and achievement scores has been long criticized (Lyon, Fletcher, Shaywitz, Wood, Schulte, & Olson, 2001). It has been well documented that a portion of students who have been identified as learning disabled do not exhibit a discrepancy between their ability and achievement scores. Across several research studies over the past several years, upwards of 25% of students with a diagnosis of learning disability do not demonstrate a severe discrepancy (Peterson, & Shinn, 2002; Ysseldyke, Algozzine, & Epps, 1983).

Although federal guidelines set forth by IDEIA suggest the use of the discrepancy analysis as one piece of evidence in a comprehensive evaluation to determine eligibility of a specific learning disability, it cannot be used in isolation. However, there are still no specific criteria to indicate how to determine a discrepancy if this model is decided on as a source of information to be integrated into a learning disability diagnosis. Several researchers have proposed different frameworks to determine the best method of discrepancy analysis. What should be noted is that the discrepancies discovered in the literature indicative of a learning disability are not always between intelligence and ability scores. Additionally, some discrepancy analysis uses scores within only one measure to identify learning disabilities.

As opposed to a severe discrepancy, alternative models have been proposed to facilitate the identification of children with learning disabilities. The Absolute Achievement Discrepancy (AAD) has been proposed as an alternative to the standard ability–achievement discrepancy model as a means of identifying children with learning disabilities. AAD views the key feature of a learning disability as severe low achievement alone. From an AAD standpoint, children with a disability demonstrate to have a tested achievement score on a standardized, norm-referenced achievement test discrepant from the national average. That is, the children meeting a diagnosis of a learning disability would be on the lower end of the normal distribution within the framework of the AAD model. It has been argued that the suggested means of identifying a child with a learning disability with a discrepancy in achievement from the national norm, as proposed by the AAD model, makes intuitive sense, as children with learning disabilities have consistently been among the lowest achieving students within the schools (Peterson, & Shinn, 2002). In their meta-analysis, Fuchs, Fuchs, Mathes, Lipsey, and Eaton (2000) found that when comparing students with a learning disability to low-achieving students (e.g., Title I students), students with a learning disability consistently scored lower than low-achieving peers. Thus, students with learning disability have clearly different academic profiles from those of typically developing and low-achieving peers.

The Relative Achievement Discrepancy (RAD) proposes yet another view of how learning disabilities can be identified. As opposed to using national norms as the comparison group, as does the AAD model, RAD draws from norms defined within the local school district itself to be used to determine a discrepancy that would warrant a diagnosis of a learning disability. A problem with the RAD is that a child who may be performing satisfactorily in a low-achieving school district may move to a higher achieving district and, as a result of the locally used norms to determine a learning disability classification, become classified as a student with a learning disability. Thus, with RAD there is no consistent way to equitably diagnose a student with a learning disability, as standards will differ by community.

Hale, Fiorello, and colleagues (2003; 2004) developed the Concordance-Discordance Model (C-DM) for use in their Cognitive Hypothesis Testing (CHT) approach to assessment and intervention. The CHT methodology, when combined with knowledge of psychological processes and intervention, can be used to develop single-subject interventions that are monitored, evaluated, and revised until treatment is successful. Preliminary results with children identified by school districts as having SLD suggest the method could help reduce the number of false positives derived using an ability–achievement discrepancy approach (Hale & Fiorello, 2004).

Naglieri (1999) recommended a Discrepancy/Consistency Model for use with the Cognitive Assessment System following methods originally proposed by Davis (1959), popularized by Kaufman (1979), and modified by Silverstein (1982, 1993). Individual scores on measures of basic psychological processes that are significantly below the child's average and substantially below normal are labeled as a cognitive weakness, and when combined with similar variability in achievement test scores yield evidence of a possible specific learning disability. That is, finding a cognitive weakness *and* an academic weakness would provide evidence that contributes to the diagnosis of SLD, especially if other appropriate conditions are also met. The effectiveness of this model has been tested by Naglieri (2000), finding that children with a weakness in one or more of the basic PASS cognitive processes earned lower scores on achievement. Additionally, the more pronounced the cognitive weakness, the lower the achievement scores, and children with a PASS cognitive weakness were more likely to have been previously identified and placed in special education. Naglieri's method, which is based on the theoretically defined PASS processes, has also been used to help determine diagnosis and

design academic interventions (Naglieri, 2005). In regard to SLD, the basic differential diagnostic task facing the evaluator is to determine whether the individual's level of achievement actually reflects his or her overall level of functioning or in fact represents a deficit or discrepancy between actual and expected functioning due to specific weaknesses. Achievement data absent any measure of intellect are valuable in designing academic programs and setting achievement goals. Intellectual measures, too, are valuable in some cases as general indicators of the potential for future functioning and, in the case of certain measures (e.g., Cognitive Assessment System, Kaufman Assessment Battery for Children, etc.), are helpful in appreciating patterns of ability strengths and weaknesses that not only contribute to achievement but in and of themselves can be targets for intervention.

A number of volumes provide thorough, in-depth models for assessment utilizing myriad tests and extended batteries. Although achievement/intelligence discrepancies are most widely used to identify specific learning disabilities, the issue of high intelligence with average achievement identified as SLD continues to be controversial. An age/achievement discrepancy, nonetheless, is a good general target for evaluators, with a standard deviation and a half below the mean used as a cutoff independent of intellectual scores.

It is suggested evaluators consider a multistep process such as the following in the evaluation of SLD:

1. Obtain a complete history. As noted in regard to the assessment of ADHD, this is not a cursory process. Sufficient time should be set aside to obtain a narrative of the child's development, behavior, extended family history, family relations, and current functioning. Within the context of the interview, efforts should be made to trace a developmental course characteristic of early risk for SLD, including weaknesses in the development of

language label, association, retrieval, and sequential skills as well as orthographic abilities. In many cases, children with SLD demonstrate a very clear history of struggles during the preschool years to master basic academic material as well as to begin to learn the monetary and time-telling systems. These latter systems require many of the same underlying skills required for efficient reading, writing, spelling, and arithmetic.

2. Data obtained from the history should be supplemented by a careful review of the child's academic records. Group achievement data should be reviewed.

3. Based on the history and a review of records, the evaluator should be able to generate a consistent set of data and a series of hypotheses to explain the child's achievement. Whenever possible, group achievement data should be reviewed.

4. We strongly recommend that evaluators in or out of a school setting make an effort to communicate directly with classroom educators concerning their impressions of the child's basic academic skills. Educators are often sensitive to the basis of children's achievement problems, in particular whether impaired achievement may be the result of lack of ability and/or the result of behavioral adversities.

5. Academic abilities should be evaluated using one of the comprehensive batteries described in this volume.

REFERENCES

Achenbach, T. M. (1996). Subtyping ADHD: The request for suggestions about relating empirically based assessment to DSM-IV. *ADHD Report, 4*, 5–9.

Altfas, J. R. (2002). Prevalence of ADHD among adults in obesity treatment. *Biomedical Psychology, 2*, 1–14.

American Psychiatric Association (2000). *Diagnostic and statistical manual of mental disorders* (4th ed.—text revision). Washington, DC: Author.

Anastopoulos, A. D., Spisto, M., & Maher, M. C. (1993). The WISC-III, third factor: A preliminary look at its diagnostic utility. *ADHD Report, 1*, 4–5.

Aylward, G. P., Verhulst, S. J., & Bell, S. (1993, September). *Inter-relationships between measures of attention deficit disorders: Same scores, different reasons*. Paper presented at the Society for Behavioral Pediatrics Meeting, Providence, RI.

Barkley, R. A. (1990). *Attention-deficit hyperactivity disorder: A handbook for diagnosis and treatment*. New York: Guilford.

Barkley, R. A. (1991). Attention-deficit hyperactivity disorder. *Psychiatric Annals, 21*, 725–733.

Binet, A., & Simon, T. (1905). New methods for the diagnosis of the intellectual level of subnormals. *L'Annee Psychologique, 11*, 191–244.

Bracken, B. A., & McCallum, R. S. (1998). *Universal nonverbal intelligence test*. Austin, TX: Pro-Ed.

Carlson, C. L., Lahey, B. B., & Neeper, R. (1986). Direct assessment of the cognitive correlates of attention deficit disorders with and without hyperactivity. *Journal of Psychopathology and Behavioral Assessment, 8*, 69–86.

Carroll, X. B. (1982). The measurement of intelligence. In R. X Sternberg (Ed.), *Handbook of human intelligence*. Cambridge, England: Cambridge University Press.

Carter, B. D., Zelko, F. A., Oas, P. T., & Waltonen, S. (1990). A comparison of ADD/H children and clinical controls on the Kaufman Assessment Battery for Children (K-ABC). *Journal of Psychoeducational Assessment, 8*, 155–164.

Caruso, J. C., & Witkiewitz, K. (2002). Increasing the reliability of ability-achievement difference scores: An example using the Kaufman Assessment Battery for Children. *Journal of Educational Measurement, 39*, 39–58.

Center for Disease Control (2005). *Morbidity and Mortality Weekly Report, 54*(34). www.cdc.gov/mmwr.

Ceci, S. J. (1990). *On intelligence … more or less: A bio-ecological treatise on intellectual development*. Englewood Cliffs, NJ: Prentice-Hall.

Ceci, S. J. (1991). How much does schooling influence general intelligence and its cognitive components? A reassessment of the evidence. *Developmental Psychology, 27*(5), 703–722.

Conners, C. K. (1994). *Conners Continuous Performance Test (version 3.0)* [User's Manual]. Toronto, ON: Multi-Health Systems.

Conners, C. K. (2008). *Conners Behavioral Rating Scales*. Toronto, ON: Multi-Health Systems.

Cowen, E.L. (1991). In pursuit of wellness. *American Psychologist, 46,* 404–408.

Cuffe, S. P., Moore, C. G., & McKeown, R. E. (2005). Prevalence and correlates of ADHD symptoms in the National Health Interview Survey. *Journal of Attention Disorders, 9*(2), 392–401.

Das, J. P., Naglieri, J. A., & Kirby, J. R. (1994). *Assessment of cognitive processes*. Needham Heights, MA: Allyn & Bacon.

Davis, F. B. (1959). Interpretation of differences among averages and individual test scores. *Journal of Educational Psychology, 50,* 162–170.

Doyle, A. E., Biederman, J., & Seidman, L. J. (2000). Diagnostic efficacy of neuropsychological test scores for discriminating boys with and without ADHD. *Journal of Consulting and Clinical Psychology, 68,* 477–488.

DuPaul, G. J. (1990). *Academic-performance rating scale and ADHD rating scale*. Worcester, MA: Department of Psychiatry, University of Massachusetts.

DuPaul, G. J., Anastopoulos, A. D., Shelton, T. L., Guevremont, D. C., & Metevia, L. (1992). Multimethod assessment of attention-deficit hyperactivity disorder: The diagnostic utility of clinic-based tests. *Journal of Clinical Child Psychology, 21,* 394–402.

Edelbrock, C. (1990). Childhood attention problems (CAP) scale. In: R. A. Barkley (Ed.), *Attention-deficit hyperactivity disorder: A handbook for diagnosis and treatment* (pp. 320–321). New York: Guilford.

Fagan, J. R. (2000). A theory of intelligence as processing: Implications for society. *Psychology, Public Policy, and Law, 6,* 168–179.

Faraone, S.V., & Biederman, J. (2005). What is the prevalence of adult Attention Deficit Hyperactivity Disorder? Results of a population screen of 966 adults. *Journal of Attention Disorders, 9,* 384–391.

Fuchs, D., Fuchs, L., Mathes, P.G., & Lipsey, M.W. (2000). Reading differences between low-achieving students with and without learning disabilities: A meta-analysis. In R. Gersten & S. Vaughn (Eds.), *Issues and research in special education* (pp. 81–104). Hillsdale, NJ: Erlbaum.

Gadow, K. D., Sprafkin, J., & Nolan, E. (2001). DSM-IV symptoms in community and clinic preschool children. *Journal of the American Academy of Child and Adolescent Psychiatry, 40,* 1383–1392.

Gardner, R. A. (1979). *The objective diagnosis of minimal brain dysfunction*. Cresskill, NJ: Creative Therapeutics.

Glutting, J. J., McDermott, P. A., Prifitera, A., & McGrath, E. A. (1992). Core profile types for the WISC-III and WIAT: Their development and application in identifying multivariate IQ-achievement discrepancies. *School Psychology Review, 23,* 619–639.

Glutting, J. J., McDermott, P. A., Prifitera, A., & McGrath, E. A. (1994). Core profile types for the WISC-III and WIAT: Their development and application in identifying multivariate IQ-achievement discrepancies. *School Psychology Review, 23,* 619–639.

Goldstein, S., & Reynolds, C. R. (1999). *Handbook of neurodevelopmental and genetic disorders in children*. New York: Guilford.

Goldstein, S., & Schwebach, A. (2009). Learning disabilities. In C. Reynolds and E. F. Janzen (Eds.), *Handbook of clinical neuropsychology*. New York: Guilford.

Gordon, M. (1993). Do computerized measures of attention have a legitimate role in ADHD evaluations? *ADHD Report, 1,* 5–6.

Greenberg, L. (1991). *Test of variables of attention (TOVA)*. St. Paul, MN: Attention Technology.

Hale, J. B., Fiorello, C. A., Bertin, M., & Sherman, R. (2003). Predicting math competency through neuropsychological interpretation of WISC-III variance components. *Journal of Psychoeducational Assessment, 21,* 358–380.

Hale, J. B., & Fiorello, C. A. (2004). *School neuropsychology: A practitioner's handbook*. New York, NY: Guilford.

Harvey, J. R., & Chernouskas, C. A. (1995, October). *Diagnosis and description of attention deficit hyperactivity disorder with the Woodcock-Johnson Psychoeducational Battery (revised)*. Paper presented at the C.H.A.D.D. National Conference, Washington, DC.

Homack, S. R., & Reynolds, C. R. (2005). Continuous performance testing in differential diagnosis of ADHD. *ADHD Report*, 13(5), 5–9.

Jensen, A. R. (1998). *The "g" factor: The science of mental ability*. Westport, CT: Praeger.

Kagan, J. (1964). The Matching Familiar Figures test. Unpublished. Harvard University, Cambridge.

Kaufman, A. S. (1979). *Intelligence testing with the WISC-R*. New York: Wiley.

Kaufman, A. S., & Kaufman, N. L. (1983). *Kaufman Assessment Battery for Children*. Circle Pines, MN: American Guidance.

Kaufman, A. S., & Kaufman, N. L. (2004). *Kaufman Assessment Battery for Children* (2nd ed.). Circle Pines, MN: American Guidance.

Levine, M. D. (1992). Commentary: Attentional disorders: Elusive entities and their mistaken identities. *Journal of Child Neurology*, 7, 449–453.

Lezak, M. D. (1983). *Neuropsychological assessment* (2nd ed.). New York: Oxford University Press.

Lynn, R., Fergusson, D. M., & Horwood, L. J. (2005). Sex differences on the WISC-R in New Zealand. *Personality and Individual Differences*, 39, 103–114.

Lynn, R., Raine, A., Venables, P. H., Mednick, S. A., & Irwing, P. (2005). Sex differences on the WISC-R in Mauritius. *Intelligence*, 33, 527–533.

Lyon, G. R., Fletcher, J. M., Shaywitz, B. A., Wood, F. B., Schulte, A., & Olson, R. (2001). *Learning disabilities: An evidenced-based conceptualization* (pp. 259–283). Washington, DC: Fordham Foundation.

McGee, R. A., Clark, S. E., & Symons, D. K. (2000). Does the Conners' Continuous Performance Test aid in ADHD diagnosis? *Journal of Abnormal Child Psychology*, 28, 415–424.

Mealer, C., Morgan, S., & Luscomb, R. (1996). Cognitive functioning of ADHD and non-ADHD boys on the WISC-III and WRAML: An analysis within a memory model. *Journal of Attention Disorders*, 1, 133–147.

Medco Health Solutions (2005). ADHD medication use growing faster among adults than children: New research. www.medco.com.

Mercer, C. D., King-Sears, P., & Mercer, A. R (1990). Learning disability definitions and criteria used by state education departments. *Learning Disability Quarterly*, 13, 141–152.

Molter, R. (1995, March). *Freedom from distractibility or auditory processing problems: A critical look at the WISC-III factor*. Paper presented at the *Learning Disabilities Association Annual Conference*, Orlando, FL.

Naglieri, J. A. (1997). *Naglieri Nonverbal Ability Test multilevel form*. San Antonio, TX: The Psychological Corporation.

Naglieri, J. A. (1999). *Essentials of CAS assessment*. New York: Wiley.

Naglieri, J. A. (2000). Can profile analysis of ability test scores work? An illustration using the PASS theory and CAS with an unselected cohort. *School Psychology Quarterly* 15, 419–433.

Naglieri, J. A. (2002). Best practices in interventions for school psychologists: A cognitive approach to problem solving. In A. Thomas & J. Grimmes (Eds.), *Best practices in school psychology* (4th ed., pp. 1373–1392). Bethesda, MD: NASP.

Naglieri, J. A. (2003). *Naglieri Nonverbal Ability Test individual form*. San Antonio, TX: The Psychological Corporation.

Naglieri, J. A., (2005). The Cognitive Assessment System. In D. P. Flanagan and P. L. Harrison (Eds.), *Contemporary intellectual assessment* (2nd ed., pp. 441–460). New York: Guilford.

Naglieri, J. A. (2008). Traditional IQ: 100 years of misconception and its relationship to minority representation in gifted programs. In J. L. Van Tassel-Baska (Ed.), *Alternative assessments with gifted and talented students* (pp. 67–88). Waco, TX: Prufrock Press.

Naglieri, J. A., & Bornstein, B. T. (2003). Intelligence and achievement: Just how correlated are they? *Journal of Psychoeducational Assessment*, 21, 244–260.

Naglieri, J. A., & Das, J. P. (1997a). *Cognitive Assessment System interpretive handbook*. Itasca, IL: Riverside

Naglieri, J. A., & Das, J. P. (1997b). The PASS cognitive processing theory. In R. F. Dillon (Ed.), *Handbook on testing* (pp. 138–163). London: Greenwood Press.

Naglieri, J. A., & Ford, D. Y. (2003). Addressing under-representation of gifted minority children using the Naglieri Nonverbal Ability Test (NNAT). *Gifted Child Quarterly*, 47, 155–160.

Naglieri, J. A., & Ford, D. Y. (2005). Increasing minority children's participation in gifted classes using the NNAT: A response to Lohman. *Gifted Child Quarterly*, 49, 29–36.

Naglieri, J. A., Goldstein, S., DeLauder, B. Y., & Schwebach, A. (2005). Relationships between the

WISC-III and the Cognitive Assessment System with Conners' rating scales and continuous performance tests. *Archives of Clinical Neuropsychology, 20*, 385–401.

Naglieri, J. A., Goldstein, S., DeLauder, B. Y., & Schwebach, A. (2006). WISC-III and CAS: Which correlates higher with achievement for a clinical sample? *School Psychology Quarterly, 21*, 62–76.

Naglieri, J. A., Goldstein, S., & Schwebach, A. (2004). Can there be reliable identification of ADHD with divergent conceptualizations and inconsistent test results? *ADHD Report, 4*, 6–9.

Naglieri, J. A., & Rojahn, J. (2004). Construct validity of the PASS theory and CAS: Correlations with achievement. *Journal of Educational Psychology, 96*, 174–181.

Naglieri, J. A., & Yazzie, C. (1983). Comparison of the WISC-Rand PPVT-R with Navajo children. *Journal of Clinical Psychology, 39*, 598–600.

National Research Council (2002). *Minority students in special and gifted education*. S. Donovan, & C. T. Cross (Eds.). National Academies Press: Washington DC.

Paolito, A. W. (1999). Clinical validation of the Cognitive Assessment System for children with ADHD. *ADHD Report, 1*, 1–5.

Peterson, K. M., & Shinn, M. R. (2002). Severe discrepancy models: Which best explains school identification practices for learning disabilities? *School Psychology Review, 31*, 459–476.

Prifitera, A., & Dersh, J. (1993). Base rates of WISC-III diagnostic subtest patterns among normal, learning disabled and ADHD samples. *Journal of Psychoeducational Assessment: WISC-III Monograph*, 43–55.

Ramsey, M. C., & Reynolds, C. R. (2003). Relations between intelligence and achievement tests. In G. Goldstein and S. Beers (Eds.), *Comprehensive handbook of psychological assessment* (pp. 25–50). New York: Wiley.

Riccio, C. A., Reynolds, C. R., & Lowe, P. A. (2001). *Clinical applications of continuous performance tests: Measuring attention and impulsive responding in children and adults*. New York: Wiley.

Rindermann, H. (2007). The bigg-factor of national cognitive ability. *European Journal of Personality, 21*(5), 767–787.

Rojahn, J., & Naglieri, J. A. (2006). Developmental gender differences on the Naglieri Nonverbal Ability Test in a nationally normed sample of 5–17 year olds. *Intelligence, 34*, 253–260.

Sattler, J. M. (1988). *Assessment of children* (3rd ed.). San Diego, CA: Author.

Siegel, L. S. (1988). IQ is irrelevant to the definition of learning disabilities. *Journal of Learning Disabilities, 22*, 469–479.

Silverstein, A. B. (1982). Pattern analysis as simultaneous statistical inference. *Journal of Consulting and Clinical Psychology, 50*, 234–240.

Silverstein, A. B. (1993). Type I, Type II, and other types of errors in pattern analysis. *Psychological Assessment, 5*, 72–74.

Slate, J. R. (1998, November). Sex differences in WISC-III IQs: Time for separate norms? *Journal of Psychology: Interdisciplinary and Applied, 132*(6), 677–679.

Szatmari, P., Offord, D. R., Siegel, L. S., Finlayson, M. A. et al. (1990). The clinical significance of neurocognitive impairments among children with psychiatric disorders: Diagnosis and situational specificity. *Journal of Child Psychology and Psychiatry & Allied Disciplines, 31*, 287–299.

Ullmann, R. K., Sleator, E. K., & Sprague, R. K. (1988). *ADD-H: Comprehensive teacher's rating scale* (2nd ed.). Champaign, IL: MetriTech, Inc.

United States Department of Education (1993). *National excellence: A case for developing America's talent*. Washington, DC: Author.

Van Zomeren, A. H. (1981). *Reaction time and attention after closed head injury*. Lisse, Switzerland: Swets & Zeitinger.

Wechsler, D. (1939). *Wechsler-Bellevue Intelligence Scale*. New York: The Psychological Corporation.

Wechsler, D. (1989). *Wechsler Intelligence Scale for Children—III*. San Antonio, TX: Psychological Corporation.

Wechsler, D. (1991). *Wechsler Intelligence Scale for Children—third edition manual*. San Antonio, TX: Psychological Corporation.

Wechsler, D. (1992). *Wechsler Individual Achievement Scale*. San Antonio, TX: Psychological Corporation.

Wechsler, D. (2003). *Wechsler Intelligence Scale for Children—IV*. San Antonio, TX: Psychological Corporation.

Wechsler, D., & Naglieri, J. A. (2006). *Wechsler Nonverbal Scale of Ability*. San Antonio, TX: Harcourt Assessment.

Wender, P. H. (1975). The minimal brain dysfunction syndrome. *Annual Review of Medicine, 26*, 45–62.

Wilson, L. R., & Cone, T. (1994). The regression equation method of determining academic discrepancy. *Journal of School Psychology, 22*, 95–110.

Ysseldyke, J., Algozzine, B., & Epps, S. (1983). A logical and empirical analysis of current practice in classifying students as handicapped. *Exceptional Children, 50*, 160–166.

PART II

Intelligence Tests Measuring Diverse Abilities

The Cognitive Assessment System

Jack A. Naglieri, Cara Conway

THEORY UNDERLYING THE CAS

The *Cognitive Assessment System (CAS)* (Naglieri & Das, 1997a) is a multidimensional measure of ability based on a cognitive and neuropsychological processing theory called *Planning, Attention, Simultaneous, and Successive (PASS)* (Naglieri, 1999a, 2005). The PASS theory described by Naglieri and Das (1997b, 2005) is a reconceptualization of intelligence largely, but not solely, based on the neuropsychological work of A. R. Luria (1966, 1973, 1980, 1982). The four processes that make up the PASS theory represent a blend of cognitive and neuropsychological constructs, such as executive functioning (Planning) and selective attention (Attention), including tests that in the past were often arguably described as nonverbal/visual-spatial (Simultaneous) and sequencing/memory (Successive) (Naglieri & Das, 2002).

The PASS theory is a different approach to understanding intelligence that not only expands the idea of what "abilities" should be measured, but also stresses the significance of basic psychological or cognitive processes. Additionally, the functions of the brain that encompass the PASS processes are considered the building blocks of ability conceptualized within a cognitive processing framework. While

the theory may have its roots in neuropsychology, "its branches are spread over developmental and educational psychology" (Varnhagen & Das, 1986, p. 130). Thus, with its connections to developmental and cognitive processing, the PASS theory offers an advantage in explanatory power over the notion of traditional general intelligence (Naglieri & Das, 2002).

PASS Defined

The four cognitive processes that make up the PASS theory are each associated with different brain regions, cognitive abilities, and behaviors (Naglieri, Conway, & Goldstein, 2007). The four processes of the PASS theory are described more fully below.

Planning is a mental activity that provides cognitive control, intentionality, organization, self-regulation and use of processes, knowledge, and skills. This includes self-monitoring and impulse control as well as generation, evaluation, and execution of a plan. This process may involve control over the other three processes, as well as providing the means to solve problems and to acquire knowledge and skills.

The essence of the construct of Planning and tests to measure it is that they provide a novel problem-solving situation for which one does not have a previously acquired strategy. This is also similar to how the concept of executive function has been described. O'Shanick and O'Shanick (1994) describe executive functions as including the abilities to formulate and set goals, assess strengths and weaknesses, plan and/or direct activities, initiate and/or inhibit behavior, monitor current activities, and evaluate results. This is very similar to the description provided by Hayes, Gifford, and Ruckstuhl (1996). Executive functions include abilities to formulate a goal, plan, carry out goal-directed behaviors effectively, and monitor and self-correct spontaneously and reliably (Lezak, 1995). These skills are essential for fulfilling most daily responsibilities and maintaining appropriate social behavior. This view is closely aligned with the definition of Planning provided by Goldberg (2001), particularly in that it includes self-regulation, skillful and flexible use of strategies, allocation of attention and memory, response inhibition, goal setting, and self-monitoring and self-correction (Eslinger, 1996).

Planning is a frontal lobe function. As one of the prominent capacities that differentiate humans from other primates, Planning is associated with the prefrontal cortex. The prefrontal cortex "plays a central role in forming goals and objectives and then in devising plans of action required to attain these goals. It selects the cognitive skills required to implement the plans, coordinates these skills, and applies them in a correct order. Finally, the prefrontal cortex is responsible for evaluating our actions as success or failure relative to our intentions" (Goldberg, 2001, p. 24). Planning helps to achieve goals by aiding in the development of strategies needed to accomplish tasks. Therefore, Planning is essential to all activities that require one to figure out how to solve a problem. This includes self-monitoring and impulse control as well as creation, assessment, and execution of a plan. Thus, Planning permits the generation of solutions, discriminating use of knowledge and skills, as well as control of Attention, Simultaneous, and Successive processes (Das, Kar, & Parrila, 1996).

Although a variety of assessment tools have been proposed to assess executive functions, the results often yield conflicting data given the very broad definition of these functions (e.g., for a review of this issue in the assessment of ADHD, see Barkley, 2003). Planning in the PASS theory offers a more finite description that may be characterized as executive function.

Attention is conceptualized (Naglieri & Das, 2005) as a mental function that provides focused, selective cognitive activity over time that is resistant to distraction. The base of the brain allows one to focus selective attention toward a stimulus over a period of time without the loss of attention to other, competing stimuli. The longer attention is needed, the more that activity requires vigilance. The process is linked with the orienting response, and is involved when one must demonstrate focused, selective, sustained, and effortful activity. Focused attention involves directed concentration toward a specific activity and selective attention is important for the inhibition of responses to distracting stimuli. Sustained attention refers to the variation of performance over time, which can affect the different amount of effort necessary to solve the test. Intentions and goals mandated by the Planning process control Attention, while knowledge and skills play an integral part in the process as well. This construct was conceptualized and operationalized similarly to the attention work of Schneider, Dumais, and Shiffrin (1984) and Posner and Boies (1971), particularly the selectivity aspect of attention, which relates to the deliberate discrimination between stimuli.

Simultaneous processing is a mental activity by which a person integrates stimuli into interrelated groups or a whole. Simultaneous processing tests typically have strong spatial aspects for this reason, but can involve both nonverbal and verbal content as long as the cognitive demand of the task requires the integration of information. This ability to identify patterns as interrelated elements is made possible by the parieto-occipital-temporal brain regions. The construct of Simultaneous processing is conceptually related to the examination of visual-spatial reasoning often seen in progressive matrices tests, such as those originally developed by Penrose and Raven (1936) and now included in nonverbal scales of intelligence tests such as the Wechsler Nonverbal Scale of Ability (Wechsler & Naglieri, 2006), the Naglieri Nonverbal Ability Test (Naglieri, 2008), and the Stanford-Binet Fifth Edition (Roid, 2003).

Successive processing is a mental activity by which a person processes stimuli in a specific serial order to form a chain-like progression. To require true Successive processing, the information must not be able to be grouped into a pattern (like the number 442558 organized into 44-2-55-8). Successive processing involves both the recognition of stimuli in sequence and the formation of sounds and movements in order. For this reason, Successive processing is involved with recall of information in order as well as the syntax of language and the phonological analysis, which it has been conceptually and experimentally related to (Das, Naglieri, & Kirby, 1994). The concept of Successive processing is similar to the concept of sequential processing included in the KABC-II (Kaufman & Kaufman, 2004).

DESCRIPTION OF THE CAS

The four PASS processes are assessed using the CAS (Naglieri & Das, 1997a), which was specifically structured according to the PASS theory. The CAS measures the four basic psychological processes using 12 subtests (three for each of the four scales) that are described in more detail below.

Planning Subtests

The three subtests that make up the Planning scale are Matching Numbers, Planned Codes, and Planned Connections. In the Matching Numbers subtest, the examiner introduces the child to four pages containing eight rows of numbers. The child is instructed to underline the two numbers that are the same in each row. The items were constructed so that children can use strategies such as locating the match by focusing on the last number as opposed to the first number (e.g., 318, 313, 381, 318, 813, 311) and omitting one option that does not begin with the same number that most of the others do (e.g., 813).

The Planned Codes subtest contains two pages with empty boxes sorted in seven rows and eight columns. At the top of each page is a legend that has a specific set of codes (e.g., A = XO; B = XX; C = OO). The child is instructed to write in the correct code beneath each corresponding letter. The letters are arranged on the page in a manner that gives the child the chance to use a strategy, or plan, of filling in all the codes. Planned Codes is a variation of similar coding subtests (e.g., Yoakum & Yerkes, 1920).

The child is directed to connect numbers in sequences that appear in a quasi-random order (e.g., 1-2-3, etc.) in the Planned Connections subtest. The child connects numbers and letters in sequential order for the last two items, alternating between numbers and letters (e.g., 1-A-2-B, etc.). A child can apply various strategies to this task, such as scanning the page for the next number or letter, and looking back to the previous step to know more easily what comes next (e.g., when the child reaches B in the sequence 1-A-2-B-3-C looking back to the number 2, the next step is more easily obtained). For a complete list of the strategies used by children on all the Planning tests, see Naglieri and Das (1997b) and for further discussion of strategy use, see Winsler and Naglieri (2003).

Planned Connections is similar to the Trial Making procedure that was originally part of the Army Individual Test of General Ability (Adjutant General's Office, 1944) and used by Armitage (1946), Reitan (1955), and Spreen and Gaddes (1969). Tests similar to Planned Connections, such as the Trail Making test (Lezak, 1995), are sometimes used to evaluate frontal lobe functioning (Naglieri & Das, 1997b).

Attention Subtests

The three subtests on the CAS that measure Attention processing are Expressive Attention, Number Detection, and Receptive Attention. For Expressive Attention, children 7 years and younger are presented pictures of animals arranged in rows. Animals that are typically small are drawn to appear large and large animals are drawn to appear small. The child is instructed to indicate the real size of the animal (e.g., if a horse was drawn to appear small, the child would respond "large"). In the Expressive Attention for children 8 years and older, the children are given three pages to finish that are similar to the well-known Stroop test (Lezak, 1995). The child reads color words (i.e., Red, Blue, Yellow, and Green) printed in black font and presented in a quasi-random order on the first page. On the second page, the child is instructed to name out loud the colors of a series of rectangles printed in the same colors that were introduced as words on the first page. On the third page, the color words are printed in different ink colors than the colors the words name (e.g., the word *Green* would appear in red ink). The child must say the color the word is printed in and resist the urge to read the name of the color.

The Number Detection subtest requires children to find the target stimuli (e.g., the numbers 1, 2, and 3 printed in an open font) among many distracters, such as the same numbers printed in a different font. This subtest is modeled after the work of Schneider, Dumais, and Shiffrin (1984) on selective attention.

The Receptive Attention subtest consists of two pages. On the first page, targets are letters that are physically the same (e.g., LL but not Ll). For the second page, targets are letters that have the same name (e.g., Ll but not Pl). This test was modeled after the attention research of Posner and Boies (1971).

SIMULTANEOUS SUBTESTS

The Simultaneous scale on the CAS contains the Nonverbal Matrices, Verbal Spatial Relations, and Figure Memory subtests. Nonverbal Matrices is a traditional progressive matrix test that includes items that have a variety of shapes and geometric designs that are connected through spatial or logical organization. The child must appreciate the interrelationships for each question and choose the best of six possible options that completes the matrix. Progressive matrix tasks have been included in PASS research since the 1970s and have been used to measure simultaneous processing in over 30 published papers (for summaries of these studies, see Das, Kirby, & Jarman, 1979, and Das, Naglieri, & Kirby, 1994). The construction of the Nonverbal Matrices was based on items that conformed to the item types found in the Matrix Analogies Test (Naglieri, 1985).

The Verbal Spatial Relations subtest measures the comprehension of logical and grammatical descriptions of spatial relationships. For this subtest, the child is shown six drawings, arranged in a specific spatial manner, and a printed question. Then, the child is told to select one of the six drawings that best answers the question. A typical item may ask: "Which picture shows a diamond below a circle?," with six options that include these and other shapes in various spatial arrangements. This test was based on the concept that Simultaneous processing underlies the understanding of what Luria (1982) explained as logical and grammatical relationships, as measured by the Token test (Lezak, 1995).

On the Figure Memory subtest, the child is presented a two- or three-dimensional geometric figure for 5 seconds and then is presented with a response page that has the original geometric figure embedded in a larger, more complex geometric pattern. The child is then asked to identify the original design. Luria (1966) utilized both copying designs and drawing from memory as measures of simultaneous processing. Both

Figure Copying (Ilg & Ames, 1964) and the Memory-for-Designs test (Graham & Kendall, 1960) served as models for the Figure Memory test.

Successive Subtests

The Successive scale on the CAS contains the subtests Word Series, Sentence Repetition, and Sentence Questions. In Word Series, the child is read a series of words and then asked to repeat the words in the same order. This subtest uses nine single-syllable, high-frequency words. The repetition of words and digits in order was recommended by Luria (1966) and has been used since 1972 as a measure of Successive processing in the PASS theory. Summaries of these studies can be found in Das, Kirby, and Jarman (1979) and Das, Naglieri, and Kirby (1994).

Twenty sentences are read to the child for the Sentence Repetition subtest. The child is then instructed to repeat each sentence exactly as presented. The sentences are composed of color words (e.g., "The blue yellows the green"), which reduces semantic meaning from the sentences.

The same type of sentences that are used in the Sentence Repetition subtest are used on the Sentence Questions; however, in this test the child is read a sentence and asked a question about it. For example, the examiner reads, "The blue yellows the green," and asks the child, "Who yellows the green?" The correct answer is "the blue." The development of both Sentence Repetition and Sentence Questions followed Luria's (1966, 1982) explanation of how Successive processing underlies a child's understanding of the syntactic organization of language.

ADMINISTRATION OF THE CAS

Appropriate Testing Conditions

The CAS, like any test, needs to be administered and scored as prescribed in the test's Administration and Scoring Manual (Naglieri &

Das, 1997c). While it is the obligation of the administrator to make sure that administration procedures are consistent with applicable professional standards, it is also assumed that examiners will create an appropriate environment for the standardized test. A description of general, good testing practices will not be reviewed here; however, one can obtain such information through such resources as Aiken (1987) and Sattler (1988). Only specific issues about the administration of the CAS are addressed here.

Seating Arrangement

Proper administration of the CAS can be obtained only if the examiner is within reach of the child and can closely observe the child's actions. This is especially important for the Planning tests that involve recording the strategies used by the child (see the section later in this chapter on Strategy Assessment). Examiners would likely find sitting across from the child or across the corner of a table most appropriate for this instrument.

Administration Directions

The CAS instructions typically involve both verbal and nonverbal instructions. Examiners need to carefully observe the gestures (indicated in parenthetical statements following or preceding the text) that correspond to the oral directions.

Administration Information

There are two places that provide information about administration of the test—the Administration and Scoring Manual (Naglieri & Das, 1997c) and the Record Form. Both sources provide the same information about various administration issues in a text box at the top of their respective sections. This information includes what pages are used in the Response or Stimulus Books, whether a stopwatch or red pencil is needed, time limits, which items to give, and so on. This redundancy provides examiners ample opportunity to obtain information about how to give the subtests.

Standard and Basic Batteries

There are two versions of the CAS. The Standard Battery contains all 12 subtests, while the Basic Battery is made up of only 8 of the subtests. Each of the two batteries is composed of Planning, Attention, Simultaneous, and Successive subtests. If the Basic Battery is administered, the first two subtests in each of the four PASS Scales are given. The subtests included in the Basic Battery are clearly noted in several ways on the Record Form and in the Administration and Scoring Manual. The subtests that form the Basic Battery appear in dark blue boxes with white lettering on the front of the Record Form. Regardless of which version is administered, both yield PASS Scale and Full Scale standard scores with a mean of 100 and *SD* of 15.

Subtest Order

To retain the integrity of the test and reduce the influence of extraneous variables on the child's performance, it is necessary that the CAS subtests be administered in the prescribed order. The Planning, Simultaneous, Attention, and Successive order was determined to maximize the validity of the scales. For example, the Planning tests are administered first because they provide the fewest restrictions on how the child may complete the task. This gives children considerable flexibility to solve the subtest in any manner they choose, which is the goal of these subtests. In contrast, the Attention subtests must be completed in the prescribed manner (e.g., left to right, top to bottom). By administering the Planning subtests before the Attention subtests, the amount of constraint increases over time. If the Attention subtests were administered before the Planning ones, some children could be inhibited by the more structured instruction. It is also strongly recommended that either the 8- or 12-subtest version be used in its entirety

rather than a smaller number of subtests being selected.

Age Partition

Instructions and, in some cases, sets of items differ for children aged 5–7 and 8–17 years. In addition, two of the Attention subtests have different types of materials so that the content of the test would be more appropriate for children in the two age groups. Specialized content was necessary to ensure that children aged 5–7 would easily understand the items and that older children (aged 8–17) would not view subtests as too simple.

All of the CAS subtests, except two, are given to all children regardless of age. The exceptions are Speech Rate, which is administered only at ages 5–7 years, and Sentence Questions, which is given only to children 8–17 years of age. This information appears in the Record Form and Administration and Scoring Manual (Naglieri & Das, 1997c). The items, which are to be given for children aged 5–7 or 8–17 years, are also indicated in the way the Record Form is graphically constructed. The form includes boxes that are arranged so that they are filled in only when the test is given to the appropriate age group.

Start and Discontinue Rules

Children aged 5–7 always begin with the first item, but children aged 8–17 typically begin with a more advanced item. The exception to this rule is for Planned Codes (all children get the same items) and Speech Rate (all items are given to children aged 5–7 years). A discontinue rule of four consecutively numbered item failures is applied to all Simultaneous subtests and all Successive subtests except Speech Rate.

Time Limits

The time limits for items vary and for that reason they are provided in the Administration

Directions Manual and in the Record Form. These limits are provided in total seconds (e.g., 150") as well as minutes and seconds (e.g., 2:30) to accommodate professionals who use digital or analog stopwatches. The point at which to begin timing is clearly indicated in the Administration and Scoring Manual (Naglieri & Das, 1997c). In those instances where time limits are not provided (e.g., Nonverbal Matrices), examiners should exercise good judgment when encouraging the child to attempt the next item.

Rates of Presentation

There are six subtests that require stimuli be presented at a specific rate or for an exact period of time. There is one successive subtest that requires administration at the rate of one word per second (Word Series), and two that are presented at the rate of two words per second (Sentence Repetition and Sentence Questions). Figure Memory involves stimuli that are presented for exactly five seconds, and there is a 30-second exposure time limit for each item in the Verbal-Spatial Relations subtest. These time limits must be followed exactly to ensure comparison to the normative sample.

Strategy Assessment

All the CAS Planning subtests include an observational phase called *Strategy Assessment*. This means that the examiner observes whether the child used strategies to complete the items. Strategy Assessment was developed to obtain information about how the child completed the items and is used to help describe the standard scores that were obtained (see the later section on interpretation). This information allows the examiner to go beyond the score and understand the methods the child used during planning. The specific strategy used is then interpreted in relation to the standard score and the percentage of children who used that strategy in the standardization sample. This can help explain a particularly high or low Planning score and

be integrated into the overall pool of data that comprises the entire evaluation.

Strategy Assessment includes two parts: Observed Strategies and Reported Strategies. Observed Strategies are those seen by the examiner through nonobtrusive means when the child completed the items. Examiners often evaluate how children complete test items through careful observation during testing. Reported Strategies are obtained following completion of the item(s) of each Planning subtest. The examiner obtains this information by saying, "Tell me how you did these," "How did you find what you were looking for?," or a similar statement or question. The strategies can be communicated by the child by either verbal or nonverbal (gesturing) means.

To facilitate recording of strategies that were both "Observed" and "Reported," a Strategy Assessment Checklist is included in the Record Form. Examiners indicate which strategy or strategies were used by placing a checkmark in the appropriate location(s) during the observation and reporting stages. Unique strategies can be recorded in a blank space provided.

Provide Help Guidelines

One of the unique features of the CAS is the opportunity to provide help. The instructions for administration of the CAS have been written to ensure that the child will understand the demands of every subtest. Several methods have been used to ensure that the child understands what is being requested. This includes sample and demonstration items as well as opportunities for the examiner to clarify the requirements of the task. For example, after the first sample in Expressive Attention, the child is asked whether he or she is ready to begin. If the child does not seem ready or appears in any way confused or uncertain, the examiner is instructed to "provide a brief explanation if necessary." This instruction is intended to give the examiner the freedom to explain what the child must do in whatever terms are considered necessary so as to ensure that the child understands the task. This interaction can be in any form, including gestures, verbal statement, or communication in any language. The intent of this instruction is to give the examiner full decision making in clarifying the demands of the subtest and to allow the examiner to be certain that the child was well informed about what to do. This instruction, however, is not intended to teach the child how to do the test, but rather to tell the child what is required.

Bilingual or Hearing-Impaired Children

The CAS instructions for administration were designed to give the examiner flexibility to interact with the child to assure that good data are obtained. It is assumed that the child has an adequate working knowledge of English so that he or she will benefit from the samples and demonstrations provided. It is, as discussed above, possible to augment the English instructions when the statement "provide additional help when needed" is given. That is, during initial introductory portions of the subtests, examiners who have the knowledge to interact with the child in his or her native language or through another means such as sign language may do so when instructed to provide assistance. The child's need for information in another language or method can become obvious when the child asks for help using another language, or if it is apparent that the child is hearing impaired, or the child does not respond to the instruction. In such instances, it is the responsibility of the examiner to decide when to use another method of communication. It is also the responsibility of the examiner to determine whether, because he or she does not know the child's other language, another examiner should evaluate the child.

Spoiled Subtests

It is possible that one of the three regularly administered subtests in the Standard Battery is spoiled. There are two options in such an instance. First, the sum of three subtests can

be estimated using a Prorating table found in Naglieri (1999a). Second, examiners could use the remaining two subtests and compute the PASS Scale using the Basic Battery norms. Because the Full Scale requires either 8 or 12 subtests, the calculation of the Full Scale would have to be computed on the basis of the Basic, not Standard, Battery. If one of the Basic Battery subtests is spoiled during administration, practitioners should give the last subtest on the scale. That subtest scaled score could be used as one of the two scores needed to obtain a Basic Battery sum of scaled scores and the Full Scale. This practice should be limited to those rare instances where limitations demand variation from the normally prescribed method of calculating scores for the Basic Battery.

SCORING THE CAS

There are two methods for scoring the CAS. First, the *CAS Rapid Score* (Naglieri, 2002) software can be used to convert all raw scores to standard scores, make comparisons among the PASS scores, compare PASS and Full Scale scores to achievement, and obtain a written description of the results. Alternatively, the CAS can be manually scored. Essentially, the sequence of events follows the pattern: Subtest raw scores are obtained, and then raw scores are converted to subtest scaled scores. After that, the PASS Scale standard scores are obtained from the sum of the respective subtest scaled scores, and, finally, the CAS Full Scale is obtained from the sum of all subtest scaled scores.

Subtest Raw Scores

The CAS subtest raw scores are calculated using four different methods based on which aspects of the child's performance are being measured. These methods include one or more of the following dimensions: (1) the number correct; (2) time to completion; (3) and number of false detections. These methods of evaluating a child's performance are used either in isolation or in combination based on the goals of the subtest. Some subtest raw scores, therefore, are based on: (1) number correct, (2) total time, (3) number correct and total time, and (4) number correct, total time, and number of false detections.

Converting Raw Scores to Subtest Scaled Scores

The CAS subtest scaled scores (mean of 10 and *SD* of 3) are obtained using age-based tables included in Appendix A.1 (pp. 99–177) of the Administration and Scoring Manual (Naglieri & Das, 1997c). The Appendix is divided according to the child's chronological age in years, months, and days. Locate the appropriate conversion table (the first page of the subtest norms section includes an index showing which pages in the manual to apply to each age group).

PASS Scale Standard Scores

Each of the four PASS Scales is derived from the sum of the subtest scaled scores. For the Standard Battery, sum all three subtest scaled scores within each PASS Scale. For the Basic Battery, sum only the first two subtests within each PASS Scale. The Full Scale is obtained from the sum of scaled scores for both the Standard and Basic Batteries and is calculated by summing the four "Sum of Subtest Scaled Scores" values found on the front page of the Record Form. The PASS Scales (mean of 100 and *SD* of 15) are derived from the sum of subtest scaled scores using Appendix B (pp. 179–191) of the Administration and Scoring Manual (Naglieri & Das, 1997c). Each PASS Scale has its own table. The table provides the standard score, percentile, and estimated true-score-based confidence intervals (90% and 95%).

Obtaining Full Scale Standard Scores

The CAS Full Scale (mean of 100 and *SD* of 15) is obtained from the sum of the scaled scores used to obtain the four PASS Scales using Appendix B (pp. 179–191) of the Administration and Scoring Manual (Naglieri & Das, 1997c). The Full Scale is computed from the sum of 8 or 12 subtests if the Basic and Standard Batteries, respectively, are given. The sum of the subtest scaled scores, which appears on the front of the Record Form, is used to obtain the standard score. Like the PASS conversion system, this table provides the standard score, percentile, and estimated true-score-based confidence intervals (90% and 95%) for all possible raw scores.

CAS Rapid Score Software

The CAS Rapid Score (Naglieri, 2002) software is uniquely designed around the CAS Record Form and functions as a portal for data entry that is graphically configured to mimic the child's responses that were recorded during administration. For example, Figure 3.1 provides the CAS Rapid Score window for entry of data for the Planned Connections and Nonverbal Matrices subtests. The configuration of the computer image is nearly identical to the configuration in the CAS Record Form. Examiners simply insert the time scores for Planned Connections and the child's response or the score for each Matrices item. The appropriate subtest raw score is automatically calculated and transferred to the front of the Record Form. Once all subtest raw scores or all raw scores are entered on the electronic version of the front of the CAS Record Form (see Figure 3.2), then the standard scores, percentile ranks, and confidence intervals are provided. These findings can be printed and attached to the original CAS Record Form.

Analysis of the differences among the four PASS Scales, subtest analysis, and comparisons of each PASS Scale and the Full Scale with a variety of achievement tests is also provided (see Figure 3.3). Finally, a narrative report of the CAS results can be obtained (see Figure 3.4) and copied and pasted into a word processing program, printed, or converted to a text file.

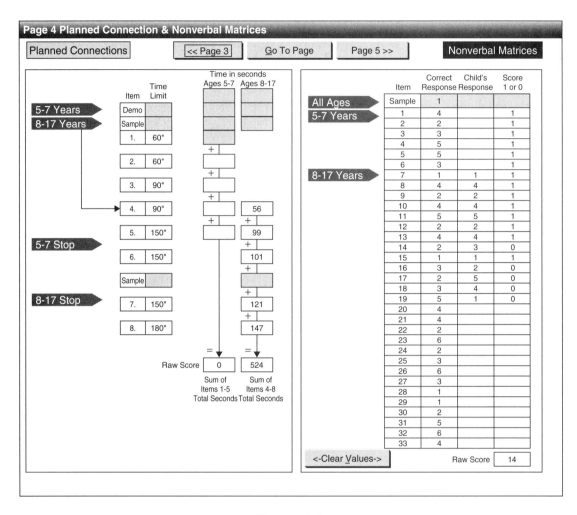

FIGURE 3.1

CAS Rapid Score Subtest Data Entry Screen

STANDARDIZATION, NORMS, AND PSYCHOMETRICS OF THE CAS

Standardization

The CAS was standardized on a sample of 2,200 children aged 5–17 years who were representative of the U.S. population on a number of important demographic variables. The sample is a nationally representative, stratified sample based on gender, race, ethnicity, region, community setting, classroom placement, and parental education (see Naglieri & Das, 1997b, for more details).

Reliability

The CAS Full Scale has a high internal reliability ranging from .95 to .97 for the different age groups. The average reliability coefficients for

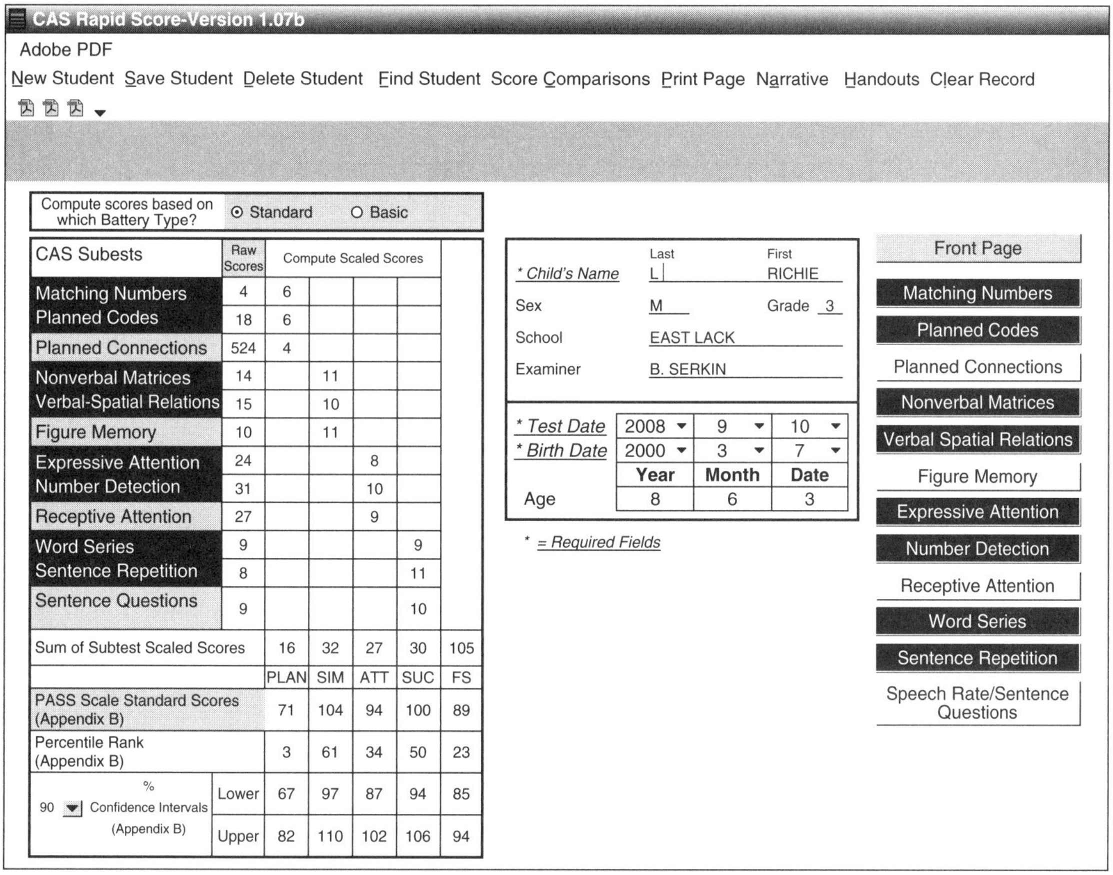

FIGURE 3.2

CAS Rapid Score Summary Page

the scales are .88 (Planning), .88 (Attention), .93 (Simultaneous processing), and .93 (Successive processing).

USE OF THE CAS

Interpretation Methods

The goal of interpreting a child's CAS is to integrate PASS scores with all other information so that a comprehensive view of the child is achieved and a thorough plan for treatment, if appropriate, can be developed, implemented,

and evaluated. The CAS interpretative methods discussed below should be applied flexibly and within the context of all available information about the child.

Steps for Interpreting CAS Results

Interpretation of CAS scores first involves examination of the PASS Scale (and secondarily subtest) variability and comparison of these results with other tests (measures of achievement, rating scales, etc.). A five-step interpretation procedure will be discussed.

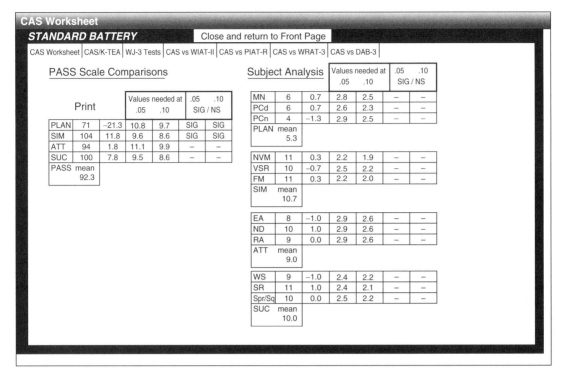

FIGURE 3.3

CAS Rapid Score Comparison of CAS Scores Screen

Step 1—CAS Full Scale and PASS Scale Standard Scores

The first step in interpreting the CAS is to describe the PASS and Full Scale standard scores using descriptive categories that can be found in Appendix C in the Administration and Scoring Manual (Naglieri & Das, 1997c). These categories qualitatively summarize the child's scores but are not intended to be diagnostic. Further description of the scores includes the confidence intervals and percentile ranks that are provided in the sum of scaled score to raw score conversion tables. The Full Scale score should be considered as a good general description of a child's cognitive processing when the four PASS Scale scores are similar. However, when there is significant variability among the PASS Scale standard scores, emphasis on the Full Scale

may obscure important relative strengths and weaknesses. When this happens, then the Full Scale score should be clarified (as a midpoint between extreme scores) and deemphasized.

The PASS and Full Scale standard scores that are associated with normal curve percentile ranks are provided in the respective norms conversion tables in Appendix B in the Administration and Scoring Manual (Naglieri & Das, 1997c). These scores can be interpreted as a ranking of a child's performance relative to those of comparable age in the standardization group.

Confidence intervals provide a way to estimate the precision of test scores and a range of values in which the child's true score is likely to fall. Estimated true-score-based confidence intervals are provided in the PASS and Full Scale standard score conversion tables (Appendix B of

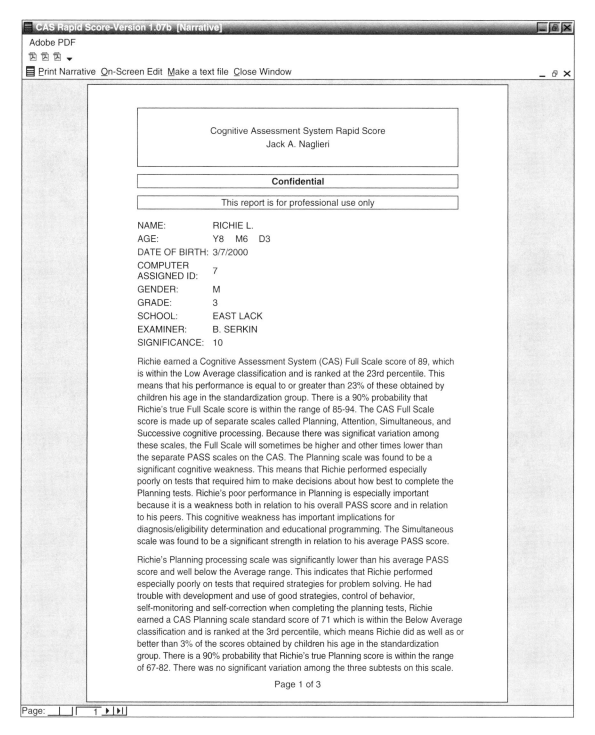

FIGURE 3.4

Narrative Report Text File

the Administration and Scoring Manual), making calculation unnecessary (Naglieri & Das, 1997c).

Step 2—Compare the Four PASS Standard Scores

One of the main purposes of the CAS is to examine the variability across PASS scores to determine whether the child has cognitive strengths or weaknesses. There are two factors to consider when PASS variation is examined. First is the statistical significance of the profile of scores, and second is the percentages of children in the standardization sample with such differences. The statistical significance of the variation in PASS scores, that is, the profile, is evaluated using an intraindividual or ipsative (Kaufman, 1994) method. These procedures help distinguish among differences that are related to error associated with reliability of the scales and when the PASS variation can be interpreted within the context of the theory, related to strategy use, and evaluated in relation to achievement tests.

PASS cognitive processing strengths (scores that are significantly greater than the child's mean score) or weaknesses (scores that are significantly lower than the child's mean score) are found if a score is significantly high or low relative to the child's own level of performance. Because the PASS scores are compared to the individual child's average (and not the normative mean of 100), this tells us about "relative" strengths or weaknesses. This approach has been used in intelligence testing (see Kaufman, 1994; Naglieri, 1993; Sattler, 1988) for some time.

The steps needed to determine whether a child's PASS profile is significant are listed below. The values needed at different levels of significance and for the Standard and Basic Batteries are shown in Figure 3.3 and the CAS Interpretive Handbook (Naglieri & Das, 1997b).

1. Calculate the average of the four PASS standard scores.

2. Subtract the mean from each of the PASS standard scores to obtain the intraindividual difference scores.

3. Compare the intraindividual difference scores (ignore the sign) to the values needed for significance. Differences equal to or greater than the tabled values are significantly different from the child's average PASS Scale standard score.

4. Label any significant score that is above the mean as a strength and those below the mean as weaknesses.

5. Any variation from the mean that is not significant should be considered chance fluctuation.

When a significant weakness in the PASS Scale profile is found, it is also important to consider the level of performance in relation to the standardization sample. For example, if a child has a significant intraindividual difference score that also falls below a score of 90 (in the low-average range or lower), then it should be labeled a cognitive weakness. In contrast, a child could have a significant weakness that still falls in the average range (90–110); this score should be viewed as relative weakness because it is low in relation to the child's mean but still in the average range of normative expectations. In this case, the finding is important for different reasons (it could explain uneven high performance for a child who typically functions very well), but it is not the same as a cognitive weakness. A cognitive weakness is a more serious finding because it represents poor performance relative to peers as well as in comparison to the child's own level.

The frequency of occurrence of PASS profiles can be determined through use of actuarial tables in Appendix D of the CAS Administration and Scoring Manual (Naglieri & Das, 1997c). These tables tell the frequency of occurrence of all possible intraindividual difference scores in the standardization sample. This can help determine how common or rare the PASS profile is and whether a pattern is typical or unusual.

Step 3—Compare Subtest Scores within Each Scale

Variation in CAS subtests, set at a mean of 10 and *SD* of 3, can be examined using the same method used for studying the PASS profile. The subtest scaled scores are compared to the child's mean subtest score and the presence of significant differences determined. In addition, the frequency of occurrence of subtest differences is compared to that found for the normal standardization sample. These variations should also be interpreted within the context of the theory, consideration of strategy use, and other relevant variables. Additionally, although this fine-grain analysis has the advantage of allowing for a more specific examination of the child's performance, it has the disadvantage of involving scores with lower reliability than the PASS Scales.

Step 4—Compare the PASS and Full Scale with Achievement Standard Scores

The CAS scores can be used to help determine whether a child's achievement is below expectations, to assist when interventions are being planned, and when eligibility for special education services is being considered. The exploration of these differences is intended to fit within a theoretical framework designed to discover whether the child has a PASS cognitive weakness and an associated academic weakness. Values for comparing PASS and Full Scale standard scores to various achievement tests are provided in the *CAS Rapid Score* program, the *CAS Interpretive Handbook* (Naglieri & Das, 1997b), and *Essentials of CAS Assessment* (Naglieri, 1999a).

The examination of differences between PASS and achievement can be used to determine whether an ability achievement discrepancy is present. Traditionally, the ability achievement discrepancy has provided information that the child's actual level of achievement is inconsistent with the level predicted by the IQ score. Such a finding, however, does not allow us to know whether there may be a cognitive explanation for the poor academic performance. Assuming that the academic weakness is not due to sensory limitations, lack of educational opportunity, and so forth, we have typically identified a child as disabled partially on the basis of not finding any cognitive problem.

The CAS allows practitioners to detect whether there may be a cognitive explanation for an academic problem. When a child's Full Scale or separate PASS Scale standard scores are significantly higher than achievement, then the discrepancy is found. However, because a child's weakness in a specific area of achievement (e.g., reading decoding) could be related to a specific weakness in a PASS area (e.g., Successive processing), the *consistency* between these two scores (Successive and reading decoding) as well as a *discrepancy* between other CAS Scales and achievement scores can be found. The consistency between successive processing and reading decoding is indicated by a nonsignificant difference between these scores. This evidence contributes to the interpretation that for an individual child Successive processing and reading decoding were related, as suggested by Kirby and Williams (1991), and such a suggestion has intervention implications.

Step 5—Compare CAS Scores over Time

It is sometimes important to administer a test of cognitive functioning on two occasions to monitor recovery or deterioration associated with neurological conditions, or to evaluate cognitive functioning that may have changed over the course of medical treatments. This may be especially important to evaluate the recovery of children who have experienced traumatic brain injury. The statistical significance of the differences between first and second Full Scale and PASS standard scores can be determined using a method described by Atkinson (1991). This involves the comparison of the first test score with a range of scores that represents the variability expected by both regression to the mean and test reliability. The method can be applied when sufficient time has elapsed, for example, 6–12 months, so that minimal practice effects are anticipated.

The ranges of scores that are used to determine when significant change has occurred were calculated for the PASS and Full Scale standard scores for the Standard and Basic Batteries separately. The values appear in Appendix G in the CAS Administration and Scoring Manual (Naglieri & Das, 1997c).

CASE EXAMPLE

This case illustration involves a young boy named Gary who attends a school for children with learning disabilities. This is a real child—one of the subjects who participated in a math intervention study summarized by Naglieri (2008). His name has been changed to protect his identity. Both CAS and actual results of the classroom intervention will be provided to illustrate how the results could be described. Additional test results that might normally accompany the CAS and K-TEA scores are not included in this example. Thus, this example is not intended to provide a complete case study with all other test data that typically would accompany a full evaluation. Instead, the goal is to show how the PASS and Full Scale results might be described and then used to identify an appropriate instructional approach, and finally how the effectiveness of the intervention is determined.

Test Results and Interpretation

Gary earned a Cognitive Assessment System (CAS) Full Scale score of 87, which falls within the Low Average classification. His Full Scale score is ranked at the 19th percentile, which is equal to or greater than 19% of the scores obtained by the children his age who were included in the standardization group. There is a 90% probability that Gary's true Full Scale score falls within the range of 83–92; however, there was significant variation among the separate scales of the CAS. This means that sometimes the Full Scale will be higher and other times lower than the separate scales in the test. For example, his Planning score is classified as Below Average and his Simultaneous scale is Low Average but his Attention and Successive standard scores are within the Average range. Thus, the Full Scale score is inconsistent with some of these scores. Importantly, Gary's Planning scale score is significantly lower than the mean of the four PASS Scales, indicating that an important weakness has been detected.

Gary earned a significantly low score on measures of Planning processing, which indicates that he has a cognitive weakness in this important area. Gary's score on the Planning scale of 75 (90% confidence interval is 71–85) reflects the difficulty he had using efficient and effective strategies for problem solving. He had trouble making good decisions about how to complete several tests and failed to monitor the quality of his work. This resulted in poor completion of tasks due to inadequate and inefficient methods for solving them.

Gary's poor performance in Planning is especially important because it is a weakness both in relation to his overall PASS score and in relation to his peers. The low Planning score suggests that Gary has an important cognitive weakness and suggests he will have difficulty in activities that demand development and/or use of strategies to solve problems, making decisions about how to do things, general control of behavior, and self-monitoring and self-correction.

Gary earned a K-TEA Mathematics Computation score that is as low as his cognitive weakness in Planning. In fact, there is no significant difference between these scores. While his Mathematics Computation score of 76 (5th percentile) is similar to his Planning score (75, 5th percentile), it is significantly lower than his Mathematics Applications score of 91 (27th percentile). Additionally, the Mathematics Computation score is significantly lower than his Simultaneous, Attention, and Successive scores (therefore, an ability achievement discrepancy has been found). In addition, the consistency between his low scores in mathematics computation and Planning processing is likely related (which can be assessed via examination of his responsiveness to intervention that will be described later in this illustration).

Gary's Attention was measured by subtests that required him to focus on specific features of test material and resist reacting to distracting parts of the tests. He was able to focus concentration and resist distractions well enough to earn a score of 102 on the CAS Attention scale, which ranks at the 55th percentile and falls within the Average classification (90% range is 94–109). Gary's score in Attention indicates that he demonstrated typical performance in both identifying targets and avoiding responses to distracting stimuli.

On the Simultaneous processing scale, Gary earned a score of 89. This ranks him at the 23rd percentile and falls at the juncture of Average and Low Average classifications. These tests involving Simultaneous processes required that he work with spatial relationships, relate parts as a group or whole, and understand relationships among words and diagrams. Gary's score on the Simultaneous scale illustrates that he can solve problems that demand integration of information into groups at a level that is close to the average range.

Gary also earned an Average score of 96 on the Successive processing scale, which ranks at the 39th percentile (90% true score interval is 90–103). His Successive processing was measured by tests that required Gary to work with information in a specific linear order. For example, these tests required him to remember the order of words spoken by the examiner and answer questions that are based on ordering of words.

Overall, Gary had important variation among the four PASS Scales. While he earned scores that ranged from 89 to 102 on the Simultaneous, Successive, and Attention scales, he earned a cognitive weakness in Planning (75). This cognitive weakness in Planning is accompanied by a similar score on the K-TEA Math Computation subtest, because both measures demand careful control of activity, selection of appropriate strategies to complete the problems, and self-monitoring (checking one's work). These results indicate that interventions that address both the academic and Planning processing demands of these tasks should be considered.

Intervention Design

In order to address the Planning component of Gary's math computation problems, an intervention described by Naglieri and Pickering (2003) from the book *Helping Children Learn* was applied. This text will be discussed more extensively in the intervention section of this chapter. The regular teacher, using math worksheets consistent with the teacher's instructional objectives and curriculum, gave the intervention to the entire class. The teacher taught in half-hour segments following the format of 10 minutes of math worksheet activity, 10 minutes of discussion, and 10 minutes of math worksheets. During the 10-minute discussion period, the teacher facilitated an interaction designed to encourage the children to consider how they completed the work and how they would go about completing the pages in the future. The teacher did not attempt to reinforce or otherwise encourage the children to complete the math in any particular manner. For example, if a child reported using a particular strategy, the teacher did not say something like "Good job" but instead encouraged the children to think about how they did the work and what methods were effective.

In general, the teacher encouraged Gary's class to describe how they did the worksheets and discuss their ideas and methods (this facilitates planning). In addition, the children were asked to explain why some methods work better. The goal was to teach the children to be self-reflective and self-evaluative when they think about what they are doing. The teacher's job in this intervention was to facilitate self-awareness and self-reflection through class interaction and not specifically instruct the children to use strategies.

Response to Intervention

Gary reported that he developed and used several methods for completing the math pages. First, Gary informed his teacher that it was very difficult to concentrate because he was sitting next to someone who was disturbing him. He moved to a quieter part of the room so he could do his work and not be distracted by this person. Second, he noticed that he needed to review his basic math facts. Gary found that making flashcards and working with one of his friends at his teacher's suggestion was an enjoyable way to review this information. Third, Gary reported that in the past he rushed through his math problems without checking his work. His work was often written in a sloppy and messy manner. This caused errors, for example, when he subtracted columns that were not aligned properly. These observations illustrate how the cognitively based intervention encouraged Gary to be self-reflective, evaluate his approach to completing the work, and make modifications to improve accuracy.

Gary's performance in math was evaluated in two different ways. First, the number of math problems he got correct on each worksheet during baseline and the intervention phases were recorded and provided in Figure 3.5. The results showed that Gary appeared to improve from baseline to intervention, more than doubling the number of problems correct per worksheet. Additional analysis was conducted to determine the magnitude of change using Gorsuch's detrended analysis method, described by Glutting and Watkins (2007). These authors describe this method (Gorsuch, 1983) as a fairly simple approach to examine change for a single subject. The procedure is similar to an analysis of covariance and yields a result expressed as Cohen's *d* statistic, which is the difference between the means during baseline and intervention phases divided by the averaged standard deviations. The result is a *d* ratio that is interpreted as follows: .20–.49 as small, .5–.79 as medium, and .80 and above as large.

Gary's response to intervention suggested that improvement was made with a cognitively based instructional method, but the longer term effectiveness of continued treatment like that described above as well as more academically focused interventions should also be determined. The effects of treatment could be further evaluated using the pre/post method described by Naglieri (1999a) and his Table 4.14. This method provides a way to test the significance of the differences between pre- and post-treatment standard scores on a standardized test. In this case, the initial K-TEA score of 76 is compared to a range of test scores that would be expected on the basis of regression to the mean and reliability. Gary's initial Math Computation score (assuming a reliability of .93) of 76 has a range of scores of 69 to 87 that are expected on the basis of psychometric issues. To obtain this value from Naglieri's (1999a) Table 4.14, enter the column labeled .93 (the reliability of the Math Computation score) and then read down the row that corresponds to the first test score and find where 76 is located. Reading across the table, the range of 69–87 is found. If Gary's score on Math Computation after academic instruction is less than 87, then no significant improvement has been made. If, however, Gary's post-intervention score is above 87, then significant improvement has been found and the intervention can be viewed as being effective.

Identification of Special Populations and the CAS

The CAS can be used in identification of special populations (Naglieri & Kaufman, 2008). Research on specific populations suggests that specific PASS profiles that are consistent with an understanding of the nature of the cognitive deficits have been found. For example, children with ADHD *hyperactive/impulsive* type earned

Gorsuch's Detrended Analysis

Sessions	Sessions Code	Time	Score	Predict	Residual
Baseline 1	0	1	14	16.2	–2.2
Baseline 2	0	2	13	16.6	–3.6
Baseline 3	0	3	17	17.0	0.0
Baseline 4	0	4	15	17.4	–2.4
Baseline 5	0	5	16	17.8	–1.8
Baseline 6	0	6	14	18.2	–4.2
Baseline 7	0	7	17	18.7	–1.7
Intervention 1	1	8	19	19.1	–0.1
Intervention 2	1	9	24	19.5	4.5
Intervention 3	1	10	20	19.9	0.1
Intervention 4	1	11	23	20.3	2.7
Intervention 5	1	12	27	20.8	6.2
Intervention 6	1	13	28	21.2	6.8
Intervention 7	1	14	23	21.6	1.4
Intervention 8	1	15	22	22.0	0.0
Intervention 9	1	16	24	22.4	1.6
Intervention 10	1	17	22	22.8	–0.8
Intervention 11	1	18	26	23.3	2.7
Intervention 12	1	19	19	23.7	–4.7
Intervention 13	1	20	25	24.1	0.9
Intervention 14	1	21	29	24.5	4.5
Intervention 15	1	22	28	24.9	3.1
Intervention 16	1	23	29	25.4	3.6
Intervention 17	1	24	20	25.8	–5.8
Intervention 18	1	25	24	26.2	–2.2
Intervention 19	1	26	22	26.6	–4.6
Intervention 20	1	27	23	27.0	–4.0

Preliminary Statistics

Slope	Intercept	r	r-square
0.418	15.738	0.393	0.155

Detrended Regression Result

$d = 0.856$

Note: Interpret d values of .2 - .49 as small, .5 - .79 as medium, and .80 above as large.

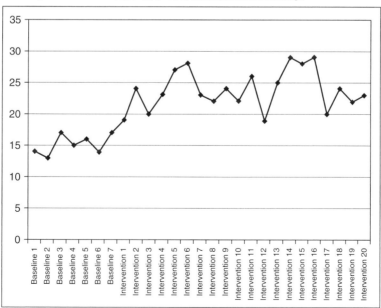

FIGURE 3.5

Example of Using Gorsuch's Detrended Analysis Method for an Individual Student

average scores except in Planning, but those with reading decoding problems show poor performance on Successive processing. As a group, these findings suggest that the PASS processing scores have utility for differential diagnosis and intervention, as well as response to intervention (Naglieri, 2003, 2005).

The profiles of the PASS scores obtained from populations of children with ADHD, mental retardation, and reading disabilities have been examined in several studies (Naglieri, 1999a, 2005). The significant finding among the various studies is that predictable and discriminating differences between the groups have emerged. That is, children with mental retardation earned low and similar PASS scores (Naglieri & Das, 1997b), while children diagnosed with ADHD earned average scores except in Planning (Dehn, 2000; Naglieri, Goldstein, Iseman, & Schwebach, 2003; Naglieri, Salter, & Edwards, 2004; Paolitto, 1999). In contrast, children with evidence of reading disabilities obtained average scores except for low Successive scores (Naglieri, 1999a). As a group, these studies provided evidence that measuring cognitive processes can give important information and suggest that the PASS processing scores have utility for differential diagnosis and intervention, as well as predicting children's response to instruction (Naglieri, 2003, 2005).

Correspondence with IDEA 2004

The PASS cognitive processing scores obtained from the CAS fit well with the movement away from ability/achievement discrepancy analysis for significant learning disability (SLD) eligibility and toward a system that better aligns the definition and the methods used. Naglieri (1999a) first argued that a model based on a discrepancy *and* a consistency would be more informative than the traditional ability/achievement discrepancy approach. He argued that intraindividual variability should be determined using the statistical method originally proposed by Davis (1959) and modified by Silverstein (1982, 1993). Sometimes

referred to as an *ipsative approach*, the method can be used to determine when variability within a child is greater than what would be expected on the basis of unreliability of the scores. This technique has been applied to a number of tests, including, for example, the CAS (Naglieri & Das, 1997a) and SB 5 (Roid, 2003). Determining whether a child has significant variability relative to his or her own average score is a useful way to determine relative strengths and weaknesses. However, Naglieri (1999a) cautioned that in order to ensure that a child has "a disorder in one or more of the basic psychological processes" necessary for SLD identification, the child's PASS profile should show significant variability (using the ipsative method) *and* the lowest score must also fall at a level that could be defended as substantially below normal. When this occurs, evidence for a disorder in one or more of the basic psychological processes, also referred to as a *cognitive weakness*, is obtained. Naglieri (1999a) further suggested that finding a cognitive weakness *and* an academic weakness would provide evidence that contributes to the diagnosis of SLD, especially if other appropriate conditions are also met.

The Consistency/Discrepancy approach (shown in Figure 3.6) is consistent with the widely held view that specific learning disabilities are defined by a dysfunction in cognitive, or neuropsychological, processes and that this processing disorder is seen as the primary causal factor. This view is apparent in the definition of SLD that appeared in IDEA 2004:

Specific learning disability *means a disorder in one or more of the basic psychological processes involved in understanding or in using language, spoken or written, which may manifest itself in the imperfect ability to listen, think, speak, read, write, spell, or do mathematical calculations. Such term includes such conditions as perceptual disabilities, brain injury, minimal brain dysfunction, dyslexia, and developmental aphasia. Such term does not include a learning problem that is primarily the result of visual, hearing, or motor disabilities, of mental retardation, of emotional*

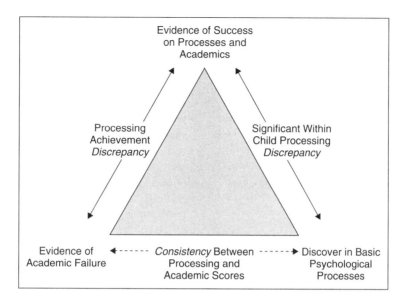

FIGURE 3.6
Illustration of Naglieri's Consistency/Discrepancy Model

disturbance, or of environmental, cultural, or economic disadvantage.

There is wide consensus, as evidenced by the 10 professional organizations that comprised the Learning Disabilities Roundtable (2002), that the "identification of a core cognitive deficit, or a disorder in one or more psychological processes, that is predictive of an imperfect ability to learn, is a marker for a specific learning disability." Documentation of the cognitive and academic status of the child is essential (Hale, Kaufman, Naglieri, & Kavale, 2006). It is logical, therefore, that assessment of "basic psychological processes" as stipulated in IDEA 2004 be a part of any comprehensive assessment designed to determine whether a child has a specific learning disability.

Naglieri (2000) tested the Consistency/ Discrepancy model and found that children with a weakness in one or more of the basic PASS cognitive processes earned lower scores on achievement and were more like to have been deemed eligible for special educational services.

Importantly, the more pronounced the cognitive weakness, the lower the achievement scores. Naglieri's (2000) findings support the view that a PASS cognitive processing disorder accompanied by academic failure could be used for the purpose of eligibility determination. Even though a cognitive approach makes sense because IDEA 2004 defines SLD as a disorder in processing, it also requires the use of a variety of assessment tools that are technically sound and nondiscriminatory to gather functional, developmental, and academic information when special education eligibility is being determined. It is always important that cognitive processing information be intergraded with other important findings about the child to ensure that a comprehensive evaluation is obtained.

VALIDITY OF THE CAS

There is considerable evidence that the CAS can be used to gain an understanding of how well the child thinks and learns (Naglieri & Rojahn,

2004); can be used to discover strengths and needs of children that can then be used for effective differential diagnosis (Naglieri, 2003, 2005); is particularly appropriate for assessment of minority children (Naglieri, Otero, DeLauder, & Matto, 2007; Naglieri, Rojahn, & Matto, 2007; Naglieri, Rojahn, Matto, & Aquilino, 2005); and can be used to select or design appropriate interventions (Naglieri, 2003, 2005; Naglieri & Pickering, 2003). More details about the validity evidence for each of these topics will be summarized below.

Relationships to Achievement

One of the functions of an ability test is to use a child's cognitive functioning scores to anticipate current and latter academic performance. Some researchers have argued that the relationship between a test of ability and achievement is one of the most important aspects of validity (Brody, 1992; Naglieri & Bornstein, 2003; Ramsey & Reynolds, 2003). Therefore, the capacity of a cognitive processing ability test to predict (typically evaluated on the basis of correlational prediction rather than prediction over time) a child's level of school performance is an important indication of validity (Brody, 1992; Ramsey, & Reynolds, 2003).

Comparing the correlations between a test of cognitive processing and a test of achievement in comparison to correlating a traditional IQ test with achievement is more complex than might initially be considered. The complication is that traditional IQ tests contain questions that are often very similar to those included on achievement tests. In contrast, tests of cognitive processing do not contain questions that are as similar to those found in achievement tests. The reason is that verbal and quantitative test questions on some traditional IQ tests are indistinguishable from questions found on tests of achievement. For example, it is not unusual to have a test of word knowledge or math word problems on an IQ test as well as an achievement test. Traditional IQ tests

also typically have some type of quantitative reasoning or arithmetic subtest. These test questions are very similar to those that appear on tests of achievement (see Naglieri, 2008b, and Naglieri & Bornstein, 2003). The similarity in content inflates the correlation between traditional IQ and school achievement tests. It should be expected, therefore, that traditional IQ tests have a content-based advantage when they are correlated with tests of achievement that tests of basic psychological processes do not (Naglieri & Ford, 2005; Suzuki & Valencia, 1997). The predication of school achievement from tests of cognitive processing that do not include achievement-like questions has the advantage of predicting concurrent, and future, performance without the interference of content overlap. Just how well does the CAS relate to academic performance?

Naglieri and Rojahn (2004) studied the relationship between the PASS processing scores from the CAS and the Woodcock-Johnson Revised (WJ-R) Tests of Achievement (Woodcock & Johnson, 1989) for a sample of 1,559 students aged 5–17 years. The sample closely represented the U.S. population on a number of demographic characteristics including gender, race, parental education, and geographic region. The CAS Full Scale correlation with the WJ-R Tests of Achievement was .71 for the Standard (all 12 subtests) and .70 for the Basic Battery score (8 subtests). In comparison to the conventional correlation between ability and traditional intelligence of .55 to .60, these findings demonstrate that the CAS correlated with achievement at least as well as tests of general intelligence (Brody, 1992; Naglieri, 1999a). The findings also provide evidence for the construct validity of the CAS, and suggest that basic psychological processes are strongly correlated with academic performance as measured by the WJ-R. Importantly, Naglieri and Rojahn (2004) also found that prediction to achievement was slightly higher for the four PASS Scales than the CAS Full Scale. These findings suggested that the four PASS Scales individually and collectively correlate higher with achievement than the four scales aggregated into the one Full Scale score. Additionally, the predictive power of the combination of the four PASS Scales was weakened when any one of the PASS Scales was excluded in the prediction equation (Naglieri & Rojahn, 2004). This suggests that each of the PASS Scales has additive value in predicting achievement.

A direct comparison of the Wechsler Intelligence Scale for Children—Third Edition (WISC-III) and CAS correlations with the Woodcock-Johnson III (WJ-III) Test of Achievement was reported by Naglieri, Goldstein, DeLauder, and Schwebach (2006). Their sample included children aged 6 to 16 who were referred for evaluation because of learning problems. The correlation of the WJ-III achievement scores with the WISC-III Full Scale IQ scores was .63; and .83 with the CAS Full Scale. The results indicate that when the same children took the two ability tests and those scores were correlated with the same achievement scores, both showed a strong relationship between ability and achievement. However, the CAS Full Scale scores correlations were significantly higher (Naglieri et al., 2006).

Naglieri, Rojahn, Matto, and Aquillino (2005) reported correlations between the CAS and achievement for samples of black children and white children from the CAS standardization sample; and Naglieri, Rojahn, and Matto (2007) examined the correlations between the CAS and achievement for samples of Hispanic children and non-Hispanic children. The correlations between the CAS scores and WJ-R Tests of Achievement were significant and similar for blacks (.70; $n = 298$) and whites (.64; $n = 1,691$) (Naglieri et al., 2005). Similarly, the median correlations between achievement and the CAS scores were significant and did not differ significantly between the Hispanic (.51; $n = 159$) and non-Hispanic (.65; $n = 1,285$) samples (Naglieri et al., 2006).

The evidence based on the research summarized here demonstrates that there is a strong correlation between the PASS processes and academic achievement without similarity in test context. This point is especially important for children who come from culturally and linguistically diverse populations, especially those who live in poverty, and those who have had a history of academic failure, and therefore could be disadvantaged on traditional intelligence tests that contain verbal and quantitative questions (Naglieri & Ford, 2005; Suzuki & Valencia, 1997).

Race, Ethnicity, and Fairness

The need for fair assessment of children has become increasingly important, as the demographics of the U.S. population continue to change. Federal law mandates that assessments must be selected and administered so as not to be discriminatory on a racial or cultural basis. One way to ensure appropriate and fair assessment of diverse populations is to decrease the amount of knowledge required to correctly answer the questions on intelligence tests. Suzuki and Valencia (1997) and Fagan (2000) have suggested that intelligence be conceptualized on the basis of psychological processes, such as the PASS theory as operationalized by the CAS, and that this approach has utility for the assessment of children from culturally and linguistically diverse populations because verbal and quantitative skills are not included. Of the assorted processing options, Suzuki and Valencia (1997) characterized the PASS theory of intelligence and the CAS used to measure that theory as "an innovative approach to traditional intelligence assessment that assesses a broader spectrum of abilities than has been previously available in IQ testing" (p. 1111).

Messick (1995) argued that the validity of a test is related to the consequences of the test scores. This is especially true if test characteristics contribute to issues such as overrepresentation of minorities in classes for children with mental retardation and underrepresentation of minorities in programs for the gifted, where the validity of the instruments should be questioned. One way to assess the impact of test scores by race is to examine mean score differences. Naglieri et al. (2005) compared CAS scores of 298 black and 1,691 white children and found that when controlling for key demographic variables, regression analyses showed an estimated CAS Full Scale mean score difference of 4.8. This difference is considerably smaller than the difference between blacks and whites of about one standardization (about 15 points) typically found on traditional IQ tests (Jensen, 1980; Fagan, 2000). Similarly, Naglieri et al. (2006) examined CAS scores for 244 Hispanic and 1,956 non-Hispanic children. They found that the two groups differed by 6.1 points when the samples were unmatched samples, 5.1 with samples matched on basic demographic variables, and 4.8 points when demographics differences were statistically controlled.

Irrelevant variance due to ethnic or cultural difference can also be a concern when examining the differences in scores on different-language versions of the same test. Naglieri, Otero, DeLauder, and Matto (2007) compared the English and Spanish versions of the CAS for bilingual Hispanic children. The children in this study earned similar Full Scale scores and deficits in Successive processing were found on both versions of the test. Importantly, 90% of children who had a cognitive weakness on one version of the CAS also had the *same* cognitive weakness on the other version of the CAS. These results suggest that the PASS scores from both the English and Spanish version of the CAS could be used as part of a comprehensive evaluation to identify a disorder in one or more of the basic psychological processes as described by current IDEA legislation for a specific learning disability (see Hale, Kaufman, Naglieri, & Kavale, 2006), and that the results would very likely be the same regardless of the language in which the CAS was administered.

Fairness and Gender

Many studies and an extensive body of literature have focused on gender differences in ability and achievement (e.g., Deaux, 1984; Fennema & Sherman, 1977; Geary, 1989, 1994, 1996; Halpern, 1997; Linn & Peterson, 1985; Maccoby & Jacklin, 1974; Voyer, Voyer, & Bryden, 1995). Some researchers have conceptualized the results of their findings within the context of verbal, quantitative, and visual-spatial abilities (Geary, 1996; Maccoby & Jacklin, 1974; Voyer et al., 1995). Halpern (1997) rejected the verbal, visual-spatial, and quantitative taxonomy domains and suggested an approach based "on underlying cognitive processes [which] offers a more fine-grained analysis of how information is retrieved from memory and what participants are doing when they are working on a cognitive task" (p. 1092). McHough, Koeske, and Frieze (1986) argued that gender differences cannot be understood adequately unless girls and boys are compared according to a theoretical model of cognitive functioning. Geary (1989) further emphasized that conceptual models of cognitive differences between the genders should provide an integration of the neurological and sociocultural components that influence the development of cognitive processes. Similarly, Fagan (2000), Sternberg (1988), and Naglieri (1999a) stressed the importance of using a theoretical approach to define and measure intelligence, which is especially important when group differences are examined, such as when genders are compared.

Naglieri and Rojahn (2004) examined gender differences in PASS scores for 1,100 boys and 1,100 girls who matched the U.S. population. They found that girls outperformed boys between the ages of 5 and 17 years on measures of Planning (d-ratio = .33), which is consistent with initial suggestions reported by Bardos, Naglieri, and Prewett (1992) and Warrick and Naglieri (1993), and on measures of Attention (d-ratio = .35), as suggested by Warrick and Naglieri (1993). A significant, formerly undetected, yet much smaller difference to the advantage of girls was also found in Successive processing. Gender differences were also found on the Woodcock-Johnson Revised Tests of Achievement Proofing, Dictation, Passage Comprehension, and Letter-Word Identification achievement subtests (especially for the 11–17-year age group). These academic tasks have strong Planning and Attention demands (Naglieri & Das, 1997a). The findings that girls and boys differed in basic PASS cognitive processes are especially important because the data were obtained using a national representative sample of school-aged children, and, therefore, generalization to the wider population is appropriate.

Empirical Support for the Test Structure

Factor structure of the CAS was first examined by Naglieri and Das (1997b) using both exploratory and confirmatory factor-analytic methods. They provided evidence that the PASS four-factor solution was the best solution based on the convergence of both factor-analytic results, clinical utility of the four separate scores, evidence of strategy use, and theoretical interpretation of the subtests. Keith and Kranzler (1999) challenged this assertion and argued that there was not sufficient support for the PASS structure. Naglieri (1999b) responded with considerable evidence and rational arguments in defense of the structure of the test and the validity of the theory. However, like many factor-analytic arguments, the outcome seemed equivocal. Factor-analytic methods are, in fact, far from decisive, and are inadequate as the sole method for establishing or discrediting the validity of any instrument. At best, the method of analyzing intercorrelations provides one piece of evidence that must be part of a balanced examination of validity. Other issues such as relationships to achievement, diagnostic utility, issues of fair assessment, and relevance to instructional interventions must be considered. This is particularly true with a neuropsychologically derived theory such as PASS, with its rich validity evidence from neuropsychology as well as cognitive and educational psychology.

The factor structure of the CAS was most recently examined using an alternative method of factor analysis that is considered more objective than the statistical approaches previously used (Blaha, 2003). This method is less subjective than the statistical approaches used in the previous studies. Blaha (2003) used an exploratory hierarchical factor-analytic method described by Blaha and Wallbrown (1996) to examine the CAS subtest assignment to the PASS Scales. It follows the data more closely, allowing for the most probable factor-analytic model (Carroll, 1993). A general factor equated to the CAS Full Scale was found and interpreted as a general intelligence factor. Two factors emerged after removal of the variance caused by the general factor. The first was comprised of the Simultaneous and Successive and the second included the Planning and Attention subtests. At the third level, four primary factors were found that consisted of each of the four PASS Scales. Blaha (2003) concluded that the results "provide support for maintaining the Full Scale as well as the Planning, Attention, Simultaneous, and Successive standard scores of the CAS" (p. 1).

Intervention Relevance

There are several resources for applying the PASS theory to academic remediation and instruction. The PASS Remedial Program (PREP; 1999) developed by J. P. Das and the Planning Strategy Instruction, also known as the Planning Facilitation Method, described by Naglieri and Pickering (2003), are two options. Other resources include Kirby and Williams's 1991 book, *Learning Problems: A Cognitive Approach*, as well as Naglieri and Pickering's (2003) book, *Helping Children Learn: Intervention Handouts for Use in School and Home*. The first two methods are based on empirical studies, while the two books contain several reasonable approaches to academic interventions. The instructional methods in the books use structured and directed instructions based on PREP, as well as minimally structured instructions based on Planning Strategy Instruction. The books vary from more general (Kirby & Williams, 1991) to more applied (Naglieri & Pickering, 2003). Based on the fact that the two books utilize the concepts of both PREP and

Planning Strategy Instruction, only PREP and Planning Strategy Instruction will be discussed in further detail.

PREP Remedial Program

PREP is a cognitive remedial program that is based on the PASS theory of cognitive functioning (Das, Naglieri, & Kirby, 1994) and is supported by a line of research beginning with Brailsford, Snart, and Das (1984), D. Kaufman and P. Kaufman (1979), and Krywaniuk and Das (1976). These researchers demonstrated that students could be trained to use Successive and Simultaneous processes more efficiently, which resulted in an improvement in "their performance on that process and some transfer to specific reading tasks also occurred (Ashman & Conway, 1997, p. 169)." PREP assumes that the information processing strategies recognized as Simultaneous and Successive processing underlie reading ability and aims to improve these two processes. At the same time, the direct teaching of word reading skills such as phoneme segmentation or blending is avoided. The tasks in the program teach children to focus their attention on the sequential nature of many tasks, including reading. This helps the children better utilize Successive processing, which is a cognitive process necessary for reading decoding. The premise that the transfer of principles is best facilitated through inductive, rather than deductive, inference is also at the foundation of PREP (Das, 2001). The program is accordingly structured so that tacitly acquired strategies are likely to be used in appropriate ways.

Support for PREP has been established by studies that examine the effectiveness of the instructional method for children with reading decoding problems. In a study by Carlson and Das (1997), children who received PREP (n = 22) were compared to those in a regular reading program (control n = 15). The samples were tested before and after intervention using the reading subtests Word Attack and

Word Identification from the Woodcock Reading Mastery Test—Revised (WRMT-R; Woodcock, 1987). The intervention was conducted in two 50-minute sessions each week for 12 weeks. Another study by Das, Mishra, and Pool (1995) involved 51 reading-disabled children who were divided into PREP (n = 31) and control (n = 20) groups. There were 15 PREP sessions given to small groups of four children. Word Attack and Word Identification tests were administered pre- and post-treatment. PREP groups outperformed the control groups in both studies.

In a study conducted by Boden and Kirby (1995), a group of learning-disabled children were randomly assigned to PREP training and compared to a control group that received regular instruction. As in previous studies, the results showed significant differences between the two groups in reading decoding of real and pseudowords. Similar results were found in a study by Das, Parrila, and Papadopoulos (2000), where children who were taught using PREP (n = 23) improved significantly more in pseudoword reading than did a control group (n = 17).

Another study by Parrila, Das, Kendrick, Papadopoulos, and Kirby (1999) was an extension of the above experiments except for three important changes. The first change was that the control condition was a competing program given to a carefully matched group of children. Second, the participants (N = 58) were beginning readers in Grade 1, which was younger than the participants in the previous studies. Finally, the training was shorter in duration than in most of the previous studies (Parrila et al., 1999). The purpose of this study was to examine the possible efficacy of PREP in comparison to a meaning-based reading program received by the control group. All of the participants were experiencing reading difficulties and were divided into two matched remediation groups of either PREP or the control condition. Results showed a significant improvement of reading (Word Identification and Word Attack) for the PREP group. Specifically, the gain in reading was greater than it was for the meaning-based control group (Parrila et al., 1999). Particular relevance to the children's CAS profiles was also demonstrated by the fact that those children with a higher level of Successive processing at the beginning of the program benefited the most from the PREP instruction but those with the most improvement in the meaning-based program were characterized by a higher level of Planning (Parrila et al., 1999).

Planning Facilitation

The research that has examined the relationship between strategy instruction and CAS Planning scores has illustrated a significant connection between Planning and intervention. These intervention studies focused on the concept that children can be encouraged to be more planful when they complete academic tasks and that the facilitation of plans positively impacts academic performance. The studies have involved both math and reading achievement scores. The initial concept for Planning Strategy Instruction was based on the work of Cormier, Carlson, and Das (1990) and Kar, Dash, Das, and Carlson (1992). These authors taught children to discover the value of strategy use without being specifically instructed to do so. This was done by encouraging the children to examine the demands of the task in a strategic and organized manner. They demonstrated that students differentially benefited from the technique that facilitated Planning. The children who demonstrated significantly greater gains were the children who performed poorly on the CAS measures of Planning. The children with higher Planning scores did not demonstrate as pronounced gains. These initial results indicated that a relationship between PASS and instruction might be possible.

Naglieri and Gottling (1995, 1997) found that Planning Strategy Instruction was shown to improve children's performance in math calculation. All children in these studies attended a special school for those with learning disabilities. In these studies, students completed mathematics worksheets in sessions over about a two-month

period. The method designed to indirectly teach Planning was applied in individual one-on-one tutoring sessions (Naglieri & Gottling, 1995) or in the classroom by the teacher (Naglieri & Gottling, 1997) about two to three times per week in half-hour blocks of time. During the intervention periods, students were encouraged to recognize the need to plan and use strategies when completing mathematic problems. The teachers provided probes that facilitated discussion and encouraged the children to consider various ways to be more successful. More details about the method can be found in Naglieri and Gottling (1995, 1997) and Naglieri and Pickering (2003).

The relationship between the PASS profiles for children with learning disabilities and mild mental impairments and Planning Strategy Instruction was studied by Naglieri and Johnson (2000). The purpose of this study was to determine whether children with cognitive weaknesses in each of the four PASS processes and children with no cognitive weaknesses showed different rates of improvement in math when given the same group Planning Strategy Instruction. The children with a cognitive weakness in Planning were shown to improve considerably over baseline rates, while those with no cognitive weakness improved only marginally. Similarly, there were substantially lower rates of Simultaneous, Successive, and Attention. The importance of this study was that the five groups of children responded very differently to the same intervention. In other words, the PASS processing scores were predictive of the children's response to this math intervention (Naglieri & Johnson, 2000).

Haddad, Garcia, Naglieri, Grimditch, McAndrews, and Eubanks (2003) conducted another study that examined the effects of Planning Strategy Instruction. An instruction designed to facilitate Planning was assessed in this study to see whether it would have differential benefit on reading comprehension, and whether improvement was related to the PASS processing scores of each child. The researchers used a sample of general-education children sorted into three groups based on each of the PASS Scale profiles from the CAS. Even though the groups did not differ by CAS Full Scale scores or pretest reading comprehension scores, children with a Planning weakness benefited substantially more from the instruction designed to facilitate Planning. In contrast, children with no PASS weakness or a Successive weakness did not benefit as much. These results further support previous research suggesting that the PASS profiles are relevant to instruction.

Planning Strategy Instruction in children with learning disabilities and ADHD was examined by Iseman (2005). Students in the experimental group engaged in Planning Strategy Instruction designed to encourage effective strategies in mathematics. Additional math instruction by the regular teacher was given to a comparison group. An analysis examined students with and students without a cognitive weakness in Planning on the CAS after the intervention. Students with a Planning cognitive weakness in the experimental group improved considerably on math worksheets. In contrast, students with a Planning cognitive weakness in the comparison group did not improve. Students with ADHD in the experimental group with a weakness in Planning improved considerably on the worksheets. In contrast, students with ADHD in the comparison group without a cognitive weakness in Planning did not improve. The results of this study showed that individuals with cognitive weaknesses in Planning, with and without ADHD, benefited more from Planning Strategy Instruction than normal instruction (Iseman, 2005).

The results of these Planning Strategy Instruction studies using academic tasks suggest that changing the way aptitude is conceptualized (e.g., as the PASS rather than traditional IQ) and measured (using the CAS) increases the probability that an aptitude-by-treatment interaction (ATI) is detected. Past ATI research suffered from inadequate conceptualizations of aptitudes based on the general intelligence model. That model and approach is very different from the basic psychological processing view represented by the PASS theory and measured by the CAS.

The summary of studies provided here is particularly different from previous ATI research, which found that students with low general ability improve little, whereas those with high general ability improve a lot to instruction. In contrast, children with a weakness in one of the PASS processes (Planning) benefited more from instruction compared to children who had no weakness or a weakness in a different PASS process. The results of these studies also indicate that the PASS profiles can help predict which children will benefit from academic instruction and which will not. As suggested by Naglieri and Pickering (2003), this offers an important opportunity for researchers and practitioners interested in the design of instruction.

SUMMARY

The CAS holds a unique position in the field of ability assessment. It is the only test explicitly constructed on a specific cognitive processing conceptualization of intelligence. The PASS theory provided the framework for the instrument and the test provided a means to evaluate the strength of the theory. The result is a well-articulated theory with a strong empirical base that supports both the PASS theory and its operationalization in the CAS (see Das, Kirby, & Jarman, 1979; Das, Naglieri, & Kirby, 1994; Naglieri, 1999b, 2003, 2005, 2008a; Naglieri & Das, 1997b, 2005). The theory is easily accessed through the well-standardized PASS measures, which are easy to administer and score and can be used for calibration of basic psychological processes. The PASS scores can also be used within the context of IDEA for specific learning disability eligibility determination and the PASS profile aids in understanding the cognitive processing deficit found in many children with ADHD. Importantly, the CAS has been shown to yield small differences between samples of whites and African Americans as well as Hispanics and non-Hispanics, yet it has very strong correlations with academic achievement.

Additionally, much research has demonstrated that PASS is relevant to academic interventions and selection of specific instructional methods. The research summarized in this chapter illustrates that the PASS theory, as operationalized by the CAS, provides a viable option to today's practitioners who are most concerned about (1) equitable assessment; (2) intervention design; and (3) detecting specific variations in ability that are related to success and failure.

REFERENCES

Adjutant General's Office. (1944). *Army Individual Test of General Ability: Manual of directions and scoring*. Washington, DC: Author.

Aiken, L. R. (1987). *Assessment of intellectual functioning*. Boston: Allyn & Bacon.

Armitage, S. G. (1946). An analysis of certain psychological tests used for the evaluation of brain injury. *Psychological Monographs, 60* (277, entire).

Ashman, A. F., & Conway, R. N. F. (1993). *Using cognitive methods in the classroom*. New York: Routledge.

Ashman, A. F., & Conway, R. N. F. (1997). *An introduction to cognitive education: Theory and applications*. London: Routledge.

Atkinson, L. (1991). Three standard errors of measurement and the Wechsler Memory Scale Revised. *Psychological Assessment, 3,* 136–138.

Bardos, A. N., Naglieri, J. A., & Prewett, P. N. (1992). Sex differences in planning, attention, simultaneous, and successive cognitive processes. *Journal of School Psychology, 30,* 293–305.

Barkley, R. A. (2003). Attention-deficit/hyperactivity disorder. In E. J. Mash & R. A. Barkley (Eds.), *Child psychopathology* (2nd ed., pp. 75–143). New York: Guilford Press.

Blaha, J. (2003). *What does the CAS really measure?: An exploratory hierarchical factor analysis of the Cognitive Assessment System*. Paper presented at the National Association of School Psychologists Convention, Chicago.

Blaha, J., & Wallbrown, F. H. (1996). Hierarchical factor structure of the Wechsler Intelligence Scale for Children—III. *Psychological Assessment, 8,* 214–218.

Boden, C., & Kirby, J. R. (1995). Successive processing, phonological coding and the remediation of reading. *Journal of Cognitive Education, 4,* 19–31.

Brailsford, A., Snart, F., and Das, J. P. (1984). Strategy training and reading comprehension. *Journal of Learning Disabilities, 17* (5), 287–290.

Brody, N. (1992). *Intelligence*. San Diego: Academic Press.

Carlson, J., & Das, J. P. (1997). A process approach to remediating word decoding deficiencies in Chapter 1 children. *Learning Disabilities Quarterly, 20,* 93–102.

Carroll, J. B. (1993). *Human cognitive abilities: A survey of factor-analytic studies*. New York: Cambridge University Press.

Cormier, P., Carlson, J. S., & Das, J. P. (1990). Planning ability and cognitive performance: The compensatory effects of a dynamic assessment approach. *Learning and Individual Differences, 2,* 437–449.

Das, J. P. (1999). *PASS reading enhancement program*. Deal, NJ: Sarka Educational Resources.

Das, J.P. (2001). *Reading difficulties and dyslexia*. Deal, N.J.: Sarka.(Distributed by Amazon.com).

Das. J. P., Kar, B. C., and Parrila, R. K. (1996). *Cognitive planning: The psychological basis of intelligent behavior*. Thousand Oaks, CA: Sage Publications.

Das, J. P., Kirby, J. R., & Jarman, R. F. (1979). *Simultaneous and successive cognitive processes*. New York: Academic Press.

Das, J. P., Mishra, R. K., & Pool, J. E. (1995). An experiment on cognitive remediation or word-reading difficulty. *Journal of Learning Disabilities, 28,* 66–79.

Das, J. P., Naglieri, J. A., & Kirby, J. R. (1994). *Assessment of cognitive processes*. Needham Heights, MA: Allyn & Bacon.

Das, J.P., Parrila, R. K., & Papadopoulos, T. C. (2000). Cognitive education and reading disability. In A. Kozulin & Y. Rand (Eds.), *Experience of mediated learning* (pp. 276–291). Amsterdam: Pergamon.

Davis, F. B. (1959). Interpretation of differences among averages and individual test scores. *Journal of Educational Psychology, 50,* 162–170.

Deaux, K. (1984). From individual differences to social categories: Analysis of a decade's research on gender. *American Psychologist, 39,* 105–116.

Dehn, M. J. (2000). Cognitive Assessment System performance of ADHD children. Paper presented at the annual *NASP Convention*, New Orleans.

Eslinger, P. J. (1996). Conceptualizing, describing, and measuring components of executive function: A summary. In G. R. Lyon & N. A. Krasnegor (Eds.), *Attention, memory and executive function* (pp. 367–396). Baltimore: Brookes.

Fagan, J. R. (2000). A theory of intelligence as processing: Implications for society. *Psychology, Public Policy, and Law, 6,* 168–179.

Fennema, E., & Sherman, J. (1977). Sex-related differences in mathematics achievement, spatial visualization, and affective factors. *American Educational Research Journal, 14,* 51–71.

Geary, D. C. (1989). A model for representing gender differences in the pattern of cognitive abilities. *American Psychologist, 44,* 1155–1156.

Geary, D. C. (1994). *Children's mathematical development: Research and practical applications.* Washington, DC: American Psychological Association.

Geary, D. C. (1996). Sexual selection and sex differences in mathematical abilities. *Behavioral and Brain Sciences, 19,* 229–247.

Glutting, J., & Watkins, M. (2007). Analysis of single subject data. Unpublished manuscript.

Goldberg, E. (2001). *The executive brain: Frontal lobes and the civilized mind.* New York: Oxford University Press.

Goldstein, S., & Mather, N. (1998). *Overcoming underachieving.* Baltimore: Brookes.

Gorsuch, R. L. (1983). Three methods for analyzing limited time-series data. *Behavioral Assessment, 5,* 141–154.

Graham, F. K., & Kendall, B. S. (1960). Memory-for-Designs test: Revised general manual. *Perceptual and Motor Skills, 11,* 147–188.

Haddad, F. A., Garcia, Y. E., Naglieri, J. A., Grimditch, M., McAndrews, A., & Eubanks, J. (2003). Planning facilitation and reading comprehension: Instructional relevance of the PASS theory. *Journal of Psychoeducational Assessment, 21,* 282–289.

Hale, J. B., Kaufman, A. S., Naglieri, J. A., & Kavale, K. A. (2006). Implementation of IDEA: Integrating response to intervention and cognitive assessment methods. *Psychology in the Schools, 43,* 753–770.

Halpern, D. F. (1997). Sex differences in intelligence. *American Psychologist, 52,* 1091–1102.

Hayes, S. C., Gifford, E. B, & Ruckstuhl, L. E. (1996). Relational frame theory and executive function: A behavioral approach. In G. R. Lyon & N. A. Krasnegor (Eds.), *Attention, memory and executive function* (pp. 279–306). Baltimore: Brookes.

Ilg, F. L., & Ames, L. B. (1964) *School readiness: Behavior tests used at the Gesell Institute.* New York: Harper & Row.

Iseman, J. S. (2005). *A cognitive instructional approach to improving math calculation of children with ADHD: Application of the PASS theory.* Unpublished doctoral dissertation, George Mason University.

Jensen, A. R. (1980). *Bias in mental testing.* New York: Free Press.

Kar, B. C., Dash, U. N., Das, J. P., & Carlson, J. S. (1992). Two experiments on the dynamic assessment of planning. *Learning and Individual Differences, 5,* 13–29.

Kaufman, A. S. (1994). *Intelligent testing with the WISC-III.* New York: Wiley.

Kaufman, A. S., & Kaufman, N. L. (2004). *Kaufman assessment battery for children* (2nd ed.). Circle Pines, MN: American Guidance Service.

Kaufman, D., & Kaufman, P. (1979). Strategy training and remedial techniques. *Journal of Learning Disabilities, 12,* 63–66.

Keith, T. Z., & Kranzler, J. H. (1999). Independent confirmatory factor analysis of the Cognitive Assessment System (CAS): What does the CAS measure? *School Psychology Review, 28,* 117–144.

Kirby, J. R., & Williams, N. H. (1991). *Learning problems: A cognitive approach.* Toronto: Kagan and Woo.

Krywaniuk, L. W., & Das, J. P. (1976). Cognitive strategies in native children: Analysis and intervention. *Alberta Journal of Educational Research, 22,* 271–280.

Learning Disabilities Roundtable, U.S. Department of Education (2002). *Specific learning disabilities: Finding common ground.* Washington, DC: U.S. Department of Education, Office of Special Education Programs, Office of Innovation and Development.

Lezak, M. (1995). *Neuropsychologcial assessment* (3rd ed.). New York: Oxford.

Linn, M. C., & Peterson, A. C. (1985). Emergence and characterization of sex differences in spatial ability: A meta-analysis. *Child Development, 56,* 1479–1498.

Luria, A. R. (1966). *Human brain and psychological processes.* New York: Harper and Row.

Luria, A. R. (1973). *The working brain.* New York: Basic Books.

Luria, A. R. (1980). *Higher cortical functions in man* (2nd ed.). New York: Basic Books.

Luria, A. R. (1982). *Language and cognition*. New York: Wiley.

Maccoby, E. E., & Jacklin, C. (1974). *The psychology of sex differences*. Stanford, CA: Stanford University Press.

McHough, M. C., Koeske, R. D., & Frieze, I. H. (1986). Issues to consider in conducting nonsexist psychological research: A guide for researchers. *American Psychologist*, *41*, 879–890.

Messick, S. (1995). Validity of psychological assessment: Validation of inferences from persons' responses and performances as scientific inquiry into score meaning. *American Psychologist*, *50*, 741–749.

Naglieri, J. A. (1985). *Matrix analogy test, expanded form*. San Antonio, TX: The Psychological Corporation.

Naglieri, J. A. (1993). Pairwise and ipsative Wisc-III IQ and Index Score comparisons. *Psychological Assessment*, *5*, 113–116.

Naglieri, J. A. (1997). *Naglieri Nonverbal Ability Test*. San Antonio: The Psychological Corporation.

Naglieri, J. A. (1999a). *Essentials of CAS assessment*. New York: Wiley.

Naglieri, J. A. (1999b). How valid is the PASS theory and CAS? *School Psychology Review*, *28*, 145–162.

Naglieri, J. A. (2000). Can profile analysis of ability test scores work? An illustration using the PASS theory and CAS with an unselected cohort. *School Psychology Quarterly*, *15*, 419–433.

Naglieri, J. A. (2002). *CAS rapid score*. Centreville, VA: NL Associates.

Naglieri, J. A. (2003). Current advances in assessment and intervention for children with learning disabilities. In T. E. Scruggs and M. A. Mastropieri (Eds.), *Advances in learning and behavioral disabilities, Vol. 16: Identification and assessment* (pp. 163–190). New York: JAI.

Naglieri, J. A. (2005). The Cognitive Assessment System. In D. P. Flanagan and P. L. Harrison (Eds.), *Contemporary intellectual assessment* (2nd ed., pp. 441–460). New York: Guilford.

Naglieri, J. A. (2008a). Best practices in linking cognitive assessment of students with learning disabilities to interventions. In A. Thomas and J. Grimes (Eds.), *Best practices in school psychology* (5th ed., pp. 679–696). Bethesda: NASP.

Naglieri, J. A. (2008b). Traditional IQ: 100 Years of misconception and its relationship to minority representation in gifted programs. In J. VanTassel-Baska (Ed.), *Critical issues in equity and excellence in gifted education series alternative assessment of gifted learners* (pp. 67–88). Waco, TX: Prufrock Press.

Naglieri, J. A., & Bornstein, B. T. (2003). Intelligence and achievement: Just how correlated are they? *Journal of Psychoeducational Assessment*, *21*, 244–260.

Naglieri, J. A., Conway, C., & Goldstein, S. (2007). Cognition and learning: Application of the PASS theory to understanding the role of intellectual processes in classroom behavior. In S. Goldstein & R. B. Brookes (Eds.), *Understanding and managing children's classroom behavior* (pp. 64–90). New York: Wiley.

Naglieri, J. A., & Das, J. P. (1997a). *Cognitive Assessment System*. Itasca: Riverside Publishing Company.

Naglieri, J. A., & Das, J. P. (1997b). *Cognitive Assessment System interpretive handbook*. Chicago: Riverside Publishing Company.

Naglieri, J. A., & Das, J. P. (1997c). *Cognitive Assessment System administration and scoring handbook*. Chicago: Riverside Publishing Company.

Naglieri, J. A., & Das, J. P. (2002). Practical implications of general intelligence and PASS cognitive processes. In R. J. Sternberg & E. L. Grigorenko (Eds.), *The general factor of intelligence: How general is it?* (pp. 855–884). New York: Erlbaum.

Naglieri, J. A., & Das, J. P. (2005). Planning, Attention, Simultaneous, Successive (PASS) theory: A revision of the concept of intelligence. In D. P. Flanagan and P. L. Harrison (Eds.), *Contemporary intellectual assessment* (2nd ed., pp. 136–182). New York: Guilford.

Naglieri, J. A., & Ford, D. Y. (2005). Increasing minority children's participation in gifted classes using the NNAT: A response to Lohman. *Gifted Child Quarterly*, *49*, 29–36.

Naglieri, J. A., Goldstein, S., Delauder, B. Y., & Schwebach, A. (2006). WISC-III and CAS: Which correlates higher with achievement for a clinical sample? *School Psychology Quarterly*, *21*, 62–76.

Naglieri, J. A., Goldstein, S., Iseman, J. S., and Schwebach, A. (2003). Performance of children with attention deficit hyperactivity disorder and anxiety/depression on the WISC-III and Cognitive Assessment System (CAS). *Journal of Psychoeducational Assessment, 21,* 32–42.

Naglieri, J. A., & Gottling, S. H. (1995). A cognitive education approach to math instruction for the learning disabled: An individual study. *Psychological Reports, 76,* 1343–1354.

Naglieri, J. A., & Gottling, S. H. (1997). Mathematics instruction and PASS cognitive processes: An intervention study. *Journal of Learning Disabilities, 30,* 513–520.

Naglieri, J. A., & Johnson, D. (2000). Effectiveness of a cognitive strategy intervention to improve math calculation based on the PASS theory. *Journal of Learning Disabilities, 33,* 591–597.

Naglieri, J. A., & Kaufman, A. S. (2008). IDEIA 2004 and specific learning disabilities: What role does intelligence play? In E. Grigorenko (Ed.), *Educating individuals with disabilities: IDEIA 2004 and beyond* (pp. 165–195). New York: Springer.

Naglieri, J. A. & Paolitto, A. W. (2005). Ipsative comparisons of WISC-IV index scores. *Applied Neuropsychology, 12,* 208–211.

Naglieri, J. A., & Pickering, E. (2003). *Helping children learn: Instructional handouts for use in school and at home.* Baltimore: Brookes.

Naglieri, J. A., Otero, T., DeLauder, B., & Matto, H. C. (2007). Bilingual Hispanic children's performance on the English and Spanish versions of the Cognitive Assessment System. *School Psychology Quarterly, 22,* 432–448.

Naglieri, J. A., & Rojahn, J. (2001). Evaluation of African-American and white children in special education programs for children with mental retardation using the WISC-III and Cognitive Assessment System. *American Journal of Mental Retardation, 106,* 359–367.

Naglieri, J. A., & Rojahn, J. R. (2004). Validity of the PASS theory and CAS: Correlations with achievement. *Journal of Educational Psychology, 96,* 174–181.

Naglieri, J. A., Rojahn, J., & Matto, H. (2007). Hispanic and non-Hispanic children's performance on PASS cognitive processes and achievement. *Intelligence.*

Naglieri, J.A., Rojahn, J. R., Matto, H. C., & Aquilino, S. A. (2005). Black/white differences in intelligence: A study of the PASS theory

and Cognitive Assessment System. *Journal of Psychoeducational Assessment, 23,* 146–160.

Naglieri, J. A., Salter, C. J., and Edwards, G. (2004). Assessment of ADHD and reading disabilities using the PASS theory and Cognitive Assessment System. *Journal of Psychoeducational Assessment, 22,* 93–105.

O'Shanick, G. J., & O'Shanick, A. M. (1994). Personality and intellectual changes. In J. M. Silver, S. C. Yudofsky, & R. E. Hales (Eds.), *Neuropsychiatry of traumatic brain injury* (pp. 163–188). Washington, DC: American Psychiatric Press.

Paolitto, A. W. (1999). Clinical validation of the Cognitive Assessment System with children with ADHD. *ADHD Report, 7,* 1–5.

Parrila, R. K., Das, J. P., Kendrick, M., Papadopoulos, T., & Kirby, J. (1999). Efficacy of a cognitive reading remediation program for at-risk children in Grade 1. *Developmental Disabilities Bulletin, 27,* 1–31.

Penrose, L. S., & Raven, J. C. (1936) A new series of perceptual tests: Preliminary communication. *British Journal of Medical Psychology, 16,* 97–104.

Posner, M. I., & Boies, S. J. (1971). Components of attention. *Psychological Review, 78,* 391–408.

Ramsey, M. C., & Reynolds, C. R. (2003). Relations between intelligence and achievement test. In G. Goldstein and S. Beers (Eds.), *Comprehensive handbook of psychological assessment* (pp. 25–50). New York: Wiley.

Reitan, R. M. (1955). The relation of the Trail Making test to organic brain damage. *Journal of Counseling Psychology, 19,* 393–394.

Roid, G. H. (2003). *Stanford-Binet Intelligence Scales—Fifth Edition, technical manual.* Austin, TX: Pro-Ed.

Sattler, J. M. (1988). *Assessment of children* (3rd ed.). San Diego: Author.

Schneider, W., Dumais, S. T., & Shiffrin, R. M. (1984). Automatic and controlled processing and attention. In R. Parasuraman & D. R. Davies (Eds.), *Varieties of attention* (pp. 1–28). New York: Academic Press.

Silverstein, A. B. (1982). Pattern analysis as simultaneous statistical inference. *Journal of Consulting and Clinical Psychology, 50,* 234–240.

Silverstein. A. B. (1993). Type I, Type II, and other types of errors in pattern analysis. *Psychological Assessment, 5,* 72–74.

Spreen, O., & Gaddes, W. H. (1969). Developmental norms for 15 neuropsychological tests ages 5 to 15. *Cortex*, *5*, 171–191.

Sternberg, R. J. (1988). *The triarchic mind: A new theory of human intelligence*. New York: Viking.

Suzuki, L. A., & Valencia, R. R. (1997). Race-ethnicity and measured intelligence. *American Psychologist*, *52*, 1103–1114.

U.S. Department of Education, Office of Special Education Programs (OSEP). (2004). Building the Legacy IDEIA 2004 website for information and resources about the law and regulations, http://IDEIA.ed.gov/.

Varnhagen, C. K., & Das, J. P. (1986). Neuropsychological functioning and cognitive processing. In J. E. Obzrut and G. W. Hynd (Eds.), *Child neuropsychology, Vol. 1: Theory and research* (pp. 117–140). New York: Academic Press.

Voyer, D., Voyer, S., & Bryden, M. P. (1995). Magnitude of sex differences in spatial abilities: A meta-analysis and consideration of critical variables. *Psychological Bulletin*, *117*, 250–270.

Warrick, P. D., & Naglieri, J. A. (1993). Gender differences in planning, attention, simultaneous, and successive cognitive processes. *Journal of Educational Psychology*, *85*, 693–701.

Wechsler, D. (1991). *Wechsler intelligence scale for children*: (3rd ed.). San Antonio, TX: The Psychological Corporation.

Wechsler, D. & Naglieri, J. A. (2006). *Wechsler nonverbal scale of ability*. San Antonio: Harcourt Assessment.

Winsler, A., & Naglieri, J. A. (2003). Overt and covert verbal problem-solving strategies: Developmental trends in use, awareness, and relations with task performance in children age 5 to 17. *Child Development*, *74*, 659–678.

Woodcock, R. W. (1987). *Woodcock Reading Mastery tests—revised*. Circle Pines, MN: American Guidance Service.

Woodcock, R. W., & Johnson, M. B. (1989). *Woodcock-Johnson revised tests of achievement: Standard and supplemental batteries*. Itasca, IL: Riverside Publishing.

Woodcock, R. W., McGrew, K. S., & Mather, N. (2001). *Woodcock-Johnson III test of achievement*. Itasca, IL: Riverside Publishing.

Yoakum, C. S., & Yerkes, R. M. (1920). *Army mental tests*. New York: Henry Holt.

CHAPTER 4

The Kaufman Assessment Battery for Children—Second Edition

Elizabeth O. Lichtenberger, Marlene Sotelo-Dynega, and Alan S. Kaufman*

HISTORY AND THEORY OF THE TEST

Historical Information

Beginning in the mid-1800s, Sir Francis Galton embarked on a quest to define and, therefore, measure intelligence Over 150 years after Galton's pioneering efforts, the quest to measure intelligence has taken a different turn. Although intelligence tests continue to be used to predict outcomes, the majority of intellectual assessments are conducted within the public school system, by school psychologists to determine whether an individual meets criteria to receive special education services under the Individuals with Disabilities Education Act (IDEA, 2004). According to a review conducted by Fagan and Wise (2007), school psychologists spend about half their time involved in the psychoeducational assessment of students. Clinicians use these assessments to acquire data to help make diagnostic decisions and to develop individualized interventions that focus on remediating the child's identified academic weaknesses.

Unfortunately, a historically documented "divide between theory and practice" (Flanagan & McGrew, 1997, p. 322) has manifested in much frustration among clinicians regarding the best applications of intelligence tests (Hale, Kaufman, Naglieri, & Kavale, 2006). Kamphaus, Winsor, Rowe, and Kim (2005) state that "the progress in the area of intellectual assessment and interpretation should be seen as an evolution, rather than a series of disjointed starts and stops. This evolution has culminated in the integration of empirical research, theory development, and test design, resulting in more accurate and meaningful test interpretation" (p. 36).

Amid the divide between theory and practice, the original Kaufman Assessment Battery for Children (K-ABC; Kaufman & Kaufman, 1983a, 1983b) emerged. It was groundbreaking in its development as it was a theory-based, empirically grounded clinical instrument that made it virtually impossible for the practitioner not to link theory with practice. The K-ABC

*Author's note: Financial Conflict-of-Interest Disclosure: Alan S. Kaufman is co-author of the Kaufman Assessment Battery for Children—Second Edition (KABC-II).

broke from tradition, as it was rooted in neuropsychological theory—Sperry's (1968) cerebral specialization approach and the Luria-Das successive–simultaneous processing dichotomy. Both the Sperry and Luria-Das models are characterized by a dual-processing approach that has been well supported by a large body of cognitive and neuropsychological research (Das et al., 1979; Neisser, 1967).

When developing the Kaufman Assessment Battery for Children—Second Edition (KABC-II; Kaufman & Kaufman, 2004a), the Kaufmans considered the perspectives of clinicians and research conducted using the K-ABC, along with needs dictated by political, social, economic, and educational concerns. The goals for the K-ABC's revision included: strengthening the theoretical foundations, increasing the number of constructs measured (especially fluid reasoning and learning ability), enhancing the test's clinical utility, developing a test that continues to fairly assess children from minority groups, and maintaining intrinsically interesting tasks for preschoolers. Upon its release in 2004, the KABC-II pioneered a new movement in assessment in that it allowed clinicians the choice between two theoretical models for test selection and interpretation. In a recent review, the KABC-II has been described as "easy to administer with practice and is inherently interesting for children, with several manipulative opportunities and brightly colored, well-designed stimuli" (Bain & Gray, 2008, p. 101).

Theory and Structure

The KABC-II is founded in two theoretical models: Luria's (1966, 1966a, 1970, 1973) neuropsychological model, featuring three blocks or functional units, and the Cattell-Horn-Carroll (CHC) theory of cognitive abilities (Carroll, 1997; Flanagan, McGrew, & Ortiz, 2000).

Luria's Neuropsychological Theory

Luria (1970) believed that the brain's basic functions could be represented by three blocks,

or functional systems, which have since been supported through empirical research (see, for example, Das, Naglieri, & Kirby, 1994; Naglieri, 1999; Naglieri & Das, 1997). These three blocks are responsible for arousal and attention (block 1); the use of one's senses to analyze, code, and store information (block 2); and the application of executive functions for formulating plans and programming behavior (block 3).

To be capable of complex behavior, such as learning and academic achievement, Luria's theory emphasizes the necessary integration and interdependence of these blocks into functional systems (Naglieri, 1999; Reitan, 1988). Furthermore, for learning to be efficient, the joint operation of several brain systems is crucial. In the development of the KABC-II, the Kaufmans focused on the integrative aspects of Luria's theory rather than on each of the blocks' specific functions.

The KABC-II was designed primarily to measure high-level, complex, intelligent behavior. Conceptually, the integration of Luria's blocks captures that complexity. Luria's theory emphasizes the integration of the incoming stimuli and the responsibility of block 2 to make connections with block 3. Thus, the KABC-II includes subtests that require synthesis of auditory and visual stimuli (e.g., Word Order, Atlantis, Rebus Learning, and Rover). To capture the linkage between blocks 2 and 3, the KABC-II includes measures of simultaneous processing that not only require the analysis, coding, and storage of incoming stimuli, but also demand executive functioning and problem solving for success (e.g., Rover, Conceptual Thinking).

Cattell-Horn-Carroll (CHC) Theory

The Cattell-Horn-Carroll (CHC) model is a psychometric theory that rests on a large body of research (Carroll, 1993, 1997, 2005; Flanagan & McGrew, 1997; Flanagan, McGrew, & Ortiz, 2000; Horn & Blankson, 2005; Horn & Noll, 1997; McGrew, 1997, 2005; McGrew & Flanagan, 1998). Thus, CHC theory is data-driven, in contrast to the distinctly clinical origins of Luria's model (although Luria's theory has also been empirically validated). CHC theory has been described as a "taxonomy for understanding specific cognitive and academic abilities" (Flanagan, Ortiz, & Alfonso, 2007, p. 275) that is organized into three levels, or *Strata*. *Stratum III* represents the general level of intelligence or *g*. *Stratum II* includes 10 broad abilities that represent the "basic constitutional and longstanding characteristics of individuals that can govern or influence a great variety of behaviors in a given domain" (Carroll, 1993, p. 634). They include: Fluid Intelligence *Gf*; Quantitative Reasoning, *Gq*; Crystallized Intelligence *Gc*; Reading and Writing, *Grw*; Short-Term Memory, *Gsm*; Visual Processing, *Gv*; Auditory Processing, *Ga*; Long-Term Storage and Retrieval, *Glr*; Processing Speed, *Gs*; and Decision/Reaction Time/Speed, *Gt*. Stratum I includes over 70 narrow abilities that are subsumed by the 10 broad abilities in *Stratum II*. Narrow abilities "represent greater specializations of abilities, often in quite specific ways that reflect the effect of experiences and learning, or the adoption of particular strategies of performance" (Carroll, 1993, p. 634). Dawn Flanagan, Kevin McGrew, and their colleagues (Flanagan et al., 2000; Flanagan & Ortiz, 2001; McGrew, Woodcock, & Ford, 2002) provide a comprehensive review of the origins and implications of CHC theory.

In applying CHC theory to the KABC-II, the *g* level is not intended as a theoretical construct but as a practical one to provide a summary score. There are five CHC Stratum II abilities (corresponding to five KABC-II scales) that are measured by the KABC-II (*Glr*, *Gsm*, *Gv*, *Gf*, and *Gc*). An additional sixth Broad Ability, Quantitative Knowledge (*Gq*), is also tapped by the KABC-II because the Narrow Ability of Mathematical Achievement is measured by two subtests as a secondary ability (Rover and Block Counting, both of which require counting). Separate measures of *Gq* and *Grw* are available on both the Brief and Comprehensive Forms of the Kaufman Test of Educational Achievement—Second Edition

(KTEA-II; Kaufman & Kaufman, 2004b, 2005). Auditory Processing (*Ga*), Processing Speed (*Gs*), and Decision/Reaction Time/Speed (*Gt*) were not included on the KABC-II because they lacked the requisite complexity for inclusion in the Kaufmans' test battery.

DESCRIPTION OF THE **KABC-II**

Structure and Organization

The KABC-II is a measure of the processing and cognitive abilities of children and adolescents between the ages of 3 years 0 months and 18 years 11 months that is organized into three levels (age 3, ages 4–6, ages 7–18). Depending on the age of the child and the interpretive model selected by the clinician, the KABC-II can generate from one to five scales (please refer to Table 4.1).

From the Luria perspective, the KABC-II scales correspond to learning ability, sequential processing, simultaneous processing, and planning ability. From the vantage point of the CHC model, the KABC-II scales measure the following Broad Abilities: Long-Term Storage and Retrieval (*Glr*), Short-Term Memory (*Gsm*), Visual Processing (*Gv*), Fluid Reasoning (*Gf*), and Crystallized Ability (*Gc*). As shown in Table 4.2, the names of the KABC-II scales reflect both the Luria process it is believed to measure and its CHC Broad Ability: Learning/*Glr*, Sequential/*Gsm*, Simultaneous/*Gv*, and Planning/*Gf*. The Knowledge/*Gc* scale reflects only CHC theory and is specifically excluded from the Luria system.

The KABC-II yields two global scores: the Mental Processing Index (MPI) and the Fluid-Crystallized Index (FCI). The key difference between these two global scores is that the MPI (reflecting Luria's theory) *excludes* measures of acquired knowledge, whereas the FCI (reflecting CHC theory) *includes* measures of acquired knowledge. The FCI offers an alternative way of viewing children's cognitive abilities that is founded in a theory that has gained much

TABLE 4.1   KABC-II Scale Structure across the Ranges

Age 3	Ages 4–6	Ages 7–18
MPI, FCI, or NVI	MPI, FCI, or NVI	MPI, FCI, or NVILearning/*Glr*Learning/*Glr*Sequential/*Gsm* Sequential/*Gsm*Simultaneous/ *Gv*Simultaneous/*Gv*
	Knowledge/*Gc*	Planning/*Gf*
		Knowledge/*Gc*

NOTE : MPI from the Luria system excludes Knowledge/*Gc* subtests (age 3) and scale (ages 4–18).

popularity among assessment-oriented psychologists (Flanagan et al., 2000; McGrew & Flanagan, 1998), is consistent with several other Kaufman tests (Kaufman & Kaufman, 1990, 1993, 2004a), and corresponds to traditional (Wechsler-Binet) views of cognitive ability. The authors of the KABC-II state in the *Manual* (Kaufman & Kaufman, 2004a, pp. 4–5) that "the CHC model should generally be the model of choice, except in cases where the examiner believes that including measures of acquired knowledge/crystallized ability would compromise the validity of the Fluid-Crystallized Index (FCI). In those cases, the Luria global score (MPI) is preferred." The examiner must choose the Luria or CHC model *prior* to administering the KABC-II based on knowledge about the child's language, cultural, and educational history. It is inappropriate to select the model once you know the child's actual scores to avoid the temptation of selecting the model that yielded the highest global score.

In addition to the MPI and FCI, and the five scales, the KABC-II has a Nonverbal Scale, composed of subtests that may be administered in pantomime and responded to motorically. The Nonverbal Scale permits valid assessment of children who are hearing impaired, limited English proficient, or with moderate to severe speech or language impairments and other disabilities that make both the MPI and FCI unsuitable.

The KABC-II includes two batteries: a Core and an Expanded. The Expanded battery offers supplementary subtests to increase the breadth of the constructs that are measured by the Core battery, to follow up hypotheses, and to provide a comparison of the child's initial learning and delayed recall of new learning. Scores earned on the supplementary subtests do *not* contribute to the child's standard scores on any KABC-II scale (except for the Nonverbal Scale).

Administration and Scoring

The standardized assessment of cognitive abilities creates predictable conditions in which to observe a child using his or her abilities and resources to solve problems, provides a comparison of individual cognitive skills with a group of same-aged children, permits the observation of naturally occurring developmental changes in cognitive ability, and allows us to determine hypotheses about individual cognitive strengths and weaknesses. The following are a list of general tips for standardized KABC-II administration.

General Administration Features

Use of Sample and Teaching Items

Like the K-ABC, the KABC-II was designed to give children every opportunity to understand what is expected of them for each task to ensure that a low score denotes limited *ability* and not the failure to understand the examiner's instructions. Sample and teaching items provide

TABLE 4.2 Definitions of Luria and CHC Terms

Name of KABC-II Scale/Subtest	Luria Term	CHC Term
Learning/*Glr*	**Learning Ability**	**Long-Term Storage & Retrieval (*Glr*)**
Atlantis Atlantis Delayed Rebus Learning Rebus Learning Delayed	Reflects an integration of the processes associated with all three blocks, placing a premium on the attention-concentration processes that are in the domain of block 1, but also requiring block 2 coding processes and block 3 strategy generation to learn and retain the new information with efficiency. Sequential and simultaneous processing are associated primarily with Luria's block 2, and pertain to either a step-by-step (sequential) or holistic (simultaneous) processing of information.	Storing and efficiently retrieving newly learned, or previously learned, information
Memory/*Gsm*	**Sequential Processing**	**Short-Term Memory (*Gsm*)**
Word Order Number Recall Hand Movements	Measures the kind of coding function that Luria labeled *successive*, and involves arranging input in sequential or serial order to solve a problem, where each idea is linearly and temporally related to the preceding one.	Taking in and holding information, and then using it within a few seconds
Simultaneous/*Gv*	**Simultaneous Processing**	**Visual Processing (*Gv*)**
Rover Triangles Conceptual Thinking Face Recognition Gestalt Closure Block Counting	Measures the second type, or simultaneous, coding function associated with block 2. For its tasks, the input has to be integrated and synthesized simultaneously (holistically), usually spatially, to produce the appropriate solution. As mentioned earlier, the KABC-II measure of simultaneous processing deliberately blends Luria's block 2 and block 3 to enhance the complexity of the simultaneous syntheses that are required.	Perceiving, storing, manipulating, and thinking with visual patterns
Planning/*Gf*	**Planning Ability**	**Fluid Reasoning (*Gf*)**
Pattern Reasoning Story Completion	Measures the high-level, decision-making, executive processes associated with block 3. However, as Reitan (1988) states, "Block 3 is involved in no sensory, motor, perceptual, or speech functions and is devoted exclusively to analysis, planning, and organization of programs for behavior" (p. 335). Because any cognitive task involves perception of sensory input and either a motor or verbal response, the KABC-II measure of planning ability necessarily requires functions associated with the other two blocks as well.	Solving novel problems by using reasoning abilities such as induction and deduction
Verbal/*Gc*	**(*This scale is not included in the Luria model*)**	**Crystallized Ability (*Gc*)**
Riddles Expressive Vocabulary Verbal Knowledge		Demonstrating the breadth and depth of knowledge acquired from one's culture

NOTE : Verbal/*Gc* is included in the CHC system for the computation of the FCI, but it is excluded from the Luria system for the computation of the Mental Processing Index (MPI). The Planning/*Gf* scale is for ages 7–18 only. All other scales are for ages 4–18. Only the MPI and FCI are offered for 3-year-olds.

the mechanism by which children are given fair opportunity to adequately learn a task during administration. Thus, when a child responds incorrectly on a Sample item or a teaching item, the examiner demonstrates the correct response, gives a second trial, and teaches the task, if necessary. All subtests, except the Knowledge/*Gc* and Delayed Recall subtests, include teaching items. The specific teaching instructions are printed on the pages of the easel.

Out-of-Level Norms

Due to the structure of the KABC-II, examiners are able to conduct "out-of-level" testing for children that are either lower or higher functioning than their respective age-level counterparts. For example, if a 5-year-old is low functioning, the 5-year-old battery may be too frustrating for the child (and may not have an adequate floor), but the core battery for 4- or 3-year-olds may be at an appropriate level of difficulty. Conversely, high-functioning children ages 3–6 may benefit from the administration of a battery designed for older children. For example, a high-functioning 6-year-old may be bored during administration of the 6-year-old battery (and may not achieve a ceiling), but will be appropriately challenged by the battery for children ages 7–12. Importantly, the out-of-level battery yields scores based on norms for the child's *own* age group.

Testing Bilingual Children

The KABC-II authors recommend the use of the Nonverbal Scale when testing bilingual children who are *not* yet fluent in English. However, when testing bilingual children who *are* proficient in English, the entire KABC-II battery may be administered. The structure of the test allows the examiner to teach *relevant* sample and teaching items, and to present subtest directions and supplementary teaching instructions in an alternative language or communication method. In addition, if the examiner is capable of doing so, credit should be given when a verbal response is provided in a foreign language

that is equivalent to the correct response in English. To facilitate this administrative option, the KABC-II easels include: lists of correct and incorrect verbal responses in Spanish and English for Expressive Vocabulary, Gestalt Closure, and Riddles, and the Spanish version of instructions to the child for all subtests with sample or teaching items.

Timing

The original K-ABC did not offer bonus points for quick, perfect performance, but the KABC-II does offer one or two extra points for speed on later items of the Triangles, Pattern Reasoning, and Story Completion subtests. This decision was based on psychometric considerations concerning the "ceiling" and reliability of the subtests for *groups* of children. However, time bonus points may be inappropriate for *individual* children, for example, those with a motor impairment. Examiners may use their professional judgment to eliminate the time bonus points in those circumstances, and are provided alternative norms for Triangles, Pattern Reasoning, and Story Completion that permit obtaining scaled scores without the influence of time points. However, whenever possible, the standard scoring method (using time points for ages 7–18) is preferred.

Querying

Querying an incomplete or ambiguous answer occurs only on Riddles, Expressive Vocabulary, and Gestalt Closure, tasks that generally require a one-word answer. Consequently, the child's KABC-II profile is not affected very much by subjective scoring, which is occasionally a problem on Wechsler's verbal tasks.

Scoring

Obtaining and Recording Scaled Scores and Index Scores

The front cover of the record form is for recording scores for ages 7–18 and the back cover is for 3- to 6-year-olds. Make sure that you have the correct cover before proceeding. Also remember that the front *inside* cover is for documenting scale index analyses and graphing scale Indexes for 7- to 18-year-olds, whereas the back *inside* cover is for 3- to 6-year-olds.

Standard Scores and Scaled Scores

The KABC-II's two global scores, the MPI and FCI, are standard scores with a mean of 100 and a standard deviation (*SD*) of 15. However, only *one* of these global scores is computed and interpreted for any child or adolescent who is evaluated, based on the examiner's choice of the Luria or CHC model for that individual. When the Nonverbal Scale is administered instead of either the CHC or Luria model, the Nonverbal Index (NVI) also has a mean of 100 and *SD* = 15; so, too, do the additional KABC-II scales (e.g., Simultaneous/*Gv*, Planning/*Gf*). Note that for 3-year-olds, the only scales offered with a mean of 100 and *SD* of 15 are the MPI, FCI, and NVI. For all ages, all KABC-II subtests have a mean of 10 and *SD* of 3. The core subtest standard scores contribute to the scales but the supplementary scaled scores do not (except some supplementary subtests are included on the special Nonverbal Scale).

Qualitative Indicators

Each of the KABC-II subtests has an optional list of Qualitative Indicators (QIs) to help guide your observations of the child's behavior during the test session. Each QI is either disruptive (–) or enhancing (+) with regard to test performance. The KABC-II record form has space on the subtest pages for recording QIs along with a summary page on the inside front cover. You can use the *Summary of Qualitative Indicators* table on page 2 of the record form to check off the types of QIs that were observed from subtest to subtest. The record of these behaviors can be a source of helpful information when interpreting scores and writing a report.

Use of Scoring and Report Writing Software

KABC-II ASSIST™

The authors of the KABC-II have created a computer software program, the KABC-II ASSIST™, that facilitates the scoring process by eliminating hand scoring. The software contains both Macintosh and Windows programs on one CD-ROM. The KABC-II ASSIST™ works on the same platform as the KTEA-II ASSIST™, so examinee information (e.g., name, date of birth, dates of testing) will be saved and can transfer from one program to the next. Relevant demographic information and raw scores are inputted and converted into standardized scores by the program. The KABC-II ASSIST™ also provides the clinician with a score summary, scale profile, achievement/ability comparisons, and additional diagnostic information for hypothesis generation. The program does not, however, interpret the results or generate a report; that is the sole responsibility of the clinician.

Psychometric Properties

Standardization

The KABC-II was standardized on a sample of 3,025 children who were chosen to match closely the 2001 U.S. Census data on the variables of age, gender, geographic region, ethnicity, and parental education. The standardization sample was divided into 18 age groups, each composed of 100–200 children. The sample was split approximately equally between boys and girls with most groups consisting of exactly 200 children.

Reliability

The average internal consistency coefficients are .95 for the MPI at ages 3–6 and ages 7–18; for the FCI, means are .96 for ages 3–6 and .97 for ages 7–18. Internal consistency values for individual subtests range from .69 for Hand Movements to .92 on Rebus for ages 3–6 and from .74 on Gestalt

Closure to .93 on Rebus at ages 7–18. The median internal consistency value for the individual subtests is .84 for ages 3–6 and .86 for ages 7–18.

The KABC-II is a fairly stable instrument with average test–retest coefficients of .86, .89, and .91 for the MPI at ages 3–5, 7–12, and 13–18, respectively. Average test–retest coefficients for the FCI were .90, .91, and .94 at ages 3–5, 7–12, and 13–18, respectively. Across the three broad age groups, the ranges of the stability values of Learning/*Glr* (.76–.81), Sequential/*Gsm* (79–.80), Simultaneous/*Gv* (.74–.78), Planning/*Gf* (.80–.82), and Knowledge/*Gc* (.88–.95) denote adequate stability.

Validity

Construct validity of the KABC-II is supported by the factor-analytic studies described in the *KABC-II Manual* (Kaufman & Kaufman, 2004a). Results of confirmatory factor analyses (CFA) across age levels supported different batteries at different age levels. At age 3, a single-factor model is the basis for the KABC-II (although CFA did yield a distinction between the Sequential/*Gsm* subtests and the rest of the battery). At age 4, the Concept Formation subtest loaded substantially on both Knowledge/*Gc* and Simultaneous/*Gv*. This dual-loading led to a nonsignificant distinction between Knowledge/*Gc* and Simultaneous/*Gv*. Despite the findings of the CFA, the final battery separates Knowledge/*Gc* and Simultaneous/*Gv* into distinct scales on the basis of the distinct content in each of the scales. The other two factors measured at age 4, Sequential/*Gsm* and Learning/*Glr*, were well supported and distinct.

From ages 5 to 8, CFA was used to determine whether Simultaneous/*Gv* and Planning/*Gf* were distinguishable. Results indicated that at ages 5 and 6 these two abilities were not in fact distinguishable. However, at ages 7 and 8, these two ability factors were significantly separate. Thus, at ages 5–6 you will note that there are more Simultaneous/*Gv* subtests than at ages 7–8, when the Planning/*Gf* scale is introduced.

At ages 7–18, distinguishing Simultaneous /*Gv* and Planning/*Gf* was still critical. Thus, CFA helped determine which subtests to place on Simultaneous/*Gv* and Planning/*Gf* to yield the best distinction between the factors. Combining Rover and Triangles at ages 7–12 and Rover and Block Counting at ages 13–18 produced a Simultaneous/*Gv* factor that was distinct from Planning/*Gf*. The KABC-II manual suggests that at ages 7–12 Block Counting is a more cognitively complex task and at ages 13–18 it is more purely visual. In addition, the older children, who were administered the most difficult Triangles items, required more reasoning ability than visualization to complete the task.

Overall results of the CFA show that the subtests have high loadings on their intended scale and they load strongly on the general factor. At each age, the core subtests model fits the data well, and the scales were adequately separate from one another.

Tim Keith and his colleagues used confirmatory factor analysis to provide evidence supporting the consistency of the KABC-II's factor structure from ages 3 to 18 (Fine, Fisher, and Low, 2007) and demonstrating its invariance for both high- and low-ability groups (in press). Furthermore, their findings demonstrate that "for school-aged children (ages 6–18) the constructs measured by the KABC-II generally match those specified by CHC theory and operationalized in the scoring structure of the test" (p. 534). In addition, a study conducted by Hunt (2007) involved the administration of the KABC-II to 200 preschoolers (ages 4 to 5 years 11 months). The results provide additional support for the construct validity of the KABC-II for this age group by demonstrating through confirmatory factor analysis that the structure of the test is best explained by a "two-tiered model of multiple cognitive abilities [i.e., Broad and Narrow Abilities]" (p. 179). In other words, CHC theory serves as a good model for the factors that are being measured by the KABC-II for children ages 4 to 5 years 11 months.

In addition to factor analyses, validity of the KABC-II is further supported by correlations with the following instruments: WISC-III, WISC-IV, WPPSI-III, KAIT, and WJ-III (Kaufman & Kaufman, 2004a, Chapter 8). Each of the global scales of these instruments correlated strongly with the KABC-II MPI and FCI. Correlations ranged from .71 to .91. The KABC-II Knowledge/*Gc* scale correlated substantially higher with the verbal scales of the WJ-III and WISC-IV (.84, .85 respectively) than it did with the reasoning, visual spatial, and memory scales of each instrument. These patterns of correlations support the convergent and discriminant validity of the KABC-II.

Use of the Test

Interpretation Methods

The KABC-II's interpretive steps have been developed to serve as a clinician's guide for identifying and understanding a child's strong and weak areas of cognitive functioning and mental processing from both *normative* (age-based) and *ipsative* (person-based) perspectives. The system, discussed in this chapter, includes the four steps described in the KABC-II manual (Kaufman & Kaufman, 2004a, Chapter 5), but also expands the system to include three additional steps described in *Essentials of KABC-II Assessment* (Kaufman, Lichtenberger, Fletcher-Janzen, & Kaufman, 2005). To best illustrate the KABC-II's interpretive system, the six steps are presented here and illustrated with data obtained from an administration of the KABC-II to a child who has autism (see the case study). The reader is encouraged to refer to *Essentials of KABC-II Assessment* as it provides easy-to-follow interpretive worksheets that facilitate the interpretive process of the KABC-II (Kaufman et al., 2005, Appendix A).

Summary of the Six KABC-II Interpretive Steps

Essential Steps

Step 1. Interpret the **global scale index**, whether the FCI (CHC model), MPI (Luria model), or Nonverbal Index (NVI) (ages 3–18).

Step 2. Interpret the child's profile of scale indexes to **identify strengths and weaknesses**, both personal (relative to the child's overall *ability*) and normative (compared to children about the same *age*) (ages 4–18).

Optional Steps

Step 3. Planned Scale Comparisons

    Step 3A: Initial Learning vs. **Delayed Recall**—Learning/*Glr* (Initial) vs. Delayed Recall (ages 5–18)

    Step 3B: Learning vs. **Acquired Knowledge**—Learning/*Glr* vs. Knowledge/*Gc* (ages 4–18)

Step 4. Supplementary Subtest Analysis

Step 5. Planned Clinical Comparisons

    Step 5A: Nonverbal Ability (NVI) vs. **Verbal** Ability (ages 3–18)

    Step 5B: Problem-Solving Ability vs. **Memory & Learning** (ages 3–18)

    Step 5C: Visual Perception of **Meaningful** Stimuli vs. **Abstract** Stimuli (ages 4–18)

    Step 5D: Verbal Response vs. **Pointing** Response (ages 4–18)

    Step 5E: Little or **No Motor** Response vs. **Gross-Motor** Response (ages 4–18)

Step 6. Generate hypotheses to explain fluctuations in two circumstances:

    Step 6A: Scales that are **Not Interpretable** (ages 4–18)

    Step 6B: Supplementary Subtests that are Inconsistent with Pertinent Core Subtests (ages 3–18)

KABC-II ILLUSTRATIVE CASE STUDY

Name:	Helena S.
Age:	4 years 11 months
Grade in school:	Kindergarten
Evaluator:	Marlene Sotelo-Dynega, PsyD

Reason for Referral

Prior to beginning her kindergarten school year, Mrs. and Mr. S. brought their daughter, Helena, to the local elementary school for a kindergarten screening. In the screening, school personnel assessed areas such as concepts, motor skills, speech, vision/hearing, English language proficiency, and social skills. Results of the school's screening showed that Helena's performance in all domains was "Potentially Delayed," which was indicative of development that was significantly below what is expected for a child her age. As a result, the kindergarten screening team referred Helena to Dr. Manuel of the Children's Neurological Associates Group for a neurological evaluation. Dr. Manuel reported that Helena "has features consistent with a diagnosis of Autistic Spectrum Disorder based on her difficulties with social interaction and pragmatic speech." Dr. Manuel and Helena's parents requested an evaluation to assess Helena's cognitive abilities to determine program placement and interventions.

Test Administered

Kaufman Assessment Battery for Children—Second Edition (KABC-II)

Background Information

Helena currently resides with her biological parents, Mr. and Mrs. S., and her brother, Daniel (3 months). All members of the S. family are Caucasian, and were born and raised in the United States and speak English. The information obtained for this interview was obtained from Helena's parents.

Mrs. and Mr. S. reported that Helena was a product of a full-term pregnancy, delivered naturally and without complication. Although Helena was born without any health issues, according to her parents, doctors were initially concerned about Helena's small head circumference. As per the doctor's request, Helena's parents brought her to frequent, scheduled doctor visits to monitor her development. All assessments were unremarkable.

Mrs. and Mr. S. reported that Helena attained all developmental milestones within age-appropriate timeframes, with the exception of her speech. Although Helena began using one-word utterances before the age of 1 year, she continued to struggle with the use of phrases and sentences until she began attending kindergarten. Mrs. and Mr. S. indicated that Helena did not attend preschool or day care, but she was exposed to social situations with other children prior to beginning kindergarten.

When asked about Helena's behavior, Mrs. and Mr. S. disclosed that Helena is an "easy child to manage." However, she can be stubborn at times, particularly when someone interrupts her when doing something that she enjoys. Her parents find that Helena can often be redirected and calmed when she is frustrated. Her parents noted that Helena loves to draw and color in her free time at home. Often she attempts to draw pictures of the cartoons that she watches on television. Her parents have also observed that Helena has adjusted very nicely to the addition of her 3-month-old baby brother, Daniel. According to her parents, Helena enjoys helping her mother take care of her brother, and loves playing with him.

Since beginning school, Mrs. and Mr. S. have noticed significant improvements in Helena's speech and social skills. Her parents stated that Helena has begun to engage in pretend play at home, where she pretends to interact with her classmates. For example, Mr. S. has heard Helena say "Hi, Samantha (a classmate), my name is Helena, do you want to play with me?" Her parents also indicated that Helena is expressing her wants and needs more effectively than before she began attending school.

Behavioral Observations

Helena, an almost 5-year-old girl of average height and weight, readily accompanied the examiner to the testing office. She was neatly and appropriately dressed, and appeared to be in overall good health. Prior to the testing, Helena was reluctant to leave her classroom with the unfamiliar examiner, but she did so with encouragement from her teacher. Once in the testing room, Helena seemed more comfortable as she sat down and began to look around at the games, toys, and pictures in the room, and smiled. Overall, rapport was easily established through casual conversation and informal play.

Helena presented as a happy, easy-going youngster with significant language difficulty, specifically with pragmatic aspects of language. Helena had trouble taking turns in conversation, staying on topic, adjusting her high-pitched, loud tone of voice, and using language for different purposes. She communicated using one-word utterances, which were difficult to understand due to articulation difficulties. The examiner observed that she did not use her oral-motor musculature effectively, which in turn affected the quality of her speech production. Furthermore, Helena could not embellish her answers even with assistance from the examiner. For instance, when asked about how she gets along with her brother, Daniel, Helena responded "baby." The examiner replied, "Yes, he is a baby, do you play with the baby?" and Helena replied "baby." Although she could verbally label many things appropriately, she could not express herself in any way other than one-word utterances and gestures. Helena also often echoed what she heard. For example, when given a direction, Helena repeated the direction aloud to herself.

Helena was able to initiate and sustain appropriate eye contact, but her range of affect was limited. Often she smiled at inappropriate times during the testing session. Throughout the assessment, Helena was attentive but showed signs of impulsivity. Her attentiveness was evident from her ability to sit in her seat without any excessive fidgeting. She was well focused and motivated to do well on all tasks. In contrast to her attentiveness, she often repeated the examiner's prompts and directions, which required the examiner to implement visual and physical prompts to help Helena listen and wait for her turn to answer. For instance, during a task that required Helena to listen to a string of numbers and then repeat them in the order that they were presented, the examiner had to put up a finger to her ear and her mouth to suggest to the student that she should be listening; then, when it was her turn, the examiner would point to Helena. Also, during a task that required the examiner to present a series of hand gestures that Helena then had to copy on her own in the same order that they were presented, the examiner had to hold her hand down on the table to indicate that she should be observing and waiting her turn. Both of these interventions were successful and allowed the examiner to administer all subtests needed for this evaluation. Due to Helena's level of cooperation and ability to understand the task demands, the results of this assessment accurately reflect her current level of cognitive functioning. (See Table 4.3.)

TABLE 4.3   Psychometric Summary for Helena: KABC-II, CHC Model

Scale	Standard/Scaled Scores Mean = 100/10; SD = 15/3	95% Confidence Interval	Percentile Rank
Sequential/*Gsm*	77	[70–86]	6
Number Recall	6		9
Word Order	6		9
Hand Movements	8		25
Simultaneous/*Gv*	83	[74–94]	13
Conceptual Thinking	5		5
Face Recognition	10		50
Triangles	7		16
Gestalt Closure	6		9
Learning/*Gf*	78	[70–88]	7
Atlantis	5		5
Rebus	7		16
Knowledge/*Gc*	88	[80–98]	21
Expressive Vocabulary	9		37
Riddles	6		9
Verbal Knowledge	7		16
Fluid-Crystallized Index (FCI)	77	[71–83]	6

NOTE : Italicized subtests are Supplementary and not included in the calculation of the indexes.

Test Results and Interpretation

Helena was administered the KABC-II, a test of intellectual and processing ability that provides scales to identify her cognitive strengths and weaknesses.

> **Model Selection**
> Although the child has moderate to severe expressive language difficulties, the examiner chose the CHC model of test selection and interpretation to get a broader view of the child's cognitive abilities that includes tests of acquired knowledge (Knowledge/*Gc*).

The KABC-II is based on a dual-theoretical foundation, Luria's neuropsychological model and the CHC psychometric theory. Given Helena's mainstream cultural background, English-speaking proficiency, and the reason for referral, the examiner chose the CHC model to guide test selection and interpretation of the KABC-II. This model yields the Fluid-Crystallized Index (FCI) as the global measure of general cognitive ability, along with four scale indexes (Sequential/*Gsm*, Simultaneous/*Gv*, Learning/*Glr*, Knowledge/*Gc*).

Helena's overall cognitive ability was within the Below Average range (6th percentile), as evidenced from her KABC-II FCI of 77. The chances are 95% that her true FCI is between 71 and 83. Her individual abilities, as measured by the four theory-based scales that compose KABC-II, ranged from the 21st percentile on her lexical development and general fund of information (Knowledge/*Gc* scale standard score of 88) to the 6th percentile on her short-term memory skills (Sequential/*Gsm* standard score of 77).

As evidenced by Helena's Knowledge/*Gc* index of 88, her language development, vocabulary skills, and base of knowledge are within the expected range for a child her age. She performed better than 21 out of 100 children her age. Helena's Knowledge/*Gc* index is consistent with her Below Average level of cognitive ability, as well as her performance on the remaining three indexes. It must be noted that although Helena's Knowledge/*Gc* index was within the average range, the tasks that compose the scale require only one-word responses. Although Helena demonstrates average language development and lexical knowledge abilities based on her performance on this scale, she is not able to use the language that she knows to express her wants and needs, to answer a question, or simply to respond to a peer's request to play. By the age of four, children are typically able to express themselves with multiword, complete sentences.

> **Step 1: Interpret the Global Scale Index**
> Analysis of the score differences between Helena's highest (Knowledge/*Gc*, 88) and lowest (Sequential/*Gsm*) Index scores suggests that the Fluid-Crystallized Index (FCI) is interpretable as there is less than a 23 point difference (1.5 standard deviations) between the two scores.

> **Step 2: Interpret the child's profile of scale indexes to identify strengths and weaknesses, both normative and personal**
> *Step 2a*, determine whether the four index scores are interpretable based on the consistency of performance on the Core subtests that comprise each scale, using a base rate criterion of less than 10%. All four of Helena's Indexes: Sequential/*Gsm* (77), Simultaneous/*Gv* (83), Learning/*Glr* (78), and Knowledge/*Gc* (88) were deemed interpretable, as she performed consistently on the tasks that comprise each separate scale.
>
> *Step 2b*, for the interpretable scales, we identify Normative Weaknesses (standard scores below 85) and Normative Strengths (standard scores above 115). Three out of Helena's four interpretable indexes were Normative Weaknesses: Sequential/*Gsm* (77), Simultaneous/*Gv* (83), Learning/*Glr* (78); her performance on the Knowledge/*Gc* scale (88) was within normal limits/average range.
>
> *Step 2c* involves the determination of whether there are any Personal Strengths or Weaknesses in the child's profile. Upon calculating the mean of the four scale indexes, each scale index is subtracted from the mean to determine if the difference between the scores is significant. Helena's performance on all four scales was consistent with her average level of cognitive ability; there were no personal strengths or weaknesses noted.
>
> *Step 2d*, if there are any Personal Strengths or Weaknesses, consider whether the difference is infrequent, or occurring in less than 10% of the population. This step is not applicable for Helena since there were no Personal Strengths or Weaknesses noted.

In contrast to her average lexical knowledge and base of knowledge, Helena's visual processing, long-term storage and retrieval, and short-term memory abilities were below average compared to her peers. These depressed abilities were notable from her performance on the Simultaneous/*Gv* (standard score = 83), Learning/*Glr* (standard score = 78), and Sequential/*Gsm* (standard score = 77) scales. Although these indexes reveal normative weaknesses because these scores were below expectation in comparison to her same-aged peers, they were consistent with her overall below-average level of cognitive ability. Helena's below-average visual processing, long-term storage and retrieval, and short-term memory abilities will likely impact the efficiency with which she learns, and may necessitate specialized interventions and instruction.

Summary and Diagnostic Impressions

Helena, an almost 5-year-old girl in kindergarten, was referred for an evaluation by her parents upon receiving a diagnosis of *autistic disorder* by Dr. Manuel of the Children's Neurological Associates Group. The goal of this evaluation was to assess Helena's cognitive abilities and to determine program placement and interventions. During the evaluation, Helena was happy and easily engaged, but struggled to express herself verbally. Her language difficulties appear to be the result of a moderate-to-severe level

Step 3: Planned scale comparisons
Step3a, if interpretable. Initial Learning (Learning/*Glr*) versus Delayed Recall (Delayed Learning/*Glr*) are compared to allow the clinician to contrast the child's initial learning of new information with their ability to retain that information about 20 minutes later. This step was not applicable for Helena, since the delayed subtests are not administered to children in her age group. *Step 3b*, if interpretable. Learning Ability (Learning/*Glr*) versus Acquired Knowledge (Knowledge/*Gc*) are compared to provide information regarding how the child learns new material during the test session versus their ability to learn verbal facts and concepts over time at home and in school. Helena's performance on both scales was compared and was not found to significantly differ, suggesting that her ability to learn is consistent with the material she has already learned.

Steps 4 and 5: Supplementary subtest analysis and planned clinical comparisons
Step 4: If a scale was deemed interpretable in *Step 2*, the clinician is able to compare each Supplementary subtest that was administered with the mean scaled score of the Core subtests on that scale. For Helena's age group (4-year-olds), Supplementary subtests from the Sequential/*Gsm* (Hand Movements), Simultaneous/*Gv* (Gestalt Closure), and Knowledge/*Gc* (Verbal Knowledge) subtests were conducted. Once again, Helena's performance on the supplementary subtests was consistent with the mean scaled score performance of the Core subtests on that scale.

Step 5: Planned clinical comparisons. The step is comprised of five planned clinical comparisons that allow the clinician to assess two different domains of information processing. *Steps 5a* and *5b* involve the comparison of "integration and storage" that will help the clinician develop and analyze hypotheses about the child's verbal and nonverbal ability (*Step 5a*) and problem solving ability vs. memory and learning (*Step 5b*). *Steps 5c, 5d,* and *5e* involve the comparison of "input and output." Hypotheses about the input and output of information involve the child's ability to process meaningful vs. abstract visual stimuli (*Step 5c*), to answer questions with verbal vs. pointing responses (*Step 5d*), and responding to problems that demand little or no motor response as opposed to a gross motor response (*Step 5e*). In Helena's case, all of the planned clinical comparisons yielded nonsignificant differences, indicating that each of these abilities is equally well developed.

of articulation difficulty, as well as a deficit in the pragmatic aspects of language. On the KABC-II, Helena's overall level of cognitive ability was in the Below Average range (she earned an FCI of 77; 6th percentile), which is consistent with her performance on the other four scales of the test, and with her results from the school's kindergarten screening that indicated that there was a "Potential Delay." Helena has evenly developed cognitive abilities with no personal strengths or weaknesses. Although Helena's strongest performance was on the Average range Knowledge/*Gc* scale (standard score of 88; 21st percentile), her performance was indicative of her

> **Step 6: Generate hypotheses to explain fluctuations in two circumstances**
>
> This step assists the clinician in generating hypotheses to explain why scales are not interpretable (*Step 6a*), and why supplemental subtests that were analyzed as part of *Step 4* were not consistent with the core subtests that they were being compared to (*Step 6b*). In Helena's case, all four indexes were interpretable and her supplementary subtest performances were consistent with her Core subtest performance; therefore, this step would not be necessary. In the event that there are noninterpretable indexes or supplementary subtests performances that are not consistent with Core subtest performance, this step should be used as a starting point for hypothesis generation. The clinician must seek corroborating data and/or observations (including *Qualitative Indicators*) to support the hypotheses that are generated from this step, which at times may require additional testing. The main guidelines are to be flexible, to seek multiple pieces of corroborating evidence, to be a vigilant clinician during the administration of all tasks, and to be knowledgeable in pertinent theory and research.

language development and lexical knowledge abilities, not of the functional aspects of language, which are clearly delayed.

Overall, Helena's performance on the KABC-II; interviews with her parents, teachers, and neurologist; and observations made by this examiner across multiple settings are consistent with a diagnosis of *autistic disorder*.

Recommendations

Helena requires a comprehensive speech and language evaluation by a speech and language pathologist that will include the assessment of receptive, expressive, and pragmatic aspects of language.

Helena requires an evaluation of her academic achievement that will be used to develop academic goals for her Individualized Education Program (IEP).

Helena would benefit from a social-skills counseling group to assist in her development of pragmatic language and appropriate play skills.

Pending the results of the abovementioned evaluations, the multidisciplinary team (including Helena's parents) must meet to determine whether a small-class placement is a more appropriate learning environment for Helena.

IDENTIFICATION OF SPECIAL POPULATIONS

The structure of the test, accompanied by the breadth and depth of the constructs measured by the KABC-II, allow the practitioner to utilize the test for a variety of applications that are based on the reason for referral. The following section includes the summaries of the clinical validity studies that were included in the KABC-II *Manual*. The studies involve the comparison of performances on the KABC-II between seven exceptional groups and a nonclinical reference group that was derived from the KABC-II standardization sample. Considering that the illustrative case study included in this chapter was of an *autistic* child, we will begin with the autistic validity study to highlight both similarities and differences between the case and the validity studies.

Autism

The KABC-II manual reports findings from a sample of 38 children with *autistic disorder* (not high-functioning autism or Asperger's disorder). The mean age for the autistic group was 13:3 (ranging from 4:3 to 18:10). The sample was 84% male and 50% Caucasian. The cognitive functioning of the autistic group was in the Below Average to Lower Extreme range of functioning across all domains. Mean KABC-II global scores spanned the narrow range of 66.9 (FCI) to 68.6 (NVI). Their mean Index profile ranged from a low of 66.1 on Knowledge/*Gc* to a high of 76.1 on Learning/*Glr*. The comparable mean standard scores on Knowledge/*Gc* and NVI indicate no difference in this sample's performance on verbal versus nonverbal tasks. However, consistent with the research showing that children with autism perform relatively well on Wechsler's Block Design and K-ABC Triangles, the sample tested on the KABC-II earned their second highest mean scaled score on Triangles (6.1); only their mean score of 6.6 on the supplementary Gestalt Closure subtest was higher. These two areas of relative strength coincide with data on the original K-ABC (Allen et al., 1991).

Helena's case provides an excellent example of the nature of autism. Similar to the clinical validity sample, Helena's cognitive ability was Below Average. On the other hand, Helena's

scale performances ranged from Average to Below Average, indicating that although she met diagnostic criteria for autism, she was clearly a "higher functioning" child with a relatively consistent cognitive profile (since no personal strengths or weaknesses were noted). In addition, although younger children were included in the clinical sample, the mean age of the group was much higher than Helena's age (4:11) and consisted mostly of males. In other words, this sample may not be representative of Helena, or the *spectrum* of autistic children.

Verbal Knowledge (3.9) and Riddles (4.0) were two of the three lowest average scaled scores. These low scores on two Knowledge/*Gc* subtests are likely a reflection of this population's overall poor communicative and language abilities, and general poor achievement in school. This finding is further supported by past research showing that children with autistic disorder perform poorly on subtests requiring verbal conceptualization, such as Wechsler's Comprehension (Barnhill et al., 2000; Ehlers et al., 1997). Unlike these two low Knowledge/*Gc* subtests, Expressive Vocabulary was not one of the lowest scores for the group, on average—perhaps because Expressive Vocabulary requires a simple naming of a pictured object, and doesn't require a higher level of abstract thinking or verbal conceptualization.

Individuals diagnosed with autistic disorder performed very poorly on Rover (3.5), a Simultaneous/*Gv* subtest that requires children to find the "quickest" path for a toy dog to reach his bone on a checkerboard-like grid. Past research has shown that children with autistic disorder typically perform relatively well on tasks that require simultaneous processing and spatial visualization (Allen et al., 1991; Tsatsanis et al., 2003). Although Rover is a Simultaneous/*Gv* subtest, it also places heavy demands on executive functioning and deductive reasoning, abilities that may not have been as well developed as visualization in the KABC-II sample of individuals with autism.

Perhaps the most interesting finding in the KABC-II study with individuals diagnosed with autism is their relative strength on the Learning/*Glr* scale (Index = 76.1). Indeed, the sample earned its highest standard score on the supplementary Delayed Recall scale (standard score = 82.8, a standard deviation higher than their mean MPI of 68.1). These scores indicate that the children with autism were able to learn new information that was taught by the examiner during the evaluation and that they were able to retain that information after an interval of about 20 minutes, despite the interference of being administered other cognitive tasks. There are four noteworthy aspects of this finding of relative strength in the learning and retention of newly learned information: (1) The component subtests involve language as well as visual stimuli, with Rebus requiring both verbalization and the learning of a new pictorial language; (2) most comprehensive batteries that have been administered to individuals with autism—such as Wechsler's scales, the Binet-4, and the original K-ABC—did not measure learning ability, so the present results are suggestive of a previously unknown cognitive strength for these children and adolescents; (3) the learning of new information ties directly to the classroom, such that these results may provide specific ideas for the educational intervention of individuals with autism; and (4) another sample of children who traditionally perform relatively poorly on tests that emphasize language—those with hearing loss—also had relative strengths in learning (mean Index = 101.6) and delayed recall (mean standard score = 101.3).

Previous research has shown a pattern of stronger simultaneous processing than sequential processing in children with autistic disorder (Allen et al., 1991), but that pattern was not found on the KABC-II. Autistic children earned similar mean Indexes of about 70 on the Sequential/*Gsm* and Simultaneous/*Gv* scales. At least two differences in the studies may explain the difference in the findings: (1) The autistic group in the original K-ABC study was higher functioning than the KABC-II sample (Mental Processing Composite of 81.3 vs. MPI of 68.1), and (2) the

Simultaneous Processing subtests have changed considerably from the K-ABC to the KABC-II (Matrix Analogies, Spatial Memory, and Photo Series were removed; Rover and Block Counting were added). Indeed, the correlation between the K-ABC Simultaneous Processing scale and the KABC-II Simultaneous/*Gv* scale is .62.

Specific Learning Disabilities

According to the Individuals with Disabilities Education Improvement Act (IDEA, 2004), a *specific learning disability (SLD)*

> *means a disorder in one or more of the basic psychological processes involved in understanding or in using language, spoken or written, that may manifest itself in the imperfect ability to listen, think, speak, read, write, spell, or to do mathematical calculations, including conditions such as perceptual disabilities, brain injury, minimal brain dysfunction, dyslexia, and developmental aphasia.*

The use of the KABC-II, in conjunction with the Kaufman Test of Educational Achievement—Second Edition (KTEA-II; Kaufman & Kaufman, 2005), allows for the comprehensive evaluation of the psychological processes, consistent with criteria described in the regulations to IDEA (2004), that may be contributing to learning issues in students. Although there are many ways of determining the cognitive functioning of a child who is experiencing difficulties in the classroom, a multifaceted approach that includes response to intervention along with a comprehensive evaluation of psychological processes and achievement is the most appropriate. There is much research evidence to demonstrate that cognitive ability tests, in the past and on their own, simply cannot carry the burden of predicting how a child with an SLD responds to academic intervention. However, cognitive ability tests that measure processing strengths and weaknesses fit very well into the comprehensive assessment paradigm (Teeter, 1997), and those measures, like the KABC-II, that have a clear delineation of process from product have a specific place in the comprehensive assessments of today and of the future.

SLD Studies with the K-ABC-II

There were three prepublication studies of children with learning disabilities conducted with the KABC-II: a reading disability study, a mathematics disability study, and a written expression disability study (Kaufman & Kaufman, 2004a). The results of the learning disability studies indicate some interesting similarities across groups. For example, all three groups had significantly different scores (p < .001) on *all* scales compared to the nonclinical reference sample. It would be reasonable to suspect that different disabilities would produce significant differences on some scales but not others. While some differences were greater than others, overall, all three groups were significantly different from the control sample for the entire set of KABC-II scales. Therefore, it would be appropriate to assume that children with learning disabilities on the whole will perform very differently on the KABC-II than their peers who do not have disabilities.

Another general observation for the three groups is that they all have mean Simultaneous/*Gv* Indexes that are slightly higher than all of the other mean Indexes. The phenomenon of the Sequential scale score being slightly lower than the Simultaneous scale score in children with SLD has been observed for years with the K-ABC, but the Learning /*Glr*, Planning/*Gf*, and Knowledge/*Gc* Scales are new and it will be interesting to see whether this relationship continues in future research studies.

Another salient overall comparison is that there was little difference in the MPI and FCI for the three groups, with standard scores ranging from 79.3 to 82.6 (see Figure 4.1). In these studies, children with learning disabilities generally performed much lower than their control peers, but these SLD samples were not necessarily different from each other. One reason for the similarity in KABC-II profiles concerns the fact that the SLD groups were in no way

"pure." Of the 96 students with math disabilities, 81% also had reading disabilities. Similarly, 34% of the students with written expression disabilities also had reading disabilities (Kaufman et al., 2005).

The performance of the three disability groups on the Learning/*Glr* scale of the KABC-II is of particular interest. The Learning/*Glr* scale was developed for the KABC-II for many reasons, but primarily to assist in the investigation of a child's learning in a dynamic/interactive way. It was designed to provide the child with an opportunity to bring a learning experience together with the help of a teacher—in this case, the KABC-II examiner.

The Learning/*Glr* scale is a demanding scale because it requires that all of the cognitive processes work together. Children must use sequential abilities to listen and organize information in a serial manner and learn in a step-by-step fashion; they must use simultaneous processing to perceive, organize, and remember visual information; and they must use planning abilities to prioritize information processing. The complexity of processes utilized for the Learning/*Glr* scale is very much like a functional symphony where the first and second functional units of the brain (measured by the Sequential/*Gsm* and Simultaneous/*Gv* scales) must interact and take direction and sustain interest from the third functional unit (measured by the Planning/*Gf* scale). A disability in any of these areas can affect scores on the respective scales, but may also affect the performance on the Learning/*Glr* scale where it all has to come together.

The KABC-II learning disability study groups demonstrated consistent difficulties in all of the scales (see Table 4.4), and the end product was commensurate performance difficulties on the Learning/*Glr* scale and its Delayed Recall counterpart. Of course, these results are group scores, and individual children with learning disabilities will inevitably show unique patterns of performance. Indeed, the research literature has not yet shown any definitive patterns of processing among all children with learning

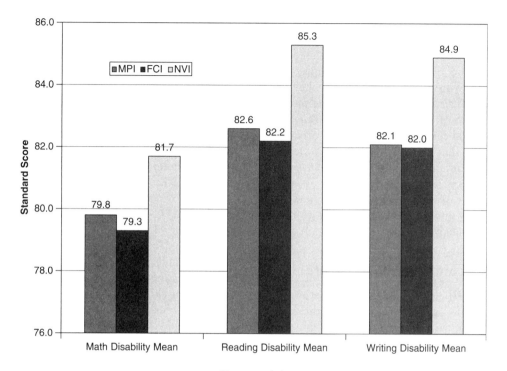

FIGURE 4.1
KABC-II MPI, FCI, and NVI for Three Learning-Disabled Groups

TABLE 4.4 Mean KABC-II Index Scores for Children with Reading, Mathematics, and Writing Disabilities

KABC-II Scale	Math Disability Mean	Reading Disability Mean	Writing Disability Mean
Sequential/*Gsm*	83.7	85.4	84.6
Simultaneous/*Gv*	84.6	88.1	87.7
Learning/*Glr*	83.7	84.3	83.9
Planning/*Gf*	82.7	86.8	86.8
Knowledge/*Gc*	82.0	84.8	85.2

NOTE: Adapted from Kaufman and Kaufman (2004a, Tables 8.31, 8.32, 8.33).

disabilities (Lichtenberger, 2001). Nonetheless, we would expect that a specific deficit would still show up in poor performance. It will be interesting to see in future research how different subtypes of learning disabilities may be evidenced on the Learning/*Glr* scale.

One point that should be mentioned is that each disability group had a Knowledge/*Gc* Index that was very similar to the other KABC-II Indexes for that group. Although the Knowledge/*Gc* scale is the closest in construct to the Achievement scale on the original K-ABC, there are notable differences. The KABC-II Knowledge/*Gc* Index does not include the conventional achievement subtests (reading and math) that were on the K-ABC, and for ages 7–18 the Knowledge/*Gc* Index is composed of one subtest that is entirely receptive in nature (Verbal Knowledge) and one that requires only one-word responses (Riddles). Ordinarily, a discrepancy would be expected for samples of children diagnosed with learning disabilities (as in an ability/achievement discrepancy). Probably, the reason for this nondiscrepancy is that the Knowledge/*Gc* scale on the KABC-II is more receptive in nature and does not require complex verbal responses from the examinee as other verbal/achievement tests have done in the past. In addition, one of the Core Knowledge/*Gc* Core subtests (Riddles) demands good fluid reasoning ability (in addition to crystallized knowledge). Also, the Kaufmans deliberately tried to measure facts and verbal concepts on all three Knowledge/*Gc* subtests that are accessible within the everyday environment, as opposed to being specifically taught in school.

Speech and Language Disorders

The KABC-II deemphasizes language and acquired knowledge in the Luria model, the model that the Kaufmans recommend be administered to children with receptive, expressive, or mixed receptive-expressive language disorders. In addition, if the examiner believes that the MPI yielded by the Luria model unfairly penalizes children with moderate-to-severe language disorders, then the NVI provides an excellent way to assess these children's global cognitive functioning.

The Knowledge/*Gc* subtests are not likely to reflect the cognitive *abilities* of children with language impairments, but are more likely to be a reflection of their areas of *impairment*. Nonetheless, when these subtests are administered as supplements to the MPI or NVI, examiners often will obtain beneficial additional information. For example, on tasks requiring simple verbal expression, such as naming a pictured object (Expressive Vocabulary) or requiring receptive understanding (Verbal Knowledge), children with language impairments do not always perform poorly (Lichtenberger & Kaufman, 2004). In contrast, on tasks that require more extensive processing of language and verbal reasoning (e.g., Riddles), children with language impairments are likely to struggle. These differences in performance on the various verbally laden *Gc*

tests may provide good behavioral observations and clinical information that will be useful for interpreting a wide range of the spectrum of abilities of children diagnosed with language disorders. To facilitate the examiner's observation of variables that may influence performance, each Knowledge/*Gc* subtest includes a list of relevant disruptive or enhancing Qualitative Indicators (QIs) on the record form.

In addition to minimal focus on verbal knowledge in the Luria model, speed of processing is not emphasized in the KABC-II. Three subtests on the KABC-II require the recording of response time (Triangles, Pattern Reasoning, and Story Completion). On these three subtests, children and adolescents aged 7–18 can obtain one or two extra points on each item that they complete rapidly. For children with language impairments (who historically have struggled on tasks that require rapid processing; Miller et al., 2001), examiners should select the alternative option offered by the KABC-II, which permits scoring these three subtests based only on correct answers (with time points excluded). Scaled scores are then based on this special procedure, deemphasizing processing speed for children who might be unfairly penalized by the need to respond quickly.

Attention Deficit Disorders

The KABC-II was administered to 56 children diagnosed with ADHD according to DSM-IV-TR criteria. The sample was 70% male and 73% Caucasian, with a mean age of 5:11. The ADHD sample was compared to a group of nonclinical children who were matched on sex, ethnicity, and parent education.

This sample of children with ADHD performed about equally well on all KABC-II indexes, but scored significantly lower than nonclinical children on all scales. They averaged about 93 on the MPI and FCI, with Scale Indexes spanning the narrow range from 92.5 on Simultaneous/*Gv* to 95.9 on both Learning/*Glr* and Knowledge/*Gc*. The Kaufmans' emphasis when revising the K-ABC and developing the second edition was to assess high-level cognitive ability on virtually all Core subtests, with an emphasis on working memory and executive functioning. Indeed, working memory is needed to succeed on the subtests that constitute each of the scales: It is needed to cope with the color interference task on Word Order (Sequential/*Gsm*); to code and store the paired associations on the Learning/*Glr* subtests; to permit children to generate and select hypotheses and perform other executive functions on the Simultaneous/*Gv* and Planning/*Gf* subtests; and to enable children to integrate different aspects of a construct to solve Riddles items (a Knowledge/*Gc* subtest).

Given the deficits in the areas of executive functioning and working memory for children with ADHD (Brady & Denckla , 1994; Mahone et al., 2002; Perugini et al., 2000; Seidman, Biederman et al., 1995, Seidman, Biederman, Faraone, Weber, & Oullette, 1997), children with ADHD may experience difficulty on all of the KABC-II scales, leading to a pattern of uniform deficits (relative to the normal control group) on all of the KABC-II scales. Similar to the small amount of variability on the five scales, the variability among the subtests was also minimal. Only 1.2 points (0.4 *SD*) separated the highest and lowest subtests for this sample. Mean scaled scores for the children with ADHD ranged from a low of 8.4 on Block Counting to a high of 9.6 on Gestalt Closure. All of the Sequential/*Gsm* subtests were among the lowest scores for the group, along with Rover.

Whether future KABC-II studies of children and adolescents diagnosed with ADHD will display characteristic profiles, or will continue to demonstrate flat profiles, is unknown. However, as Barkley (1998) has emphasized, cognitive test profiles have not proven especially useful for ADHD diagnosis. What comprehensive test batteries offer most to clinicians are standardized observations of how children approach different tasks, especially if they have to cope with attentional problems.

The KABC-II, by virtue of its emphasis on executive functioning and working memory, offers clinicians a rich source of behavioral observations. In particular, Rover, the two Learning/*Glr* subtests, and the two Planning/*Gf* subtests put children with ADHD into sink-or-swim situations in which they must employ working memory and cope with a bombardment of stimuli while solving each item. The supplementary Delayed Recall scale affords the opportunity to assess how a child's attentional problems might interfere with retention of newly learned information about 20 minutes later in the evaluation (i.e., do the intervening tasks make it unusually difficult for individuals with attentional problems to retain the paired associations?). In addition, when assessing children with ADHD, the KABC-II provides the examiner with a structured method for observing relevant behaviors. The Qualitative Indicators (QIs) that are located on the record form for each respective subtest include items such as *fails to sustain attention*, *impulsively responds incorrectly*, *does not monitor accuracy*, and *repeatedly breaks rules*.

All of these aspects of the KABC-II suggest its value for specific *individuals* referred for a known or suspected attentional disorder. Nonetheless, much additional *group* data based on samples of children diagnosed with ADHD are needed to facilitate and more fully understand the applications of the KABC-II in clinical practice. Especially valuable will be studies in which children with ADHD are assessed both on and off their therapeutic doses of medication. Test data obtained while the children are on medication will most accurately reflect their actual competence (rather than having results of questionable validity because of a significant amount of distractibility, hyperactivity, or impulsivity).

Deaf and Hard of Hearing

During the standardization process, three skilled school psychologists (fluent in direct communication skills and experienced in working with deaf and hard-of-hearing children) administered the KABC-II to 27 children who were classified in special education as hearing impaired. These children ranged in age from 6:8 to 17:7 (mean 12 1/2 years) and were educated in either a state residential school for the deaf (CA) or a local education program (VA). The scores of these children were compared to a nonclinical reference group that was matched for age, gender, race/ethnicity, and parent education. The hearing impaired children earned an average NVI of 95.7 (SD = 17.1), which was 8.7 points lower than the reference group. The Nonverbal subtest scores ranged from 8.5 (Block Counting) to 9.6 (Hand Movements, Triangles, and Story Completion). Children with hearing impairment did not perform significantly differently from the reference group on either Hand Movements or Triangles, but did perform significantly lower on Block Counting (.7 SD), Pattern Reasoning (.5 SD), and Story Completion (.4 SD).

Although the NVI is the most appropriate score to interpret when assessing deaf and hard-of-hearing children, this clinical sample was administered the full KABC-II battery during standardization for statistical analyses. Qualified and trained examiners may find other KABC-II subtests of use in assessments as well. As expected, hearing impaired children performed most poorly on the Knowledge/Gc scale (mean standard score of 80.9). This scale is primarily verbally based and requires verbal expression and understanding as well as verbal reasoning, so for children who are hearing impaired, the requisite skills needed to succeed are often hindered by virtue of their disability. The Knowledge/Gc scale also contained the lowest subtest scaled score for this clinical group: Expressive Vocabulary (the mean scaled score of 4.5 was more than 2 SDs below the average score for the reference group).

Similar to findings reported on the original K-ABC (Ullssi, Brice, & Gibbons, 1985) and on Wechsler's tests (Braden, 1984; Slate & Fawcett, 1995; Sullivan & Montoya, 1997), children with hearing impairment also struggled on the Sequential/Gsm scale (with the exception of Hand Movements). Overall, children scored 20 points lower than the reference group on the Sequential/Gsm scale (mean Index = 83.2). Apparently, the Low Average Sequential/Gsm Index was primarily a function of the auditory stimuli (numbers and words spoken by the examiner) on the two Core Sequential/Gsm subtests. In contrast to the mean scaled scores of about 7 on the Core subtests, the sample of children with hearing loss earned a mean scaled score of 9.6 on the supplementary Hand Movements subtest. That average performance suggests intact sequential processing and short-term memory for children with hearing loss when language is eliminated from the tasks.

In contrast to the Low Average Knowledge/Gc and Sequential/Gsm Indexes, the sample of children with hearing loss scored solidly within the Average Range on the Simultaneous/Gv Index (mean = 94.6), Planning/Gf Index (mean = 97.6), and Learning/Glr Index (mean = 101.6). The latter result is extremely noteworthy because both Core Learning/Glr subtests require the child to understand words spoken by the examiner (that are paired with visual stimuli), and Rebus also requires verbal expression. Despite these considerable language demands, the Learning/Glr Index indicates that the group of children with hearing loss was able to demonstrate intact learning ability—comparable to the normal control group—when faced with structured storage-and-retrieval tasks requiring integration of visual and auditory stimuli.

On the various Core and supplementary subtests that are included on the Simultaneous/Gv and Planning/Gf scales, only one subtest places demands on verbal expression—Gestalt Closure. That subtest yielded a mean scaled score of 7.9 for the children with hearing loss, undoubtedly a finding that is related more to the children's verbalizations than to their visual processing.

As indicated, children with hearing impairments performed most similarly to the normative mean (and to the nonclinical reference group) on the Learning/Glr scale. Hearing impaired children performed similarly on the two Learning/*Glr* subtests (Atlantis and Rebus), and also performed equally well on the Delayed Recall portion of the tests. Many hearing impaired children have experience with visual languages (i.e., ASL or other signed languages), which may contribute to their ability to learn tasks like Rebus and Atlantis that require mapping language onto a visual format.

Mental Retardation

The *KABC-II Manual* (Kaufman & Kaufman, 2004a) reports the results of a study of 42 children diagnosed with mild mental retardation. The mean age of the group was 11:2, and their mean FCI was 64.5 ($SD = 13.6$). This SD is larger than is typically found in samples diagnosed with mental retardation. In general, SDs for such samples are restricted in range in large part because strict cutoff scores (e.g., < 70) are used to make the diagnosis. All children in the KABC-II sample had a diagnosis of mental retardation when initially assessed (typically on a Wechsler scale). When previously diagnosed children are assessed again, their scores will tend to regress to the mean, especially when using a different instrument than the one used for the diagnosis. Hence, the SDs on the FCI and other KABC-II Indexes are larger than usual.

Like the group's mean FCI, their mean MPI (64.8) and NVI (65.6) were also in the mid-60s, consistent with expectations. The group's scale profile showed some variability with mean Indexes ranging from about 65 on the two problem-solving scales (Simultaneous/*Gv* and Planning/*Gf*) to 72.4 on the Learning/*Glr* scale. The group's mean NVI of 65.6 was slightly lower than its mean Knowledge/*Gc* Index (69.1), indicating about equal functioning on the traditional nonverbal–verbal comparison.

Although specific subtest patterns have not historically characterized the performance of children with mental retardation, we examined the highest and lowest KABC-II subtests for these children. Two Simultaneous/*Gv* subtests

were among the three lowest for this group: Rover and Triangles. Although both Rover and Triangles measure visual processing, Rover has a distinct executive functioning and fluid reasoning component, exemplified by one of its CHC Narrow Abilities (General Sequential Reasoning, also referred to as *deductive reasoning*). Also among the three lowest subtests was Pattern Reasoning, a Planning/*Gf* subtest that also measures higher-level executive functioning and fluid reasoning abilities and assesses the CHC Narrow Ability of Induction (or *inductive reasoning*).

In contrast, the three highest subtests for this group of children with mental retardation called on acquired knowledge, memory, and visual closure speed. The highest subtests came from three separate scales: Expressive Vocabulary (Knowledge/*Gc*), Gestalt Closure (Simultaneous/*Gv*), and Atlantis (Learning/*Glr*).

Some of the limitations that were noted for using the first-edition K-ABC with children who have mental retardation were addressed in the creation of the KABC-II. For example, Kamphaus and Reynolds (1987) noted that the K-ABC lacked enough easy items for developmentally delayed children, creating a poor floor for these children. Also, the K-ABC's Mental Processing Composite did not extend below a standard score of 55, which made the diagnosis of moderate (IQ range: 35–55) or severe (IQ range: 20–40) levels of mental retardation difficult. The KABC-II extended the floor on many subtests and allows out-of-level testing for children with known or suspected cognitive delays. The MPI, FCI, and NVI all yield scores that are three to four standard deviations below the normative mean of 100 (the lowest standard scores range from 40 to 49). The five indexes yield equally strong floors at all ages, with the lowest standard scores ranging from 40 to 51. These floors are lower than the original K-ABC, making it useful for diagnosing children with more extreme levels of mental retardation.

Another benefit of using the KABC-II in assessing children with mental retardation is the availability of sample and teaching items, as well as the reduced emphasis on verbal expression and school-learned knowledge. In addition to ensuring that children understand a task, teaching items allow examiners to see how children respond to instruction, which is useful in developing educational recommendations. Response to feedback is also a built-in aspect of the Learning/*Glr* subtests. During the administration of Atlantis, the child is corrected every time a mistake is made. On Rebus, although mistakes are not corrected, virtually all symbol-word associations are presented a second time to ensure that children are able to correct any mistakes they might have made.

Gifted

A gifted group study of 95 students was reported in the *KABC-II Manual* (Kaufman & Kaufman, 2004a). The children's schools identified students in the sample as "high performing or talented in one or more academic, artistic, or leadership categories" (p. 130). The mean age of the sample was 12:11 (ranging from 7:4 to 18:11). The KABC-II scores for these children were compared to a nonclinical reference group that controlled for the influence of sex, ethnicity, and parent education. The gifted sample scored significantly higher than the nonclinical reference group on all KABC-II indexes, composites, and subtests. However, the mean index scores of the gifted sample were generally only 1 to 1 1/3 standard deviations above the test's mean of 100. Typically, one would expect intellectually gifted children to score higher. However, lower than expected scores are not unusual in studies of gifted children with new tests (e.g., see Volker & Phelps, 2004, regarding the WISC-IV, and Roid, 2003, pp. 96–97, regarding the SB5). A variety of factors may explain this result for the KABC-II, including regression to the mean upon being tested for a second time and the inclusion in the sample of numerous children who were selected based on nonintellective factors (e.g.,

artistic and leadership qualities, as noted in the manual).

The gifted sample scored highest on the FCI ($M = 120.1$) compared to mean scores of 118.7 for the MPI and 116.8 for the NVI. Among the factor composites or scales, Knowledge/*Gc* was the highest ($M = 118.4$), which led to the slightly higher score on the FCI than MPI. The other KABC-II factor composite scores were very similar to each other (113–114). Taken together, these results support use of the CHC model, which includes the Knowledge/*Gc* scale, when testing most intellectually gifted children. However, this support is predicated on the absence of cultural, linguistic, or disability factors that would make use of the Knowledge/*Gc* scale inappropriate. Overall, given the limitations of this one sample of gifted children with the KABC-II, further research on the instrument with this population is recommended to clarify its utility.

Those who administer and interpret cognitive ability tests as part of the gifted identification process must do so with the following issues in mind: (1) The cognitive ability tests selected should have strong psychometric properties for the population involved (e.g., high reliability, strong construct validity, appropriately high test ceilings, etc.); (2) cognitive ability tests should be selected, administered, and interpreted with sensitivity to the child's cultural and linguistic background (Kaufman & Harrison, 1986; Pfeiffer, 2001, 2002), emotional needs (Pfeiffer, 2002), and disability status (McCoach, Kehle, Bray, & Siegle, 2001); (3) score interpretations should take into account errors in measurement (Kaufman & Harrison, 1986); (4) examiners should be sensitive to variability in the score profiles or expressions of intelligence in children that may render composite scores less interpretable (Hale & Fiorello, 2001; Kaufman & Kaufman, 1993; Sparrow & Gurland, 1998); and (5) cognitive ability tests vary in their emphasis on speed of performance, which should be taken into account when assessing more reflective children (Kaufman, 1994a).

As noted by Lichtenberger and colleagues (2006), the KABC-II addresses each of the above issues: (1) It has strong psychometric properties, including reliability, validity, and appropriately high ceilings; (2) it is sensitive to cultural and linguistic differences and minimizes the effect of these differences; (3) its dual theoretical base and qualitative indicators help in the interpretation of the results; (4) its five scales allow for interpretation of profiles that have significant variability; and (5) its minimal emphasis on speed of performance is a plus when assessing high-functioning children with reflective styles of responding. Thus, when used as part of a multidimensional battery for assessing giftedness, the strengths of the KABC-II make it a useful tool in measuring the cognitive abilities of intellectually high-functioning children.

Interventions Based on Test Results

Table 4.5 was created to provide the reader with a small sampling of easy-to-implement interventions that can assist in the training or the compensation of weaknesses in any of the five domains that are assessed by the KABC-II.

Relationships between Ability and Achievement

To evaluate the relationship of the KABC-II scores to the key criterion of academic achievement, the KABC-II was correlated with the KTEA-II for 2,475 students between pre-K and grade 12 (Kaufman & Kaufman, 2004b), and with a total of 401 children on the WJ III Achievement battery, the WIAT-II, and the PIAT-R (Kaufman & Kaufman, 2004a). For the KTEA-II, FCI correlated .79, on the average, with KTEA-II Composite Achievement Composite, with the MPI correlating slightly lower (.75). These coefficients with the co-normed KTEA-II are similar in magnitude to the mean values of .75 (FCI) and .71 (MPI) with the other achievement batteries. Values in the .70s are comparable to the *best* coefficients reported by Naglieri and Bornstein

(2003) in their summary of a vast number of correlational studies between diverse cognitive and achievement batteries: "For the large studies, the ability/achievement composite correlations for the K-ABC (.74) followed by the CAS and WJ III (both .70) were top ranked" (Naglieri & Bornstein, 2003, p. 244). The WISC-III coefficients were lower (.63) in that study, although a recent correlation between WISC-IV Full Scale IQ and WIAT-II Total Achievement was substantial (.87) (Psychological Corporation, 2003, Table 5.15).

For the younger group, the MPI was equivalent to the FCI as a correlate of KTEA-II achievement composites. For 4$\frac{1}{2}$- to 6-year-olds, MPI correlated a bit higher with Written Language, FCI correlated a bit higher with Oral Language, and they correlated about the same with Reading, Math, and the Comprehensive Achievement Composite. For ages 7–18, FCI was consistently a higher correlate than MPI of each academic domain, as reflected in the coefficient with Comprehensive Achievement (.80 vs. 74).

For both age groups, FCI and MPI correlated lowest with Oral Language (.57–.67) and highest with Reading and Math (.67–.74). The NVI correlated with Math at almost the same level as the MPI and FCI (.65–.67 vs. .68–.71), but otherwise correlated substantially lower than MPI and FCI with other academic areas. For example, NVI correlated about .60 with Reading, whereas the other two global scores correlated about .70. Therefore, KABC-II examiners who opt to administer the Nonverbal Scale need to be aware that prediction of the child's academic achievement will suffer (except for prediction of mathematics).

Nonetheless, despite the lower correlations of NVI with Achievement (relative to MPI and FCI), and correlations in the .50s and .60s with Oral Language, all of the coefficients for the KABC-II global scores compare favorably with the values yielded by global scores on other tests (Naglieri & Bornstein, 2003), and reflect strong support for the KABC-II's criterion-related validity.

TABLE 4.5   Interventions Based on KABC-II Assessment Domains

KABC-II Domain	Interventions
Sequential/*Gsm*	• Keep oral directions short and simple[a] • Check for understanding after directions have been presented[a] • Provide compensatory aids (e.g., write directions, procedures, and assignments on board or paper, provide lecture notes, provide a study guide) [a] • Teach memory strategies (e.g., chunking, verbal rehearsal, visual imagery)[a] • Teach the student how to organize things in steps as a strategy for completing tasks[b] • Teach poems and songs[b] • Arrange items or repeat events from a story or occasion in order[b]
Simultaneous/*Gv*	• Provide activities with manipulatives[a] • Provide copying, tracing, drawing activities[a] • Verbally describe graphics and visually based concepts[a] • Play matching and categorization games that include opposites[b] • Ask the student to provide missing details from stories • Encourage rhyming[b] • Have students work on puzzle, hidden picture worksheets, and building three-dimensional objects[b]
Learning/*Glr*	• Provide overlearning, review, and repetition[a] • Teach memory aids such as verbal mediation or rehearsal, and mnemonic strategies[a] • Provide multi-sensory learning: use visual, kinesthetic, vocal, and auditory channels as appropriate[a] • Provide context and meaning-based instruction[a] • Limit the number of new facts, words, concepts presented in one session[a] • Use of the keyword method (See Naglieri & Pickering, 2003, pp. 47-48)[b] • Use graphic organizers to link new information to learned information[b]
Planning/*Gf*	• Teach problem-solving strategies in the contexts in which they are most likely to be applied[a] • Use real objects and manipulatives to develop concepts[a] • Teach strategies to increase understanding and retention of concepts (e.g., self-talk, lists of procedures or steps)[a] • Teach planning skills by developing classroom and homework activities that require the students to be engaged in a planning process (See Naglieri & Pickering, 2003, pp. 37-38)[b]
Knowledge/*Gc*	• Relate new information to acquired knowledge[a] • Assess prior knowledge before introducing new topics, concepts[a] • Pre-teach relevant vocabulary or background knowledge[a] • Incorporate interests and prior knowledge areas into instruction[a]

SOURCE : [a]From Mather, N., & Jaffe, L. (2002). *Woodcock-Johnson III: Reports, Recommendations, and Strategies*. New York: Wiley. [b]From Naglieri, J.A., & Pickering, E.B. (2003). *Helping Children Learn: Intervention Handouts for Use in School and at Home*. Baltimore, MD: Brookes.

FAIRNESS: SEX, RACE, AND ETHNIC DIFFERENCES

The original K-ABC was acclaimed for yielding smaller mean differences among ethnic minority groups (Campbell, Bell, & Keith, 2001; Davidson, 1992; Fourqurean, 1987; Kaufman & Kaufman, 1983b; Valencia, Rankin, & Livingston, 1995; Vincent, 1991; Whitworth & Chrisman, 1987). The Kaufmans hoped to both preserve and improve this quality of fairness in the KABC-II. The test authors, however, did not develop any new subtests for the KABC-II based on this consideration. Instead, all new tasks had to meet two main criteria: (1) They had to measure one of the basic theoretical constructs measured by the KABC-II, and (2) they had to capture the interest of children and adolescents across a broad age range. Gender and race and ethnic biases were thoroughly evaluated during both the try-out and standardization phases of the KABC-II development.

Sex Differences

The KABC-II standardization data for males and females were analyzed according to age group: preschool (ages 3–6) and school-age (ages 7–18). Within the preschool group, females scored higher on all global scales and scales with the exception of the Knowledge/*Gc* scale, in which there were no sex differences. This finding is consistent with the observation that young females' cognitive development is advanced relative to that of boys of the same age.

Analyses of sex differences in the school-age group (7–18) reveal that males and females tended to perform at very similar levels with a few exceptions. Males performed significantly higher than females on the Simultaneous/*Gv* scale (.27 *SD*), whereas females outperformed males on Rebus (.2 *SD*) and Story Completion (.17 *SD*). Overall, these differences between school-aged males and females offset one another as the FCI, MPI, and NVI do not show statistically significant sex differences.

Reynolds, Keith, Ridley, and Patel (in press) conducted a study of sex differences using the 6- to 18-year-old standardization sample of the KABC-II to assess the mean level differences of *g* and the five CHC broad factors measured by the KABC-II. When controlling for *g*, males consistently demonstrated higher scores on the Simultaneous/*Gv* scale (all ages studied, 6–18) and the Knowledge/*Gc* scale (except ages 17 and 18). In addition, although the females consistently obtained higher scores on the FCI at all ages, they were only significantly higher than males at the ages of 15 and 16.

Race and Ethnic Differences

As a result of the varied distribution of parental education levels among ethnic groups in the national population, the KABC-II authors controlled for the effects of parental educational level and sex for the analyses involving race and ethnic differences (the *Manual* also provides unadjusted results). The Kaufmans add that controlling for parental education level provides only a partial adjustment for socioeconomic status (SES) differences among groups but was chosen because it could be measured objectively, has a plausible causal relationship to the intellectual development of the child, and has been found to have a relatively strong relationship to performance on cognitive ability tests (Centers for Disease Control and Prevention, 1993; McKenzie & Crowcroft, 1994; Wong et al., 2000).

Adjusted mean KABC-II global scores (MPI, FCI, and NVI) for the normative sample for ages 3–6 are close to the normative mean of 100 for African American and Hispanic children (means of about 97 to 100); white children ages 3–6 averaged about 101. For ages 7–18, means are about 95 ± 5 for African American, Hispanic, American Indian, Asian, and white children. (Means are not provided at ages 3–6 for American Indians and Asians because of small sample sizes.)

For children ages 7–18, African American children earned their highest mean Index (adjusted for sex and SES) on the Sequential/*Gsm* scale (100) followed closely by the Learning/*Glr* scale (98). In contrast, for that same age range, Hispanic children scored highest on the Simultaneous/*Gv* and Planning/*Gf* Indexes (99); the Simultaneous/*Gv* Index was highest for American Indian children (101) and Asian children (105) (Kaufman & Kaufman, 2004a, Table 8.8).

Most of the adjusted Indexes for Hispanic children were close to 100 except for the Sequential/*Gsm* scale (95), where the language load on Word Order and Number Recall may have interfered with performance. This observation is consistent with K-ABC data and other tests that have verbal–nonverbal distinctions (Kaufman, 1994a; Kaufman & Lichtenberger, 2005).

Differences between whites and African Americans are smaller on the KABC-II than for the Wechsler scales (Kaufman & Lichtenberger, 2005). Without adjustment for background variables such as SES, school-age African American children and adolescents scored about $1/2$ *SD* higher on the KABC-II FCI (94.0) and MPI (94.8) than on the WISC-III Full Scale IQ (88.6), with the WISC-IV Full Scale IQ falling about midway in between (91.7). When adjusted for background variables such as SES, whites and African Americans in the entire KABC-II standardization sample differed by 6.5 points (FCI) and 5 points (MPI), with the white group scoring higher. These values are comparable to the values reported for the entire standardization sample for the Luria-based Cognitive Assessment System (CAS; Naglieri & Das, 1997), but are smaller than differences reported for the entire standardization samples of the WISC-III (11 points) and WISC-IV (9 points). (CAS data are from Naglieri, Rojahn, Aquilino, & Matto, 2005; WISC-III data are from Prifitera, Weiss, & Saklofske, 1998; and WISC-IV data are from Prifitera, Saklofske, & Weiss, 2004.)

Results of these analyses of ethnic differences, both with and without adjustment for background variables, indicate that the KABC-II continues to have small differences between white children and children from ethnic minority backgrounds. One finding of extreme interest concerns Fletcher-Janzen's (2003) study of Taos Pueblo Indian children of New Mexico. She tested 46 children on the KABC-II (mean age = 7:8) and retested 30 of these children on the WISC-IV about 18 months later (mean age = 9:3). Global scores on the two instruments correlated about .85, but the mean standard scores differed substantially: Taos Pueblo Indian children scored higher on the KABC-II global scores than the WISC-IV Full Scale IQ, with the FCI averaging 7.4 points higher (.49 *SD*) and the MPI averaging 8.4 points higher (.56 *SD*).

The KABC-II appears to be continuing the tradition set by the K-ABC for smaller global score differences between Euro-American and other ethnic groups. While the KABC-II seems to be highly correlated with other tests of ability, the global scores that clinicians seek to obtain on a daily basis will be higher for ethnic minority students on the KABC-II than nearly all other ability batteries. This result was by design.

One other factor that might assist the cultural validity of the KABC-II is that sample items, instructions, and teaching can be done in the child's native language. In addition, examiners can accept verbal responses that are spoken in the child's native language as long as they are correct. Not only will this process allow for ease of administration, but it also demonstrates that the KABC-II is adept at obtaining information about the child's cognitive processes, not cognitions confounded by problems with language interpretation.

The lowest Index for all of the ethnic minority groups was on the Knowledge/*Gc* Scale and was most likely related to language and educational variables. As might be expected, the Knowledge/*Gc* Scale accounted for quite a bit of the SES variance for ages 3–6 (22.2%) and 7–18 (17.6%). In addition, the FCI was slightly lower for all ethnic minority groups than the MPI, again reflecting the influence of the Knowledge/*Gc* Scale and supporting the use of the MPI rather than the FCI for some populations.

Ethnic versus Socioeconomic Differences

Overall, as demonstrated, the ethnic group differences are modest on the KABC-II. Indeed, compared to the amount of variance accounted for by SES (mother's education level), the amount of variance accounted for by ethnicity is much smaller. At ages 3–6, ethnic differences account for less than 1–2% of the variance in both the MPI and FCI, in contrast to a huge 18–22% of the variance accounted for by SES (mother's education). At ages 7–18, the percents are 4–5% (ethnic differences) versus 11–14% (SES). The profile of KABC-II Scale Indexes reflects the same general weighting for SES over ethnic differences in determining children's scores. Notably, and consistent with the Kaufmans' recommendation that the Luria model is the model of choice for children from bilingual and nonmainstream backgrounds, the Knowledge/*Gc* Index produced the highest percents of variance at ages 3–18 for both ethnicity (6–7%) and SES (18–22%).

One clear trend is that both the 3–6 and 7–18 age groups scored progressively higher as mother's education increased. These data are consistent with a wide array of data on other instruments (Kaufman & Lichtenberger, 2005, Chapter 4), including the original K-ABC (Kaufman & Kaufman, 2004a, Tables 4.34 and 4.35), and suggest an overall pattern that is understandable in light of the major role that the home environment and parental modeling have in the cognitive development and knowledge acquisition of children.

SUMMARY

The KABC-II's structure, organization, and psychometric properties make it a particularly valuable instrument for the cognitive assessment of children and adolescents. The test's dual-theoretical foundation allows the clinician to select and interpret results based on the model that corresponds with the child's background characteristics and the reason for referral. In addition to the dual-theoretical model, the KABC-II also allows the clinician to administer a Nonverbal Scale to children that are limited English proficient, have hearing loss, or have moderate-to-severe speech or language disabilities. The KABC-II measures a wide range of abilities that are relevant to understanding children who are having educational or psychological problems in a way that reduces score differences between ethnic and cultural groups, and in a way that allows the clinician to consider the effect of specific test-taking behaviors that are relevant to interpretation. The interpretation of KABC-II allows the clinician to link assessment results to intervention through careful study of the child's cognitive strengths and weaknesses. That being said, the KABC-II is aesthetically pleasing, engaging, and thoroughly enjoyable for children of all ages. In a recent review of the KABC-II, Bain & Gray (2008) state that the addition of the dual theoretical model has provided examiners much-needed broad and narrow ability measures for younger children and "recommend that examiners who are not familiar with the Kaufmans' cognitive test review the KABC-II for themselves, practice it, and use it a few times. Who knows? The examiner may become addicted to using the test" (p. 101).

REFERENCES

Allen, M. H., Lincoln, A. J., & Kaufman, A. S. (1991). Sequential and simultaneous processing abilities of high-functioning autistic and language-impaired children. *Journal of Autism and Developmental Disorders, 21,* 483–502.

American Psychiatric Association. (2000). *Diagnostic and statistical manual of mental disorders* (4th ed., text rev.). Washington, DC: Author.

Bain, S. K., & Gray, R. (2008). Review of Kaufman Assessment Battery for Children—Second edition. *Journal of Psychoeducational Assessment, 26*, 92–101.

Barkley, R. A. (1998). *Attention-deficit hyperactivity disorder: A handbook for diagnosis and treatment* (2nd ed.). New York: Guilford Press.

Barnhill, G., Hagiwara, T., Myles, B. S., & Simpson, R. L. (2000). Asperger syndrome: A study of 37 children and adolescents. *Focus on Autism and Other Developmental Disabilities, 15*(3), 146–153.

Braden, J. P. (1984). The factorial similarity of the WISC-R Performance Scale in deaf and hearing samples. *Personal and Individual Differences, 5*(4), 403–409.

Brady, K. D., & Denckla, M. B. (1994). Performance of children with attention deficit hyperactivity disorder on the Tower of Hanoi task. Unpublished manuscript, Johns Hopkins University School of Medicine.

Campbell, J. M., Bell, S. K., & Keith, L. K. (2001). Concurrent validity of the Peabody Picture Vocabulary test-third edition—as an intelligence and achievement screener for low SES African American children. *Assessment, 8*, 85–94.

Carroll, J. B. (1993). *Human cognitive abilities: A survey of factor-analytic studies*. Cambridge, England: Cambridge University Press.

Carroll, J. B. (1997). The three-stratum theory of cognitive abilities. In D. P. Flanagan, J. L. Genshaft, & P. L. Harrison (Eds.), *Contemporary intellectual assessment: Theories, tests, and issues* (pp. 122–130). New York: Guilford.

Carroll, J. B. (2005). The three-stratum theory of cognitive abilities. In D. P. Flanagan, J. L. Genshaft, & P. L. Harrison (Eds.), *Contemporary intellectual assessment: Theories, tests, and issues* (pp. 69–76). New York: Guilford.

Centers for Disease Control and Prevention. (1993). Use of race and ethnicity in public health surveillance summary of the *CDC/ATSDR Workshop. MMWR Weekly* (No. RR-10). Washington, DC: Author.

Das, J. P., Kirby, J. R., & Jarman, R. F. (1979). *Simultaneous and successive cognitive processes*. New York: Academic Press.

Das, J. P., Naglieri, J. A., & Kirby, J. R. (1994). *Assessment of cognitive processes*. Needham Heights, MA: Allyn & Bacon.

Davidson, K. L. (1992). A comparison of Native American and white students' cognitive strengths as measured by the Kaufman Assessment Battery for Children. *Roeper Review, 14*, 111–115.

Ehlers, S., Nyden, A., & Gillberg, C. (1997). Asperger syndrome, autism, and attention disorders: A comparative study of the cognitive profiles of 120 children. *Journal of Child Psychology and Psychiatry and Allied Disciplines, 38*(2), 207–217.

Fagan, T. K., & Wise, P. S. (2007). *School psychology: Past, present, and future* (3rd ed.). Bethesda, MD: National Association of School Psychologists.

Flanagan, D. P., & McGrew, K. S. (1997). A cross-battery approach to assessing and interpreting cognitive abilities: Narrowing the gap between practice and cognitive science. In D. P. Flanagan, J. L. Genshaft, & P. L. Harrison (Eds.), *Contemporary intellectual assessment: Theories, tests, and issues* (pp. 314–325). New York: Guilford.

Flanagan, D. P., McGrew, K. S., & Ortiz, S. O. (2000). *The Wechsler intelligence scales and CHC theory: A contemporary approach to interpretation*. Boston: Allyn & Bacon.

Flanagan, D. P., & Ortiz, S. O. (2001). *Essentials of cross-battery assessment*. New York: Wiley.

Flanagan, D. P., Ortiz, S. O., & Alfonso, V. C. (2007). *Essentials of cross-battery assessment* (2nd ed.). Hoboken, NJ: Wiley.

Fletcher-Janzen, E. (2003). *A validity study of the KABC-II and the Taos Pueblo Indian children of New Mexico*. Circle Pines, MN: American Guidance Service.

Fourqurean, J. M. (1987). A K-ABC and WISC-R comparison for Latino learning disabled children of limited English proficiency. *Journal of School Psychology, 25*, 15–21.

Hale, J. B., & Fiorello, C. A. (2001). Beyond the academic rhetoric of "g": Intelligence testing guidelines for practitioners. *School Psychologist, 55*(4), 113–117, 131–135, 138–139. New York: Wiley.

Hale, J. B., Kaufman, A, Naglieri, J. A., & Kavale, K. A. (2006). Implementation of IDEA: Integrating response to intervention and cognitive assessment methods. *Psychology in the Schools, 43*(7), 753–770.

Horn, J. L., & Blankson, N. (2005). Foundations for better understanding of cognitive abilities. In D. P. Flanagan & P. L. Harrison (Eds.), *Contemporary intellectual assessment: Theories, tests, and issues* (2nd ed., pp. 136–182).

Horn, J. L., & Noll, J. (1997). Human cognitive capabilities: *Gf-Gc* theory. In D. P. Flanagan, J. L. Genshaft, & P. L. Harrison (Eds.), *Contemporary intellectual assessment: Theories, tests, and issues* (pp. 53–91). New York: Guilford.

Hunt, M. S. (2007). A joint confirmatory factor analysis of the Kaufman Assessment Battery for Children, Second Edition, and the Woodcock-Johnson Tests of Cognitive Abilities, Third Edition, with preschool children. Ph.D. dissertation, Ball State University, Indiana. Retrieved March 7, 2008, from ProQuest Digital Dissertations database. (Publication No. AAT 3288307).

Individuals with Disabilities Education Act of 2004 (IDEA), 20 U.S.C. § 1400 *et seq.*

Individuals with Disabilities Education Improvement Act (IDEA) of 2004, Title 34 Code of Federal Register, Part 300.

Kamphaus, R. W., & Reynolds, C. R. (1987). *Clinical and research applications of the K-ABC*. Circle Pines, MN: American Guidance Service.

Kamphaus, R. W., Winsor, A. P., Rowe, E. W., & Kim, S. (2005). A history of intelligence test interpretation. In D. P. Flanagan & P. L. Harrison (Eds.), *Contemporary intellectual assessment: Theories, tests, and issues* (2nd ed., pp. 23–38). New York: Guilford.

Kaufman, A. S. (1994a). *Intelligent testing with the WISC-III*. New York: Wiley.

Kaufman, A. S. (1994b). Practice effects. In R. J. Sternberg (Ed.), *Encyclopedia of intelligence* (Vol. II, pp. 828–833). New York: Macmillan.

Kaufman, A. S., & Harrison, P. L. (1986). Intelligence tests and gifted assessment: What are the positives? *Roeper Review*, *8*, 154–159.

Kaufman, A. S., & Kaufman, N. L. (1983a). *Kaufman Assessment Battery for Children (K-ABC) administration and scoring manual*. Circle Pines, MN: American Guidance Service.

Kaufman, A. S., & Kaufman, N. L. (1983b). *K-ABC interpretive manual*. Circle Pines, MN: American Guidance Service.

Kaufman, A. S., & Kaufman, N. L. (1990). *Administration and scoring manual for the Kaufman Brief Intelligence Test* (K-BIT). Circle Pines, MN: American Guidance Service.

Kaufman, A. S., & Kaufman, N. L. (1993). *Manual for Kaufman Adolescent and Adult Intelligence Test* (KAIT). Circle Pines, MN: American Guidance Service.

Kaufman, A. S., & Kaufman, N. L. (2004a). *Kaufman Assessment Battery for Children—Second Edition manual* (KABC-II). Circle Pines, MN: American Guidance Service.

Kaufman, A. S., & Kaufman, N. L. (2004b). *Kaufman Test of Educational Achievement—Second Edition brief form* (KTEA-II Brief). Circle Pines, MN: American Guidance Service.

Kaufman, A. S., & Kaufman, N. L. (2005). *Kaufman Test of Educational Achievement—Second Edition brief form manual*. Circle Pines, MN: AGS.

Kaufman, A. S., Lichtenberger, E. O., Fletcher-Janzen, E., & Kaufman, N. (2005). *Essentials of KABC-II assessment*. Hoboken, NJ: Wiley.

Lichtenberger, E. O. (2001). The Kaufman tests: K-ABC and KAIT. In A. S. Kaufman & N. L. Kaufman (Eds.), *Specific learning disabilities and difficulties in children and adolescents* (pp. 97–140). New York: Cambridge University Press.

Lichtenberger, E. O., & Kaufman, A. S. (2004). *Essentials of WPPSI-III assessment*. New York: Wiley.

Lichtenberger, E. O., Volker, M., Kaufman, A. S., & Kaufman, N. L. (2006). Assessing gifted children with the Kaufman Assessment Battery for Children—Second Edition. *Gifted Education International*, *21*, 99–126.

Luria, A. R. (1966). *Human brain: An introduction to neuropsychology*. New York: Basic Books.

Luria, A. R. (1966a). *Higher cortical functions in man*. New York: Basic Books.

Luria, A. R. (1970). The functional organization of the brain. *Scientific American*, *222*, 66–78.

Luria, A. R. (1973). *The working brain: An introduction to neuro-psychology*. London: Penguin Books.

Mahone, E. M., Hagelthron, K. M., Cutting, L. E., Schuerholz, L. J., Pelletier, S. F., Rawlins, C., et al. (2002). Effects of IQ on executive function measures in children with ADHD. *Child Neuropsychology*, *8*(1), 52–65.

Mather, N. & Jaffe, L. E. (2002). *Woodcock-Johnson III: Reports, recommendations and strategies*. New York: Wiley.

McCoach, D. B., Kehle, T. J., Bray, M. A., & Siegle, D. (2001). Best practices in the identification of gifted students with learning disabilities. *Psychology in the Schools*, *38*, 403–411.

McGrew, K. S. (1997). Analysis of the major intelligence batteries according to a proposed comprehensive *Gf-Gc* framework. In D. P. Flanagan, J.

L. Genshaft, & P. L. Harrison (Eds.), *Contemporary intellectual assessment: Theories, tests, and issues* (pp. 151–180). New York: Guilford.

McGrew, K. S. (2005). The Cattell-Horn-Carroll theory of cognitive abilities: Past, present, and future. In D. P. Flanagan & P. L. Harrison (Eds.), *Contemporary intellectual assessment: Theories, tests, and issues* (2nd ed., pp. 136–182).

McGrew, K. S., & Flanagan, D. P. (1998). *The intelligence test desk reference (ITDR): Gf-Gc cross-battery assessment*. Boston: Allyn & Bacon.

McGrew, K. S., Woodcock, R., & Ford, L. (2002). The Woodcock-Johnson Battery—Third Edition. In A. S. Kaufman & E. O. Lichtenberger (Aus.), *Assessing adolescent and adult intelligence* (2nd ed., pp. 561–628). Boston: Allyn & Bacon.

McKenzie, K. J., & Crowcroft, N. S. (1994). Race, ethnicity, culture, and science. *British Medical Journal*, *39*, 286–287.

Miller, C., Kail, R., Leonard, L., & Tomblin, J. B. (2001). Speed of processing in children with specific language impairment. *Journal of Speech, Language, and Hearing Research*, *44*, 416–433.

Naglieri, J. A. (1999). *Essentials of CAS assessment*. New York: Wiley.

Naglieri, J. A., & Bornstein, B. T. (2003). Intelligence and achievement: Just how correlated are they? *Journal of Psychoeducational Assessment*, *21*, 244–260.

Naglieri, J. A., & Das, J. P. (1997). *Cognitive Assessment System interpretive manual*. Chicago: Riverside Publishing.

Naglieri, J. A. & Pickering, E. B. (2003). *Helping children learn: Handouts for use in school and at home*. Baltimore, MD: Paul H. Brookes.

Naglieri, J. A., Rojahn, J., Aquilino, S. A., & Matto, H. C. (2005). Black-white differences in intelligence: A study of the PASS theory and Cognitive Assessment System. *Journal of Psychoeducational Assessment*, *23*, 146–160.

Neisser, U. (1967). *Cognitive psychology*. New York: Appleton-Century-Crofts.

Perugini, E. M., Harvery, E. A., Lovejoy, D. W., Sandstrom, K., & Webb, A. H. (2000). The predictive power of combined neuropsychological measures for attention deficit hyperactivity disorder in children. *Child Neuropsychology*, *6*(2), 101–114.

Pfeiffer, S. L. (2001). Professional psychology and the gifted: Emerging practice opportunities. *Professional Psychology, Research and Practice*, *32*(2), 175–180.

Pfeiffer, S. L. (2002). Identifying gifted and talented students: Recurring issues and promising solutions. *Journal of Applied School Psychology*, *19*(1), 31–50.

Prifitera, A., Saklofske, D. H., & Weiss, L. G. (2004). *WISC-IV clinical use and interpretation: Scientist-practitioner perspectives*. Burlington, MA: Academic Press.

Prifitera, A., Weiss, L. G. & Saklofske, D. H., (1998). The WISC-III in context. In A. Prifitera & D. H. Saklofske (Eds.), *WISC-III clinical use and interpretation: Scientist-practitioner perspective* (pp. 1–38). San Diego: Academic Press.

Psychological Corporation. (2003). *WISC-III technical and interpretive manual*. San Antonio, TX: The Psychological Corporation.

Reitan, R. M. (1988). Integration of neuropsychological theory, assessment, and application. *The Clinical Neuropsychologist*, *2*, 331–349.

Reynolds, M. R. & Keith, T. Z. (in press). Spearman's law of diminishing returns in hierarchical models of intelligence for children and adolescents. *Intelligence*.

Reynolds, M. R., Keith, T. Z., Fine, J. G., Fisher, M. E., Low, J. A. (2007). Confirmatory factor structure of the Kaufman Assessment Battery for Children—Second Edition: Consistency with Cattell-Horn-Carroll theory. *School Psychology Quarterly*, *22*(4), 511–539.

Reynolds, M. R., Keith, T. Z., Ridley, K. P., & Patel, P. G. (in press). Sex differences in latent general and broad cognitive abilities for children and youth: Evidence from higher-order MG-MACS and MIMIC models. *Intelligence*.

Roid, G. H. (2003). *Stanford-Binet Intelligence Scales—Fifth Edition, technical manual*. Austin, TX: Pro-Ed.

Seidman, L. J., Biederman, J., Faraone, S. V., & Milberger, S. (1995). Effects of family history and comorbidity on the neuropsychological performance of children with ADHD: Preliminary findings. *Journal of the American Academy of Child and Adolescent Psychiatry*, *34*(8), 1015–1024.

Seidman, L. J., Biederman, J., Faraone, S. V., Weber, W., & Ouellette, C. (1997). Toward defining a neuropsychology of attention deficit-hyperactivity disorder: Performance of children and adolescents from a large clinically referred sample. *Journal of Consulting and Clinical Psychology*, *65*, 150–160.

Slate, J. R., & Fawcett, J. (1995). Validity of the WISC-III for deaf and hard of hearing persons. *American Annals of the Deaf*, *140*(4), 250–254.

Sparrow, S. S., & Gurland, S. T. (1998). Assessment of gifted children with the WISC-III. In A. Prifitera & D. Saklofske (Eds.), *WISC-III clinical use and interpretation: Scientist-practitioner perspectives* (pp. 59–72). San Diego, CA: Academic Press.

Sperry, R. W. (1968). Hemisphere deconnection and unity in conscious awareness. *American Psychologist*, *23*, 723–733.

Sullivan, P. M., & Montoya, L. M. (1997). Factor analysis of WISC-III with deaf and hard of hearing children. *Psychological Assessment*, *9*(3), 317–321.

Teeter, P. A. (1997). Neurocognitive interventions for childhood and adolescent disorders: A transactional model. In C. R. Reynolds & E. Fletcher-Janzen (Eds.), *The handbook of clinical child neuropsychology* (2nd ed., pp. 387–417). New York: Kluwer-Plenum.

Tsatsanis, K. D., Dartnall, N., Cicchetti, D., Sparrow, S. S., Kiln, A., & Volkmar, F. R. (2003). Concurrent validity and classification accuracy of the Leiter and Leiter-R in low-functioning children with autism. *Journal of Autism & Developmental Disorders*, *33*(1), 23–30.

Ulissi, S. M., Brice, P. J., & Gibbons, S. (1985, April). *The use of the KABC with the hearing impaired*. Paper presented at the meeting of the National Association of School Psychologists, Las Vegas, NV.

Valencia, R. R., Rankin, R. J., & Livingston, R. (1995). K-ABC content bias: Comparisons between Mexican American and white children. *Psychology in the Schools*, *32*, 153–169.

Vincent, K. R. (1991). Black/white IQ differences: Does age make the difference? *Journal of Clinical Psychology*, *47*, 266–270.

Volker, M. A., & Phelps, L. (2004). Identification of gifted students with the WISC-IV. In D. P. Flanagan & A. S. Kaufman (Eds.), *Essentials of WISC-IV assessment* (pp. 216–224). Hoboken, NJ: Wiley.

Wechsler, D. (2003). *The Wechsler Intelligence Scale for Children—Fourth Edition* (WISC-IV). San Antonio, TX: The Psychological Corporation.

Whitworth, R. H., & Chrisman, S. M. (1987). Validation of the Kaufman Assessment Battery for Children comparing Anglo and Mexican-American preschoolers. *Educational and Psychological Measurement*, *47*, 695–702.

Wong, T. M., Strickland, T. L., Fletcher-Janzen, E., Ardila, A., & Reynolds, C. R. (2000). Theoretical and practical issues in neuropsychological assessment and treatment of culturally dissimilar patients. In E. Fletcher-Janzen, T. L. Strickland, & C. R. Reynolds (Eds.), *Handbook of cross-cultural neuropsychology*. New York: Kluwer-Plenum.

Woodcock, R. W., & Johnson, M. B. (1977). *Woodcock-Johnson Tests of Cognitive Ability: Standard and supplemental batteries*. Chicago: Riverside Publishing.

Woodcock, R. W., & Johnson, M. B. (1989). *Woodcock-Johnson Tests of Cognitive Ability: Standard and supplemental batteries*. Chicago: Riverside Publishers.

Woodcock, R. W, McGrew, K. S., & Mather, N. (2001). *Woodcock-Johnson III Tests of Cognitive Abilities*. Chicago: Riverside Publishing.

CHAPTER 5

Development and Application of the Reynolds Intellectual Assessment Scales (RIAS)

Cecil R. Reynolds, R. W. Kamphaus*

This chapter provides the reader with an extensive introduction to the RIAS (Reynolds & Kamphaus, 2003), a recently published measure of intelligence for children and adults. A brief overview of the tests is provided, followed by a review of the theory and structure of the RIAS, framed primarily around its goals for development. A more extensive description is then provided of the subtests and their administration and scoring. Psychometric characteristics of the RIAS are next presented along with guidelines for interpretation. Clinical applications of the RIAS are discussed, followed by a brief review of the characteristics and use of the Reynolds Intellectual Screening Test (RIST). The chapter closes with a case study using the RIAS as the featured measure of intelligence.

The RIAS is an individually administered test of intelligence appropriate for ages 3–94 years with a co-normed, supplemental measure of memory. The RIAS includes a two-subtest Verbal Intelligence Index (VIX) and a two-subtest

Nonverbal Intelligence Index (NIX). The scaled sums of T scores for the four subtests are combined to form the Composite Intelligence Index (CIX), which is a summary estimate of global intelligence. Administration of the four intelligence scale subtests by a trained, experienced examiner requires approximately 20 to 25 minutes. A Composite Memory Index (CMX) is derived from the two supplementary memory subtests, which require approximately 10 to 15 minutes of additional testing time. The Composite Intelligence Index and the Composite Memory Index represent the combination of both verbal and nonverbal subtests. Table 5.1 provides an overview of the indexes and subtests of the RIAS.

For those who consider memory to be an important element in the determination of IQ, the *RIAS Professional Manual* as well as the RIAS scoring and interpretive software includes all necessary psychometric and normative information for creating intelligence indexes that combine

*Portions of this chapter are adapted with permission of PAR, Inc. from Reynolds and Kamphaus (2003). We also wish to disclose that we are the authors of the RIAS.

the VIX, NIX, and CMX subtests into Total Battery Indexes.

THEORY AND STRUCTURE

The RIAS was designed to meld practical and theoretical aspects of the assessment of intelligence. While the models of Cattell and Horn (Horn & Cattell, 1966; Kamphaus, 2001) and Carroll (1993) were the primary theoretical guides, the RIAS also followed closely the division of intelligence into verbal and nonverbal domains, due to the practical benefits of assessing verbal and nonverbal intelligence. The latter are closely related to concepts of *fluid* and *crystallized intelligence* (aka the Cattell-Horn-Carroll or CHC approach) but are clearly not entirely cognate concepts. Memory was included as a separate scale on the RIAS due to the growing importance of working memory in models of intelligence and the practical aspects of memory to everyday diagnostic questions faced by the practitioner (e. g., see Bigler & Clement, 1997; Goldstein & Reynolds, 1999; Reynolds & Bigler, 1994; Reynolds & Fletcher-Janzen, 1997). To understand the theoretical underpinnings of the RIAS as well as its practical aspects and structure, a review of the goals for development of the test provides a strong heuristic.

Development Goals

Reynolds and Kamphaus (2003) describe a set of eight primary goals for development of the RIAS, derived based on their experiences over the years in teaching, administering and interpreting, and researching intelligence tests (for more extensive review and discussion, see Reynolds & Kamphaus, 2003, especially Chapters 1 and 6).

Goal 1: Provide reliable and valid measurement of g and its two primary components, verbal and nonverbal intelligence, with close correspondence to crystallized and fluid intelligence. The general intelligence factor, g, is the most reliable component present in any multifactorial view of intelligence (Jensen, 1998). In the Cattell-Horn model (Horn & Cattell, 1966; Kamphaus, 2001) of intelligence, g is the dominant factor in the hierarchy of multiple abilities, with the next two dominant facets being crystallized and fluid intelligence. The RIAS includes subtests that match both approaches closely in order to share in the theoretical support of the Cattell-Horn model of crystallized and fluid intelligence, while taking advantage of the very practical division of intelligence into verbal and nonverbal components. Verbal and nonverbal components of intelligence also have strong support from factor-analytic work (e.g., Kaufman, 1994) and the brain sciences (e.g., Reynolds, Castillo, & Horton, 2008; Riccio & Hynd, 2000).

Goal 2: Provide a practical measurement device in terms of efficacies of time, direct costs, and information needed from a measure of intelligence. Time, cost, and efficiency have always been necessary considerations in the delivery of effective psychological and psychoeducational services, but the advent of managed care in the 1990s (for private practice and clinical settings) and the explosion of services for children with disabilities in schools has made time a crucial consideration for practitioners. A useful intelligence test needs to provide an objective, reliable, and valid assessment of the major constructs that underlie psychometric intelligence. Intellectual assessment can be done efficiently and at a significantly lower cost than is often the case with other tests. One goal for the RIAS was for it to provide an efficient measure of intelligence that, at the same time, meets regulatory guidelines for the Individuals with Disabilities Educational Improvement Act and other rules.

Goal 3: Allow continuity of measurement across all developmental levels from ages 3 through

94 years for both clinical and research purposes. Individuals frequently require reevaluation of intellectual function over a period of years. As they age, different versions of intelligence tests may be required, and these various tests have different subtests, measure different aspects of intelligence, were normed in different years, and may have sample stratifications that do not match. Thus, scores obtained over time may not be comparable due to measurement artifact and not to any real changes in the individual's cognitive level or structure (Sattler, 2001). There is clinical utility in having a common set of subtests and a common reference group for such comparisons.

Goal 4: Substantially reduce or eliminate dependence on motor coordination and visual-motor speed in the measurement of intelligence. The majority of current individually administered intelligence tests rely heavily on visual-motor coordination and motor speed for accurate assessment of intelligence. However, many children referred to special education services have visual-motor difficulties or frank motor impairment or they may have other neurodevelopmental disorders that produce motor-related problems (Goldstein & Reynolds, 1999). Individuals with traumatic brain injury or central nervous system disease commonly have motor problems of various forms, including fine motor, gross motor, and strength problems (Reynolds & Fletcher-Janzen, 1997). In older populations, the incidence of tremor and related motor problems is quite high. To attempt to measure the intelligence of such individuals (who form a significant portion of referrals involving intellectual assessments) with tasks that require rapid manipulation of blocks, small cardboard pieces, or even pencil markings where speed and accuracy of performance are substantial contributors to the resulting IQ or cognitive index seems inappropriate. It is

our view that intelligence tests should emphasize thinking, reasoning, and problem solving.

Goal 5: Eliminate dependence on reading in the measurement of intelligence. Tasks where the ability to read the English language facilitates individual item performance confound the measurement of intelligence with school instruction. Certainly intelligence cannot be assessed completely independent of prior knowledge despite many failed attempts to do so (e.g., culture-free tests; see Anastasi & Urbina, 1997; Kamphaus, 2001; Reynolds, Lowe, & Saenz, 1999). However, to confound intellectual assessment with clues obtained from the ability to read a vocabulary card or to fill in blanks within printed words (which also adds a confound with the ability to spell) makes such tests inappropriate for nonreaders or those with limited English-reading skills. Reading tasks also penalize individuals with visual impairments whose intellectual functioning is assessed traditionally via verbal tasks.

Goal 6: Provide for accurate prediction of basic academic achievement at levels that are at least comparable to that of intelligence tests twice its length. Prediction of academic achievement and acquired knowledge in such areas as reading, language, and math is an important function for intelligence tests. Prediction of achievement should remain a function of any new intelligence test.

Goal 7: Apply familiar, common concepts that are clear and easy to interpret, coupled with simple administration and scoring. Formal intelligence testing via Binet-type tasks is more than a century old. During this time, innumerable tasks have been devised to measure intelligence and related abilities. Many of these tasks are quite good at the measurement of intellectual function and possess long histories in psychology and education. The use of familiar, well-researched tasks has many advantages over the use of novel, less-well-established tasks. Many of these tasks are simple and easy to administer despite the complex mental functions required for deriving a correct solution. Objective scoring can be facilitated by avoiding tasks that require lengthy verbal responses or split-second timing for awarding bonus points. Tasks that are simple to administer and objective to score nearly eliminate administration and scoring errors.

Goal 8: *Eliminate items that show differential item functioning (DIF), associated with gender or ethnicity.* The problem of cultural bias has long produced debate in psychology, in education, and in the lay press (e.g., Brown, Reynolds, & Whitaker, 1999; Reynolds, Lowe, & Saenz, 1999). Following years of debate, a host of methods for detecting test items that function differentially across nominally defined groups have been devised (Reynolds, 2000). Despite the importance of this issue, it is seldom discussed in significant detail in test manuals. However, in view of the availability of sound statistical approaches for identifying such test items, all intelligence test items should be scrutinized during development and standardization to determine whether any are in fact biased.

The RIAS provides a more reliable assessment of memory, both verbal and nonverbal, than other intelligence tests, and also treats memory function as a separate scale. The RIAS includes assessment of memory function because it is crucial to the diagnostic process for numerous disorders of childhood (Goldstein & Reynolds, 1999; Reynolds & Fletcher-Janzen, 1997) and adulthood (Goldstein & Reynolds, 2005), particularly in later adulthood (Bigler & Clement, 1997). In fact, assessment of memory function provides a better window into the integrity of brain function than does the assessment of intelligence (e.g., see Adams & Reynolds, 2009). Memory functions are more easily disrupted than

general intellectual skill in the face of central nervous system (CNS) compromise due to trauma or disease. Although intelligence will often suffer under such conditions (Joseph, 1996), memory will suffer sooner and is typically more affected. The RIAS CMX does not provide a comprehensive memory assessment, but it does cover the two areas of memory historically assessed by intelligence tests, which are considered by many to be the two most important memory functions to assess (e.g., Bigler & Clement, 1997; Reynolds & Bigler, 1994): memory for meaningful verbal material and visual memory.

There is also utility in having memory tests co-normed with a measure of intelligence on a fully overlapping sample. This co-norming presents the best possible scenario for contrasting test scores (Reynolds, 1984–1985), allowing the clinician directly to compare the examinee's IQ with these key memory functions.

Theory

The RIAS was designed to measure four important aspects of intelligence—general intelligence (of which the major component is *fluid* or *reasoning abilities*), verbal intelligence (sometimes referred to as *crystallized abilities*, which is a closely related though not identical concept), nonverbal intelligence (referred to in some theories as *visualization* or *spatial abilities* and closely allied with fluid intelligence), and memory (subtests comprising this ability have been labeled variously as *working memory*, *short-term memory*, or *learning*). These four constructs are measured by combinations of the six RIAS subtests (see Table 5.1).

The RIAS subtests were selected and designed to measure intelligence constructs that have a substantial history of scientific support. In addition, Carroll's (1993) seminal and often-cited three-stratum theory of intelligence informed the creation of the RIAS by demonstrating that many of the latent traits tapped by intelligence tests were test-battery independent.

TABLE 5.1 Structure and Components of the RIAS

Composite Intelligence Index (CIX)

Subtests of the Verbal Intelligence Index (VIX)

Guess What. Examinees are given a set of 2 or 3 clues and asked to deduce the object or concept being described. This subtest measures verbal reasoning in combination with vocabulary, language development, and overall fund of available information.

Verbal Reasoning. Examinees listen to a propositional statement that essentially forms a verbal analogy and are asked to respond with one or two words that complete the idea or proposition. This subtest measures verbal-analytical reasoning ability but with fewer vocabulary and general knowledge demands than Guess What.

Subtests of the Nonverbal Intelligence Index (NIX)

Odd Item Out. Examinees are presented with a picture card containing five to seven pictures or drawings and asked to designate which one does not belong or go with the others. This subtest measures nonverbal reasoning skills but will also require the use of spatial ability, visual imagery, and other nonverbal skills on various items. It is a form of reverse nonverbal analogy.

What's Missing. A redesign of a classic task present on various ability measures, examinees are shown a picture with some key element or logically consistent component missing and are asked to identify the missing essential element. This subtest assesses nonverbal reasoning wherein the examinee must conceptualize the picture, analyze its Gestalt, and deduce what essential element is missing.

Composite Memory Index (CMX)

Verbal Memory Index (VMX). This scale consists of a single verbal memory subtest. Depending on the examinee's age, a series of sentences or brief stories are read aloud by the examiner and then recalled by the examinee. This task assesses the ability to encode, store briefly, and recall verbal material in a meaningful context where associations are clear and evident.

Nonverbal Memory Index (NMX). This scale consists of a single visual memory subtest. It contains a series of items in which a stimulus picture is presented for five seconds, following which an array of pictures is presented. The examinee must identify the target picture from the new array of six pictures. It assesses the ability to encode, store, and recognize pictorial stimuli that are both concrete and abstract or without meaningful referents.

He clearly demonstrated, for example, that numerous tests measured the same crystallized, visual-perceptual, and memory abilities. However, Kamphaus (2001) concluded that these same test batteries did not measure fluid abilities to a great extent.

The RIAS focuses on the assessment of stratum-three and stratum-two abilities from Carroll's (1993) three-stratum theory. Stratum three is composed of one construct only, *g*. Psychometric *g* accounts for the major portion of variance assessed by intelligence test batteries. More important, however, is the consistent finding that the correlations of intelligence tests with important outcomes, such as academic achievement and occupational attainment, are related to the amount of *g* measured by the test battery. In other words, so-called *g*-saturated tests are better predictors of important outcomes than are tests with low *g* saturation. Although the nature of *g* is yet to be fully understood, the scores from *g*-saturated tests have known utility, especially in terms of prediction.

The second stratum in Carroll's (1993) hierarchy consists of traits that are assessed by combinations of subtests, or stratum-one measures. A stratum-one measure is typically a single subtest that measures the trait of interest. Combinations of stratum-one subtests, such as those used to form VIX and NIX, are considered stratum-two measures and should result in enhanced measurement of complex traits such as verbal and nonverbal intelligence. Combining stratum-two index measures into an overarching composite measure, such as CIX, allows for the measurement of a complex stratum-three trait, such as general intelligence.

There are, however, several stratum-two traits to choose from. These second-stratum traits include fluid intelligence, crystallized intelligence, general memory and learning, broad visual perception, broad auditory perception, broad retrieval ability, broad cognitive speed, and processing speed (i.e., reaction time or decision speed). Of importance, however, is the finding, from hundreds of investigations, suggesting that these abilities are ordered by their assessment of g (Kamphaus, 2001). Specifically, subtests that tap reasoning abilities are excellent measures of g, making the first few stratum-two factors the best for inclusion in an intelligence test like the RIAS, especially one that seeks to be a time-efficient test.

Any test of g must measure so-called *higher-order cognitive abilities*, those associated with fluid abilities, such as general sequential reasoning, induction, deduction, syllogisms, series tasks, matrix reasoning, analogies, quantitative reasoning, and so on (Carroll, 1993). Kamphaus (2001) advocated the following definition of reasoning: "that which follows as a reasonable inference or natural consequence; deducible or defensible on the grounds of consistency; reasonably believed or done" (Oxford Press, 1999). This definition emphasizes a central cognitive requirement to draw inferences from knowledge. This characteristic of general intelligence is measured best by two RIAS subtests, Verbal Reasoning and Odd Item Out, although all of the subtests have substantial g saturation (see Reynolds & Kamphaus, 2003, especially Chapter 6).

Kamphaus (2001) has suggested that the term *crystallized* for this second-order factor does not fully capture the centrality of language processes involved in successful performance on subtests typically associated with this ability. He proposed the term *verbal* to describe the latent construct tapped by subtests like those selected for the RIAS.

Nonverbal tests have come to be recognized as measures of important spatial and visual-perceptual abilities—abilities that may need to be assessed for a variety of examinees, including those with brain injuries. In the 1963 landmark *ETS Kit of Factor-Referenced Cognitive Tests*, spatial ability was defined as "the ability to manipulate or transform the image of spatial patterns into other visual arrangements" (as cited in Carroll, 1993, p. 316). The RIAS What's Missing and Odd Item Out subtests follow in this long tradition of tasks designed to measure visuospatial abilities.

Digit recall, sentence recall, geometric design recall, bead recall, and similar measures loaded consistently on a "general memory and learning" stratum-two factor identified by Carroll (1993) in his numerous analyses. The RIAS Verbal Memory and Nonverbal Memory subtests are of this same variety, although more complex than simple confrontational memory tasks such as pure digit recall. Carroll's findings suggest that the RIAS Verbal Memory and Nonverbal Memory subtests should be good measures of the memory construct that has been identified previously in so many investigations of a diverse array of tests. Carroll described memory span as "attention to a temporally ordered stimulus, registration of the stimulus in immediate memory, and output of its repetition" (p. 259). This operational definition is an accurate description of the RIAS memory subtests and composite. Memory is typically considered a complex trait with many permutations, including visual, verbal, long term, and short term. Carroll's analysis of hundreds of data sets supports the organization of the RIAS, in that he found ample evidence of a general memory trait that may be further subdivided for particular clinical purposes.

Description of Subtests

Subtests with a familiar look and feel and with essentially long histories in the field of intellectual assessment were chosen for inclusion on the RIAS. There are a total of four intelligence subtests and two memory subtests. The intelligence subtests were chosen also due to their complex nature—each assesses many intellectual functions and requires their integration for successful performance (also see Reynolds & Kamphaus, 2003, Chapter 6, under the heading of "evidence based on response processes"). The memory subtests were chosen not only for complexity but also due to their representation of the primary content domains of memory.

Guess What

This subtest measures vocabulary knowledge in combination with reasoning skills that are predicated on language development and fund of information. For each item, the examinee is asked to listen to a question that contains clues presented orally by the examiner and then to give a verbal response (typically one or two words) that is consistent with the clues.

Verbal Reasoning

The second verbal subtest, Verbal Reasoning, measures analytical reasoning abilities. More difficult items of necessity also require advanced vocabulary knowledge. For each item, the examinee is asked to listen to an incomplete sentence, presented orally by the examiner, and then to give a verbal response, typically one or two words, that completes the sentence, most commonly completing a complex analogy. Completion of the sentences requires the examinee to evaluate the various conceptual relationships that exist between the physical objects or abstract ideas contained in the sentences.

Odd Item Out

This subtest measures general reasoning skills emphasizing nonverbal ability in the form of a reverse analogy. For each item, the examinee is presented with a picture card containing from five to seven figures or drawings. One of the figures or drawings on the picture card has a distinguishing characteristic, making it different from the others.

What's Missing

This subtest measures nonverbal reasoning skills through the presentation of pictures in which some important component of the pictured object is missing. Examinees must understand or conceptualize the pictured object, assess its gestalt, and distinguish essential from nonessential components. For each item, the examinee is shown a picture card and asked to examine the picture and then to indicate, in words or by pointing, what is missing from the picture. Naming the missing part correctly is not required so long as the examinee can indicate the location of the missing component correctly.

Verbal Memory

This subtest measures the ability to encode, briefly store, and recall verbal material in a meaningful context. Young children (ages 3–4) are asked to listen to sentences of progressively greater length as each is read aloud by the examiner and then asked to repeat each sentence back to the examiner, word for word, immediately after it is read aloud. Older children and adults are asked to listen to two stories read aloud by the examiner and then to repeat each story back to the examiner, word for word, immediately after it is read aloud. The sentences and stories were written to provide developmentally appropriate content and material of interest to the targeted age group. Specific stories are designated for various age groups.

Nonverbal Memory

This subtest measures the ability to encode, briefly store, and recall visually presented material, whether the stimuli represent concrete objects or abstract concepts. For each item, the examinee is presented with a target picture for five seconds and then a picture card containing the target picture and an array of similar pictures. The examinee is asked to identify the target picture among the array of pictures presented on the picture card. For each item, the examinee is given two chances to identify the target picture. The pictures are, at the upper levels, primarily abstract, and at the lower age levels, common objects. The use of naming and related language strategies, however, is not helpful due to the design of the distractors. For example, one early item presents as a target stimulus a picture of a cat. On the recall page, six cats are presented, each different (save one) in some characteristic from the target stimulus.

Scales and Structure

The six RIAS subtests are divided into four composite indexes as depicted in Tables 5.1 and 5.2: the Verbal Intelligence Index (VIX), the Nonverbal Intelligence Index (NIX), the Composite Intelligence Index (CIX, composed of the VIX + NIX), and the Composite memory Index (CMX). Interpretations of these indexes are discussed in a later section.

Administration and Scoring

The RIAS was specifically designed to be easy to administer and objective to score. For all subtests except Verbal Memory, there are clear objective lists of correct responses for each test item and seldom are any judgment calls required. Studies of the interscorer reliability of these five subtests produced interscorer reliability coefficients of 1.00 by trained examiners (Reynolds & Kamphaus, 2003). On Verbal Memory, some judgment is required when examinees do not give verbatim responses; however, the scoring

TABLE 5.2   RIAS Subtest Composition of IQ and Index Scores

| Subtests Mean = 50 SD = 10 | Indexes Mean = 100   SD = 15 | | | |
	VIX	NIX	CIX	CMX
GWH	%		%	
VRZ	✓	%		
OIO		%	%	
WHM		%	%	
VRM				%
NVM				%

NOTE : VRZ = Verbal Reasoning; GWH = Guess What; OIO = Odd Item Out; WHM = What's Missing; VRM = Verbal Memory; NVM = Nonverbal Memory; VIX = Verbal Composite Index; NIX = Nonverbal Composite Index; CIX = RIAS Composite Index; CMX = Composite Memory Index.

criteria provide clear examples and guidelines for such circumstances, making the Verbal Memory subtest only slightly more difficult to score. The interscorer reliability study of this subtest produced a coefficient of .95.

The time required to administer the entire RIAS (including the intelligence and the memory subtests) averages 30 to 35 minutes once the examiner has practiced giving the RIAS and has become fluent in its administration. Basal and ceiling rules along with age-designated starting points were employed to control the administration time and each was derived empirically from the responses of the standardization sample. A detailed description of the methods used for setting these administration parameters is given in Chapter 2 of Reynolds and Kamphaus (2003). Also, to facilitate ease of administration and to make it more efficient, the RIAS record form contains all of the instructions and examiner guides necessary to administer the test.

Experienced examiners as well as graduate students have consistently reported that the RIAS is surprisingly easy to administer and score.

SCORING AND INTERPRETIVE SOFTWARE

There are two separately available computerized scoring and interpretive programs related to the RIAS. One is the RIAS-IR (Reynolds & Kamphaus, 2007a), a scoring and interpretive program devoted just to the RIAS (and the RIAST), and the RIAS/WRAT-4-DIR (Reynolds & Kamphaus, 2007b), which analyzes discrepancies between the RIAS and the WRAT4 scores of examinees based on a linking sample between the two measures.

The RIAS-IR (Scoring and Interpretive Report)

The unlimited-use RIAS-IR is designed to assist clinicians with scoring, profiling, and interpreting the performance of individuals (ages 3–94) on the RIAS and the Reynolds Intellectual Screening Test (RIST; only the RIAS features are discussed here). After manual entry of an examinee's raw scores into the software, the RIAS-IR can generate up to three Score Reports, two Feedback Reports (for parents/guardians of minors, teachers, or adult examinees after a discussion of the test results), and two Interpretive Reports. Program functionality includes report editing. Report options for the RIAS and the RIST include:

RIAS Score Report

After input of all four subtest scores, the RIAS Score Report includes the examinee's demographic information, the RIAS Score Summary Table, the RIAS Profile, brief interpretive text, and an Extended Score Summary Table.

RIAS Total Battery Score Report

After input of all six subtest scores, the RIAS Total Battery Score Report includes the examinee's demographic information, the RIAS Total Battery Score Summary Table, a Total Battery Profile, and brief interpretive text.

Feedback Reports

RIAS Feedback Report

After input of all four subtest scores, the RIAS Feedback Report provides easy-to-understand information about the examinee's performance on the RIAS written in lay terms for parents/guardians, teachers, or an adult examinee.

RIAS Total Battery Feedback Report

After input of all six subtest scores, the RIAS Total Battery Feedback Report provides easy-to-understand information about the examinee's performance on the RIAS Total Battery written in lay terms for parents/guardians, teachers, or an adult examinee.

Interpretive Reports

RIAS Interpretive Report

After input of either four or all six subtest scores, the RIAS Interpretive Report includes the examinee's demographic information, the RIAS Score Summary Table, the RIAS Profile, an Extended Score Summary Table, and extensive interpretive text with intervention and additional testing recommendations. This report also provides clinicians with the option to include the Total Battery scores (i.e., Total Test Battery, Total Verbal Battery, Total Nonverbal Battery).

The RIAS-IR provides clinicians with greater flexibility to obtain the report they desire by enabling the selection of specific report components for inclusion and by providing built-in report-editing features that also allow clinicians to cut-and-drop features into their own word processing programs. It also provides flexibility within the Interpretive Reports to generate setting-specific feedback and recommendations (i.e., school, employment, long-term care [assisted living, nursing home]) in addition to the software's default general feedback and recommendations.

Aptitude–Achievement Discrepancy Software: RIAS/WRAT4-DIR

The RIAS/WRAT4-DIR addresses the evaluation of discrepancies between intelligence test performance and achievement test performance by providing and evaluating discrepancies between scores on the Reynolds Intellectual Assessment Scales (RIAS)/Reynolds Intellectual Screening Test (RIST) and on the Wide Range Achievement Test 4 (WRAT4). By comparing general ability levels as assessed by the RIAS to achievement levels as obtained by the WRAT4, the RIAS/WRAT4-DIR provides the information necessary for assisting in the determination of special education eligibility and the presence of specific learning disabilities in individuals in cases where discrepancy analyses are useful or necessary. Although evaluation of such discrepancies is now optional in school settings, many other settings continue to adhere to a requirement of aptitude–achievement discrepancies for learning disability determination.

Two types of scoring methodologies are used to derive the discrepancy scores and to evaluate the statistical significance of the score and its prevalence within the population. The simple difference method examines the difference between an obtained RIAS score and an obtained WRAT4 score. The predicted-achievement method uses the individual's obtained RIAS score to predict his or her performance on the WRAT4. It then examines the difference between the predicted WRAT4 score and the individual's obtained WRAT4 score. Using these methods, three types of discrepancy reports that contain a total of 40 discrepancy scores are generated by the software:

1. *RIST/WRAT4 Discrepancy Interpretive Report*: provides discrepancy scores and analysis

between the RIST index score and each WRAT4 subtest/composite score (i.e., Word Reading, Sentence Comprehension, Spelling, Math Computation, Reading Composite)

2. *RIAS/WRAT4 Discrepancy Interpretive Report*: provides discrepancy scores and analysis between each RIAS Index score (i.e., VIX, NIX, CIX, CMX) and each WRAT4 subtest/composite score

3. *RIAS/WRAT4 Total Battery Discrepancy Interpretive Report*: provides discrepancy scores and analysis between the RIAS Total Battery Index scores (i.e., TTB, TVB, TNB) and each WRAT4 subtest/composite score

The *RIAS/WRAT4-DIR Professional Manual Supplement* provides normative data about the separate linking sample developed specifically for derivation of this interpretive program. It consisted of 410 participants ages 5–24 and was matched to U.S. Bureau of the Census population data for gender, ethnicity, and educational attainment. The Professional Manual Supplement also provides overviews of the RIAS and the WRAT4, including original standardization information, descriptions of the two different scoring methods, and suggestions for the interpretation of the discrepancy scores. It is unlimited-use software that generates discrepancy scores and interpretive reports based on a clinician's entry of an individual's raw scores and provides an efficient file-handling system that enables the user to create examinee files where all protocols and report files for each examinee are managed.

PSYCHOMETRIC PROPERTIES

The psychometric characteristics of any measurement device and its scores are certainly crucial in determining its utility. In this section, a review of the standardization procedures and the scaling of the RIAS is presented, followed by a summary of the reliability of the scores derived from the instrument and evidence related to the validity of score interpretations. Due to the length restrictions in a single book chapter, a discussion of the developmental process of the test simply cannot be provided. However, the RIAS underwent years of development, including tryout and review of the items on multiple occasions by school, clinical, and other psychologists, including neuropsychologists. Items were written to conform to clear specifications consistent with the goals for development of the test as given previously in this chapter. Items were reviewed by panels of expert psychologists for content and construct consistency and by expert minority psychologists, as well, to ascertain the cultural saliency of the items and any potential problems of ambiguity or offensiveness in various settings. The developmental process speaks directly to the psychometric characteristics of the tests and is described in far more detail in Reynolds and Kamphaus (2003) and should be considered carefully in any full evaluation of the instrument.

Standardization

The RIAS was normed on a sample of 2,438 participants residing in 41 states between the years 1999 and 2002. United States Bureau of the Census projected characteristics of the U.S. population, initially to the year 2000 and then updated through 2001, were used to select a population proportionate sample. Age, gender, ethnicity, educational level (parent educational level was used for ages 3–16 and the participants' educational level was used at all other ages), and region of residence were used as stratification variables. To facilitate some of the analyses of cultural bias in the item pool, minorities were oversampled in some cells, particularly at the early ages. The resulting norms for the RIAS were calculated on a weighted sampling that provided a virtually perfect match to the census data. The overall sample was a close match to the population statistics in any regard (see Reynolds & Kamphaus, 2003, especially Tables 4.2–4.5).

Norm Derivation and Scaling

Starting Points and Basal/Ceiling Rules

During standardization, starting points and basal/ceiling rules were set to ensure that participants received the maximum number of items they would be expected to receive on the final version. Once the final RIAS items were determined (after standardization), they were reordered by ascending item difficulty index. An iterative process of item selection and various basal and ceiling rules was then applied to locate the points that captured the performance of most (over 90% across all ages) of the examinees had they been administered all items on the test. The reliability of scores obtained under the basal and ceiling rules that best fit these criteria were then examined to be certain accuracy of score estimation was not adversely impacted across examinees by applying a particular set of rules. Finally (after scaling was completed using the chosen rules), the scores of all examinees were compared under the application of the chosen basal/ceiling rules and under the condition of taking all items as a final check to ascertain the impact on the scores of individual examinees. It was rare under the final rules for any examinee's subtest scaled score to be affected by more than one point and most were in fact unaffected. Once the basal and ceiling rules were established, the raw score distributions were determined and the various scaled scores derived.

Scaling Methods

All standard scores for the RIAS were derived via a method known as *continuous norming*. Continuous norming is a regression-based methodology used to mitigate the effects of any sampling irregularities across age groupings and to stabilize parameter estimation. An important feature of continuous norming is that it uses information from all age groups, rather than relying solely on the estimates of central tendency, dispersion, and the shape of the distributions of a single age grouping for producing the norms at each chosen age interval in the normative tables for a particular test (Zachary & Gorsuch, 1985). As such, the continuous norming procedure maximizes the accuracy of the derived normative scores and has become widespread in its application to the derivation of test norms over the last 20 years.

T-scores were chosen for the RIAS subtests over the more traditional mean = 10 scaled scores popularized by Wechsler (e.g., Wechsler, 1949) due to the higher reliability coefficients obtained for the RIAS subtest scores and expanded item pools. With high degrees of reliability of test scores, the use of scales that make finer discriminations among individuals is possible, producing a more desirable range of possible scores. For the convenience of researchers and examiners who wish to use other types of scores for comparative, research, or other purposes, the RIAS Manual (Reynolds & Kamphaus, 2003, Appendix B) provides several other common types of scores for the RIAS indexes, including percentiles, T-scores, z-scores, normal curve equivalents (NCEs), and stanines, along with a detailed explanation of each score type.

Score Reliability

Since the RIAS is a power test, the internal consistency reliability of the items on the RIAS subtests was investigated using Cronbach's coefficient alpha. Alpha reliability coefficients for the RIAS subtest scores (Cronbach, 1951) and the Nunnally reliability estimates (see Nunnally, 1978, p. 249, formula 7-15) for the index scores are presented in Reynolds and Kamphaus (2003) for 16 age groups from the total standardization sample. The reliability estimates are rounded to two decimal places and represent the lower limits of the internal consistency reliability of the RIAS scores.

According to the tables in Chapter 5 of Reynolds and Kamphaus (2003), 100% of the alpha coefficients for the RIAS subtest scores reach .84, or higher, for every age group. The median alpha reliability estimate for each RIAS subtest across age equals or exceeds .90. This

point is important because many measurement experts recommend that reliability estimates above .80 are necessary and those above .90 are highly desirable for tests used to make decisions about individuals. All RIAS subtests meet these recommended levels. As shown in Table 5.2 of Reynolds and Kamphaus (2003, p. 78), the reliability estimates for all RIAS indexes have median values across age that equal or exceed .94. These reliability estimates are viewed as excellent and often exceed the reliability values presented for the composite indexes or IQs of tests two or three times the length of the RIAS. Thus, one can have strong confidence in the relative reliability and accuracy of both subtest and index scores derived from standardized administration of the RIAS.

One cannot always assume that because a test is reliable for a general population, it will be equally reliable for every subgroup within that population. It is thus instructive to view the various reliability estimates for the RIAS (or any test) for smaller, meaningful subgroups of a population (Reynolds, 2003). When calculated separately for male and female examinees, the reliability coefficients are high and relatively uniform (see Table 5.3 of Reynolds & Kamphaus, 2003, for the full table of values) with no significant differences in test score reliability at any age level as a function of gender.

TABLE 5.3 Uncorrected (and Corrected) Pearson Correlations between Reynolds Intellectual Assessment Scales (RIAS) Indexes and WJ-III Scores for a Referral Sample

RIAS Index	WISC-III			WAIS-III		
	VIQ	PIQ	FSIQ	VIQ	PIQ	FSIQ
VIX	.86	.44	.78	.71	.61	.70
NIX	.60	.33	.60	.67	.71	.71
CIX	.81	.42	.76	.74	.70	.75
CMX	.67	.40	.66	.76	.76	.79

Reliability estimates were also calculated separately for whites and African Americans. These values are reported in Chapter 5 of the RIAS Manual. Although the reliability estimates across ethnic groups display more variability than across gender, the values are consistently high except for several instances. Of the 320 values calculated, only five drop below .80 (i.e., range from .66 to .79). When the values are tested for the presence of statistically significant differences (again using the Feldt technique, see Reynolds, 2003) and the Bonferroni correction is applied (as recommended in the APA task force on statistical significance testing official report; Wilkinson & Task Force on Statistical Inference, 1999), no significant differences are found. Thus, the RIAS shows uniformly high internal consistency reliability estimates across age (3–94) and across gender and across ethnicity.

Test score stability (sometimes referred to as *error due to time sampling*) refers to the extent to which an individual's test performance is constant over time and is usually estimated by the test–retest method. The stability of RIAS scores over time was investigated using the test–retest method with 86 individuals ages 3–82. The intervals between the two test administrations ranged from 9 to 39 days, with a median test–retest interval of 21 days. The correlations for the two testings, along with mean scores and standard deviations, are reported in detail in the RIAS Manual (Reynolds & Kamphaus, 2003) in Tables 5.7–5.11 for the total test–retest sample and for four age groups: 3–4 years, 5–8 years, 9–12 years, and 13–82 years.

The obtained coefficients are of sufficient magnitude to allow confidence in the stability of RIAS test scores over time. In fact, the values are quite good for all of the subtests, but especially for the index scores. Both the uncorrected coefficients and the corrected, or disattenuated, coefficients are reported (the corrected coefficients being corrected for the alpha for each subtest). The uncorrected coefficients are all higher than .70, and 6 of the 10 values are in the .80s. The corrected values are even more impressive, with all but two values ranging from .83 to .91. When viewed across age groups, the values are generally consistent with the values obtained for the total test–retest sample. The test–retest stability coefficients for scores on the RIAS subtests and indexes are quite strong and provide evidence of more than sufficient short-term temporal stability of the scores to allow examiners to be confident in the obtained results.

Validity of RIAS Test Scores as Measures of Intelligence

According to the *Standards*, *validity*, in this context, refers to "the degree to which evidence and theory *support the interpretations of test scores* entailed by proposed users of tests" (emphasis added, p. 9). Reynolds (1998) defined *validity* similarly, arguing that validity refers to the appropriateness and accuracy of the interpretation of performance on a test, with such performance usually expressed as a test score. Validation of the meaning of test scores is also a process, one that involves an ongoing, dynamic effort to accumulate evidence for a sound scientific basis for proposed test score interpretations (AERA, APA, & NCME, 1999; Reynolds, 1998). Validity as such will always be a relative concept because the validity of an interpretation will vary according to the purpose for which test scores are being used, the types of individuals or populations being examined, and the specific interpretations being made.

The *Standards* (AERA et al., 1999, pp. 11–17) suggests a five-category scheme for organizing sources of evidence to evaluate proposed interpretations of test scores, although clearly recognizing that other organizational systems may be appropriate. What follows is a summary of the currently available validity evidence associated with the RIAS/RIST scores as measures of intelligence organized according to the recommendations just noted.

Evidence Based on Test Content

The *Standards* states that "test content refers to the themes, wording, and format of the items, tasks, or questions . . . as well as guidelines . . . for administration and scoring" (p. 11). In discussing the types of evidence that may be appropriate in this context, the Standards concludes that evidence related to test content may be logical or empirical, and that expert judgments of the relationship between the test and the intended constructs to be assessed are appropriate.

Subtests with familiar formats were chosen for the various intelligence and memory subtests of the RIAS. Although the individual items of the RIAS are unique, each of the formats for the four intelligence and two memory tasks has a long history in the field of psychological assessment. Tasks similar in format and cognitive processing requirements to What's Missing and Verbal Reasoning, for example, can be traced to the early efforts of Alfred Binet at the turn of the twentieth century (Binet & Simon, 1905) and also to Yerkes (1917) and his team of psychologists, who built aptitude measures for the U.S. military early in the last century. Verbal analogies such as those represented on Verbal Reasoning are present on many tests of verbal ability, including early and modern versions of the SAT and GRE examinations, the Miller Analogies Test (Miller, 1926), as well as many individually administered intelligence tests (e.g., McCarthy, 1972). Item formats corresponding to those of Guess What and Odd Item Out appear shortly after these early types and are common formats on various tests of general information and matrix reasoning. Validity evidence for these item formats as measures of intellectual skill is voluminous and reviewed in a variety of sources, the most readily accessible being Eliot and Smith (1983), Kamphaus (2001), Kaufman (1990, 1994), and Sattler (2001).

Likewise, the two memory tasks chosen for inclusion in the RIAS have long, rich histories in the field of psychological testing, dating back to the 1920s and 1930s (e.g., Kamphaus, 2001; Reynolds & Bigler, 1994). Over many decades, similar tasks have been included on a variety of tests designed to measure memory function (see Benton, 1974; Reynolds & Bigler, 1994; Wechsler, 1997b).

Additionally, during the first item tryout, a panel of psychologists representing a variety of ethnic, cultural, and linguistic groups, all with experience in assessment, reviewed all RIAS items for appropriateness as measures of their respective constructs and for applicability across various U.S. cultures. Items questioned or faulted by this panel were eliminated from the RIAS item pool or were revised. Another panel of five psychologists with doctoral degrees in school psychology, clinical psychology, clinical neuropsychology, and measurement also reviewed all items in the item pool for appropriateness. Items questioned or found faulty by this group were either eliminated outright or modified.

Evidence Based on Response Processes

Evidence based on the response processes of the tasks is concerned with the fit between the nature of the performance or actions in which the examinee is actually engaged and the constructs being assessed. The four RIAS intelligence subtests are designed to measure general intelligence in the verbal and nonverbal domains. As such, the tasks are complex and require the integration of multiple cognitive skills, thereby avoiding contamination by irrelevant, noncognitive response processes.

Because of their relationship to crystallized intelligence, the two verbal subtests invoke vocabulary and language comprehension. However, clearly academic or purely acquired skills such as reading are avoided. The response process requires integration of language and some general knowledge to deduce relationships; only minimal expressive language is required. One- or two-word responses are acceptable for virtually all items. The response process also is not contaminated by nonintellectual processes such as motor acuity, speed, and coordination. Rather, problem solving through the processes of deductive and inductive reasoning is emphasized.

Likewise, the two nonverbal tasks avoid contamination by extraneous variables such as motor acuity, speed, and coordination. Examinees have the option of responding by pointing or with a one- or two-word verbal indication of the correct answer. As with any nonverbal task, some examinees might attempt to use verbal encoding to solve these tasks, and some will do so successfully. However, the tasks themselves are largely spatial and are known to be more affected by right—rather than by left—hemisphere impairment (e.g., Joseph, 1996; Reynolds, Castillo, & Horton, 2008), a finding that supports the lack of verbal domination in strategies for solving such problems. When examiners suspect that verbal strategies are being applied, they should question the examinee regarding his or her strategies after all the subtests have been administered in order to gain relevant information for the interpretation of the examinee's test performance.

Response processes of the two RIAS memory subtests also avoid contamination from reading and various aspects of motor skills. Although good language skills undoubtedly facilitate verbal memory, it is not the dominant skill involved. The RIAS memory tasks are very straightforward, with response processes that coincide with their content domain—verbal in verbal memory and nonverbal in nonverbal memory. Even so, in the latter case, examinees who have severe motor problems may give a verbal indication of the answer they have selected.

Evidence Based on Internal Structure

Analyses of the internal structure of a test provide information about the interrelationships of the items or subtests of a larger test and can reveal how this structure might conform to the hypothesized construct(s) being assessed (AERA, APA, & NCME, 1999). Such an examination of evidence requires both empirical and logical analyses. Here, evidence from studies of internal consistency and studies of the factor structure are reviewed in the context of proposed interpretations of RIAS scores.

Evidence based on the internal structure of the RIAS is provided from two sources—item coherence (or internal consistency) and factor analyses of the intercorrelations of the subtests. The internal consistency evidence has been reviewed in the section on the reliability of test scores derived from the RIAS, and the evidence for coherence is certainly strong for each of the subtests as well as the composite scores. Factor analysis is another method of examining the internal structure of a scale that lends itself to assessing the validity of recommended score interpretations.

Two methods of factor analysis have been applied to the intercorrelation matrix of the RIAS subtests, first with only the four intelligence subtests examined and then with all six subtests examined under both techniques of analysis. Exploratory analyses were undertaken first and were followed by a set of confirmatory analyses to assess the relative goodness-of-fit of the chosen exploratory results to mathematically optimal models.

For purposes of factor analyses of the RIAS subtest's intercorrelations, the sample was divided into five age groups (rather than one-year interval groups) to enhance the stability and the generalizability of the factor analyses of the RIAS scores. These age groupings reflect common developmental stages. The five age groupings were early childhood, ages 3–5; childhood, ages 6–11; adolescence, ages 12–18; adulthood, ages 19–54; and senior adulthood, ages 55–94.

When the two-factor and three-factor solutions were subsequently obtained, the two-factor varimax solution made the most psychological and psychometric sense both for the set of four intelligence subtests and for all six RIAS subtests. In the four-subtest three-factor solution, no variables consistently defined the third factor across the four age groupings. In the six-subtest three-factor solutions, singlet factors (i.e., factors with a single salient loading) appeared, commonly representing a memory subtest; What's Missing tended to behave in an unstable manner as well. Summaries of the two-factor varimax solutions are presented in Reynolds and Kamphaus, 2003 for the four-subtest and six-subtest analyses. In each case, the first, unrotated factor is a representation of g as measured by the RIAS.

The g factor of the RIAS is quite strong. Only the intelligence subtests have loadings that reach into the .70s and .80s. All four intelligence subtests are good measures of g; however, of the four, the verbal subtests are the strongest. Odd Item Out and What's Missing follow, the latter being the weakest measure of g among the four intelligence subtests. The strength of the first unrotated factor is, however, indisputable and indicates that first and foremost the RIAS intelligence subtests are measures of g and that the strongest interpretive support is given, in these analyses, to the CIX.

At the same time, the varimax rotation of the two-factor solution clearly delineates two components of the construct of g among the RIAS intelligence subtests. For every age group, the verbal and nonverbal subtests clearly break into two distinct factors that coincide with their respective indexes, VIX and NIX. The six-subtest solution also breaks along content dimensions, with Verbal Memory joining the two verbal intelligence subtests on the first rotated factor and Nonverbal Memory joining the two nonverbal intelligence subtests on the second rotated factor. However, in view of the analysis of the content and response processes as well as other evidence presented throughout this manual, we continue to believe that the separation of the Verbal Memory and Nonverbal Memory subtests into a separate memory index (i.e., CMX) is more than justified. Memory is clearly a component of intelligence. The two memory tasks that were chosen for the RIAS are relatively complex, and both are strong predictors of broader composites of verbal and nonverbal memory (Reynolds & Bigler, 1994), characteristics that are at once an asset and a liability. Although these two memory tasks are good measures of overall, or general, memory skill, they tend to correlate more highly with intelligence test scores than do very simple,

confrontational measures of working memory, such as forward digit repetition. Given the purpose of providing a highly reliable assessment of overall memory skill, such a compromise is warranted.

The stability of the two-factor solution across other relevant nominal groupings and the potential for cultural bias in the internal structure of the RIAS were also assessed. For this purpose, the factor analyses were also calculated separately for males and females and for whites and African Americans, according to recommendations and procedures outlined in detail by Reynolds (2000). Tables 6.3 through 6.6 in Reynolds and Kamphaus (2003) present these results for each comparison. The similarity of the factor-analytic results across gender and across ethnicity was also assessed. Two indexes of factorial similarity were calculated for the visually matched rotated factors and for the first unrotated factor, the coefficient of congruence (r_c), and Cattell's (1978) salient variable similarity index (s), as recommended in several sources (e.g., Reynolds, 2000). In all cases, the factor structure of the RIAS was found to be highly consistent across gender and ethnicity.

Subsequent to the exploratory factor analyses, a series of confirmatory factor analyses were conducted to examine the fit of our choice of exploratory analyses to a more purely mathematical model. Based on the theoretical views of the structure of the RIAS discussed earlier in this chapter, three theoretical models were tested. The models were defined as follows: Model 1, The RIAS is a measure of general intellectual abilities; Model 2, The RIAS is a measure of verbal and nonverbal abilities; and Model 3, The RIAS is a measure of verbal, nonverbal, and memory abilities.

The resulting chi square (O^2), residuals, root mean square error of approximation (RMSEA), and other model-fit statistics were then compared using the LISREL-VI program (Joreskog & Sorbom, 1987) to test the relative fit of the three models. Model 1, general intelligence, clearly fit better when only the four intelligence subtests were included ($\chi^2 = 8.17$–20.57 and RMSEA ranging from .10 to .14 depending on the age range studied) than when six subtests were included. Although these models suggest, much in the same way as the exploratory factor analyses showed, that the RIAS is dominated by a large first factor, the RMSEAs were still high enough to suggest that Models 2 and 3 should be explored.

Model 2 was a very good fit to the data particularly when four subtests were included in the model versus six subtests. For the model that included four subtests, the chi-square values were between .22 and 1.49. Similarly, the RMSEAs were less than .01 for the first four age groups (i.e., 3–54 years) and .04 for ages 55 and older, values suggesting that two factors explained virtually all of the variance between the four subtests. These findings indicated that the fit of a three-factor model was not likely to be as good, and in fact Model 3 with six subtests included ($\chi^2 = 14.14$–37.48 and RMSEA ranging from .01 to .09) did not fit nearly as well as Model 2.

In summary, the results of the confirmatory factor analyses suggest that the CIX, VIX, and NIX possess evidence of factorial validity. The CMX in particular requires further research with a variety of clinical and nonclinical samples.

Evidence Based on Relations with Other (External) Variables

Another important area in the validation process is the evaluation of the relationship of scores on the instrument of interest to variables that are external to the test itself. A variety of external variables were chosen for investigation with the RIAS, including developmental variables (e.g., age), demographic variables, relations with other tests, and clinical status.

Developmental Trends

As a developmental construct, intellectual ability grows rapidly in the early years, begins to plateau in the teens but with some continued growth (particularly in verbal domains), and eventually declines in the older years. This decline generally begins sooner and is more dramatic for nonverbal, or fluid, intelligence (Kaufman, McLean, Kaufman-Packer, & Reynolds, 1991; Kaufman, Reynolds, & McLean, 1989; Reynolds, Chastain, Kaufman, & McLean, 1987). If raw scores on the tasks of the RIAS reflect such a developmental process or attribute, then relationships with age should be evident. The relationship between age (a variable external to the RIAS) and performance on the RIAS was investigated in two ways.

First, the correlation between age and raw score for each subtest was calculated for the primary developmental stage, ages 3–18, for the entire sample and for a variety of ethnic groups and by gender. The correlations for all groups are uniformly large, typically exceeding .80 and demonstrating that raw scores on the RIAS increase with age and in a relatively constant manner across subtests. When the values for each subtest are compared across nominal groupings (gender and ethnicity), there are very small differences observed, none being statistically significant or clinically meaningful, indicating common developmental patterns across all groups to the extent correlational data can reveal such trends. Second, to examine the issue in more detail, lifespan developmental curves were generated for each subtest from ages 3 through 94. These curves are presented in the RIAS Manual (Reynolds & Kamphaus, 2003) and show a consistent pattern of score increases and declines (with aging) across all groups.

Correlations with the Wechsler Scales

Measures of intelligence generally should correlate well with one another if they are measuring g and related constructs. Thus, to understand a new measure and its appropriate interpretations, it is instructive to assess the relationship of the new measure to other measures of intelligence. For children (ages 6–16), the best known and most widely researched scale over the years and one that has maintained a reasonably consistent structure is the Wechsler Intelligence Scale for

Children, in its third edition (WISC-III; Wechsler, 1991) when the RIAS was published, and now in its fourth.

WISC-IV   Edwards (2006) reported on correlations between the RIAS and the WISC-IV factor indexes for two referral samples. In the first group of 83 children ages 7–9, the correlations reported were: RIAS VIX-WISC-IV VCI r = .83, NIX-PRI r = .42, CIX-WMI r = .58, CIX-PSI r = .36, and CIX-FSIQ r = .75. In a sample of 121 children and adolescents ages 6–16, Edwards reported the same set of correlations as: RIAS VIX-WISC-IV VCI r = .83, NIX-PRI r = .54, CIX-WMI r = .62, CIX-PSI r = .45, and CIX-FSIQ r= .79.

In another study, Edwards and Paulin (2007) reported on another referral sample, of 26 boys and 24 girls ranging in age from 6–12 years, administered both the RIAS and the WISC-IV. In this study, some additional correlations were reported and the correlations were generally larger as well. Edwards and Paulin reported correlations between related constructs of: RIAS VIX-WISC-IV VCI r = .90, NIX-PRI r = .72, and CIX-FSIQ r = .90. They also reported a correlation between the RIAS CIX and the WISC-IV GAI of .90. The RIAS composite scores are thus seen to be very highly correlated with the cognate composite scores on the WISC-III and WISC-IV, except for the PRI, which on the Wechsler Scales is confounded by motor and speed of performance—factors eliminated as confounds on the RIAS and factors less confounding in the assessment of adults.

WISC-III   Table 5.4 summarizes RIAS correlations with the WISC-III and WAIS-III. The RIAS indexes all correlate highly with the WISC-III Full Scale IQ (FSIQ), with correlations ranging from a low of .60 (NIX to FSIQ) to a high of .78 (VIX to FSIQ). The relatively lower correlations between the RIAS NIX and the WISC-III IQs are most likely attributable to the increased emphasis on motor and language skills on the WISC-III Performance IQ (PIQ)

relative to that in the RIAS. The WISC-III PIQ subtests also rely on sequencing (e.g., Picture Arrangement and Coding), whereas the RIAS has no subtest in which sequencing is crucial to the task. Speed of performance and motor skills are also less important on the RIAS, taking away confounds in the measurement of nonverbal intelligence present on the Wechsler Scales at the child level. For adults, these are far less salient issues. With this one exception, the pattern of correlations is much as was predicted, namely, the highest correlations were between those aspects of the tests most closely associated with g (from their respective factor analyses).

WAIS-III   A group of 31 adults were administered the RIAS and the Wechsler Adult Intelligence Scale—Third Edition (WAIS-III; Wechsler, 1997a) in a counterbalanced design. All but two of the correlations exceed .70; the VIX-PIQ correlation was the lowest at .61. All of the RIAS indexes correlate at or above .70 with the WAIS-III FSIQ (see Table 5.3).

Correlations with Measures of Academic Achievement

One of the major reasons for the development of the early, individually administered intelligence tests was to predict academic achievement levels. Intelligence tests have done well as predictors of school learning, with typical correlations in the mid .50s and .60s (see Kamphaus, 2001, and Sattler, 2001, for summaries). To evaluate the relationship between the RIAS and academic achievement, 78 children and adolescents were administered the RIAS and the Wechsler Individual Achievement Test (WIAT; Wechsler, 1992).

School learning is fundamentally a language-related task, and this fact is clearly evident in the data presented in Reynolds and Kamphaus (2003). Although all of the RIAS indexes correlate well with all of the WIAT composite scores, the highest correlations are consistently between the VIX and CIX and the WIAT composites. These correlations are

TABLE 5.4 Correlations between RIAS Indexes and WISC-III and WAIS-III IQs

	RIAS Index		
WJ-III Score	**VIX**	**NIX**	**CIX**
Reading Composite	.88 (.85)	.74 (.75)	.88 (.86)
Basic Reading Composite	.79 (.74)	.59 (.60)	.76 (.73)
Comprehension	.88 (.86)	.74 (.75)	.87 (.85)
Low Identification	.85 (.81)	.62 (.64)	.81 (.78)
Reading Fluency	.37 (.33)	.06 (.06)	.26 (.24)
Passage Comprehension	.85 (.81)	.71 (.72)	.85 (.82)
Math Composite	.80 (.75)	.70 (.71)	.82 (.79)
Calculation Composite	.72 (.67)	.57 (.58)	.72 (.68)
Math Reasoning	.86 (.83)	.85 (.86)	.90 (.88)
Calculation	.76 (.72)	.63 (.64)	.76 (.72)
Math Fluency	.68 (.63)	.55 (.56)	.66 (.63)
Applied Problems	.79 (.75)	.76 (.77)	.84 (.81)
Written Language Composite	.56 (.51)	.33 (.34)	.54 (.50)
Written Expression Composite	.58 (.53)	.55 (.57)	.64 (.60)
Writing Fluency	.50 (.45)	.34 (.35)	.49 (.45)
RIAS Mean	94	99	96
RIAS *SD*	17	14	16

NOTE : *N* varies by subtests. Not all were administered to all children. Total *N* = 121, but most correlations in this table are based on *N*s from 50 to 81. Corrections are for the population estimated of the *SD*s of the scores.
SOURCE : Data courtesy of Charles Szasz of West Virginia.

predominantly in the .60s and .70s, indicating that the RIAS has strong predictive value for educational achievement as measured by the WIAT.

Reynolds and Kamphaus (2007b) report on a correlational study between the RIAS and the WRAT4, based on a sample of 410 nonreferred individuals ranging in age from 5 to 24 years. The majority of the 16 correlations reported were in the .50s and .60s, with the VIX correlating highest overall with the WRAT4 achievement variables of Sentence Comprehension, Word Reading, and the Reading Composite. Correlations with the Math Computation scores were mostly in the .40s. The RIAS CMX correlated

in the .40s and .50s with all of the WRAT4 variables. When the RIAS Total Battery scores are used, the correlations increase, some reaching into the .70s. In another study, Reynolds and Kamphaus (2007c), including over 2,000 children and adults, reported the RIAS to correlate in the .40s and .50s with a simple measure of rapid word calling.

Beaujean et al. (2006) reported the RIAS to be a significant predictor of SAT scores as well. Correlations of .58 were determined in a very-high-achieving sample (mean SAT > 1.5 *SD*s above the population mean) between the CIX and the SAT using two methods of centering SAT scores as described therein.

In an unpublished study conducted for a school district, Szasz (2006, personal communication) reported correlations between the RIAS and the Woodcock-Johnson-III for a sample of 121 students referred for potential special education placement. Table 5.4 provides the correlation table from this study. In general, the correlations for the RIAS and the WJ-III scores trend higher than with other achievement tests, some reaching into the high .80s. Indeed, most of the correlations with reading achievement, especially complex reading tasks such as comprehension, are quite high. These correlations indicate the RIAS has strong predictive value for educational achievement as measured by the WJ-III as well as a wide range of other academic achievement tests and across all age levels, predicting achievement well for children, adolescents, and adults.

Performance of Clinical Groups

Examination of performance on the RIAS by groups of clinically identified individuals (wherein the RIAS was not a component of the process of clinical diagnosis) can also be instructive. For example, individuals with mental retardation (MR), dementia, and related cognitive problems associated with intellectual impairment should earn lower scores on the RIAS than the normally functioning examinees in the RIAS standardization sample. In interpreting such scores of preselected samples, however, especially when those samples are selected on the basis of extreme scores on a cognitive measure, one must always consider the problem of regression to the mean on a second testing. Thus, scores obtained from a sample with MR will typically be higher on such a testing, but the scores should still be well below the population mean.

During the standardization of the RIAS, 15 different clinical groups were identified, and their scores on the RIAS analyzed to supplement the validation of the interpretation of RIAS scores as reflecting intelligence and memory processes. In each instance, the primary diagnosis given by the agency serving the examinee was accepted, and no independent review or diagnosis was undertaken. The samples included those with traumatic brain injury (TBI), dementia, and stroke/CVA, mental retardation, deaf and hearing impaired, learning disabilities, and a variety of others. The various impairments represented a variety of organic deficits within each category, along with diffuse brain lesions. There were samples of children with learning disabilities (LD) and attention-deficit/hyperactivity disorder (ADHD) as well as the cognate adult samples, which came from more than one source. In reviewing the outcomes of testing with the RIAS with these 15 clinical samples, Reynolds and Kamphaus concluded that all of the various clinical groups in these studies demonstrated some levels of deviation from the population mean on the RIAS. Although most deviations are small decrements, as is commonly found in the literature, the samples with more severe disorders showed greater decrements in performance. Again, however, the purpose for presenting these data is not to make definitive statements about these clinical groups but to describe how the RIAS scores function for each group. Moreover, these data are preliminary and not definitive as to any score patterns on the RIAS that may emerge for clinical groups. Replication with larger and more carefully defined samples will be necessary before firm conclusions can be drawn. The evidence thus far is quite supportive because the score patterns do conform well to known patterns in the related literature and can be reviewed in detail in Reynolds and Kamphaus (2003), Chapter 6.

Evidence Based on the Consequences of Testing

This area of the validation process is the most controversial of all the aspects of the process as presented in the standards. It is most applicable to tests designed for selection and may deal with issues of bias or loss of opportunity. How these applications should be evaluated for clinical diagnostic tests is largely unclear. However, accurate diagnosis might be one anticipated consequence of testing and should be the key to evaluating the "consequential" validity of a clinical instrument. The evidence reviewed in the preceding sections demonstrates the ability of the RIAS to provide an accurate estimate of intellectual ability and certain memory skills and to do so accurately across such nominal groupings as gender and ethnicity. Cultural biases in the format and content of tests, when apparent, have also been found to produce undue consequences of testing. Evidence pointing toward a lack of cultural bias in the RIAS is extensive for male and female examinees, whites, African Americans, and Hispanic Americans. This evidence has been reviewed previously in this chapter and is discussed in detail in Chapters 4–6 of the RIAS Manual. Studies of potential cultural bias in the RIAS items were extensive in both objective and subjective formats and resulted in the removal of many items and modification of others. Evaluation of the mean scores of different ethnic groups from the RIAS standardization sample indicated that mean score differences across groups for whites, African Americans, and Hispanic Americans were about half the size typically reported in the research literature for traditional intelligence tests such as the Wechsler and the Binet series.

In evaluating evidence for test score interpretations, examiners must always consider their purposes for using objective tests. Evidence clearly supports the use of the constructs represented on the RIAS. The potential consequences of knowing how an individual's performance compares to that of others are many and complex and not always anticipated. The RIAS was designed to eliminate or minimize any cultural biases in the assessment of intelligence and memory for individuals reared and educated in the United States (who are fluent in the English language). The data available to date indicate the RIAS precludes undue consequences toward minority groups and women who fit the target population. Examiners must nevertheless act wisely, consider the need for objective testing of intelligence and memory, and work to minimize or eliminate unsupported interpretations of scores on such tests.

APPLICATIONS OF THE RIAS

As a measure of intelligence, the RIAS is appropriate for a wide array of purposes and should be useful when assessment of an examinee's intellectual level is needed. The RIAS will be useful with preschool and school-aged children for purposes of diagnosis and educational placement and for diagnosis of various forms of childhood psychopathology (especially developmental disorders) where intellectual functioning is an issue. Diagnosis of specific disorders, such as mental retardation, learning disabilities, the various dementias, and the effects of central nervous system injury or compromise, most often calls for the use of an intelligence test as a component of patient evaluation, and the RIAS is appropriate for such applications. Clinicians who perform general clinical and neuropsychological evaluations will find the RIAS very useful when a measure of intelligence is needed. Practitioners will also find the RIAS useful in disability determinations under various state and federal programs, such as the Social Security Administration's disability program and Section 504 regulations.

Intelligence tests, including the RIAS, have many additional uses and perform certain functions particularly well. Performance on an intelligence test predicts a host of outcomes. For example, the relationship between intelligence and persistence and success in school and related academic environments is one of the most widely, soundly documented relationships in all of psychology (Jensen, 1998). Intellectual level predicts a plethora of other quite varied outcomes as well, such as job performance in numerous occupations and professions and recovery following traumatic brain injury (Golden, Zillmer, & Spiers, 1992).

Although the RIAS is rapid to administer relative to the majority of other comprehensive measures of intelligence, it is not an abbreviated measure or a short form of intellectual assessment. The RIAS is a comprehensive measure of verbal and nonverbal intelligence and of general intelligence, providing the same level of useful information often gleaned from other intelligence tests much greater in length. When the memory subtests are also administered, the RIAS can provide even more useful information than typical intelligence tests currently used. The major clinical uses of intelligence tests are generally classification (most commonly, diagnostic) and selection. The RIAS has broad applicability in each of these areas. Some of the more common uses in these areas are discussed here.

Learning Disability

For the evaluation of a learning disability, assessment of intelligence is a common activity. However, when children and adults are evaluated for the possible presence of a learning disability, both verbal and nonverbal intelligence should be assessed. Individuals with a learning disability may have spuriously deflated IQ estimates in one or the other domain due to the learning disability itself. Lower verbal ability is most common in the school population and among adjudicated delinquents (Kaufman, 1994). However, the concept of the nonverbal learning disability is gaining momentum. For individuals with nonverbal learning disability, verbal ability will often exceed nonverbal ability. The assessment of functioning in both areas is important and the RIAS provides a reliable assessment of these domains as well as a composite intelligence index. The three RIAS intelligence index scores (i.e., VIX, NIX, and CIX) allow for an accurate estimation of intelligence simultaneously with the diagnosis of learning disability.

Mental Retardation

Most definitions, including those of the American Association on Mental Retardation (2002) and the *Diagnostic and Statistical Manual of Mental Disorders*—Fourth Edition, Text Revision (DSM-IV-TR; American Psychiatric Association, 2000), require the administration of an individually administered test of intelligence for diagnosis of mental retardation. The RIAS is applicable to the diagnosis of mental retardation for which the evaluation of verbal and nonverbal intelligence as well as adaptive functioning is necessary. Mental retardation is a pervasive intellectual problem and not limited to serious problems in only the verbal or nonverbal domain. The range of scores available on the RIAS will also make it useful in distinguishing levels of severity of mental retardation. Lower levels of functioning such as profound mental retardation are difficult to assess accurately on nearly all tests of intelligence, and this is likewise true of the RIAS. Although normed on children as young as 3 years of age, the RIAS also has limited discriminative ability below mild levels of mental retardation in the 3-year-old age group.

Intellectual Giftedness

Many definitions of giftedness include reference to superior levels of performance on measures of intelligence. Here again, measures of both the verbal and nonverbal domains are useful due to the influences of schooling and educational opportunity on verbal intelligence. The RIAS also has eliminated issues of motor skill and timing to enhance the assessment of intelligence free of irrelevant confounds, which makes it especially useful for identifying high-IQ children (see Bruegeman, Reynolds, & Kamphaus, 2006, for a detailed discussion of these issues). The range of index scores available on the RIAS (up to index scores of 160, four *SD*s above the mean) is adequate at all ages for identifying persons with significantly above-average levels of overall intellectual function as well as in the verbal and nonverbal domain.

Visual Impairment

Individuals with significant visual impairments that are uncorrected should not be administered the RIAS nonverbal subtests. The verbal subtests, however, should be useful with such individuals.

Hearing Deficiency

Individuals with significant hearing impairment may require examination by specially trained examiners. In such instances, the examiner must judge whether the particular individual's impairment makes any portion of the RIAS more or less useful. Because of the extreme variability in the levels and types of hearing impairments and the communication skills (both form and level) of individuals with significant hearing impairments, no general rule for applicability is offered. Judgments of applicability should be made on a case-by-case basis by examiners with special training and experience with these populations.

Physical/Orthopedic Impairment

The RIAS will be particularly useful in the evaluation of intellectual functioning among in-dividuals with any significant degree of physical or motor impairment. The RIAS has no real demands for speed or accuracy of fine motor movements. If necessary, the pointing responses by the examinee on the RIAS nonverbal tasks can all be replaced with simple verbal responses, designating the location of the chosen response. It is, however, very important for examiners to have knowledge of the physical impairments of any examinee and to make any necessary modifi-cations in the testing environment, doing so in a manner consistent with appropriate professional standards (e.g., Standards for Educational and Psychological Testing; American Educational Research Association [AERA], American Psycho-logical Association [APA], & National Council on Measurement in Education [NCME], 1999).

Neuropsychological Impairment

The RIAS can form one central component of the neuropsychological evaluation of children and adults. Assessment of general intelligence levels is important in establishing comparison levels for the interpretation of the highly specific tasks that are commonly used by neuropsychologists. The RIAS has been shown to be sensitive to intellectual decline in the various dementias and in cerebrovascular accident and traumatic brain injury (Reynolds & Kamphaus, 2003). The brevity of the RIAS also makes it attractive in the context of neuropsychological assessment, in view of the extensive length of such evaluations. The RIAS can provide strong and efficient measurement of general intelligence and create more time for the neuropsychologist to assess the many specific cognitive and psychomotor functions that are desirable components of the comprehensive neuropsychological examination. The RIAS memory subtests also can provide a preliminary indication of the need for a more extensive memory evaluation.

Memory Impairment

The information gleaned from evaluating mem-ory functions can provide valuable clinical infor-mation above and beyond what is traditionally assessed using IQ measures. Memory is gener-ally recognized as a focal or discrete subset of cognitive functions and as such is often quite vul-nerable to central nervous system (CNS) trauma and various other CNS events. Disturbances of memory and attention are the two most frequent complaints of children and adults following trau-matic brain injury at all levels of severity as well as other forms of CNS compromise (e.g., viral meningitis, AIDS-dementia complex, and other systemic insults). Therefore, it is not unusual for memory functioning to be affected even when there is little or no impact on general intellectual ability. The memory measures on the RIAS offer clinicians valuable assessment tools with which to evaluate recent or more immediate memory functioning in both the auditory (i.e., Verbal Memory) and visual (i.e., Nonverbal Memory) modalities.

For both children and adults, memory deficits can occur in a broad range of cognitive and psychiatric disorders. For example, memory dysfunction is often seen in individuals diagnosed with learning disability (LD), attention deficit/hyperactivity disorder (ADHD), traumatic brain injury, and stroke/cerebrovascular accident (CVA). Many of the common neurodevelopmental and genetic disorders of children have memory and/or attention problems as an element of the symptom complex (Goldstein & Reynolds, 1999; Reynolds & Fletcher-Janzen, 1997). One significant value of including memory measures in an assessment is that it allows the examiner to expand the scope of available information to include clinically meaningful measures that pertain to the examinee's current functioning in daily activities such as learning and memory.

The RIAS memory measures add important information in terms of the ecological validity of the evaluation. For example, the ability to focus attention and learn new information is critical for academic success. The verbal and nonverbal memory measures can give the examiner a very good preliminary indication of a student's ability to learn and remember material. This can lead to more meaningful and better informed evaluation recommendations and remediation strategies.

It is important to note that the RIAS does not provide memory measures to assess delayed memory. Delayed memory functioning (e.g., recall and retrieval) can be affected adversely even though an examinee performs at expected levels on immediate or short-term memory measures. As such, the RIAS does not provide a comprehensive measure of all memory domains.

Emotional Disturbance

Individuals with various forms of emotional and/or psychotic disturbance (e.g., depression, schizophrenia) may exhibit cognitive impairments to varying degrees. Often clinicians do not assess the intelligence of such individuals due to the time required. The RIAS offers the clinician a more efficient means of gathering information on the psychometric intelligence of individuals with emotional problems. Often, especially in the case of children, other cognitive disorders, such as LD, may contribute to the emotional problems observed. An intellectual assessment can be helpful in identifying cognitive and intellectual difficulties in such cases. Level of intellectual function may also influence the choice of appropriate treatments. For example, cognitive behavioral therapies and analytic/insight-oriented approaches to treatment would not be appropriate for individuals with borderline levels of intellectual function and, in some cases, even low average intelligence. Knowledge of the intellectual level of a referred child or adult with emotional problems as the primary complaint can provide a broader context for treatment, and the RIAS seems especially well suited for use in such referrals.

Job Performance

In personnel settings, IQ tests are sometimes used to predict success in job training programs and, in other instances, lower limits are set on IQ levels for specific jobs. The RIAS and the RIST are strong predictors of academic performance, and the tasks involved and constructs assessed on these instruments match up well with known predictors of job performance in the form of other IQ tests. When intelligence level is a question in such situations, the RIAS and the RIST are appropriate choices.

SUMMARY OF A CASE STUDY

This case summary is an illustration of the use of RIAS results. While a much more extensive evaluation was conducted, this section highlights only the findings most relevant to the use of the RIAS and does not present the entire case due to space limitations.

Brad is a 9-year-old boy referred for difficulties in learning to read. Brad was born following a full-term, uneventful pregnancy. Currently, Brad is in good physical health. Overall, Brad presented himself as well behaved and cooperative during testing. He seemed engaged in most testing procedures and appeared to put forth his best effort. Results of the evaluation are viewed as valid estimates of Brad's intellectual abilities, academic achievement, and social-emotional adjustment. Achievement testing as well as consultation with the school confirmed grade-level performance in math but very poor reading skills.

On testing with the RIAS, Brad earned a Composite Intelligence Index (CIX) of 88. On the RIAS, this level of performance falls within the range of scores designated as below average and exceeds the performance of 21% of individuals at Brad's age. Brad earned a Verbal Intelligence Index (VIX) of 78, which falls within the moderately below-average range of verbal intelligence skills and exceeds the performance of 7% of individuals Brad's age. Brad earned a Nonverbal Intelligence Index (NIX) of 103, which falls within the average range of nonverbal intelligence skills and exceeds the performance of 58% of individuals Brad's age. Brad earned a Composite Memory Index (CMX) of 75, which falls within the moderately below-average range of working memory skills. This exceeds the performance of 5% of individuals Brad's age. On testing with the RIAS, Brad earned a Total Test Battery (TTB) score of 80. This level of performance on the RIAS falls within the range of scores designated as below average and exceeds the performance of 9% of individuals at Brad's age. Brad's Total Verbal Battery (TVB) score of 75 falls within the range of scores designated as moderately below average and exceeds the performance of 5% of individuals his age. The chances are 90 out of 100 that Brad's true TVB falls within the range of scores from 71 to 81.

Brad's Total Nonverbal Battery (TNB) score of 91 falls within the range of scores designated as average and exceeds the performance of 27% of individuals his age.

RIAS Discrepancy Score Summary Table

Discrepancy Score	Score Difference	Statistically Significant?	Prevalence in Standardization Sample
VIX < NIX	25	yes	9.20%
CIX > CMX	13	yes	40.00%
VRM > NVM	1	no	94.60%
TVB < TNB	16	yes	28.30%

VIX is the Verbal Intelligence Index, NIX is the Nonverbal Intelligence Index, CIX is the Composite Intelligence Index, CMX is the Composite Memory Index, VRM is the Verbal Memory Subtest, NVM is the Nonverbal Memory Subtest, TVB is the Total Verbal Battery Index, and TNB is the Total Nonverbal Battery Index.

Discrepancy Norm-Referenced Interpretations

Although the CIX is a good estimate of Brad's general intelligence, a statistically significant discrepancy exists between his NIX of 103 and his VIX of 78, demonstrating better-developed nonverbal intelligence or spatial abilities. The magnitude of the difference observed between these two scores is potentially important and should be considered when drawing conclusions about Brad's current status. A difference of this size is relatively uncommon, occurring in only 9% of cases in the general population. In such cases, interpretation of the CIX or general intelligence score may be of less value than viewing Brad's verbal and nonverbal abilities separately.

When compared to Brad's measured level of general intelligence as reflected in Brad's CIX, it can be seen that his CMX falls significantly below his CIX. This result indicates that Brad is able to engage in intellectual problem solving and general reasoning tasks at a level that significantly exceeds his ability to use immediate recall and working memory functions. Although the size of the observed difference is reliable and indicates a real difference in these two cognitive domains, the magnitude of the difference observed is relatively common, occurring in 40% of the population. Within the subtests making up the CMX, Brad's performance was substantially equivalent on verbal and nonverbal memory tasks. This result indicates that Brad functions about equally well when called on to engage in recall or use working memory functions in either the verbal or nonverbal domain.

School Feedback and Recommendations

Brad's CIX score of 88 and TTB score of 80 indicate mild deficits in overall development of general intelligence relative to others at Brad's age. Individuals earning general intelligence scores in this range frequently experience at least some difficulty acquiring information through traditional educational methods provided in the classroom setting.

The TTB measures the same general construct as the CIX with the exception that six tests are included rather than four. Evidence in the RIAS/RIST Professional Manual (Reynolds & Kamphaus, 2003) documents the equivalence of these two scores based on evidence that a first-factor solution is defensible at all age levels of the RIAS whether four or six subtests are used. There also is evidence from a variety of intelligence tests to suggest the "indifference of the indicator." In other words, general intelligence may be assessed using a variety of cognitive tests, providing further evidence that for most individuals the TTB and CIX will be interchangeable. There will be exceptions to this well-documented scientific finding, in the case of severe brain injury, for example, where significant memory impairment may be present, but these cases will be exceptions rather than the rule.

Since most instructional programs presume at least average intellectual ability and involve lecture, note taking, and other typical instructional approaches, with the exception of demonstrative and repetitive methods commonly used with young children, difficulties in acquiring information when these methods are used is anticipated. Given Brad's deficits, special teaching methods might be considered, including special class placement for severe deficits in general intellectual development. Teachers should prepare an individualized curriculum designed for students who learn at a slower rate than others of the same age and grade level. Alternative methods of instruction should be considered that involve the use of repeated practice, spaced practice, concrete examples, guided practice, and demonstrative techniques. Individuals with general intelligence scores in this range often benefit from repeated practice approaches to training because of problems with acquisition and long-term retrieval, as well as an individualized instructional method that differs significantly from that of their age-mates. It also will be important to assist Brad in developing strategies for learning and studying. Although it is important for all students to know *how* to learn and not just what to learn, low scores on general intelligence indices make the development of learning and study strategies through direct instruction even more important. If confirmed through further testing, co-occurring deficits in adaptive behavior and behavioral problems should be added to the school intervention program.

Brad's VIX score of 78 and TVB score of 75 indicate moderate deficits in the development of verbal intellect relative to others at Brad's age. Verbal memory problems of varying severity levels are commonly evident in this group of individuals, and special attention to Brad's VRM score is necessary.

Verbal ability is important for virtually every aspect of activity because language is key to nearly all areas of human endeavor. A multitude of research investigations have documented the importance of verbal ability for predicting important life outcomes. *Verbal ability* should be considered equivalent to the term *crystallized intelligence*. As assessed by the RIAS, verbal ability (like crystallized intelligence) is highly related to general intelligence, and as such its relationship to important life outcomes is easily correlated. Verbal ability also is the foundation for linguistic knowledge, which is necessary for many types of learning.

With the exception of the early grades, along with Kindergarten and pre-K settings, school is principally a language-oriented task. Given Brad's relative verbal deficits, special teaching methods might be considered, including special class placement in the case of severe deficits in verbal intellectual development. The examiner should also consider either conducting, or making a referral for, an evaluation for the presence of a language disorder. Alternative methods of instruction that emphasize "show me" rather than "tell me" techniques, or as a minimum pair these two general approaches, are preferred.

Although linguistic stimulation likely cannot counteract the effects of verbal ability deficits that began in infancy or preschool years, verbal stimulation is still warranted to improve adaptation or at least prevent an individual from falling further behind peers. Verbal concept and knowledge acquisition should continue to be emphasized. A simple word-for-the-day program may be beneficial for some students. Verbal knowledge builders of all varieties may be helpful, including defining words, writing book reports, a book reading program, and social studies and science courses that include writing and oral expression components. Alternatively, assistive technology (e.g., personal digital assistance devices, tape recorders, MP3 players, or iPods) may be used to enhance functioning in the face of the extensive verbal demands required for making adequate academic progress.

In addition, teachers should rely more heavily on placing learning into the student's experiential context, giving it meaning and enabling Brad to visualize incorporating each newly learned task or skill into his life experience. The use of visual aids should be encouraged and made available to Brad whenever possible. Academic difficulties are most likely to occur in language-related areas (e.g., the acquisition of reading), especially early phonics training. The acquisition of comprehension skills also is aided when the verbal ability falls into this level by the use of language experience approaches to reading, in particular. Frequent formal and informal assessment of Brad's reading skills, as well as learning and study strategies (the latter with an instrument, e.g., the School Motivation and Learning Strategies Inventory—SMALSI; Stroud & Reynolds, 2006) is recommended. This should be followed by careful direct instruction in areas of specific skill weaknesses and the use of high-interest, relevant materials. It also will be important to assist Brad in developing strategies for learning and studying. Although it is important for all students to know how to learn and not just what to learn, low scores within the verbal intelligence domains make the development of learning and study strategies through direct instruction even more important.

Brad's CMX of 75 falls within the moderately below-average range and indicates moderate difficulties with recall of verbal and visual/spatial information relative to others Brad's age. Individuals who score in this range frequently experience consternation in the acquisition of new information and may need some assistance in developing strategies for the day-to-day recall of verbal and visual/spatial information.

Students with deficits in memory ability relative to others their age can benefit from special accommodations in the classroom and from instruction on developing better memory techniques. The use of multiple modalities is typically recommended to increase retention, such as routinely pairing visual/spatial stimuli with verbal stimuli in order to enhance recall. The use of lists, visual, oral language, and written language directions, and verbal and visual reminders may be especially helpful. Repetition of information during learning is often helpful along with review of important material at regular intervals after initial instruction to improve retention.

Memory is a complex function that heavily involves attention. Brad's low performance on the CMX most likely reflects complex difficulties with memory as well as difficulties with attention to at least some degree. Although specific instructional strategies must await a comprehensive assessment of memory functions as noted in subsequent sections, some general recommendations for classroom management of Brad's memory problems can be provided. For example, students referred for learning problems who score 75 on the CMX should be seated near the front of the classroom to ensure that the teacher can obtain the maximum degree of attention to classroom instruction and directions for completing work. The instructions, particularly for younger students, should be specific, simple, and given one at a time. The teacher may wish to stand close to Brad when giving instruction and directions in the classroom. Brad's teacher should ensure that homework assignments are provided in writing or are written down by Brad prior to leaving the classroom for the day. It would be helpful to have the teacher check to ensure that any homework instructions or instructions for any other projects to be completed are written accurately and completely. Maintenance of a daily calendar and instruction in the use of general types of memory strategies also will be helpful to most students with this level of performance on the CMX. Instruction in the use of such memory strategies as rehearsal, chunking, visualization, and related mnemonic aides also can be useful in improving memory function.

Brad's VRM score of 35 suggests that he will experience moderate difficulties in learning and recall of verbal material, even when presented in a meaningful or experiential context, which should be performed because it aids recall. When presenting verbal information to Brad, cues for future recall should be provided and a discussion of strategies for the recall of verbal information would be helpful. Moderate attentional difficulties also are common with VRM scores at this level.

Students with verbal memory deficits relative to others their age may benefit from instruction on developing better memory techniques as related to verbal material. Students such as Brad should be seated near the classroom instructor, who should be sure to ascertain that he or she has Brad's attention during any form of lecture or verbal presentation. Direct instruction in reading and study strategies also may be quite helpful. Memory strategies can be taught, including strategies such as rehearsal, chunking, and skill in making verbal associations. Calling Brad's name prior to giving instructions or other verbal information that will need to be recalled may be helpful along with the use of other techniques to assure his specific attention to the material being presented. Pairing verbal information with visual presentations including pictures or demonstrations of what is expected or what is to be recalled also may be quite useful. A determination of existing strategies employed for learning verbal material can be obtained from administration of the School Motivation and Learning Strategies Inventory for students beginning at age 8 years (Stroud & Reynolds, 2006).

Brad's NVM score of 34 suggests that he will experience moderate difficulties in the learning and recall of visual/spatial material, including maps, figures, graphs, drawings, locations, the arrangement of items in a written work, signs, faces, and directions that require visualization. These difficulties will likely occur even when Brad is presented material in a meaningful or experiential context, which should be performed because the use of concrete objects often aids recall.

Discrepancy Feedback and Recommendations

The magnitude of discrepancy between Brad's VIX score of 78 and NIX score of 103 is relatively unusual within the normal population. Although this is the most common pattern within referral populations, the magnitude of the discrepancy occurring for Brad makes the difference noteworthy. In general, this pattern represents substantially disparate skills in the general domains of verbal and nonverbal reasoning with clear superiority evident in the nonverbal domain. Relative to their verbal reasoning and general language skills, individuals who display this pattern will experience greater success in tasks involving spatial reasoning, visualization skills, the use of mental rotation, reading of nonverbal cues, and related aspects of nonverbal reasoning and communication that usually includes nonverbal and visual memory skills. Nonverbal ability is less influential in others' appraisal of general intellectual functioning. Because NIX is greater than VIX, Brad's general intellectual functioning may appear lower than is reflected by his CIX score. Whenever possible, one should take advantage of Brad's relatively higher levels of performance in the nonverbal domain by always providing visual cues and an explanation of tasks, expectations, or a demonstration of what is expected to be learned (where possible). Experiential learning is typically superior to traditional lecture and related pedagogical methods for individuals with this score pattern. The synthesis of information as opposed to the analysis of information is often a relative strength.

Teaching should emphasize the use of visual images, spatial representations of relationships, experiential learning, and the synthesis of information as opposed to methods of deduction in learning. Difficulties are likely to occur with traditional pedagogical styles such as lecturing and the completion of reading and written assignments. An emphasis on the spatial relationships of numbers and the construction of problems is likely to be the most effective means for teaching math versus the memorization and the learning of step-by-step rules for calculation. A heavy emphasis on learning by example and by demonstration is likely to be most effective with students with this intellectual pattern. Also common are problems with sequencing, including sequential memory and, in the early grades, mastery of phonics when synthesizing word sounds into correct words. Emphases on holistic methods of learning are likely to be more successful in addition to experiential approaches. The practical side of learning and the application of knowledge can be emphasized to enhance motivation in these students.

Often, these students do not have good study, learning, and test-taking strategies. It is often useful to assess the presence of strategies with a scale such as the School Motivation and Learning Strategies Inventory and then to target deficient areas of learning strategies for direct instruction (Stroud & Reynolds, 2006).

Recommendations for Additional Testing

In cases where the CMX falls below 90, additional follow-up assessment with a more comprehensive memory battery often provides additional clues and insights into appropriate instructional practices as well as rehabilitative exercises that may be most useful. Follow-up evaluation with a comprehensive memory battery should be given even stronger consideration when the CMX is below 90 and also falls at a level that is significantly below the CIX. Evaluation with a comprehensive memory battery such as the Test of Memory and Learning—Second Edition (TOMAL-2; Reynolds & Voress, 2007) is recommended for such assessments because of the high degree of variability in performance produced by even small changes in memory tasks.

Brad's NIX score of 103 is significantly higher than his VIX score of 78. As such, follow-up evaluation may be warranted. Although this is the most common pattern in referral populations, additional information is almost always helpful in making a diagnosis, in treatment planning, and/or in making vocational recommendations. Evaluations that consider disturbances in language and verbal functions in general (including receptive and expressive language) and other left-hemisphere-related tasks may prove helpful. Although empirical research at this point is lacking, clinical experience with the RIAS indicates that when the VIX score is significantly below the NIX score and the absolute value of the VIX is less than 90, there is a high probability of the presence of a language disorder that may have an adverse impact on academic attainment or success in any academically related vocational training program. When this pattern occurs, as in the case of Brad, screening for a language disorder is recommended at a minimum, and a more comprehensive language assessment should be considered.

SUMMARY

The RIAS was devised from theories of intelligence that have practical value and empirical support. Therefore, the RIAS indexes are firmly rooted in modern intelligence test theory of the 1990s, thus making the results interpretable. In addition, usage of modern test theories means that the most important and predictive intellectual abilities are assessed. More than this, however, the RIAS is designed to promote empirically supported practice in intellectual assessment. The practices of the past that lack empirical support, most prominently subtest level profile analysis of IQ-tests, have been the principal reason for giving lengthy subtest batteries of intelligence. The RIAS is steeped in empirical research that not only fails to support such practices, but also refutes their utility. The RIAS takes advantage of well-known and well-researched tasks to provide the examiner with measurement of the constructs of primary utility when questions of intelligence need to be answered.

The RIAS was developed with special attention to well-reasoned modern standards for psychological and educational assessment (AERA, APA, NCME, 1999). Consistent with these standards, the RIAS provides many opportunities for validation research to uncover new or unforeseen and contraindicated inferences based on test scores.

REFERENCES

Adams, W., & Reynolds, C. R. (2009). *Essentials of memory assessment with the WRAML2 and the TOMAL-2*. Hoboken, NJ: John Wiley & Sons.

American Association on Mental Retardation. (2002). *Mental retardation: Definition, classification, and systems of supports* (10th ed.). Washington, DC: Author.

American Educational Research Association, American Psychological Association, and National Council on Measurement in Education. (1999). *Standards for educational and psychological testing*. Washington, DC: American Psychological Association.

American Psychiatric Association. (2000). *Diagnostic and statistical manual of mental disorders* (4th ed., text revision). Washington, DC: Author.

Anastasi, A., & Urbina, S. (1997). *Psychological testing* (7th ed.). Upper Saddle River, NJ: Prentice Hall.

Beaujean, A., Firmin, M., Knoop, A., Michonski, J., Berry, T., & Lowrie, R. (2006). Validation of the Frey and Detterman (2004) IQ prediction equations using the Reynolds Intellectual Assessment Scales. *Personality and Individual Differences*, *41*, 353–357.

Benton, A. L. (1974). *Benton visual retention test* (rev. ed.). New York: The Psychological Corporation.

Bigler, E. D., & Clement, P. F. (1997). *Diagnostic clinical neuropsychology* (3rd ed.). Austin, TX: University of Texas Press.

Binet, A., & Simon, T. (1905). New methods for the diagnosis of the intellectual level of subnormals. *L'Année Psychologique*, *11*, 191–244.

Brown, R. T., Reynolds, C. R., & Whitaker, J. S. (1999). Bias in mental testing since bias in mental testing. *School Psychology Quarterly*, *14*(3), 208–238.

Bruegemann, A., Reynolds, C. R., & Kamphaus, R. W. (2006). The Reynolds Intellectual Assessment Scales (RIAS) and assessment of intellectual giftedness. *Gifted Education International*, *21*, 122–136.

Carroll, J. B. (1993). *Human cognitive abilities: A survey of factor analytic studies*. New York: Cambridge University Press.

Cattell, R. B. (1978). Matched determiners vs. factor invariance: A reply to Korth. *Multivariate Behavioral Research*, *13*(4), 431–448.

Cronbach, L. J. (1951). Coefficient alpha and the internal structure of tests. *Psychometrika*, *16*, 297–334.

Edwards, O. (2006). *WISC-IV VS. RIAS: Will the real IQ please stand up!!* Paper presented at the annual meeting of the Florida Association of School Psychologists, Orlando, FL.

Edwards, O. & Paulin, R. V. (2007). Referred students' performance on the Reynolds Intellectual Assessment Scales and the Wechsler Intelligence Scale for Children—Fourth Edition. *Journal of Psychoeducational Assessment*, *25*(4), 334–340.

Eliot, J., & Smith, I. M. (1983). *An international dictionary of spatial tests*. Windsor, Berks, England: Nefer-Nelson.

Golden, C. J., Zillmer, E., & Spiers, M. (1992). *Neuropsychological assessment and intervention*. Springfield, IL; England: Charles C. Thomas.

Goldstein, S., & Reynolds, C. R. (1999). *Handbook of neurodevelopmental and genetic disorders in children*. New York: Guilford Press.

Goldstein, S., & Reynolds, C. R. (2005). *Handbook of neurodevelopmental and genetic disorders in adults*. New York: Guilford Press.

Horn, J. L., & Cattell, R. B. (1966). Refinement and test of the theory of fluid and crystallized general intelligences. *Journal of Educational Psychology*, *57*(5), 253–270.

Jensen, A. (1998). The suppressed relationship between IQ and the reaction time slope parameter of the Hick function. *Intelligence*, *26*(1), 43–52.

Joreskog, K., & Sorbom, D. (1987). *LISREL 6.13: User's reference guide*. Chicago: Scientific Software.

Joseph, R. (1996). *Neuropsychiatry, neuropsychology, and clinical neuroscience: Emotion, evolution, cognition, language, memory, brain damage, and abnormal behavior* (2nd ed.). Baltimore: Williams & Wilkins.

Kamphaus, R. W. (2001). *Clinical assessment of child and adolescent intelligence* (2nd ed.). Boston: Allyn and Bacon.

Kamphaus, R. W., & Reynolds, C. R. (2003). *Reynolds intellectual screening test*. Odessa, FL: PAR, Inc.

Kaufman, A. S. (1990). *Assessing adolescent and adult intelligence*. Needham Heights, MA: Allyn & Bacon.

Kaufman, A. S. (1994). *Intelligent testing with the WISC-III*. New York: Wiley.

Kaufman, A. S., McLean, J. E., Kaufman-Packer, J., & Reynolds, C. R. (1991). Is the pattern of intellectual growth and decline across the adult lifespan different for men and women? *Journal of Clinical Psychology*, *47*(6), 801–812.

Kaufman, A. S., Reynolds, C. R., & McLean, J. E. (1989). Age and WAIS-R intelligence in a national sample of adults in the 20 to 74 year range: A cross-sectional analysis with education level controlled. *Intelligence*, *13*(3), 235–253.

McCarthy, D. (1972). *McCarthy scales of children's abilities*. New York: The Psychological Corporation.

Miller, W. S. (1926). *Miller Analogies Test*. New York: The Psychological Corporation.

Nunnally, J. C. (1978). *Psychometric theory* (2nd ed.). New York: McGraw-Hill.

Oxford Press. (1999). New shorter Oxford English dictionary. Oxford: author.

Reynolds, C. R. (1984–1985). Critical measurement issues in learning disabilities. *Journal of Special Education*, *18*, 451–476.

Reynolds, C. R. (1997). Measurement and statistical problems in neuropsychological assessment of children. In C. R. Reynolds & E. Fletcher-Janzen (Eds.), *Handbook of clinical child neuropsychology* (2nd ed., pp. 180–203). New York: Plenum Press.

Reynolds, C. R. (1998). Fundamentals of measurement and assessment in psychology. In A. Bellack & M. Hersen (Series Eds.) & C. R. Reynolds (Vol. Ed.), *Comprehensive clinical psychology: Vol. 4. Assessment* (pp. 33–56). Oxford, England: Elsevier Science.

Reynolds, C. R. (2000). Methods for detecting and evaluating cultural bias in neuropsychological tests. In E. Fletcher-Janzen, T. Strickland, & C. R. Reynolds (Eds.), *Handbook of cross-cultural neuropsychology* (pp. 249–286). New York: Plenum.

Reynolds, C. R., & Bigler, E. D. (1994). *Test of memory and learning*. Austin, TX: PRO-ED.

Reynolds, C. R., Castillo, C. L. & Horton, A. M., Jr. (2008). Neuropsychology and intelligence: An overview. In A. M. Horton, Jr. and D. Wedding (Eds.), *The neuropsychology handbook* (3rd ed., pp. 69–86). New York: Springer.

Reynolds, C. R., Chastain, R. L., Kaufman, A. S., & McLean, J. E. (1987). Demographic influences on adult intelligence at ages 16 to 74 years. *Journal of School Psychology, 25*(4), 323–342.

Reynolds, C. R., & Fletcher-Janzen, E. (Eds.). (1997). *Handbook of clinical child neuropsychology* (2nd ed.). New York: Plenum Press.

Reynolds, C. R., & Kamphaus, R. W. (2003). *Reynolds intellectual assessment scales*. Odessa, FL: PAR, Inc.

Reynolds, C. R., Kamphaus, R. W., & PAR Staff (2007a). *Reynolds Intellectual Assessment Scales Interpretive Report*. Lutz, FL: Psychological Assessment Resources.

Reynolds, C. R., & Kamphaus, R. W. (2007b). *Reynolds Intellectual Assessment Scales/Wide Range Achievement Test 4 Discrepancy Interpretive Report professional manual supplement*. Lutz, FL: Psychological Assessment Resources.

Reynolds, C. R., & Kamphaus, R. W. (2007c). *Test of irregular word reading efficiency*. Lutz, FL: Psychological Assessment Resources.

Reynolds, C. R., Lowe, P. A., & Saenz, A. (1999). The problem of bias in psychological assessment. In C. R. Reynolds and T. B. Gutkin (Eds.), *Handbook of school psychology* (3rd ed., pp. 549–595). New York: Wiley.

Reynolds, C. R., & Voress, J. (2007). *Test of memory and learning* (2nd ed.). Austin, TX: Pro-Ed.

Riccio, C. A., & Hynd, G. W. (2000). Measurable biological substrates to verbal-performance differences in Wechsler scores. *School Psychology Quarterly, 15*(4), 386–399.

Sattler, J. M. (2001). *Assessment of children: Cognitive applications* (4th ed.). La Mesa, CA: Author.

Stroud, K., & Reynolds, C. R. (2006). *School motivation and learning strategies inventory (SMALSI)*. Los Angeles: Western Psychological Services.

Wechsler, D. (1949). *Wechsler Intelligence Scale for Children*. San Antonio, TX: The Psychological Corporation.

Wechsler, D. (1991). *Wechsler Intelligence Scale for Children—Third Edition*. San Antonio, TX: The Psychological Corporation.

Wechsler, D. (1992). *Wechsler Individual Achievement Test*. San Antonio, TX: The Psychological Corporation.

Wechsler, D. (1997). *Wechsler Adult Intelligence Scale—Third Edition*. San Antonio, TX: The Psychological Corporation.

Weinberg, R. A. (1989). Intelligence and IQ: Landmark issues and great debates. *American Psychologist, 44*(2), 98–104.

Wilkinson, L., & Task Force on Statistical Inference. (1999). Statistical methods in psychology journals: Guidelines and explanations. *American Psychologist, 54*(8), 594–604.

Yerkes, R. M. (1917). The Binet versus the Point scale method of measuring intelligence. *Journal of Applied Psychology, 1*, 11–122.

Zachary, R., & Gorsuch, R. (1985). Continuous norming: Implications for the WAIS-R. *Journal of Clinical Psychology, 41*, 86–94.

Assessment of Intellectual Strengths and Weaknesses with the Stanford-Binet Intelligence Scales—Fifth Edition (SB5)

Gale H. Roid, Seth M. Tippin

The *Stanford-Binet Intelligence Scales—Fifth Edition* (SB5) was designed to assess individuals in the age range of 2 through 85+ years with a comprehensive set of 10 subtests. SB5 is well known in the field of psychology and education, with roots in the first clinical measure of intelligence (Binet & Simon, 1905). This intelligence battery has been employed for decades as the standard of intellectual assessment. The Stanford-Binet name comes from the Stanford University affiliation of Lewis Terman (1916) and from the original developer—Alfred Binet (Binet & Simon, 1916). Terman adapted and expanded the foundational work of Binet for use in North America. Terman continued to work on the second and third editions of the scale through 1956 (Terman & Merrill, 1937, 1960). The first three editions of the test were organized into clusters of items (usually 6 each) at various age or developmental levels, with the vocabulary test used as a placement device to adapt the level of the test to the individual. Thorndike, Hagen, and Sattler (1986) authored the fourth edition (SB4) and changed the format of the test to a point-scale format (where each subtest has a series of items

from easy to difficult, with age-appropriate starting points and stopping rules based on number of errors). The SB5 combined features of the earlier editions (employing both point-scale and developmental level formats) to make the battery more useful for current assessment needs in schools and clinics. SB5 has many modern features, expanded age range and ability-range (e.g., from extremely low to extremely gifted), and many new psychometric enhancements. Also, the SB5 assists the practitioner in the analysis of cognitive "strengths and weaknesses" as specified in the guidelines for the reauthorized *Individuals with Disabilities Education Act* (IDEA, 2004), in the identification of learning disabilities and other conditions. The SB5 includes an expanded nonverbal section (one-half of the test) compared to previous editions. The nonverbal section is especially useful for evaluating individuals with non-English backgrounds, and those with communication disorders, preschool learning difficulties, and the various special needs at any age. Each of the features of SB5 will be described in the following sections of this chapter.

Theory Underlying the Test

The SB5 was developed on the basis of widely employed hierarchical models of intellectual and cognitive abilities. These models were developed by researchers such as Cattell (1943), Horn (1965), Gustafsson (1984), and Carroll (1993). Originally, the models emphasized the distinction between fluid and crystallized abilities (Horn & Cattell, 1966). Later, the models included an overall general ability (g) at the highest level and multiple factors at the second and third levels of the model (Carroll, 1993). These models were later called the *Cattell-Horn-Carroll (CHC) theory* by McGrew and Flanagan (1998) and Flanagan and Ortiz (2001). The CHC theory has become popular as the basis for several published cognitive tests, including the *Kaufman Adolescent and Adult Intelligence Scale* (KAIT; Kaufman & Kaufman, 1993), the *Leiter International Performance Scale—Revised* (Roid & Miller, 1997; see Chapter 10 on Leiter in this book), and the *Woodcock-Johnson III Tests of Cognitive Abilities* (Mather & Woodcock, 2001b). The SB5 was designed to measure several cognitive factors from CHC theory: fluid reasoning, crystallized general knowledge, quantitative reasoning, visual-spatial ability, and working memory (Baddeley, 1986). The foundation of the SB5 on CHC theory allows the assessment professional to compare the individual's performance on other tests measuring the same cognitive factors through the process of cross-battery assessment (Flanagan and Ortiz, 2001), increasing diagnostic power of the evaluation.

The definition of general intellectual ability employed by the SB5 is based on the Cattell-Horn-Carroll theoretical model—that intelligence is a multifaceted array of cognitive abilities with a general (g) overarching ability, composed of several dimensions (fluid, crystallized, quantitative, visual, and memory). For the SB5, the operational and empirical definition of *intelligence* is presented here.

Roid (2003a) defined *intelligence* as a cluster of related abilities in reasoning, visual and auditory ability, short- and long-term memory, speed of information processing, and other cognitive skills, which function to employ accumulated knowledge, life experiences, and cognitive strategies to solve problems and adapt to one's environment. The addition of the final phrase in the definition, concerning problem solving, and adapting to the environment makes the SB5 compatible with other major intelligence measures such as the Wechsler (1991, 1997) scales.

Description of the Test

The SB5 is distributed in two forms: (1) the standard full-range battery covering all ability levels for ages 2 through 85+, and (2) an alternative kit for early childhood assessment (ages 2–7) that includes a more narrow range of ability. The early childhood version was designed for younger children (Roid, 2005a) for use by professionals working with preschool assessment. The early childhood version could also be used for very-low-functioning individuals (e.g., those below 80 IQ), regardless of chronological age. The SB5 is the first intellectual assessment battery to measure five cognitive factors in both the nonverbal (reduced vocal language) domain and the verbal (vocal language required) domain. As shown in Figure 6.1, and based on the CHC theory discussed above, the SB5 measures a global ability (g) estimated from the Full Scale IQ. The SB5 also measures five cognitive factors, each assessed by one verbal and one nonverbal subtest for Fluid Reasoning (FR), Knowledge (KN), Quantitative Reasoning (QR), Visual-Spatial Processing (VS), and Working Memory (WM). The Nonverbal IQ and the Verbal IQ are derived from the respective five subtests in each domain. At the fundamental level, each subtest (e.g., Nonverbal FR, Verbal FR) is available for individual interpretation or in combination with all 10 subtest profile scores.

ADMINISTRATION AND SCORING

Test Administration

The standard order of administration of SB5 begins with Item Book 1 (the spiral-bound book with a built-in easel containing the items and pictures for examinees and directions for the examiner), containing the two routing subtests: Nonverbal Fluid Reasoning (Object-Series Matrices) and Verbal Knowledge (Vocabulary). The SB5 Record Form directs the examiner to administer these scales in point-scale format, beginning with the age-level of the examinee. The start points are either chronological age or estimated intellectual functioning level. Scores on the nonverbal subtest determine at what level in the remaining nonverbal sections (Item Book 2) the examinee will continue. Similarly, the verbal routing subtest determines the continuation into Item Book 3 (Figure 6.1).

Simple tables of raw scores for the routing subtests direct the examiner to one of the six color-coded levels in Item Books 2 and 3. Each level of the item books is identified by a colored stripe along the bottom of each page to facilitate finding the beginning of each level.

New users of SB5 should find Item Book 1, and begin to experiment using items in the routing tests. All the procedures, scoring guides, and spoken examiner prompts are printed on the examiner pages of the item books. The separate Record Form also provides reminders of start and stop rules, scoring methods for each subtest, procedures for routing, and basal and ceiling rules. The names and brief descriptions of the 10 SB5 subtests are listed in Table 6.1.

The use of initial routing tests has been a tradition in Stanford-Binet assessment, based on the Vocabulary subtest. The addition of Object-Series/Matrices helps to tailor the test to the examinee's level of ability, whether verbal or nonverbal. This adaptive method, based on the same technology as computer-adaptive testing (Wainer, 1990), will give you a more precise assessment of ability in a shorter time. Thus, the extra effort to learn and understand the simple routing procedures is well invested.

Nonverbal and Verbal Sections of SB5

Following the routing tests of Item Book 1, the standard administration proceeds to the four subtests in the nonverbal domain (Item Book 2) and concludes with the four subtests in the verbal domain (Item Book 3). In the unusual case where the examiner is completely familiar with the background of the examinee, it may be clear that the individual has conditions or deficits that prevent him or her from performing well in either the nonverbal domain (e.g., individuals with blindness) or the verbal domain (having very limited English-language or reading ability, or severe verbal delay from brain injury, communication disorder, deafness, etc.). In such cases, the SB5 can still be valuable because it measures all five of the CHC cognitive factors in either domain. You would proceed to administer

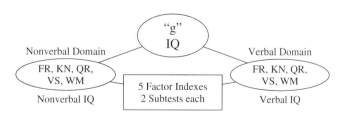

FIGURE 6.1
Hierarchical Structure of the SB5 Scoring System

TABLE 6.1   Subtests of the SB5

Subtest	Description (Activities at Various Levels)
Nonverbal	
Fluid Reasoning	Object-Series/Matrices. A point-scale used for routing. Includes new sequential reasoning items and matrices.
Knowledge	Procedural Knowledge. A new type of item involving gestures to identify the function of illustrated objects. This is followed by Picture Absurdities, where the examinee looks for odd or silly features.
Quantitative Reasoning	Nonverbal quantitative items tapping number concepts, problem solving, figural/geometric and measurement/estimation problems.
Visual-Spatial Reasoning	Formboard items for the lower levels followed by the new Form Patterns (making designs from an expanded set of formboard pieces).
Working Memory	Delayed Response (e.g., hiding an object under a cup) at the lower levels followed by the new block tapping procedure (Block Span).
Verbal	
Fluid Reasoning	Early Reasoning items (e.g., picture reasoning) followed by Verbal Absurdities and Verbal Analogies.
Knowledge	Vocabulary: A point-scale used for routing. Includes identification of body parts, toys, child-card and word definitions.
Quantitative Reasoning	Verbal quantitative items tapping number concepts, problem solving, figural/geometric and measurement/estimation problems.
Visual-Spatial Reasoning	Innovative new Position and Direction items that include: verbal spatial problems requiring explanation of directions, identifying spatial relations in pictures, understanding complex statements of spatial orientation.
Working Memory	Sentence Memory followed by an innovative Last Word procedure requiring memory of the last word of series of questions.

SOURCE : Adapted by permission from Roid and Barram (2004).

only Item Book 2 or 3 to complete the assessment (Table 6.1).

Nonverbal Level Subtests

The nonverbal section is designed as a series of item clusters called "testlets" (brief tests with 3 to 6 related items that form a mini-scale). Each level of the SB5 (except Level 1) has four sets of testlets measuring the four nonverbal abilities (knowledge, quantitative, visual, and working memory). The standard administration sequence follows the method of reading a two-column newspaper—beginning with the Knowledge testlet in the upper-left corner of the Record Form, then Quantitative Reasoning in the lower left, then Visual-Spatial Processing in the upper right, and, finally, Working Memory in the lower right. Only Level 1 (for extremely low scores of 0–6 on Object-Series/Matrices) has two testlets, for Visual-Spatial and Working Memory, due to children's restricted fund of knowledge and quantitative concepts in the 2-year-old range. Subtests are, therefore, composed of a series of testlets located across levels (raw scores will be added together for the total subtest raw score). Most examiners only test about two levels (two complete pages of the Record Form), and, possibly, one or two additional testlets at a third level. Reversal to the previous level (when testlet raw scores are less than 3 points, or less than 4 points at Level 5) rarely occurs because the starting levels have been designed to occur below the examinees' actual level of ability.

Verbal Level Subtests

Use Item Book 3 to administer the verbal portion of SB5, based on the raw score obtained from the Vocabulary subtest. As in the nonverbal levels, each page has four testlets, representing four cognitive factors. Fluid Reasoning in the upper-left corner of the Record Form is given first, then Quantitative Reasoning in the lower left, then Visual-Spatial Processing in the upper right, and Working Memory in the lower right. Unlike the nonverbal section, Fluid Reasoning now occurs in the upper left because Verbal Knowledge was previously measured by the Vocabulary routing subtest. Note that there is no Level 1 for the verbal section, because verbal abilities are not well developed in the typical 2-year-old or low-functioning individual.

Tips for Examiners

Some examiners who are unfamiliar with the age-level design of the Stanford-Binet early editions have expressed concern about the functional levels in Item Books 2 and 3. Many examiners have years of testing experience with point-scales where each subtest forms a separate array of items that span the ages. Thus, examiners new to SB5 have the urge to administer all the testlets across levels for each subtest to create point scales. However, field trials with the functional level format of SB5 showed that children were engaged and attentive to testing when there was variety at each age level (among the four testlets) as compared to the point-scale format used in the SB5 tryout edition.

Additionally, new users of the SB5 often have questions about two sections of the SB5 that have not appeared in other batteries: (1) the Nonverbal Working Memory subtest (Levels 3–6, Block Span task), and (2) the Verbal Fluid Reasoning subtest (Early Reasoning, Level 3, Sorting Chips task). For Block Span, the best results are obtained when the examiner does two things: (1) taking time to practice the tapping sequences (mentally) by imagining the pattern of movements across the block layout, and (2) exaggerating the "hopping" movements of the block tapping and tapping loudly with one of the corners of the examiner block. Of course, having the complete attention of the examinee is also vitally important. For the Sorting Chips task, practice in advance by grouping the chips yourself into classifications of three chips each and do not be concerned that the sample item (using the three red-colored picture chips) will cause the examinee to perseverate on color groupings. If the examinee (typically a child) continues to use color, remember that one red grouping (repeated from your sample even) is acceptable. And, only one grouping is allowed for each color (e.g., red, yellow, green), and if this is continued, the score will be lower than when the examinee uses "functional" groupings (e.g., all writing implements). Color is the first conceptual category to develop in young children, so the task begins at that level. Examinees who stay with color only may be stuck at an earlier developmental and conceptual level.

How to Score the Test

The SB5 provides two choices for the estimation of global intellectual ability—the Verbal and Nonverbal IQ, each consisting of five subtests based on CHC theory cognitive abilities. Each of the IQ and factor index scores are normalized standard scores with a mean of 100 and a standard deviation of 15 for comparability with other achievement and cognitive batteries. All 10 subtest scores are also normalized standard scores with a mean of 10 and a standard deviation of 3.

After presenting each item in each testlet at the appropriate levels of Item Books 2 and 3, score the responses using the answer key or directions included on the examiner direction pages of the item books (and repeated in brief form on the Record Form). Sum the item scores for each testlet and place the testlet raw score in the white box provided on the front (Summary) page of the Record Form. The maximum score possible is nearly always 6 points (except for the two testlets at Nonverbal Level 1, which have 4 points each). Use the four raw score totals on each page of the Record Form, combined with the raw score totals from the routing subtests, to obtain the total raw scores for each of the 10 subtests of SB5.

Follow the directions on the Record Form to convert raw scores to standardized scaled scores (similar to Wechsler scaled scores) for each subtest. Each IQ or Factor Index score is first derived from the sum of the subtest scaled scores needed for each scoring combination. Sums of scaled scores are converted to normalized IQ-type standard scores.

Use of the Scoring Software

The SB5 has an optional computer scoring program, called the *SB5 Scoring Pro* (Roid, 2003c). The program is distributed on computer disk (CD, IBM-compatible format) for use on a given computer for unlimited numbers of cases. By entering raw scores into the program, all of the normative and supplemental scores described above can be derived for a given examinee. Also, a descriptive report with graphs and analyses of score differences can be generated, copied to a word processor, and edited by the examiner. One of the main advantages of computer scoring is that the conversion of raw scores is done rapidly and with complete accuracy, as compared to manually finding each of the conversion tables in the various test manuals. And, many of the SB5 profiles are reproduced and plotted by the computer in a form nearly identical to the hand-scoring sections of the Record Form. Also, all of the analyses of score differences can be calculated quickly without hand calculations or retrieval of critical values for significant differences. Differences within the SB5 would include those between IQ scores or among Factor Indexes or between all 10 subtest scaled scores. In addition, differences between SB5 scores and scores on the *Woodcock-Johnson III Tests of Achievement* (WJ III Achievement; Mather & Woodcock, 2001a) are also programmed into the system. Thus, the calculation of ability–achievement discrepancies (the regression-based prediction method) for assessment of learning disabilities can be done by the program and entered into a computerized report for the user. Examiners are encouraged to edit the report and add their own commentary, analysis, interpretation, and recommendations for each case.

STANDARDIZATION, NORMS, DEVELOPMENT, AND PSYCHOMETRICS

The SB5 was standardized on a nationally representative sample of 4,800 subjects, from ages 2 years, 0 months through the category of 85+ years (the oldest subject being 96). Demographics of the normative sample closely matched the 2000 Census statistics for stratification groups based on age (2–21), gender, ethnicity (Asian-, African-, Hispanic-, non-Hispanic Caucasian-, and Native-American), geographic region (northeast, mid-central, south, and west), and parental education (less than high school, high school or GED, and 13+ years). Extensive reliability, validity, and fairness studies were conducted for the Field-Test edition and the final Standardization edition of the scale (Roid, 2003d), and these are summarized in the sections below.

Development of the Scale

The original editions of the Stanford-Binet (Terman, 1916; Terman & Merrill, 1937, 1960, 1973) employed a global mental age scoring system—ratio IQ at first and standard deviation IQ after 1960. The revision project for SB5 included seven years of intensive research (Roid, 2003d). The revision of the scale involved a complex, multiyear, data-based project. After three years of literature research, three pilot studies, and expert review, a field-testing version containing various combinations of four or five subtests for each cognitive factor (including SB4 subtests) was tested on a national sample of 600 individuals (typical children and adolescents without disabilities and small groups with various cognitive or communication disabilities, as well as intellectual giftedness). More than 60 professional examiners were trained to administer the tests and gave extensive feedback leading to the revision of the tests and dropping of several subtests that showed limited psychometric quality or did not fit the factor model or the item response theory (Rasch, 1980) requirements. Extensive psychometric item and scale analyses were conducted using conventional and item-response theory (IRT; Rasch, 1980; Wright & Linacre, 1999) methods, differential item functioning (DIF; Holland & Wainer, 1993; Mantel & Haenszel, 1959) fairness studies, confirmatory factor analysis, and criterion-related evidence. Any deficient subtests retained for the Standardization edition were revised by adding, deleting, and revising various items and examiner directions.

The final published SB5 was derived from the Standardization edition, which was administered to 4,800 typical children and adolescents from all four Census regions of the United States. The demographics of this normative sample matched the 2000 Census percentages (U. S. Census Bureau, 2001) of gender, race/ethnicity, socioeconomic level (number of years of education completed by parents or by adult examinees), and geographic region. The norm sample included students receiving special education services (6.8%) and students attending officially designated intellectual giftedness programs (2%). Extensive quality-control procedures were used to collect, screen, score, computerize, and verify each of the normative cases, employing a large team of clerical and testing specialists at the headquarters of the publisher. The standardization data was collected over a 12-month period in 2001 and 2002 by nearly 600 experienced and carefully selected professional examiners, many being school- or clinical-psychologists and educational diagnosticians. In addition, the standardization study included various clinical or special comparison groups (number of subjects in parentheses) consisting of individuals with ADHD (104; Barkley, 1990) autism (108), developmental delay (114; ages 2–6), English-language learners (76; ELL, ESL, or LEP), intellectually gifted (202; official school program enrollees), learning disabilities (373; several subgroups depending on specific academic area), severe motoric/orthopedic impairment (26), mental retardation (154), documented speech/language impairment (128), deafness or hard-of hearing conditions (36), and serious emotional disturbance (44).

Psychometrics: Reliability of the Scales

The subtests of the SB5 show excellent levels of internal consistency reliability (Roid, 2003d), with average across-age coefficients of .84–.89 among the 10 subtests. Table 6.2 shows the names of the subtests, composite scores, and IQ indexes of the SB5, along with the average internal consistency (split half coefficients) or composite reliability (Nunnally, 1967, p. 229) of the scores.

Clearly, Table 6.2 shows a high level of reliability for all the IQ and composite scores, and a level of reliability for the subtests that exceeds those of subtests in other published intelligence tests. Complete listings of all the reliability coefficients for subtests, IQ, and factor index scores are given in Roid (2003d) for each year of age (2–16) or age categories up to 80+. One of the routing subtests, Nonverbal Fluid Reasoning (NVFR; Object-Series/Matrices) had only 4 age categories (out of 23) with internal consistency coefficients below .80 (age 10, .79; age 13, .72; and ages 21–39, .73–.78), but otherwise ranged from .81 to .94, with an average of .86. Standard errors of measurement (SEM) for each age category, IRT-based test information curves, test–retest stability coefficients, and interscorer reliabilities are also presented in the SB5 technical manual (Roid, 2003d).

Table 6.2 shows one of the composite scores developed as special diagnostic composites using the method of Tellegen and Briggs (1967), which has been widely used with the Wechsler scales (Kaufman, 1994). Roid and Carson (2004) developed a wide range of these diagnostic composites and these were further elaborated by Roid and Barram (2004). The Learning Disability—Reading (LD-R) composite shown in Table 6.2 was developed, based on extensive regression analyses (Roid, 2003b), to predict the risk for early emergence of learning disabilities. The composite uses four subtests—the knowledge subtests (NVKN and VKN) plus the working memory subtests (NVWM and VWM)—in a sum of scaled scores converted to the IQ scale (mean 100, SD 3). This conversion was done by calculating the sum of scaled scores in the normative sample (N = 4,800) and using the normative mean and standard deviation of the sum to transform the sum into an IQ scale. The LD-R composite has a reliability of .95 (Roid & Carson, 2004).

The technical manual for the SB5 (Roid, 2003d) includes tables of significant differences between and among the subtests and composite scores of the batteries, and the frequencies of differences in the normative sample. Also, formulas and appendix tables for the calculation of ability–achievement discrepancies are also included in Roid (2003d). Examples of the use

TABLE 6.2   Average Reliability of SB5 Scores across All Age Groups

IQ Scores		Nonverbal Subtests	
Full Scale IQ	.98	Fluid Reasoning	.86
Nonverbal IQ	.95	Knowledge	.85
Verbal IQ	.96	Quantitative Reasoning	.86
Abbreviated IQ	.91	Visual-Spatial Reasoning	.87
		Working Memory	.88
Factor Index Scores		**Verbal Subtests**	
Fluid Reasoning	.90	Fluid Reasoning	.86
Knowledge	.92	Knowledge	.89
Quantitative Reasoning	.92	Quantitative Reasoning	.87
Visual-Spatial Processing	.92	Visual-Spatial Reasoning	.88
Working Memory	.92	Working Memory	.84

SOURCE : Summarized from Roid (2003d).

of difference scores are provided in the section below on Interpretive Strategies.

A surprising strength of the SB5 was identified by the test–retest reliability studies reported in Roid (2003d). First, the correlations between administrations of the IQ measures at four age levels showed high coefficients (corrected for restricted variance) ranging from .87 to .95 (ages 2–5), .84 to .93 (ages 6–20), .88 to .95 (ages 21–59), and .85 to .95 (ages 60+), with most coefficients above .90. Second, the practice effects (measured by the score difference between initial and repeated testing) on the SB5 were smaller than expected. For example, the nonverbal IQ of SB5 showed shifts of only 2–5 IQ points, which compares favorably with the standard error of measurement, which is approximately 3 IQ points. The lower shift and, thus, practice effect, for SB5 is even more notable, given the short retest period (5–8 days). Research usually shows that the shorter the retest period the greater the practice effect because the examinee remembers the details of the test items and directions in the shorter time period. The implication of the lower practice effect on SB5 is that retesting can be done earlier on SB5 than on other IQ batteries, perhaps as soon as 6 months rather than the typical one-year delay.

Uses and Interpretive Strategies for the SB5

Uses of SB5

The SB5 has been widely used for decades for preschool children because of the toys and materials included in the testing kit and the sensitivity of the scales to cognitive development in young children. Also, the Stanford-Binet editions have traditionally been widely used for identifying students with intellectual giftedness. Clinicians and assessment professionals have used the SB5 for a wide variety of evaluations, including qualifications for special education (e.g., for learning disabilities, mental retardation, and traumatic brain injury), worker's compensation, social security evaluations, and many other adolescent and adult conditions that affect cognitive performance (e.g., brain injury, dementia, and stroke). The newly expanded nonverbal sections of SB5 will assist professionals in the evaluation of individuals with communication difficulties, autism, and deafness/hard-of-hearing, as well as non-English speakers.

Eight-Step Interpretive Strategy

The test manual for the SB5 (Roid & Miller, 1997) outlines a seven-step interpretive strategy that begins with background information and the global level of IQ scores and proceeds through the composite scores, growth scores, subtests,

TABLE 6.3 Steps in SB5 Interpretation: The 8-Step System

Step 1: Purpose and Context

Step 2: Comparison of NVIQ and VIQ

Step 3: Global IQ Evaluation

Step 4: Factor Index and Composite Score Comparisons

Step 5: Growth Score Analysis

Step 6: Subtest Scores and Profile Analysis

Step 7: Cross-Battery Assessment

Step 8: Qualitative Analysis

and special diagnostic indexes. This chapter adds an additional step and explains the process of interpretation (see Table 6.3). The eight steps are based on the hierarchical strategies typically used on the Wechsler scales (Kaufman, 1994; Kaufman & Lichtenberger, 1999), and other intellectual assessments (e.g., Sattler, 2001). Each of these interpretive systems begins at the highest level (IQ) and proceeds to study the patterns and significant differences between composite and subtest scores so that a comprehensive view of the individual's cognitive strengths and weaknesses can be reported. The overall purpose of these strategies is to generate clinical hypotheses to explain the cognitive strengths and weaknesses that impact the individual's performance (e.g., in school or work). Hypotheses are then verified (or not verified) by collecting additional information from a broad range of sources such as parent, teacher, care-giver, or peer observations, additional test data on achievement, behavior, and social-emotional variables, interviews, medical and school records, and so on. In addition, considerations of the current IDEA (2004) recommendation to explore cognitive strengths and weaknesses (to enhance the use of intellectual ability batteries and supplement global information from IQ measures alone), methods of profile analysis, and score-difference significance are also included in the interpretive steps.

Step 1: Purpose and Context. The examiner's purpose for the assessment and the ethnic, cultural, medical, or environmental context of the examinee can greatly impact (and even invalidate) the interpretation of findings from testing. The AERA/APA/NCME (1999) ethical guidelines for professional examiners caution that the validity of tests depends on the specific purposes, uses, and interpretation of tests, and that validity evidence for specific uses or interpretations may not be available or included in a test manual. For example, most standardized intellectual batteries have documented and excellent validity for using the global IQ score in identifying high levels of giftedness or low levels of mental retardation, but IQ scores themselves are less able to accurately identify the variations of conditions such as autism, learning disabilities, and ADHD, without supplemental assessment of all subtests and social and behavioral variables. Also, the AERA/NCME/APA guidelines require consideration of many other examinee characteristics, including the match between the individual's characteristics and the nature of the normative sample of the test being used. Clearly, the interpretation of normative scores depends on such a match. Some of the major considerations in modern multicultural society are (1) whether the examinee can comprehend and speak in the language employed by the test, and (2) whether the examinee has recently immigrated to a country and is not fully acculturated (Dana, 2005) to the society and especially to the requirements of standardized tests. A thorough assessment would measure acculturation levels, for example, degree of activities in the majority culture as compared to isolation in previous culture, and not just the number of years in the United States (Paniagua, 2005). Fortunately, nonverbal (nonvocal) batteries such as the SB5 provide an alternative to batteries that require extensive verbal

and expressive language ability. However, even with the SB5, the examiner must pause and reflect on the purpose (e.g., look at the validity evidence available for that use of the test) and the context (e.g., the ethnic, cultural, language-proficiency, and acculturation level) of the examinee before beginning the analysis of scores, score differences, profile patterns, and so forth.

Table 6.4 shows a case study of a 7-year-old boy (called "Sean" for this

TABLE 6.4 Case Study of SB5 Scores for Sean, a 7-Year-Old Male Student with Documented Reading Learning Disability

Composite Scores

IQ Scores		*Factor Index Scores*	
Nonverbal IQ (NVIQ)	90	Fluid Reasoning (FR)	100
Verbal IQ (VIQ)	87	Knowledge (KN)	97
Full Scale IQ (FSIQ)	93	Quantitative Reasoning (QR)	94
		Visual-Spatial Ability (VS)	91
Diagnostic Cluster			
LD Reading Composite	81		
		Working Memory (WM)	74

Subtests

Nonverbal Subtests		*Verbal Subtests*	
Fluid Reasoning (NVFR)	11	Fluid Reasoning (VFR)	9
Knowledge (NVKN)	9	Knowledge (VKN)	10
Quantitative Reasoning (NVQR)	10	Quantitative Reasoning (VQR)	8
Visual-Spatial Ability (NVVS)	9	Visual-Spatial Ability (VVS)	8
Working Memory (NVWM)	6	Working Memory (WM)	5

example) who was administered the SB5 as part of a verification of qualification for special-education services when he moved to a new school district in another state in the southern area of the United States. His majority-ethnic background (Anglo-Caucasian, non-Hispanic) and other demographics suggested that he matched the expected characteristics of the SB5 normative sample. Also, knowing that he has a history of learning disabilities, the SB5 is a good choice because it was standardized with a large concurrent sample (N = 472) of students who took the WJ III Achievement tests in reading (Mather & Woodcock, 2001a). Thus, tables of comparison between the SB5 and WJ III Achievement are available in the technical manual (Roid, 2003d).

The Learning Disability Reading Composite (LD Reading) shown in Table 6.4 was developed by Roid (2003b). In the tradition of other composites used to generate clinical hypotheses (e.g., Kaufman, 1994), scaled scores for specific SB5 subtests are summed and the total transformed to the metric of IQ (mean 100, *SD* 15). For LD Reading, the two Knowledge subtests and two Working Memory subtests are added together (the total is 30 for the case study in Table 6.4) and transformed by multiplying 1.875 times the sum, adding 25 points, and then rounding the result. The multiplier and constant were derived by studying the distribution of the sum in the SB5 normative sample (N = 4800) to find a transformation that would provide a nationally normed mean of 100 and *SD* of 15 (Roid, 2003b; Roid & Carson, 2004). Applying the transformation to the case study data in Table 6.4 resulted in an LD Reading composite of 81 (56.25 + 25, rounded). Comparing the 81 to Sean's Full Scale IQ of 93 shows a statistically significant 12-point difference.

The evidence for the validity of the LD Reading composite and other composites was presented by Roid (2003b, 2003d). Roid (2003d) presented means for 212 students (ages 5–19) with documented learning disabilities in reading (official enrollment in special education for LD in reading, and ability and achievement scores for documentation). Significantly lower scores were found for the Knowledge and Working Memory factor indexes. Inspection of the SB5 profile subtest scores of students with learning disabilities in reading (LD—reading) showed the lowest profile scores on the Vocabulary and Verbal Working Memory subtests (means of 7.88 and 8.23, respectively, with standard deviations of 2.7 and 3.0). When compared to a normative control sample of 256 students (ages 5–19, matched approximately for ethnicity, educational level of parents, and gender), these subtest scores in the LD—reading group were significantly different (t-tests significant at $p < .001$ and standardized mean difference effect sizes of .82 and .64 respectively). Pomplun and Custer (2005) also found that SB5 factor indexes of Knowledge and Working Memory were significant predictors of Woodcock-Johnson III Reading scores (correlations in the .40–.45 range in a sample of 472 students ages 6–19). Finally, Roid (2003b) examined the classification accuracy of using the LD—reading composite score from the SB5 to classify students as LD versus non-LD. Results showed a fairly high rate of accurate identification (81%), with few LD cases misidentified using a cutoff of 89 points or lower, but with a sizeable false positive rate (17% of the normative non-LD cases were identified as LD). Thus, examiners should use caution in applying the LD—reading composite as a single measure of LD, but should always collect multiple sources of evidence for learning disabilities from other tests, parent and teacher ratings, observations, and so on.

Step 2: Comparison of Nonverbal and Verbal IQ. Unlike other interpretive systems (e.g., Sattler, 1988) that begin interpretation with the Full Scale (FS) IQ, the multicultural nature of current society suggests that examiners look at the difference between NVIQ and VIQ before interpreting the FSIQ. If the difference is highly significant and rare in the population, examiners should interpret the Full Scale IQ with caution because it may not truly estimate latent general ability. When the examinee has a non-English-language background or is a recent immigrant to an English-speaking community, the Nonverbal IQ may be a closer estimate of true potential. If the examinee has sensory disabilities such as blindness, the VIQ may provide a better estimate. In either case, more testing with other instruments may be needed. The test manual for the SB5 provides appendix tables containing the numerical values for two important methods of comparing differences among the IQ composites—statistical significance of the difference and frequency (rarity) of the magnitude of differences. Both the significance and rarity of the difference between IQs, factor index scores, and subtest scores have been recommended in most of the interpretive systems for cognitive tests (e.g., Kaufman, 1994; Sattler, 2001). Both methods are important because statistical significance alone may not indicate that the difference is truly unusual and clinically significant given that most examinees taking cognitive tests have existing differences of various magnitudes among their scores.

Roid (2003d) showed that differences between the nonverbal and verbal IQ of about 10 points would reach statistical significance for all ages (actual range is from about 7.2 for adults to 10.2 for adolescents). In terms of the frequency of differences in the normative population, at least 14-point differences are required at the 15% level and 18-point differences for the more-infrequent differences in only 5% of the population. For the case study of Sean (Table 6.4), the difference of 3 points is clearly not significant or infrequent.

Step 3: Global IQ Evaluation. Table 6.4 shows the Full Scale IQ for Sean was 93, placing him in the average range (90–109; Roid, 2003b). Given that his reading achievement scores were much lower (in the 75–80 range), the identification of a specific learning disability was justified, using the traditional discrepancy method. In Step 4, the strengths and weaknesses in Sean's performance will be examined to identify the cognitive deficits that are associated with learning disabilities.

Step 4: Factor Index and Composite Score Comparisons. For the clinical evaluation of cognitive strengths and weaknesses (as requested in the guidelines of IDEA, 2004), factor indexes and composite scores were designed to combine clusters of subtests to measure specific diagnostic constructs. The factor indexes and one of the composite scores (LD—reading) of the SB5 are shown in Table 6.4 for the case study of Sean. The score of 81 for the LD—reading composite was obtained by summing the subtest scaled scores for the Knowledge (NVKN and VKN) and Working Memory (NVWM and VWM), multiplying the sum by 1.875 and adding 25 points to the final total (rounded from 81.25 to 81), as described by Roid and Carson (2004) and Roid and Barram (2004). Because the difference between the LD—reading composite (81) and Full Scale IQ (93) is 12 points, the difference is statistically significant and further evidence of the presence of a learning disability as explained in Step 1 above. Because the LD—reading composite contains the Vocabulary subtest along with the memory subtests, and because these subtests can be given to young children before Kindergarten, the composite shows potential for early identification of reading disabilities, even though reading achievement is difficult to measure. The early identification of LD, prior to grade 3, was a goal of the reauthorized IDEA (2004).

Another score comparison that is relevant for Sean's case (Table 6.4) is the contrast between the Working Memory Factor Index score and all the other four factor indexes of the SB5 (multiple pairwise comparisons, as explained in Roid, 2003d, Appendix Table B1). Clearly, Sean's WM score of 74 is far lower (17–26 points) than the other indexes, and 19 points lower than his Full Scale IQ (93). Tables of score differences would confirm these differences to be both statistically significant and infrequent in the normative sample (Roid, 2003d). Another approach to score differences is to contrast the factor index with the mean of all five indexes, as recommended in the technical bulletin by Roid (2005b), available online. So, for Sean's profile, we have a mean of 91.2 and subtracting WM of 74 gives a difference of 17.2. According to Roid (2005b), this difference is both statistically significant at the .05 level and rare in the normative sample (5%). Thus, Sean shows strengths in Fluid Reasoning particularly, and a striking weakness in working memory processes. This means that Sean has difficulty sorting, scanning, and transforming information stored in both his verbal and his visual-spatial memory (Baddeley, 1986). This finding is also consistent with research by Coltheart (1987) linking working memory to reading comprehension. Also, Sean's deficit in working memory could be easily explained to his teacher and parents for purposes of planning interventions that would help him compensate for his deficit (e.g., using written lists and visual prompts to recall complex information in the classroom).

Step 5: Growth Score Analysis. The SB5 has an optional series of scores called *change sensitive scores (CSSs)*, derived from IRT transformations of raw score totals (Roid, 2003a, 2003b, 2003d; Roid & Barram, 2004). The scores are similar to the W-scores of the *Woodcock-Johnson* (McGrew & Woodcock, 2001), being based on item response theory (Rasch, 1980; Wright & Linacre, 1999), and showing similar growth curves across ages to those on the *WJ III Tests of Cognitive Abilities* (Mather & Woodcock, 2001b). You can detect small improvements across time if the SB5 is repeated (e.g., annually). The CSS scale is fine-grained and small increments of raw score improvement will be noticeable. Similar to the WJ III, the SB5 Growth Scores range between approximately 425 and 570, centered at 500 for age 10 years, 0 months, with an expansion factor of 9.1024 (used to calculate the W-scale from a Rasch ability estimate; Woodcock & Dahl, 1971). Woodcock (1999) discusses more detailed specifications and uses of these Rasch-based scales. These scores are not standardized by age nor are they norm-referenced, as with IQ or subtest scaled scores. Instead they are criterion-referenced (by age and task difficulty) and follow the age-related growth pattern of children, increasing quickly from ages 2 to 8 (approximately) and increasing more gradually from ages 9 to 20. A typical standard deviation within various age groups would be approximately 10.0 for the NVIQ, VIQ, and Full Scale change sensitive scores. For the case study of Sean, the lowest CSS was Working Memory (WM CSS at 469, age equivalent 5 years, 8 months) and the highest was Fluid Reasoning (FR CSS at 491, age equivalent 8 years, 2 months). Clearly, the 22-point difference between the WM and FR change sensitive scores was highly significant, with more than 2 years of age equivalence difference, and shows the potential improvement that might be possible with an effective memory-training intervention (see section on Links to Instruction).

In addition to the standard IQ indexes, an Extended IQ (EXIQ) was derived from the CSS transformation of the raw scores that compose the Full Scale IQ (e.g., all 10 subtests, 358 raw score points in total) by Roid (2003b). This allows the IQ scale to extend to a high of 225 for profound intellectual giftedness and a low of 10 for profound cognitive deficiencies. Using a standard method of creating norms, the age-group means and standard deviation of the CSS for the full-scale raw score were smoothed and used to derive the EXIQ scores. The standard linear transformation was used to convert the CSS to EXIQ values (M = 100, SD = 15). Data analyses to verify the close relationship between EXIQ and the conventional IQ were completed along with extensive tables of EXIQ values by Roid (2003b). Users who work with individuals having extreme giftedness or extreme mental retardation should obtain the Interpretive Manual for the SB5 (Roid, 2003b) to employ the EXIQ as a valuable guide to placement of these rare cases.

Roid (2003b) presented construct-related evidence of the validity of EXIQ, and Roid (2003d) presented evidence of the reliability of the change sensitive scores (CSSs) that form the basis of the EXIQ. Correlations between EXIQ and conventional Full Scale IQ scores were calculated for all examinees in the standardization sample (N = 4,800) divided into 30 age groups across ages 2–85. The median correlation between EXIQ and FSIQ was .99, with a range of .94–.99 (with 17 of the age groups showing correlations of .99). Also, the numerical differences between EXIQ and FSIQ were calculated across the standardization sample, showing an average of 0.23 with no consistent pattern of positive or negative differences within age groups. Extensive studies of the fit of

the SB5 items to the Rasch item response theory model (Roid, 2003d) provide evidence for the reliability of the EXIQ scores. Test information curves (showing the precision of measurement at each score point based on Rasch standard errors of the ability estimates) show low measurement error within the range of 400–550 on the CSS Rasch-based scale (similar to the W-score of the Woodcock-Johnson, with 500 centered at age 10 years, 0 months). Scores within this range show a standard error (for their particular score level) of 3 points or less. The 3-point error magnitude corresponds to the traditional standard error of measurement for the SB5 IQ scores (2.30 for FSIQ, 3.26 for Nonverbal IQ, and 3.05 for Verbal IQ). An inspection of the total validation sample collected for the SB5 project (N = 7,340—all normative and special cases including mental retardation and gifted) shows only 0.1 percent (about 7 people) below 400 (corresponding to raw score totals of less than 5 out of 358 points and EXIQ of 10) and no persons scoring above 550 (raw scores of 350 or more; EXIQ of 174 or more).

Step 6: Subtest Comparisons and Profile Analysis. The comparison of cognitive strengths and weaknesses among the subtests of cognitive batteries can be a complex and lengthy process if carried to the full extent suggested by Kaufman (1994), Sattler (2001), and most intellectual-ability test manuals. Therefore, the reader is referred to the SB5 test manual (Roid, 2003a, 2003b) or to the book by Roid and Barram (2004) for more details on subtest definitions, research, comparisons, and profile pattern analysis. A brief summary of some of the major steps and guidelines in subtest analysis is as follows:

1. *Recognize the limits of measurement error.* The first step in subtest profile analysis is to recognize that some subtests have

lower reliability than others, sometimes at certain age levels, so the experienced examiner should consult the test manual tables of reliability values to discover which subtests dip below a reliability of .80 at certain age levels where the use of individual scores becomes more problematic. Because composite scores and IQ measures combine several subtests, they are often more reliable indicators of strengths and weaknesses. However, when a clear pattern across all 10 SB5 subtests emerges, the patterns of subtests gain an enhanced reliability from their joint usage. For example, in the profile pattern of Sean (Table 6.4), the patterns of scores in both the nonverbal and verbal area are similar—high FR or KN subtests and very low WM scores—*increasing the likelihood that the pattern shows a true cognitive deficit.*

2. *Examine subtest scatter.* One of the quickest ways to see strengths and weaknesses is through the time-tested method of calculating *profile scatter.* Scatter is simply the difference between the lowest and highest scaled scores for the profile. The profile for Sean (Table 6.4) shows a difference of 6 points (NVFR versus VWM). According to the table of scatter frequencies for 10 subtests supplied in the test manual appendices, a scatter of 6 points occurs in about 61% of normative-sample profiles. Thus, the scatter is not a rarity.

3. *Examine statistical significance and frequency of score differences among the subtests.* Extensive tables for the statistical significance of differences, the significance of differences between the individual subtest and the mean of all the subtests, and the frequency (rarity) of the difference magnitude are all provided in the SB5 test manual appendices (Roid, 2003d), and guidelines are also mentioned by Roid and Barram (2004).

As a rule-of-thumb, a difference of 4 points between any of the SB5 subtests will reach statistical significance at the .05 level. For Sean, NVWM differs from NVFR and NVQR by 4 points or more and VWM differs from VFR and VKN by the 4 points. These confirmed differences help to verify the importance of the low Working Memory (WM) scores for Sean.

4. *Compare the entire subtest profile to the core profiles derived from the normative sample.* The study of common profile patterns in a normative sample was initiated by the work of McDermott, Fantuzzo, & Glutting (1990), who studied profile patterns on the WISC-R. Since that time, a number of tests have included normative profile analyses (e.g., Roid, 2003b, for the SB5). The method of deriving accurate profile patterns from cluster analysis must be correctly applied, including the use of subjects with clinical conditions (to allow for the variability that occurs in clinical practice) and the use of accurate cluster-analysis methods (Roid, 1994). Without careful analysis, the early conclusion of McDermott et al. (1990) was to abandon profile analysis because of an apparent lack of profile differentiation (dominance of profiles by a general level—"flat profiles" with little scatter) in one of the Wechsler normative data sets. Roid (1994, 2003b) has found that the guidelines of Aldenderfer and Blashfield (1984) are critical to finding true profile patterns (occurring in as much as 40% of the population) instead of the undifferentiated flat profiles originally identified by McDermott et al. The key was to employ Pearson correlations as the similarity measure in SPSS cluster analysis (Norusis, 1990) with Ward's (1963) method of hierarchical clustering in the first stage (R. K. Blashfield, personal

communication, February 22, 1992). The preferred data-analysis procedures are outlined in Chapter 10 on Nonverbal Intellectual and Cognitive Assessment with the Leiter International Performance Scale—Revised (Leiter-R), by Roid, Pomplun, and Martin in this book.

For the SB5, 10 types of normative subtest profile patterns were discovered by Roid (2003b). Four of the patterns were "flat" (nearly uniform subtest means) at different levels (high ability, above average, below average, and low ability). These level profiles represented 53% of the normative sample. The other 47% of the sample had various differentiated profiles with high or low verbal or unique pairs of subtests (high QR, high or low FR, and high KN). Users of the SB5 should check these profile patterns first before concluding that their individual has an uncommon profile pattern. Also, the user can examine the patterns of mean scores for the various clinical groups (e.g., LD, ADHD, autism, ESL) included in the validation studies of the technical manual (Roid, 2003d) to see if their case fits one of those patterns.

Step 7: Cross-Battery Comparisons (Composites and Subtests). As explained by Flanagan and Ortiz (2001), another approach to test interpretation is to compare measures of major constructs (e.g., the cognitive factors in CHC theory) across different cognitive batteries. The first comparison for the SB5 would be the WJ III Tests of Cognitive Abilities (Mather & Woodcock, 2001b), which were correlated as part of a construct-related, cross-battery factor analysis in Roid (2003d). Both batteries have subtests that measure each of the five factors of the SB5. Comparisons between SB5 factor index scores and WJ III subtests would be as follows:

1. Fluid Reasoning with Analysis-Synthesis

2. Knowledge with Verbal Comprehension

3. Quantitative Reasoning with Applied Problems

4. Visual-Spatial Processing with Spatial Relations

5. Working Memory with Auditory Memory

Next, we would range more widely to find specific comparisons with other cognitive batteries that have been analyzed from a CHC-theory perspective (e.g., most of the major intelligence and cognitive batteries, such as Wechsler scales, the Kaufman batteries, the Stanford-Binet, and the Woodcock-Johnson cognitive tests included in McGrew & Flanagan, 1998). For additional cross-battery suggestions, see Flanagan and Ortiz (2001).

Step 8: Qualitative Observations. Additional qualitative observations of test-taking behavior by the child can be collected, sequences of item responses examined, and the process of "testing the limits" used after the standardized testing is completed. Each of these will be discussed in turn. Initially, the experienced examiner looks for inattention, distraction, oppositional behavior, depression, anxiety, or fatigue and illness in the individual taking the test. Also, the strategies used by the individual to complete tasks, especially any unexpected or unusual styles of responding, should be noted. These behaviors are noted on the Record Form and must be used to temper conclusions or hypotheses derived from analysis of SB5 scores and patterns. Sattler (2001) has a wealth of suggestions for noting behaviors, and, if necessary in special cases, instruments such as the Test Observation Form (McConaughy & Achenbach, 2004) may be helpful.

Next, the examiner looks for portions of subtests where the individual's behavior was unexpected or significantly different from other portions of the battery or that specific subtest. For example, in a student with ADHD, inattention or distraction can cause the student to incorrectly answer easy questions but correctly answer more difficult ones. By studying the string of answers (because all SB5 items within testlets or routing tests are organized from easy to hard), the examiner can identify unusual response patterns that may be diagnostic.

Finally, the examiner can return to subtests after the standardized administration is completed and change the tasks for diagnostic purposes. For example, in cases of brain injury or memory-loss, the individual may do poorly with the standard directions on the memory subtests. Cases of moderate memory loss may require only one repetition of sentences in the Last Word task (VWM), but severe cases may require two or three repetitions. Such procedures provide a qualitative assessment of degree of deficit severity.

Links to Instruction

The technical report by Roid (2006) provides a beginning source of information for applying results from the Stanford-Binet Intelligence Scales—Fifth Edition (SB5; Roid, 2003b) to the planning of instruction and intervention by teachers, parents, and others who work with children. The recommendations are particularly aimed at professionals working with children and adolescents (especially ages 2–16) who have cognitive delays and disabilities, specific learning disabilities, and other conditions that affect school learning. To identify areas of cognitive weakness, look for two possible patterns: (1) The child scores *more than one standard deviation below national norms* (e.g., scores below 85) on one or more of the five cognitive factor index scores of SB5, or (2) the child shows a significantly low factor index score, *within*

his or her own profile (*intrapersonal or* ipsative *comparisons*), based on differences among the five factor scores. Because these patterns were found in the case of Sean (Table 6.4), some suggestions for intervention with working memory are as follows:

There are many educational toys and games that require short-term memory, recall, and lots of working memory. Toys and blocks, and so forth, can be hidden from small children and require a search-and-find solution. You can use a mixture of yellow, red, and blue plastic poker-style chips that are put into a box (out of sight) one by one in random order. The child must remember how many of each color has been placed in the box to practice working memory.

Many card games and board games require short-term, long-term, and working memory to keep track of all the cards/pieces. Chess is an example, because the many moves possible or in future steps must be examined mentally.

Older children would be asked to remember and recall all the numbers embedded in phone calls or media commercials, for example. Shopping lists and to-do lists can be real-life lists from which certain elements are required for recall (e.g., "What were all the vegetables we needed?").

The various assessments used in Reading have various word lists and prose passages that could be used to practice/evaluate selected recall (working memory for verbal material), for example, by reading a word list and then later recalling all the words that begin with W or certain words in meaningful categories such as animals or nouns.

Older students could be asked to visit "visually rich" environments such as museums, science/industry locations, art exhibits, or beautiful scenic locations, and later asked to draw or map the locations of various objects, to test the nonverbal "visual" sketch-pad of working memory.

An important short-term retention memory paradigm is the Brown-Peterson Technique (Baddeley, 1986; Peterson, 1966). Sets of printed letters (3 consonants, such as *RXT*) are presented for the person to remember. However, during a delay (varied by the examiner from 3 to 18 seconds, in subsequent trials), the person must count backwards from a large number. So, if we present *RXT*, we then ask you to count backwards from 45 (44, 43, 42, ...). At the end of the delay period, the response is recorded to see whether the letter sequence is remembered exactly. The span of memory and control of memory functions can be trained over time by gradually increasing the time delay and increasing the size of the number (go up into the hundreds).

VALIDITY

Numerous studies providing content-, criterion-, construct-, and consequence-related evidence of validity were included in lengthy sections (41 pages with 22 tables of validity results and another 10 pages of fairness studies) in the Technical Manual (Roid, 2003d). Also, the supplementary Interpretive Manual (Roid, 2003b) has another 33 pages and about 20 tables or figures showing validity-related data. Highlights of these studies are listed below.

Content-Related Evidence

Three types of content-related evidence were presented—expert judgment, coverage of theoretical constructs, and data-based item analysis. An advisory panel of 18 experts reviewed the pilot studies, Tryout edition, and Standardization edition designs, items, and materials. More than 600 examiners gave very specific feedback on wording of items and examiner directions on the Tryout and Standardization. A panel of 19 fairness reviewers, representing gender, ethnic, and religious issues, reviewed the Standardization edition. A few items or illustrations identified as problematic for gender, ethnic, or religious concerns were edited prior to standardization or deleted for the final published version.

Extensive studies of the match between items and the constructs of the CHC model (Flanagan & Ortiz, 2001) were conducted. Drs. Woodcock and McGrew (McGrew & Woodcock, 2001)

personally examined all the items from previous editions of Stanford-Binet and draft items for new subtests and assigned CHC factor codes to each item or cluster of similar items. Factor analyses of Form L confirmed the presence of CHC factors in the original Terman (1916) and Terman and Merrill (1937) editions of the scale (Roid, 2003d). Additional confirming factor analyses were conducted on pilot, Tryout, and Standardization data.

Also, extensive item analyses (classical and item-response theory—IRT—methods) were conducted, including differential item functioning (DIF; item bias analysis; Holland & Wainer, 1993), and any problematic items were deleted or changed. Extensive studies of the fit of each item to the IRT model (Wright & Linacre, 1999; Rasch, 1980) and to each composite scale were conducted, and, as described by Kamphaus (2001), provide content-related evidence of validity.

Fairness studies included DIF studies of items, and consistency of internal reliability and intercorrelations across groups (Roid, 2003d). Roid (2003b) reported extensive studies of fairness of predicting achievement across gender, ethnic (Hispanic), and educational-level groups, finding no significantly different slopes in the prediction of WJ III achievement cluster scores.

Criterion-Related Evidence

Studies of mean differences between normative and special/clinical groups were conducted for the SB5. Validity study groups included children with severe speech/language, motor (orthopedic) delays, developmental delays, intellectual deficiency (mental retardation), ADHD, intellectual giftedness, learning disabilities, severe emotional disturbance, and English-as-second-language (ESL). Also the SB5 IQ was correlated in separate studies with the SB4 (.90, $n = 104$), the Stanford-Binet L-M form (Terman & Merrill, 1960) (.85, $n = 80$), the WISC-III Full Scale IQ (.84, $n = 66$), the WAIS-III (.82, $n = 87$), and a five-factor composite from the WJ III (Mather & Woodcock, 2001b) cognitive battery (.90, $n = 145$; Roid & Barram, 2004). In terms of correlation with achievement, the SB5 Full Scale IQ correlated with the *Wechsler Individual Achievement Test—Second Edition* (WIAT-II; Harcourt Assessment, 2001) and the WJ III (Mather & Woodcock, 2001b). Correlations for WIAT-II ranged from .53 (Writing) to .67 (Reading) and .79 (Math). Correlations for the WJ III ranged from .66 to .84, very high compared to the typical IQ measure (achievement correlations averaging in the .60 range as summarized by Naglieri and Bornstein, 2003).

Construct-Related Evidence

Studies of the cross-sectional trends in age-level means for the raw scores and the IRT-based CSS scores of the SB5 showed a growth curve pattern very similar to that found with the WJ-R and WJ III W-scale scores across ages 2–80 (Roid, 2003d). The CSS for the Knowledge Factor Index showed increases in performance all the way to age 60, whereas the other factors showed the expected decrease in performance in adult cross-sectional data. Extensive studies of the factor structure of SB5 were conducted, including confirmatory factor analyses using LISREL 8.3 (Joreskog & Sorbom, 1999). The factor analyses were calculated for five successive age groups (2–5, 6–10, 11–16, 17–50, and 51+), comparing factor models with 1, 2, 3, 4, and 5 factors. Split-half scores (scores for odd- and even-numbered items in each of the 10 subtests) were employed to provide more stable estimates of each factor in the maximum likelihood analyses. The five-factor models showed superior fit including the non-normed fit (NNFI) index (ranging from .89 to .93), comparative fit index (CFI) ranging from .91 to .93, and root mean square error of approximation (RMSEA) ranging from .076 to .088. A second series of confirmatory analyses was conducted with LISREL using conventional full-length subtests across two

batteries: SB5 and the WJ III (Mather & Woodcock, 2001b). Again, the five-factor model showed the best fit with the fluid, knowledge, quantitative, visual, and memory factors aligning across the SB5 and WJ III as predicted.

Consequential Validity

Roid (2003b) reported on several studies of classification accuracy of using the SB5 to identify special groups with specific cut-points on SB5 scales. The most accurate classification creating the fewest consequential errors of identification is the use of SB5 to identify intellectual deficiency (mental retardation). A sample of 119 individuals, ages 5–18, previously identified and qualified for special education in school districts (based on IQ from other assessments, adaptive behavior, and direct observation) was contrasted with a matching control sample of 1,743 cases from the SB5 normative sample. Results showed that the traditional cut-point of 70 IQ accurately identified a total of 94.3% of the subjects, with 0.1% false negatives (true MR cases not identified) and 4.8% false positives (control subjects identified as MR). Sensitivity (proportion of only the true MR cases correctly identified) was 83.7%. These classification statistics are quite high compared to the similar studies by Roid (2003b) on giftedness (6.1% false positive, 70.1% sensitivity) or reading LD cases (17.2% false positive, 66.7% sensitivity).

Recent Published Validity Evidence

In a study of concurrent and construct validity of the working memory subtests in SB5, Pomplun and Custer (2005) found significant correlations between SB5 WM scores and reading achievement.

The association of this type of low-WM profile pattern with reading LD is consistent with the research of Reid, Hresko, and Swanson (1996). Also, the case study of Sean (Table 6.4) showed this pattern of low working memory subtests. The predictive power of the SB5 working memory scales for mathematics achievement was studied by Roid and Pomplun (2005) in a series of regression studies with WJ III mathematics scores (Mather & Woodcock, 2001a) as the criterion. The study found that the Working Memory Factor Index of SB5 added a significant increment of predictive power (2% to 4% based on squared multiple correlations) over and above the use of the Quantitative Reasoning (QR) Factor Index of SB5. Roid and Pomplun (2005) also found evidence that working memory measures are most powerful in predicting mathematics reasoning scores for students with below-average QR scores.

Dissertation Research Using the SB5

Two recent studies were completed under the supervision of Dr. Roid using the SB5 standardization and special-groups data: Tippin (2007) and McClellan and Roid (2007). In the Tippin (2007) study, learning disability cases were compared to normative control subjects (ages 5–13 years) using the 10 subtests of the SB5. The study included a sample of 129 students who were diagnosed with a reading LD. A total of 292 normative participants were selected from the SB5 standardization sample and used as a control group. This group was created by approximating the LD group on the stratification variables: gender, education level, and ethnicity. For example, 23.9% of the LD cases had parents with less than high school education, and the control sample was matched with 24%. Table 6.5 shows the means and standard deviations of the reading LD and control samples. Because the SB5 subtests have an expected mean of 10 and standard deviation of 3, the control group means are all in the 9–10 range.

Table 6.5 shows that the group with reading learning disabilities has low scores (relative weaknesses) on Nonverbal Quantitative Reasoning (7.88), Verbal Knowledge (7.88), and Nonverbal Fluid Reasoning (7.91). The highest group scores

TABLE 6.5   Means, Standard Deviation, and Effect Sizes for SB5 Subtest Scores in the Comparison of Learning Disability Cases to Controls

SB5 Subtests	Reading LD	Control	Effect Size
Nonverbal Fluid Reasoning	7.91 (3.10)	9.66 (3.06)	.57
Nonverbal Knowledge	8.41 (2.64)	9.84 (2.52)	.55
Nonverbal Quantitative Reasoning	7.88 (2.16)	9.72 (2.40)	.81
Nonverbal Visual-Spatial Processing	8.80 (3.02)	10.01(2.67)	.42
Nonverbal Working Memory	8.01 (3.00)	9.42 (2.60)	.50
Verbal Fluid Reasoning	8.35 (2.77)	9.82 (2.55)	.55
Verbal Knowledge	7.88 (2.67)	9.73 (2.54)	.71
Verbal Quantitative Reasoning	8.27 (2.31)	9.93 (2.30)	.72
Verbal Visual-Spatial Processing	8.86 (2.42)	9.99 (2.69)	.46
Verbal Working Memory	8.03 (3.10)	9.94 (2.26)	.70

(relative strengths) are Verbal Visual-Spatial Processing (8.86), Nonverbal Visual-Spatial Processing (8.80), and Nonverbal Knowledge (8.41). The effect sizes (standardized mean differences) ranged from four-tenths to eight-tenths of a standard deviation, considered as moderate to large in size (Cohen, 1988). The largest effects (all .70 or more) were for NVQR, VKN, VQR, and VWM, again showing the importance of verbal working memory and knowledge (vocabulary) in reading learning disabilities. A statistically significant group-mean difference between groups was identified using a multivariate analysis of variance (MANOVA; $F = 5.48$, $df = 20, 822$, $p < .001$).

McClellan and Roid (2007) conducted a study that included individuals aged 3–18 from four types of samples collected as part of the standardization of the SB5: (1) 22 individuals with documented orthopedic disabilities (9 with cerebral palsy, and 12 with other motor disabilities, identified by physicians), (2) 54 individuals with developmental delays, (3) 104 individuals with documented mental retardation, and (4) 211 normative cases from a stratified random sample of the United States (selected from the 4,800 cases in the SB5 standardization sample) selected to match the disability samples for age, gender, ethnicity, and parental education level. These special groups had higher proportions of males (63%) than females, more nonmajority ethnic origins (60% versus about 40% in the U.S. population), and fewer cases with college-level parental education (35%) as compared to the U.S. population (about 55%). Overall the 10 subtests of the SB5 significantly separated the four samples (Wilk's Lambda and F-tests from discriminant function analyses were significant below the .001 level). Compared to national average scaled scores of 10 (standard deviation of 3.0), the control sample averaged about 9.6 (average SD 2.8), the orthopedic sample 7.6 (SD 2.3), the developmental delay sample 6.5 (SD 3.2), and MR sample 3.6 (SD 2.4). Thus, effect sizes for sample differences were 1–3 SD units—extremely large affects due to the disability conditions. Findings suggest that

SB5 subtests and tasks that most clearly differentiate the orthopedic cases from DD or MR and control cases were those emphasizing speed of performance and manipulation of forms (Nonverbal Visual-Spatial, including the placement of pieces in a formboard or form completion using tangram-style pieces, and Nonverbal Working Memory, involving the tapping of blocks).

The current trend in cognitive and intellectual assessment has been to minimize the role of speeded performance, and to separate the measurement of processing speed into separate subtests. The separation of speed from general ability is crucial for the fair assessment of individuals with physical disabilities (Braden & Elliott, 2003). In designing or selecting accommodations to testing procedures, it is important to distinguish between "target" abilities and "access abilities" (Braden & Elliott, 2003). *Target* abilities are the content of the cognitive factors such as fluid reasoning in the SB5 subtests of that factor. *Access* abilities include seeing, feeling, writing, manipulating, and responding quickly to test questions. Obviously, accommodations must be designed to adjust the latter without affecting the former, if national norms are to be used in interpretation. Details of recommended accommodations are provided in Braden and Elliott (2003) and in Roid (2003b).

SUMMARY

The fifth edition of the Stanford-Binet Intelligence Scales revived many of the features considered strengths in previous editions—toys for children, functional age levels, and expanded ranges of scores for low- and high-functioning examinees. The SB5 was designed to meet the needs of educators and psychologists working with special education, preschool assessment, evaluation of individuals with mental retardation, gifted assessment, and other applications of previous editions of Stanford-Binet tests. A new emphasis was placed on assessment for adults and the elderly by extending the normative age range above 85 years old. This emphasis had surprising benefits to school-aged assessment of learning disabilities by bringing increased attention to working memory, a highly effective predictor of learning difficulties.

The seven years of SB5 development encompassed numerous complex steps including pilot studies of new items and subtests, nationwide testing of a very comprehensive Tryout edition, extensive normative data collection involving hundreds of examiners, and extensive reliability and validity studies. The age range of SB5, from age 2 to above 85 (with the oldest subject being 96), exceeded any of the previous editions and is also somewhat unique for a cognitive battery, except, again, for the WJ III Cognitive. The large normative sample (N = 4,800) also shows excellent match to the ethnic and socioeconomic characteristics of the U.S. population (U. S. Census Bureau, 2001).

The SB5 employed extensive fairness reviews by experts from various religious perspectives as well as those from representative ethnic, gender, and disability groups. Reviews of items, illustrations, and procedures were conducted by assessment professionals representing Buddhism, Christianity (both conservative and liberal denominations), Hinduism, Islam, and Judaism. Reviews were also conducted from the viewpoint of examinees with deafness and various disabilities. Ethnic perspectives were addressed by reviewers representing African American, Asian American or Pacific Islander, Hispanic American, and Native American or Alaskan Native populations.

Continuing the long tradition begun by Terman (1916), the SB5 shows high reliability among the IQ and Factor Index scores (.90–.98) and among the subtests (.84–.89) as compared to other tests. Correlations in the .80–.90 range with other IQ measures helped to verify the validity of the SB5 Full Scale IQ (Roid, 2003d). The five cognitive factors were shown to be related to other measures of the CHC factors in a cross-battery factor analysis of the SB5 and the WJ III Cognitive scales, verifying the theoretical basis of the factor design.

As discussed in the case study of Sean, who has a learning disability in reading, the SB5 was designed to allow for the prediction of early emerging learning disabilities (LD). Research has shown that several composites consisting of the Knowledge, Quantitative Reasoning, and Working Memory scores may be predictive of LD risk in ages 5–7 (Roid, 2003b), although additional research is needed. As discussed previously in this chapter, the composite scores and the Vocabulary (VKN) and Working Memory (VWM especially) are helpful in identifying LD prior to the beginning of schooling and the consequences of early academic failure. The SB5 scores do not *diagnose* LD, of course, but may be used as screening devices. The advantage of their use is that they can be used to assess cognitive strengths and weaknesses as required by the new IDEA (2004) reauthorization, without using the conventional discrepancy model. Further discussion of some of the issues of SB5 use can be found in the documented author interview by Roid, Shaughnessy, and Greathouse (2005).

REFERENCES

Achenbach, T. M. (2000). *Achenbach System of Empirically Based Assessment*. Burlington, VT: ASEBA.

Aldenderfer, M. S., & Blashfield, R. K. (1984). *Cluster analysis*. Newbury Park, CA: Sage.

American Academy of Pediatrics. (2000). Clinical practice guideline: Diagnosis and evaluation of children with attention-deficit/hyperactivity disorder. *Pediatrics, 105*, 1158–1170.

American Psychiatric Association (2000). *Diagnostic and statistical manual of mental disorders* (DSM-IV-TR) (4th ed.) (Text Revision). Washington, DC: Author.

AERA/APA/NCME: American Educational Research Association, American Psychological Association & National Council on Measurement in Education (1999). *Standards for educational and psychological testing*. Washington, DC: Author.

Baddeley, A. D. (1986). *Working memory*. Oxford: Clarendon Press.

Bannatyne, A. (1974). Diagnosis: A note on recategorization of the WISC scaled scores. *Journal of Learning Disabilities*, 7, 2.

Barkley, R. A. (1990). *Attention deficit hyperactivity disorder: A handbook for diagnosis and treatment*. New York: Guilford Press.

Binet, A., & Simon, T. (1905). Méthodes nouvelles pour le diagnostic du niveau intellectual des anormaux. *L'Année psychologique*, *11*, 191–336.

Binet, A., & Simon, T. (1916). *The development of intelligence in children*. (Translated by Elizabeth Kite). Baltimore: Williams & Wilkins.

Bracken, B. A., & McCallum, R. S. (1998). *The Universal Nonverbal Intelligence Test*. Austin, TX: Pro-Ed.

Braden, J. P., & Elliott, S. N. (2003). Accommodations on the Stanford-Binet Intelligence Scale—Fifth Edition (Assessment Service Bulletin No. 2). Rolling Meadows, IL: Riverside.

Butter, E. M., Mulick, J. A., & Metz, B. (2006). Eight case reports of learning recovery in children with pervasive developmental disorders after early intervention. *Behavioral Interventions*, *21*, 227–243.

Carr, J. (2005). Stability and change in cognitive ability over the life span: A comparison of populations with and without Down's syndrome. *Journal of Intellectual Disability Research*, *49*(12), 915–928.

Carroll, J. B. (1993). *Human cognitive abilities: A survey of factor-analytic studies*. Cambridge; New York: Cambridge University Press.

Cattell, R. B. (1943). The measurement of intelligence. *Psychological Bulletin*, *40*, 153–193.

Cohen, J. (1988). Statistical power analysis for the behavioral sciences (2nd ed.). Mahwah, NJ: Erlbaum.

Coltheart, M. (Ed.) (1987). *Attention and performance. Volume 12: The psychology of reading*. London: Erlbaum/Routledge.

Dana, R. H. (2005). *Multicultural assessment* (2nd ed.). Mahwah, NJ: Erlbaum.

Daneman, M., & Carpenter, P. A. (1980). Individual differences in working memory and reading. *Journal of Verbal Learning and Verbal Behavior*, *19*, 450–466.

Dunn, L. M., & Dunn, L. M. (1997). *Peabody Picture Vocabulary Test—Third Edition*. Circle Pines, MN: American Guidance Service/Pearson Assessments.

Dunn, L. M., Dunn, L. M., & NFER-Nelson (1997). *British Picture Vocabulary Scale—Second Edition*. London, UK: NFER-Nelson.

Farrant, B. M., Fletcher, J., & Maybery, M. T. (2006). Specific language impairment, theory of mind, and visual perspective taking: Evidence for simulation theory and the developmental role of language. *Child Development*, *77*(6), 1842–1853.

Feuerstein, R., Rand, Y., & Hoffman, M. D. (1979). *The dynamic assessment of retarded performers: The Learning Potential Assessment Device*. Baltimore: University Park Press.

Flanagan, D. P., & Ortiz, S. O. (2001). *Essentials of cross-battery assessment*. New York: Wiley.

Flemmer, D. D., & Roid, G. H. (1997). Nonverbal intellectual assessment of Hispanic and speech-impaired adolescents. *Psychological Reports*, *80*, 1115–1122.

Flynn, J. R. (1987). Massive IQ gains in 14 nations: What IQ tests really measure. *Psychological Bulletin*, *101*, 171–191.

Glenn, S., & Cunningham, C. (2005). Performance of young people with Down syndrome on the SB5 and British Picture Vocabulary Scales. *Journal of Intellectual Disability Research*, *49*(4), 239–244.

Gustafsson, J. E. (1984). A unifying model for the structure of intellectual abilities. *Intelligence*, *8*, 179–203.

Harcourt Assessment (1995). *Stanford Achievement Tests (SAT)*. San Antonio, TX: Author.

Harcourt Assessment (2001). *Wechsler Individual Achievement Test—Second Edition (WIAT-II)*. San Antonio, TX: Author.

Holland, P. W., & Wainer, H. (Eds.). (1993). *Differential item functioning*. Mahwah, NJ: Erlbaum.

Horn, J. L. (1965). *Fluid and crystallized intelligence*. Unpublished doctoral dissertation, University of Illinois, Urbana-Champaign.

Horn, J. L. (1985). Remodeling old models of intelligence. In B. B. Wolman (Ed.), *Handbook of intelligence* (pp. 267–300). New York: Wiley.

Horn, J. L. (1994). Theory of fluid and crystallized intelligence. In R. J. Sternberg (Ed.), *Encyclopedia of human intelligence* (pp. 443–451). New York: Macmillan.

Horn, J. L., & Cattell, R. B. (1966). Refinement and test of the theory of fluid and crystallized general intelligences. *Journal of Educational Psychology*, *57*, 253–270.

Horst, D. P., Tallmadge, G. K., & Wood, C. T. (1975). *A practical guide to measuring project impact on student achievement.* Washington, DC: U.S. Department of Education.

IDEA: Individuals with Disabilities Education Improvement Act (2004). Public Law No. 108-446, §632, 118 Stat. 2744.

Joreskog, K. G., & Sorbom, D. (1999). *LISREL 8: User's reference guide.* Chicago: Scientific Software.

Kamphaus, R. W. (2001). *Clinical assessment of child and adolescent intelligence* (2nd ed.). Boston: Allyn & Bacon.

Kaufman, A. S. (1994). Intelligent testing with the WISC-III. New York: Wiley.

Kaufman, A. S., & Kaufman, N. (1993). *Kaufman Adult Intelligence Test (KAIT).* Circle Pines, MN: American Guidance Service/Pearson Assessment.

Kaufman, A. S., & Lichtenberger, E. O. (1999). *Essentials of WAIS-III assessment.* New York: Wiley.

Leslie, L., & Caldwell, J. (2001). *Qualitative Reading Inventory—3 (QRI-3).* New York: Addison-Wesley Longman.

Lezak, M. D. (1995). *Neuropsychological assessment.* (3rd ed.). New York: Oxford University Press.

Lord, F. M. (1980). *Applications of item response theory to practical testing problems.* Mahwah, NJ: Erlbaum.

Mantel, N., & Haenszel, W. (1959). Statistical aspects of the analysis of data from retrospective studies of disease. *Journal of the National Cancer Institute, 22,* 719–748.

Mather, N., & Woodcock, R. W. (2001a). *WJ III Tests of Achievement examiner's manual.* Rolling Meadows, IL: Riverside.

Mather, N., & Woodcock, R. W. (2001b). *WJ III Tests of Cognitive Abilities examiner's manual.* Rolling Meadows, IL: Riverside.

McClellan, M., & Roid, G. H. (2007, August). *Comparison of developmental delay, mental retardation, and orthopedic disability groups with the Stanford-Binet 5 subtests.* Paper presented at the meetings of the American Psychological Association, San Francisco.

McConaughy, S. H., & Achenbach, T. M. (2004). *Manual for the Test Observation Form for Ages 2–18.* Burlington, VT: ASEBA.

McDermott, P. A., Fantuzzo, J. W., & Glutting, J. J. (1990). Just say no to subtest analysis: A critique on Wechsler theory and practice. *Journal of Psychoeducational Assessment, 8,* 290–302.

McGrew, K. S., & Flanagan, D. P. (1998). *The intelligence test desk reference (ITDR): Cf-Gc cross battery assessment.* Boston: Allyn & Bacon.

McGrew, K. S., & Woodcock, R. W. (2001). *Woodcock-Johnson III: Technical manual.* Rolling Meadows, IL: Riverside.

Naglieri, J. A., & Bornstein, B. T. (2003). Intelligence and achievement: Just how correlated are they? *Journal of Psychoeducational Assessment, 21,* 244–260.

Norusis, M. J. (1990). *SPSS base system user's guide.* Chicago: SPSS.

Nunnally, J. C. (1967). *Psychometric theory.* New York: McGraw-Hill.

Paniagua, F. A. (2005). *Assessing and treating culturally diverse clients: A practical guide* (3rd ed.). Thousand Oaks, CA: Sage.

Peterson, L. R. (1966). Short-term memory. *Scientific American, 215,* 90–95.

Pomplun, M. & Custer, M. (2005). The construct validity of the Stanford-Binet 5 measures of working memory. *Assessment, 10*(10), 1–9.

Rasch, G. (1980). *Probabilistic models for some intelligence and attainment tests.* Chicago: University of Chicago Press.

Reid, D. K., Hresko, W. P., & Swanson, H. L. (1996). *Cognitive approaches to learning disabilities.* Austin, TX: Pro-Ed.

Roid, G. H. (1994). Patterns of writing skills derived from cluster analysis of direct-writing assessments. *Applied Measurement in Education, 7*(2), 159–170.

Roid, G. H. (2003a). *Stanford-Binet Intelligence Scales —Fifth Edition, Examiner's manual.* Rolling Meadows, IL: Riverside.

Roid, G. H. (2003b). *Stanford-Binet Intelligence Scales —Fifth Edition, Interpretive manual.* Rolling Meadows, IL: Riverside.

Roid, G. H. (2003c). *Stanford-Binet Intelligence Scales —Fifth Edition (SB5), Scoring pro.* [Computer software]. Rolling Meadows, IL: Riverside.

Roid, G. H. (2003d). *Stanford-Binet Intelligence Scale —Fifth Edition, Technical manual.* Rolling Meadows, IL: Riverside.

Roid, G. H. (2005a). *Stanford-Binet Intelligence Scales for Early Childhood—Fifth Edition manual.* Rolling Meadows, IL: Riverside.

Roid, G. H. (2005b). Interpretation of SB5 or early SB5 factor index scores. Technical bulletin (available at www.stanford-binet.com). Rolling Meadows, IL: Riverside.

Roid, G. H. (2006). Linking SB5 assessment to instruction and intervention for children, Ages 2 to 16: SB5 Technical Note #01-2006 (available from Riverside).

Roid, G. H., & Barram, R. A. (2004). *Essentials of Stanford-Binet Intelligence Scales (SB5) assessment*. Hoboken, NJ: Wiley.

Roid, G. H., & Carson, A. D. (2004). Special composite scores for the SB5: Assessment Service Bulletin #4. Rolling Meadows, IL: Riverside.

Roid, G. H., & Miller, L. J. (1997). *Leiter International Performance Scale—Revised*. Wood Dale, IL: Stoelting.

Roid, G. H., & Miller, L. J. (1999). *Stoelting Brief Intelligence Scale manual*. Wood Dale, IL: Stoelting.

Roid, G. H., & Pomplun, M. (2005). Interpreting the Stanford-Binet Intelligence Scales—Fifth Edition. In D. P. Flanagan & P. L. Harrison (Eds.), *Contemporary intellectual assessment: Theories, tests, and issues* (pp. 325–343). New York: Guilford.

Roid, G. H., Prifitera, A., & Weiss, L.G. (1993). Replication of the WISC-III factor structure in an independent sample. *Journal of Psychoeducational Assessment*, *11*, 6–21.

Roid, G. H., Shaughnessy, M. F., & Greathouse, D. (2005). An interview with Gale Roid about the Stanford-Binet 5. *North American Journal of Psychology*, 7(3), 493–504.

Sattler, J. M. (1988). *Assessment of children* (3rd ed.). San Diego: Author.

Sattler, J. M. (2001). *Assessment of children: Cognitive applications* (4th ed.). La Mesa, CA: Author.

Tellegen, A., & Briggs, P. F. (1967). Old wine in new skins: Grouping Wechsler subtests into new scales. *Journal of Consulting Psychology*, *31*, 499–506.

Terman, L. M. (1916). *The measurement of intelligence: An explanation of and a complete guide for the use of the Stanford revision and extension of the Binet-Simon Scale*. Boston: Houghton Mifflin.

Terman, L. M., & Merrill, M. A. (1937). *Measuring intelligence*. Boston: Houghton Mifflin.

Terman, L. M., & Merrill, M. A. (1960). *Stanford-Binet Intelligence Scale: Manual for the Third Revision Form L-M*. Boston: Houghton Mifflin.

Terman, L. M., & Merrill, M. A. (1973). *Stanford-Binet Intelligence Scale: Manual for the Third Revision Form L-M. (1972 Norm Tables by R. L. Thorndike)*. Boston: Houghton Mifflin.

Thorndike, R. L., Hagen, E. P., & Sattler, J. M. (1986). *The Stanford-Binet Intelligence Scale—Fourth Edition guide for administering and scoring*. Rolling Meadows, IL: Riverside Publishing.

Tippin, S. M. (2007). *Stanford-Binet Profile differences between normative children and those with learning disabilities or ADHD*. Unpublished doctoral dissertation, George Fox University.

Tsatsanis, K. D., Dartnall, N., Cicchetti, D., Sparrow, S. S., Klin, A., & Volkmar, F. R. (2003). Concurrent validity and classification accuracy of the Leiter and Leiter-R in low-functioning children with autism. *Journal of Autism and Developmental Disorders*, *33*(1), 23–30.

U. S. Census Bureau. (2001). *Census 2000 Summary File 1 United States*. Washington, DC: Author.

Wainer, H. (Ed.). (1990). *Computerized adaptive testing: A primer*. Hillsdale, NJ: Erlbaum.

Ward, J. (1963). Hierarchical grouping to optimize an objective function. *Journal of the American Statistical Association*, *56*, 236–244.

Webster, P. E., Plante, A. S., & Couvillion, L. M. (1997). Phonological impairment and prereading: Update on a longitudinal study. *Journal of Learning Disabilities*, *30*(4), 365–375.

Wechsler, D. (1991). *Wechsler Intelligence Scale for Children—Third Edition*. San Antonio, TX: The Psychological Corporation.

Wechsler, D. (1992). *Wechsler Individual Achievement Test (WIAT)*. San Antonio, TX: The Psychological Corporation.

Wechsler, D. (1997). *Wechsler Adult Intelligence Scale—Third Edition*. San Antonio, TX: The Psychological Corporation.

Wechsler, D. (2003). *Wechsler Intelligence Scale for Children—Fourth Edition*. San Antonio, TX: The Psychological Corporation.

Woodcock, R. W. (1999). What can Rasch-based scores convey about a person's test performance? In S. E. Embretson & S. L. Hershberger (Eds.), *The new rules of measurement: What every psychologist and educator should know* (pp. 105–128). Mahwah, NJ: Erlbaum.

Woodcock, R. W., & Dahl, M. N. (1971). A common scale for the measurement of person ability and test item difficulty (AGS Paper #10). Circle Pines, MN: American Guidance Service.

Woodcock, R. W., & Johnson, M. B. (1989). *Woodcock-Johnson—Revised, Tests of Achievement*. Rolling Meadows, IL: Riverside.

Woodcock, R. W., & Mather, N. (1989). *Woodcock-Johnson—Revised, Tests of Cognitive Abilities*. Rolling Meadows, IL: Riverside.

Wright, B. D., & Linacre, J. M. (1999). *WINSTEPS: Rasch analysis for all two-facet models*. Chicago: MESA Press.

The Wechsler Intelligence Scale for Children—Fourth Edition

Louise O'Donnell

THEORY UNDERLYING THE WISC-IV

The Wechsler Intelligence Scales are the most well known and widely used measures of cognitive abilities. The Wechsler Intelligence Scale for Children—Fourth Edition (WISC-IV; Wechsler, 2003a, b) is the latest version of an individually administered instrument designed to measure the cognitive functioning of children between the ages of 6 years, 0 months and 16 years, 11 months. The WISC-IV has lengthy historical roots that can be traced back to two group-administered examinations (Army Alpha and Beta) and the Wechsler-Bellevue Form I and II, published by David Wechsler in 1939 and 1946 respectively, and to the more direct predecessors of the WISC-IV, the Wechsler Intelligence Scale for Children (WISC), published in 1949, followed by two subsequent revisions: the Wechsler Intelligence Scale for Children—Revised (WISC-R), in 1974, and the Wechsler Intelligence Scale for Children—Third Edition (WISC-III), in 1991. Other Wechsler cognitive assessment lines include a preschool measure for children ages

2 years, 6 months to 7 years, 3 months (current version: Wechsler Preschool and Primary Scale of Intelligence—Third Edition; Wechsler, 2002) and an adult assessment instrument for persons ages 17 years, 0 months to 89 years, 11 months (latest version: Wechsler Adult Intelligence Scale—Third Edition; Wechsler, 1997).

The Army Alpha and Beta instruments were developed by a task force of experimental psychologists, headed by Robert Yerkes, to screen World War I military recruits. The Army Alpha exam required that the examinee read test instructions, whereas Army Beta did not require English literacy. Although the item content has been updated, the basic task demands of the Army Beta subtests are similar to a number of current WISC-IV subtests. For example, on both the Army Beta subtest and the WISC-IV Picture Completion subtest, the examinee looks at a set of pictures, each with a critical part missing, and, whereas the examinee drew in the missing element on the Army Beta, on the Picture Completion subtest the examinee is required to point to the missing element. The Coding and Block Design subtests can also trace their beginnings to the Army Beta (Tulsky, Saklofske, & Ricker, 2003), and early versions of the Digit Span, Information, and Arithmetic subtests are found in the Army Alpha (Wasserman & Tulsky, 2005).

Employment of a summary measure of intelligence (the Full Scale IQ score) and utilization of tasks that sample a range of cognitive abilities, scale aspects present in the WISC-IV, reflect the theoretical influences of Charles Spearman and Edward Thorndike, respectively. These individuals were promoting two distinctly different approaches to intelligence and its measurement when Wechsler developed his Wechsler-Bellevue scales. According to Spearman, the construct of intelligence consisted of a general factor, g, that was a mediating influence on behavior. Wechsler viewed intelligence as a "global entity aggregated of specific abilities that are qualitatively different" (Zhu & Weiss, 2005). He also defined *intelligence* as "the aggregate or global capacity of the individual to act purposefully, to think rationally and to deal effectively with his environment" (Wechsler, 1939). Use of the FSIQ score operationalized the measurement of g or *global ability*.

Test design or structure influences the types of assessment interpretations possible. Kamphaus, Winsor, Rowe, and Kim (2005) trace the history of the Wechsler scales through four distinct interpretation periods: classification, clinical profile analysis, factor-based analysis, and theory-driven interpretation. In the first wave, the main emphasis was on classification into distinct intellectual groups ranging from defective to superior based on summary IQ scores. While Wechsler recognized that the summary score (Full Scale IQ) was psychometrically robust, he also cautioned users to keep in mind that IQ scores do not represent absolute quantities, and that when using summary scores for classification or diagnostic purposes it was important to consider multiple sources of information (Wechsler, 1958).

The Wechsler-Bellevue subtests were divided into either verbal or performance measures. This verbal–performance dichotomy reflected Wechsler's view that general intelligence could be measured using two types of tests: those that were

verbal and those that were nonverbal in content. According to Flanagan and Kaufman (2004), the main purpose of the second (profile analysis) phase was to identify common clinical profiles based on verbal and performance subtest scatter and even patterns of responses to individual items. This approach, typified by Rapaport, Gill, and Schafer (1968), was soon criticized on the grounds that the clinically intuitive profiles did not reliably differentiate clinical groups from one another and from typically developing children.

The third phase of Wechsler interpretation (factor-based analysis) was fueled by simultaneous advances in computer technology and inferential statistics. Cohen (1959) challenged the verbal–performance discrepancy method of interpretation with his factor analysis of the WISC standardization data. Based on a sample of 200 children from three age groups, he identified five factors, three of which had significant loadings: Factor I—Verbal Comprehension, Factor II—Perceptual Organization, and Factor III—Freedom from Distractibility. Kaufman (1979) is credited with developing a systematic method of factor-based interpretation to replace the traditional verbal–performance IQ strengths and weaknesses approach. These factors and their corresponding labels were maintained across the WISC-R and WISC-III, though the WISC-III added a fourth factor: Processing Speed.

The search for a distinct pattern of Wechsler subtests that could reliably differentiate clinical groups from one another and from typically developing children continued with the WISC-R and to some degree with the WISC-III. For example, Dykman, Ackerman and Oglesby (1980) found lower WISC-R mean scores on the Arithmetic, Coding, Information, and Digit Span (ACID) subtests in a group of children with *attention deficit hyperactivity disorder (ADHD)*. Using the WISC-III standardization sample, Prifitera and Dersh (1993) found that the ACID profile was very rare (1.1%) in the typically developing children who comprised the standardization sample but was more common in clinical groups of children with learning disabilities (5.1%) and

ADHD (12.3%). They concluded that, although the ACID profile did not distinguish children with ADHD from children with learning disabilities, the ACID profile was useful in discriminating clinical and nonclinical performance.

The fourth and current phase involves the incorporation of theory-driven constructs drawn from research advances in human cognition and information processing. With the addition of new subtests and refinement of existing constructs, the WISC-IV joins the ranks of theory-driven assessment instruments such as the Differential Abilities Scales—Second Edition (Elliott, 2007), Cognitive Assessment System (Das & Naglieri, 1997), and the Woodcock-Johnson-III (Woodcock, McGrew, & Mather, 2001).

The Cattell-Horn-Carroll (CHC) theory of cognitive abilities provides a useful model from which to appreciate the construct modifications in the WISC-IV. CHC theory is the result of an integration of the Cattell-Horn Gf-Gc theory (Horn & Blankson, 2005) with Carroll's three-stratum theory (Carroll, 1993). Catell divided cognitive abilities into two general areas: those that drew on *fluid* intelligence (novel, *in-vivo* problem-solving abilities) and those that tapped *crystallized* intelligence (acquired knowledge). Horn expanded the model, adding quantitative knowledge (Gq), visual perception (Gv), short-term memory (Gsm), long-term storage and retrieval (Glr), speed of processing (Gs), auditory processing ability (Ga), correct decision speed (CDS), and reading/writing (Grw) (Alfonso, Flanagan, & Radwan, 2005). Carroll's three-stratum theory is based on factor analysis of 460 data sets of cognitive abilities. He found evidence for stratum III general intelligence or *g* factor, and stratum II, which consisted of eight broad categories of cognitive abilities: fluid intelligence, crystallized intelligence, general memory and learning, broad visual perception, broad auditory perception, broad retrieval ability, broad cognitive speediness, and decision/reaction time. Stratum I consists of narrow abilities or subsets of the stratum II abilities.

For example, speech sound and general sound discrimination are specific abilities that are part of the broad auditory perception construct—a stratum II ability.

DESCRIPTION OF THE TEST

Subtest Background and Structure

The WISC-IV has a total of 15 subtests that are divided into 10 core subtests and 5 supplemental subtests. Table 7.1 provides a brief description of what the child is asked to accomplish for each of the subtests.

Scales the Test Yields

In addition to Full Scale IQ, the WISC-IV interpretive foundation consists of four factor indices: Verbal Comprehension Index (VCI), Perceptual Reasoning Index (PRI), Working Memory Index (WMI), and Processing Speed Index (PSI).

Verbal comprehension is defined as a measure of verbal concept formation, verbal reasoning, and knowledge acquired from one's environment (Wechsler, 2003b, p. 14).

The WISC-IV (VCI) consists of the following core subtests: Similarities, Vocabulary, and Comprehension. The Information and Word Reasoning subtests are supplemental subtests. According to CHC theory, *crystallized intelligence/knowledge* (Gc) is defined as acquired knowledge, information, and concepts specific to a culture. It is a store of verbal or language-based declarative (knowing what) and procedural knowledge (knowing how) based on experience.

The *Perceptual Reasoning Index* (PRI) includes the Block Design, Picture Concepts, and Matrix Reasoning subtests. Picture Completion is a supplemental subtest. The label change from perceptual *organization* index (WISC-III) to perceptual *reasoning* index (PRI) "reflects the increased emphasis on fluid reasoning abilities in

TABLE 7.1   Description of the WISC-IV Subtests

Subtest	Description
Block Design	While viewing a constructed model or a picture in the Stimulus Book, the child uses red-and-white blocks to re-create the design within a specified time limit.
Similarities	The child is presented two words that represent common objects or concepts and describes how they are similar.
Digit Span	For Digit Span Forward, the child repeats numbers in the same order as presented aloud by the examiner. For Digit Span Backward, the child repeats numbers in the reverse order of that presented aloud by the examiner.
Picture Concepts	The child is presented with two or three rows of pictures and chooses one picture from each row to form a group with a common characteristic.
Coding	The child copies symbols that are paired with simple geometric shapes or numbers. Using a key, the child draws each symbol in its corresponding shape or box within a specified time limit.
Vocabulary	For Picture Items, the child names pictures that are displayed in the Stimulus Book. For Verbal Items, the child gives definitions for words that the examiner reads aloud.
Letter-Number Sequencing	The child is read a sequence of numbers and letters and recalls the numbers in ascending order and the letters in alphabetical order.
Matrix Reasoning	The child looks at an incomplete matrix and selects the missing portion from five response options.
Comprehension	The child answers questions based on his or her understanding of general principles and social situations.
Symbol Search	The child scans a search group and indicates whether the target symbol(s) matches any of the symbols in the search group within a specified time limit.
Picture Completion	The child views a picture and then points to or names the important part missing within a specified time limit.
Cancellation	The child scans both a random and a structured arrangement of pictures and marks target pictures within a specified time limit.
Information	The child answers questions that address a broad range of general knowledge topics.
Arithmetic	The child mentally solves a series of orally presented arithmetic problems within a specified time limit.
Word Reasoning	The child identifies the common concept being described in a series of clues.

this index" (Wechsler, 2003b, pg. 14). Fluid reasoning involves the use of mental operations to solve novel tasks. These mental operations include making inferences and the use of inductive and deductive reasoning strategies.

The *Working Memory Index* (WMI) includes the Digit Span and Letter–Number Sequencing subtests. The Arithmetic subtest is a supplemental subtest. A number of the researchers (Denckla, 1994; Pennington & Ozonoff, 1996) have defined working memory as the temporary holding of representations for the duration of a task. Working Memory is viewed as the process that controls retrieval and utilization of acquired knowledge and allows the individual to act on the basis of represented rather than immediately presented information.

The *Processing Speed Index* (PSI) includes the Coding and Symbol Search Subtests with the Cancellation subtest as optional. Within the CHC framework, these subtests tap speed of processing (Gs) functioning.

Other Relevant Issues

For school and clinical practitioners who need to compare current WISC-IV performance with previous WISC-III scores, the issue of FSIQ and index score comparability is relevant. To understand this issue, it is necessary to examine a number of influences that can contribute to score differences. At the most basic level, if all items including subtest administration and scoring instructions on the WISC-III remained unchanged, and the instrument was given to a new age-appropriate cohort of children, there would be score differences due to the Flynn effect (Flynn, 1998). The *Flynn effect* refers to the systematic rise in IQ scores over time due to better performance of subsequent typically developing populations on the test. Prifitera, Weiss, Saklofske, and Rolfhus (2005) report, based on the performance of children who took WISC-IV and WISC-III in counterbalanced order, that on average there was a 2.5 higher score difference for WISC-III. Although 10 of the subtests from

WISC-III are present in the WISC-IV, there has been modification in item content, artwork, and administration and scoring instructions—all of which contribute to subtest and ultimately Full Scale score differences between the two instruments. The third and most significant change has been in the makeup of the factor indices, as discussed previously, and the inclusion of all core subtests from the Working Memory (WMI) and Processing Speed Indices (PSI) in the calculation of the WISC-IV FSIQ score. To assist examiners with interpretation of current WISC-IV factor and Full Scale IQ scores compared with corresponding WISC-III scores, Wechsler (2003b, p. 63) provides ranges of expected scores. Because of the major changes in the composition of the WISC-IV PR index compared with the WISC-III Perceptual Organization Index, it is not unreasonable to expect more variability. In contrast, the VCI and PS indices are relatively unchanged, so it is expected that the two scores will be more similar, although not identical to each other.

In response to examiner concerns over the increased contributions of the WMI and PSI in the WISC-IV FSIQ score, the General Ability Index (GAI) score was developed as an alternative. The GAI equivalents of sums of scales scores are available in the WISC-IV General Ability Index Technical Report #4. The GAI score will be discussed in more detail in the next section.

The WISC-IV yields four index scores (VCI, PRI, WMI, PSI), a Full Scale IQ (FSIQ) score and, as an alternative to FSIQ, the General Ability Index (GAI). Figure 7.1 lists these four factor composites and the subtests and supplemental subtests that comprise each factor.

The factor indices have replaced the traditional Verbal IQ (VIQ) and Performance IQ (PIQ) scores. As can be seen by the comparisons between the subtests that contribute to the WISC-IV factor scores and the WISC-III factor and verbal–performance scores, (Tables 7.2 and 7.3), the Interpretive focus is now squarely centered on the factor-based scores rather than

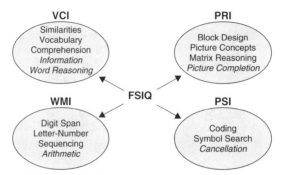

Note: Supplemental Subtests are shown in italics

Source: Administration and Scoring Manual of the Wechsler Intelligence
Scale for Children—Fourth Edition. Copyright © 2003 by NCS Pearson,
Inc. Reproduced with permission. Portions of this report are protected
by copyright. Copyright © 2005 by Harcourt Assessment, Inc.
Normative Data copyright © 2004, 2003 by Harcourt Assessment, Inc.

FIGURE 7.1

WISC-IV Test Framework

TABLE 7.2   WISC-IV, WISC-III VCI, and VIQ Comparisons

WISC-IV VCI	WISC-III VCI	WISC-III VIQ
Similarities	Similarities	Similarities
Vocabulary	Vocabulary	Vocabulary
Comprehension	Comprehension	Comprehension
*Information	Information	Information
*Word Reasoning		Arithmetic
		**Digit Span

*Supplemental subtest.
**Substitute for Arithmetic only.

TABLE 7.3   WISC-IV PRI, WISC-III POI, and PIQ Comparisons

WISC-IV PRI	WISC-III POI	WISC-III PIQ
Block Design	Block Design	Block Design
Picture Concepts	Picture Arrangement	Picture Arrangement
Matrix Reasoning	Object Assembly	Object Assembly
*Picture Completion	Picture Completion	Picture Completion
		Coding
		**Symbol Search

*Supplemental subtest.
**Substitute for Coding only.

on the multifactorial VIQ or PIQ scores. The WISC-III VIQ score included subtest scores from the Freedom from Distractibility (Working Memory) factor and the WISC-III PIQ score included scores from the Processing Speed factor.

The practice of combining total scores on Digit Span Forward and Digit Span Backward to form the Digit Span subtest score used in generating the WMI composite has continued, although separate scaled score information for

each of the two tasks is available to aid interpretation. The Cancellation subtest has two items (random and structured) whose combined raw score total is used to generate scaled score information if the subtest is substituted for either Symbol Search or Coding in the Processing Speed index. Separate scaled score information for each Cancellation item, however, is available to evaluate performance separately.

The WISC-IV yields an FSIQ score consisting of scores from each of the 10 core subtests (see Table 7.4). The inclusion of scores from all four core Working Memory and Processing Speed subtests places the working memory skills and processing speed abilities on equal psychometric footing with verbal and nonverbal reasoning skills in measuring intelligence. Recent research (Colom, Rebello, Palacios, Juan-Espinosa, & Kyllonen, 2004; Fry & Hale, 1996, 2000; Heinz-Martin, Oberauer, Wittman, Wilhelm, & Schulze, 2002) has affirmed the contributions of these two factors to overall *g*.

In response to examiner concerns over the increased contributions of the WMI and PSI in the WISC-IV FSIQ score, the General Ability Index (GAI) score was developed as an alternative. The GAI equivalents of sums of scales scores are available in the WISC-IV General Ability Index Technical Report #4 (Raiford, Weiss, Rolfhus, & Coalson, 2005), available free-of-charge from the website: harcourtassessment.com. Consisting of scores from the three core subtests from the Verbal Comprehension index and three core subtests from the Perceptual Reasoning index, the General Ability Index (GAI) is available for practitioners to use if there is significant variability between working memory and verbal comprehension scores, between processing speed and perceptual reasoning, or between working memory and processing speed, and/or significant scatter within the working memory or processing speed indices.

ADMINISTRATION AND SCORING

Tips on Administration

A reliable and valid administration requires the successful coordination of a number of key elements. The examiner must enlist and maintain the child's cooperation and provide a favorable testing environment where the child feels capable of demonstrating his or her best efforts. These interactions form the emotional context of the assessment process and set the stage for the procedural elements. Procedural elements include adherence to instructions so that administration is standard, along with maintaining an adequate pace while observing test session behavior and accurately recording all responses. The interested reader should consult Sattler (2008) for a discussion of general testing guidelines applicable across cognitive, psychoeducational, and behavioral assessments. Administration of the WISC-IV is straightforward and with practice is easy to administer in a standardized fashion. The following tips are offered to aid in the administration process:

Materials

1. Check to make sure the test kit is complete. Table 2.1 (p. 19) of the *WISC-IV Administration and Scoring Manual* (Wechsler, 2003a) contains a list of materials included in the WISC-IV test kit.

2. Examiners should supply a stopwatch, which is used for subtests with time limits (Block

TABLE 7.4 FSIQ and GAI Comparisons

WISC-IV FSIQ	WISC-IV GAI	WISC-III FSIQ
Similarities	Similarities	Similarities
Vocabulary	Vocabulary	Vocabulary
Comprehension	Comprehension	Comprehension
Block Design	Block Design	Block Design
Picture Concepts	Picture Concepts	Information
Matrix Reasoning	Matrix Reasoning	Arithmetic
Digit Span		Picture Arrangement
Letter–Number Sequencing		Object Assembly
Coding		Coding
Symbol Search		Picture Completion

Design, Coding, Symbol Search, and Cancellation).

3. Examiners should also plan to use a clipboard during administration because the WISC-IV Record Form contains the correct responses for a number of the subtests and attaching the record form to the clipboard and holding it in your lap will prevent the child from glimpsing answers.

4. It is fairly common practice for school psychologists to provide assessment services to multiple schools and, unlike private practice where the child and family come to the office for services, school psychologists travel to the school where the child is enrolled. In the interest of saving space and weight, the *WISC-IV Technical and Interpretive Manual* (Wechsler 2003b) can be left in the home office because it is not required for administration and scoring activities. All other materials listed in Table 2.1 are necessary.

5. The *WISC-IV Administration and Scoring Manual* contains crackback binding that allows it to be freestanding during administration. It is recommended that the examiner bend the crackback binder a number of times to work out the stiffness so that it is able to easily stand and to prevent unexpected toppling when first used.

6. Arrange materials so that you have easy access to them during administration. This will contribute to a smooth testing pace and make it easier to keep the child engaged in the process. Fumbling for materials wastes time, and with a child who is easily distracted, may require multiple redirection efforts.

Practice

1. Be familiar with the administration procedures so that you are able to make eye contact while reading instructions verbatim. Prior to testing, read Chapters 2 and 3 of the *Administration and Scoring Manual*. The instructions

are straightforward with spoken text clearly highlighted in green ink.

2. Conduct a practice administration. Read the instructions verbatim, use the stimulus book, and time and record responses. Be sure to include sample items and items that have additional trials in the practice testing.

3. Know the general scoring principals and become familiar with the sample item responses for the verbal subtests. Being familiar with the range of sample responses associated with an item will help you maintain an even administration pace and know when to query for more information with ambiguous responses and when to apply discontinue rules.

Administration

1. Do not allow children to turn the stimulus book pages as rough handling may cause the pages to rip. Instead provide other opportunities where the child can be helpful. The child, for example, could place the Block Design blocks into the container when the subtest is finished.

2. Review Chapter 2 of the *WISC-IV Administration and Scoring Manual* as it provides detailed information on start points, reverse rules, and discontinue rules. See Table 7.5 in this chapter for a summary of the start points and reverse and discontinue rules. As in previous editions, children with suspected cognitive impairment may begin subtests with earlier items. Administration rules are also located on the Record Form.

3. On the majority of the subtests, administration is discontinued when the child fails a specified number of items consecutively. If it was necessary to reverse items to obtain a basal, these items should be included in the discontinue criteria. There are, however, three exceptions to the consecutive failure rule. Items 1–3 of the Block Design subtest and the Digit Span subtest require failure on two trials before an item is counted as a failed

TABLE 7.5 Summary of WISC-IV Start Points and Reverse and Discontinue Rules

Summary of Start Points, Reverse Rules, and Discontinue Rules

Subtest	Start Point	Reverse Rule	Discontinue Rule
BD	6–7: Item 1 8–16: Item 3	8–16: Score of **0** or **1** on *either* of the first two items given, administer preceding items in reverse order until two consecutive perfect scores are obtained.	After **3** consecutive scores of 0
SI	6–8: Sample, then Item 1 9–11: Sample, then Item 3 12–16: Sample, then Item 5	9–16: Score of **0** or **1** on *either* of the first two items given, administer preceding items in reverse order until two consecutive perfect scores are obtained.	After **5** consecutive scores of 0
DS	6–16: Forward: Item 1 Backward: Sample, then Item 1	None	Forward: After scores of 0 on *both trials* of an item Backward: After scores of 0 on *both trials* of an item
PCn	6–8: Samples A & B, then Item 1 9–11: Samples A & B, then Item 5 12–16: Samples A & B, then Item 7	9–16: Score of **0** on *either* of the first two items given, administer preceding items in reverse order until two consecutive perfect scores are obtained.	After **5** consecutive scores of **0**
CD	6–7: Coding A Sample Items, then Test Items 8–16: Coding B Sample Items, then Test Items	None	After **120** seconds
VC	6–8: Item 5 9–11: Item 7 12–16: Item 9	6–16: Score of **0** or **1** on *either* of the first two items given, administer preceding items in reverse order until two consecutive perfect scores are obtained.	After **5** consecutive scores of **0**
LN	6–7: Qualifying Items, Sample Item, then Item 1 8–16: Sample Item, then Item 1	None	If the child is unable to respond correctly to either Qualifying Item *or* after scores of **0** on *all three trials* of an item.

SOURCE : *Wechsler Intelligence Scale for Children—Fourth Edition.* Copyright © 2003 by NCS Pearson, Inc. Reproduced with permission. All rights reserved.

and the Letter–Number Sequencing subtest requires failure on all three trials.

4. Know the subtest substitution rules so that you can apply them successfully if the need arises:

   a. Either the Information or Word Reasoning subtests can be substituted for one of the following Verbal Comprehension subtests: Similarities, Vocabulary, or Comprehension.

   b. The Picture Completion subtest can replace one of the Perceptual Reasoning subtests (Block Design, Picture Concepts, or Matrix Reasoning).

   c. The Arithmetic subtest can be substituted for either the Digit Span or Letter–Number Sequencing subtests and the Cancellation subtest can replace either one of the Coding or Symbol Search subtests.

   d. Although there is the possibility of substitution in each one of the four indices, when calculating a Full Scale IQ score, no more than two substitutions are allowed.

5. The following subtest suggestions cover subtle administration issues that the examiner may overlook:

   a. *Block Design:* It is important to present the blocks so that a variety of colors are facing up. Initial presentation of blocks for the four-block items should have only one red-and-white side facing up and for 9-block items should have two red-and-white sides facing up. Additionally, be sure to scramble the blocks between items.

   b. *Similarities, Picture Concepts, Matrices, and Word Reasoning:* Regardless of the child's starting point, be sure to administer the sample item(s).

   c. *Digit Span:* Present the digits at the rate of one per second. Avoid chunking the

digits, which is easy to do inadvertently with long strings of numbers.

   d. *Coding:* For children who are left-handed and whose hand partially blocks the key during the sample items, be sure to place an extra Response Booklet to the right of the child and have the child practice the items using this key.

   e. *Vocabulary:* Be sure to say "Listen carefully, what does [insert item] mean?" if the child has misheard the word.

   f. *Letter–Number Sequencing:* Regardless of the child's age, if you are unsure whether the child knows the alphabet or is able to count sequentially, administer the two qualifying items before subtest administration.

   g. *Comprehension:* For items marked with an asterisk on the Record Form and in the *Administration Manual*, ask for a second response if the child's response contains only one idea.

   h. *Symbol Search:* If the child skips an item, say "Do them in order. Don't skip any."

   i. *Picture Completion:* Be sure to provide the following prompts and queries only once during the subtest. If the child names the object instead of identifying the missing part, say "Yes, but what is missing?" If the child mentions a part that is off the page, say "A part is missing in the picture. What is it that is missing?" If the child identified an unessential part, say "Yes, but what is the most important part missing?"

   j. *Cancellation:* Be sure to correct errors during the practice item.

   k. *Information:* Pay close attention to the additional queries required for items marked with an asterisk in the *Administration and Scoring Manual*.

   l. *Arithmetic:* Note that when the child asks for a repetition of an item, timing continues.

How to Score the Test

Accurate score generation and comprehensive recording of responses go hand-in-hand. This is especially important if scoring is not done immediately after administration.

While scoring of the WISC-IV is uncomplicated, it is easy to make computation and other scoring errors.

Suggested Subtest Scoring Tips
to Reduce Errors

1. Because the WISC-IV subtest normative information is presented in four-month intervals, it is important to calculate the child's age at testing, including year, month, and day. Also note that all months are assumed to have 30 days and that there is no rounding of days up to the next month.

2. When determining subtest raw score totals, be sure to credit items below the basal item or starting point. Also do not give credit for items correctly answered after the discontinue rule has been met.

3. On the Picture Concepts and Matrix Reasoning subtests, make sure that each circled item response matches the corresponding item score. The same procedure applies to the recorded responses and corresponding scores for the Digit Span, Letter–Number Sequencing, Picture Completion, Information, and Arithmetic subtests.

4. On the Block Design subtest make sure that items receiving credit have been correctly completed within the allotted time.

5. Note that the first two items of the Similarities subtest and the Picture items of the Vocabulary subtest are scored 0 or 1, whereas all other subtest items on these two subtests are scored 0, 1, or 2 points.

6. Consult the sample responses sections of the Similarities, Vocabulary, and Comprehension subtests to verify scoring.

7. To prevent error and reduce scoring time, use the scoring keys for the Coding, Symbol Search, and Cancellation subtests.

Generating Summary Score Information

1. Check to make sure that you have accurately calculated the subtest raw score information and correctly transferred this information to the front of the record form.

2. To generate the scaled score equivalents for the subtests, use Appendix A, Table A.1 of the *Norms and Conversion Tables* found in the *WISC-IV Administration and Scoring Manual* (Wechsler, 2003a). Be sure to use the correct age grouping and record the standard score information for the subtests on the WISC-IV Record Form section marked "Total Raw Score to Scaled Score Conversions."

3. If desired, the subtest scaled score information can be recorded in the scaled score profile portion of the Record Form. The subtest scaled score information ranges from 1 to 19 and has a mean of 10 and standard deviation of 3.

4. Generate a sum of scaled scores for each of the four factor scores and the Full Scale IQ score if needed. Check to make sure that you have accurately calculated the sum of scaled score information. If a supplemental subtest has been administered but no subtest substitution is required, do not include the supplemental subtest scaled score information in the sum of scaled scores calculation.

5. Transfer the sum of scaled score information to the "Sum of Scaled Scores to Composite Score Conversions" section found on the front of the WISC-IV Record Form.

6. Although the appendices have a tab separating them from the Subtest Administration section of the manual, the individual appendices and tables within each appendix do not. Because it is necessary to use Appendix A, Tables A.2–A.6, to generate the composite score indices, it is suggested that examiners mark this section for easy access. In addition

to the composite score information, these tables also contain percentile rank and confidence interval (90% and 95%) information.

7. If desired, the composite profile information can be recorded in the Composite Score profile portion of the Record Form. The composite score information ranges from 40 to 160 and has a mean of 100 and standard deviation of 15.

8. Process Score information is available for the Block Design, Digit Span, and Cancellation subtests.

   • If the Block Design subtest was administered with no time bonus (BDN), it is important to note that the maximum raw score total possible is 50 points (a maximum of 2 points possible for items 1–3 and a maximum of 4 points possible for items 4–14). Record the raw score total on page 2 of the Record Form in the section marked "Profile Analysis." Use Appendix Table A.8 to generate the raw score to scaled score information.

   • Also use Appendix Table A.8 to generate Digit Span Forward and Digit Span Backward scaled score information and record on page 2 of the Record Form in the section marked "Profile Analysis." Use Table B.7 to obtain base rate information for the longest correctly recalled span of digits for each of the two tasks.

   • Process Analysis is also available for the two Cancellation tasks (random and structured). Use Appendix Table A.8 to generate the scaled score information and record it on page 2 of the Record Form in the section marked "Profile Analysis."

Use of the Scoring and Report Writing Software

A number of Psychcorp computer software products support the WISC-IV. Two of the most common include the WISC-IV Scoring Assistant™ and WISC-IV Writer™. The WISC-IV Scoring Assistant™ is a user-friendly scoring program where the examiner provides demographic information (name, age, grade, gender, and ethnicity of the child) and enters subtest raw score information. The Scoring Assistant report provides:

Composite Score Information

• Summary Table of Composite Scores, Percentile Ranks, 95% confidence intervals, and qualitative descriptions

• Graph of the Composite Score profile including standard error of measurement (SEM) information associated with each composite

• A table of each of the four composites and corresponding subtest raw scores, scaled scores, test age equivalents, and percentile ranks

Subtest Profile

• Graph of the Subtest Scaled Score profile with SEM information for each subtest

• A table of WISC-IV Total Raw Score information

Score Differences

• A table of Composite score discrepancy comparisons including the scaled score difference between the two composites, .05 critical value information, Yes/No significant difference indication, and overall sample base rate information

• A table of subtest score discrepancy comparisons within each composite that includes .05 critical values information, Yes/No significant difference indication, and base rate information

• Differences between individual subtests and mean of subtest scores within each composite with .05 critical values, strength and weakness, and base rate information

Process Summary and Discrepancy Analysis

• A table of raw and scaled score information is provided for the process measures: Block

Design with no time bonus, Digit Span Forward and Backward, Longest Digit Span Forward and Backward, and Cancellation—Random and Structured.

The WISC-IV Scoring Assistant™ also provides a WISC-IV Test Score report to parents in either English or Spanish. This score report combines quantitative and qualitative information in clear, nontechnical language. Figure 7.2 is an example of the WISC-IV Test Score report for parents or guardians.

The WISC-IV Writer™ includes all the features described above in the Scoring Assistant™ with the addition of interpretation of assessment results. The examiner has the option of providing the following background information:

- Reason for referral
- Family living situation including education level of parents and current family stressors
- Language
- Acquisition of developmental milestones
- Sensory/motor status
- Medical/psychiatric/neurological status
- Medication and substance abuse
- Educational history
- Behavioral observations

The interpretation rationale is based on a successive levels approach to test interpretation and proceeds from the global to the specific with the examiner selecting appropriate recommendations.

STANDARDIZATION, NORMS, AND RELIABILITY

Characteristics of the Standardization Sample

Trained recruiters and independent examiners identified 2,200 children ages 6:0–16:11 who met standardization sample inclusion criteria. Informed consent was obtained from the parent or legal guardian, and when possible, assent was obtained from the child. All participants, including standardization examiners, received compensation for participation. Children who comprised the standardization sample were required to be fluent in English, able to communicate verbally, free from any upper-extremity disorder that would reduce motor performance, free from uncorrected visual or hearing impairment, not taking any medication that could reduce performance (e.g., anticonvulsants, antidepressants, antipsychotics, anxiolytics), and not diagnosed with any physical condition that might depress performance (e.g., traumatic brain injury). Additionally, participants could not have taken any intelligence measure in the previous six months.

A stratified sampling plan based on the March 2000 U.S. Bureau of Census population parameters was developed using the following demographic variables: age, sex, race, parental education level, and geographic region. The 2,200 children were divided into 11 age groups with 200 (100 males and 100 females) children in each age group. Within each age group, the proportions of African-American, Asian, Hispanic, Other, and White children were matched to the race/ethnic-group 2000 Census proportions. The Other Census category includes children of Native American, Eskimo, and Pacific Islander descent. Parent education level was based on the number of years of schooling completed by the parent(s) or guardian(s) and, if the parents were not residing in the same household, the education level of the parent who lived with the child the majority of the time was utilized. The five categories of parent educational attainment were defined as 0–8 years, 9–11 years, 12 years (high school degree or equivalent), 13–15 (some college or associate's degree), and 16 or more (college or advanced degree). For children who resided with two parents or guardians, an average of both persons' educational attainment was used with partial levels rounded up to the next highest category. The standardization process utilized the same four geographic regions (Northeast, South, Midwest, and West) as specified in the

WISC-IV Test Scores
Report to Parents/Guardians

EXAMINEE:	Hayley Keller	REPORT DATE:	2/15/2005
AGE:	12 years 11 months	GRADE:	6th
DATE OF BIRTH:	2/18/1992	ETHNICITY:	White not Hispanic Origin
EXAMINEE ID:	9494949	EXAMINER:	Emily Martinez
GENDER:	Female		

Tests Administered: WISC-IV Core/Supplemental (6/12/2003)
WISC-IV Process Approach (6/12/2003)

Age at Testing: (11 years 3 months)
(11 years 3 months)

Is this a retest? No

Reason for Testing

Hayley was referred for testing.

About the WISC-IV

Hayley was administered the Wechsler Intelligence Scale for Children– Fourth Edition (WISC–IV) on 6/12/2003. The WISC–IV is used to assess the general thinking and reasoning skills of children aged 6 years to 16 years. This test has five main scores: Verbal Comprehension score, Perceptual Reasoning score, Working Memory score, Processing Speed score, and Full Scale score.

The Verbal Comprehension score indicates how well Hayley did on tasks that required her to listen to questions and give spoken answers to them. These tasks evaluate her skills in understanding verbal information, thinking and reasoning with words, and expressing thoughts as words.

The Perceptual Reasoning score indicates how well Hayley did on tasks that required her to examine and think about things such as designs and pictures, and to solve problems without using words. These tasks evaluate her skills in solving nonverbal problems, sometimes using eye-hand coordination, and working quickly and efficiently with visual information.

The Working Memory score indicates how well Hayley did on tasks requiring her to learn and retain information in memory while utilizing the learned information to complete a task. These tasks measure her skills in attention, concentration, and mental reasoning. This skill is closely related to learning and achievement.

The Processing Speed score indicates how well Hayley did on tasks requiring her to quickly scan symbols and make judgments about them. These tasks measure her skills in speed of mental problem-solving, attention, and eye-hand coordination. This skill may be important to her development in reading, and ability to think quickly in general.

FIGURE 7.2
WISC-IV Test Score Report to Parents/Guardians

WISC-IV Test Scores
Report to Parents/Guardians

The Full Scale score is derived from the combination of the Verbal Comprehension, Perceptual Reasoning, Working Memory, and Processing Speed scores. The WISC–IV Full Scale score is one way to view Hayley's overall thinking and reasoning skills.

How WISC-IV Scores are Reported

The scores show how well Hayley performed compared to a group of children the same age from across the United States. The highest possible score is 160 and the lowest possible score is 40. Half of all children will score less than 100, and half of all children will score more than 100. Scores from 90 to 109 are average.

A percentile rank is also given. This shows your child's rank in the national comparison group. If the percentile rank were 45, for example, it would mean that she scored higher than approximately 45 out of 100 children her age.

When reviewing Hayley's scores, remember that no test is perfectly accurate. Any child might score slightly higher or lower if tested again on a different day.

WISC-IV Test Scores

Scale	Score	Percentile Rank	Qualitative Range
Verbal Comprehension (VCI)	112	79	High Average
Perceptual Reasoning (PRI)	79	8	Borderline
Working Memory (WMI)	102	55	Average
Processing Speed (PSI)	91	27	Average

Hayley's Verbal Comprehension score is 112. She scored higher than approximately 79 out of 100 children her age on tasks that require listening to questions and giving verbal responses. Generally speaking, Hayley's skills in understanding verbal information, thinking with words, and expressing thoughts in words are in the High Average range. Her skills in solving verbal problems are much better developed than her skills in solving nonverbal problems.

Her Perceptual Reasoning score is 79. Hayley scored higher than approximately 8 out of 100 children her age on tasks that require her to examine and think about designs and pictures, and solve problems without using words. In general, her skills in solving nonverbal problems quickly and efficiently with visual information are in the Borderline range.

Hayley's Working Memory score is 102. She scored higher than approximately 55 out of 100 children her age on tasks that require learning and retaining information in memory while utilizing the learned information to complete a task. In general, her skills in attention, concentration, and mental reasoning are in the Average range.

FIGURE 7.2

(Continued)

2000 Census report. Figure 7.3 presents the WISC-IV standardization sample percentages for the demographic stratification variables of parent education level, race/ethnicity, and geographic region compared to the percentages present in the U.S. population. Because the WISC-IV standardization sample very closely matches the population of U.S. children on these key demographic variables, the examiner can have confidence that WISC-IV normative information is based on a sample representative of children in the United States between ages 6 and 16.

scaled scores range from 1 to 19 with mean of 10 and a standard deviation of 3. The composite scores (VCI, PRI, WMI, PSI, FSIQ, and GAI) are based on sums of age-corrected scaled scores generated from each child in the standardization sample. Because there were no significant differences in scaled score sums across ages, the age groups were combined to form a single table of composite score equivalents for each of the six composites with a mean of 100 and a standard deviation of 15.

Normative Information

The *WISC-IV Administration and Scoring Manual* presents the scaled score equivalents of total raw scores for the 15 subtests by age group divided into four-month intervals. The subtest

Reliability of the Scales

The WISC-IV consists of a set of subtests designed to describe children's cognitive functioning with performance quantified according to a set of scoring procedures. Reliability refers to

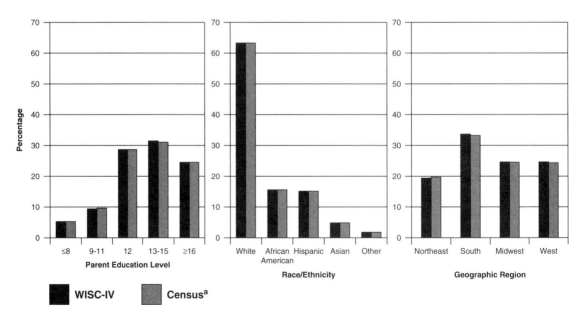

a U.S. Population data are from Current Population Survey, March 2000: School Enrollment Supplemental File [CD-ROM] by U.S. Bureau of the Census, 2000, Washington, DC: U.S. Bureau of the Census (Producer/Distributer).

Source: From Comprehensive Test of Nonverbal Intelligence—Second Edition, by Donald Nils Pearson, and J. Lee Wiederholt, 2009. Austin: PRO-ED, Inc. Copyright © 2009 by PRO-ED, Inc. Reprinted with Permission

FIGURE 7.3
Demographic Characteristics of the Standardization Sample Compared to the U.S. Population

the consistency of these measurements when the assessment is repeated (American Educational Research Association, 1999).

Evidence of Internal Consistency

Internal consistency measures provide a measurement of how homogeneous or internally consistent a subtest is. Internal consistency of each of the WISC-IV subtests was evaluated using the split-half method, where the reliability coefficient is the correlation between the total scores of the two half-tests corrected by the Spearman-Brown formula (Crocker & Algina, 1986). Overall, the WISC-IV has good reliability, with the composite indices evidencing higher reliability than the individual subtests as the composite indices reflect multiple measurements of the construct. (See *WISC-IV Technical and Interpretive Manual*, Table 4.1, p. 34.) Average internal consistency reliabilities calculated from the nonclinical standardization WISC-IV sample participants are .92 or above for four of the five composite indices (see Table 7.6). The average reliability across the 11 age groups for the Verbal Comprehension Index is .94 with a range of .91–.95, the Perceptual Reasoning and Working Memory indices are .92 with a range of .90–.93, and Full Scale is .97 with a range of .96–.97. Because the subtests that comprise the Processing Speed Index reflect performance under speeded conditions, the test–retest coefficient (explained in the section on evidence of test–retest stability, below) was used in place of the split-half method. The average reliability for the Processing Speed Index is .88 with a range of .81–.90. Although lower than the other composite indices, it is important to note that only the two youngest age groups have average reliabilities below .88. The average General Ability Index reliability estimate for ages 6–11 is .95 and for ages 12–16 is .96 (Saklofske, Prifitera, Weiss, Rolfhus, & Zhu, 2005).

Average subtest reliability estimates for the nonclinical standardization sample range from

TABLE 7.6   Reliability Coefficients of WISC-IV Subtests and Composite Scales

Subtest/ Composite	Average WISC-IV r_{xx}[a]	WISC-IV Average with Special Groups r_{xx}
Block Design	.86	.90
Similarities	.86	.90
Digit Span	.87	.87
Picture Concepts	.82	.88
Coding	.85	–
Vocabulary	.89	.92
Letter-Number Seq.	.90	.93
Matrix Reasoning	.89	.93
Comprehension	.81	.87
Symbol Search	.79	–
Picture Completion	.84	.89
Cancellation	.79	–
Information	.86	.89
Arithmetic	.88	.92
Word Reasoning	.80	.85
Block Design No Time Bonus	.84	.89
Digit Span Forward	.83	.82
Digit Span Backward	.80	.84
Cancellation Random	.70	–
Cancellation Structured	.75	–
Verbal Comprehension	.94	
Perceptual Reasoning	.92	
Working Memory	.92	
Processing Speed	.88	
Full Scale	.97	

[a]Average reliability coefficients were calculated with Fisher's z transformation.

Source : Modified from *WISC-IV Technical Report #2, Psychometric Properties*. Copyright © 2003 by NCS Pearson, Inc. Reproduced with permission. All rights reserved.

.79 for Symbol Search and Cancellation to .90 for Letter–Number Sequencing.

The WISC-IV also includes reliability coefficients for 12 of the 15 subtests averaged across a total of 16 clinical groups (N = 661 children). As shown in Table 7.6, the average subtest reliability coefficients for the clinical groups are identical or better than the subtest coefficients from the standardization sample. These reliability coefficients range from .85 for Word Reasoning to .93 for Letter–Number Sequencing and Matrices. Because it was not possible for the clinical groups to participate in test–retest sampling, no information is available regarding reliability estimates for the speeded subtests (Coding, Symbol Search, and Cancellation).

Evidence of Test–Retest Stability

The stability of a test refers to the degree to which it gives the same general, though not numerically identical, results with repeated administrations. The WISC-IV was administered twice to a group of 243 children with an average of one month between the first and second assessment sessions. The first set of scores was correlated with the second set of scores with the test–retest subtest coefficients ranging from .76 for Picture Concepts subtest to .92 for the Vocabulary subtest and the composite coefficients ranging from .86 for the Processing Speed Index and .93 for Verbal Comprehension and the Full Scale Index. Table 7.7 reveals that the WISC-IV subtest and composite scores have good-to-excellent stability and the process scores have adequate stability. As expected, because children's performance often improves with repeated exposure, the WISC-IV average scores are somewhat higher for the second testing compared with the initial session. Average score differences between the two sessions due to practice effects are very minor for the Verbal Comprehension Index (2.1) and the Working Memory Index (2.6) and more pronounced for the Perceptual Reasoning (5.2) and Processing Speed Index (7.1).

USE OF THE TEST

Interpretation Methods

The WISC-IV score information should be interpreted, not in isolation, but within the context of the reason for referral and background information, and in comparison with other assessment information (e.g., performance on other individually administered instruments and/or parent, teacher, and self-report questionnaires). The information contained in the reason for referral and background history sections of a report are the result of an information gathering process with parents, the school, and/or other non-school professionals. In the school setting, in addition to meeting with parents, it is important to discuss referral concerns with teachers, including ones where the child is not experiencing difficulties, and to observe the child in structured and unstructured settings. Although more time intensive than reliance on questionnaires alone, these activities can assist with the development of succinct referral questions and provide added background information. As part of gathering background history, examiners routinely conduct a clinical interview with referral sources. Many examiners find it helpful to employ a structured interview format such as the one offered with the *Behavioral Assessment System for Children—Second Edition* (Reynolds & Kamphaus, 2004). Along with developmental, medical, social, and educational history, it is also important to detail what interventions and accommodations have been employed and the associated degree of success or failure. For example, in *Functional assessment intervention system: Improving school behavior* (Stoiber, 2003), the assessment team systematically identifies concerns, defines behavioral objectives, and develops and monitors interventions.

To interpret the test scores obtained from the WISC-IV, the following steps are suggested:

1. Generate a table of WISC-IV summary score information. Also included in this table are

TABLE 7.7   Stability Coefficients of the WISC-IV Subtests and Process and Composite Scales

All Ages Subtest/Process Score/Composite	First Testing		Second Testing		r_{12}[b]	Corrected r[a]	Standard Difference
	Mean	SD	Mean	SD			
Block Design	10.0	3.0	11.2	2.9	.81	.82	.41
Similarities	10.1	2.6	10.7	2.5	.81	.86	.24
Digit Span	9.9	2.9	10.4	2.7	.81	.83	.18
Picture Concepts	10.1	2.7	10.9	2.8	.71	.76	.29
Coding	10.4	2.7	11.8	3.1	.81	.84	.48
Vocabulary	10.1	2.3	10.4	2.4	.85	.92	.13
Letter-Number Seq.	10.3	2.5	10.7	2.6	.75	.83	.16
Matrix Reasoning	10.2	2.5	10.8	2.7	.77	.85	.23
Comprehension	10.1	2.5	10.3	2.4	.72	.82	.08
Symbol Search	10.4	2.5	11.5	2.8	.68	.80	.41
Picture Completion	10.3	2.9	12.1	3.1	.82	.84	.60
Cancellation	10.2	3.0	11.3	3.0	.78	.79	.37
Information	10.0	2.5	10.4	2.5	.83	.89	.16
Arithmetic	10.1	2.8	10.7	2.5	.75	.79	.23
Word Reasoning	10.2	2.5	11.0	2.6	.75	.82	.31
Block Design No Time Bonus	10.1	2.9	11.2	2.7	.76	.78	.39
Digit Span Forward	9.9	2.9	10.3	2.8	.72	.76	.14
Digit Span Backward	10.1	2.7	10.5	2.7	.67	.74	.15
Cancellation Random	10.0	2.9	11.0	2.9	.68	.72	.34
Cancellation Structured	10.2	2.8	11.0	2.8	.73	.76	.29
Verbal Comprehension	100.0	11.7	102.1	11.7	.89	.93	.18
Perceptual Reasoning	100.7	13.1	105.9	13.9	.85	.89	.39
Working Memory	99.8	13.1	102.4	13.3	.85	.89	.20
Processing Speed	102.4	12.6	109.5	15.2	.79	.86	.51
Full Scale	101.0	11.7	106.6	12.5	.89	.93	.46

[a]Correlations were corrected for the variability of the standardization sample (Allen & Yen, 1979; Magnusson, 1967).
[b]Average stability coefficients across the five age bands were calculated with Fisher's z transformation.
SOURCE : *WISC-IV Technical Report #2, Psychometric Properties.* Copyright © 2003 by NCS Pearson, Inc. Reproduced with permission. All rights reserved.

the WISC-IV Process Scores and summary scores from other instruments administered during the assessment.

2. Begin WISC-IV interpretation with the factor indexes. Determine whether there are significant differences between the indexes and evaluate how common or rare are the differences.

3. Decide how to summarize overall cognitive ability, choosing either the FSIQ score or the GAI score.

4. Determine whether there are significant differences among the subtests within each index

and determine base rate of occurrence. Determine strengths and weaknesses using either the overall mean or Verbal Comprehension and Perceptual Reasoning means as the basis for comparison.

5. Evaluate subtest-level discrepancy comparisons if needed.

6. Conduct a Process Analysis, if information on the forward and backward trials of the Digit Span subtest, the structured and random trials of the Cancellation subtest, and Block Design No Time Bonus adds further explanatory power.

CASE STUDY

This case study of an 11-year-11-month-old boy who is enrolled in the 6th grade illustrates the six WISC-IV interpretive steps and the integration of these results into a written report.

Background Information

Reason for Referral
Zach was referred for a psychoeducational evaluation by his parents (Tim and Elizabeth Wood) and his 6th-grade team of teachers. His parents identified the following concerns: problems with focusing and sustaining attention, low frustration tolerance, and poor planning and organization skills. Both his parents and teachers reported that his grades range from A's/B's when he turns in his work to F's because of missing and late homework assignments, though his math teacher indicated that Zach continues to have trouble with retrieval of basic math information. She also indicated that on two occasions, problems with impulsivity and emotional outbursts (yelling) have resulted in brief removal from the classroom. Other teachers indicated that although Zach often blurts out answers or makes jokes, he is able to be redirected and no behavioral escalation has occurred.

History
Zach's background history was developed from a clinical interview with Zach and his mother separately and a developmental history questionnaire completed by his mother, along with interviews and academic and behavioral information supplied by the teaching team. Zach was observed during his math and English classes and at lunch in the school cafeteria.

Zach is a young boy who resides with his parents and a brother (age 13) and sister (age 8). He is enrolled in the 6th grade at a Middle School in Texas. His mother reports that she most enjoys Zach's concern and caring for others' feelings. She indicates that his emotional outbursts and "forgetfulness" are a daily challenge. No risk factors related to pregnancy and delivery were noted. Acquisition of motor and language skills was within typical age parameters. Zach's early infant temperament was described as irritable. He was oversensitive to noise and continues to have difficulty tolerating unexpected change. His current physical health is reported as good with no history of serious accidents or injuries. No vision, hearing, or sleep difficulties are reported.

Zach participates in a wide variety of activities. His parents report that he enjoys playing all sports and is currently on the school basketball team, though he at times struggles to remain on the team due to failing grades. Discipline techniques the parents employ to reduce emotional outbursts include timeout and removal of privileges, though they report being inconsistent in the application of these techniques. No formal intervention procedures other than the requirement of keeping track of his assignments in a day planner have been implemented. Zach indicated that he often forgets to record the information. He also added that he does not have time to record all the needed information before the class lesson starts and that if he waits to the end of class to record the assignments, he will be late for his next class. During a 30-minute-each observation of Zach in English and math class, he was frequently off-task (dropping his pencil, talking to peers, staring in space) and required redirection by the teachers. In the cafeteria, Zach was observed joking and interacting appropriately with peers.

Behavioral Observations

The assessment was conducted over two sessions. Zach presented as a friendly child who was easy to engage in the testing process. Although he was cooperative and attempted all tasks, his attention span was short and he was often restless, constantly moving and shifting in his chair. His problem-solving approach on non-challenging tasks was fast and fairly accurate, though, for example, on the WISC-IV Matrix Reasoning subtest, he often chose an answer without carefully considering all possible response choices. He did, however, at times self-correct. On tasks he found challenging such as the WISC-IV Letter–Number Sequencing and the Digit Backwards trial of the Digit Span subtests, he gave up at the first sign of difficulty. Overall, he required fairly constant redirection back to the activities and was never able to independently refocus himself, though his off-task conversation was engaging and socially appropriate. The obtained test results are considered to represent a reliable picture of Zach's current level of functioning.

WISC-IV Score Interpretation for Zach

Step 1: Generate a table of WISC-IV summary score information. Include standard score, percentile rank, and confidence interval information for the four factor indexes and the Full Scale or GAI score. To assist with easy interpretation, group the WISC-IV subtests under their respective factors and provide scaled score and percentile rank information. Be sure to note whether any supplemental subtests were administered and whether they were included in the calculation of the factor indexes. Table 7.8 presents the WISC-IV assessment results for Zach.

Step 2: Examine the factor indexes. Determine whether there are significant differences between the indexes and evaluate how common or rare are the differences.

Use the analysis page of the WISC-IV record form and complete the information needed for the index level discrepancy comparisons. As shown in Table 7.9, Zach's performance on the Verbal Comprehension subtests did not differ significantly from his performance on the Perceptual Reasoning subtests and the 4-point scaled score difference between the two indexes was common in the standardization sample. His VCI performance also did not differ significantly from his performance on the Processing Speed (PSI) subtests and the 9-point difference occurred frequently (base rate 27.6%). On two of the index comparisons, there were significant differences (PRI-PSI and WMI-PSI), though the base rate information suggested that the point differences (13 and 14 points respectively) occurred fairly frequently. There were significant differences in performance between the VCI and WMI (23 points) and the PRI and

TABLE 7.8   WISC-IV Assessment Results for Zach Wood

	Standard Score	Percentile Rank	95%
Verbal Comprehension	100	50	93–107
Perceptual Reasoning	104	61	96–111
Working Memory	77	06	71–88
Processing Speed	91	27	83–103
Full Scale IQ	93	32	88–98
GAI Score	102	55	96–108

	Scaled Score	Percentile Rank
Verbal Comprehension		
Similarities	10	50
Vocabulary	11	63
Comprehension	10	50
Perceptual Reasoning		
Block Design	11	63
Picture Concepts	11	63
Matrix Reasoning	10	50
Working Memory		
Digit Span	6	09
Letter–Number Sequencing	6	09
Arithmetic*	7	16
Processing Speed		
Coding	6	09
Symbol Search	11	63
Cancellation*	7	16

Process Scores

	Scaled Score
Digit Span Forward	9
Digit Span Backward	5
Cancellation—Random	7
Cancellation—Structured	7

*Not included in calculation of Working Memory index score.
**Not included in calculation of Processing Speed index score.
Source : *Wechsler Intelligence Scales for Children—Fourth Edition* (WISC-IV).

TABLE 7.9   WISC-IV Index Discrepancy Comparisons

Index	Score 1	Score 2	Difference	Critical Value	Significant Difference	Base Rate
VCI-PRI	VCI 100	PRI 104	4	11	N	39.5%
VCI-WMI	VCI 100	WMI 77	23	11.38	Y	4.1%
VCI-PSI	VCI 100	PSI 91	9	12	N	27.6%
PRI-WMI	PRI 104	WMI 77	27	11.3	Y	3.5%
PRI-PSI	PRI 104	PSI 91	13	12.12	Y	19.9%
WMI-PSI	WMI 77	PSI 91	14	12.46	Y	20.4%

WMI (27 points) factors and these score differences occurred infrequently in the standardization sample.

Naglieri and Paolitto (2005) remind the examiner that the six pairwise comparisons of index scores increases the error rate from .05 to .265 and increases the chance of a Type I error (incorrectly rejecting the null hypothesis of no difference between scores). They suggest utilizing an ipsative method, which consists of three simple steps. First, generate an overall mean using the four factor scores; second, subtract this mean from each of the indexes; and third, compare the obtained differences with the set of critical values. Table 7.10 contains an ipsative comparison of Zach's factor scores. Using this approach reveals that Zach's working memory skills are an area of significant weakness.

Step 3: Summarize overall cognitive ability. Prifitera et al. (2005) suggest that the FSIQ score be used when performance on the factor indexes is uniform and no significant differences are present. When these criteria are not met and when performance on the working memory and processing speed indexes lowers the FSIQ, as is the case with many children with ADHD and SLD, use of the GAI score is recommended (Raiford et al., 2005). In the case example, given Zach's discrepant factor index performance, the GAI score is used.

TABLE 7.10   WISC-IV Ipsative Comparisons of the Factor Scores

Comparison	Observed Difference	Critical Value	Significant Difference	Strength or Weakness
VCI—Mean 100–93.5	6.5	8.8	No	No
PRI—Mean 104–93.5	10.5	8.8	Yes	Relative Strength
WMI—Mean 77–93.5	16.5	9.2	Yes	Weakness
PSI—Mean 91–93.5	2.5	9.9	No	No

He attained a Full Scale IQ score of 93 based on 10 core subtests and a GAI score of 102 based on the 6 core subtests of the Verbal Comprehension and Perceptual Reasoning subtests.

Step 4: Evaluate strengths and weaknesses. Page 108 of the *Technical and Interpretative Manual* (Wechsler, 2003b) stresses the following: "In general, if there is no significant discrepancy among the composite scores, the mean of ten core subtests should be used for the strength and weakness analysis." Use Appendix Table B.5 to determine whether there are significant differences among the subtests either overall or within the Verbal Comprehension and Perceptual Reasoning indexes. Also determine base rate of occurrence of observed differences. In our case example, we would not conduct a profile analysis of strengths and weaknesses for two reasons. The first is that there were significant differences between factor score performance; second (see Table 7.8), verbal inspection of Zach's performance on the Verbal Comprehension and Perceptual Reasoning subtests reveals relatively uniform performance within these two indexes.

Step 5: Evaluate subtest-level discrepancy comparisons if needed. This step can be used when specific pairwise comparisons are needed to assist with hypothesis testing. In the case example, to evaluate whether the Processing Speed subtest scores are significantly different from each other, use Appendix Tables B.3 and B.4 to determine the base rate of these differences. Using these tables, the 5-point scaled score difference between Zach's performance on the Coding and Symbol Search subtests was significant (P =.05) and occurred fairly infrequently (6.3% of the standardization sample).

Step 6: Conduct a Process Analysis. Zach attained a Digit Forward raw score of 8, which, using Table A.8, translates into a scaled score of 9, whereas his Digit Backward raw score of 4 translates to a scaled score of 5. The scaled score difference of 4 points is statistically significant at the .05 confidence level (use Appendix Table B.9) and is occurred in 9% of the standardization sample. On the Cancellation Task the raw scores of 27 on the random task and 34 on the structured task translated into scaled scores of 7 with no additional discrepancy information needed.

WISC-IV Summary Information *for Zach*

The Wechsler Intelligence Scales for Children—Fourth Edition (WISC-IV) provides a measure of cognitive development. The WISC-IV evaluates a child's ability to understand language, solve problems, and interpret visual information. Zach achieved an overall score of 102 (55th percentile), which, when compared with same-age peers, places his estimated general conceptual ability within the average range of cognitive functioning. However, given the significant discrepancies between his average verbal comprehension and perceptual reasoning skills and his significantly weaker verbal working memory functioning (23 and 27 points respectively), an examination of his verbal comprehension, perceptual reasoning, processing speed, and verbal working memory skills individually will result in a more complete portrayal of Zach's cognitive profile.

Zach's verbal comprehension and perceptual reasoning skills are average when compared with same age peers. He appeared to enjoy defining words, explaining rules, and describing common attributes of objects and concepts. He also appeared to enjoy the cognitive challenge the nonverbal reasoning subtests presented. In sharp contrast, his verbal working memory performance was significantly below average (Standard score = 77, 6th percentile). He had great difficulty recalling a string of numbers and then reversing the numerical sequence (Digit

Span Backward scaled score = 5, 5th percentile). Zach's performance on measures of processing speed varied significantly. His performance was average compared with same age peers on a task that required him to quickly visually scan and mark items, whereas his performance was slower (low average compared with peers) on a more complicated task that, in addition to visual scanning and motor demands, also taxes working memory to a greater degree.

Identification of Special Populations

Children with Specific Learning Disabilities

The Individuals with Disabilities Education Act (IDEA) of 2004 defines *specific learning disability (SLD)* as "a disorder in one or more of the basic psychological processes involved in understanding or using language, spoken or written, which may manifest itself in the imperfect ability to listen, think, speak, read, write, spell or do mathematical calculations" (20 U.S.C 1401[30]). This illustrates that SLD is still defined as a processing disorder in which the learning problem does not stem from visual, hearing, or motor disabilities, mental retardation, or emotional disturbance and cannot be attributed to environmental, cultural, or economic disadvantage. Hale, Fiorello, Kavanagh, Holdnack and Aloe (2007) succinctly summarize the process when they say, "Diagnosis ... requires determination of a deficit in the basic psychological processes in the presence of cognitive integrities." The qualifying diagnostic requirement that a severe discrepancy exist between scores on individually administered measures of intelligence and an achievement has been removed. This frees the examiner from strict eligibility criteria in determining SLD. Because of the psychometric rigor inherent with the predicted achievement method and the base-rate information, the examiner may, however, still find the ability-achievement information useful when evaluating performance. Appendix B of the *WISC-IV Technical and Interpretive Manual* (Wechsler, 2003b) provides information on using the predicted and simple-difference methods to compare score differences on the WISC-IV (FSIQ, VCI, PRI) and all scores on the Wechsler Individual Achievement Test—Second Edition

(WIAT-II) (Psychological Corporation, 2002). The same information for the General Ability Index can be found in the WISC-IV Technical Report # 4 General Ability Index (Raiford, Weiss, Rolfhus, & Coalson, 2005). In our case example (see Table 7.11), compared with same-age peers, Zach has significant weaknesses in math and written expression. Prior to IDEA 2004, if Zach lived in a state that required a discrepancy of 22 points to qualify for special education, he would have had difficulty receiving services.

Five groups of children with SLD are included in the WISC-IV clinical validity studies (Wechsler, 2003b). These include 56 children who met diagnostic criteria for reading disability (RD), 35 children with a dual diagnosis of reading and writing disability (RW), 33 children with math disability alone (MD), 42 children with reading, writing, and math disability (RWMD), and 45 children with learning disability and co-morbid ADHD (LD/ADHD). The children's WISC-IV performance in each clinical group was compared with children from the standardization sample matched by gender, race-ethnicity, parent education level, and geographic region. The factor index results of these studies will be summarized here, though the interested reader is referred to the *WISC-IV Technical and Interpretive Manual* (Wechsler, 2003b) for detailed subtest information. The majority of clinical groups of children attained significantly lower WISC-IV mean index and FSIQ scores than did their matched control counterparts, with two exceptions: a nonsignificant difference between the reading and writing disability group and controls on the PRI and the math disability group and controls on the PSI. In four of the five clinical groups (RD, RW, MD, and LD/ADHD) the effect sizes for

TABLE 7.11   Zach's WISC-IV GAI and WIAT-II Results

(age-based norms)

GAI score = 102

Predicted Method

	Obtained Score	Expected Score	Sign (.05)	Base RT
Word Reading	105	101	no	NA
Reading Comprehension	99	102	no	NA
Numerical Operations	89	101	yes	15%
Math Reasoning	86	102	yes	05%
Spelling	100	101	no	NA
Written Expression	88	101	yes	13–15%

SOURCE: Wechsler Individual Achievement Test—Second Edition.

the mean WMI factor score differences ranged from moderate to large, and for two groups (RW and LD/ADHD) the effect sizes for the mean PSI factor score differences were also moderate to large.

Children with Attention Deficit Disorders

In addition to the group of children with co-morbid LD and ADHD, a second group of children with ADHD alone were included in the WISC-IV clinical studies (Wechsler, 2003b). The WISC-IV scores of 89 children were compared with a demographically matched group of children from the standardization sample. Although the index and FSIQ scores were significantly lower than the matched control group of children, when compared to children in the LD/ADHD group, small effect sizes were obtained for the WMI. Consistent with the LD/ADHD group, the effect size for the PSI was moderate to large. It is interesting to note that in both groups approximately 65% of the children were on medication at the time of testing. A follow-up study comparing the WISC-IV performance of those on and off medication with the matched control group would more clearly assess the impact of ADHD medication.

Children Who Are Cognitively Gifted

The WISC-IV scores of a group of 63 children who were classified as intellectually gifted by their respective school districts and who met the inclusionary criteria for the study (2 SDs above the mean on an individually administered measure of ability) were compared with the WISC-IV scores of a demographically matched control group of children (Wechsler, 2003b). Table 7.12 lists the mean factor and FSIQ performance of these two groups. (Williams, Weiss, & Rolfhus, 2003b). As expected, the gifted sample performed significantly better on all measures than the control sample with the differences in performance most pronounced on the VCI and PRI factors. Similar to findings with the WISC-III (Wechsler, 1991), the differences between the two groups on the WMI and PSI factors were more modest (on average 9.5 and 7.8 points respectively).

Identification of Individuals with Mental Retardation

The DSM-IV-TR (American Psychiatric Association, 2000) diagnostic criteria for mental

TABLE 7.12   Mean Performance of Intellectually Gifted and Matched Control Groups

| Composite | Intellectually Gifted | | Matched Control Group | | | Group Mean Comparison | | | |
	Mean	SD	Mean	SD	N	Difference	t value	p value	Effect Size
VCI	124.7	11.0	106.6	14.2	63	−18.14	−9.04	<.01	−1.43
PRI	120.4	11.0	105.6	13.0	63	−14.87	−7.79	<.01	−1.24
WMI	112.5	11.9	103.0	13.7	60	−9.43	−4.99	<.01	−.74
PSI	110.6	11.5	102.8	14.8	62	−7.84	−4.03	<.01	−.59
FSIQ	123.5	8.5	106.7	13.5	59	−16.80	−10.33	<.01	−1.49

SOURCE: *Technical and Interpretive Manual* (Wechsler, 2003b) and the *WISC-IV Technical Report #3, Clinical Validity* (Williams, Weiss, & Rolfhus, 2003b). NCS Pearson, Inc. Reproduced with permission. All rights reserved.

retardation are straightforward: an IQ of approximately 70 or below on an individually administered IQ test, and concurrent adaptive and behavior deficits in at least two of the following areas: communication, self-care, home living, social/interpersonal skills, use of community resources, self-direction, functional academic skills, work, leisure, and health and safety. Onset must occur before age 18. The inclusion criteria for children in the WISC-IV special group study were as follows: meets DSM-IV-TR criteria for mild or moderate retardation or has scores between 2 and 4 SDs below the mean and has adaptive functioning impairments in at least two areas identified by DSM-IV-TR. Table 7.13 presents the WISC-IV factor score information for individuals with mild cognitive disability compared to a matched control group and Table 7.14 includes the WISC-IV score information for children with severe mental retardation again compared to matched controls. As expected, all children with mental retardation performed significantly poorer than nonimpaired matched controls and children with moderate mental retardation performed worse than those children with mild mental retardation. Additionally, for children with mild mental retardation, processing speed was an area of relative strength when compared with their other factor scores.

Other Groups

The *WISC-IV Technical and Interpretive Manual* (Wechsler, 2003b) offers preliminary validity data on seven additional clinical groups. These include children with language disorders (expressive and mixed receptive and expressive language problems), children who had experienced head trauma (open head injury or closed head injury), children with autism spectrum disorders (autism and Asperger's disorder), and children with motor impairment. Although the total number of children in each of these seven groups is less than the primary clinical validity studies of children with attention and learning difficulties, all seven groups present data compared with that of a demographically matched sample. To better understand the specifics of each clinical group and to assess comparability with their own clinical population, the interested reader is referred to the inclusion criteria for participation in the clinical validity studies found in Appendix D of the *WISC-IV Technical and Interpretive Manual* (Wechsler, 2003b).

Interventions Based on Test Results

The following interventions are based on the case study clinical impressions.

TABLE 7.13   Mean Performance of Children with Mild Mental Retardation

Composite	Mental Retardation -Mild Severity		Matched Control Group		N	Group Mean Comparison			
	Mean	SD	Mean	SD		Difference	t value	p value	Effect Size
VCI	67.1	9.1	98.7	12.5	58	31.62	13.94	<.01	2.90
PRI	65.5	10.3	98.7	15.2	63	33.16	14.01	<.01	2.55
WMI	66.8	11.1	99.4	13.8	62	32.61	14.39	<.01	2.60
PSI	73.0	11.6	98.3	13.5	61	25.36	11.48	<.01	2.01
FSIQ	60.5	9.2	99.2	13.6	56	38.64	16.59	<.01	3.33

SOURCE : Technical and Interpretation Manual (Wechsler, 2003b) and the WISC-IV Technical Report #3, Clinical Validity (Williams, Weiss, & Rolfhus, 2003b). NCS Pearson, Inc. Reproduced with permission. All rights reserved.

TABLE 7.14   Mean Performance of Children with Moderate Mental Retardation

Composite	Mental Retardation -Moderate Severity		Matched Control Group		N	Group Mean Comparison			
	Mean	SD	Mean	SD		Difference	t value	p value	Effect Size
VCI	52.3	7.5	97.2	14.1	55	44.93	19.07	<.01	3.97
PRI	52.5	9.2	99.2	15.2	57	46.63	19.14	<.01	3.72
WMI	57.0	9.5	98.9	14.6	53	41.85	15.80	<.01	3.41
PSI	58.2	11.0	97.3	12.3	51	39.12	15.20	<.01	3.36
FSIQ	46.4	8.5	98.0	14.5	47	51.62	18.32	<.01	4.35

SOURCE : Technical and Interpretation Manual (Wechsler, 2003b) and the WISC-IV Technical Report #3, Clinical Validity (Williams, Weiss, & Rolfhus, 2003b). NCS Pearson, Inc. Reproduced with permission. All rights reserved.

In addition to problems with verbal working memory and slow visual processing speed, Zach has problems with impulse and attention regulation, and math and writing deficits (lower-than-expected basic math computation, reasoning, and written composition skills).

Problems Sustaining Attention

Zach had difficulty sustaining attention. The implication of this finding is that following directions for school and home activities and sustained listening in class will be harder for him than same-age peers, despite his average verbal and nonverbal reasoning abilities. Because of his short attention span, he may miss important information. Although his good cognitive abilities will help him learn, his ability to refocus independently when off-task is developmentally immature compared with same-age peers.

Academic Concerns

Zach's knowledge of basic math facts (addition and subtraction) is not yet automatic or solidly in his memory. He also has trouble with a number of the sequential steps in addition and subtraction. His math difficulties represent low performance compared with children his age in 6th grade and are an area of unexpected weakness when compared with his cognitive abilities.

Improving Classroom Attention and Engagement

1. Zach will benefit from instruction that is interesting, challenging, and engaging. He appears to enjoy verbal and nonverbal reasoning and problem-solving activities.

2. Allow Zach to demonstrate what he knows verbally and separate mechanical aspects of writing from his written communication of ideas and information.

3. Some children are better able to learn and recall information when moving around. For Zach to remain still, it appears to require effort, which reduces his ability to attend and process information. Consequently, allowing him some freedom of movement will facilitate his learning and memory.

4. Additional classroom modifications might include frequent breaks for physical activity. Try to structure the day so that activities that require more intensive academic concentration are scheduled in the morning and activities that require Zach to sit quietly are interspersed with activities where he can move around.

5. Take short breaks. Have Zach finish a set amount of work, take a break, and then work again.

6. His problems with inattention may cause him to miss or have incomplete information.
   a. Modifications in the classroom might include: minimizing distractions, preferential seating, and reduction of background noise to insure that Zach can hear oral instructions.
   b. Zach should be encouraged to ask for additional information or clarification when he is unclear about something the teacher has said.

7. Questions teachers can use to help insure Zach's attention and engagement:
   - Could Zach see and hear me clearly?
   - Did he understand the purpose of the lesson?
   - Could he tell me what he had to do?
   - Was there some time in the lesson when he could feel confident and successful?
   - Have I left him with appropriate memory triggers to allow him to recall well?
   - Did I use pictures and imagery to aid his memory?
   - Can I find positive things to say when I mark his work or when I provide feedback?
   - Did I offer sufficient reassurance and support in the lesson?
   - Was the pace of work achievable throughout the lesson?
   - Did my teaching use visual, auditory, and kinesthetic strategies?
   - Was any part of the lesson funny to help him remember it later?
   - Did I do plenty of varied repetitions?
   - Did I summarize the main points in logical, easy-to-understand words?

Improving Attention at Home and Engagement in the Classroom

1. Be sure you have his attention before speaking.
2. Make eye contact or gently touch his shoulder to get his attention.
3. Initially, give one direction at a time and be specific about what you want completed. It is important to check for understanding before continuing.

Check for Understanding

4. Use visual cues and gestures when you give verbal directions.
5. Break a complex job into smaller parts.

6. Be prepared to repeat your request. You may need to rephrase it to make sure Zach understands what you are asking him to do.

7. Reward progress and praise his efforts.

8. Encourage Zach to slow down on his tasks and assignments.

Improving Working Memory

1. It is important to teach Zach recall strategies and rules (e.g., spelling rules) so that he can use his good reasoning abilities rather than focusing entirely on memorization. It will be important to practice for short intervals (5 minutes), take a break, and then return to the task. This break allows Zach time to process the information and reduces cognitive interference and helps reduce frustration.

2. Help Zach learn information in context. Make sure he understands the *whys* and *hows*. This will give him a cognitive framework from which he can retrieve information. Information learned in isolation and without context is more easily forgotten. Given Zach's variable attention and concentration, it will be especially important to validate his understanding.

3. Break the content into small understandable parts. This reduces working memory load by giving Zach time to process the information and relate it to what he already knows.

4. Link new content to familiar material. Doing this makes the linkage to the already-existing knowledge explicit.

Dealing with Homework

1. Homework and review of classroom material should not exceed 30 minutes a day.

2. Take short breaks. Have Zach finish a set amount of work, take a break, and then work again.

3. Have Zach play teacher and have him explain the material or lesson to you. Show interest in how he obtains an answer. When the answer is correct, have him explain why; conversely, when an answer is incorrect, help him understand why and what is needed for it to be correct.

4. Teaching strategies that can support your homework efforts can be found in the following materials: *Homework success for children with ADHD: A family–school intervention program* (Thomas J. Power, James L. Karustis, and Dine F. Habboushe, Guilford Press, ISBN 1-57230-616-5), and *How to reach and teach ADD/ADHD children: Practical techniques, strategies and interventions for helping children with attention problems and hyperactivity* (Sandra F. Rief, Center for Applied Research in Education, ISBN 0-87628-413-6).

Academic

1. Because of Zach's problems with processing speed, working memory, and attention, it is important for the school team to keep in mind that note taking and other handwriting activities are difficult for Zach. The following accommodations should be considered:

   a. Basic lecture outlines when requested

   b. The option of taking notes and examinations on a laptop computer

   For example, if a lesson is presented in a lecture format, from an overhead projector, or in a small group where Zach is expected to record information quickly or the information exceeds a few sentences, it is important that he be provided with a "shell outline." With a shell outline, he can follow along and add additional notes but would not be responsible for writing all the notes.

2. Zach could profit from:

   - Review of basic math facts

   - Use of a calculator for homework assignments and examinations

- Use of a math fact sheet for homework and examinations
- Review of step-by-step procedures for:
  - Two- and three-digit subtraction
  - Two- and three-digit multiplication and division
  - Adding, subtracting, multiplying, and dividing fractions
  - Percentages
3. When preparing for a math examination, it will be important to test Zach's understanding of the problems in multiple ways. Have him explain the steps and have him devise possible test problems. He may also need some assistance on how to study for specific types of tests (multiple choice, essay, word problems).

VALIDITY

Relationships between Ability and Achievement

Evidence suggests that IQ is a good predictor of educational achievement (Kaufman, 1994; Wechsler, 1991) as well as predicting response to educational intervention (Berninger, O'Donnell, & Holdnack, 2008; Shaywitz, Fletcher, Holahan, & Shaywitz, 1992). The *WISC-IV Technical and Interpretive Manual* Tables B.14 and B.15 provide correlation results for the WISC-IV/WIAT-II linking sample. Similar to the WISC-III-WIAT results, FSIQ was more highly correlated with the four WIAT-II achievement composites than were the other three factor indices. For example, in children ages 6:0–11:11, FSIQ correlates .76 with the WIAT-II Reading Composite, .78 with the Math Composite, .76 with the Written Expression Composite, and .73 with the Oral Expression Composite, whereas the PSI factor ranges from .49 with the Oral Expression Composite to .58 with the Math Composite.

Fairness: Sex and Race/Ethnic Difference

The issues of test fairness based on sex and race and ethnic difference were addressed throughout the development of the WISC-IV. Beginning with the development of the blueprint and continuing throughout all development phases (pilot studies, national tryout, standardization, and final development), expert and statistical examination of test items was a primary goal. Appendix E of the *WISC-IV Technical and Interpretive Manual* provides a list of Advisory Panels, Test Reviewers, and Consultants who lent their expertise to the five-year development process. Items during the pilot and tryout phases were revised and deleted based on their feedback. During the national tryout, in addition to the 1,270 children who were stratified according to age, sex, race, parent education, and geographic parameters, an additional sample of 252 African American and 186 Hispanic children were included to allow for examination of item bias using IRT methods. All items in the standardization sample were evaluated for gender, race, and parent-education-level bias. Items were also evaluated for content redundancy and degree of difficulty with approximately three items dropped from every subtest. Face validity issues were also addressed. For example, item artwork depicts both males and females as well as individuals with varying racial and ethnic backgrounds.

Although Reynolds & Kaiser (2003) in their review of the Wechsler series found no evidence of test bias, there continues to be concern regarding ethnic and racial bias with intelligence tests in general, including the Wechsler series. In a discussion of test bias, Prifitera et al. (2005) caution that it is important to avoid simplistic explanations of the consistent finding that African American groups on average score 15 FSIQ points below white groups on IQ tests. The authors assert that sample stratification variables such as social economic status (SES) and education level contribute to these differences because minority groups have a larger proportion of persons with lower SES levels. For example, on the WISC-IV, when SES level is controlled, the following average point differences between the two groups were obtained: FSIQ (10), VCI and PRI (9), WMI (5), and PSI (4) (Prifitera et al., 2005).

Profiles of Abilities and Their Relationship to Diagnosis

Currently the field of cognitive ability assessment and diagnosis is one characterized by strongly held, and sometimes acrimonious, philosophical differences. The use of intelligence tests, and of the Wechslers' specifically, has been viewed as contributing little to the diagnosis of and intervention in learning disabilities (Reschly & Ysseldyke, 2002), with proponents of the response-to-intervention approach (RTI) advocating use of curriculum-based interventions instead of intelligence assessment results. See Hale, Kaufman, Naglieri, and Kavale (2006) for a cogent approach to integrating RTI and cognitive assessment procedures. Although not rejecting the use of ability measures when evaluating learning differences, a second group of researchers see limited utility in interpretation beyond global or FSIQ (McDermott, Fantuzzo, & Glutting, 1990; Watkins, 2000). In counterpoint to those who see limited utility of the ability measures, are recent contributions from brain imaging and neuropsychological assessment studies (see Semrud-Clikeman, 2005, for a review of the literature). For example, processing speed differentiated fluent from nonfluent readers (Semrud-Clikeman, Guy, & Griffin, 2000) and working memory is an essential component of both word recognition and reading comprehension (Teeter & Semrud-Clikeman, 1997). Mayes and Calhoun (2007) found the combination of WMI and PSI indexes important to determining co-morbid LD in children with ADHD.

Empirical Support for the Test Structure

The *WISC-IV Technical and Interpretive Manual* (Wechsler, 2003b) presents intercorrelation information on the subtest and composite scores and factor-analytic studies as evidence of the instrument's internal structure. Four a priori hypotheses were made regarding correlation patterns: (1) All subtests would have low-to-moderate correlations with each other as all subtests are presumably measuring general intelligence (*g*). Table 7.15 presents the intercorrelations of subtests and composites for all ages combined. As Table 7.15 demonstrates, all subtests and composites are at least moderately correlated with each other. (2) Subtests within each of the factor indexes would correlate more highly with each other than with subtests from other factor indexes. This hypothesis is also supported by the data in Table 7.15. For example, the scores on the Block Design subtest correlate more highly with scores on the Matrix Reasoning subtest (.55) than with scores on the Coding subtest (.34). (3) Subtests with the highest *g* loadings would correlate with each other, independent of scale membership. It was expected that the Block Design, Similarities, Vocabulary, and Picture Completion subtests would be highly correlated. Table 7.15 supports this expectation (Block Design and Similarities correlate .50 and Vocabulary and Similarities correlate .74). (4) Because of split-factor analytic loadings, two subtests (Picture Completion and Word Reasoning) would correlate with the Verbal Comprehension and Perceptual Reasoning subtests as successful performance on these subtests involves a combination of verbal and nonverbal reasoning skills. Picture Completion correlates .77 with scores on the Perceptual Reasoning factor and .47 with scores on the Verbal Comprehension factor and Word Reasoning correlates .63 and .62 with scores on the VCI and PRI factors respectively.

The *WISC-IV Technical and Interpretive Manual* (Wechsler 2003b) presents both exploratory and confirmatory factor-analytic

TABLE 7.15 Intercorrelations of Subtests and Composites for All Ages

Intercorrelations of the Subtests and Sums of Scaled Scores for Composites: All Ages

Subtest/Composite	BD	SI	DS	PCn	CD	VC	LN	MR	CO	SS	PCm	CA	IN	AR	WR	VCI	PRI	WMI	PSI	FSIQ
BD																	.56			.61
SI	.50															.74				.70
DS	.35	.39																.49		.51
PCn	.41	.45	.30														.50			.55
CD	.34	.28	.23	.29															.53	.46
VC	.48	.74	.42	.42	.30											.79				.72
LN	.38	.47	.49	.36	.34	.50												.49		.60
MR	.55	.49	.38	.47	.30	.49	.42										.61			.64
CO	.36	.62	.36	.40	.30	.68	.43	.42								.70				.63
SS	.45	.39	.30	.34	.53	.38	.40	.42	.34										.57	.53
PCm	.54	.50	.26	.39	.29	.51	.34	.46	.44	.37										
CA	.19	.16	.10	.14	.40	.14	.11	.14	.11	.32	.14									
IN	.48	.70	.40	.40	.31	.75	.48	.50	.62	.38	.50	.11								
AR	.55	.56	.47	.42	.36	.59	.51	.54	.52	.43	.41	.17	.62							
WR	.44	.62	.35	.41	.25	.66	.42	.41	.58	.35	.47	.13	.62	.48						
VCI	.50	.89	.44	.47	.34	.91	.52	.52	.86	.42	.55	.15	.77	.63	.70					
PRI	.81	.59	.42	.77	.40	.58	.48	.84	.49	.50	.57	.20	.57	.62	.52	.62				
WMI	.42	.50	.86	.39	.30	.53	.86	.46	.46	.40	.35	.12	.51	.57	.45	.56	.52			
PSI	.45	.38	.30	.36	.88	.39	.40	.44	.37	.87	.39	.41	.39	.45	.35	.43	.51	.40		
FSIQ	.70	.77	.62	.64	.57	.79	.69	.72	.71	.66	.60	.26	.73	.72	.65	.85	.86	.76	.70	
Mean	10.0	10.0	10.0	10.0	10.0	10.0	10.1	10.0	10.0	10.0	10.0	10.0	10.1	10.0	10.1	30.0	30.0	20.0	20.0	100.0
SD	3.0	3.0	3.0	3.0	3.0	3.0	3.0	3.0	3.0	3.0	3.0	3.0	3.0	2.9	3.0	7.9	7.2	5.2	5.2	20.6

NOTE. Uncorrected coefficients appear below the diagonal, and corrected coefficients appear above the diagonal in the shaded area.

SOURCE: *Wechsler Intelligence Scale for Children—Fourth Edition.* Copyright © 2003 by NCS Pearson, Inc. Reproduced with permission. All rights reserved.

TABLE 7.16   Exploratory Factor Pattern Loadings of Core Subtests

All Ages (N = 2,200)

Subtest	Factor			
	Verbal Comprehension	Perceptual Reasoning	Working Memory	Processing Speed
Similarities	**.74**	.19	−.03	−.06
Vocabulary	**.84**	.02	.03	−.02
Comprehension	**.78**	−.11	.03	.08
Block Design	.01	**.66**	−.02	.08
Picture Concepts	.13	**.45**	.03	.03
Matrix Reasoning	.00	**.69**	.06	.01
Digit Span	.00	.07	**.62**	−.06
Letter-Number Sequencing	.09	−.02	**.62**	.06
Coding	.02	−.01	−.04	**.68**
Symbol Search	−.01	.09	.04	**.65**

SOURCE : *Wechsler Intelligence Scale for Children—Fourth Edition.* Copyright © 2003 by NCS Pearson, Inc. Reproduced with permission. All rights reserved.

evidence. Table 7.16 presents the exploratory factor loadings for the core and supplemental subtests based on 1,525 test participants. A series of confirmatory factor analyses were also performed with the four-factor model providing the most parsimonious explanation of the data. The interested reader is referred to the *WISC-IV Technical and Interpretive Manual* (Wechsler, 2003b) for an in-depth discussion.

Other Evidence of Validity

As additional evidence of validity, four studies were conducted where children's WISC-IV performance was compared with their performance on one of four measures of ability (Wechsler, 2003b). In all WISC-IV comparison studies (WISC-III, WPPSI-III, WAIS-III, and WASI), order of administration was counterbalanced and careful attention was paid to the sample characteristics (sex, race/ethnicity, parent education,

and region) to insure adequate representation. Table 7.17, for example, presents the correlations between the WISC-IV and WISC-III Composite scores for 244 children. The high correlations (.89 for FSIQ and .88 for VCI to .72 for WMI-FDI and PRI-POI) provide validity evidence that the WISC-IV is assessing similar intelligence constructs as the WISC-III. Additional validity study evidence examining relationships between the WISC-IV and an individually administered measure of memory and parent or teacher ratings of emotional intelligence, adaptive behavior, and giftedness can be found in the *WISC-IV Technical and Interpretive Manual* (Wechsler, 2003b).

SUMMARY

This chapter has provided the user with a combination of practical and essential administration,

TABLE 7.17   Correlations between Composite Scores on the WISC-IV and WISC-III

Composite	WISC-IV			WISC-III			r_{12}[b]	Corrected r_{12}[b]	Standard Difference[c]
	Mean[a]	SD	N	Mean[a]	SD	N			
VCI-VIQ	103.0	12.3	239	105.4	13.8	239	.83	.87	.18
PRI-PIQ	103.9	14.0	242	107.3	14.9	242	.73	.74	.24
WMI-FDI	101.5	15.3	240	103.0	15.9	240	.74	.72	.10
PSI-PSI	102.7	15.1	232	108.2	16.3	232	.81	.81	.35
FSIQ-FSIQ	104.5	14.0	233	107.0	14.4	233	.87	.89	.18
VCI-VCI	102.9	12.3	238	106.0	13.6	238	.85	.88	.24
PRI-POI	103.9	14.0	241	106.9	14.6	241	.70	.72	.21

NOTE : Correlations were computed separately for each order of administration in counterbalance design and corrected for the variability of the WISC-IV standardization sample (Guilford & Fruchter, 1978).
[a]The values in the Mean columns are the average of the means of the two administration orders.
[b]The weighted average across both administration orders was obtained with Fisher's z transformation.
[c]The Standard Difference is the difference of the two test means divided by the square root of the pooled variance, computed using Cohen's (1996) Formula 10.4.

scoring, and Interpretive tips, framed by solid psychometric and test construction information. The latest version of the Wechsler series, WISC-IV (Wechsler, 2003a), blends features that have stood the test of time (e.g. Vocabulary, Similarities, and Block Design) with modifications and changes in test interpretation and advances in cognitive neuroscience and intelligence theory. As the field of school psychology shifts from the ability–achievement discrepancy model of LD identification toward incorporation of RTI and process assessment in the identification and treatment of children with neurodevelopmental disorders, the WISC-IV with its strong psychometrics and improved theoretical foundation is well suited to assist with this diagnostic clarification process.

REFERENCES

Alfonso, V. C., Flanagan, D. P., & Radwan, S. (2005). The impact of the Catell-Horn-Carroll theory on test development and interpretation of cognitive and academic abilities. In D. P. Flanagan & P. L. Harrison (Eds.), *Contemporary intellectual assessment: Theories, tests and issues* (pp. 185–202). New York: Guilford Press.

Allen, M. J., & Yen, W. M. (1979). *Introduction to measurement theory.* Monterey, CA: Brooks/Cole.

American Educational Research Association. (1999). *Standards for educational and psychological testing.* Washington, DC: Author.

American Psychiatric Association. (2000). *Diagnostic and statistical manual of mental disorders* (4th ed., Text Revision). Washington, DC: Author.

Berninger, V. W., O'Donnell, L., & Holdnack, J. (2008). Research-supported differential diagnosis of specific learning disabilities and implications for instruction and response to instruction. In A. Prifitera, D. Saklofske, & L. Weiss (Eds.), *WISC-IV Clinical Assessment and Intervention* (2nd ed., pp. 69–108). London: Elsevier Academic Press.

Crocker, L., & Algina, J. (1986). *Introduction to classical and modern test theory.* Fort Worth, TX: Harcourt Brace Javanovich College.

Carroll, J. (1993). *Human cognitive abilities: A survey of factor-analytic studies*. Cambridge, England: Cambridge University Press.

Cohen, J. (1959). The factorial structure of the WISC at 7-7, 10-6, and 13-6. *Journal of Consulting Psychology*, *23*, 285–299.

Colom, R. Rebello, L., Palacios, A., Juan-Espinosa, M., & Kyllonen, P. C. (2004). Working memory is (almost) perfectly predicted by g. *Intelligence*, *32*, 277–296.

Das, J. P., & Naglieri, J. A. (1997). *Cognitive Assessment System*. Itasca, IL: Riverside.

Delis, D., Kaplan, E., & Kramer, J. (2001). *Delis-Kaplan Executive Function System*. San Antonio, TX: Psychological Corporation.

Denckla, M. B. (1994). Measurement of executive function. In G. R. Lyon (Ed.), *Frames of reference for the assessment of learning disabilities: New views on measurement issues* (pp. 117–142). Baltimore: Brookes.

Dykman, R. A., Ackerman, P. T., & Oglesby, D. M. (1980). Correlates of problem solving in hyperactive, learning disabled, and control boys. *Journal of Learning Disabilities*, *13*, 309–318.

Elliott, C. D. (2007). *Differential Abilities Scales—Second Edition*. San Antonio, TX: Harcourt Assessment.

Flanagan, D. P., & Kaufman, A. S. (2004). *Essentials of WISC-IV assessment*. Hoboken, NJ: Wiley.

Flavell, J. H. (1985). *Cognitive development* (2nd ed.). Englewood Cliffs, NJ: Prentice-Hall.

Flynn, J. R. (1998). IQ gains over time: Toward finding the causes. In U. Neisser (Ed.), *The rising curve: Long term gains in IQ and related measures* (pp. 25–66). Washington, DC: American Psychological Association.

Fry, A. F., & Hale, S. (1996). Processing speed, working memory, and fluid intelligence: Evidence for a developmental cascade. *Psychological Science*, *7*, 237–241.

Fry, A. F., & Hale, S. (2000). Relationships among processing speed, working memory, and fluid intelligence in children. *Biological Psychology*, *54*, 1–34.

Hale, J. B., Fiorello, C. A., Kavanagh, J. A., Holdnack, J. A., & Aloe, A. M. (2007). Is the demise of IQ interpretation justified?: A response to Special Issue authors. *Applied Neuropsychology*, *14*, 37–51.

Hale, J. B., Kaufman, A. S., Naglieri, J. A., & Kavale, K. A. (2006). Implementation of IDEA: Integrating response to intervention and cognitive assessment models. *Psychology in the Schools*, *43*, 753–770.

Heinz-Martin, S., Oberauer, K., Wittman, W. W., Wilhelm, O., & Schulze, R. (2002). Working memory capacity explains reasoning ability—and a little more. *Intelligence*, *30*, 261–288.

Horn, J. L., & Blankson, N. (2005). Foundations for better understanding of cognitive abilities. In D. P. Flanagan & P. L. Harrison (Eds.), *Contemporary intellectual assessment: Theories, tests and issues* (pp. 41–68). New York: Guilford Press.

Individuals with Disabilities Education Improvement Act of 2004 (IDEA), Pub. L. No. 108–446, 118 Stat. 2647 (2004). [Amending 20 U.S.C. §§ 1400 et seq.].

Kamphaus, R. K., Winsor, A. P., Rowe, E. W., & Kim, S. (2005). A history of intelligence test interpretation. In D. P. Flanagan & P. L. Harrison (Eds.), *Contemporary intellectual assessment: Theories, tests and issues* (pp. 23–38). New York: Guilford Press.

Kaufman, A. S. (1979). *Intelligent testing with the WISC-R*. New York: Wiley.

Kaufman, A. S. (1994). *Intelligent testing with the WISC-III*. New York: Wiley.

Magnusson, D. (1967). *Test theory*. Reading, MA: Addison-Wesley.

Mayes, S. D., & Calhoun, S. L. (2007). Wechsler Intelligence Scale for Children—Third and Fourth Editions: Predictors of academic achievement in children with attention-deficit/hyperactivity disorder. *School Psychology Quarterly*, *22*, 234–249.

McDermott, P. A., Fantuzzo, J. W., & Glutting, J. J. (1990). Just say no to subtest analysis: A critique on Wechsler theory and practice. *Journal of Psychoeducational Assessment*, *8*, 290–302.

Naglieri, J. A., & Paolitto, A. W. (2005). Ipsative comparisons of the WISC-IV Index scores. *Applied Neuropsychology*, *12*, 208–211.

Pennington, B. F., & Ozonoff, S. (1996). Executive functions and developmental psychopathology. *Journal of Child Psychology and Psychiatry*, *37*(1), 51–87.

Prifitera, A., & Dersh, J. (1993). Base rates of WISC-III diagnostic subtest patterns among normal, learning-disabled, and ADHD samples. *Journal of Psychoeducational Assessment: WISC-III Monograph*, 43–55.

Prifitera, A., Weiss, L. G., Saklofske, D. H., & Rolfhus, E. (2005). In A. Prifitera, D. H. Saklofske, & L. G. Weiss (Eds.), *WISC-IV clinical use and interpretation* (pp. 3–32). London: Elsevier Academic Press.

Psychological Corporation. (2002). *Wechsler Individual Achievement Test—Second Edition*. San Antonio: Author.

Raiford, S. E., Weiss, L. G., Rolfhus, E., & Coalson, D. (2005) *WISC-IV technical report # 4: General ability index*. San Antonio, TX: Harcourt Assessment Inc.

Rapaport, D., Gill, M. M., & Schafer, R (1968). *Diagnostic psychological testing*. New York: International Universities Press.

Reschly, D. J., & Ysseldyke, J. E. (2002). Paradigm shift: The past is not the future. In A. Thomas & J. Grimes (Eds.), *Best practices in school psychology IV: Vol. I*. Bethesda, MD: National Association of School Psychologists.

Reynolds, C. R., & Kaiser, S. M. (2003). Bias in the assessment of aptitude. In C. R. Reynolds & R. W. Kamphaus (Eds.), *Handbook of psychological and educational assessment of children* (2nd ed., 519–562). New York: Wiley.

Reynolds, C. R., & Kamphaus, R. W. (2004). *Behavior assessment system for children—Second Edition*. Bloomington, MN: Pearson Assessments.

Saklofske, D. H, Prifitera, A., Weiss, L. G., Rolfhus, E., & Zhu, J. (2005). In A. Prifitera, D. H. Saklofske, & L. G. Weiss (Eds.), *WISC-IV clinical use and interpretation* (pp. 33–65). London: Elsevier Academic Press.

Sattler, J. M. (2008). *Assessment of children: Cognitive foundations* (5th ed.). San Diego, CA: Author.

Semrud-Clikeman, M. (2005). Neuropsychological aspects for evaluating learning disabilities. *Journal of Learning Disabilities*, 38, 563–568.

Semrud-Clikeman, M., Guy, K. A., & Griffin, J. (2000). Rapid automatized naming in children with reading disabilities and attention deficit hyperactivity disorder. *Brain and Language*, 74, 70–83.

Shaywitz, B. A., Fletcher, J. M., Holahan, J. M., & Shaywitz, S. E. (1992). Discrepancy compared to low achievement definitions of reading disability: Results from the Connecticut Longitudinal Study. *Journal of Learning Disabilities*, 25, 639–648.

Stoiber, K. C. (2003). *Functional assessment and intervention system: Improving school behavior*. San Antonio, TX: Psychological Corporation.

Teeter, P. A., & Semrud-Clikeman, M. (1997). *Child neuropsychological assessment and intervention*. Boston: Allyn & Bacon.

Tulsky, D., Saklofske, D., & Ricker, J. (2003). Historical overview of intelligence and memory: Factors influencing the Wechsler scales. In D. S. Tulsky et al. (Eds.), *Clinical interpretation of the WAIS-III and the WMS-III* (pp. 7–41). San Diego: Academic Press.

U.S. Bureau of the Census, (2000). *Current population survey, March 2000: School Enrollment Supplement File* [CD-Rom]. Washington, DC: U.S. Bureau of the Census (producer/distributor).

Wasserman, J. D., & Tulsky, D. S. (2005). A history of intelligence assessment. In D. P. Flanagan & P. L. Harrison (Eds.), *Contemporary intellectual assessment: Theories, tests and issues* (pp. 3–22). New York: Guilford Press.

Watkins, M. (2000). Cognitive profile analysis: A shared professional myth. *School Psychology Quarterly*, 15, 465–479.

Wechsler, D. (1939). *Wechsler-Bellevue Intelligence Scale*. New York: Psychological Corporation.

Wechsler, D. (1946). *Wechsler-Bellevue Intelligence Scale—Form II*. New York: Psychological Corporation.

Wechsler, D. (1949). *Wechsler Intelligence Scale for Children*. New York: Psychological Corporation.

Wechsler, D. (1958). *The measurement and appraisal of adult intelligence* (4th ed.). Baltimore: Williams and Wilkins.

Wechsler, D. (1974). *Wechsler Intelligence Scale for Children—Revised*. New York: Psychological Corporation.

Wechsler, D. (1991). *Wechsler Intelligence Scale for Children—Third Edition*. San Antonio, TX: Psychological Corporation.

Wechsler, D. (1997). *Wechsler Adult Intelligence Scale—Third Edition*. San Antonio, TX: Psychological Corporation.

Wechsler, D. (2002). *Wechsler Preschool and Primary Scale of Intelligence for Children—Third Edition*. San Antonio, TX: Psychological Corporation.

Wechsler, D. (2003a). *Wechsler Intelligence Scale for Children—Fourth Edition (WISC-IV): Administration and scoring manual*. San Antonio, TX: Psychological Corporation.

Wechsler, D. (2003b). *Wechsler Intelligence Scale for Children—Fourth Edition (WISC-IV): Technical and Interpretive manual*. San Antonio, TX: Psychological Corporation.

Wechsler, D. (2003c). WISC-IV Scoring Assistant™. San Antonio, TX: Psychological Corporation.

Wechsler, D. (2003d). WISC-IV Writer™. San Antonio, TX: Psychological Corporation.

Williams, P., Weiss, L., & Rolfhus, E. (2003a). WISC-IV technical report #2: *Psychometric properties*. San Antonio, TX. Psychological Corporation.

Williams, P., Weiss, L., & Rolfhus, E. (2003b). WISC-IV technical report #3: *Clinical validity*. San Antonio, TX. Psychological Corporation

Woodcock, R. W., McGrew, K. S., Mather, N. (2001). *Woodcock-Johnson-III Tests of Cognitive Abilities*. Itasca, IL: Riverside.

Zhu, J., & Weiss, L. (2005). The Wechsler scales. In D. P. Flanagan & P. L. Harrison (Eds.), *Contemporary intellectual assessment: Theories, tests and issues* (pp. 297–324). New York: Guilford Press.

CHAPTER 8

Woodcock-Johnson III Tests of Cognitive Abilities

Barbara J. Wendling, Nancy Mather, and Fredrick A. Schrank

THEORETICAL FOUNDATIONS OF THE WJ III

A Brief History of the WJ III

The *Woodcock-Johnson III Tests of Cognitive Abilities* (WJ III COG; Woodcock, McGrew, & Mather, 2001) provides measures of general intellectual ability, as well as broad and narrow cognitive abilities across the lifespan (from 2 to 90+ years). An important element of the WJ III COG is its focus on measurement of various cognitive processes that can help provide a clearer picture of an individual's strengths and weaknesses. The first edition of the Woodcock-Johnson was published in 1977; it was subsequently revised in 1989 and the third edition was published in 2001. A normative update to the WJ III COG was made available in 2007 (Woodcock, McGrew, Schrank, & Mather, 2007). The *Woodcock-Johnson III Diagnostic Supplement to the Tests of Cognitive Abilities* (Diagnostic Supplement) (Woodcock, McGrew, Mather, & Schrank, 2003) provides additional cognitive measures and interpretive options and is designed to be used in conjunction with the WJ III COG. In addition, the WJ III COG was co-normed with the WJ III Tests of Achievement (WJ III ACH) and is part of a family of related assessments that includes the parallel Spanish version, the *Batería III Woodcock-Muñoz Pruebas de habilidad cognitiva* (Muñoz-Sandoval, Woodcock, McGrew, & Mather, 2005).

CHC Theory

The theoretical model that underlies the development and organization of the WJ III COG is referred to as the Cattell-Horn-Carroll (CHC) theory. This data-based theory is derived from the merging of two theoretically similar psychometric theories of intelligence: the Cattell-Horn *Gf-Gc* theory (Horn & Noll, 1977) and Carroll's three-stratum theory (Carroll, 1993). Both of these theories conceptualize intelligence as involving multiple broad and narrow cognitive abilities. An in-depth description of CHC theory is provided in McGrew (2005) and McGrew and Woodcock (2001). CHC theory rests on a foundation of validity evidence (Kranzler & Keith, 1999; McGrew & Flanagan, 1998; McGrew & Woodcock, 2001). Additionally, empirical studies have shown that the CHC structure of intelligence is invariant across the lifespan (Bickley, Keith, & Wolfe, 1995) and across gender and ethnic groups (Carroll, 1993; Keith, 1997, 1999). When discussing CHC theory, Flanagan and Ortiz (2001) stated, " … it is currently the most researched, empirically supported, and comprehensive descriptive hierarchical psychometric framework from which to organize thinking about intelligence-test interpretation" (p. 25).

CHC theory was used as the blueprint for development of the WJ III COG. Each of the WJ III COG and Diagnostic Supplement tests provides a norm-referenced measure of one or more narrow, or specific, psychometrically defined cognitive abilities. Each cluster, or composite, measuring a broad ability or construct, includes a minimum of two tests that measure different specific, narrow abilities. Table 8.1 summarizes the broad and narrow abilities represented in the WJ III COG and the Diagnostic Supplement.

Within the CHC framework, the WJ III COG measures seven broad cognitive abilities and a number of narrow abilities. The seven broad CHC abilities measured are: Comprehension-Knowledge (*Gc*), Long-Term Retrieval (*Glr*), Visual-Spatial Thinking (*Gv*), Auditory Processing (*Ga*), Fluid Reasoning (*Gf*), Processing Speed (*Gs*), and Short-Term Memory (*Gsm*). The uppercase *G* indicates a measure of cognitive ability, and the subsequent lowercase initials are used to specify the type (e.g., *Gsm* represents the cognitive ability of short-term memory). A brief description of each of these abilities follows.

Comprehension-Knowledge (*Gc*)

This CHC broad ability is sometimes referred to as *crystallized intelligence*, *cultural knowledge*, or *verbal ability*. *Gc* is typically viewed as a store of acquired knowledge that is primarily language-based. *Gc* includes vocabulary knowledge, general and specific knowledge, and listening comprehension.

Long-Term Retrieval (*Glr*)

The CHC broad ability of Long-Term Retrieval (*Glr*) involves the cognitive processes of acquiring, storing, and retrieving information. *Glr* reflects the efficiency with which information is initially stored and later retrieved. Thus, this ability measures a person's facility in storing and recalling associations.

Visual-Spatial Thinking (*Gv*)

Visual-Spatial Thinking (*Gv*) involves visual perception (the process of extracting features from visual stimuli) and includes the processes involved in generating, storing, retrieving, and transforming visual images.

Auditory Processing (*Ga*)

Auditory Processing (*Ga*) is a CHC broad ability that involves auditory perception (the process of extracting features from auditory stimuli) and includes a wide range of abilities that are needed to discriminate, analyze, synthesize, comprehend, and manipulate sounds. *Ga* includes phonological awareness, an important ability underlying reading and spelling development.

Fluid Reasoning (*Gf*)

Reasoning is a complex, hierarchical cognitive function that can rely on many other cognitive processes, depending on the nature and requirements of the task. Certain narrow abilities have been identified by CHC theory based on different types of reasoning processes. Inductive and deductive reasoning are the hallmarks of this CHC broad ability. Reasoning also often relies on novel problem solving or determining methods and strategies for solving unfamiliar problems.

Processing Speed (*Gs*)

This CHC broad ability represents the fluency and automaticity with which cognitive tasks are performed, especially when under pressure to maintain attention and concentration. Efficiency

TABLE 8.1   Broad and Narrow CHC Abilities Represented in the WJ III COG and Diagnostic Supplement

CHC Broad Ability	WJ III COG Standard Battery *Primary Narrow Abilities Measured*	WJ III COG Extended Battery *Primary Narrow Abilities Measured*	WJ III Diagnostic Supplement *Primary Narrow Abilities Measured*
Comprehension-Knowledge (*Gc*)	1. Verbal Comprehension *Lexical knowledge* *Language development*	11. General Information *General (verbal) information*	31. Bilingual Verbal Comprehension *Lexical knowledge* *Language development*
Long-Term Retrieval (*Glr*)	2. Visual-Auditory Learning *Associative memory* 10. Visual Auditory Learning—Delayed *Associative memory*	12. Retrieval Fluency *Ideational fluency*	21. Memory for Names *Associative memory* 30. Memory for Names—Delayed *Associative memory*
Visual-Spatial Thinking (*Gv*)	3. Spatial Relations *Visualization* *Spatial relations*	13. Picture Recognition *Visual memory* 19. Planning *Spatial scanning* *Deduction reasoning*	22. Visual Closure *Closure speed* 28. Block Rotation *Visualization* *Spatial relations*
Auditory Processing (*Ga*)	4. Sound Blending *Phonetic coding* 9. Incomplete Words *Phonetic coding*	14. Auditory Attention *Speech-sound discrimination* *Resistance to auditory stimulus distortion*	23. Sound Patterns—Voice *Sound discrimination* 29. Sound Patterns—Music *Sound discrimination*
Fluid Reasoning (*Gf*)	5. Concept Formation *Inductive reasoning*	15. Analysis-Synthesis *Deductive reasoning* 19. Planning (see *Gv*)	24. Number Series *Quantitative reasoning* 25. Number Matrices *Quantitative reasoning*
Processing Speed (*Gs*)	6. Visual Matching *Perceptual speed*	16. Decision Speed *Semantic processing speed* 18. Rapid Picture Naming *Naming facility* 20. Pair Cancellation *Attention/concentration*	26. Cross Out *Perceptual speed*
Short-Term Memory (*Gsm*)	7. Numbers Reversed *Working memory* 8. Auditory Working Memory *Working memory*	17. Memory for Words *Memory span*	27. Memory for Sentences *Auditory memory span* *Listening ability*

of cognitive processing is based partly on the speed of mental activity. For many years, cognitive speediness, or mental quickness, has been considered an important aspect of intelligence (Nettelbeck, 1994; Vernon, 1983). Kail (1991) explained the importance of *Gs* to performance of tasks: "In the face of limited processing resources, the speed of processing is critical because it determines in part how rapidly limited resources can be reallocated to other cognitive tasks" (p. 152).

Short-Term Memory (*Gsm*)

Short-Term Memory (*Gsm*) is the ability to apprehend and maintain awareness of elements of information within a short timeframe (the last minute or so). *Gsm* is defined as a limited-capacity system because most typical adults can only hold seven bits or chunks of information (plus or minus two chunks) for a matter of seconds before it is acted upon, lost, or stored. In the WJ III COG, the *Gsm* cluster includes a memory span task, which involves repeating information verbatim, and a working memory task, which involves apprehending the information but then rearranging it, such as hearing a string of numbers or words and then saying them in a reversed order.

In the context of CHC theory, two additional broad abilities are measured within the co-normed WJ III Tests of Achievement: Quantitative Knowledge (*Gq*), which includes mathematical understanding and reasoning, and Reading and Writing Ability (*Grw*). When used together, the WJ III COG, Diagnostic Supplement, and the WJ III ACH provide a wide breadth of coverage of the continuum of human abilities as defined by CHC theory.

DESCRIPTION

The WJ III COG and Diagnostic Supplement have a total of 31 tests organized into three test easels: Standard, Extended, and Diagnostic Supplement (see Table 8.1). Various combinations of these 31 tests measure general intellectual ability, broad and narrow cognitive abilities, and aspects of executive functioning. The Selective Testing Table (see Figure 8.1 for the WJ III COG and Figure 8.2 for the Diagnostic Supplement) illustrates which tests are required for each cluster, or interpretive option.

Measures of Intelligence

When a global estimate of intellectual ability is necessary, practitioners may select from a number of options on the WJ III COG: standard, extended, brief, early development, or bilingual. A low verbal broad cognitive ability score is also available. Some of the options require tests from the WJ III COG only (Tests 1–20), while others require additional tests from the Diagnostic Supplement (Tests 21–31).

All General Intellectual Ability (GIA) options are first principal-component measures of general intellectual ability (*g*). The tests are differentially weighted so that high *g* tasks (e.g., *Gc* or *Gf*) contribute more toward the global score than do the low *g* tasks (e.g., *Gs* or *Ga*). Appendix C in the *Technical Manual for the WJ III Normative Update* (McGrew, Schrank, & Woodcock, 2007) provides complete information about the *g* weights for the tests in each GIA option. An examination of the *g* weights reveals that they vary little as a function of age.

General Intellectual Ability (GIA)—Standard or Extended

These two options for obtaining a comprehensive estimate of ability include measures of all seven abilities. GIA—Standard requires administration of 7 tests (Tests 1–7), one for each ability. GIA—Extended requires administration of 14 tests (Tests 1–7 and Tests 11–17), two tests for each of the seven broad CHC abilities. An advantage of the GIA—Extended is that these same 14 tests create the seven CHC broad

Selective Testing Table

Figure 8.1 — Selective Testing Table for the WJ III Tests of Cognitive Abilities. Column groups: **Intellectual Ability** = General Intellectual Ability (Std); General Intellectual Ability (Ext); Brief Intellectual Ability; Verbal Ability (Std); Verbal Ability (Ext). **Cognitive Categories** = Thinking Ability (Std); Thinking Ability (Ext); Cognitive Efficiency (Std); Cognitive Efficiency (Ext). **CHC Factors** = Comprehension-Knowledge (Gc); Long-Term Retrieval (Glr); Visual-Spatial Thinking (Gv); Auditory Processing (Ga); Fluid Reasoning (Gf); Processing Speed (Gs); Short-Term Memory (Gsm). **Clinical Clusters** = Phonemic Awareness; Working Memory; Broad Attention; Cognitive Fluency; Executive Processes; Delayed Recall; Knowledge.

Tests of Cognitive Abilities	GIA (Std)	GIA (Ext)	Brief Intel.	Verbal (Std)	Verbal (Ext)	Thinking (Std)	Thinking (Ext)	Cog. Eff. (Std)	Cog. Eff. (Ext)	Gc	Glr	Gv	Ga	Gf	Gs	Gsm	Phonemic Aware.	Working Mem.	Broad Atten.	Cog. Fluency	Exec. Processes	Delayed Recall	Knowledge
Standard Battery																							
1. Verbal Comprehension	■	■	■	■	■					■													
2. Visual-Auditory Learning	■	■				■	■				■												
3. Spatial Relations	■	■				■	■					■											
4. Sound Blending	■	■				■	■						■				■						
5. Concept Formation	■	■	■			■	■							■							■		
6. Visual Matching	■	■	■					■	■						■								
7. Numbers Reversed	■	■						■	■							■		■	■				
8. Incomplete Words													■										
9. Auditory Working Memory																		■	■				
10. Visual-Auditory Learning-Delayed																						■[1]	
Extended Battery																							
11. General Information		■			■					■													■[2]
12. Retrieval Fluency		■					■				■									■			
13. Picture Recognition		■					■					■											
14. Auditory Attention		■					■						■						■				
15. Analysis-Synthesis		■					■							■									
16. Decision Speed		■							■						■					■			
17. Memory for Words		■							■							■							
18. Rapid Picture Naming																				■			
19. Planning																					■		
20. Pair Cancellation																			■		■		

[1] Also includes Test 12 Story Recall–Delayed from the *WJ III Tests of Achievement*.

[2] Also includes Test 19 Academic Knowledge from the *WJ III Tests of Achievement*.

Source: From the WJ III Tests of Congnitive Abilities, by R.W. Woodcock, K.S. McGrew, and N. Mather, 2001, Rolling Meadows, IL: Riverside Publishing. Copyright © 2001 by the Riverside Publishing Company. Used with Permission.

FIGURE 8.1
Selective Testing Table for the WJ III Tests of Cognitive Abilities

ability clusters, resulting in rich interpretive information.

GIA—Early Development

The GIA—Early Development (*GIA-EDev*) is designed to be used with preschool children or individuals of any age with severe developmental delays. It requires six tests, three from the WJ III COG and three from the Diagnostic Supplement. GIA-EDev does not include a measure of fluid reasoning.

GIA—Bilingual

The GIA—Bilingual (*GIA-Bil*) is designed for English-dominant bilingual individuals. It includes seven tests, five from the WJ III COG and two from the Diagnostic Supplement. Uniquely, the GIA-Bil allows practitioners to combine the

Selective Testing Table

Tests of Cognitive Abilities		General Intellectual Ability	General Intellectual Ability–Early Dev	General Intellectual Ability–Bilingual	Broad Cognitive Ability–Low Verbal	Visual-Spatial Thinking-3	Fluid Reasoning-3	Numerical Reasoning	Associative Memory	Associative Memory–Delayed	Visualization	Sound Discrimination	Auditory Memory Span	Perceptual Speed
		Intellectual Ability				**Broad CHC Clusters**		**Narrow CHC Clusters**						
Standard Battery	Test 1. Verbal Comprehension	▪	▪											
	Test 2. Visual-Auditory Learning								▪					
	Test 3. Spatial Relations		▪	▪	▪						▪			
	Test 4. Sound Blending													
	Test 5. Concept Formation		▪	▪			▪							
	Test 6. Visual Matching	▪	▪	▪										▪
	Test 7. Numbers Reversed		▪	▪										
	Test 8. Incomplete Words	▪												
	Test 9. Auditory Working Memory													
	Test 10. Visual-Auditory Learning-Delayed									▪				
Extended Battery	Test 11. General Information													
	Test 12. Retrieval Fluency													
	Test 13. Picture Recognition					▪								
	Test 14. Auditory Attention													
	Test 15. Analysis-Synthesis						▪							
	Test 16. Decision Speed													
	Test 17. Memory for Words												▪	
	Test 18. Rapid Picture Naming													
	Test 19. Planning													
	Test 20. Pair Cancellation													
Diagnostic Supplement	Test 21. Memory for Names	▪	▪	▪					▪					
	Test 22. Visual Closure	▪			▪									
	Test 23. Sound Patterns–Voice		▪	▪								▪		
	Test 24. Number Series							▪						
	Test 25. Number Matrices						▪	▪						
	Test 26. Cross Out													▪
	Test 27. Memory for Sentences	▪											▪	
	Test 28. Block Rotation										▪			
	Test 29. Sound Patterns–Music											▪		
	Test 30. Memory for Names–Delayed									▪				
	Test 31. Bilingual Verbal Comprehension English/Spanish		▪											

Source: From the WJ III Diagnostic Supplement, by R.W. Woodcock, K.S. McGrew, N. Mather, & F.S. Schrank, 2003, Rolling Meadows, IL: Riverside Publishing. Copyright © 2003 by the Riverside Publishing Company. Used with Permission.

FIGURE 8.2
Selective Testing Table for the WJ III Diagnostic Supplement

individual's English knowledge with knowledge in his or her first language for the *Gc* test, Verbal Comprehension (Test 1). Practitioners may use Test 31: Bilingual Verbal Comprehension in place of Test 1 if the individual speaks English and Spanish. If the individual's first language is something other than Spanish, practitioners may be able to substitute the appropriate score from the Bilingual Verbal Ability Test (BVAT) (Muñoz-Sandoval, Cummins, Alvarado, & Ruef, 1998).

Brief Intellectual Ability (BIA)

When a quick estimate of overall ability is needed, practitioners may administer three tests (Tests 1, 5, 6) to obtain the BIA. This option is ideal for screening, reevaluations, or research. Should further testing be needed, the practitioner may simply administer additional tests to obtain a more comprehensive GIA or diagnostic information. The BIA is an equally weighted composite.

Broad Cognitive Ability—Low Verbal

Designed as a broad measure of cognitive ability that has relatively low overall receptive and expressive verbal requirements, the Broad Cognitive Ability—Low Verbal (*BCA-LV*) includes six tests, four from the WJ III COG and two from the Diagnostic Supplement. It does not include a *Gc* measure. The BCA-LV is an equally weighted composite.

Measures of Broad and Narrow Abilities

Each test in the WJ III COG and Diagnostic Supplement measures a narrow ability. However, several narrow ability clusters are also available for interpretation. Practitioners may obtain cluster-level information on the following: working memory (the ability to hold information in immediate awareness and then transform, or manipulate it), numerical reasoning (the ability to reason with mathematical

concepts involving the relationships and properties of numbers), associative memory (the ability to store and retrieve associations), associative memory—delayed (the ability to recall associations that were previously learned from 30 minutes to 8 days), visualization (the ability to picture objects or patterns in space by perceiving how the object would appear if presented in an altered form), sound discrimination (the ability to distinguish between pairs of voice-like or musical sound patterns), auditory memory span (the ability to listen to sequentially ordered information and then recall it immediately), and perceptual speed (the ability to scan and compare visual symbols quickly).

The seven CHC broad abilities and working memory are available from tests within the WJ III COG. The narrow ability clusters for numerical reasoning and sound discrimination are available from tests in the Diagnostic Supplement. All other narrow abilities require tests from both the WJ III COG and the Diagnostic Supplement. In addition, when using the Diagnostic Supplement with the WJ III COG, practitioners have access to broader measures of fluid reasoning (Fluid Reasoning 3) and visual-spatial thinking (Visual-Spatial Thinking 3).

Practitioners may obtain three additional, clinical clusters: Broad Attention, Executive Processes, and Cognitive Fluency. Information from these clusters can help provide information about an individual's unique cognitive characteristics. The Selective Testing Table (see Figure 8.1) identifies the tests needed to obtain each cluster.

Broad Attention

The Broad Attention cluster is comprised of four tests, each of which measures a different cognitive aspect of attention: attentional capacity, sustained attention, selective attention, and the ability to manipulate information placed in short-term memory. The purpose of this cluster is to examine the underlying cognitive components of attention and, therefore, it may not identify attention-deficit disorders, which are attributed primarily with behavioral problems of impulse control and/or behavioral self-regulation.

Executive Processes

This cluster measures aspects of the central executive system such as planning, response inhibition, and cognitive flexibility. Executive processing requires mental forethought and flexibility, as well as impulse control and self-monitoring behaviors.

Cognitive Fluency

This cluster measures automaticity with simple cognitive tasks and includes naming facility, semantic processing speed, and ideational fluency. All three tests are timed. Comparing performance on this cluster to performance on the WJ III ACH Academic Fluency cluster can provide important information regarding a need for accommodations or certain instructional strategies.

ADMINISTRATION AND SCORING

The WJ III COG and Diagnostic Supplement use easel-style test books for the administration of all tests. The easels contain the examiner directions, administration instructions, and for many of the tests, the actual test items. Nine of the tests, six in the WJ III COG and three in the Diagnostic Supplement, require use of an audio recording to administer items. Six of the tests, five in the WJ III COG and one in the Diagnostic Supplement, are timed. With the exception of the timed tests, all of the other tests use estimated starting points with basal and ceiling rules. In addition, three tests in the WJ III COG require the use of a Subject Response Booklet (SRB) so examinees may record their responses to the test items. Two tests, Test 6 (Visual Matching) and Test 26 (Cross Out), include examinee response pages within the examiner's test record.

Order of Administration

Although many examiners administer tests in the order in which they appear in the easel, beginning with the Standard Battery, the tests may be administered in any order. Because the WJ III encourages practitioners to follow the principle of selective testing, examiners may select the specific tests that are most relevant to the referral question and purpose of testing. In these situations, the examiner must use professional judgment in determining the administration order. One sequence is to maintain the numeric order, but skip the tests that will not be administered to the examinee.

Administration Formats

The WJ III tests have several different formats: standard, standard with sample/training items, audio-recorded presentation, controlled learning, timed, and special scoring procedures. Table 8.2 presents the tests organized by type of format. These formats are described briefly in the following.

Standard Format

These tests have straightforward administration rules and have starting points and basal/ceiling rules, but no other special administration features. This format is the easiest to learn.

Standard Format with Samples/Training

These tests are simple to administer, but require the use of samples or training items. Examiners must be diligent about administering the samples as directed and providing the appropriate feedback and training opportunities to each examinee.

Audio-Recorded Presentation

Once the introduction is completed live-voice, as well as any items that are administered orally, the remainder of the test is administered by using the audio-recording that comes with the test. Some

TABLE 8.2 WJ III COG and Diagnostic Supplement Tests Organized by Test Format

Standard with or without Samples	Audio-Recorded	Controlled-Learning	Timed	Special Scoring
1. Verbal Comprehension	4. Sound Blending	2. Visual-Auditory Learning	12. Retrieval Fluency	19. Planning
3. Spatial Relations	7. Numbers Reversed	5. Concept Formation	6. Visual Matching	
13. Picture Recognition	8. Incomplete Words	10. VAL—Delayed	16. Decision Speed	
11. General Information	9. Auditory Working Memory	15. Analysis-Synthesis	18. Rapid Picture Naming	
22. Visual Closure	14. Auditory Attention	21. Memory for Names	20. Pair Cancellation	
24. Number Series	17. Memory for Words	30. MFN—Delayed	26. Cross Out	
25. Number Matrices	27. Memory for Sentences			
28. Block Rotation	23. Sound Patterns—Voice			
31. Bilingual Verbal Comprehension	29. Sound Patterns—Music			

practice is required in locating the various tests on the CD for quick, efficient administration.

Controlled Learning

The tests with this format are the most demanding to learn. They require study and practice for fluent administration. Examiners must be consistent when teaching each examinee and when providing corrective feedback.

Timed

Once the directions and any allowable practice items have been completed, the examinee works independently until the task is finished or the time limit has been reached.

Special Scoring

One test, Planning, requires the examiner to observe carefully while the examinee is responding to each item so that appropriate directions can be provided when any errors are made.

Administration Tips

All of the necessary information for learning how to administer the WJ III COG and Diagnostic Supplement are located in the Examiner's Manuals and test easels. Another helpful resource for using and interpreting the WJ III COG is the *Essentials of WJ III Cognitive Abilities Assessment* (Schrank, Flanagan, Woodcock, & Mascolo, 2002). In the Essentials book, Chapter 2 reviews key administration points and Chapter 3 provides reminders for scoring each test. A summary of test-specific administration tips is presented in Table 8.3. Additional administration tips and common examiner errors are presented in the chapter on the WJ III ACH (see Chapter 19).

Scoring the Test

The WJ III COG requires the examiner to record the item-level scores (usually 1 or 0) and to calculate raw scores. With the exception of three tests that use the number of errors

TABLE 8.3   Test-Specific Administration Tips for WJ III COG and Diagnostic Supplement

Test 1 Verbal Comprehension	Points to correct picture or part as indicated
	Administers any samples correctly
	Reads items from Test Book, not Test Record
	Completes all queries
Test 2 Visual-Auditory Learning	Ensures that examinee repeats each item during introductions
	Provides immediate corrective feedback
	Scores synonyms as incorrect
Test 3 Spatial Relations	Scores the last response(s) given by examinee
	Discontinues testing when a cutoff criterion is met
Test 4 Sound Blending	Accepts only words pronounced smoothly as correct
	Gives reminder to say the whole word smoothly only once
	Does not repeat any items
Test 5 Concept Formation	Ensures exact administration (controlled learning)
	Provides corrective feedback as indicated
	Accepts synonyms as correct (e.g., *small* for *little*)
Test 6 Visual Matching	Adheres to appropriate time limits for version administered
	Uses the response pages for Version 2 in the Test Record
Test 7 Numbers Reversed	Pauses 1 second between numbers when presenting orally
	Follows guidelines for recorded tests
	Adheres to basal/ceiling rules of a group of items
Test 8 Incomplete Words	Reminds examinee to say the whole word on each item if needed
Test 9 Auditory Working Memory	Ensures that things are named before numbers for any credit
	Ensures order is correct to receive credit
	Accepts similar sounding or rhyming words for targets
Test 10 VAL—Delayed	Administers only if all of Test 2 was administered
	Provides corrective feedback as directed
Test 11 General Information	Administers both subtests 11A and 11B
	Accepts correct responses in any language
Test 12 Retrieval Fluency	Provides credit for different types of the same food, name, or animal or brand names
	Accepts correct responses in any language (no duplicates)
Test 13 Picture Recognition	Scores last response(s) given
	Shows stimulus page for only 5 seconds
Test 14 Auditory Attention	Administers all training items providing corrective feedback
	Retrains any incorrect training items
	Uses audio-recording for all test items
	Does not replay any test items

TABLE 8.3 (Continued)

Test 15 Analysis-Synthesis	Ensures exact administration (controlled learning)
	Provides corrective feedback as indicated
Test 16 Decision Speed	Adheres to 3-minute time limit
	Accepts marks other than circles (e.g., fine motor difficulties)
Test 17 Memory for Words	Ensures words are in exact order to be correct
	Accepts rhyming or similar-sounding words for targets
Test 18 Rapid Picture Naming	Turns page immediately after last item on page
	Accepts correct responses in any language
Test 19 Planning	Monitors examinee performance closely and provides feedback as directed
	Attends carefully to scoring rules
	Counts number of errors for the raw score
Test 20 Pair Cancellation	Completes Practice Exercise and error correction procedure
	Ensures that circled pairs are in the same row to be correct
Test 21 Memory for Names	Ensures exact administration (controlled learning)
	Ensures that examinee points to each creature when introduced
Test 22 Visual Closure	Scores the response as "0" if not within 30 seconds
Test 23 Sound Patterns—Voice	Pauses audio-recording if more time is needed
	Does not take a break or converse during test
Test 24 Number Series	Allows 1 minute for each item
	Provides more time if examinee is actively trying to solve
Test 25 Number Matrices	Allows 1 minute for each item
	Provides more time if examinee is actively trying to solve
Test 26 Cross Out	Uses examinee response pages in the Test Record
	Adheres to 3-minute time limit
Test 27 Memory for Sentences	Scores with 2 points for an exact repetition
	Scores with 1 point for only one error
Test 28 Block Rotation	Attends to pointing instructions in the Introduction and Sample Items
	Does not allow examinee to touch drawings with finger or pencil
Test 29 Sound Patterns—Music	Pauses audio-recording if more time is needed
Test 30 Memory for Names—Delayed	Administers Test 21 (Memory for Names) in its entirety
Test 31 Bilingual Verbal Comprehension—English/ Spanish	Ensures that the examiner is fluent in Spanish. Administers English items first and then readministers incorrect items in Spanish

as the raw score (Visual-Auditory Learning, Visual-Auditory Learning—Delayed, and Planning), the raw score is the total number correct. Once the raw score has been obtained, examiners may consult the scoring tables that appear in the test record to determine estimated age and grade equivalents. They are referred to as *estimated* because the computer scoring provides more precise calculations, particularly for tests with subtests. This immediate information can be helpful in cases where little is known about the examinee's ability levels. After testing is completed, the raw scores are then entered into the computer-scoring software program, Compuscore, which comes with the test kit. All derived scores and profiles are generated by Compuscore. Because of the complexity of the WJ III and the numerous scoring options, hand-scoring scoring options do not exist.

In many instances, practitioners should also write down the examinee's actual responses for incorrect items so that these errors can be reviewed and analyzed after testing is completed. Additionally, the examiner should write down any pertinent observations or comments made during the testing. This type of qualitative information can often be helpful in guiding further assessment options or developing individual program plans.

Interpretation of Scores

The WJ III COG provides a wide array of derived scores that includes raw scores, W scores, age equivalents, grade equivalents, standard scores, percentile ranks, relative proficiency indexes, standard score/percentile rank profiles, age/grade profiles, instructional zones, and CALP levels. Many of these scores are familiar to practitioners (e.g., percentile ranks and standard scores). Some scores, however, such as the W score, relative proficiency index (RPI), instructional ranges, age/grade profiles, and CALP levels, are not as common, or are unique

to the Woodcock family of tests, and thus require additional explanation. To avoid redundancy, these scores are explained in the "Interpreting the Scores" section of Chapter 19 in this book. Also, the "Step-by-Step Guide to Interpreting the WJ III COG" section of this chapter provides guidance for the interpretation of these scores.

For school children, adolescents, and college students, an important part of the evaluation is linking assessment results to instructional planning. To facilitate this step, practitioners may wish to use an optional software program, the Woodcock Interpretation and Instructional Interventions Program (WIIIP; Schrank, Wendling, & Woodcock, 2008). This program includes a bank of evidence-based educational interventions that are related to performance on the WJ III broad and narrow abilities and cognitive processes. Based on the individual's performance on the WJ III tests and clusters, the program presents specific interventions from the bank for consideration by the practitioner. The WIIIP generates scores, profiles, narrative reports, and instructional interventions based on the individual's performance on the WJ III COG and ACH. Additional recommendations and educational strategies can also be found in *WJ III: Recommendations, Reports, and Strategies* (Mather & Jaffe, 2002).

STANDARDIZATION, NORMS, AND PSYCHOMETRICS

The WJ III COG and Diagnostic Supplement were co-normed with the WJ III Tests of Achievement (WJ III ACH). To avoid duplicating the information, the descriptions of the standardization and norming procedures are provided within Chapter 19 in this book. Additional information about development, standardization, norms construction, normative update, reliability, and validity is available in the

Technical Manual for the Woodcock-Johnson III Normative Update (McGrew, Schrank, & Woodcock, 2007).

Reliability

Reliability statistics were calculated for all WJ III COG and Diagnostic Supplement tests across their range of intended use and included all of the norming subjects. The reliabilities for all tests but the speeded tests and tests with multiple-point scoring were calculated using the split-half procedure and corrected for length using the Spearman-Brown correction formula. The reliabilities for the speeded tests and those with multiple-point scoring systems were calculated using Rasch analysis procedures. The WJ III COG tests and clusters typically meet or exceed the benchmarks typically used for reliability: .80 or higher for the tests; 90 or higher for the clusters. Table 8.4 provides a summary of the median reliabilities for the WJ III COG tests and clusters.

USE OF THE TEST

Because of the comprehensive nature of the WJ III COG, it can be used for a variety of purposes, including determining an individual's present cognitive performance levels, identifying an individual's cognitive strengths and weaknesses, comparing an individual's performance to age or grade peers, investigating need for special services, monitoring cognitive abilities across the years, and assisting with instructional and program planning. For example, with the changes in the Individuals with Disabilities Education Improvement Act of 2004 (IDEA, 2004), examiners may use the WJ III to focus on understanding an individual's learning strengths and weaknesses and use the evaluation data to help develop educational plans. In cases where the referral question involves exploring the presence of a specific learning disability, the WJ III COG provides measurement of a number of important cognitive processes that may help explain the individual's learning difficulties. Also, the co-normed WJ III ACH provides measures of the eight academic areas of eligibility listed in IDEA 2004.

Interpretation Methods

The WJ III provides information at four different interpretive levels (see Chapter 19). The skilled practitioner must integrate information from these levels as well as from a variety of other sources to develop a more complete understanding of each case. When making high-stakes decisions, like special education eligibility, practitioners often use cluster-level information because of higher reliabilities and broader coverage of the construct. The examiner should, however, also consider performance on the narrow abilities so that the person's strengths and weaknesses are clearly understood. If an examiner looks only at performance on the broad clusters, which are composed of numerous abilities, he or she may not fully grasp the specific nature of the problem, such as a problem only in perceptual speed rather than a broader-based processing speed problem. When planning an appropriate instructional program, information from the clusters, the individual tests, and even item-level information can be useful in interpreting and explaining performance.

The WJ III COG provides several variation procedures for determining an individual's intra-individual strengths and weaknesses in performance. Under IDEA (2004), documentation of the pattern of strengths and weaknesses can be used to provide evidence that an individual has a specific learning disability.

Intra-Cognitive Variation Procedures

The intra-cognitive variation procedures allow practitioners to analyze intra-individual differences, identifying strengths and weaknesses

TABLE 8.4   Median Reliabilities for WJ III COG and Diagnostic Supplement Clusters

Category	Cluster	Median Reliability
Global Intelligence/ Cognitive Clusters	GIA—Standard	.97
	GIA—Extended	.98
	GIA—Bilingual	.96
	GIA—Early Development	.94
	BCA—Low Verbal	.96
	BIA	.95
Cognitive Performance Clusters	Verbal Ability—Standard	.92
	Verbal Ability—Extended	.95
	Thinking Abilities—Standard	.95
	Thinking Abilities—Extended	.96
	Thinking Abilities—Low Verbal	.95
	Cognitive Efficiency—Standard	.92
	Cognitive Efficiency—Extended	.93
CHC Broad Ability Clusters	Comprehension-Knowledge	.95
	Long-Term Retrieval	.88
	Visual-Spatial Thinking	.81
	Visual-Spatial Thinking 3	.85
	Auditory Processing	.91
	Fluid Reasoning	.95
	Fluid Reasoning 3	.96
	Processing Speed	.93
	Short-Term Memory	.88
Clinical Clusters	Broad Attention	.92
	Working Memory	.91
	Cognitive Fluency	.96
	Executive Processes	.93
	Delayed Recall	.92
	Knowledge	.94
	Phonemic Awareness	.90
	Phonemic Awareness 3	.90

TABLE 8.4   (Continued)

Category	Cluster	Median Reliability
Narrow Ability Clusters	Associative Memory	.92
	Associative Memory—Delayed	.94
	Visualization	.83
	Sound Discrimination	.96
	Auditory Memory Span	.88
	Perceptual Speed	.91
	Numerical Reasoning	.94

that may exist within cognitive performance. Discrepancy norms are used in determining the significance and frequency of the individual's variations in performance. Three different options are available when using this procedure, depending on which tests and clusters are administered.

BRIEF   This procedure requires administration of COG Tests 1–7; it provides an analysis of strengths and weaknesses among seven tests, each representing a different broad cognitive ability. Examiners may use this procedure to determine whether strengths and weaknesses exist at the test level. This procedure provides the greatest level of detail among the seven component tests. In addition, it is often useful for determining whether additional cognitive testing is needed.

STANDARD   This procedure also requires administration of the first seven tests (COG 1–7) and provides a profile of strengths and weaknesses based on three broad categories of abilities: verbal ability, thinking abilities, and cognitive efficiency.

EXTENDED   This procedure requires administration of 14 tests (1–7 and 11–17) and provides a profile of strengths and weaknesses based on the seven broad CHC factors. When additional tests are administered, clusters representing up

to eight different narrow abilities can be included in this variation procedure.

Ability/Achievement Discrepancy Procedures

Two ability/achievement discrepancy procedures use scores from the WJ III COG as the basis for predicted performance. These procedures use either the GIA or the Predicted Achievement as the ability score. Although both scores are based on the WJ III COG, their derivation and purpose differ. The GIA/achievement discrepancy procedure uses the examinee's general intellectual ability as the predictor of achievement. The evaluator may use the GIA—Standard, based on Tests 1–7, or the GIA—Extended, based on Tests 1–7 and 11–17. Comparisons are then made between the examinee's GIA score and his or her achievement in reading, writing, and math.

The Predicted Achievement/achievement discrepancy procedure, based on WJ III COG Tests 1–7, uses the examinee's aptitude for each achievement domain as the predictor. The Predicted Achievement scores might best be understood as specialized aptitude scores. Instead of providing the best estimate of global intelligence, like the GIA, the Predicted Achievement scores provide the best estimate of ability for the specific achievement areas. Through multiple regression procedures, the optimal weighted combination of

Tests 1–7 is derived to provide the most accurate prediction of each of the WJ III ACH clusters. This score is a weighted score with more important abilities getting greater weight at various developmental levels. For example, in predicting Basic Reading Skills in first grade, Sound Blending and Visual Matching have higher weights, but by high school, Verbal Comprehension has more weight. This procedure is used to establish whether the individual's most relevant cognitive abilities can help explain his or her current levels of academic performance. For example, if the person's reading aptitude (Predicted Achievement) is low and his reading achievement is also low, a discrepancy will not exist. In this case, the individual's low cognitive abilities for reading help explain the poor reading achievement.

GIA/Cognitive Cluster Discrepancies

Examiners can determine whether a discrepancy exists between an individual's general intellectual ability (GIA—Standard) score and any specific broad or narrow cognitive ability cluster measured by the WJ III COG. Some examiners use this procedure to provide evidence of a specific processing disability when compared to overall intellectual ability.

STEP-BY-STEP GUIDE TO INTERPRETING THE WJ III COG

Interpretation of the WJ III COG can be enhanced by considering the following five steps: (1) interpretation of clusters and tests; (2) interpretation of the intra-cognitive variation procedure; (3) interpretation of criterion-referenced information; (4) interpretation of qualitative information; and, if the WJ III ACH is also being used, (5) interpretation of ability/achievement discrepancy procedures. Each step is described in detail and illustrated using Bart's case study data, which appear in the next section of this chapter.

Step 1: Interpretation of Clusters and Tests

Step 1A: Interpretation of Clusters

The first step is interpreting the *clusters*, which are composites created by administering two or more tests. Clusters contain two measures of a broad or narrow ability and are more reliable than individual tests. Clusters are recommended when making broad generalizations about an individual's performance. They provide comprehensive, norm-referenced measures of the cognitive abilities. When performance is consistent on the tests that comprise the cluster, interpretation may be focused at the cluster level.

Step 1B: Interpretation of Tests

Each of the WJ III COG tests measures a distinctive narrow ability. The narrow abilities provide operational definitions of what is specifically being measured by each test. The definitions of the narrow abilities are consistent with a cognitive processing perspective that can be related to educational interventions (Schrank & Wendling, 2008). For many purposes, interpretation at the test level provides a useful link to planning interventions and educational accommodations.

At times, significant differences may exist between the tests that comprise each cluster. When these differences exist, the reasons for the differences should be clarified, which may require further testing. Significant differences can be determined by examining the confidence bands for the tests within each cluster. The Standard Score/Percentile Rank Profile (SS/PR Profile) provides a graphic representation of these bands, making it easy to see whether significant differences exist among the clusters and the tests.

Three basic rules exist for interpreting these bands: If the bands overlap, there is no significant difference; if a separation exists between the two bands but it is not as wide as either band, a probable difference exists; if the separation between the two bands is wider than either

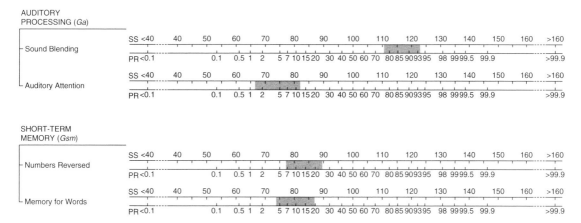

Note: Profiles generated by the Woodcock-Johnson III Normative Update Compuscore and Profiles Program (Version 3.1), 2008, Riverside Publishing.

FIGURE 8.3
Bart's SS/PR Profile for Selected Cognitive Tests within Broad CHC Clusters

band, it is likely that a real difference exists. Figure 8.3 illustrates Bart's SS/PR Profile for the tests that comprise two of the CHC broad abilities, Auditory Processing and Short-Term Memory. A review of the tests that comprise the Auditory Processing cluster reveals that the confidence bands of the two tests do not overlap. Additionally, the distance between the two bands is wider than either band, indicating that a significant difference exists between Bart's performance on Sound Blending and on Auditory Attention. This significant difference requires explanation and possibly further assessment by the practitioner. In contrast, the tests within the Short-Term Memory cluster (Numbers Reversed and Memory for Words) do not show a significant difference. The bands overlap, so interpretation may be focused at the cluster level.

Step 2: Interpretation of the Intra-Cognitive Variation Procedure

The second step helps determine whether any significant strengths or weaknesses exist within the individual's cognitive performance. Bart's Intra-Cognitive Variation (shown

in Table 8.5) uses the seven broad CHC clusters. Results of the procedure indicate that he has a significant intra-cognitive strength in Comprehension-Knowledge (*Gc*) and a significant intra-cognitive weakness in Processing Speed (*Gs*). His variation percentile rank of 99 indicates that Bart scored as high, or higher, than 99 out of 100 age-mates with the same predicted score on Comprehension-Knowledge. In other words, only 1% of age-mates with the same predicted score obtained a higher score on Comprehension-Knowledge. The variation percentile rank of .2 on Processing Speed indicates that only two out of a thousand age-mates with the same predicted score would have scored as low, or lower, than Bart. Bart's performance in Comprehension-Knowledge was significantly and unusually higher than predicted, whereas his performance in Processing Speed was significantly and unusually lower than predicted.

Step 3: Interpretation of Criterion-Referenced Information

Step 3 helps practitioners interpret the WJ III COG from a criterion-referenced perspective.

TABLE 8.5   Bart's Intra-Cognitive Variation Procedure

| | Standard Scores | | | Variation | | Significant at |
Variations	Actual	Predicted	Difference	PR	SD	+ or −1.50 SD(SEE)
Intra-Cognitive (Ext)						
Comp-Knowledge (*Gc*)	112	86	26	99	+2.30	Yes
L-T Retrieval (*Glr*)	80	91	−11	15	−1.04	No
Vis-Spatial Think (*Gv*)	92	93	−1	46	−0.11	No
Auditory Process (*Ga*)	102	90	12	83	+0.94	No
Fluid Reasoning (*Gf*)	99	88	11	83	+0.95	No
Process Speed (*Gs*)	60	96	−36	0.2	−2.86	Yes
Short-Term Mem (*Gsm*)	77	93	−16	12	−1.18	No

The Relative Proficiency Index (RPI) and the Age/Grade Profile, described in the Scores section of Chapter 19, provide valuable information. The RPI and Age/Grade Profiles are applications of the W difference (W Diff) score, representing the difference, in W units, between the person's performance and the median performance of the person's age- or grade-peers. The relationship between the W Diff, the RPI, proficiency levels, and practical implications is outlined in Table 8.6.

The RPI is especially helpful in describing a person's proficiency on tasks and can provide insights that would otherwise be indistinguishable when using peer comparison scores alone. For example, Bart obtained a standard score of 86 on Retrieval Fluency indicating low average standing relative to age peers. However, his RPI of 86/90 indicates his proficiency on this task is average. That is, the relative quality of Bart's performance (obtained from the W Diff) was actually closer to the median performance of age-peers than was indicated by his standard score. In contrast, on Numbers Reversed, Bart obtained a standard score of 83 indicating low average standing relative to age peers, but his RPI of 41/90 indicates limited proficiency on the task. In this example, the quality of Bart's performance

was actually quite different from the median performance of age peers than would be indicated by his obtained standard score. The RPI often yields a more accurate description of the individual's actual performance, or proficiency on the task. Examiners can obtain descriptive labels that describe the person's proficiency with tasks on the Compuscore (Schrank & Woodcock, 2008) or WIIIP (Schrank, Wendling, & Woodcock, 2008). See Table 8.7.

Implications derived from a person's performance on similar age- or grade-level tasks are described in the comprehensive report from the WIIIP (Schrank, Wendling, & Woodcock, 2008). Additionally, for persons with limited-to-average proficiency and below, the WIIIP provides a bank of instructional objectives that are linked to each WJ III test score. In Bart's case, a bank of instructional objectives or accommodations are available that are related to Bart's limitations on Visual-Auditory-Learning, Spatial Relations, Visual Matching, Numbers Reversed, Auditory Attention, Decision Speed, Memory for Words, and Rapid Picture Naming. Table 8.8 contains a bank of possible instructional interventions and accommodations from the WIIIP that are related to Bart's limited proficiency on these WJ III COG tests.

TABLE 8.6   Relationship between W Diff, RPIs, Proficiency Levels, and Implications

W Diff	RPI	Proficiency Level	Implications for Performance: This person will find similar age- or grade-level tasks . . .
+31 and above	100/90	Very Advanced	. . . extremely easy.
+14 to +30	98/90 to 100/90	Advanced	. . . very easy.
+7 to +13	95/90 to 98/90	Average to Advanced	. . . easy.
−6 to −6	82/90 to 95/90	Average	. . . manageable.
−13 to −7	67/90 to 82/90	Limited to Average	. . . difficult.
−30 to −14	24/90 to 67/90	Limited	. . . very difficult.
−50 to −31	3/90 to 24/90	Very Limited	. . . extremely difficult.
−51 and below	0/90 to 3/90	Negligible	. . . impossible.

TABLE 8.7   Bart's Proficiency on Each of the WJ III COG Tests

Test	W	AE	Proficiency	RPI	SS (68% Band)	W Diff
Verbal Comprehension	500	10-1	avg to adv	95/90	108 (103–114)	8
Visual-Auditory Learning	488	6-9	lmtd to avg	75/90	82 (78–86)	−10
Spatial Relations	490	6-7	lmtd to avg	80/90	88 (83–93)	−8
Sound Blending	512	14-2	advanced	98/90	117 (111–123)	14
Concept Formation	489	8-1	average	83/90	95 (90–99)	−6
Visual Matching	465	6-2	limited	31/90	60 (56–64)	−27
Numbers Reversed	470	6-6	limited	41/90	83 (77–89)	−23
General Information	505	10-8	avg to adv	97/90	114 (108–120)	13
Retrieval Fluency	496	7-1	average	86/90	86 (79–93)	−3
Picture Recognition	496	8-7	average	89/90	99 (93–104)	−1
Auditory Attention	487	6-0	lmtd to avg	70/90	75 (67–82)	−12
Analysis-Synthesis	498	9-7	average	93/90	104 (99–110)	4
Decision Speed	474	6-0	limited	54/90	67 (62–72)	−19
Memory for Words	470	5-9	limited	34/90	81 (74–87)	−26
Rapid Picture Naming	465	4-6	limited	28/90	67 (65–69)	−29

TABLE 8.8   Bank of WIIIP Instructional Interventions and Accommodations Related to Bart's Proficiency on WJ III COG Tests

---

Attending to and thinking about the material to be learned (active learning) is necessary for acquisition of new knowledge. Interventions that emphasize active engagement in the learning process, rather than being a passive recipient of instruction, may be especially helpful for Bart.

Repetition is an important factor in building speed. Repeated and extensive practice may enable Bart to perform some tasks in a more automatic fashion to increase speeded performance. Activities can be teacher-directed or student-directed; related computer programs or games can provide opportunities to practice responding quickly.

Speed drills focus performance on completing a task quickly. When Bart's performance on familiar tasks is timed and progress monitored, speed may increase. For example, Bart might be asked to count aloud, or say the letters of the alphabet, as quickly as he can for 10 seconds. The number of numerals or letters named is recorded. The speed drill is repeated at regular intervals, recording the number of items named each time. Allowing Bart to chart his progress can provide additional motivation. Speed drills can be teacher-directed, student-directed, or make use of technology, such as computerized programs or tachistoscopes.

Accommodations that may help compensate for Bart's limitations in processing speed might include providing extended time, reducing the quantity of work required (breaking large assignments into two or more component assignments), eliminating or limiting copying activities, and increasing *wait times* after questions are asked as well as after responses are given.

To increase Bart's fluency of retrieval and oral production of names of recognized objects (lexical retrieval), have him compete against himself by timing how fast a series of pictured objects can be named. Encourage Bart to increase his speed each time.

Mnemonics are strategies that provide helpful cognitive cues to enhance the encoding and recall of new information. They can be especially helpful in learning rules, patterns, and word lists. Examples of mnemonic strategies include acronyms, acrostics, keyboards, rhymes, and songs. For example, the acronym *HOMES* can be used to recall the names of the Great Lakes (**H**uron, **O**ntario, **M**ichigan, **E**rie, **S**uperior).

Rehearsal is an important factor in learning. Repeated and extensive practice may enable Bart to perform some tasks in a more automatic fashion, lessening the demand on short-term memory.

Accommodations may be useful in compensating for Bart's limitations in short-term memory. Some examples include keeping oral directions short and simple, asking Bart to paraphrase directions to ensure understanding, and providing visual cues for directions or steps to be followed.

Figure 8.4 illustrates several of the cognitive clusters from Bart's Age Profile. This profile provides a graphic representation of Bart's developmental ranges for selected cognitive areas. For example, the developmental zones for Cognitive Efficiency, Processing Speed, and Short-Term Memory fall below Bart's chronological age (shown by the vertical line), indicating areas of concern. The developmental zone for Comprehension-Knowledge falls entirely above Bart's age, indicating that verbal ability is a developmental strength.

Step 4: Interpretation of Qualitative Information

Step 4 focuses on integrating informal and observational information that was gathered during the evaluation process. The WJ III COG provides a framework for recording behavioral observations by including a Test Sessions Observation Checklist on the first page of each Test Record. In addition, an evaluator should note how the examinee approaches each task, observing things such as speed of response and strategies employed. When possible, the evaluator should record an

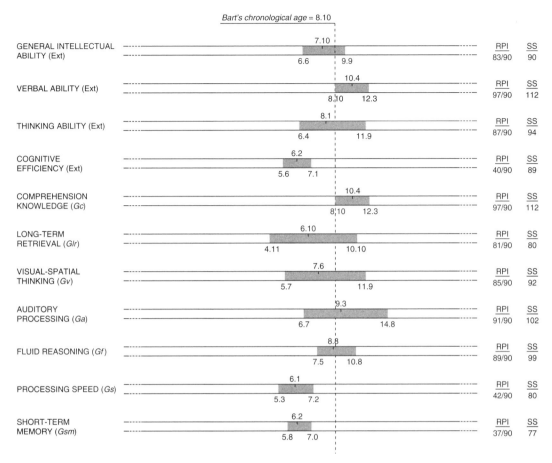

Note: Profiles generated by the Woodcock-Johnson III Normative Update
Compuscore and Profiles Program (Version 3.1), 2008, Riverside Publishing.

FIGURE 8.4

Bart's Age Profile for Selected Cognitive Clusters

examinee's errors and then later analyze those errors for patterns and instructional implications. The type of errors an individual makes often helps to inform instructional planning. For example, during the WJ III COG evaluation, Bart's conversational proficiency was rated as advanced for his age. Although he was willing to attempt all tasks, on several tests when he perceived that the questions or problems were becoming too difficult, he elected not to persist, making statements such as: "These are getting way too hard for me" or "I don't think I can do any more of these." When Bart was encouraged, he would usually persist, but on two tests, he insisted he could not do any more after only making one error. Bart appeared to not want to take risks if he was not certain of a response. His current approach to tasks and his reluctance to attempt tasks he perceives as too difficult suggest that the initial instruction must be carefully sequenced so that Bart will experience success as his skills improve.

Step 5: Interpretation of the GIA and/or the Predicted Achievement/Achievement Discrepancy Procedure

The fifth step involves determining whether significant discrepancies exist between the individual's general intellectual ability and academic performance and predicted achievement and academic performance. These procedures help document whether the individual's achievement is commensurate with general intellectual ability (GIA) or his aptitude for the predicted academic area (Predicted Achievement). Table 8.9 illustrates Bart's GIA/Achievement discrepancy procedure. Bart has significant discrepancies between his ability, represented by the

GIA—Extended score, and his Broad Reading, Reading Comprehension, Brief Reading, and all Written Language clusters. For example, his discrepancy percentile rank of 1 indicates that only 1% of age-mates with the same predicted score would have scored as low, or lower, than Bart in Reading Comprehension. Only 3 out of 1,000 (.3) age-mates with the same predicted score would have scored as low, or lower, than Bart on Broad Written Language. Conversely, Bart does not exhibit any discrepancies between his GIA score and achievement in math, oral language, or academic knowledge.

Table 8.10 illustrates Bart's Predicted Achievement/Achievement discrepancy procedure. This procedure compares Bart's aptitude for each academic area to his achievement. In

TABLE 8.9   Bart's GIA/Achievement Discrepancy Procedure

Discrepancies	Standard Scores			Discrepancy		Significant at
	Actual	Predicted	Diff	PR	SD	−1.50 SD (SEE)
*Intellectual Ability/Achievement Discrepancies**						
Broad Reading	73	93	−20	3	−1.85	Yes
Basic Reading Skills	84	94	−10	19	−0.87	No
Reading Comp	70	93	−23	1	−2.21	Yes
Broad Math	93	94	−1	46	−0.09	No
Math Calc Skills	81	95	−14	15	−1.05	No
Math Reasoning	99	93	6	72	+0.59	No
Broad Written Lang	58	94	−36	0.3	−2.80	Yes
Basic Writing Skills	68	94	−26	1	−2.32	Yes
Written Expression	69	94	−25	2	−2.13	Yes
Oral Language (Ext)	122	92	30	>99.9	+3.15	No
Oral Expression	116	93	23	98	+2.07	No
Listening Comp	122	93	29	99.7	+2.73	No
Academic Knowledge	120	93	27	99	+2.50	No
Brief Reading	74	94	−20	5	−1.65	Yes
Brief Math	97	94	3	60	+0.26	No
Brief Writing	67	94	−27	1	−2.28	Yes

*These discrepancies compare WJ III GIA (Ext) with Broad, Basic, Brief, and Applied ACH clusters.

TABLE 8.10   Bart's Predicted Achievement/Achievement Discrepancy Procedure

| Discrepancies | Standard Scores | | | Discrepancy | | Significant at |
	Actual	Predicted	Diff	PR	SD	+ or −1.50 SD (SEE)
*Predicted Achievement/Achievement Discrepancies**						
Broad Reading	73	91	−18	4	−1.78	Yes
Basic Reading Skills	84	93	−9	21	−0.79	No
Reading Comp	70	97	−27	0.4	−2.69	Yes
Broad Math	93	85	8	75	+0.68	No
Math Calc Skills	81	82	−1	47	−0.07	No
Math Reasoning	99	90	9	82	+0.90	No
Broad Written Lang	58	87	−29	1	−2.46	Yes
Basic Writing Skills	68	86	−18	4	−1.70	Yes
Written Expression	69	90	−21	5	−1.70	Yes
Oral Language (Ext)	122	94	28	99	+2.50	Yes
Oral Expression	116	97	19	94	+1.54	Yes
Listening Comp	122	93	29	99	+2.46	Yes
Academic Knowledge	120	103	17	96	+1.78	Yes
Brief Reading	74	93	−19	4	−1.78	Yes
Brief Math	97	87	10	79	+0.80	No
Brief Writing	67	89	−22	3	−1.89	Yes

*These discrepancies compare predicted achievement scores with Broad, Basic, Brief, and Applied ACH clusters.

other words, only the most relevant cognitive abilities, rather than a global intelligence score, are used to make the prediction. If a significant discrepancy exists, it may be due to factors other than the underlying cognitive abilities. For example, Bart demonstrates a significant discrepancy between his reading aptitude and his reading comprehension. He appears to have average aptitude for reading comprehension as indicated by the predicted score of 97. His reading comprehension score of 70 is significantly below that as indicated by his discrepancy percentile rank of .4 and his −2.69 *SD* (SEE). Only 4 out of 1,000 age-mates with the same aptitude (predicted) score for reading comprehension would have scored as low, or lower, than Bart. These findings suggest that Bart's

reading comprehension should be better than it is based on his performance on the cognitive and linguistic abilities that are most related to reading comprehension. One may surmise that the reason for Bart's low scores on the reading comprehension cluster is poor basic reading skills, not verbal comprehension (a strength). In contrast, a review of Bart's math clusters reveals that his achievement is not significantly below the predicted level. His aptitude for math and his achievement in math are similar.

An important part of evaluation is integrating cognitive results with achievement results to create a comprehensive, meaningful picture of the individual. This step would be critical in cases where an evaluator is attempting to document the presence and severity of a specific learning disability. The co-normed cognitive and achievement batteries from the WJ III facilitate the integration of results. Sharing a common norm group ensures that observed differences between cognitive and achievement performance are not due simply to differences in the norm groups. An additional benefit of co-norming is that the exact correlations between the predictor scores and academic scores are known so that discrepancy norms can be created from the actual discrepancy scores.

Planned comparisons between cognitive abilities and achievement areas, such as comparing an individual's GIA or Predicted Achievement to his or her achievement (described previously), are included in the interpretive framework for the WJ III. Exploring the relationship between cognitive abilities and academic performance is key to understanding the individual's learning difficulties. In addition, the intra-individual variation procedure illustrates the person's pattern of strengths and weaknesses across the factors and clusters of both the WJ III COG and WJ III ACH. These procedures are illustrated in the following Case Study.

CASE STUDY

This brief case study of Bart, a third-grade student, is provided to illustrate several of the interpretive features of the WJ III COG. The reason for referral, background information, behavioral observations, instructional recommendations, and Bart's complete achievement test results are presented in Chapter 19 on the WJ III ACH. Age norms were used when scoring both the WJ III COG and the WJ III ACH to facilitate comparisons. Bart's WJ III COG Compuscore Table of Scores, including the interpretive procedures requiring both the cognitive and achievement results, is shown in Table 8.11.

Assessments

Woodcock-Johnson III: Tests of Cognitive Abilities (WJ III COG)

Tests #1–7, 9, 11–18

Woodcock-Johnson III: Tests of Achievement (WJ III ACH)[1]

Cognitive Abilities

An examination of Bart's performance on each of the CHC cognitive ability clusters and test scores reveals variable performance. Bart's standard scores are in the high-average range for Comprehension-Knowledge (*Gc*), and the average range for Auditory Processing (*Ga*), Visual-Spatial Thinking (*Gv*), and Fluid Reasoning (*Gf*). His standard scores are in the low to low-average range for Long-Term Retrieval (*Glr*) and Short-Term Memory (*Gsm*) and his score for Processing Speed (*Gs*) is very low. His standard scores on the seven cognitive factors range from a high of 112 (*Gc*) to a low of 60 (*Gs*).

---

[1]See Chapter 19 for complete WJ III ACH results.

TABLE 8.11 Bart's Compuscore Score Report

Table of Scores

Woodcock-Johnson III Normative Update Tests of Cognitive Abilities

Norms based on age 8–10.

Cluster/Test	W	AE	Proficiency	RPI	SS (68% Band)	PR
GIA (Ext)	490	7-10	average	83/90	90 (88-93)	26
Verbal Ability (Ext)	503	10-4	avg to adv	97/90	112 (107–116)	78
Thinking Ability (Ext)	494	8-1	average	87/90	94 (91–97)	35
Cog Efficiency (Ext)	470	6-2	limited	40/90	69 (65–73)	2
Comp-Knowledge (*Gc*)	503	10-4	avg to adv	97/90	112 (107–116)	78
L-T Retrieval (*Glr*)	492	6-10	lmtd to avg	81/90	80 (76–85)	9
Vis-Spatial Think (*Gv*)	493	7-6	average	85/90	92 (87–96)	29
Auditory Process (*Ga*)	499	9-3	average	91/90	102 (95–109)	56
Fluid Reasoning (*Gf*)	493	8-8	average	89/90	99 (94–104)	47
Process Speed (*Gs*)	470	6-1	limited	42/90	60 (57–64)	0.4
Short-Term Mem (*Gsm*)	470	6-2	limited	37/90	77 (72–83)	6
Cognitive Fluency	478	5-5	limited	58/90	60 (57–63)	0.4
Verbal Comprehension	500	10-1	avg to adv	95/90	108 (103–114)	71
Visual-Auditory Learning	488	6-9	lmtd to avg	75/90	82 (78–86)	12
Spatial Relations	490	6-7	lmtd to avg	80/90	88 (83–93)	21
Sound Blending	512	14-2	advanced	98/90	117 (111–123)	87
Concept Formation	489	8-1	average	83/90	95 (90–99)	37
Visual Matching	465	6-2	limited	31/90	60 (56–64)	0.4
Numbers Reversed	470	6-6	limited	41/90	83 (77–89)	13
General Information	505	10-8	avg to adv	97/90	114 (108–120)	83
Retrieval Fluency	496	7-1	average	86/90	86 (79–93)	18
Picture Recognition	496	8-7	average	89/90	99 (93–104)	47
Auditory Attention	487	6-0	lmtd to avg	70/90	75 (67–82)	5
Analysis-Synthesis	498	9-7	average	93/90	104 (99–110)	61
Decision Speed	474	6-0	limited	54/90	67 (62–72)	1
Memory for Words	470	5-9	limited	34/90	81 (74–87)	10
Rapid Picture Naming	465	4-6	limited	28/90	67 (65–69)	1

(Continues)

TABLE 8.11   (Continued)

Variations	Standard Scores			Variation		Significant at + or
	Actual	Predicted	Diff	PR	SD	− 1.50 SD (SEE)
Intra-Cognitive (Ext)						
Comp-Knowledge (*Gc*)	112	86	26	99	+2.30	Yes
L-T Retrieval (*Glr*)	80	91	−11	15	−1.04	No
Vis-Spatial Think (*Gv*)	92	93	−1	46	−0.11	No
Auditory Process (*Ga*)	102	90	12	83	+0.94	No
Fluid Reasoning (*Gf*)	99	88	11	83	+0.95	No
Process Speed (*Gs*)	60	96	−36	0.2	−2.86	Yes
Short-Term Mem (*Gsm*)	77	93	−16	12	−1.18	No

Variations	Standard Scores			Variation		Significant at + or
	Actual	Predicted	Diff	PR	SD	− 1.50 SD (SEE)
Intra-Individual (Ext/Ext)						
Comp-Knowledge (*Gc*)	112	88	24	99.8	+2.85	Yes
L-T Retrieval (*Glr*)	80	92	−12	11	−1.25	No
Vis-Spatial Think (*Gv*)	92	95	−3	40	−0.24	No
Auditory Process (*Ga*)	102	93	9	77	+0.75	No
Fluid Reasoning (*Gf*)	99	90	9	76	+0.72	No
Process Speed (*Gs*)	60	96	−36	0.2	−2.91	Yes
Short-Term Mem (*Gsm*)	77	93	−16	11	−1.24	No
Basic Reading Skills	84	91	−7	24	−0.69	No
Reading Comp	70	91	−21	1	−2.35	Yes
Math Calc Skills	81	93	−12	16	−0.99	No
Math Reasoning	99	89	10	86	+1.08	No
Basic Writing Skills	68	92	−24	1	−2.54	Yes
Written Expression	69	93	−24	1	−2.42	Yes
Oral Expression	116	90	26	99	+2.37	Yes
Listening Comp	122	89	33	99.9	+3.03	Yes
Academic Knowledge	120	89	31	>99.9	+3.13	Yes
Knowledge	119	88	31	>99.9	+3.39	Yes

TABLE 8.11 (Continued)

Discrepancies	Standard Scores			Discrepancy		Significant at
	Actual	Predicted	Diff	PR	SD	−1.50 SD (SEE)
Intellectual Ability/Achievement Discrepancies*						
Broad Reading	73	93	−20	3	−1.85	Yes
Basic Reading Skills	84	94	−10	19	−0.87	No
Reading Comp	70	93	−23	1	−2.21	Yes
Broad Math	93	94	−1	46	−0.09	No
Math Calc Skills	81	95	−14	15	−1.05	No
Math Reasoning	99	93	6	72	+0.59	No
Broad Written Lang	58	94	−36	0.3	−2.80	Yes
Basic Writing Skills	68	94	−26	1	−2.32	Yes
Written Expression	69	94	−25	2	−2.13	Yes
Oral Language (Ext)	122	92	30	> 99.9	+3.15	No
Oral Expression	116	93	23	98	+2.07	No
Listening Comp	122	93	29	99.7	+2.73	No
Academic Knowledge	120	93	27	99	+2.50	No
Brief Reading	74	94	−20	5	−1.65	Yes
Brief Math	97	94	3	60	+0.26	No
Brief Writing	67	94	−27	1	−2.28	Yes

Discrepancies	Standard Scores			Discrepancy		Significant at + or
	Actual	Predicted	Diff	PR	SD	− 1.50 SD (SEE)
Predicted Achievement/Achievement Discrepancies**						
Broad Reading	73	91	−18	4	−1.78	Yes
Basic Reading Skills	84	93	−9	21	−0.79	No
Reading Comp	70	97	−27	0.4	−2.69	Yes
Broad Math	93	85	8	75	+0.68	No
Math Calc Skills	81	82	−1	47	−0.07	No
Math Reasoning	99	90	9	82	+0.90	No
Broad Written Lang	58	87	−29	1	−2.46	Yes
Basic Writing Skills	68	86	−18	4	−1.70	Yes
Written Expression	69	90	−21	5	−1.70	Yes
Oral Language (Ext)	122	94	28	99	+2.50	Yes
Oral Expression	116	97	19	94	+1.54	Yes

(Continues)

TABLE 8.11   (Continued)

| Discrepancies | Standard Scores | | | Discrepancy | | Significant at |
	Actual	Predicted	Diff	PR	SD	− 1.50 SD (SEE)
Listening Comp	122	93	29	99	+2.46	Yes
Academic Knowledge	120	103	17	96	+1.78	Yes
Brief Reading	74	93	−19	4	−1.78	Yes
Brief Math	97	87	10	79	+0.80	No
Brief Writing	67	89	−22	3	−1.89	Yes

*These discrepancies compare WJ III GIA (Ext) with Broad, Basic, Brief, and Applied ACH clusters.
**These discrepancies compare predicted achievement scores with Broad, Basic, Brief, and Applied ACH clusters.
NOTE : Scores generated by the Woodcock-Johnson III Normative Update Compuscore and Profiles Program (Version 3.1), 2008, Riverside Publishing.

On the Processing Speed (*Gs*) cluster, Bart worked slowly on both tests: scanning rows of numbers to find the two that matched, and scanning rows of pictures to find the two that were most similar conceptually. Despite his accuracy on all items he attempted, his test results indicated that his speed on simple tasks involving visual scanning was in the bottom 1% of his age-peers (PR = .4). His RPI of 42/90 indicates that his processing speed is limited. Similarly, Bart's limited proficiency on Rapid Picture Naming indicated that he has difficulty with rapid retrieval of familiar words.

Bart's proficiency on the Long-Term Retrieval (*Glr*) and Short-Term Memory (*Gsm*) clusters suggest that he will find tasks involving storing and retrieving associations to be difficult, and tasks involving remembering and manipulating information to be very difficult. In addition, Bart's Cognitive Efficiency (a combination of processing speed and short-term memory) and Cognitive Fluency (a combination of three speeded tests with simple demands) fell within the very low range of standard scores, further substantiating his slow performance on speeded tasks, as well as his relative weakness performing memory tasks.

One cognitive cluster, Auditory Processing (*Ga*), had significant variation between the two tests that comprise the cluster. Bart performed well on blending sounds but had difficulty on a test requiring discriminating sounds within increasing background noise. His proficiency on Sound Blending was advanced (RPI = 98/90), but was limited-to-average (RPI = 70/90) on Auditory Attention. Although the factor score falls within the average range of standard scores, the significant differences observed indicate that caution is necessary when discussing Bart's auditory processing abilities.

Variation Procedures

Bart's unique pattern of strengths and weaknesses are also apparent on the two variation procedures that use the WJ III COG results: the Intra-Cognitive (Extended) Variation Procedure (based on Tests 1–7 and 11–17), and the Intra-Individual Variation Procedure (based on results from both the WJ III COG and WJ III ACH).

Intra-Cognitive Variation Procedure

On the WJ III COG, the intra-cognitive variation procedure illustrates a person's significant strengths and weaknesses. Among his cognitive abilities, Bart has a significant strength in Comprehension-Knowledge. When Bart's Comprehension-Knowledge (*Gc*) cluster score (SS = 112) was compared to his other cognitive abilities, it was significantly higher than predicted (SS = 86). Bart's variation percentile rank score (PR = 99) indicates that his performance exceeded 99 out of 100 individuals with similar predicted scores, or only 1 out of 100 people with the same predicted score would have a score as high or higher. In contrast, when Bart's Processing Speed (*Gs*) score (SS = 60) was compared to his predicted score (SS = 96), only 2 out of 1,000 students with a similar predicted score would obtain a score as low (variation percentile rank = .2). Thus, Processing Speed is a significant intra-cognitive weakness for Bart.

Intra-Individual Variation Procedure

The *intra-individual variation procedure* combines results from the CHC cognitive factors and the WJ III ACH clusters. Significant strengths were noted in Bart's verbal comprehension, knowledge, and oral language abilities. Significant weaknesses were present in processing speed, reading comprehension, and all facets of written language. Bart's strength in oral language corroborates his strength in verbal ability. It appears that verbal ability and oral language are not the reasons for Bart's difficulties in reading comprehension and written language.

Ability/Achievement Discrepancy Procedures

The WJ III provides two procedures for exploring the relationship between Bart's cognitive and academic performance. Two ability/achievement discrepancies compare aspects of cognitive functioning to achievement: the General Intellectual Ability/Achievement Discrepancy and the Predicted Achievement/Achievement Discrepancy.

General Intellectual Ability/Achievement Discrepancy.

The General Intellectual Ability (GIA)/Achievement discrepancy procedure compares the person's performance on the GIA—Extended (or Standard) cluster to his or her performance in oral language, reading, writing, and mathematics. When Bart's GIA—Extended score (SS = 90) was compared to his scores in reading, both the Broad Reading (Discrepancy Percentile = 3) and Reading Comprehension (Discrepancy Percentile = 1) clusters were significantly lower than predicted. Similar results were obtained with measures of written language. When Bart's GIA-Ext is compared to his performance on the Broad Written Language cluster, only 3 out of 1,000 students would have a discrepancy of this size. These findings indicate that Bart's reading and writing abilities are significantly lower than would be predicted by his general overall ability, GIA-Ext score. No significant discrepancies were noted between Bart's general intellectual ability and his achievement in oral language, mathematics, or academic knowledge, suggesting his learning difficulties are more specific to reading and writing.

Predicted Achievement/Achievement Discrepancy.

The Predicted Achievement/Achievement Discrepancy (based on COG tests 1–7) is designed to compare a person's aptitude or most relevant cognitive abilities to his or her actual academic performance. Similar to the results of the GIA-Ext Ability/Achievement comparisons, the Predicted Achievement scores indicated that Bart's obtained scores were lower than predicted in reading and written language. In contrast, his performances in all aspects of oral language were higher than predicted (e.g., Oral Language, Academic Knowledge). These findings suggest that Bart's low performance in reading and writing cannot be solely attributed to low cognitive and linguistic abilities. That is, several of his abilities related to being a successful reader are even above average (e.g., Verbal-Comprehension and Sound Blending). Thus, the Predicted Achievement score suggests that his levels of reading and writing performance should be higher than they actually are.

Summary of Diagnostic Impressions

Current test results indicate that Bart has slow processing speed, a cognitive ability that provides a critical foundation for processing information quickly and efficiently. This finding suggests that Bart may need more time when processing, responding to, and learning new information. Bart's moderate weaknesses in short-term memory and associative memory, a narrow ability of long-term retrieval, contribute further to his reading and writing problems. His slow and nonautomatic processing quickly overloads the limited-capacity system of short-term memory. His weaknesses in associative memory make it more difficult for him to recall the sounds and symbols with ease. The effects of these cognitive weaknesses are evident in Bart's low performances in basic reading and writing skills.

In sharp contrast to these processing weaknesses, Bart's verbal abilities and knowledge of general world information are above average when compared to his age-peers. Up until third grade, knowledge and information are learned primarily through oral language encounters and experiences. From fourth grade on, however, children are expected to begin to learn world knowledge and new vocabulary from reading. Children with reading difficulties often lag behind in their development of knowledge and vocabulary in relation to their peers, because of more limited exposures to texts. Consequently, specialized, intensive academic instruction for Bart is critical at this point. (See Chapter 19 for specific instructional recommendations.)

The results of this evaluation indicate that Bart has significant discrepancies among his cognitive and linguistic abilities that have affected his development in reading and writing. Despite having above-average verbal abilities and having received systematic instruction, he continues to struggle to learn to read and write. Bart has difficulty processing and producing visual symbols quickly. His significant weakness in processing speed, combined with his limits in short-term memory, and associative memory help explain his present academic difficulties. The findings of this evaluation indicate that Bart has a specific learning disability that has impacted his abilities to learn to read and write. This neurodevelopmental disorder is often referred to as *dyslexia*, or a specific reading disability. Bart requires specialized instruction with a teacher who has expertise in teaching children with specific reading disabilities.

SELECTION OF INTERVENTIONS BASED ON TEST RESULTS

Practitioners must consider a variety of factors when determining appropriate educational interventions for a person—other than just the test scores. Examples of pertinent information would include the person's age, prior history of interventions, the success of previous interventions, the type of educational environment, the training of the personnel, the motivation and persistence of the person, the severity of the problem, as well as the available resources in the setting. As long as test results are viewed along with consideration of these additional factors, the WJ III COG can provide valuable information for selecting appropriate educational

TABLE 8.12 Educational Interventions Related to the WJ III COG Tests

Test	Related Educational Interventions
Test 1: Verbal Comprehension	Creating a vocabulary-rich learning environment, particularly reading aloud to a young child and discussing new words; text talks; directed vocabulary thinking activities; explicit teaching of specific words; semantic feature analysis; semantic maps; use of computer technology to develop word knowledge; association of key words to prior knowledge; reading for a variety of purposes; independent word-learning strategies
Test 2: Visual-Auditory Learning	Active, successful learning experiences; rehearsal; overlearning; organizational strategies; mnemonics; illustrate or visualize content
Test 3: Spatial Relations	Multisensory teaching techniques; private speech; graphic organizers
Test 4: Sound Blending	Early exposure to language sounds; promoting phonological awareness; direct instruction in sound blending; practice blending sounds into words
Test 5: Concept Formation	Categorize using real objects; develop skills in drawing conclusions; hands-on problem-solving tasks; make meaningful associations; concrete examples of grouping objects
Test 6: Visual Matching	Emphasize speediness; build cognitive speed via repetition, speed drills, use of technology
Test 7: Numbers Reversed	Chunking strategies; rehearsal; mnemonics; visual cues
Test 8: Incomplete Words	Promote phonological awareness; read aloud; games that focus on sounds and words
Test 9: Auditory Working Memory	Rehearsal; mnemonics; active learning
Test 10: Visual-Auditory Learning—Delayed	Active, successful learning experiences; rehearsal; overlearning; organizational strategies; mnemonics; illustrate or visualize content
Test 11: General Information	Text talks; semantic maps
Test 12: Retrieval Fluency	Oral elaboration
Test 13: Picture Recognition	Activities designed to discriminate/match visual features and recall visual information
Test 14: Auditory Attention	Reduce distracting noise; modifications to listening environment
Test 15: Analysis-Synthesis	Deductive reasoning using concrete objects; hands-on problem solving tasks; metacognitive strategies
Test 16: Decision Speed	Emphasize speediness; build cognitive speed via repetition
Test 17: Memory for Words	Mnemonics; rehearsal; provide visual cues
Test 18: Rapid Picture Naming	Increase fluency through self-competition
Test 19: Planning	Use of puzzles, pegboards, dot-to-dot drawings; multisensory teaching techniques; private speech
Test 20: Pair Cancellation	Speed drills; repetition
Test 21: Memory for Names	Active, successful learning experiences; rehearsal; overlearning; organizational strategies; mnemonics; illustrate or visualize content
Test 22: Visual Closure	Accommodations to enhance visual stimuli (e.g., enlarge, use color overlays)

(Continues)

TABLE 8.12   (Continued)

Test	Related Educational Interventions
Test 23: Sound Patterns—Voice	Auditory training; enhancements/modifications to listening environment
Test 24: Number Series	Develop number sense; count by increments; manipulatives
Test 25: Number Matrices	Seriation; patterns; explicit instruction in number reasoning skills
Test 26: Cross Out	Emphasize speediness; build cognitive speed via repetition
Test 27: Memory for Sentences	Associate new information with prior knowledge; rehearsal
Test 28: Block Rotation	Use of puzzles, pegboards, dot-to-dot drawings; multisensory teaching techniques; private speech
Test 29: Sound Patterns—Music	Auditory training; enhancements/modifications to listening environment
Test 30: Memory for Names—Delayed	Interventions/accommodations to help recall previously learned information
Test 31: Bilingual Verbal Comprehension— English/Spanish	See Test 1: Verbal Comprehension

SOURCE : From *Educational Interventions and Accommodations Related to the Woodcock-Johnson III Tests of Cognitive Abilities*, by F. A. Schrank & B. J. Wendling, 2008 (Assessment Service Bulletin No. 10). Rolling Meadows, IL: Riverside Publishing. Copyright © 2008 by the Riverside Publishing Company. Adapted with permission.

interventions. Table 8.12 provides a brief summary of evidence-based interventions that have been related to each of the WJ III COG tests. Additional information on educational interventions can be found in *Educational Interventions and Accommodations Related to the Woodcock-Johnson III Tests of Cognitive Abilities* (Schrank & Wendling, 2008), and the *Woodcock Interpretation and Instructional Interventions Program* (Schrank et al., 2008), as well as *Woodcock-Johnson III: Recommendations, Reports, and Strategies* (Mather & Jaffe, 2002).

VALIDITY

Test validity refers to the degree to which theory and empirical evidence support the use and interpretation of the test (AERA, APA, & NCME, 1999). The WJ III is based on the empirically based and well-documented CHC theory.

Understanding the relationship between the WJ III tests, CHC theory, and related cognitive processing research may be useful when analyzing the nature of an individual's performance (Schrank & Wendling, 2008). Table 8.13 summarizes the relevant cognitive processes for each of the WJ III COG tests. The primary broad and narrow CHC abilities measured in each test were presented in Table 8.1.

Developmental Growth Curves

Another form of validity evidence supporting the CHC abilities measured in the WJ III is the distinct developmental patterns of the tests and clusters. Developmental growth curves illustrate that the unique abilities measured by the WJ III typically follow different developmental paths over the life span covered by the test. These divergent growth curves provide evidence of the existence of unique abilities (Carroll, 1983, 1993). The

TABLE 8.13 Cognitive Processes Involved in Performance on the WJ III COG Tests

Test	Cognitive Process(es)
Test 1: Verbal Comprehension	Object recognition and re-identification; semantic activation, access, and matching; verbal analogical reasoning
Test 2: Visual-Auditory Learning	Paired-associative encoding, storage and retrieval
Test 3: Spatial Relations	Visual perception (feature detection); manipulation of visual images in space (visualization); matching
Test 4: Sound Blending	Synthesis of acoustic, phonological elements in immediate awareness; matching the sequence of elements to stored lexical entries; lexical activation and access
Test 5: Concept Formation	Rule-based categorization; rule-switching; induction/inference
Test 6: Visual Matching	Speeded matching of numbers
Test 7: Numbers Reversed	Span of apprehension and recoding in working memory
Test 8: Incomplete Words	Analysis of a sequence of acoustic, phonological elements in immediate awareness; activation of a stored representation of the word from an incomplete set of phonological features
Test 9: Auditory Working Memory	Recoding of acoustic, verbalizable stimuli held in immediate awareness
Test 10: Visual-Auditory Learning—Delayed	Retrieval and re-identification; associative encoding (for relearning)
Test 11: General Information	Semantic activation and access from store of acquired knowledge
Test 12: Retrieval Fluency	Recognition, fluent retrieval, and oral production of examples of a semantic category
Test 13: Picture Recognition	Formation of iconic memories and matching of visual stimuli to stored representations
Test 14: Auditory Attention	Selective auditory attention
Test 15: Analysis-Synthesis	Algorithmic, or step-by-step, sequential reasoning; deduction
Test 16: Decision Speed	Speeded matching of pictures in a category
Test 17: Memory for Words	Auditory sequential memory of unrelated words; memory span
Test 18: Rapid Picture Naming	Speed/fluency of retrieval and oral production of recognized objects
Test 19: Planning	Means–end analysis
Test 20: Pair Cancellation	Controlled, focal attention; vigilance
Test 21: Memory for Names	Associative encoding via directed spotlight attention, storage, and retrieval
Test 22: Visual Closure	Object identification from a limited set of features
Test 23: Sound Patterns—Voice	Prelexical, perceptual analysis of speech patterns
Test 24: Number Series	Representation and manipulation of points on a mental number line; identifying and applying an underlying rule/principle to complete a numerical sequence

(Continues)

TABLE 8.13   (Continued)

Test	Cognitive Process(es)
Test 25: Number Matrices	Access to verbal–visual numeric codes; transcoding verbal and/or visual representations of numeric information into analogical representations; determining the relationship between/among numbers on the first part of the structure and mapping (projecting) the structure to complete the analogy
Test 26: Cross Out	Speeded matching of geometric shapes and patterns
Test 27: Memory for Sentences	Formation of memories aided by a semantic, meaning-based code
Test 28: Block Rotation	Visual–spatial manipulation
Test 29: Sound Patterns—Music	Prelexical, perceptual analysis of auditory waveform patterns
Test 30: Memory for Names—Delayed	Re-identification of the names of figures
Test 31: Bilingual Verbal Comprehension—English/Spanish	Object re-identification; semantic activation, access, and matching; verbal analogical reasoning

SOURCE : From *Specification of the Cognitive Processes Involved in Performance on the Woodcock-Johnson III*, by F. A. Schrank, 2006 (Assessment Service Bulletin No. 7). Rolling Meadows, IL: Riverside Publishing. Copyright © 2006 by the Riverside Publishing Company. Adapted with permission.

pattern varies noticeably among the seven broad CHC abilities. For example, long-term retrieval (*Glr*) demonstrates the least amount of developmental change. Comprehension-knowledge (*Gc*) demonstrates the greatest amount of change as well as the slowest rate of decline compared to the other abilities. Developmental patterns for the narrow abilities provide further validity evidence for the narrow abilities comprising the broad abilities (see Chapter 4 of the Technical Manual for the WJ III NU for a review).

Clinical Samples

Studies reflecting the performance of various special populations on selected WJ III tests and clusters offer additional validity evidence. Individuals with various types of developmental, educational, and neuropsychological disabilities were administered different combinations of the WJ III tests. The purpose of these studies was to determine whether the WJ III differentiates

between special populations. For example, the gifted sample was expected to have a higher mean GIA score than the sample for individuals with mental retardation. Table 8.14 summarizes information for clinical samples comprised of individuals younger than 19 years of age. Table 8.15 summarizes the information for clinical samples comprised of adults 19 years of age or older.

Relationships between Ability and Achievement

Research has shown that the CHC broad and narrow abilities differentially predict performance on academic tasks (Evans, Floyd, McGrew, & Leforgee, 2002; Floyd, Evans, & McGrew, 2003; Floyd, McGrew, & Evans, 2008). Understanding the relationship between cognitive abilities and academic performance is a key to determining the presence of a specific learning disability (IDEA, 2004) and underlies the process of using assessment to inform instructional planning.

TABLE 8.14   Performance of Special Populations Younger Than 19 Years of Age on Selected WJ III COG Clusters

Reference Sample	GIA	Gc	Glr	Gv	Ga	Gf	Gs	Gsm
WJ III Norm Group	(*Std*)							
n	2834	3593	3102	3693	3256	3971	3975	4453
Median (SS)	101	101	100	101	99	101	101	101
Clinical Samples								
Anxiety Spectrum Disorders								
n	87	31	—	66	—	144	61	52
Median (SS)	91	96	—	100	—	97	91	90
ADHD								
n	259	177	209	240	183	712	254	250
Median (SS)	99	97	92	100	96	96	91	93
Autism Spectrum								
n	101	80	71	98	71	118	87	85
Median (SS)	95	97	97	99	100	94	86	94
Depressive Spectrum								
n	73	26	—	71	—	149	51	46
Median (SS)	93	96	—	101	—	96	95	93
Gifted								
n	124	40	40	125	39	125	40	124
Median (SS)	116	116	103	107	113	115	114	108
Language Disorders								
n	91	82	69	98	66	120	74	72
Median (SS)	81	87	87	96	96	82	89	90
Math Disorders								
n	115	98	105	99	86	149	111	105
Median (SS)	92	95	93	100	101	93	96	95
Mental Retardation								
n	93	51	31	121	31	105	32	83
Median (SS)	58	62	56	77	75	58	61	67
Reading Disorders								
n	284	203	238	175	138	352	254	224
Median (SS)	92	94	90	100	99	97	91	92
Written Expression Disorders								
n	238	198	216	174	152	314	224	205
Median (SS)	96	101	94	101	98	100	94	94

NOTE : See Chapter 4 of the Technical Manual for the WJ III NU for complete information.

TABLE 8.15   Performance of Special Populations 19 Years of Age or Older on Selected WJ III COG Clusters

Reference Sample	GIA	Gc	Glr	Gv	Ga	Gf	Gs	Gsm
WJ III Norm Group	(Std)							
n	1350	1564	1415	1688	1356	1740	2030	2188
Median (SS)	104	104	105	103	101	105	102	102
Clinical Samples								
Anxiety Spectrum Disorders								
n	170	44	44	137	41	372	136	138
Median (SS)	88	96	90	99	105	94	96	95
ADHD								
n	49	39	44	56	43	117	47	53
Median (SS)	93	95	91	98	99	101	91	95
Depressive Spectrum								
n	159	79	80	147	77	297	139	42
Median (SS)	89	95	87	99	103	95	93	94
Head Injury								
n	290	147	152	307	147	386	177	293
Median (SS)	93	97	85	99	100	96	86	95
Math Disorders								
n	77	68	75	89	72	106	77	91
Median (SS)	103	107	103	100	106	100	102	104
Reading Disorders								
n	75	44	74	120	74	178	75	121
Median (SS)	101	100	103	101	99	104	98	101
Written Expression Disorders								
n	103	81	101	129	98	166	103	129
Median (SS)	105	107	105	103	99	106	98	101

NOTE: See Chapter 4 of the Technical Manual for the WJ III NU for complete information.

For children and adolescents, Comprehension-Knowledge (*Gc*) is moderately to strongly related to reading (Evans et al., 2002), mathematics (Floyd et al., 2003), and writing (Floyd et al., 2008) achievement. In a recent study using structural equation modeling on the WJ III normative sample, Benson (2008) found that *Gc* had a strong direct effect on reading comprehension that increased with age. Oral language ability, an aspect of Comprehension-Knowledge (*Gc*), serves as the foundation for, and is positively related to, subsequent success in reading and writing (Glazer, 1989; Stanovich, 1986; Strickland & Feeley, 1991; Wiig & Semel, 1984). Research indicates significant relationships among level of oral vocabulary (Baumann & Kame'enui, 1991), background knowledge (Anderson & Pearson, 1984), and reading ability.

Long-Term Retrieval (*Glr*) is related to reading achievement during the elementary school years (Evans et al., 2002), to mathematics achievement during the same period (Floyd et al., 2003), and to writing achievement in the early elementary school years (Floyd et al., 2008). Naming facility is a narrow ability subsumed by *Glr*. A deficit in rapid naming has been found to be a good predictor of poor reading achievement across the lifespan (e.g., Bowers, Sunseth, & Golden, 1999; Bowers & Wolf, 1993: Denckla & Cutting, 1999; Manis, Seidenberg, & Doi, 1999; Scarborough, 1998).

While the ability to make sense of visual information is important to school success, the research has not established strong connections between the visual processing and visual-spatial tasks found on most intelligence tests and achievement (Evans et al., 2002; Floyd et al., 2003; Floyd et al., 2008). In clarifying the relationship between visual processing and reading, Berninger (1990) points out that these visual perceptual abilities should not be confused with the orthographic code processing abilities important during reading and spelling. In addition, a few research studies have indicated a relationship between visual processing and higher-level math achievement, such as geometry or calculus (Hegarty & Kozhevnikov, 1999).

Auditory Processing is related to reading achievement in the elementary school years (Evans et al., 2002). In particular, phonological awareness, an aspect of auditory processing, is an important prerequisite to competence in basic reading skills (Adams, 1990). Fluid Reasoning (*Gf*) is related to mathematics achievement (Floyd et al., 2003), reading comprehension (Evans et al., 2002), and to writing ability (Floyd et al., 2008; McGrew & Knopik, 1993). Both Processing Speed (*Gs*) and Short-Term Memory (*Gsm*) are also related to reading (Benson, 2008; Evans et al., 2002), mathematics (Floyd et al., 2003), and writing achievement (Floyd et al., 2008). In some cases, slow *Gs* appears to

be a correlate of reading disability (McGrew, Schrank, & Woodcock, 2007). In a recent study using structural equation modeling on the WJ III normative sample, Benson (2008) found that the effect of *Gs* on reading fluency increased with age.

SUMMARY

The WJ III COG and Diagnostic Supplement are useful diagnostic tools for exploring an individual's present performance levels in seven broad CHC abilities and a number of narrow abilities. In addition, the WJ III COG is helpful to practitioners who need to determine whether an individual has a specific learning disability. IDEA 2004 addresses the need to document a pattern of strengths and weaknesses between cognitive abilities and academic performance. The WJ III COG provides unique variation and discrepancy procedures that can be helpful to practitioners in quantifying a pattern of strengths and weaknesses and understanding the nature of the problem.

This battery of cognitive tests is often used in conjunction with the *Woodcock-Johnson III Tests of Achievement* (WJ III ACH), which is described in Chapter 19. Because the WJ III COG and the WJ III ACH were co-normed using a single sample, together they provide a comprehensive diagnostic system for identifying an individual's strengths and weaknesses among specific cognitive, linguistic, and academic abilities. The discrepancy and variation procedures provide additional ways to demonstrate patterns of performance. Once an individual's strengths and the specific areas of concern have been identified, the evaluator can then select the most appropriate instructional recommendations.

REFERENCES

Adams, M. J. (1990). *Beginning to read: Thinking and learning about print.* Cambridge, MA: MIT Press.

American Educational Research Association (AERA), American Psychological Association (APA), &

National Council on Measurement in Education (NCME). (1999). *Standards for educational and psychological testing*. Washington, DC: American Educational Research Association.

Anderson, R. C., & Pearson, P. D. (1984). A schema-theoretic view of basic processes in reading. In P. D. Pearson, R. Barr, M. L. Kamil, & P. Mosenthal (Eds.), *Handbook of reading research* (pp. 255–291). White Plains, NY: Longman.

Baumann, J. F., & Kame'enui, E. J. (1991). Research on vocabulary instruction. In J. Flood, J. M. Jensen, D. Lapp, & J. R. Squire (Eds.), *Handbook of research on teaching the English language arts* (pp. 604–632). New York: Macmillan.

Benson, N. (2008). Cattell-Horn-Carroll cognitive abilities and reading achievement. *Journal of Psychoeducational Assessment, 26*(1), 27–41.

Berninger, V. W. (1990). Multiple orthographic codes: Key to alternative instructional methodologies for developing the orthographic phonological connections underlying word identification. *School Psychology Review, 19*, 518–533.

Bickley, P. G., Keith, T. Z., & Wolfe, L. M. (1995). The three-stratum theory of cognitive abilities: Test of the structure of intelligence across the life span. *Intelligence, 22*, 311–326.

Bowers, P. G., Sunseth, K., & Golden, J. (1999). The route between rapid naming and reading progress. *Scientific Studies of Reading, 3*, 31–53.

Bowers, P. G., & Wolf, M. (1993). Theoretical links between naming speed, precise timing mechanisms, and orthographic skill in dyslexia. *Reading and Writing: An Interdisciplinary Journal, 5*, 69–85.

Carroll, J. B. (1983). Studying individual differences in cognitive abilities: Through and beyond factor analysis. In R. F. Dillon (Ed.), *Individual differences in cognition* (Vol. 1, pp. 1–33). New York: Academic Press.

Carroll, J. B. (1993). *Human cognitive abilities: A survey of factor-analytic studies*. New York: Cambridge University Press.

Denckla, M. B., & Cutting, L. E. (1999). History and significance of rapid automatized naming. *Annals of Dyslexia, 49*, 29–42.

Evans, J. J., Floyd, R. G., McGrew, K. S., & Leforgee, M. H. (2002). The relations between measures of Cattell-Horn-Carroll (CHC) cognitive abilities and reading achievement during childhood and adolescence. *School Psychology Review, 31*, 246–262.

Flanagan, D. P., & Ortiz, S. O. (2001). *Essentials of cross-battery assessment*. New York: Wiley.

Floyd, R. G., Evans, J. J., & McGrew, K. S. (2003). Relations between measures of Cattell-Horn-Carroll (CHC) cognitive abilities and mathematics achievement across the school-age years. *Psychology in the Schools, 40*, 155–171.

Floyd, R. G., McGrew, K. S., & Evans, J. J. (2008). The relative contribution of the Cattell-Horn-Carroll cognitive abilities in explaining writing achievement during childhood and adolescence. *Psychology in the Schools, 45*, 132–144.

Glazer, S. M. (1989). Oral language and literacy. In D. S. Strickland & L. M. Morrow (Eds.), *Emerging literacy: Young children learn to read and write* (pp. 16–26). Newark, DE: International Reading Association.

Hegarty, M. & Kozhevnikov, M. (1999). Types of visual-spatial representations and mathematical problem-solving. *Journal of Educational Psychology, 91*, 684–689.

Horn, J. L., & Noll, J. (1977). Human cognitive capabilities: Gf-Gc theory. In D. P. Flanagan, J. L. Genshaft, & P. L. Harrison (Eds.), *Contemporary intellectual assessment: Theories, tests, and issues* (pp. 53–91). New York: Guilford Press.

Individuals with Disabilities Education Improvement Act of 2004. (PL No. 108-446, 20 USC 1400).

Kail, R. (1991). Development of processing speed in childhood and adolescence. *Advances in Child Development and Behavior, 23*, 151–184.

Keith, T. Z. (1997). Using confirmatory factor analysis to aid in understanding the constructs measured by intelligence tests. In D. P. Flanagan & P. L. Harrison (Eds.), *Contemporary intellectual assessment: Theories, tests and issues* (pp. 373–402). New York: Guilford Press.

Keith, T. Z. (1999). Effects of general and specific abilities on student achievement: Similarities and differences across ethnic groups. *School Psychology Quarterly, 14*, 239–262.

Kranzler, J. H., & Keith, T. Z. (1999). Independent confirmatory factor analysis of the Cognitive Assessment System (CAS): What does the CAS measure? *School Psychology Review, 28*, 117–144.

Manis, F. R., Seidenberg, M. S., & Doi, L. M. (1999). See Dick RAN: Rapid naming and the longitudinal prediction of reading subskills in first and second graders. *Scientific Studies of Reading, 3,* 129–157.

Mather, N., & Jaffe, L. (2002). *Woodcock-Johnson III: Recommendations, reports, and strategies*. New York: Wiley.

McGrew, K. S. (2005). The Cattell-Horn-Carroll Theory of Cognitive Abilities: Past, present, and future. In D. P. Flanagan & P. L. Harrison (Eds.), *Contemporary intellectual assessment: Theories, tests and issues* (pp. 136–182). New York: Guilford Press.

McGrew, K. S., Dailey, D., & Schrank, F. A. (in press). *WJIII/NU score differences; What the user can expect and why.* (Assessment Service Bulletin). Rolling Meadows, IL: Riverside.

McGrew, K. S., & Flanagan, D. P. (1998). *The intelligence test desk reference (ITDR): Gf-Gc cross battery assessment*. Boston: Allyn & Bacon.

McGrew, K. S. & Knopik, S. N. (1993). The relationship between the WJ-R Gf-Gc cognitive clusters and writing achievement across the life-span. *Journal of Psychoeducational Assessment, 13,* 21–38.

McGrew, K. S., Schrank, F. A., & Woodcock, R. W. (2007). *Technical manual: Woodcock-Johnson III normative update*. Rolling Meadows, IL: Riverside.

McGrew, K., & Woodcock, R. (2001). *Technical manual: Woodcock-Johnson III*. Rolling Meadows, IL: Riverside.

Muñoz-Sandoval, A. F., Cummins, J., Alvarado, C. G., & Ruef, M. L. (1998; 2005). *Bilingual verbal ability tests normative update*. Rolling Meadows, IL: Riverside.

Muñoz-Sandoval, A. F., Woodcock, R. W., McGrew, K. S., & Mather, N. (2005). *Batería III Woodcock-Muñoz: Pruebas de habilidad cognitiva*. Rolling Meadows, IL: Riverside.

Nettlebeck, T. (1994). Speediness. In R. J. Sternberg (Ed.), *Encyclopedia of human intelligence* (pp. 1014–1019). New York: Macmillan.

Scarborough, H. S. (1998). Predicting the future achievement of second graders with reading disabilities: Contributions of phonemic awareness, verbal memory, rapid naming, and IQ. *Annals of Dyslexia, 48,* 115–136.

Schrank, F. A. (2006). *Specification of the cognitive processes involved in performance on the Woodcock-Johnson III* (Assessment Service Bulletin No. 7). Rolling Meadows, IL: Riverside.

Schrank, F. A., Flanagan, D. P., Woodcock, R. W., & Mascolo, J. T. (2002). *Essentials of WJ III cognitive abilities assessment*. New York: Wiley.

Schrank, F. A., & Wendling, B. J. (2008). *Educational interventions and accommodations related to the Woodcock-Johnson III Tests of Cognitive Abilities* (Assessment Service Bulletin No. 10). Rolling Meadows, IL: Riverside.

Schrank, F. A., Wendling, B. J., & Woodcock, R. W. (2008). *Woodcock Interpretation and Instructional Interventions Program (WIIIP)*. Rolling Meadows, IL: Riverside.

Schrank, F. A., & Woodcock, R. W. (2008). Woodcock-Johnson III Normative Update Compuscore and Profiles Program (version 3.1) [computer software]. *Woodcock-Johnson III normative update*. Rolling Meadows, IL: Riverside.

Stanovich, K. E. (1986). Matthew effects in reading: Some consequences of individual differences in the acquisition of literacy. *Reading Research Quarterly, 21,* 360–407.

Strickland, D. S., & Feeley, J. T. (1991). Development in the early school years. In J. Flood, J. M. Jensen, D. Lapp, & J. R. Squire (Eds.), *Handbook of research on teaching the English language arts* (pp. 529–535). New York: Macmillan.

Vernon, P. A. (1983). Speed of information processing and general intelligence. *Intelligence, 7,* 53–70.

Wiig, E. H., & Semel, E. M. (1984). *Language assessment and intervention for the learning disabled* (2nd ed.). Columbus, OH: Charles E. Merrill.

Woodcock, R. W., McGrew, K., & Mather, N. (2001). *Woodcock-Johnson Tests of Cognitive Abilities and Tests of Achievement* (3rd ed.). Rolling Meadows, IL: Riverside.

Woodcock, R. W., McGrew, K. S., Mather, N., & Schrank, F. A. (2003). *Woodcock-Johnson III diagnostic supplement to the Tests of Cognitive Abilities*. Rolling Meadows. IL: Riverside.

Woodcock, R. W., McGrew, K. S., Schrank. F. A., & Mather, N. (2007). *Woodcock-Johnson III normative update*. Rolling Meadows, IL: Riverside.

Nonverbal Intelligence Tests

Comprehensive Test of Nonverbal Intelligence—Second Edition

Donald D. Hammill, Nils A. Pearson

The *Comprehensive Test of Nonverbal Intelligence—Second Edition* (CTONI-2; Hammill, Pearson, & Wiederholt, 2009) is a norm-referenced test that uses nonverbal formats to estimate general intelligence of children and adults whose performances on traditional tests might be adversely affected by subtle or overt impairments involving language or motor abilities. The CTONI was published originally in 1996; a second edition was published in 2009. This chapter will briefly describe the test's theoretical foundation, basic structure, standardization and reliability characteristics, uses, and validity.

THEORY UNDERLYING THE CTONI-2

Neither the CTONI nor the CTONI-2 was built to conform to any particular theory. Instead, when building the first edition of CTONI, we were guided by the results of a review of the nature, content, and formats of 36 "nonverbal" measures of reasoning or problem solving that existed in 1996. We found that the authors of these tests had built five times more language-reduced tests (i.e., tests that used

simple oral instruction) than nonlanguage tests (i.e., tests that used pantomime instructions), had chosen to measure analogical, categorical, and sequential reasoning in about equal numbers, and had employed pictured objects and geometric contexts (i.e., formats) also in equal numbers.

Based on this review, we decided to build a test that would provide both simple oral instructions for general use and pantomime instructions for use in those few cases where they are appropriate. Therefore, the test can be either a language-reduced nonverbal test or a nonlanguage nonverbal test depending on the type of administration opted for by the examiner. We also decided that the test would measure analogical, categorical, and sequential reasoning in both pictorial and geometric contexts (i.e., formats).

Although the CTONI-2 adheres to no particular theory, its content is consistent with that of most other tests of intelligence. In their text, *Assessment in Inclusive and Special Education*, Salvia, Ysseldyke, and Bolt (2007) list 13 abilities measured by most intelligence tests. The CTONI-2 measures all but 3 of these abilities. The exceptions are general information, vocabulary, and motor behavior. The first two of these are inherently verbal in nature and, thereby, inappropriate content for a "nonverbal" test; the last ability, motor behavior, is also inappropriate content because the CTONI-2 was designed to be motor reduced as well as language reduced.

Finally, even though the underpinnings of the CTONI-2 are theoretically eclectic and pragmatic in design, its contents can be readily identified with current theories of intelligence, for example, Cattell and Horn's (Horn & Cattell, 1966) *fluid intelligence* construct; Das's (1972) *simultaneous processing or successive processing* contructs; Jensen's (1980) *associative level* construct; and Wechsler's (2003) *performance scale* on the WISC-IV.

DESCRIPTION OF THE CTONI-2

A description of the CTONI-2 is provided in this section. Included is a description of the subtests and composites, a summary of the reviews of CTONI, and a listing of the new features of CTONI-2.

Subtests and Composites

The subtests and composites that make up CTONI and CTONI-2 are identical. Their relationship to the abilities and contacts in the test model is displayed in Table 9.1. The six subtests that make up the CTONI-2 are described briefly below, followed by a description of the three composites.

Subtest 1. Pictorial Analogies
Subtest 2. Geometric Analogies

Both the Pictorial Analogies and Geometric Analogies subtests use a 2 × 2 matrix format to measure this highly complex cognitive ability. To pass the items, the test-takers must understand that *this is to that* (the upper two boxes in the matrix) as *this is to what* (the lower two boxes in the matrix). They must demonstrate knowledge by pointing to the one of the choice items that goes into the blank box. Example items from

TABLE 9.1   Relationship of CTONI-2 Subtests to the Test Model

Ability	Context	
	Pictorial Objects	**Geometric Designs**
Analogical Reasoning	Pictorial Analogies	Geometric Analogies
Categorical Reasoning	Pictorial Categories	Geometric Categories
Sequential Reasoning	Pictorial Sequences	Geometric Sequences

the Pictorial Analogies and Geometric Analogies subtests are found in Figure 9.1.

Subtest 3. Pictorial Categories
Subtest 4. Geometric Categories

The Pictorial Categories and Geometric Categories subtests require the test-takers to deduce the relationship between two stimulus figures and to select from the choice items the one that shares the same relationship with the stimulus figures. They have to figure out *which of these is related to those*. Example items from each subtest are found in Figure 9.1.

Subtest 5. Pictorial Sequences
Subtest 6. Geometric Sequences

The Pictorial Sequences and Geometric Sequences subtests use a problem-solving progression format. Test-takers are shown a series of boxes that contain different figures that bear some sequential relationship to one another; the last box is blank. After viewing an array of choices, they point to the one that completes the progression in the previously displayed series of figures. They must recognize *the rule that is guiding the progression of figures*. Example items for each subtest are found in Figure 9.1.

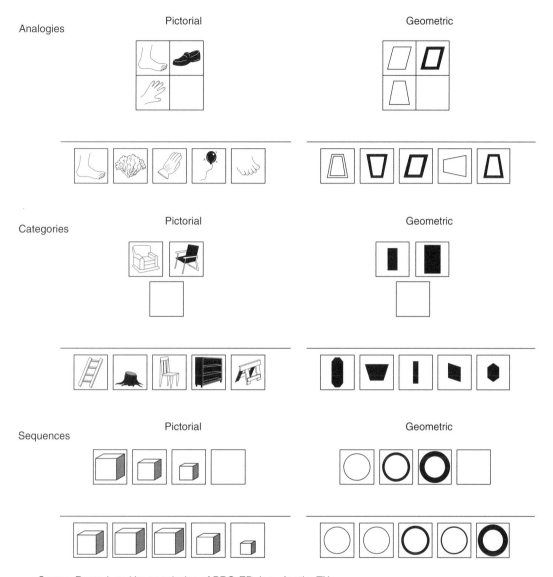

Source: Reproduced by permission of PRO-ED, Inc., Austin, TX

FIGURE 9.1

Examples of items from CTONI-2

In addition to the subtests, the CTONI-2 also has three composites. Two composites represent the contexts used to measure the abilities (Pictorial Scale and Geometric Scale). The third composite, the Full Scale, is the overall

ability score on the test). All three composites measure general intelligence. Each composite is described next.

The *Pictorial Scale* is formed by combining the scaled scores of the three subtests that use pictures of objects (i.e., Pictorial Analogies, Pictorial Categories, and Pictorial Sequences). The *Geometric Scale* is formed by combining the scaled scores of the three subtests that use images involving points, lines, angles, surfaces, and solids (i.e., Geometric Analogies, Geometric Categories, and Geometric Sequences). The *Full Scale* composite is the best representation of general intelligence because it is the most reliable score on the CTONI-2. Because it is formed by combining the scaled scores of all six CTONI-2 subtests, the index for the Full Scale is also the best estimate of Spearman's (1923) global factor *g* in that it reflects status on a wide array of cognitive abilities.

We conclude this description of the CTONI-2 subtests and composites by calling attention to the fact that the simple act of pointing is the method of response required for all subtests. We purposely avoided complex motor responses because we did not want to bias our test against individuals who have motor impairments (e.g., people with cerebral palsy or apraxia, people recovering from stroke or other brain anomalies, or people who are simply awkward). In his description of nonverbal tests, Levin (1987) observed that the presence of complicated motor responses unnecessarily penalizes many people with disabilities. We might add that requiring complicated motor responses on a test of intelligence can be as biasing as requiring sophisticated oral (i.e., verbal) responses.

Reviewers' Comments about the CTONI

From the start, the CTONI was very popular with professionals in psychology and education. Because of its popularity, the CTONI was reviewed extensively. These reviews were published in a volume of the *Mental Measurements Yearbook*, in books devoted to current assessment practices, in guides to tests in special and deaf education, and in the test review sections of respected professional journals. Excerpts from these reviews follow.

This CTONI is one of the most up-to-date tests of nonverbal intelligence available; it is based on a well-constructed model and promises to provide valuable information in this area (Taylor, 2003, p. 523).

The test is designed and documented to be unbiased with regards to gender, race, and disability. The test directions can be administered orally or through pantomime. The test can be individually administered in less than 60 minutes. There is strong evidence of good reliability (Pierangelo & Giuliani, 2002, pp. 182–183).

The CTONI can be a useful adjunct to the psychologist's and educational diagnostician's tools. ... the CTONI represents a good positive attempt to measure nonverbal ability, and does fill a void (Nicholson, 1998–1999, pp. 67–68).

The CTONI, although it has no norms for deaf individuals and measures particular aspects of intelligence, looks to be a good addition to the very limited battery of tests that are appropriate for deaf or hard of hearing individuals (Spragins, 1997–1998, p. 40).

The CTONI presents a welcome addition to measure of nonverbal intelligence, and the reviewer is excited about its appearance on the market (van Lingen, 1998, p. 83).

In summary, the CTONI has several distinct advantages. The use of both pictorial and geometric content, and the separation of the processes involved into analogies, categories, and sequences are useful in the overall evaluation of nonverbal intelligence. The type of nonverbal skills are of the "higher order" nature, namely, they do not rely solely on concrete properties of objects (size, color, shape) or perception/perceptual-motor integration (Aylward, 1998, p. 82).

The CTONI manual provides detailed, yet clear, directions for administration, scoring, and interpretation of subtest and composite scores (Drossman & Maller, 2000, p. 300).

Thus, the CTONI is a welcome addition to tests available for students who have difficulty with language or in making fine motor responses. It is well normed and easy to give (Bradley-Johnson, 1997, p. 291).

Athanasiou (2002) compared the internal consistency reliability of six nonverbal tests [CTONI, General Ability Measure for Adults (GAMA; Naglieri & Bardos, 1997), Leiter International Performance Scale-Revised (LEITER-R; Roid & Miller, 1997),

Test of Nonverbal Intelligence *(TONI-3; Brown, Sherbenou, & Johnsen, 1997), and* Universal Nonverbal Intelligence Test *(UNIT; Bracken & McCallum, 1998)]. He concluded that "the CTONI is the only instrument that exceeds the standard of .90 at every age level"* (p. 214). *He also found the CTONI's test-retest reliability coefficients to be even larger (i.e., above 90).*

Although the reviewers were generous in praising the CTONI, they also expressed some valid criticisms and made many useful suggestions for improving the test. These are summarized below.

- The most frequently mentioned criticisms focused on issues related to validity. For example, the reviewers thought that we needed to provide more evidence for predictive validity and to use larger numbers and types of subjects in our supportive studies (Bracken & Naglieri, 2003; Cohen & Spenciner, 1998; Drossman & Maller, 2000; Pierangelo & Guiliani, 2002; Rossen, Shearer, Penfield, & Kranzer, 2005; Salvia & Ysseldyke, 2001); they wanted the means and standard deviations to be included in the validity studies.
- Relative to reliability, Bradley-Johnson (1997) and Salvia and Ysseldyke (2001) felt that the status of our test–retest reliability evidence was questionable due to the small number of subjects in our study.
- Bracken and Naglieri (2003), Bradley-Johnson (1997), Di Cerbo and de Barona (2001), Nicholson (1998–1999), Sattler (2001), and van Lingen (1998) noted the presence of floor effects at the younger ages.
- Some reviewers wanted more information related to the deaf and hard-of-hearing population (Bradley-Johnson, 1997; Spragins, 1997–1998), especially item bias data for this group (Drossman & Maller, 2000).
- Comments by Aylward (1998) and Drossman and Maller (2000) about interpreting profiles and subtest and composite discrepancies

indicated that we had not provided enough direction on this and related topics.
- Bracken and Naglieri (2003), Drossman and Maller (2000), Rossen et al. (2005), and Salvia and Ysseldyke (2001) wanted to know how many people in the normative sample were tested with the oral instructions and how many were tested with the pantomime instructions.
- Drossman and Maller (2000) wanted to know what to do when the test-taker fails one or two of the practice items.
- Rossen et al. (2005) wanted to know the relationship between CTONI and tests of school achievement.
- Nicholson (1998–1999) thought it would be helpful if we provided space on the record form for recording the standard errors of measurement (SEM).

These criticisms and suggestions for improvement seemed valid to us and were very useful in designing the CTONI-2. We addressed all of them in the current edition.

Characteristics of the CTONI-2

The test reviews, comments, and queries from individuals who used the test, and our own ideas for improving the test, were all considered in the development of CTONI-2. This second edition of the test has been improved in many ways. Some of the most important changes are listed below.

1. All new normative data were collected in 2007 and 2008. The demographic characteristics of the sample conform to those of the population by the *U.S. Census Bureau* (www.census.gov) and are thereby representative of the U.S. population.
2. The floor effects present in the first edition have been eliminated.
3. The study of item bias has been expanded.

4. New oral instructions have been provided for common non-English languages spoken in the United States.

A major effort has been made to show conclusively that CTONI-2 is both reliable and valid. This effort involved the addition of more studies with larger numbers of subjects than were used in the first edition. Further, we have subjected CTONI-2 to a particularly rigorous technique for establishing validity called *positive predictive outcome analysis* (i.e., the computation of a test's sensitivity index, specificity index, and positive predictive value).

The overall look of the test has been updated and enhanced (e.g., some items have been redrawn and all of the pictured items have been colored to make them more appealing).

ADMINISTRATION AND SCORING PROCEDURES

The information in this section includes (1) guidelines for giving the CTONI-2, (2) ceiling rules for the subtests, (3) testing time, and (4) recommendations concerning the use of oral and pantomime instructions.

Guidelines

The CTONI-2 is appropriate for use with individuals between the ages of 6:0 and 89:11 who can understand the instructions, who are capable of making a pointing response, who are familiar with printed pictures and forms, and especially who can pass at least one of the practice items on a subtest. The CTONI-2 should not be administered to people who have serious visual problems.

Only examiners with formal training in assessment should administer the CTONI-2. They should have a basic understanding of measurement statistics; procedures governing test administration, scoring, and interpretation; and specific information about mental ability evaluation. This special knowledge can be obtained

from numerous sources. Most often, it can be acquired by enrolling in college courses devoted to assessment. Such courses frequently are found in departments of school psychology, special education, speech pathology, reading, and counseling, among others. Workshops sponsored by local school agencies or private consultants are other sources that are helpful. Examiners with such experience should have little difficulty in mastering the procedures necessary to give, score, and interpret the CTONI-2 properly.

Before actually giving the CTONI-2, examiners should consult local school policies, state regulations, and position statements of their respective professional organizations regarding test administration, interpretation, and issues of confidentiality. This is especially the case when the purpose of testing is to diagnose handicapping conditions and to qualify individuals for special programs.

Ceilings

The CTONI-2 subtests have no basals. Testing begins with item 1 and proceeds until the subject misses 3 items in a row (the ceiling). Scoring is simple; the test-taker earns 1 point for each item passed before reaching the ceiling. Because scoring is so simple, no scoring software is necessary.

Testing Time

No time limits are imposed on this test. The time required to give all six subtests varies from 40 to 60 minutes. Individual subtests rarely take more than 5 to 10 minutes to administer.

Method of Administration

When administering the CTONI-2, we prefer that whenever feasible you use the simple English-language instructions provided in this manual or the oral instructions (provided in an appendix) for other languages frequently spoken in the United States. Our reasons for providing *both* verbal and nonverbal instructions are the same as those given by Snijders, Tellegen, and Laros (1989) in their manual and research report for the *Snijder-Oomen Non-Verbal Intelligence Test*. They wrote that when administering a nonverbal test "to a hearing subject, not speaking creates a strange and disturbing situation. For many hearing-disabled, not speaking is also unusual. Therefore we have developed both verbal and nonverbal instructions for each subtest" (p. 2). And we are not alone in providing both verbal and nonverbal instructions (see *Test of Nonverbal Intelligence—Fourth Edition* [TONI-4; Brown, Sherbenou, & Johnsen, 2009]; *Wechsler Nonverbal Scale of Ability* [WNV; Wechsler & Naglieri, 2006]; among others).

When testing people who are deaf or who have serious hearing impairments, examiners may use American Sign Language (ASL), Manually Coded English (MCE), Aural/Oral English (oral English without signs, usually with some form of auditory amplification), or Signs-Supported Speech (the use of spoken English with signs).

The optional pantomime instructions should be used only in those few cases where you think the subject might not understand the oral instructions.

STANDARDIZATION, NORMS, AND PSYCHOMETRICS

This section discusses three topics related to the CTONI-2's standardization: characteristics of the normative sample, description of the normative scores provided, and reliability of the test's subtest and composite scores.

Characteristics of the Standardization Sample

The CTONI-2 was normed on a sample of 2,827 persons in 10 states: Alabama, California, Georgia, Louisiana, Minnesota, North Dakota, New York, Texas, Virginia, and Washington. The majority of the normative sample was tested in the fall and winter of 2007 and the spring of 2008. Major testing sites were set up in the South (Birmingham, *Alabama*; Corpus Christi, Lubbock, *Texas*), West (Burbank, Manteca, Pleasant Grove, Ripon, *California*), Northeast (Rochester, *New York*), and Midwest (Bismarck, Mandan, *North Dakota*).

A site coordinator with experience in collecting standardization data was selected for each location and trained with the CTONI-2. Personnel experienced with assessment were contracted by the site coordinator to administer the test. At each site, participating schools were selected on the basis that the demographic characteristics of the subjects closely matched those of the region as a whole. Additional examiners were located by accessing the PRO-ED customer files and asking current users of the CTONI whether they would participate in the norming effort. The examiners who responded were asked to test 20 individuals between the ages of 6 and 89 years old. They were sent enough materials to test individuals in their area whose demographic makeup matched that of their community. Ninety-seven percent of the normative data were collected from the major sites. At least 95% of the normative sample was tested using the English oral instructions; the remaining 5% were tested using the pantomime instructions. Because the non-English option has been recently added to the test, no individuals in the normative sample were tested using a language other than English or pantomime.

The procedures described above resulted in a normative sample that is representative of the nation as a whole. The characteristics of the sample with regard to gender, geographic region, race, Hispanic status, exceptionality status, family income, and educational level of parents are reported as percentages in Table 9.2. The percentages for these characteristics were compared with those reported by the U.S. Census Bureau (www.census.gov) for the school-aged and adult populations. A comparison of the percentages demonstrates that the sample is representative. To further demonstrate the representativeness of the sample, selected demographic information

TABLE 9.2   Demographic Characteristics of the Normative Sample ($n = 2,827$)

Characteristics	Percentage of School-Aged Sample	Percentage of School-Aged Population	Percentage of Adult Sample	Percentage of Adult Population
Geographic Region[a]				
Northeast	19	18	20	19
South	36	36	36	36
Midwest	22	22	21	22
West	23	24	23	23
Gender[b]				
Male	51	51	48	49
Female	49	49	52	51
Ethnicity[c]				
White	75	76	82	82
Black/African American	15	16	12	12
Asian/Pacific Islander	4	4	2	4
Two or more	4	3	2	1
Other	2	1	1	1
Hispanic[c]				
Yes	16	19	13	13
No	84	81	87	87
Parent Education/Education[d]				
Less than Bachelor's Degree	77	70	73	72
Bachelor's Degree	16	20	18	19
Advanced Degree	7	10	9	9
Income[e]				
Under $10,000	8	5	8	5
$10,000 to $14,999	4	4	4	4
$15,000 to $24,999	10	11	10	11
$25,000 to $34,999	11	11	10	11
$35,000 to $49,999	15	15	15	15
$50,000 to $74,999	20	20	21	20
$75,000 and above	32	34	32	34

TABLE 9.2   (Continued)

Characteristics	Percentage of School-Aged Sample	Percentage of School-Aged Population	Percentage of Adult Sample	Percentage of Adult Population
Exceptionality Status[f]				
Specific Learning Disabilities	2	5	1	NA
Mental Retardation	<1	1	1	NA
Hearing Impaired	1	<1	1	NA
Other Health Impairments	<1	1	2	NA
Attention Deficit Disorder	3	NA	1	NA
Other Disability	2	4	1	NA

[a]SOURCE : U.S. Census Bureau, "Age and Sex for States and for Puerto Rico: April 1, 2000 to July 1, 2005"; published 4 August 2006;<http://www.census.gov/popest/states/asrh/SC-EST2005-02.html>. My INTERNET LINK http://www.census.gov/compendia/statab/tables/07s0021.xls

[b]SOURCE : U.S. Census Bureau, Current Population Reports, P25-1095; "Table US-EST90INT-04-Intercensal Estimates of the United States Resident Population by Age Groups and Sex, 1990–2000: Selected Months"; published September 13, 2002; <http://www.census.gov/popest/archives/EST90INTERCENSAL/US-EST90INT-04.html>; and "Table 1: Annual Estimates of the Population by Sex and Five-Year Age Groups for the United States: April 1, 2000 to July 1, 2005"; published 10 May 2006; <http://www.census.gov/popest/national/asrh/NC-EST2005/NC-EST2005-01.xls>.

[c]SOURCE : U.S. Census Bureau, "Annual Estimates of the Population by Sex, Age and Race for the United States: April 1, 2000 to July 1, 2005(NC-EST2005-04)"; published 10 May 2006; http://www.census.gov/popest/national/asrh/NC-EST2005-asrh.html>.

[d]SOURCE : U.S. Census Bureau, Current Population Survey. Data are available on the Internet at <http://www.census.gov/population/www/socdemo/educ-attn.html>. INTERNET LINK http://www.census.gov/population/ www/socdemo/educ-attn.html My link http://www.census.gov/compendia/statab/tables/07s0216.xls

[e]SOURCE : U.S. Census Bureau, Income, Poverty, and Health Insurance 2004, Current Population Report, P60–229; and Internet site at http://pubdb3.census.gov/macro/032005/faminc/new07_000.htm (revised 31 January 2006). My INERNET LINK http://www.census.gov/hhes/www/income.html http://www.census.gov/compendia/statab/tables/07s0675.xls

[f]SOURCE : U.S. Census Bureau, Current Population Survey. Data are available on the Internet at <http://www.census.gov/compendia/statab/cats/education.html>. My links <http://www.census.gov/compendia/statab/tables/08s0231.xls> and <http://www.census.gov/compendia/statab/tables/08s0255.xls>.

was stratified by age. The stratified variables conform to national expectations at each age group covered by the test's norms.

Normative Scores and Their Interpretation

The CTONI-2 yields four types of normative scores: age equivalents, percentile ranks, scaled scores, and composite indexes. Information about how these scores were derived and how to interpret them is discussed in this section.

Age Equivalents

These scores are usually labeled according to the content of the test. Thus, age equivalents associated with tests of reading, vocabulary, and mental ability are called *reading ages*, *vocabulary ages*, and *mental ages*, respectively. The age equivalents for the CTONI-2 are referred to as *mental ages*. These scores are derived by calculating the average normative group's score at each 6-month interval. Through the process of interpolation, extrapolation, and smoothing, age equivalents are generated for each raw score point achieved on a subtest.

The use of age equivalents has been criticized extensively; most authorities have advocated discontinuing these scores and have even encouraged test publishers to stop reporting test scores as age equivalents. The main arguments against their use are that their statistical properties are inadequate and that their results are often misleading. Salvia et al. (2007) and Reynolds, Livingston, and Willson (2009) provide detailed discussions of the difficulties associated with age equivalents. Nonetheless, schools and state education agencies frequently mandate the use of these scores for administrative purposes. For this reason alone, we provide them (reluctantly) and only for use with school-age subjects.

Percentile Ranks

Percentile ranks, also called *percentile scores* or *percentiles*, are another type of normative score provided for the CTONI-2. On a scale ranging from 0 to 100, these ranks indicate the percentage of the distribution of the standardization sample that is equal to or below any particular percentile. For example, a percentile rank of 76 means that 76% of the standardization sample scored at or below that percentile. Percentiles are used often by practitioners to share test results with others and are understood easily if one remembers that the differences between the successive percentile ranks do not represent equal amounts of the information measured. The distance between two percentile ranks becomes much greater as those ranks are located farther from the mean or average (i.e., the 50th percentile). Although percentile ranks are convenient and popular, examiners should be familiar with their advantages and disadvantages, as explained by Aiken and Groth-Marnat (2006), McLoughlin and Lewis (2005), and Salvia et al. (2007).

Scaled Scores for the Subtests

Norms for the subtests are presented in terms of scaled scores (a type of standard score), which have a mean of 10 and a standard deviation of 3. We chose to use the 10:3 distribution for calculating the subtest scaled scores (and the 100:15 distribution for the composite scores, discussed in the next section) because this distribution is widely used in other tests of intellectual abilities (e.g., the *Wechsler Intelligence Scale for Children—Fourth Edition*) (WISC-IV; Wechsler, 2003), the *Stanford-Binet Intelligence Scales—Fifth Edition* (SBIS-5; Roid, 2003), the *Kaufman Assessment Battery for Children—Second Edition* (KABC-2; Kaufman & Kaufman, 2004), the *Detroit Test of Learning Aptitude—Fourth Edition* (DTLA-4; Hammill, 1998), the *Universal Nonverbal Intelligence Test* (UNIT; Bracken & McCallum, 1998), the *Test of Nonverbal Intelligence—Fourth Edition* (TONI-4; Brown, Sherbenou, & Johnsen, 2009), and *Cognitive Assessment System* (CAS; Naglieri & Das, 1997).

These subtest scaled scores were developed by using a continuous norming procedure. This method used polynomial regression to fit the progression of means, standard deviations, skewness, and kurtosis across ages. These fitted values were estimated at each age interval. Given the fitted values of skewness and kurtosis from the regression, the shape of the distribution of the scores was determined and percentiles were derived. These percentiles were then converted into scaled scores at each age interval. The resulting data were smoothed somewhat to allow for a consistent progression across age levels. As a result of these procedures, none of the CTONI-2 subtests have floor effects. A few of the subtests have some minor ceiling effects at the older ages, which is not seen as a problem because the CTONI-2 is mostly used to identify persons who have cognitive difficulties and not to differentiate between degrees of proficiency among persons who are gifted and talented intellectually. Also worth noting is that none of the indexes have floor or ceiling effects.

Unlike raw scores, which cannot be meaningfully compared, scaled scores provide a clear indication of an individual's subtest performance because examiners can make comparisons across subtests. For example, a scaled score of 10 on two subtests means that the individual is performing equally well on both subtests (i.e., average).

Subtest findings should be interpreted only in terms of the specific content and skills measured. To facilitate interpretation, we briefly describe the abilities measured by the subtests.

Pictorial Analogies

This measures the ability to recognize the relationship of two objects to each other and to find the same relationship between two different objects.

Geometric Analogies

This measures the ability to recognize the relationship of two geometric designs to each other and to find the same relationship between two different geometric designs.

Pictorial Categories

This measures the ability to select from a set of different pictures the one that is the most similar to two other related pictures.

Geometric Categories

This measures the ability to select from a set of different geometric designs the one that is most similar to two other related geometric designs.

Pictorial Sequences

This measures the ability to select from a set of pictures the one that completes a sequence of actions shown in three pictures.

Geometric Sequences

This measures the ability to select from a set of geometric designs the one that completes a sequence of action shown in three designs.

Indexes for the Composites

Normative scores for the composites are called *indexes* (another type of standard score). They were calculated by applying a direct linear transformation to the sums of scaled scores to obtain a distribution with a mean of 100 and a standard deviation of 15. The resulting data across age levels were smoothed somewhat to allow for a consistent progression.

The indexes for the composites are the most clinically useful scores on the CTONI-2 because they are the most reliable scores on the test. Guidelines for interpreting these important scores are discussed next. To reiterate, these composites are Full Scale, Pictorial Scale, and Geometric Scale.

The index for the *Full Scale* composite is formed by combining the subscales of all six subtests. Because of this, it is the CTONI-2's best, most comprehensive estimate of a person's overall, general intellectual ability.

Average to high indexes (i.e., 90 and above) indicate that the person tested has attained at least a minimal level of reasoning and problem solving that is expected for his or her age. He or she can see logical and abstract relationship, reason without words, solve mental puzzles that involve progressive elements, and form meaningful associations between objects and designs. Usually, people with high scores do well in academic subjects, especially mathematics.

Low indexes (i.e., below 90) indicate that the person tested has performed below a level that is expected for a person his or her age. He or she probably has trouble managing nonverbal information, perceiving visual data, organizing spatially oriented material, and mastering abstract properties of visual symbols. Usually, people with low scores will also struggle academically in school.

People are relatively consistent in their cognitive abilities. That is to say, individuals who are good (or poor) in one cognitive ability tend to be more or less good (or poor) in other cognitive abilities, including their achievement abilities. Because of this, examiners could expect that an individual's CTONI-2 Full Scale Index would closely resemble his or her Full Scale, Verbal Scale, and Performance Scale quotients on the *Wechsler Intelligence Scale for Children—Fourth Edition* (Wechsler, 2003) or their Reading, Spelling, and Arithmetic standard scores from the *Wide Range Achievement Test—Fourth Edition* (Glutting & Wilkinson, 2006). Worth noting is the fact that persons with strong nonverbal reasoning ability often excel in mathematics, geometry, engineering, mechanics, art, and music.

The discussion of high and low Full Scale indexes is equally appropriate to the discussion of the meaning of the Pictorial Scale and the Geometric Scale indexes. All three scales measure general intellectual ability.

The index for the *Pictorial Scale* is formed by combining the subscales of the three subtests that use familiar pictured objects in their test formats. Because the pictured objects have names, examinees will likely verbalize to some extent while taking the subtests that contribute to this index. By verbalize, we mean that the examinees will talk about particular items while responding to them or silently think in words while pondering the items. In either case, most persons being tested will probably enlist their verbal skills to reach an answer for the items. Because of this, verbal ability may influence performance on the Pictorial Scale to some unknown degree. Although individuals could score high on this index without any verbal mediation at all, this is not likely in most cases.

The index for the *Geometric Scale* is formed by combining the subscales for the three subtests that use *unfamiliar designs* as stimuli. Because examinees have no names for the designs, any tendency to verbalize about the items is inhibited considerably. The formats of subtests that contribute to this index were specially selected to avoid verbal contamination and therefore yield results that are the purest possible estimates of intelligence when evaluated by means of nonverbal formats. Although verbalization cannot be eliminated entirely from any test (i.e., no test format can completely keep an individual examinee from using words while thinking), the selected formats do reduce the probability that incidental verbalization (oral or silent) might influence a person's answers to any appreciable extent.

In the vast majority of circumstances, these two indexes will be approximately equal (i.e., the difference between them will be inconsequential). Where large differences do occur, we suspect that the Pictorial Scale Index will be the higher index because of the mitigating influence of language ability. At this time, we cannot say for certain exactly what clinical connotations are implied by the presence of a significant difference between the two indexes. To date, some evidence exists that the Geometric Scale may be by far the better predictor of math ability than the Pictorial Scale (see Table 9.12).

Test Reliability

Unreliable tests yield inaccurate results. For tests such as the CTONI-2, reliability coefficients must approximate or exceed .80 in magnitude to be considered minimally reliable; coefficients of .90 or higher are considered most desirable (Aiken & Groth-Marnat, 2006; Nunnally & Bernstein, 1994; Salvia et al., 2007). Anastasi and Urbina (1997) describe three sources of error variance (content, time, and scorer). We calculated three types of correlation coefficients—coefficient alpha, test–retest, and scorer difference—to measure these three sources of error.

Coefficient Alpha

Content sampling error (i.e., internal consistency reliability) was investigated by applying Cronbach's (1951) coefficient alpha method. Coefficient alphas for the subtests and composites were calculated at 19 age intervals using data from the entire normative sample. Coefficient alphas for the composites were derived using Guilford's (1954, p. 393) formula. The averages of the 19 age-interval coefficients were in the .80s for the subtests and in the .90s for the composites. The coefficients were averaged using the Fisher z-transformation technique. The standard error of measurement (SEM) is 1 for all the subtests, 3 for the Full Scale Index, and 5 for the other two indexes.

Test–Retest

The subjects for the test–retest analysis were 101 individuals (63 students attending regular classes in Llano, Texas and 38 mostly adult individuals from Mandan, North Dakota). These subjects were divided into three age groups (42 aged 8 or 9; 33 aged 10–16; 26 aged 17–60). These subjects were tested twice; the time interval between testing was 2–4 weeks. The resulting coefficients were almost identical. At all age levels, the coefficients for the subtests were in the .80s; those for the composites were in the .80s or .90s. The means and standard deviations between the testings were tested for significant difference at each of the three age levels and none were found to be significantly different at the .05 level.

Scorer Differences

Scorer difference reliability refers to the amount of test error due to examiner variability in scoring. Unreliable scoring is usually the result of clerical errors or improper application of standard scoring criteria on the part of an examiner. Scorer error can be reduced considerably by availability of clear administration procedures, detailed guidelines governing scoring, and opportunities to practice scoring.

Nevertheless, test constructors should demonstrate statistically the amount of error in their tests due to different scorers. To do this, Anastasi and Urbina (1997), Rathvon (2004), and Reynolds et al. (2009), among others, recommend that two trained individuals score a set of tests independently. The correlation between scorers is a relational index of agreement.

In the case of the CTONI-2, two PRO-ED staff members independently scored the same 50 protocols drawn from children in the normative sample. The scorers learned to score the test by reading the test manual and Examiner Record Booklet. The sample represented a broad range of ability and ranged in age from 6 to 60. Twenty-five were males, and 25 were females; all subjects were from the South or Midwest. The results of the scorings were correlated. The resulting coefficients all exceed .90 in magnitude. These coefficients provide strong evidence supporting the test's scorer reliability.

Summary of Reliability Results

The CTONI-2's overall reliability is summarized in Table 9.3, which shows the test's status relative to three types of reliability coefficients and three sources of test error: content, time, and scorer differences. The coefficients depicting content sampling are the average coefficients across 19 age intervals described earlier. Those relating to time sampling are the test–retest coefficients for the entire 101 sample. The coefficients relating to scorer differences were described in the previous section.

The CTONI-2 scores satisfy the most demanding of standards for reliability, including those of Nunnally and Bernstein (1994), Reynolds et al. (2009), and Salvia et al. (2007). These authors recommend that when important decisions are to be made for individuals the minimum standard for a reliability coefficient should be .90. For the most part, coefficients for the CTONI-2 indexes meet this rigorous standard. These results strongly suggest that the test possesses little test error and that its users can have confidence in its results.

USES OF THE TEST

In this section, we will discuss the primary purposes of the CTONI-2, present a case study showing how to interpret the results of the test, and comment on the test's uses in identifying special populations and interventions based on its results.

TABLE 9.3 Summary of CTONI-2's Reliability Relative to Three Types of Reliability (Decimals Omitted)

CTONI-2 Scores	Type of Reliability Coefficient		
	Internal Consistency	**Test–Retest**	**Scorer**
Subtests			
Pictorial Analogies	83	85	98
Geometric Analogies	87	86	95
Pictorial Categories	82	81	99
Geometric Categories	87	80	98
Pictorial Sequences	84	85	99
Geometric Sequences	86	86	98
Composites			
Pictorial Scale	90	87	99
Geometric Scale	91	86	98
Full Scale	95	90	99
Sources of Test Error[a]	Content Sampling	Time Sampling	Interscorer Agreement

[a]These sources are from *Psychological Testing* (7th ed.), by A. Anastasi and S. Urbina, 1997, Upper Saddle River, NJ, Prentice Hall.

Purposes of the CTONI-2

The CTONI-2 has two principle uses. The *first use* is to estimate the intelligence of people for whom traditional ability tests might be inappropriate. For such persons, the heavy language content or the complicated motor response demands of most mental ability tests can result in a serious underestimation of their intelligence. This often leads to misidentifications, faulty diagnoses, erroneous placements, low expectations, and other undesirable consequences. Use of the CTONI-2 will avoid many of the hazards that are frequently encountered when testing people who have a variety of disabilities (traumatic brain injury, post-stroke syndrome, deafness, aphasia, autism, or other language disorders) or come from cultural, linguistic, educational, or socioeconomic backgrounds that might negatively influence their performance on ability tests. The CTONI-2's *second use* is to provide researchers with a tool that they can use to study the nature of intelligence, the interaction of verbal and nonverbal abilities, and the role of nonverbal formats in assessing thinking and academic subject matter.

A CASE STUDY: PEDRO RAMIREZ

Pedro Ramirez is a recent immigrant to the United States of America from Nueva Leon, Mexico. His mother is bilingual; his father speaks little English. Pedro speaks English (as well as Spanish) but is not yet comfortable engaging in prolonged conversations in English. Pedro was diagnosed at birth as having mild-to-moderate cerebral palsy. His gait and catching skills appear to be normal but he shuns sports activities on the playground and is rarely picked by peers to participate in team games (e.g., kickball). His vision and hearing seem to be normal. He has mild athetoid tremors in both arms (barely noticeable), which may be the cause of his poor handwriting. He has no difficulty, however, in using a cell phone. His speech is mildly dysarthric. On November 20, 2008, John Davis, the School Psychologist, administered the WISC-IV with the following results.

Verbal Comprehension	79
Perceptual Reasoning	71
Working Memory	71
Perceptual Speed	62
Full Scale	65

Mr. Davis felt that Pedro's intelligence might be higher than the WISC-IV results indicated. This suspicion was based on Mr. Davis's interaction with Pedro during the WISC-IV administration, conversations with his teacher, and on the possibility that cultural, linguistic, speech, and fine motor factors might have negatively influenced Pedro's test performance.

For these reasons, Mr. Davis decided to give Pedro the CTONI-2, a test that uses nonverbal formats and simple pointing responses to measure general intelligence. The findings of this evaluation are recorded in Figure 9.2. The results for the CTONI-2 composites in Section 3 of the figure are the most important scores on the test. Pedro's indexes are all in the average range, though they trend toward the lower limits of average. Any question that Pedro might be mentally retarded or even borderline should be abandoned at this point. One can only speculate as to why Pedro's scores were so low on the WISC-IV. We do know, however, that people who are mentally retarded are not likely to attain CTONI-2 index scores in the 90s.

Though at this time little is known about Pedro's prior educational history, he appears capable of learning to read, write, and calculate at levels expected of students his age. If he should fail to attain at least a low average level of achievement in basic school subjects, the reason will probably be something other than insufficient intelligence (e.g., socioeconomic factors, educational opportunity, lack of motivation).

Pedro's case is dramatic and it is also fictitious. We made up Pedro in order to illustrate in a single student the kinds of factors that cause some people to make low scores on most traditional tests of intelligence. In Pedro's case, these factors are low socioeconomic status, possible inadequate prior instruction, English emerging as a second language, mild-to-moderate motor problems, and a mild speech disorder. For Pedro, tests like CTONI-2 are ideal in that their formats are both language and motor reduced, and their contents are relatively culturally neutral.

Using the CTONI-2 to Diagnose and Plan Programs

The CTONI-2 is a measure of general intelligence that uses nonverbal formats and pointing responses. The goal of diagnosis is to find out why a person has scored low on the CTONI-2 (i.e., 89 or below). Generally, low scores can result from:

- Disinterest in taking the test, lack of cooperation
- Visual impairment (e.g., strabismus, field defect, double vision, reduced acuity

Comprehensive Test of Nonverbal Intelligence–Second Edition

CTONI-2

Examiner Record Form

Donald D. Hammill   Nils A. Pearson   J. Lee Wiederholt

FPO

Section 1. Identifying Information

Name: **Pedro Ramirez**   Female ☐ Male ☑   Grade **6**
(if appropriate)

	Year	Month	Day
Date Tested	2009	12 11	2 32

School: **Covert Avenue School**
(if appropriate)

Date of Birth: 1998   7   15   Examiner's Name: **John Davis**

Age*: 11   4   17   Examiner's Title: **School Psychologist**

*When accessing the normative tables, use years and months. Do not round up.

Administration Method   English ☑   Other ☐ _____

Sign ☐   Pantomime ☐

Section 2. Subtest Performance

Subtest	Raw Score	Age Equivalent	%ile Rank	Scaled Score	SEM	Descriptive Term
1. Pictorial Analogies (PA)	14	10-6	37	9	1	Average
2. Geometric Analogies (GA)	13	9-6	25	8	1	Average
3. Pictorial Categories (PC)	13	9-9	37	9	1	Average
4. Geometric Categories (GC)	15	10-6	37	9	1	Average
5. Pictorial Sequences (PS)	17	11-0	50	10	1	Average
6. Geometric Sequences (GS)	13	10-3	37	9	1	Average

Section 3. Composite Performance

Composite	PA	GA	PC	GC	PS	GS	Sum of Scaled Scores	%ile Rank	Descriptive Term	SEM	Composite Index	Difference Score
Pictorial Scale	9		9		10		28	37	Average	5	95	
Geometric Scale		8		9		9	26	27	Average	5	91	4
Full Scale	9	8	9	9	10	9	54	30	Average	3	92	

● Not important

○ Statistical
13 or above

○ Clinical
18 or above

Section 4. Descriptive Terms

Scaled Score	1–3	4–5	6–7	8–12	13–14	15–16	17–20
Descriptive Term	Very Poor	Poor	Below Average	Average	Above Average	Superior	Very Superior
Index Score	<70	70–79	80–89	90–110	111–120	121–130	>130

FIGURE 9.2

Sample page 1 of Examiner Record Form for Pedro Ramirez

- Visual attention (short-term memory deficit)
- Visual agnosia (functional blindness)
- Autism, Asperger's, or another pervasive developmental disorder
- Mental retardation or delayed cognitive development

The diagnostic effort should focus on deciding which of the above conditions is the likely cause for the low scores on CTONI-2. Obviously, this effort will require the involvement of other professionals and additional testing, including tests of verbal ability and school achievement.

The CTONI-2 results in of themselves have little to contribute to program planning unless, as in the case of Pedro, the results alert school personnel to the fact that he is not mentally retarded or a candidate for a special class. The results are most helpful when they are combined with the results of other tests and observations to form a comprehensive evaluation. Such an evaluation can lead to special placements and alternative instructional programming or to a referral to professionals who specialize in sight or vision problems (if not done so earlier).

VALIDITY

In the CTONI-2 test manual, we provide numerous studies that pertain to validity, including correlations with age, intercorrelations among the subtests, and factor analogies. In this section, however, we want to discuss the three most important topics that pertain to CTONI-2's validity: the steps taken to control for test bias, the relationship between CTONI-2 and other tests of intelligence, and the relationship of CTONI-2 to tests of school achievement.

Controlling for Test Bias

We were particularly interested in controlling for any test bias in CTONI-2. To this end, we included mainstream, minority, and disability groups in CTONI-2's normative sample and provided separate reliability information for these groups (Table 9.4). We have gone further and shown that the actual average performance of different gender and ethnic groups (see Table 9.5) is within the normal range. In this way, we have demonstrated that the CTONI-2 is valid for these subgroups.

We also used the Swaninathan and Rogers (1990) logistical regression approach to test the CTONI-2 items for bias. The results of this analysis, summarized in Table 9.6, provide convincing evidence that the CTONI-2 items contain little or no bias. Finally, because timed tests depress test performance of some groups, none of the CTONI-2 subtests are timed.

Relationship of CTONI-2 to Other Tests of Intelligence

To be valid, the CTONI-2, a test that uses nonverbal formats to measure intelligence, should be strongly related to other tests of intelligence, especially those that use nonverbal formats. To date, 11 studies have correlated the CTONI or CTONI-2 to criterion measures. The demographic characteristics of the samples used in the 11 studies are described in Table 9.7.

Ten of these studies investigated the relationship of CTONI/CTONI-2 to intelligence (which is the focus of this section) and four relate to the relationship to school achievement (which is the focus of the next section). Three of these studies used CTONI-2; eight used CTONI. We are discussing the CTONI findings because its items are essentially the same as those on the CTONI-2 and because they contribute to an accumulating body of research pertaining to the test. Of the 11 studies, 4 were conducted by the CTONI-2 authors; the other 7 were done by independent researchers.

The evidence relating to criterion-prediction validity has been organized into three sections: (1) a review of the correlations between CTONI/CTONI-2 and the criterion measures

TABLE 9.4 Coefficient Alphas for Selected Subgroups on the CTONI-2

| Subgroup | Subtests | | | | | | Composites | | |
| | Analogies | | Categories | | Sequences | | Pictorial | Geometric | Full |
	PA	GA	PC	GC	PS	GS	Scale	Scale	Scale
Male (*n* = 1416)	90	92	86	89	88	91	93	95	96
Female (*n* = 1411)	87	91	85	88	86	88	92	94	96
European American (*n* = 2189)	89	91	85	89	86	90	92	95	96
African American (*n* = 385)	90	92	85	86	88	90	93	93	96
Hispanic American (*n* = 440)	87	90	88	89	85	89	93	94	96
Asian American (*n* = 102)	90	92	85	88	89	92	93	95	96
Gifted and Talented (*n* = 78)	85	93	85	88	78	88	92	95	96
Attention-Deficit/Hyperactivity Disorder (*n* = 64)	92	93	89	90	80	87	93	94	96
Learning Disability (*n* = 53)	90	91	73	82	85	87	91	92	95
Deaf (*n* = 91)	89	92	83	92	89	92	94	95	97
Mentally Retarded (*n* = 50)	91	93	90	89	86	83	94	94	96

NOTE: PA = Pictorial Analogies; GA = Geometric Analogies; PC = Pictorial Categories; GC = Geometric Categories; PS = Pictorial Sequences; GS = Geometric Sequences.

of intellect, (2) a comparison of the means between CTONI/CTONI-2 and these criterion measures, and (3) the results of a series of positive predictive outcome analyses pertaining to CTONI-2's sensitivity, specificity, and positive predictive value.

Correlations with Criterion Measures

In this investigation of criterion-predictive validity, we report correlation coefficients showing the relationship of CTONI/CTONI-2 to 12 criterion measures of intelligence. These criterion tests are listed here:

- *Leiter International Performance Scale—Revised* (Leiter-R; Roid & Miller, 1997)
- *Primary Test of Nonverbal Intelligence* (Ehrler & McGhee, 2008)
- *Peabody Picture Vocabulary Test—Revised* (PPVT-R; Dunn & Dunn, 1981)

- *Reynolds Intellectual Assessment Scales* (RIAS; Reynolds & Kamphaus, 2003)
- *Test of Nonverbal Intelligence—Second, Third, Fourth Editions* (TONI-2, TONI-3, TONI-4; Brown, Sherbenou, & Johnsen, 1990, 1997, unpublished)
- *Universal Nonverbal Intelligence Test* (UNIT; Bracken & McCallum, 1998)
- *Wechsler Intelligence Scale for Children—Third, Fourth Editions.* (WISC-III, WISC-IV; Wechsler, 1991, 2003)
- *Woodcock-Johnson III, Tests of Cognitive Abilities*; Visual-Spatial and Fluid Reasoning subtests (WJ III; Woodcock, McGrew, & Mather, 2001)

The correlation between the CTONI/CTONI-2 and the criterion measures is reported in Table 9.8. In this analysis, we are asking a theoretical question: Does the CTONI/CTONI-2 actually measure general intelligence?

TABLE 9.5 Standard Score Means for Normative Sample and Different Gender and Ethnic Subgroups (Decimals Omitted, Rounded Values)

	Subgroups							
CTONI-2 Scores	Normative Sample (N=2827)	Male (n=1416)	Female (n=1411)	European American (n=2189)	African American (n=385)	Two or More Races (n=91)	Asian Pacific Islander (n=102)	Hispanic American (n=440)
Subtests								
Pictorial Analogies	10	10	10	10	9	10	10	10
Geometric Analogies	10	10	10	10	9	10	10	10
Pictorial Categories	10	10	10	10	9	10	10	10
Geometric Categories	10	10	10	10	9	10	10	10
Pictorial Sequences	10	10	10	10	9	10	10	10
Geometric Sequences	10	10	10	10	9	10	10	10
Composites								
Pictorial Scale	100	100	101	102	94	103	102	99
Geometric Scale	100	100	101	102	94	100	103	100
Full Scale	100	100	101	102	94	101	102	100

TABLE 9.6 Number of CTONI-2 Items with Significant Effect Sizes (and Moderate DIF Results) for Subgroups

Total Number of Items	Male/ Female	African American/ Non-African American	Hispanic American/ Non-Hispanic American
150	0(14)	0(24)	0(14)

NOTE : Numbers in parentheses represent the number of statistically significant items for each subgroup; the other numbers represent the number of moderate effect sizes detected for each subgroup.

Because the question is theoretical, it is necessary to attenuate the coefficients for any lack of reliability in the criterion test (but not in the CTONI/CTONI-2) and to correct coefficients to account for any range effects that might artificially *repress* or *inflate* the size of the coefficients. Where it is possible to do so, both corrected and uncorrected coefficients are reported in Table 9.8 (uncorrected coefficients appear in parentheses). Blank spaces in the table occur because the researchers did not report the statistics or they were otherwise not available.

TABLE 9.7 Demographic Characteristics of the Samples Used in the Validity Studies

Sample characteristics		1	2	3	4	5	6	7	8	9	10	11
								Sample					
Criterion Tests		TONI-4, TOSWRF, TOSCRF	RIAS, SAT, ACT, WRAT-3	PTONI	WISC-III, TONI-2, PPVT-R	WISC-III	TONI-3	UNIT, Leiter-R, WJ-III	WISC-III, WIAT-II	WISC-III, WISC-IV	KAIT	WJ-III
Source of Study		Hammill et al. (2009)	Firmin (2009)	Ehrler & McGhee (2008)	Hammill et al. (1997)	Hammill et al. (1997)	Hammill et al. (1997)	McCallum & Hooper (2001)	Wiseley (2001)	Launey (2005)	Lassiter et al. (2001)	Rosen et al. (2005)
Total number of Participants		72	197	82	43	32	568	26	50	33	97	46
Age range		6–17	18–22	6–9	7–17	8–18	18–80	6–13	7–16	8–16	19–54	6–10
Location		Austin, TX	Cedarville, OH	Georgia	Dallas, TX	Corpus Christi & McAllen, TX	United States	Tennessee	Arizona	North Carolina	"SE state"	Florida
Sample Type		Normal	College	Normal	Learning Disability	Deaf	Normal	Normal	Navajo	Mentally Retarded	College	Normal
Gender												
Male		40	78	43	29	14	235	nr	40	18	45	25
Female		32	119	39	14	18	333		10	15	52	22
Race												
European American		53	194	62	42	4	468	nr		10	74	27
African American		16	2	13	1		34			23	12	17
American Indian/Eskimo							1		50		1	
Asian/Pacific Islander			1				4				5	
Two or more												
Other		3		7		28	61				2	2

252

Hispanic						nr	nr	nr	nr	3	2
Yes	42	7	1	28	33						
No	30	75	42	4	535					94	44
Exceptionality Status						nr	nr	nr	nr		
No disability	68	69	0	0	546						46
Disability	4	13	43	32	22						0

NOTE: nr = not reported
KAIT = *Kaufman Adolescent & Adult Intelligence Test* (Kaufman & Kaufman, 1993)
Leiter-R = *Leiter International Performance Scale—Revised* (Roid & Miller, 1997)
PTONI = *Primary Test of Nonverbal Intelligence* (Ehrler & McGhee, 2008)
RIAS = *Reynolds Intellectual Assessment Scales* (Reynolds & Kamphaus, 2003)
TONI-2 = *Test of Nonverbal Intelligence—Second Edition* (Brown, Sherbenou, & Johnsen, 1990)
TONI-3 = *Test of Nonverbal Intelligence—Second Edition* (Brown, Sherbenou, & Johnsen, 1997)
TONI-4 = *Test of Nonverbal Intelligence—Second Edition* (Brown, Sherbenou, & Johnsen, in preparation)

TOSCRF = *Test of Silent Contextual Reading Fluency* (Hammill, Wiederholt, & Allen, 2006)
TOSWRF = *Test of Silent Word Reading Fluency* (Mather, Hammill, Allen, & Roberts, 2004)
UNIT = *Universal Nonverbal Intelligence Test* (Bracken & McCallum, 1998)
WIAT-II = *Wechsler Individual Achievement Test—Second Edition* (The Psychological Corporation, 2001)
WISC-III = *Wechsler Intelligence Scale for Children—Third Edition* (Wechsler, 1991)
WISC-IV = *Wechsler Intelligence Scale for Children—Fourth Edition* (Wechsler, 2003)
WJ III = *Woodcock-Johnson-III Tests of Cognitive Abilities* (Woodcock, McGrew, & Mather, 2001)

253

TABLE 9.8 Correlation between CTONI and CTONI-2 and Criterion Intelligence Tests (Decimals Omitted)

Criterion Test	Score	Sample(s)	N	Type of Sample	Composites Pictorial Scale	Composites Geometric Scale	Composites Full Scale	Magnitude[b]
TONI-4	Total	1	72	Normal	(70) 74	(70) 73	(75) 79	Very Large
RIAS	Verbal	2	197	College	(32)76	(22)62	(31)76	Very Large
RIAS	Nonverbal	2	197	College	(31)72	(29)71	(35)78	Very Large
RIAS	Composite	2	197	College	(38)84	(32)79	(40)86	Very Large
PTONI	Total	3	82	Normal	(86)84	(85)83	(86)81	Very Large
WISC-III	Verbal	4	43	LD	59	56	76	Large
WISC-III	Performance	4	43	LD	51	55	70	Large
WISC-III	Full Scale	4	43	LD	64	64	81	Very Large
TONI-2	Total	4	43	LD	43	84	82	Very Large
PPVT-R	Total	4	43	LD	66	41	74	Very Large
WISC-III	Performance	5	32	Deaf	87	85	90	Nearly Perfect
TONI-3	Total (Form A)	6	550	Normal	75	65	77	Very Large
TONI-3	Total (Form B)	6	550	Normal	75	65	75	Very Large
UNIT	Full Scale	7	26	Normal			(54)60	Large
Leiter-R	Full Scale	7	26	Normal			(64)72	Very Large
WJ-III	Visual Spatial	7	26	Normal			(58)72	Very Large
WJ-III	Fluid Reasoning	7	26	Normal			(44)63	Large
WISC-III	Verbal	8	50	Navajo	(36)67	(29)50	(38)69	Large
WISC-III	Performance	8	50	Navajo	(37)66	(48)71	(50)79	Very Large
WISC-III	Full Scale	8	50	Navajo	(43)77	(45)73	(51)83	Very Large
WISC-III	Full Scale	9	33	Mentally Retarded			(49)80	Very Large
WISC-IV	Full Scale	9	33	Mentally Retarded			(59)83	Very Large
KAIT	Composite IQ	10	97	College	(51)70	(44)62	(54)72	Very Large
				Average[a]	72	69	77	Very Large
				Magnitude[b]	Very Large	Large	Very Large	

[a]Fisher's average of coefficients across samples.
[b]Magnitude of corrected coefficients; based on Hopkins's (2002) criteria for interpreting correlation coefficients.
NOTE: Samples 1–3 used CTONI-2, samples 4–9 used CTONI.
NOTE: Values in parentheses are observed correlation coefficients; all others are corrected for attenuation due to range restriction and reliability of the criterion. LD = Learning Disability; PA = Pictorial Analogies; GC = Geometric Categories; PS = Pictorial Sequences; GS = Geometric Sequences.
Blank space in the table indicates that the researcher did not report the data or that it was otherwise unavailable.
KAIT=Kaufman Adolescent & Adult Intelligence Test (Kaufman & Kaufman, 1993)
Leiter-R=*Leiter International Performance Scale—Revised* (Roid & Miller, 1997)
PPVT-R=*Peabody Picture Vocabulary Test—Revised* (Dunn & Dunn, 1981)
PTONI=*Primary Test of Nonverbal Intelligence* (Ehrler & McGhee, 2008)
RIAS=*Reynolds Intellectual Assessment Scales* (Reynolds & Kamphaus, 2003)
TONI-2=*Test of Nonverbal Intelligence—Second Edition* (Brown, Sherbenou, & Johnsen, 1990)
TONI-3=*Test of Nonverbal Intelligence—Second Edition* (Brown, Sherbenou, & Johnsen, 1997)
TONI-4=*Test of Nonverbal Intelligence—Second Edition* (Brown, Sherbenou, & Johnsen, in preparation)
UNIT=*Universal Nonverbal Intelligence Test* (Bracken & McCallum, 1998)
WISC-III=*Wechsler Intelligence Scale for Children—Third Edition* (Wechsler, 1991)
WISC-IV=*Wechsler Intelligence Scale for Children—Fourth Edition* (Wechsler, 2003)
WJ-III=*Woodcock-Johnson-III Tests of Cognitive Abilities* (Woodcock, McGrew, & Mather, 2001)

In interpreting the magnitude of these coefficients, we are guided by Hopkins (2002). He suggested that coefficients between .00 and .09 are Very Small or Trivial; coefficients between .10 and .29 are Small; coefficients between .30 and .49 are Moderate; coefficients between .50 and .69 are Large; coefficients between .70 and .89 are Very Large; and coefficients between .90 and 1.00 are Nearly Perfect. Because all of these criterion tests measure intelligence, one would expect that the relationship between the CTONI/CTONI-2 and the criterion tests would be Large or Very Large.

The coefficients listed in the shaded column at the right side of the table are very important because they show the relationship between the criterion tests and the CTONI/CTONI-2 Full Scale Index, which is a composite of all six subtests. The corrected coefficients in this column range from .60 (Large) to .90 (Nearly Perfect); the average of these coefficients is .78 (Very Large).

The averaged coefficients in the shaded row at the bottom of the table are equally important because they show the overall relationship of the criterion measures to the CTONI/CTONI-2 subtests and composites. The coefficients for the subtests range from .57 (Large) to .70 (Very Large); those for the composites (.72, .69, .77) are much higher, all being Very Large in magnitude.

In another analysis involving data in Table 9.8, the 23 coefficients for the Full Scale Index were assigned to one of three groups depending on whether the criterion test measured Verbal Intelligence ($N = 4$), Nonverbal Intelligence ($N = 13$), or Full Scale Intelligence ($N = 6$). The average of the coefficients in each grouping was .74, .75, and .81, respectively; all these coefficients were Very Large in magnitude. Particularly noteworthy is the observation that the CTONI/CTONI-2 Full Scale composite correlates about equally well with the criterion tests that used verbal formats (.74) or nonverbal formats (.75). This reinforces the idea that CTONI-2 might be a good measure of general intelligence. The size of the correlation (.81)

with the average of the Full Scale Intelligence group is even larger and suggests that CTONI-2 might correlate as well with these criterion tests as they correlate with themselves in test–retest situations.

From a validity point of view, one can conclude that the size of the coefficients in Table 9.8 provides ample evidence for the CTONI-2 predictive validity. This analysis involved different criterion tests, diverse samples of subjects, and independent researchers. Regardless of the criterion test employed or the sample studied, the coefficients that were reported are uniformly high. The results pertaining to the composites were particularly encouraging.

Comparisons of CTONI/CTONI-2 and Criterion Test Means and Standard Deviations

When two tests are highly correlated, they are likely to be measuring the same or a similar ability. This does not necessarily mean, however, that the tests yield the same results. For example, one test may consistently score higher than another test even though they correlate well with each other. The validity of both tests is supported when the two tests produce similar means as well as correlate highly with each other.

The standard score means, standard deviations, and comparative information for the two editions of CTONI and the criterion intelligence tests are presented in Table 9.9. The differences between the means of the Full Scale Index and the corresponding composite scores from the criterion tests were analyzed using the t-test (Guilford & Fruchter, 1978) and effect size correlation methods (Hopkins, 2002; Rosenthal, 1994).

Conclusions based on the contents of this table are rather straightforward. In 13 of the 17 comparisons, the differences between the means of the CTONI or CTONI-2 and those of the criterion measures are either Small or Trivial. The median for the 17 composites is 100 for CTONI/CTONI-2 and 101.5 for the criterion tests; the average is 97 and 98, respectively. Because all of the criterion tests represent general

TABLE 9.9   Standard Score Means (and Standard Deviations) and Related Statistics for the CTONI/CTONI-2 and Criterion Tests

CTONI Comparisons/ Criterion Tests	Sample(s)	N	Mean	(SD)	Descriptive Terms	t	Effect Size Correlations[a]
CTONI-2 Full Scale	1	72	100	(15)	Above Average	−0.40 (ns)	.03 Trivial
TONI-4 Nonverbal			101	(15)	Above Average		
CTONI-2 Full Scale	2	197	117	(09)	Above Average	4.92**	.24 Small
RIAS Composite Intelligence			113	(07)	Above Average		
CTONI-2 Full Scale	3	82	91	(18)	Average	−3.62**	.27 Small
PTONI Nonverbal			98	(17)	Average		
CTONI Full Scale	4	43	100	(10)	Average	−2.83**	.29 Small
WISC-III Full Scale			105	(13)	Average		
CTONI Full Scale	4	43	100	(10)	Average	−1.97*	.21 Small
TONI-2 Total Quotient			104	(16)	Average		
CTONI Full Scale	4	43	100	(10)	Average	−2.95**	.31 Moderate
PPVT-R Verbal Intelligence			106	(16)	Average		
CTONI Full Scale	5	32	88	(11)	Average	−0.56 (ns)	.07 Trivial
WISC-III Performance			90	(17)	Average		
CTONI Full Scale	6	551	102	(14)	Average	0.00 (ns)	.00 Trivial
TONI-3 Form A			102	(13)	Average		
CTONI Full Scale	6	551	102	(14)	Average	0.00 (ns)	.00 Trivial
TONI-3 Form B			102	(13)	Average		
CTONI Full Scale	7	26	100	(13)	Average	−0.51 (ns)	.07 Trivial
UNIT Full Scale			102	(15)	Average		
CTONI Full Scale	7	26	100	(13)	Average	0.53 (ns)	.08 Trivial
Leiter-R			98	(14)	Average		
CTONI Full Scale	7	26	100	(15)	Average	−1.88 (ns)	.26 Small
WJ-III Visual-Spatial			105	(12)	Average		
CTONI Full Scale	7	26	100	(15)	Average	0.00 (ns)	.00 Trivial
WJ-III Fluid Reasoning			100	(11)	Average		
CTONI Full Scale	8	50	90	(10)	Average	3.00**	.29 Small
WISC-III Full Scale			84	(10)	Below Average		
CTONI Full Scale	9	33	77	(09)	Low	12.02**	.83 Very Large
WISC-III Full Scale			61	(06)	Very Low		
CTONI Full Scale	9	33	77	(09)	Low	7.22**	.67 Large
WISC-IV Full Scale			61	(09)	Very Low		
CTONI Full Scale	10	97	103	(10)	Average	−4.39**	.30 Moderate
KAIT Composite IQ			109	(09)	Average		

[a]Values of the magnitude of the effect size between CTONI-2 Nonverbal Intelligence composite and criterion tests according to Hopkins's (2002) criteria.

intelligence, one might suppose that CTONI-2 is also a valid measure of general intelligence. Three of the comparisons, however, were not Small; they were Moderate, Large, and Very Large and should not be ignored.

The Moderate effect size resulted when the CTONI was compared to the PPVT-R, a measure of verbal intelligence; in every other case in the table, the CTONI or CTONI-2 was compared either to another nonverbal test (e.g., TONI) or to a composite score that included nonverbal subtests (e.g., WISC-III, RAIS). That the CTONI mean would vary somewhat from that of a verbal test while at the same time correlating highly (.74; see Table 9.8) with that verbal test is not surprising.

The Large and Very Large effect sizes resulted from a comparison of CTONI's Full Scale Index with the Full Scales of the WISC-III and WISC-IV using 33 subjects diagnosed as having mental retardation. In Table 9.9, the Full Scale WISC mean is 61; the CTONI mean is 77, which is precisely what we would expect in cases where the sample is mentally retarded. In Wechsler's (2003a) *Technical and Interpretive Manual*, a table (5.23) is provided that shows the mean performance of 120 noninstitutionalized children who had been diagnosed as having mild to moderate mental retardation. In their sample, the Full Scale mean was 60.5 and the Processing Speed Scale (a measure of nonverbal ability) was 73. Wechsler's means are almost identical to those reported in Table 9.9 (i.e., 61 for the WISC-IV Full Scale and .77 for its nonverbal scale). For this reason, the Large and Very Large differences associated with Sample 9 in Table 9.8 are offered as evidence of CTONI's validity as well as the validity of CTONI-2.

The findings reported in Table 9.9 support the idea that for all practical purposes, regardless of the samples' characteristics or the criterion test administered, the standard scores that result from giving the CTONI-2 will be similar to those obtained from giving the criterion tests.

Positive Predictive Outcome Analyses

To examine the effectiveness of the CTONI-2 in predicting other tests of intelligence, a series of positive predictive outcome analyses was conducted. These analyses, which are described by J. Bernstein and Weiler (2000), Gredler (1997), and Mausner and Kramer (1985), involve calculating three statistics: the sensitivity index, the specificity index, and the positive predictive value. In the current context, the *sensitivity index* reflects the ability of a test to correctly identify individuals who have cognitive problems. The *specificity index* reflects the ability of a test to correctly identify individuals who do not have cognitive problems. The *positive predictive value* reflects the proportion of individuals who truly have a cognitive problem among all those whom the measure identifies as having a cognitive problem.

On both the CTONI-2 and the criterion tests, standard scores that are below 90 are considered Below Average, and scores of 90 or above are considered Average or Above Average. Using an index of 90 as the cutoff, we divided the individuals who were given the tests of intelligence into two groups—Below Average and Average or Above Average. We then created two 2 × 2 frequency matrixes, one for the TONI-4/CTONI-2 analysis, and one for the PTONI/CTONI-2 analysis. The matrix using the TONI-4 and the CTONI-2 is found in Table 9.10 and the matrix for PTONI and CTONI-2 is found in Table 9.11. Subjects for this analysis were individuals in Samples 1 and 3 described in Table 9.7 who had been given CTONI-2. We could not perform this analysis on the other group that had been given CTONI-2 (i.e., Sample 2) because it was comprised of college students, none of whom had scores below 90.

In both tables, the numbers of individuals correctly identified by the CTONI-2 are represented by cells a and d. Cell a represents true-positives and cell d represents true-negatives. The number of individuals who were not correctly identified is represented by

TABLE 9.10 Positive Predictive Matrix Demonstrating CTONI-2's Ability to Predict TONI-4

CTONI-2 Full Scale	TONI-4 Score		Total
	Below Average	**Average or Above**	
Below Average	20^a	8^b	28
Average or Above	8^c	36^d	44
Total	28	44	72

NOTE: $N = 72$;
Percent agreement $= (20 + 36) / (20 + 8 + 8 + 36) = .78$
Positive predictive value $= 20 / (20 + 8) = .71$
Sensitivity $= 20 / (20 + 8) = .71$
Specificity $= 36 / (36 + 8) = .82$
[a]True-positives.
[b]False-positives (overreferrals).
[c]False-negatives (underreferrals).
[d]True-negatives.

TABLE 9.11 Positive Predictive Matrix Demonstrating CTONI-2's Ability to Predict PTONI

CTONI-2 Full Scale	PTONI Score		Total
	Below Average	**Average or Above**	
Below Average	21^a	9^b	30
Average or Above	2^c	50^d	52
Total	23	59	82

NOTE: $N = 82$;
Percent agreement $= (21+50) / (21+9+2+50) = .87$
Positive predictive value $= 21 / (21+9) = .70$
Sensitivity $= 21 / (21+2) = .91$
Specificity $= 50 / (50+2) = .96$
[a]True-positives.
[b]False-positives (overreferrals).
[c]False-negatives (underreferrals).
[d]True-negatives.

cells b and c. Cell b represents false-positives (overreferrals). Cell c represents false-negatives (underreferrals).

The *sensitivity index* is calculated by dividing the number of true-positives (cell a) by the sum of true-positives and false-negatives (cell a + cell c). The *specificity index* is calculated by dividing the number of true-negatives (cell d) by the sum of true-negatives and false-positives (cell d + cell b). The *positive predictive value* is calculated by dividing the number of true-positives (cell a) by the sum of true-positives and false-positives (cell a + cell b).

Authorities vary regarding how large a test's sensitivity index, specificity index, and positive predictive value should be to justify its use for identification purposes. Wood, Flowers, Meyer, and Hill (2002) hold that the sensitivity and specificity indexes should reach .70 but are willing to tolerate high false-positive rates (i.e., they accept positive predictive values below .70). Jansky (1978) suggested that the sensitivity index, specificity index, and positive predictive value should all equal or exceed .70. Carran and Scott (1992), Gredler (2000), and Kingslake (1983) recommended a more rigorous standard of .75 or higher for all three values.

In an effort to clarify these criteria for acceptability, Hammill, Wiederholt, and Allen (2006) developed a ranking system for designating the level of acceptability:

Sensitivity and specificity \ .70

Level I-B: Sensitivity and positive predictive value \ .70

Level II: Sensitivity, specificity, and positive predictive value \ .70

Level III: Sensitivity, specificity, and positive predictive value \ .75

Researchers agree that at least two indexes should be .70 or greater and that the sensitivity index should be one of them, but the ambiguity lies in which of the other indexes is the most important. Although Level III should be strived for, Level I is probably acceptable for most purposes.

The results of the predictive outcome analysis demonstrating CTONI-2's ability to predict criterion measures of intelligence were presented in Tables 9.10 and 9.11. The results demonstrate that the CTONI-2 met acceptability Level II when predicting both the TONI-4 and the PTONI.

Relationship of CTONI/CTONI-2 to Tests of School Achievement

Most professionals agree that intelligence and school achievement are significantly related. If true, one way of demonstrating that an intelligence test is valid would be to show that it is correlated to school achievement tests, though one would not expect the correlation to be as high as when that test is correlated with other tests of intelligence. This being the case, how large should be the correlation between the CTONI-2 and measures of reading and mathematics in order for the test to be considered valid?

A simple answer to the question might be that the CTONI-2 coefficients should be statistically significant and similar in size to those reported by other researchers who have studied the relationship of intelligence to school achievement, specifically to reading and mathematics.

To learn what size coefficients researchers have found from correlating intelligence tests to reading and mathematics tests, we consulted the manuals of six tests of intelligence (that had included both reading and mathematics as a variable among their validity studies) and four broad-based school achievement batteries (that had included tests of intelligence among their validity studies). These tests are listed here:

- *Detroit Test of Learning Aptitude—Fourth Edition* (DTLA-4; Hammill, 1998)
- *Diagnostic Achievement Battery—Third Edition* (DAB-3; Newcomer, 2001)
- *Hammill Multiability Achievement Test* (HAMAT; Hammill, Hresko, Ammer, Cronin, Quinby, 1998)
- *Kaufman Assessment Battery for Children—Second Edition* (KABC-II; Kaufman & Kaufman, 2004)
- *Stoelting Brief Nonverbal Intelligence Test* (S-BIT; Roid & Miller, 1997)
- *Test of Nonverbal Intelligence—Third Edition* (TONI-3; Brown, Sherbenou, & Johnsen, 1997)

- *Wechsler Individual Achievement Test—Second Edition* (WIAT-II; Psychological Corporation, 2001)
- *Wechsler Nonverbal Scale of Ability* (WNV; Wechsler & Naglieri, 2006)
- *Wechsler Intelligence Scale for Children—Fourth Edition* (WISC-IV; Wechsler, 2003)
- *Woodcock-Johnson III* (Woodcock, McGrew, & Mather, 2001)

The authors of these tests reported a large number of correlation coefficients that represented the relationship of intelligence to reading and mathematics. The average of these coefficients should set a criterion level for our study

of CTONI-2's validity (i.e., the correlation between the CTONI or CTONI-2 and measures of reading and mathematics should approximate the average of those found in the manuals of the 10 tests reviewed). In conducting our analysis, we gave preference to coefficients that had been corrected for restricted range.

Our review of the manuals yielded 82 suitable coefficients that represented the relationship of intelligence to reading and 71 for mathematics. Because the 10 test batteries differed markedly in the number of useable coefficients, the coefficients were averaged for each test battery (e.g., the KABC-II manual yielded four coefficients for reading [.62, .57, .49, .76] and four for mathematics [.61, .80, .65, .59]; the average of these was .61 for reading and .66 for mathematics). In

TABLE 9.12   Correlation of CTONI and CTONI-2 and Criterion Measures of Reading (Decimals Omitted)

Criterion Test	Score	Sample(s)	N	Type of Sample	Composites Pictorial Scale	Geometric Scale	Full Scale	Magnitude[a]
TOSCRF	Total	1	72	Normal	(54) 70	(54) 70	(57) 73	Very Large
TOSWRF	Total	1	72	Normal	(41) 48	(42) 49	(43) 50	Large
WRAT-3	Reading	2	197	College	(26) 63	(20) 54	(26) 65	Large
ACT	Reading	2	197	College	(24) 52	(13) 32	(21) 49	Moderate
SAT	Reading	2	197	College	(20) 43	(13) 32	(19) 42	Moderate
WIAT-II	Reading	8	50	Navajo	(29) 64	(18) 38	(33) 69	Large
WJ-III	Broad Reading	11	46	Normal	(21) 29	(26) 33	(31) 37	Moderate
		Average of the corrected coefficients[b]			54	45	57	Large
				Magnitude	Large	Moderate	Large	

[a] Fisher's average of coefficients across samples.

[b] Magnitude of corrected coefficients; based on Hopkins's (2002) criteria for interpreting correlation coefficients.

NOTE: Values in parentheses are observed correlation coefficients; all others are corrected for attenuation due to range restriction and reliability of the criterion.

NOTE: Samples 1 and 2 used CTONI-2, samples 8 and 10 used CTONI.

TOSCRF=*Test of Silent Contextual Reading Fluency* (Hammill, Wiederholt, & Allen, 2006)

TOSWRF=*Test of Silent Word Reading Fluency* (Mather, Hammill, Allen, & Roberts, 2004)

WRAT-3=*Wide Range Achievement Test—Third Edition* (Wilkinson, 1993)

ACT=ACT (2008)

SAT=College Board (2008)

WIAT-II=*Wechsler Individual Achievement Test—Second Edition* (The Psychological Corporation, 2001)

WJ-III=*Woodcock-Johnson-III Tests of Achievement* (Woodcock & McGrew, 2001) this manner, each of the 10 batteries had 2 averaged coefficients: one for reading and one for mathematics. In all, there were 10 coefficients for reading and 10 for mathematics. When averaged, the resulting coefficients for reading and mathematics were .58 and .62, respectively. These two coefficients represented the collective findings from the 10 test manuals studied.

These two coefficients also provide an answer to the question raised in the end of the first paragraph in this section. That is, for the CTONI-2 to be valid, its correlation with reading should approximate .58 and to mathematics should approximate .62.

To date, the relationship of CTONI and CTONI-2 to school achievement has been the subject of four independent investigations. The samples for these studies were described earlier in Table 9.7 (see Samples 1, 2, 8, and 11). In these studies, the researchers have correlated either the CTONI or the CTONI-2 with seven criterion tests and have used a diverse variety of subjects. Their results are reported in Table 9.12 (for reading) and Table 9.13 (for mathematics).

The three averaged coefficients at the bottom of these tables display the findings most clearly. In Table 9.12 (*reading*), these coefficients are either Moderate or Large in size and compare favorably with the criterion coefficient (.58) that resulted from the study of the 12 tests described earlier. In fact, the .57 for the Full Scale Index is almost identical to the criterion coefficient. In Table 9.13 (*mathematics*), the coefficients are equally encouraging because their magnitude is Large or Very Large in all cases (.53, .72, .65) and they also compare favorably with the .62 criterion coefficient from the 12 studies. The findings provide additional evidence in support of the CTONI's validity.

TABLE 9.13 Correlation of CTONI and CTONI-2 and Criterion Measures of Mathematics (Decimals Omitted)

| Criterion Test | Score | Sample(s) | N | Type of Sample | Composites | | | Magnitude[a] |
					Pictorial Scale	Geometric Scale	Full Scale	
WRAT-3	Arithmetic	2	197	College	(13) 31	(18) 43	(18) 43	Moderate
ACT	Math	2	197	College	(16) 36	(38) 73	(31) 64	Large
SAT	Math	2	197	College	(29) 45	(35) 92	(37) 56	Large
WIAT-II	Math	8	50	Navajo	(59) 86	(47) 70	(62) 87	Very Large
WJ-III	Math	11	46	Normal	(39) 84	(58) 58	(53) 60	Large
			Average of the corrected coefficients[b]		53	72	65	Large
				Magnitude	Large	Very Large	Large	

[a]Fisher's average of coefficients across samples.

[b]Magnitude of corrected coefficients; based on Hopkins's (2002) criteria for interpreting correlation coefficients.

NOTE: Values in parentheses are observed correlation coefficients; all others are corrected for attenuation due to range restriction and reliability of the criterion.

NOTE: Sample 2 used CTONI-2, samples 8 and 11 used CTONI.

WRAT-3=*Wide Range Achievement Test—Third Edition* (Wilkinson, 1993)

ACT=ACT (2008)

SAT=SAT (College Board, 2008)

WIAT-II=*Wechsler Individual Achievement Test—Second Edition* (The Psychological Corporation, 2001)

SUMMARY

For many examiners, the CTONI-2 has become an essential complement to tests of nonverbal intelligence. Numerous studies have shown it to be reliable, valid, and unbiased with regard to gender, race, and disability. Because of this, examiners can have confidence that the CTONI-2 scores estimate the intelligence of at-risk or culturally different populations with little fear of contamination from social, ethnic, or disability bias. The test is appropriate for a wide range of ages. In addition to the psychometric integrity of the CTONI-2, many examiners have praised the test format because they have found that most test-takers seem to enjoy the challenge of solving picture puzzles with no time limit.

REFERENCES

Aiken, L. R., & Groth-Marnat, G. (2006). *Psychological testing and assessment* (12th ed.). Boston: Pearson Educational Group.

Anastasi, A., & Urbina, S. (1997). *Psychological testing* (7th ed.). Upper Saddle River, NJ: Prentice Hall.

Athanasiou, M. S. (2002). Current nonverbal instruments. *Journal of Psychoeducational Assessment, 18,* 211–229.

Aylward, G. P. (1998). Review of the Comprehensive Test of Nonverbal Intelligence. In J. C. Impara & B. S. Plake, (Eds.), *The thirteenth mental measurements yearbook* (pp. 310–312). Lincoln, NE: Buros Institute of Mental Measurements, University of Nebraska Press.

Bernstein, J. H., & Weiler, M. D. (2000). "Pediatric neuropsychological assessment" examined. In G. Goldstein & M. Hersen (Eds.), *Handbook of psychological assessment* (3rd ed., pp. 263–300). Kidlington, Oxford: Pergamon.

Bracken, B. A., & McCallum, R. S. (1998). *Universal Nonverbal Intelligence Test.* Austin, TX: Pro-Ed.

Bracken, B. A., & Naglieri, J. A. (2003). Assessing diverse populations with nonverbal tests of general intelligence. In C. R. Reynolds & R. W. Kamphaus (Eds.), *Handbook of psychological and educational assessment of children* (2nd ed., pp. 243–274). Thousand Oaks, CA: Sage.

Bradley-Johnson, S. (1997). Review of the Comprehensive Test of Nonverbal Intelligence. *Psychology in the Schools, 34,* 289–292.

Brown, L., Sherbenou, R. J., & Johnsen, S. K. (1990). *Test of Nonverbal Intelligence—Second Edition.* Austin, TX: Pro-Ed.

Brown, L., Sherbenou, R. J., & Johnsen, S. K. (1997). *Test of Nonverbal Intelligence* (3rd ed.). Austin, TX: Pro-Ed.

Brown, L., Sherbenou, R. J., & Johnsen, S. K. (2009). *Test of Nonverbal Intelligence* (4th ed.). Austin, TX: Pro-Ed.

Carran, D. T., & Scott, K. G. (1992). Risk assessment in preschool children: Research implications for the early detection of educational handicaps. *Topics in Early Childhood Special Education, 12,* 196–211.

Cohen, L. G., & Spenciner, L. J. (1998). *Assessment of children and youth.* New York: Longman.

Cronbach, L. J. (1951). Coefficient alpha and the internal structure of tests. *Psychometrika, 16,* 297–334.

Das, J. P. (1972). Patterns of cognitive ability in nonretarded and retarded children. *American Journal of Mental Deficiency, 77,* 6–12.

DiCerbo, K. E., & de Barona, M. S. (2001). Test reviews. *Journal of Psychoeducational Assessment, 19,* 175–180.

Drossman, E. R., & Maller, S. J. (2000). Comprehensive Test of Nonverbal Intelligence. *Journal of Psychoeducational Assessment, 18,* 293–301.

Dunn, L. M., & Dunn, L. M. (1965). *Peabody Picture Vocabulary Test—Revised.* Circle Pines, MN: American Guidance Service.

Dunn, L. M., & Dunn, L. M. (1981). *Peabody Picture Vocabulary Test—Revised.* Circle Pines, MN: American Guidance Service.

Ehrler, D. J., & McGhee, R. L. (2008). *Primary Test of Nonverbal Intelligence.* Austin, TX.: Pro-Ed.

Firmin, M. W. (2009). *Comparison of college students' performance on the CTONI-2, the RIAS, and three measures of school achievement.* An independent unpublished study done at Cedarville University, Cedarville, OH.

Glutting, J. J., & Wilkinson, G. S. (2006). *Wide Range Achievement Test* (4th ed.). Lutz, FL: Psychological Assessment Resources.

Gredler, G. R. (1997). Issues in early childhood screening and assessment. *Psychology in the Schools, 34,* 99–106.

Gredler, G. R. (2000). Early childhood screening for developmental and educational problems. In B. A. Bracken (Ed.), *The psychoeducational assessment of preschool children* (pp. 399–411). Boston: Allyn & Bacon.

Guilford, J. P. (1954). *Psychometric methods* (2nd ed.). New York: McGraw-Hill.

Guilford, J. P., & Fruchter, B. (1978). *Fundamental statistics in psychology and education* (6th ed.). New York: McGraw-Hill.

Hammill, D. D. (1998). *Detroit Test of Learning Aptitude* (4th ed.). Austin, TX: Pro-Ed.

Hammill, D. D., Hresko, W. P., Ammer, J. J., Cronin, M. E., & Quinby, S. S. (1998). *Hammill Multiability Achievement Test*. Austin, TX: Pro-Ed.

Hammill, D. D., Pearson, N. A., & Wiederholt, J. L. (1997). *Comprehensive Test of Nonverbal Intelligence*. Austin, TX: Pro-Ed.

Hammill, D. D., Pearson, N. A., & Wiederholt, J. L. (2009). *Comprehensive Test of Nonverbal Intelligence* (2nd ed.). Austin, TX: Pro-Ed.

Hammill, D. D., Wiederholt, J. L., & Allen, E. A. (2006). *Test of Silent Contextual Reading Fluency*. Austin, TX: Pro-Ed.

Hopkins, W. G. (2002). A scale of magnitudes for effect statistics. In *A new view of statistics*. Retrieved July 14, 2005, from http://www.sportsci .org/resource/stats/effectmag.html.

Horn, J. L., & Cattell, R. B. (1966). Refinement and test of the theory of fluid and crystallized intelligence. *Journal of Educational Psychology*, *57*, 253–270.

Jansky, J. J. (1978). A critical review of some developmental and predictor precursors of reading disabilities. In A. L. Benton & D. Pearl (Eds.), *Dyslexia: An appraisal of current knowledge* (pp. 412–516). New York: Oxford University Press.

Jensen, A. R. (1980). *Bias in mental testing*. New York: Free Press.

Kaufman, A. S., & Kaufman, N. L. (1993). *Kaufman Adolescent & Adult Intelligence Test*. Circle Pines, MN: American Guidance Service.

Kaufman, A. S., & Kaufman, N. L. (2004). *Kaufman Assessment Battery for Children* (2nd ed.). Minneapolis, MN: AGS Publishing/Pearson Assessments.

Kingslake, B. J. (1983). The predictive (in)accuracy of on-entry to school screening procedures when used to anticipate learning difficulties. *British Journal of Special Education*, *10*, 24–26.

Lassiter, K. S., Harrison, T. K., Mathews, T. D., & Bell, N. L. (2001). The validity of the Comprehensive Test of Nonverbal Intelligence as a measure of fluid intelligence. *Assessment*, *8*, 95–103.

Launey, K. B. (2005). *Validity of the WISC-IV and CTONI: Interpretation of IQ scores for students classified as educable mentally disabled*. Dissertation in Psychology, Waldon University, Minneapolis, Minnesota.

Levin, M. D. (1987). *Developmental variation and learning disorders*. Cambridge, MA: Educators Publishing Service.

Mather, N., Hammill, D. D., Allen, E. A., & Roberts, R. (2004). *Test of Silent Word Reading Fluency*. Austin, TX: Pro-Ed.

Mausner, J. S., & Kramer, S. K. (1985). Screening in the detection of disease. In J. S. Mausner & S. K. Kramer (Eds.), *Mausner and Bahn epidemiology: An introductory test* (2nd ed., pp. 214–238). Philadelphia: Saunders.

McCallum, S., & Hooper, V. S. (2001). McCallum and Hooper—Grades K through 8 Normal Sample (pp. 74–76). In K. S. McGrew & R. W. Woodcock (Eds.), *Woodcock-Johnson III: Technical Manual*. Itasca, IL: Riverside.

McLoughlin, J. A., & Lewis, R. B. (2005). *Assessing special students* (6th ed.). Columbus, OH: Merrill.

Naglieri, J. A., & Bardos, A. N. (1997). *General Ability Measure for Adults*. Minneapolis, MN: National Computer Systems.

Naglieri, J. A., & Das, J. P. (1997). *Das-Naglieri Cognitive Assessment System*. Austin, TX: Pro-Ed.

Newcomer, P. L. (2001). *Diagnostic Achievement Battery* (3rd ed.). Austin, TX: Pro-Ed.

Nicholson, C. L. (1998–1999). Comprehensive Test of Nonverbal Intelligence (CTONI). *Diagnostique*, *24*, 57–68.

Nunnally, J. S., & Bernstein, I. H. (1994). *Psychometric theory* (3rd ed.). Baltimore: Williams & Wilkins.

Pierangelo, R., & Giuliani, G. A. (2002). *Assessment in special education*. Boston: Allyn & Bacon.

Psychological Corporation. (2002). *Wechsler Individual Achievement Test* (2nd ed.). San Antonio, TX: Author.

Rathvon, N. (2004). *Early reading assessment*. New York: Guilford Press.

Reynolds, C. R., & Kamphaus, R. (2003). *Reynolds Intellectual Assessment Scales*. Lutz, FL: Psychological Assessment Resources.

Reynolds, C. R., Livingston, R. G., & Willson, V. (2009). *Measurement and assessment in education* (2nd ed.). Boston: Allyn & Bacon.

Roid, G. H. (2003). *Stanford-Binet Intelligence Scales—Fifth Edition, technical manual*. Austin, TX: Pro-Ed.

Roid, G. H., & Miller, L. J. (1997). *Leiter International Performance Scale—Revised*. Wood Dale, IL: Stoelting.

Rosenthal, R. (1994). Parametric measures of effect size. In H. Cooper & L. V. Hedges (Eds.), *Handbook of research synthesis* (pp. 231–244). New York: Sage.

Rossen, E. A., Shearer, D. K., Penfield, & Kranzer, J. H. (2005). Validity of the Comprehensive Test of Nonverbal Intelligence (CTONI). *Journal of Psycho-educational Assessment, 23,* 161–172.

Salvia, J., & Ysseldyke, J. E. (2001). *Assessment* (8th ed.). Boston: Houghton-Mifflin.

Salvia, J., Ysseldyke, J. E., & Bolt, S. (2007). *Assessment in special and inclusive education* (10th ed.). Boston: Houghton-Mifflin.

Sattler, J. M. (2001). *Assessment of children: Cognitive applications* (4th ed.). San Diego: Jerome M. Sattler.

Snijders, J. Th., Tellegen, P. J., & Laros, J.A. (1989). *Snijders-Oomen Non-Verbal Intelligence Test.* [S.D.N.-R 5½-17]. Manual and research report. Groningen, The Netherlands: Wolter-Noordhoff.

Spearman, C. E. (1923). *The nature of intelligence and the principles of cognition*. New York: Macmillan.

Spragins, A. (1997–1998). Reviews of four types of assessment instruments used with deaf and hard of hearing students: Cognitive assessment. *Text/Reviews*. Washington, DC: Gallaudet Research Institute (http://gri.gallaudet.edu/~catraxle/reviews.html).

Swaminathan, H., & Rogers, H. J. (1990). Detecting differential item functioning using logistic regression procedures. *Journal of Educational Measurement, 26,* 55–66.

Taylor, R. L. (2003). *Assessment of exceptional students* (6th ed.). Boston: Allyn & Bacon.

U.S. Bureau of the Census. (2007). *Statistical abstract of the United States* (126th ed.). Washington, DC: Author.

van Lingen, G. (1998). Review of the Comprehensive Test of Nonverbal Intelligence. In J. C. Impara & B. S. Plake (Eds.), *The thirteenth mental measurements yearbook* (pp. 312–314). Lincoln, NE: Buros Institute of Mental Measurements, University of Nebraska Press.

Wechsler, D. (1991). *Wechsler Intelligence Scale for Children—Third Edition*. San Antonio: Psychological Corporation.

Wechsler, D. (2003). *Wechsler Intelligence Scale for Children—Fourth Edition*. San Antonio: Psychological Corporation.

Wechsler, D. (2003a). *Technical and interpretive manual*. San Antonio: Psychological Corporation.

Wechsler, D., & Naglieri, J. A. (2006). *Wechsler Nonverbal Scale of Ability*. San Antonio, TX: Psychological Corporation.

Wilkinson, G. S. (1993). *Wide Range Achievement Test* (3rd ed.). Wilmington, DE: Wide Range.

Wiseley, M. C. (2001). *Non-verbal intelligence and Native-American Navajo children: A comparison between the CTONI and the WISC-III*. Dissertation to the Graduate College, University of Arizona, Tucson.

Wood, F., Flowers, L., Meyer, M., & Hill, D. (2002, November). *How to evaluate and compare screening tests: Principles of science and good sense*. Paper presented at the meeting of the International Dyslexia Association, Atlanta.

Woodcock, R. W., McGrew, K. S., & Mather, N. (2001). *Woodcock-Johnson III: Tests of Cognitive Abilities*. Itasca, IL: Riverside.

CHAPTER 10

Nonverbal Intellectual and Cognitive Assessment with the Leiter International Performance Scale—Revised (Leiter-R)

Gale H. Roid, Mark Pomplun, and Jamie J. Martin

The *Leiter International Performance Scale— Revised* (Leiter-R; Roid & Miller, 1997) is a battery of 20 nonverbal cognitive tests measuring reasoning, visualization, attention, and memory using pictures and pantomime instructions. The battery is individually administered to ages 2–21. The design and response mode of the Leiter-R allows the test to be administered without vocal directions by the examiner or expressive language by the examinee and allows for a wide range of cognitive, attention, and memory factors to be measured. Thus, the assessment is useful for children and adolescents with communication difficulties, autism-spectrum disorders, hard-of-hearing or deafness conditions, severe cognitive delay, learning disabilities, poor expressive language, English as a second language, orthopedic impairments, traumatic brain injury, ADHD (Barkley, 1990), and other neuropsychological difficulties (Lezak, 1995).

THEORY UNDERLYING THE TEST

The Leiter-R was developed on the basis of widely employed hierarchical models of intellectual and cognitive abilities. Development began with the Gustafsson (1984) and Carroll (1993) fluid-crystallized models of cognitive abilities that posit an overall general ability (*g*) at the highest level and multiple factors at the second and third levels of the model. The content of the scale was later compared to the combined Cattell-Horn-Carroll cognitive model (CHC; Cattell, 1943; Carroll, 1993; Horn, 1994; Horn & Cattell, 1966) by McGrew and Flanagan (1998). The CHC model has become extremely popular as the basis for several published cognitive tests including the *Kaufman Adolescent and Adult Intelligence Scale* (KAIT; Kaufman & Kaufman, 1993), the *Stanford-Binet Intelligence*

Scales—Fifth Edition (SB5; Roid, 2003b), and the *Woodcock-Johnson III Tests of Cognitive Abilities* (Mather & Woodcock, 2001). The Leiter-R was designed to measure several cognitive factors from CHC theory: fluid reasoning, visual-spatial ability, some aspects of crystallized general knowledge (e.g., visual matching of familiar objects, figures, and animals), short-term memory, long-term retrieval, and processing speed. The foundation of the Leiter-R on the CHC model allows the assessment professional to compare the individual's performance on other tests that measure the same theoretical cognitive factors. One approach to factor-based comparisons is the cross-battery approach of Flanagan and Ortiz (2001). Roid and Miller (1997), for example, presented cross-battery data on the combinations of Leiter-R and Woodcock-Johnson (WJ-R) cognitive tests, and the Leiter-R with the WISC-III. The first combination showed the convergence of the fluid reasoning factors in Leiter-R and WJ-R (e.g., correlations of .50 to .77 with Analysis-Synthesis in WJ-R). The second combination showed convergence of the visual-spatial factors in Leiter-R and WISC-III performance subtests, based on factor analyses of the combined subtests of both measures. The definition of *general intellectual ability* employed by the Leiter-R is based on the Cattell-Horn-Carroll theoretical model—that intelligence is a multifaceted array of cognitive abilities with a general (*g*) overarching ability, composed of at least 8 major dimensions (fluid, crystallized, quantitative, short- and long-term memory, auditory, processing speed, and other factors such as decision speed and language development, depending on the investigator). For the Leiter-R, the operational and empirical definition of *intelligence* is "the general ability to perform complex nonverbal mental manipulations related to conceptualization, inductive reasoning, and visualization" (Roid & Miller, 1997, p. 103), for purposes of solving problems and adapting to one's environment. The addition of the final phrase concerning problem solving and adapting comes from the definition provided by Wechsler (1991).

As stated by the original author of the scale (Leiter, 1966), the term *nonverbal* is somewhat imprecise because individuals responding to the tests probably use subvocal language and verbally guided thinking to solve the visually presented tasks in the scale. Thus, the examinee probably uses a number of unspoken verbal abilities on the items of the scale. This nonvocal administration style of the scale, however, makes it highly useful in special education, for assessment of children with various delays, disorders, and limited English, because it does not require expressive language. However, to be precise, the Leiter (1979) and the Leiter-R should be described as measuring *nonvocal* cognitive abilities although it is classified as a nonverbal assessment in common professional terminology.

DESCRIPTION OF THE TEST

The Leiter-R uses manipulatives (foam pieces and small, pictorial response cards) and an easel design (examinee stimuli on one side; examiner directions on the other). The three easels are constructed with a slotted "porch" at table height to simulate the block and slotted-frame style of the original Leiter (1979). The examinee places the response cards in the appropriate slot as directed by the task (e.g., to match a figure in the easel picture), or uses the card (or finger) to point to the correct portion of the easel pictures. Figure 10.1 shows the approximate layout of an item from the Leiter-R Repeated Patterns subtest. The item shows a pattern of black square, open square, black circle, a repeat of the first two squares, and two empty locations to be completed by response-card placement. The correct answers are shown in the bottom line of the figure.

Two groupings of subtests are provided: (1) the Visualization and Reasoning (VR) battery with 10 cognitive subtests (see Table 10.1), and (2) the Attention and Memory (AM) battery with two attention and eight memory subtests

Leiter-R easel picture

Leiter-R card slots at base of easel

Correct Leiter-R response card content

!?   #?

FIGURE 10.1

Example of Easel and Card-Response Layout for Leiter-R Repeated Patterns

TABLE 10.1 Brief Descriptions of the 10 Subtests in the Leiter-R Visualization and Reasoning Battery

Subtest Names	Description of the Subtest
Figure Ground (FG)	Find embedded objects within brightly colored pictures.
Form Completion (FC)	Place shape-pieces or match card showing separated parts of object to the examiner's model or the picture on the easel.
Sequential Order (SO)	Place pieces or match cards to show the correct sequence of objects, pictures, or geometric figures; complete the series.
Repeated Patterns (RP)	Complete the repeating pattern of pieces or pictures/figures by moving pieces or matching cards to correct slot.
Matching (M)	Discriminate and match pieces or cards to illustrations.
Picture Context (PC)	Recognize a missing object or portion of illustration from the context clues in a display or picture.
Classification (C)	Categorize objects (pieces) by color, shape, or geometric designs.
Design Analogies (DA)	Matrix analogies; complete patterns of pieces, 2×2 or 4×2 and complex matrices. Difficult items have figure rotations.
Paper Folding (PF)	Mentally fold an object displayed unfolded in 2 dimensions.
Figure Rotation (FR)	Mentally rotate increasingly complex 2- or 3-D objects/figures.

(see Table 10.2). Also included in the standardization of the battery were four rating scales (Examiner, Parent, Self, and Teacher) to provide multidimensional behavioral information about the examinee on dimensions such as attention, activity level, sociability, emotionality, and maladaptive behaviors. Examiners have the option of giving any one subtest, several brief combinations of subtests, or the VR or AM batteries separately. Administration time would vary from

TABLE 10.2   Brief Descriptions of the 10 Subtests in the Leiter-R Attention and Memory Battery

Subtest Names	Description of the Subtest
Associated Pairs (AP)	Remember pairs of pictured objects shown for 5–10 secs on an easel page; find matching object in pair on second easel page.
Immediate Recognition (IR)	Remember an array of pictured objects shown for 5 secs; identify present/absent objects shown on cards in second step of task.
Forward Memory (FM)	Repeat a sequence of touches to a series of pictures on the easel.
Attention Sustained (AS)	Paper-and-pencil *cross-out* or *cancellation* tasks; three levels of complexity by age; find and mark the targeted object; timed.
Reverse Memory (RM)	Examiner touches pictures in sequence; examinee touches in reverse order (analogous to digits-backward memory tasks).
Visual Coding (VC)	Nonverbal version of symbol/digit tasks; use target code to identify each picture/symbol/number; double-step coding in the most difficult items, tapping working memory.
Spatial Memory (SM)	Objects in a matrix shown for 10 secs; those objects on cards are placed in proper location in matrix on response sheet.
Delayed Pairs (DP)	Recognition of the pairs in AP, presented after 30 minutes elapses.
Delayed Recognition (DR)	Some objects shown in IR are repeated in new displays after 30 minutes elapse. (No mention in IR that objects will be repeated.)
Attention Divided (AD)	An experimental subtest; may require brief spoken directions; examinee is supposed to shift attention between a display with moving slots revealing pictured objects and a set of numbered cards to be sorted in order; timed task.

about 25 minutes for a brief assessment (e.g., 4 subtests) to the range of 40 to 60 minutes for a full-scale assessment (VR or AM batteries separately; 90 minutes for selected subtests of both batteries).

Some examiners find it helpful to supplement the six subtests used to estimate full-scale IQ (VR battery) with one or two subtests from the AM battery (e.g., Attention Sustained, a paper-and-pencil search-and-mark task measuring speed of information processing, and Forward Memory, a task involving touching pictures in sequence to tap memory span). These two subtests would add factors shown to be present in multiple data sets as documented by Carroll (1993). Carroll showed the presence of multiple factors in intelligence (including memory and speed of processing) in

more than 400 data sets. Also, the complete CHC model includes memory and processing speed.

Materials provided in the Leiter-R test kit include the test manual and materials for both the VR and AM batteries, including Easel Books, response cards, manipulative response shapes, Rating Scales, and Record Forms. There are two Easel Books for the VR battery. For the AM Battery, there is one Easel Book and response booklets and scoring keys for the Attention Sustained subtest, colored picture sheets used for Attention Divided, and a Response Grid for the Spatial Memory subtest. In addition to the brief descriptions in Tables 10.1 and 10.2, more details of each of the 10 VR battery subtests, the 10 AM battery subtests, and the interpretive meanings of each subtest and the composite and

IQ scores derived from Leiter-R are given in the test manual (Roid & Miller, 1997). Additional information is contained in the study by Roid, Nellis, and McLellan (2003), and in the book on nonverbal assessment by McCallum, Bracken, and Wasserman (2001).

ADMINISTRATION AND SCORING

The Leiter-R provides two choices for the estimation of global intellectual ability: (1) The Brief IQ Screener is comprised of the four core Visualization and Reasoning cognitive subtests: Figure Ground (FG), Form Completion (FC), Sequential Order (SO), and Repeated Patterns (RP). The Brief IQ Screener can be used as a rapid (25-minute) estimate of global intellectual functioning. (2) The Full Scale IQ, comprised of six subtests, offers a full-scale estimate of global intellectual functioning with high reliability. This measure takes approximately 40 minutes to administer and is beneficial for identification, classification, or placement decisions. The Easel Books provide the main stimulus materials for the examinee (and directions for examiners on the opposite side of the easel) for each of the VR and AM battery subtests.

Although the full complement of 20 subtests in both batteries may seem a challenging task to learn for the new examiner, you can begin with the four-subtest Brief IQ screener, appropriate for the full age range (2–20 years), which provides an easy introduction to the scales. Adding two subtests from the AM battery, Forward Memory (or Associative Memory) and Attention Sustained, provides an easy introduction to the AM scales. Examiner directions are clear, scoring is objective, and children easily engage with the materials.

The subtests administered within each battery vary for different age groups (2–3, 4–5, 6–10, and 11–20 years of age). It is important to closely follow the administration instructions located in the manual, on the Record Form, and on the Easel Books for age-appropriate starting points with teaching trials. However, if the child cannot independently provide correct answers, even after teaching, the examiner should turn to the starting point for the preceding age group. Standard stop rules are based on cumulative, rather than consecutive errors, and each subtest has its own stop rule.

The Leiter-R does not require expressive language (speaking) by the examinee, and the subtests' directions are communicated by gesture, demonstration, and various nonverbal cues. Although some reviews (e.g., McCallum, Bracken, & Wasserman, 2001) have claimed that the Leiter-R is not fully nonverbal, all but one (Attention Divided; AD) are consistently administered with gestures and no spoken directions by the examiner. And, the AD is not used for IQ estimation, nor does it take a critical role in most of the composite scores for the battery. Extensive surveys of 174 professional examiners who participated in the development and standardization of the Leiter-R showed that the test can be consistently administered without vocalization by examiner or examinee. Another frequently mentioned concern about administration was echoed by Glenn and Cunningham (2005) and Tsatsanis, Dartnall, Cicchetti, Sparrow, Klin, and Volkmar (2003)—that some children (e.g., those with autism) find it unusual for the examiner not to speak. As explained in the Leiter-R test manual, rapport-building conversation before beginning the test, and in between subtests, is perfectly acceptable. For children with autism spectrum disorders, Tsatsanis et al. (2003) found it effective to use very brief examiner vocalizations ("touch," "point") to supplement gestures during test administration.

Subtests within each battery should be administered in standardized order according to the manual and the Record Form. Exceptions would be special cases of variation for the purpose of facilitating a child's performance on the test. For example, if a child refuses to participate on a certain subtest, or loses interest after starting, it may be appropriate to move forward to a subtest that is more interactive and uses manipulatives.

Return to the subtest that presented difficulties; however, every reasonable effort should be made to complete a subtest when started. All changes in order of administration should be noted on Examiner's Rating Scales.

The majority of subtests are not timed by the examiner. Time bonuses are given only on various difficult items, which are specified with a picture of a watch next to the item on the record form, in the manual, and on the easel page. The child is awarded bonus points at 0–30 seconds, 31–60 seconds, and 61–180 seconds. At two minutes to go, the examiner should point to the watch and hold up two fingers and at one minute to go, point to the watch and hold up one finger. It is valuable to use a rotating motion with both index fingers pointing toward one another to indicate "speed up."

How to Score the Test

Scoring of each item on each subtest of Leiter-R is defined in the examiner directions printed on the Easel Books and on the Record Form. Even when Leiter-R items require more than one response (e.g., two or more cards placed correctly in a sequence), each response is scored. In other words, partial completion of a sequence is credited for most subtests. For example, on Subtest 2 (Design Analogies; DA) of the Visualization and Reasoning battery, the DA item number 12 is worth a total of three points. A child may place 1, 2, or 3 cards correctly. There are only three subtests within the Attention and Memory battery (Forward Memory, Reverse Memory, and Spatial Memory) where the child must get the entire sequence correct to be awarded one point.

After tallying scores for each subtest on the Visualization and Reasoning battery, raw scores are converted to scaled scores, from appendices provided in the back of the Manual. Calculation of composite and IQ scores on the Leiter-R follows the procedures of summing scaled scores and converting the sum to standard scores as done on most of the widely used intelligence tests. Scaled scores (mean 10, standard deviation 3) in each column on the Summary Sheet (front page) of the Record Form (Fluid Reasoning, Brief IQ, Fundamental Visualization, Spatial Visualization, and Full IQ) are added and the sum of scaled scores used to calculate standard scores in an IQ-style of metric (mean 100, standard deviation 15). Percentile ranks and confidence intervals for each of the composite scores are also available in the test manual appendices.

The Attention and Memory battery and each of the optional rating scales (Self, Parent, Teacher, and Examiner) are scored in the same way. In some cases, items on the rating scales may be too revealing or uncomfortable (e.g., "I feel jittery and nervous") for the respondent to answer. In this case, for researchers interested in correcting for missing data, the blank responses can be replaced by the median response within the subdomain. There are several different subdomains that combine to form one of two core domains: Cognitive/Social and Emotions/Regulation. Subdomain scores are converted to scaled scores by accessing the child's age-appropriate norm table in the test manual appendices for the Examiner rating scale, the Parent rating scale, the Self rating scale, and the Teacher rating scale. Clinical attention should be paid to scores of four or less (two standard deviations below the mean) and some attention paid to scores of five and six (one standard deviation below the mean). Standardized composite scores for domains in each rating form can be converted by using norm tables in the test manual appendices (mean of 100, with a standard deviation of 15).

Raw scores for each subtest, composite, and IQ estimate can be converted to growth scores as a way to plot development and measure growth on specific and global skills over time. The growth score provides an index sensitive to the rate at which the child is growing. A growth-profile map allows examiners to plot a growth value for each item on both batteries. Values are also provided explaining the relative item difficulty for each item passed or failed. Age equivalents are provided, but yield information regarding only typical performance in a specific age group; therefore, it is strongly recommended that they be used only when required to determine eligibility for a specific placement decision.

Use of the Scoring Software

The Leiter-R *Computer Scoring Software System* (Roid & Madsen, 1998) is available as an alternative to scoring by hand. The software automates the process of scoring, beginning with entry of raw scores for each subtest followed by conversion of raw scores to composites, IQ indexes, and growth scores by automated access to the norm tables for the examinee's age group. The software also calculates statistical significance of differences between IQ and Composite Scores, and calculates and reports all scores for special diagnostic scales. The software program makes scoring much quicker and provides a comprehensive profile report. Examiners are encouraged to edit the report and add their own commentary, analysis, interpretation, and recommendations for each case.

STANDARDIZATION, NORMS, DEVELOPMENT, AND PSYCHOMETRICS

The Leiter-R VR battery was standardized on a nationally representative sample of 1,719 subjects, ages 2 years, 0 months through 20 years, 11 months. The AM battery was co-normed on a subset of 763 subjects with the same age range and national representativeness of the VR battery. Demographics of the normative sample closely matched the 1993 Census statistics for stratification groups based on age (2–21), gender, ethnicity (Asian-, African-, Hispanic-, Non-Hispanic Caucasian-, and Native-American), geographic region (northeast, mid-central, south, and west), and parental

education (less than high school, HS or GED, and 13+ years). Extensive reliability, validity, and fairness studies were conducted for the Field-Test edition and the final Standardization edition of the scale (Roid & Miller, 1997), and these are summarized in the sections that follow.

Development of the Scale

The original Leiter (1979) was first developed in 1929 and subsequently revised editorially in 1934, 1936, 1938, 1940, and 1948. This widely used scale had a very heavy assortment of wooden blocks that fit into a wooden frame with slots for a series of blocks. The original scale employed a global mental age scoring system. Although still a popular method of assessment, the wooden blocks presented some hygienic and health issues (concern for coatings and inability to sterilize wood products). Also, the Leiter was badly in need of a national standardization and providing updated norms, expanded coverage of the number of cognitive factors assessed, and development of multiple-profile subtest scaled scores, composite standard scores, and standardized IQ indexes.

The revision of the scale involved a complex, multiyear, data-based project supported by funding from the publisher and the National Institutes of Mental Health. After a year of literature research and expert review, a preliminary field-testing version containing 24 subtests was tested on a national sample of 550 children and adolescents (225 typical children without disabilities, and 325 with various cognitive, communication, or motor delays or disabilities, or English-as-Second-Language status). More than 60 professional examiners were trained to administer the tests and gave extensive feedback leading to the revision of the tests and dropping of four subtests that showed limited psychometric quality or required some expressive language. Extensive psychometric item and scale analyses were conducted using conventional and item-response theory

(IRT; Lord, 1980; Rasch, 1980) methods, differential item functioning (DIF; Holland & Wainer, 1993) fairness studies, confirmatory factor analysis, and criterion-related evidence. For example, the preliminary versions of the subtests showed significant differences between typical-normative subjects and atypical-disability subjects, and correlations of .55 to .75 for subtests with corresponding *Stanford-Binet—Fourth Edition* (Thorndike, Hagen, & Sattler, 1986) and *WISC-III* (Wechsler, 1991) subtests. The majority of the preliminary subtests showed excellent potential with most age levels having internal consistency reliabilities in the .73–.95 range. Any deficient subtests retained for the final version of the Leiter-R were revised by adding, deleting, and revising various items and examiner directions.

The final published Leiter-R was further refined after the final version was administered to 1,719 typical children and adolescents from all four Census regions of the United States in the standardization study. In addition, the standardization study included various comparison groups (number of subjects in parenthesis), consisting of speech/language impairment (98), severe hearing impairment (69), severe motoric delay (61), cognitive delay (123), ADHD (112), intellectually gifted (67), students with documented learning disabilities (68), and English-as-second-language (73 with Spanish; 26 others). The AM battery was standardized on a subset of 763 normative cases, and the Examiner and Parent Rating scales were standardized on a subset of 785 normative cases.

Psychometrics: Reliability of the Scales

Table 10.3 shows the names of the subtests, composite scores, and IQ indexes of the Leiter-R VR battery, along with the average internal consistency (or composite) reliability of the scores. Raw scores for subtests were converted to standard scaled scores (similar to Wechsler, 1991,

scales with mean 10, and standard deviation 3), and sums of scaled scores used to derive composite and IQ standard scores (mean 100, *SD* 15). A combination of four subtests, Figure Ground, Form Completion, Sequential Order, and Repeated Patterns, functions as a consistent estimate of IQ for the full range of ages 2–21. As with many scales developed to span a wide age range, the remaining composite scores were designed for developmentally appropriate combinations of subtests that function well within certain age limits. On the VR battery, for example, the Full IQ is composed of five subtests at ages 2–5 (where Matching provides a basic visualization scale), and six subtests for ages 6–20 (where Design Analogies—a measure of matrix-style fluid reasoning—and Paper Folding work well).

Table 10.4 shows the names of the subtests and composite scores of the Leiter-R AM battery, along with the average internal consistency (or composite) reliability of the scores (Tellegen & Briggs, 1967). Raw scores for subtests were converted to standard scaled scores and sums of scaled scores converted to composite scores in the same manner as the VR battery. Unlike the VR battery where a global ability (*g*) composite is suggested by the Carroll and CHC models, assessment professionals typically keep attention and memory dimensions separate, while employing various combinations of subtests as reflected in the composites shown in Table 10.2. A rich variety of contrasts are possible within the AM battery, such as immediate versus delayed (i.e., short-term and long-term memory) scores. Two subtests span the full age range of 2–20 years—Associated Pairs and Forward Memory—and can be combined to form the Memory Screener composite score. Validity studies of the AM composites showed that the Memory Span and Memory Process composites for older children and adolescents (ages 6–20) had significantly lower scores for students with learning disabilities (means of 100 normative versus 87 approximately for

TABLE 10.3 Internal Consistency Reliability Estimates for Subtest and Composite Scores in the Leiter-R Visualization and Reasoning Battery by Age Groupings

Subtest Scaled Scores	2–20	2–5	6–10	11–20
Figure Ground (FG)	.75	.75	.78	.74
Form Completion (FC)	.88	.90	.88	.83
Sequential Order (SO)	.75	.72	.80	.70
Repeated Patterns (RP)	.76	.80	.74	.75
Matching (M)	—	.92	.74	—
Picture Context (PC)	—	.90	—	—
Classification (C)	—	.84	—	—
Design Analogies (DA)	—	—	.84	.81
Paper Folding (PF)	—	—	.75	.82
Figure Rotation (FR)	—	—	—	.82
Composite or IQ Scores				
Brief IQ (FG + FC + SO + RP)	.89	.88	.90	.89
Full Scale IQ (Ages 2–5; Brief IQ + M)	—	.92	—	—
Full Scale IQ (Ages 6–20; Brief IQ + DA + PF)	—	—	.91	.93
Fundamental Visualization (M + PC)	—	.92	—	—
Spatial Visualization (PF + FR)	—	—	—	.91
Fluid Reasoning (SO + RP*)	.89	.88	.89	.89
Visualization (from SBIT; FG + FC)	.86	—	.87	.84

NOTE : *The Fluid Reasoning composite is weighted with SO plus two times RP. The RP subtest is weighted more than SO in this composite because of its higher reliability in young children and factor analysis evidence showing its uniqueness on a reasoning factor at ages 2–5 particularly. All reliability estimates were calculated using Cronbach's (1951) coefficient alpha formula. Sample sizes were 736 (ages 2–5), 494 (6–10), 489 (11–20), and 1,719 overall. Average reliability was calculated using the Fisher-Z transformation for correlations (Guilford & Fruchter, 1978). Composite reliabilities were calculated from the formula by Nunnally (1978; p. 246).

LD groups—nearly a full standard deviation lower). Clinical hypotheses of memory process deficits could be examined by administering the four-subtest Brief IQ of the VR battery along with the three-subtest Memory Process composite of the AM battery. The test manual for the Leiter-R (Roid & Miller, 1997) includes tables of significant differences between and among the subtests and composite scores of the batteries, and shows that a difference of 15 points or more between Brief IQ and Memory Process scores would be significant at the .05 level.

USES AND INTERPRETIVE STRATEGIES FOR THE LEITER-R

Uses of Leiter-R

The authors' original intentions for uses of the Leiter-R were especially focused on children and

TABLE 10.4   Internal Consistency Reliability Estimates for Subtest and Composite Scores in the Leiter-R Attention and Memory Battery by Age Groupings

Subtest Scaled Scores	2–20	2–3	4–5	6–10	11–20
Associated Pairs (AP)	.69	.77	.72	.78	.74
Immediate Recognition (IR)	.84	—	.88	.81	—
Forward Memory (FM)	.81	.89	.85	.79	.77
Attention Sustained (AS)	.87	.83	.83	.83	.92
Reverse Memory (RM)	.84	—	—	.85	.83
Visual Coding (VC)	.85	—	—	.89	.79
Spatial Memory (SM)	.84	—	—	.82	.85
Delayed Pairs (DP)	.68	—	—	.70	.65
Delayed Recognition (DR)	.78	—	.86	.73	—
Attention Divided (AD)	.67	—	—	.68	.66
Composite or IQ Scores					
Memory Screener (AP + FM)	.80	.88	.85	.76	.75
Recognition Memory (IR + DR)	.91	—	.93	.87	—
Associative Memory (AP + DP)	.80	—	—	.81	.79
Memory Span (FM + RM + SM)	.88	—	—	.88	.89
Attention (AS + AD)	.81	—	—	.79	.83
Memory Process (FM + VC + SM)	.87	—	—	.86	.88

NOTE : All reliability estimates were calculated using Cronbach's (1951) coefficient alpha formula. Sample sizes for the AM battery were 168 (ages 2–3), 156 (4–5), 218 (6–10), and 221 (11–20), and 763 overall. Average reliability was calculated using the Fisher-Z transformation for correlations (Guilford & Fruchter, 1978). Composite reliabilities were calculated from the formula by Nunnally (1978; p. 246).

adolescents with communication difficulties and non-English speakers. For many years, the original Leiter was widely used in autism assessment (Tsatsanis et al., 2003) because it required no expressive language and included interesting tasks. In recent years, the Leiter-R has taken an increasingly visible role in the assessment of cognitive functioning in children with autism spectrum disorders (ASD), including low-functioning children with ASD (Tsatsanis et al., 2003), and those with the DSM-IV (American Psychiatric Association, 2000) designation of Pervasive Developmental Disorders, Not Specified (PDD-NOS; Butter, Mulick, & Metz, 2006).

Other uses of the Leiter-R for communication-related difficulties include cases of severe language impairment, hearing impairment, and English-as-second-language (ESL, or ELL for English Language Learner). Farrant, Fletcher, and Mayberry (2006) used the Leiter-R to measure nonverbal IQ in Australian children with and without specific language impairments (SLI), finding that the Leiter-R provided a comparable IQ (97.0) in the SLI as compared to that of similar children (ages 4–6) with typical development (IQ 101.1). Koehn (1998) found close similarity between the Leiter-R IQ (93.6) and WISC-III Performance IQ (94.0) in a sample of 28 Hispanic-American children with ESL designations in school districts. Flemmer and Roid (1997) found evidence for ethnic fairness among the Leiter-R subtests between

Hispanic-American and Euro-American samples matched for socioeconomic level (parental education). Mean differences were not significantly different between groups for 7 of the 10 subtests and there was less than one-third standard deviation (SD) for all subtests. Small differences between groups (e.g., effect sizes less than one-third SD) are important in this context given past guidelines defining effect sizes in the one-fifth SD range as *small* (Cohen, 1988, p. 25) and effect sizes of less than one-third SD as *not educationally significant* (Horst, Tallmadge, & Wood, 1975; p. 53).

The Leiter-R and the original Leiter have often been used in the assessment of mental retardation (MR) and cognitive developmental delays. Roid and Miller (1997) showed good classification accuracy in differentiating cases of mental retardation ($n = 120$, documented by medical and school records) from a normative control group from the VR battery standardization ($n = 1719$), using cutting scores of 70 IQ (Full Scale or Brief IQ). Overall classification accuracy (correct identification of both MR and normative subjects) was about 96%, with specificity (correct identification of normative subjects) about 98%, sensitivity (correct identification of MR) 84% for Full Scale IQ or 75% for Brief IQ, and small rates of false-negative or false-positive classification (1% to 2.6% for Full Scale or Brief IQ). Similar percentages of classification accuracy were obtained in a cross-validation with the AM battery subsample (with 40 MR and 724 normative cases).

Recently, Glenn and Cunningham (2005) showed that the Leiter-R estimates the expected, lower mean scores of individuals with Down syndrome on a sample of 25 individuals (ages 16–24). The study showed the mean IQ to be below 70 ($M = 62.4$, Brief IQ) as expected for a sample with Down syndrome or MR. The study also showed a correlation of .61 between the Leiter-R Brief IQ and the standard score from the British Picture Vocabulary Scales (BPVS; Dunn, Dunn, & NFER-Nelson, 1997), an adaptation of the Peabody Picture Vocabulary Test (Dunn & Dunn, 1997). Carr (2005) also used the BPVS and the original Leiter to study longitudinal changes in verbal and performance abilities in a sample of individuals with Down syndrome. In a related commentary, Kamphaus (2001) reviewed the Leiter-R and stated that "the Leiter-R did an excellent job of differentiating mental retardation from normality" (p. 453).

There are numerous other clinical and educational applications of the Leiter-R for various categories of children in special education, including attention deficit and hyperactivity disorder (ADHD; Nordlund, 1998; Roid & Miller, 1997), learning disabilities (Olson, 1998; Roid & Miller, 1997), and traumatic brain injury (Quinn, 1999). The study by Webster, Plante, and Couvillion (1997), although employing the original Leiter rather than Leiter-R, is an example of research that uses the Leiter nonverbal IQ to study children (ages 3–6) with overt phonological impairments (disordered speech) associated with pre-reading achievement. Quinn (1999) used the Field edition of the Leiter-R to study a group of 18 children and adolescents (ages 6–21) with traumatic brain injury (TBI) in comparison to a matched control sample ($n = 87$) and found significant differences, as expected. The Quinn study found that Leiter-R subtests such as Repeated Patterns and Sequential Order were particularly low for TBI cases, as expected by clinical impressions that individuals with TBI have difficulty integrating complex information to solve problems. In contrast, the TBI cases showed relative strengths in visualization skills measured by Picture Context, Figure Ground, and Classification subtests—all involving more immediate perceptual identification tasks compared to the working memory demands of complex problem solving.

The Leiter-R should also be valuable for the analysis of cognitive "strengths and weaknesses" as specified in the guidelines for the reauthorized Individuals with Disabilities Education Act (IDEA, 2004). The Leiter-R is especially useful for students with non-English backgrounds and those with the various conditions described earlier. For these reasons, the interpretive strategy described in the following was designed to analyze the cognitive strengths and weaknesses of individuals with potential delays and disabilities.

Seven-Step Interpretive Strategy

The test manual for the Leiter-R (Roid & Miller, 1997) outlines a five-step interpretive strategy that begins at the global level of IQ scores and proceeds through the composite scores, growth scores, subtests, and special diagnostic indexes. This chapter expands the five-step process to seven steps (see Table 10.5). The seven steps are based on the hierarchical strategies typically used on the Stanford-Binet (SB5; Roid, 2003a), the Wechsler scales (Kaufman, 1994; Kaufman & Lichtenberger, 1999), and other intellectual assessments (e.g., Sattler, 2001). Each of these interpretive systems begins at the highest level (IQ) and proceeds to study the patterns and significant differences between composite and subtest scores so that a comprehensive view of the individual's cognitive strengths and weaknesses can be reported. The overall purpose of these strategies is to generate clinical hypotheses to explain the cognitive strengths and processing deficits that impact the individual's performance (e.g., in school or work). Hypotheses are then verified (or not verified) by collecting additional information from a broad range of sources such as parent, teacher, caregiver, or peer observations,

TABLE 10.5   Steps in Leiter-R Interpretation: The Seven-Step System

---

STEP 1: Purpose and Context

STEP 2: Global IQ Evaluation

STEP 3: Composite Scores Comparisons

STEP 4: Growth Score Analysis

STEP 5: Subtest Comparisons and Profile Analysis

STEP 6: Cross-Battery Comparisons (Composite and Subtests)

STEP 7: Qualitative Observations and Rating Scale Analysis

---

additional test data on achievement, behavior, and social-emotional variables, interviews, medical and school records, and so forth. In addition, considerations of the current IDEA (2004) recommendation to explore cognitive strengths and weaknesses (to enhance the use of intellectual ability batteries and supplement global information from IQ measures alone), methods of profile analysis, and score-difference significance are also included in the interpretive steps.

Step 1: Purpose and Context

The examiner's purpose for the assessment and the context (the ethnic, cultural, medical, or environmental context) of the examinee can greatly impact (and even invalidate) the interpretation of findings from testing. The AERA/APA/NCME ethical guidelines for professional examiners (American Educational Research Association, 1999) caution that the validity of tests depends on the specific purposes, uses, and interpretation of tests. Also, the user should be aware that validity evidence for specific uses or interpretations might not be available or included in a test manual. For example, most standardized intellectual batteries have documented and excellent validity for using the global IQ score in identifying high levels of giftedness or low levels of mental retardation, but IQ scores themselves are less able to accurately identify the variations of conditions such as autism, learning disabilities, and ADHD, without supplemental assessment of all subtests and social and behavioral variables (Roid, 2003a). The AERA/NCME/APA guidelines require consideration of many other examinee characteristics, including the match between the individual's characteristics and the nature of the normative sample of the test being used. Clearly, the interpretation of normative scores depends on such a match. Two of the major considerations in modern multicultural society are (1) whether the examinee can comprehend and speak in the language employed by the test, and (2) whether the examinee has recently immigrated to a country and is not fully acculturated (Dana, 2005) to the society and especially to the requirements of standardized tests. Fortunately, nonverbal (non-vocal) batteries such as the Leiter-R provide an excellent alternative to other batteries that require extensive verbal and expressive language ability. However, even with the Leiter-R, the examiner must pause and reflect on the purpose (e.g., look at the validity evidence available for that use of the test) and the context (e.g., the ethnic, cultural, language-proficiency, and acculturation level) of the examinee before beginning the analysis of scores, score differences, profile patterns, and so on.

Table 10.6 shows a case study of a female student we will call "Malissa," age 14 years, 9 months, from the northeastern United States with an official diagnosis of learning disabilities based on low reading and writing scores compared to her Full Scale IQ. As part of a school district experiment, Malissa participated in an experimental reading intervention project, with frequent progress-monitoring tests of reading, based on the *Qualitative Reading Inventory* (Leslie & Caldwell, 2001). The project showed that Malissa responded very poorly (with small improvements) to the reading intervention. Malissa's lack of response to this reading intervention is the evidence of "response to validated instruction" required by the new IDEA (2004) regulations. The experienced examiner who gave her the WISC-III and some other tests in response to teacher referrals for learning disability evaluation also knew her family background. The family was Anglo-American (Caucasian) and lived in a moderate-income section of the city. Malissa's mother completed high school and her father completed two years of post-secondary training in a technical college. Both mother and father worked full-time jobs, lacked extended family support, had experienced severe medical conditions, and had little time or resources to help Malissa with schoolwork. Also, due to financial constraints, the family could not provide materials (e.g., books) or experiences (e.g., preschool or kindergarten) that might have increased her language and vocabulary development. For these reasons, and based on teacher comments, the examiner expected some deficits in verbal ability and chose to employ a nonverbal test (Leiter-R) as well as the standard WISC-III (Wechsler, 1991) referral battery of the school district to ensure an accurate estimation of intellectual ability.

Step 2: Global IQ Evaluation

Table 10.5 shows the Full Scale IQ for Malissa to be 105 (based on six subtests) and a Brief IQ of 103 (based on four subtests). The Leiter-R showed excellent agreement with the WISC-III Full Scale IQ (106). However, it should be noted from Table 10.5 that the WISC-III also showed a highly significant difference between verbal and performance IQ, with the PIQ much higher (120) than the full scale and the VIQ much lower (92). Given that some practitioners use the perceptually oriented PIQ to contrast with achievement scores, the WISC-III PIQ would have overestimated general ability level compared to the Full Scale IQ of either WISC-III or Leiter-R. As originally stated in the Theory section near the beginning of this chapter, the Leiter-R provides a way to assess subvocal (unspoken) verbal thinking that seems to operate when examinees solve the sequential or patterned series of the Leiter-R. This can be seen from the subtest scores of Sequential Order, 10, and Repeated Patterns, 7—average or lower scores that are lower than the more visual Leiter-R subtests (Figure Ground, 12, and Form Completion, 13—above-average scores). Thus, the subtest score pattern on the Leiter-R seems to follow the pattern of apparent differences on the WISC-III subtests if we can assume subvocal verbal thinking on the Leiter-R.

Step 3: Composite Score Comparisons

For clinical evaluations, composite scores were designed to combine clusters of subtests to document specific diagnostic hypotheses. Such hypotheses may be particularly useful in the

TABLE 10.6   Composite and Subtest Scores for the Case Study of Malissa, Age 14, Diagnosed with Learning Disabilities and Tested with the Leiter-R and WISC-III

Leiter-R VR	Scores	Leiter-R AM	Scores	WISC-III	Scores
Composites:		*Composites:*		*Composites:*	
Full Scale IQ	105	Memory Screen	87	Full Scale IQ	106
Brief IQ	103	Associative Memory	76	Verbal IQ	92
Fluid Reasoning	88	Memory Span	108	Performance IQ	120
Spatial Visualization	113	Attention	111	*Subtests:*	
Visualization (SBIT)	115[b]	Memory Process	107	Picture Completion	14
Subtests:		Recognition Memory	—[c]	Information	7
Figure Ground	12	*Subtests:*		Coding	17
Form Completion	13	Associated Pairs	5	Similarities	9
Sequential Order	10	Immediate Recognition	—[c]	Picture Arrangement	12
Repeated Patterns	7	Forward Memory	11	Arithmetic	11
Matching	—[a]	Attention Sustained	13	Block Design	17
Picture Context	—[a]	Reverse Memory	11	Vocabulary	7
Classification	—[a]	Visual Coding	10	Object Assembly	8
Design Analogies	12	Spatial Memory	12	Comprehension	9
Paper Folding	10	Delayed Pairs	6	Symbol Search	16
Figure Rotation	14	Delayed Recognition	—[c]	Digit Span	7
		Attention Divided	11	Retention Ability (Horn, 1985)	IN 7 AR 11 DS 7
		Associated Memory Familiar vs. Unfamiliar	6 vs. 13	Bannatyne (1974) Acquired Knowledge Composite	IN 7 AR 11 VO 7

[a]**Note**: Leiter-R VR subtests for ages 2–10 (M, PC, and C) were not included due to Malissa's age of 14.
[b]**Note**: The SBIT is the *Stoelting Brief Intelligence Scale* (Roid & Miller, 1999), which included the derivation, interpretation, and normative tables for the Visualization composite.
[c]**Note**: The Leiter-R AM subtests of Immediate Recognition and Delayed Recognition are not used for children aged 11–20, as shown in Table 10.4.

evaluations of cases of suspected learning disabilities. The guidelines of the IDEA (2004) suggest in section 300.311(a)(5) that cognitive ("performance") measures can be used to show that "the child exhibits a pattern of strengths and weaknesses in performance, achievement, or both, relative to age, State-approved grade level standards or intellectual development."

The names and subtests for each of the three composites in the Leiter-R VR battery and the six composites in the AM battery are shown in Tables 10.3 and 10.4, respectively. There are two important methods of comparing differences among the composites—statistical significance of the difference and frequency (rarity) of the magnitude of differences. Both the significance and rarity of the difference between IQs, composite scores, and subtest scores have been recommended in most of the interpretive systems for cognitive tests (e.g., Kaufman, 1994; Sattler, 2001). Both methods are important because statistical significance alone may not indicate that the difference is truly unusual and clinically significant given that most examinees taking cognitive tests have existing differences of various magnitudes among their scores.

Four of the composite-score comparisons that may be most widely used are described below in reference to the case study of Malissa (see scores in Table 10.6):

1. *Reasoning vs. Visualization.* The two major cognitive factors in the Leiter-R IQ measures are Reasoning (SO and RP subtests) and Visualization (M + PC for young children, ages 2–5, or PF + FR for ages 11–20). For the case study of Malissa (see Table 10.6), the Spatial Visualization composite was quite high (113 on the usual IQ scale with mean 100 and *SD* of 15) in comparison to the Fluid Reasoning composite (88). The Leiter-R test manual (Roid & Miller, 1997) shows that a difference of 13.15 (rounded to 13) is required for statistical significance at the .05 level and the difference of 25 points is found only in 8.5% of the normative sample. Although the difference is not extremely rare, its frequency is less than the clinical standard of 15% used by Wechsler (1991). The difference is probably caused by Malissa's low score (7, on the scale with mean 10, *SD* 3) on Repeated Patterns and average performance on SO. Perhaps the cognitive processes causing her learning disabilities are reflected in the inability to process the complex information of difficult series and patterns. A possible clinical hypothesis is that short-term working memory may be disrupted in Malissa, as seen in some of the most significant Attention and Memory composites presented below.

2. *Associative Memory vs. Memory Span.* Malissa showed a low Associative Memory composite score of 76 compared to a Memory Span composite of 108, a highly significant and infrequent (6.5% of normative cases) difference of 32 points (see Table 10.6). Both on the short-term Associated Pairs subtest (score of 5) and on the 20-minute delayed equivalent subtest, Delayed Pairs (score of 6), Malissa was more than one full standard deviation below average, causing the composite (AP + DP) to be nearly two *SD*s below average. The clinical hypothesis suggested by this contrast is that Malissa has a relative strength in short-term memory of picture series (and sequences of touching pictures) but a weakness in meaningful association of pairs of pictures (a type of working memory; Baddeley, 1986).

3. *Memory Screener vs. Attention.* Malissa showed a significant difference of 24 points between the composite FM + RM (forward and reverse touching picture sequences) and the Attention composite AS + AD (Sustained plus Divided Attention). This 24-point difference occurred in 18% of the normative population, so the difference is not considered rare. However, the comparison highlights an important aspect of Malissa's cognitive abilities—the fact that attention deficits do not appear to be present. Given the commonly high co-occurrence of learning disabilities and ADHD (American Academy of Pediatrics, 2000), Malissa appears to be an exception. The tentative conclusion would be the hypothesis that Malissa's cognitive weaknesses center around associative and working memory and not short-term visual memory or attention processes.

4. *Associative Memory vs. Attention.* Malissa showed a significant and clinically meaningful difference between the Associative Memory composite (76) and the Attention composite (111). The difference of 34 points is found only in 8% of the normative sample, and thus, by virtue of being below 15%, is considered clinically significant.

Step 4: Growth Score Analysis

The Leiter-R has an optional series of scores derived from raw score totals on the VR battery. The scores are similar to the W-scores of the *Woodcock-Johnson* (McGrew & Woodcock, 2001), being based on item response theory (Rasch, 1980; Wright & Linacre, 1999), and show similar growth curves across ages as those on the *WJ III Tests of Cognitive Abilities* (Mather & Woodcock, 2001). Similar to the WJ III, the Leiter-R Growth Scores range between approximately 425 and 570, centered at 500 for age 10 years, 0 months, with an expansion factor of 9.1024 (used to calculate the W-scale from a Rasch ability estimate; Woodcock & Dahl, 1971). Woodcock (1999) discusses more detailed specifications and uses of these Rasch-based scales. These scores are not standardized by age, nor are they norm-referenced, as with IQ or subtest scaled scores. Instead they are criterion-referenced (by age and task difficulty) and follow the age-related growth pattern of children, increasing quickly from ages 2 to 8 (approximately) and increasing more gradually from ages 9 to 20. A typical standard deviation is approximately 9.0 for the Brief and Full Scale Growth scores, and 10.0–11.0 for the other composites within each year of age. Across the most frequent school population involved in assessments (ages 6–16), the standard deviations range from 14.0 (IQ composites) to 16.0 (Reasoning and Visual composites) on average. For the case study of Malissa (Table 10.6), the Growth scores range from 502 (Fluid Reasoning composite Growth score) to 515 (Spatial Visualization composite Growth score). The Growth scores are particularly powerful for tracking long-term change, response to intervention, and progress of students in special education. The Brief IQ with four subtests can be repeated each academic year, for example, and show longitudinal progress. Because some special education students remain at low percentiles on normative scores, the positive changes in Growth scores could be the best indicator to parents and guardians that real progress is being made by educators and clinicians. The Leiter-R test manual shows that a highly significant increase in Growth scores (at the .05 level) is any magnitude of change that exceeds approximately 12 points. For example, if Malissa (Table 10.6) increased from her current Brief IQ Growth score, which is 510, to 522 by her senior year of high school, we would consider her special education experience to be significantly effective. However, some parents would like to see any amount of change—even 1 point! Much more detail concerning Growth scores can be obtained from the Leiter-R test manual (Roid & Miller, 1997) and from use of the *Growth Score and Rating Scales Profile and Record Form*, available from the Stoelting Company. This Record Form has several useful graphs and displays for Growth scores that relate student performance to specific age levels and certain tasks within the test battery.

Step 5: Subtest Comparisons and Profile Analysis

The comparison of cognitive strengths and weaknesses among the subtests of cognitive batteries can be a complex and lengthy process if carried to the full extent suggested by Kaufman (1994), Sattler (2001), and most intellectual-ability test manuals. Therefore, the reader is referred to the Leiter-R test manual (Roid & Miller, 1997) or to the helpful book by McCallum, Bracken, and Wasserman (2001) for more details on subtest definitions, research, comparisons, and profile pattern analysis. A brief summary of some of the major steps in subtest analysis is provided by the following list of suggested steps and guidelines:

1. *Recognize the limits of measurement error.* The first step in subtest profile analysis is to recognize that some subtests have lower reliability than others, sometimes at certain age levels, so the experienced examiner should consult the test manual tables of reliability values to discover which subtests dip below a reliability of .80, where use of individual scores becomes more problematic. Because composite scores and IQ measures combine several subtests, they are often more reliable indicators of strengths and weaknesses. However, when a clear pattern across all 10 subtests of either the Visualization and Reasoning (VR) battery or the Attention-Memory (AM) battery emerges (e.g., where many memory subtests are low and all attention subtests are high), the patterns of clusters of subtests become similar to composite score comparisons. Subtests of the VR battery are generally above .75–.80 for most age levels, with the exception of ages 2–4 for Figure Ground (FG) and Sequential Order (SO), the upper age range for Matching (ages 7–10), the upper age range for FG, SO, and Repeated Patterns (ages 14–20), and the lower age ranges for Paper Folding (ages 6–8), where the reliabilities reach into the .67–.74 range.

2. *Examine subtest scatter.* One of the quickest ways to see strengths and weaknesses is through the time-tested method of calculating *profile scatter*. *Scatter* is simply the difference between the lowest and highest scaled scores for the profile. Scatter is shown in Table 10.6 for the case of Malissa. Malissa's VR subtests ranged from a low of 7 (Repeated Patterns; RP) to a high of 14 (Figure Rotation; FR), resulting in a scatter of 7 points. According to the table of scatter frequencies for VR supplied in the test manual appendices, a scatter of 7 points occurs in about one-third (33%) of normative-sample profiles. Thus, the scatter is not a rarity, but does confirm findings derived from the comparison of composites showing significant differences

between Malissa's reasoning and visualization abilities.

On the AM battery, Malissa's scores ranged from a low of 5 for Associated Pairs (AP) to a high of 13 for Attention Sustained (AS). This scatter value of 8 points is found in about 25% of the normative population, so, again, the scatter is not particularly rare. However, the pattern of differences resulted in the significant difference between the Associative Memory and Attention composites discussed earlier.

Because the WISC-III results were also available for Malissa, we can see in Table 10.6 that scatter for the Wechsler scale was 10 points (low of 7 for three subtests and high of 17 on the Coding subtest). Surprisingly, according to the WISC-III manual (Wechsler, 1991), a scatter value of 10 occurs in 26% of the normative population when 12 subtests have been administered and compared. Interestingly, however, Kaufman (1994) considers that the Information, Vocabulary, and Comprehension subtests (the three subtests with scores of 7 each), along with Picture Arrangement (score of 12), reflect cultural learning opportunities in the home. The low scores on three of these four subtests seem to provide objective evidence for the examiner's impression that Malissa's home environment did not encourage reading and other activities that contribute to early learning. Also, as shown in Table 10.6, the Acquired Knowledge composite proposed by Bannatyne (1974) and the Retention Ability composite proposed by Horn (1985) also showed two out of three subtests very low.

3. *Examine statistical significance and frequency of score differences among the subtests.* Extensive tables for the statistical significance of differences, the significance of differences between the individual subtest and the mean of all the subtests, and the frequency (rarity) of the difference magnitude are all provided in the Leiter-R test manual appendices, and guidelines are also mentioned by

McCallum et al. (2001). As a rule-of-thumb, a difference of approximately 4 points between most of the subtests on either the VR or AM battery of the Leiter-R will reach statistical significance at the .05 level. For Malissa, this would include differences between Repeated Patterns and four other subtests of the VR battery, and between Associated Pairs and all the other subtests except Delayed Pairs.

4. *Compare the entire subtest profile to the core profiles derived from the normative sample.* The study of common profile patterns in a normative sample was initiated by the work of McDermott, Fantuzzo, and Glutting (1990), who studied profile patterns on the WISC-R. Since that time, a number of tests have included normative profile analyses (e.g., Roid, 2003a, for the SB5). The method of deriving accurate profile patterns from cluster analysis must be correctly applied, including the inclusion of subjects with clinical conditions (to allow for the variability that occurs in clinical practice) and the use of accurate cluster-analysis methods (Roid, 1994). Without careful analysis, the early conclusion of McDermott et al. (1990) was to abandon profile analysis because of an apparent lack of profile differentiation (dominance of profiles by a general level—"flat profiles" with little scatter) in one of the Wechsler normative data sets. Roid (1994; 2003a) has found that the guidelines of Aldenderfer and Blashfield (1984) are critical to finding true profile patterns (occurring in as much as 40% of the population) instead of the undifferentiated flat profiles originally identified by McDermott et al. The key was to employ Pearson correlations as the similarity measure in SPSS cluster analysis (Norusis, 1990) with Ward's (1963) method of hierarchical clustering in the first stage (R. K. Blashfield, personal communication, February 22, 1992). For these reasons, a new cluster analysis of Leiter-R VR profiles was prepared especially for this chapter.

DESCRIPTION OF CLUSTER AND PROFILE ANALYSIS PROCEDURE   The analyses were conducted in two stages for the six subtests of Leiter-R that occur for individuals ages 6–20, where the most complete data were available from the Leiter-R standardization sample. In the first stage, exploratory hierarchical cluster analysis along with correlational analysis was conducted to identify initial profiles. These profiles were then used as the initial input in the second stage of nonhierarchical cluster analysis (Roid, 1994), following the procedures recommended by Aldenderfer and Blashfield (1984).

The first stage began with an inspection of correlations between the subtest scores. Then, subtest z-scores were input into a hierarchical cluster analysis (Norusis, 1990). In the hierarchical cluster analysis, the average-linkage method with Pearson correlations as similarity measures was employed. This combination was used because of the moderately positive intercorrelations among the subtest scores in the study and a desire to detect patterns of differentiated scores (Roid, 1994). The average-linkage method uses the average distance between pairs of scores, one pair for each of the scores, as the distance between two examinees or profiles.

To determine the number of profiles, the number of profiles was graphed against the agglomeration coefficient between the two examinees or profiles merged to form the last or newest profile (Aldenderfer & Blashfield, 1984). This test is a variant of the scree test developed by Cattell (1966) for factor analysis. A marked flattening in the graph (or an "elbow") suggests that relatively different examinees or profiles were merged in the last profile. Nine profiles were identified in the first stage of hierarchical analysis.

The nine profiles identified in the above analyses were then used in the second stage of nonhierarchical cluster analysis to classify the full sample of examinees. Specifically, the profiles identified in the first stage were used as cluster-centered mean scores to perform the nonhierarchical clustering conducted with K-Means cluster analysis (Norusis, 1990). This K-Means method uses squared Euclidean distances as the distance measure. The measure of practical significance used was that each profile had to represent at least 5% of the examinees. No profiles were dropped because they represented less than 5% of the examinees. As a result, nine profiles were identified for the final analysis, as shown in Table 10.7.

Several interesting patterns emerged, and users of the Leiter-R VR battery should note their values. About 35% of the profiles showed "flat" patterns of Very High (with a high average parental education of 16 years and the highest mean child IQ), Low Average, and Very Low (with the lowest parental education levels). One high-average profile, with 9% of the sample, showed emphasis on slightly higher visualization scores (FG 12 and PF 14) and parental education being 15 years of education (near-completion of college). Another high-average profile, with

12% of the sample, showed emphasis on slightly higher Reasoning scores (DA 12, SO 13, RP 12) in comparison to Visualization (FG 9 and PF 11) and fairly high parental education and child IQ averages. There were four profile patterns that showed a single subtest lower than the others (DA, RP, PF, or FC) as examples of subtest-specific variations, representing a total of 44% of the sample.

Step 6: Cross-Battery Comparisons (Composites and Subtests)

Flanagan and Ortiz (2001) have suggested a strategy for comparing measures that assess the same major constructs (e.g., the cognitive factors in CHC theory) across different cognitive batteries. The *cross-battery* approach is based on the concept of *construct validation* originating in the article by Campbell and Fiske (1959), still in use today, showing how to establish *convergent validity* using multiple measures of

TABLE 10.7 Average Subtest Scaled Scores for Nine Core Normative-Population Profile Patterns Based on Six Leiter-R VR Profile Scales, Including Percent of Sample for Each Pattern, Average IQ, and Average Years of Education Completed by Parents for Each Pattern

Profile	%	Subtests Scale Scores						IQ	MED	FED
		FG	DA	FC	SO	RP	PF			
Very High	10	14	14	13	13	13	12	125	16	16
High Average Visualization	9	12	12	10	10	12	14	114	15	15
High Average Reasoning	12	9	12	12	13	12	11	112	16	16
Low DA	10	11	8	11	11	12	11	105	14	14
Low RP	13	10	11	12	10	7	11	101	17	17
Low PF	9	10	10	12	10	10	6	99	15	15
Low FC	12	10	9	6	10	10	8	92	14	14
Low Average	12	7	9	9	7	10	9	89	13	14
Very Low	13	7	6	7	6	6	8	77	12	13

NOTE : *N* = 983 (ages 6–20) from the Leiter-R normative sample. % = percentage of subjects matching the pattern; IQ = average Leiter-R Full Scale IQ. Average home educational backgrounds were estimated from Mother's (MED) and Father's (FED) number of years of education completed. Subtest abbreviations are DA = Design Analogies, RP = Repeated Patterns, PF = Paper Folding, FC = Form Completion.

the same trait, ideally with different modes of assessment (e.g., methods such as self-ratings compared to peer ratings). The first comparison for the Leiter-R would be the contrast between the VR and AM batteries. Next, contrasts could be extended to comparisons with other cognitive batteries that have been analyzed from a CHC-theory perspective (e.g., most of the major intelligence and cognitive batteries, such as the Wechsler scales, the Kaufman batteries, the Stanford-Binet, and the Woodcock-Johnson cognitive tests included in McGrew & Flanagan, 1998). Each contrast among pairs of cognitive tests would use the Campbell and Fiske logic of comparing measures of the same construct (e.g., fluid reasoning) across tests created by different authors using different types of items or tasks.

1. *Full IQ vs. Memory Screener or Memory Process.* The AM battery provides six composites (see Table 10.4), and two of them (Memory Screener and Memory Process) have been studied (Roid & Miller, 1997) in terms of comparisons to overall IQ on the VR battery. The test manual appendices show that a difference of 16.63 (rounded to 17) is required for statistical significance at the .05 level. Malissa had a Full IQ estimate of 105 and a Memory Screener composite of 87, producing a difference of 18 points. This significant difference, due to the very low Associated Pairs (AP) score of 5, seems to reflect disruptions in Malissa's memory processes. Inspection of her AM subtest scores will show (see Table 10.6) that the subtests in the Memory Process composite (FM, VC, and SM) are all in the average, 10–12 scaled score range, and thus would not show a difference when contrasted with Malissa's average-level IQ of 105.

2. *Leiter-R vs. other cognitive battery composites.* The Leiter-R test manual reported concurrent validity studies of Leiter-R correlated with WISC-III (Wechsler, 1991), Stanford-Binet—Fourth Edition (SB4;

Thorndike et al., 1986), and WJ-R Cognitive Tests (Woodcock & Mather, 1989). Cross-battery comparisons can be made (see McGrew & Flanagan, 1998) based on the major cognitive factors measured by the Leiter-R—Nonverbal Reasoning (Fluid composite, SO & RP in the VR battery), Visualization (Visualization composites or FG, FC, PF, FR in the VR battery), Memory (composites or AP, FM, RM, SM, etc.), and Attention (AS being the preferred marker subtest for this factor). Fluid Reasoning can be compared to the Matrices subtest in SB4 and the nonverbal portion of the SB5 (Roid, 2003b), Matrix Reasoning in WISC-IV (Wechsler, 2003), and Analysis-Synthesis of the WJ-R or *WJ III Tests of Cognitive Abilitie*s (Mather & Woodcock, 2001). Visualization on Leiter-R can also be compared to the Nonverbal Visual-Spatial subtest of SB5, the Perceptual Reasoning Index of WISC-IV, and the Spatial Relations subtest of WJ III. Additional cross-battery comparisons are presented in Flanagan and Ortiz (2001) and McGrew and Flanagan (1998).

Step 7: Qualitative Observations and Rating Scale Analysis

Additional qualitative observations of test-taking behavior by the child can be conducted along with analyses of certain clusters of subtest items, the results of the rating scales, and the process of "testing the limits" after the standardized testing is completed. Each of these will be discussed in turn. Initially, the experienced examiner looks for inattention, distraction, oppositional behavior, depression, anxiety, or fatigue and illness in the child taking the test. These behaviors are noted on the Record Form and must be used to temper conclusions or hypotheses derived from analysis of Leiter-R scores and patterns. Sattler (2001) has a wealth of suggestions for noting behaviors, and, if necessary in special cases, instruments such as the Test Observation Form (McConaughy & Achenbach, 2004) may be helpful. Second, the examiner looks for portions of subtests where the child's behavior was unexpected or significantly different from other portions of the battery or that specific subtest. For example, as shown in Table 10.6, the Leiter-R manual separates the pairs of pictures in Associated Pairs (AM battery) that depict familiar pairings (e.g., cat and kitten) from other random pairings. Malissa did surprisingly better on the random pairings compared to the familiar ones (of course, her overall performance on the AP subtest was very low—scaled score of 6—perhaps because she did poorly on pairs familiar to other children).

Third, the examiner can complete the Examiner Rating Scale included at the end of the Record Form, after the Leiter-R has been completed. Also, a parent or teacher can be asked to give the Parent- or Teacher-Rating Scales. For older children (ages 9–20), a Self-Rating scale is also available. These scales have some areas of content in common, such as items covering attention, activity level, impulsivity, emotionality, sociability, and severed behaviors. The scales are designed for special sensitivity to the lower-functioning (more negative) range of these separate categories of behaviors, and standardized for the lower end of the scaled score distribution. Therefore, the scores in the lower end of the scale—1 through the mean of 10—are provided to identify children with problematic behaviors. In addition, all of the scales (Examiner, Parent, Teacher, or Self) have composite scores for two major contrasting areas—Cognitive/Social, and Emotions/Self-Regulation. These composites are scored on an IQ-like standard score (mean 100, *SD* 15) and are valuable for showing strengths and weaknesses in the behavioral, social, and emotional realms. One important use of the Examiner ratings reported in the test manual (Roid & Miller, 1997) is employing the Cognitive/Social composite score to assist in identifying learning disabilities or attention-deficit conditions. Also, it should be noted that Nordlund (1998) found higher correlations between the Parent and Self ratings of children with learning disabilities or ADHD as compared to the correlations between Examiner and Parent ratings. This suggests placing more weight on the Parent scales in evaluating behavior, which certainly makes common sense.

VALIDITY

Numerous studies providing content-, criterion-, and construct-related evidence of validity were included in the test manual (Roid & Miller, 1997). Highlights of these studies are listed below, and are also listed in McCallum, Bracken, and Wasserman (2001).

Content-Related Evidence

Two types of evidence were presented—expert judgment and data-based item analysis. The 174 examiners and ethnic- and gender-issue experts reviewed all of the items, pictures, and directions for each of the 20 Leiter-R subtests, and adjustments were made between the Tryout (Field) edition and the Standardization edition, and for the final published edition. Any items or material problematic for either gender or any of the ethnic minority groups were edited prior to standardization or deleted for the final published version. Items were written or selected for the Leiter-R based on expert matching of the content and task of each item to the detailed specifications for cognitive factors in Carroll (1993) and the CHC theory. Also, extensive item analyses (classical and item-response theory—IRT—methods) were conducted, including differential item functioning (item bias analysis; Holland & Wainer, 1993), and any problematic items were deleted or changed. Extensive studies of the fit of each item to the IRT model (Wright & Linacre, 1999; Rasch, 1980) and to each composite scale were conducted, and, as described by Kamphaus (2001), provide content-related evidence of validity.

Criterion-Related Evidence

Extensive studies of mean differences between normative and special/clinical groups were conducted for the Leiter-R. Validity studies included 9 groups of children—those with communication disorders, deafness, orthopedic delays, traumatic brain injury, intellectual deficiency (mental retardation), ADHD, intellectual giftedness, learning disabilities, and English-as-second language (ESL). Also the Leiter-R IQ was correlated in separate studies with the original Leiter (.85, $n = 124$), the WISC-III Full Scale IQ (.86, $n = 121$), and various subtests of the SB4 and WJ-R. In terms of correlation with achievement, the Leiter-R Brief and Full Scale IQ were correlated with the *Wechsler Individual Achievement Test* (WIAT; Wechsler, 1992) and the *Woodcock-Johnson—Revised Tests of Achievement* (Woodcock & Johnson, 1989). Correlations for WIAT ranged from .69 to .83 for predicting achievement with a nonverbal instrument. Correlations for the WJ-R ranged from .79 to .82 compared to the typical correlations between IQ and achievement, which are in the .60 range as summarized by Naglieri and Bornstein (2003). Also, the Leiter-R Full Scale IQ predicted group-achievement scores in mathematics (.67) and reading (.70) for the Stanford Achievement Test (Harcourt Assessment, 1995).

Construct-Related Evidence

Studies of the cross-sectional trends in age-level means for the raw scores and the Growth scores of the Leiter-R showed a growth curve pattern very similar to that found with the WJ-R and WJ-III W-scale scores across ages 24 months to 240 months. An experimental intervention, using a test–retest design and the mediated instruction method of Feuerstein, Rand, and Hoffman (1979) was successful in showing growth on four Leiter-R subtests (given before and after the instruction), as evidence of Leiter-R sensitivity to growth in problem-solving ability.

Extensive exploratory and confirmatory factor analyses of both the Tryout and Final editions of the Leiter-R confirmed four or five major factors measured by the combined VR and AM batteries (Reasoning, Visualization, Associative and Recognition Memory, and Attention). For example, confirmatory analyses with LISREL (Joreskog & Sorbom, 1999) showed excellent fit (1.84 and 1.63 chi-square divided by degrees of freedom, and goodness-of-fit indexes of .896 and .924) for the five-factor models at ages 6–10 or 11–20 respectively. At ages 4–5, the two memory factors were confirmed as merged into a general memory factor.

Recently Published Validity Evidence

In a study of concurrent validity, Hooper and Bell (2006) found a correlation of .72 between the Leiter-R Full Scale IQ and the Universal Nonverbal Intelligence Test (UNIT; Bracken & McCallum, 1998; McCallum et al., 2001) for a sample of 100 students (6–14 years old) from a southeastern part of the United States. In another concurrent validity study, Tsatsanis, et al. (2003) showed that the Leiter-R correlated with the original Leiter .87 (Brief IQ) or .97 (Full Scale IQ) in a sample of 26 children (ages 4–16) with autism. The Leiter-R and Leiter were also similar in classification (Kappa coefficient was .83) of the level of functioning (MR, borderline, low average, average, high average). Also, the study showed that Leiter scores were somewhat higher than Leiter-R IQs (expected by the historical shift in normative samples; Flynn, 1987). Glenn and Cunningham (2005) found significant differences between Leiter-R Brief IQ subtests for 46 young people with Down syndrome (ages 16–24), with the Reasoning subtests (SO and RP) being lower than the Visualization subtests (FG and FC), as would be expected in this form of intellectual deficiency.

Dissertations Using the Leiter-R

Several studies presenting validity evidence for the Leiter-R have appeared as unpublished doctoral dissertations. Bos (1995) conducted factor analyses on the Field edition of Leiter-R confirming the major factors and Bay (1996) conducted an exploratory factor analysis that also verified the internal structure of the VR battery. Nordlund (1998) presented evidence for the validity of the rating scales to reveal strengths and weaknesses in children with learning disabilities and ADHD. Several dissertations applied the Leiter-R to special groups (Head, 1996, and Nordlund, 1998, for ADHD; Koehn, 1998, for ESL—Spanish; Nordland, 1998, and Olson, 1998, for learning disabilities; Quinn, 1999, for TBI).

SUMMARY

The Leiter-R provides a comprehensive assessment of nonverbal cognitive abilities, ranging from Full Scale IQ to specific reasoning, visualization, memory, and attention tests. The Visualization and Reasoning (VR) battery of 10 subtests (4 subtests in a Brief IQ or 6 subtests in a Full Scale IQ) is widely used in current research on autism, intellectual deficiency, and evaluation of exceptionalities (special education and giftedness education) for students with limited English proficiency (known by the acronyms ESL, ELL, LEP, etc.), communication difficulties, hard-of-hearing and deafness, and speech and motor delays and disabilities. Given the multicultural nature of western society, the Leiter-R appears to be essential as an additional tool for the school-based and clinical assessment professional. The subtests of the Leiter-R show an excellent pattern of common, specific, and error variance (as documented by factor analysis), with a pattern of 46%, 34%, and 20% respectively for the three types of variance. In practical terms, this means that examiners can be confident that subtests share enough in common to accurately estimate global ability (IQ), have enough specific variation to provide a profile of strengths and weaknesses (e.g., as required in the new IDEA, 2004), and have limited degrees of error of measurement. Recently published articles show the advantages of the Leiter-R as a comprehensive, diagnostic battery for the assessment of children with special needs such as autism, speech impairment, and intellectual deficiency.

REFERENCES

Achenbach, T. M. (2000). *Achenbach system of empirically based assessment*. Burlington, VT: ASEBA.

AERA/APA/NCME: American Educational Research Association, American Psychological Association, and National Council on Measurement in Education (1999). *Standards for educational and psychological testing*. Washington, DC: Author.

Aldenderfer, M. S., & Blashfield, R. K. (1984). *Cluster analysis*. Newbury Park, CA: Sage.

American Academy of Pediatrics. (2000). Clinical practice guideline: Diagnosis and evaluation of children with attention-deficit/hyperactivity disorder. *Pediatrics, 105,* 1158–1170.

American Psychiatric Association. (2000). *Diagnostic and statistical manual of mental disorders* (DSM-IV-TR) (4th ed.) (Text Revision). Washington, DC: Author.

Baddeley, A. D. (1986). *Working memory*. Oxford: Clarendon Press.

Bannatyne, A. (1974). Diagnosis: A note on recategorization of the WISC scaled scores. *Journal of Learning Disabilities, 7,* 2.

Barkley, R. A. (1990). *Attention deficit hyperactivity disorder: A handbook for diagnosis and treatment*. New York: Guilford Press.

Bay, M. (1996). *An exploratory factor analysis of the Leiter-R*. Unpublished doctoral dissertation, George Fox University, Newberg, Oregon.

Bos, J. S. (1995). *Factor structure of the field edition of the Leiter International Performance Scale—Revised*. Unpublished doctoral dissertation, George Fox University, Newberg, Oregon.

Bracken, B. A., & McCallum, R. S. (1998). *The Universal Nonverbal Intelligence Test*. Austin, TX: Pro-Ed.

Butter, E. M., Mulick, J. A., & Metz, B. (2006). Eight case reports of learning recovery in children with pervasive developmental disorders after early intervention. *Behavioral Interventions*, *21*, 227–243.

Campbell, D. T., & Fiske, D. W. (1959). Convergent and discriminant validation by the multitrait-multimethod matrix. *Psychological Bulletin*, *56*, 81–105.

Carr, J. (2005). Stability and change in cognitive ability over the life span: A comparison of populations with and without Down's syndrome. *Journal of Intellectual Disability Research*, *49*(12), 915–928.

Carroll, J. B. (1993). *Human cognitive abilities: A survey of factor-analytic studies*. Cambridge; New York: Cambridge University Press.

Cattell, R. B. (1943). The measurement of intelligence. *Psychological Bulletin*, *40*, 153–193.

Cattell, R. B. (1966). The scree test for the number of factors. *Multivariate Behavioral Research*, *1*, 245–276.

Cohen, J. (1988). *Statistical power analysis for the behavioral sciences* (2nd ed.). Mahwah, NJ: Erlbaum.

Dana, R. H. (2005). *Multicultural assessment* (2nd ed.). Mahwah, NJ: Erlbaum.

Dunn, L. M., & Dunn, L. M. (1997). *Peabody Picture Vocabulary Test—Third Edition*. Circle Pines, MN: American Guidance Service/Pearson Assessments.

Dunn, L. M., Dunn, L. M., & NFER-Nelson (1997). *British Picture Vocabulary Scale—Second Edition*. London, UK: NFER-Nelson.

Farrant, B. M., Fletcher, J., & Mayberry, M. T. (2006). Specific language impairment, theory of mind, and visual perspective taking: Evidence for simulation theory and the developmental role of language. *Child Development*, *77*(6), 1842–1853.

Feuerstein, R., Rand, Y., & Hoffman, M. D. (1979). *The dynamic assessment of retarded performers: The Learning Potential Assessment Device*. Baltimore, MD: University Park Press.

Flanagan, D. P., & Ortiz, S. O. (2001). *Essentials of cross-battery assessment*. New York: Wiley.

Flemmer, D. D., & Roid, G. H. (1997). Nonverbal intellectual assessment of Hispanic and speech-impaired adolescents. *Psychological Reports*, *80*, 1115–1122.

Flynn, J. R. (1987). Massive IQ gains in 14 nations: What IQ tests really measure. *Psychological Bulletin*, *101*, 171–191.

Glenn, S., & Cunningham, C. (2005). Performance of young people with Down syndrome on the Leiter-R and British Picture Vocabulary Scales. *Journal of Intellectual Disability Research*, *49*(4), 239–244.

Guilford, J. P., & Fruchter, B. (1978). *Fundamental statistics in psychology and education*. New York: McGraw-Hill.

Gustafsson, J. E. (1984). A unifying model for the structure of intellectual abilities. *Intelligence*, *8*, 179–203.

Harcourt Assessment (1995). *Stanford Achievement Tests (SAT)*. San Antonio, TX: Author.

Head, J. J. (1996). *Assessment of nonverbal cognitive processes in children with attention deficit hyperactivity disorder*. Unpublished doctoral dissertation, George Fox University, Newberg, Oregon.

Holland, P. W., & Wainer, H. (Eds.). (1993). *Differential item functioning*. Mahwah, NJ: Erlbaum.

Hooper, V. S., & Bell, S. M. (2006). Concurrent validity of the UNIT and Leiter-R. *Psychology in the Schools*, *43*(2), 143–148.

Horn, J. L. (1985). Remodeling old models of intelligence. In B. B. Wolman (Ed.), *Handbook of intelligence* (pp. 267–300). New York: Wiley.

Horn, J. L. (1994). Theory of fluid and crystallized intelligence. In R. J. Sternberg (Ed.), *Encyclopedia of human intelligence* (pp. 443–451). New York: Macmillan.

Horn, J. L., & Cattell, R. B. (1966). Refinement and test of the theory of fluid and crystallized general intelligences. *Journal of Educational Psychology*, *57*, 253–270.

Horst, D. P., Tallmadge, G. K., & Wood, C. T. (1975). *A practical guide to measuring project impact on student achievement*. Washington, DC: U.S. Department of Education.

IDEA: Individuals with Disabilities Education Improvement Act (2004). Public Law No. 108-446, §632, 118 Stat. 2744.

Joreskog, K. G., & Sorbom, D. (1999). *LISREL 8: User's reference guide*. Chicago: Scientific Software.

Kamphaus, R. W. (2001). *Clinical assessment of child and adolescent intelligence* (2nd ed.). Boston: Allyn & Bacon.

Kaufman, A. S. (1994). *Intelligent testing with the WISC-III*. New York: Wiley.

Kaufman, A. S., & Kaufman, N. (1993). *Kaufman Adult Intelligence Test (KAIT)*. Circle Pines, MN: American Guidance Service/Pearson Assessment.

Kaufman, A. S., & Lichtenberger, E. O. (1999). *Essentials of WAIS-III assessment*. New York: Wiley.

Koehn, R. D. (1998). *WISC-III and Leiter-R assessments of intellectual abilities in Hispanic-American children with English-as-a-second language*. Unpublished doctoral dissertation, George Fox University, Newberg, Oregon.

Leiter, R. G. (1966). Development of the Leiter International Performance Scale. Unpublished audio tape by Thomas K. Fagan, School Psychology Program, University of Memphis, TN.

Leiter, R. G. (1979). *Instruction manual for the Leiter International Performance Scale*. Wood Dale, IL: Stoelting.

Leslie, L., & Caldwell, J. (2001). *Qualitative Reading Inventory—3 (QRI-3)*. New York: Addison-Wesley Longman.

Lezak, M. D. (1995). *Neuropsychological assessment* (3rd Ed.). New York: Oxford University Press.

Lord, F. M. (1980). *Applications of item response theory to practical testing problems*. Mahwah, NJ: Erlbaum.

Mather, N., & Woodcock, R. W. (2001). *WJ III Tests of Cognitive Abilities examiner's manual*. Rolling Meadows, IL: Riverside.

McCallum, R. S., Bracken, B. A., & Wasserman, J. D. (2001). *Essentials of nonverbal assessment*. New York: Wiley.

McConaughy, S. H., & Achenbach, T. M. (2004). *Manual for the Test Observation Form for Ages 2–18*. Burlington, VT: ASEBA.

McDermott, P. A., Fantuzzo, J. W., & Glutting, J. J. (1990). Just say no to subtest analysis: A critique on Wechsler theory and practice. *Journal of Psychoeducational Assessment*, 8, 290–302.

McGrew, K. S., & Flanagan, D. P. (1998). *The intelligence test desk reference (ITDR): Cf-Gc cross battery assessment*. Boston: Allyn & Bacon.

McGrew, K. S., & Woodcock, R. W. (2001). *Woodcock-Johnson III: Technical Manual*. Itasca, IL: Riverside.

Naglieri, J. A., & Bornstein, B. T. (2003). Intelligence and achievement: Just how correlated are they? *Journal of Psychoeducational Assessment*, 21, 244–260.

Nordlund, C. B. (1998). *An examination of behavior ratings and rater differences of ADHD subjects on the Leiter-R rating scales*. Unpublished doctoral dissertation, George Fox University, Newberg, Oregon.

Norusis, M. J. (1990). *SPSS base system user's guide*. Chicago: SPSS.

Nunnally, J. C. (1978). *Psychometric theory (2nd ed.)*. New York: McGraw-Hill.

Olson, R. C. (1998). *Subtypes of learning disabilities on a nonverbal cognitive instrument*. Unpublished doctoral dissertation, George Fox University, Newberg, Oregon.

Quinn, D. C. (1999). *Nonverbal cognitive performance of children with traumatic brain injury using the Leiter-R Tryout Edition*. Unpublished doctoral dissertation, George Fox University, Newberg, Oregon.

Rasch, G. (1980). *Probabilistic models for some intelligence and attainment tests*. Chicago: University of Chicago Press.

Roid, G. H. (1994). Patterns of writing skills derived from cluster analysis of direct-writing assessments. *Applied Measurement in Education*, 7(2), 159–170.

Roid, G. H. (2003a). *Stanford-Binet Intelligence Scales—Fifth Edition, Interpretive Manual*. Austin, TX: Pro-Ed.

Roid, G. H. (2003b). *Stanford-Binet Intelligence Scales—Fifth Edition, Technical Manual*. Austin, TX: Pro-Ed.

Roid, G. H., & Madsen, D. M. (1998). *Leiter International Performance Scale—Revised: Computer scoring manual*. Wood Dale, IL: Stoelting.

Roid, G. H., & Miller, L. J. (1997). *Leiter International Performance Scale—Revised*. Wood Dale, IL: Stoelting.

Roid, G. H., & Miller, L. J. (1999). *Stoelting Brief Intelligence Scale manual*. Wood Dale, IL: Stoelting.

Roid, G. H., Nellis, L., & McLellan, M. (2003). Use of the Leiter-R and S-BIT. In R. S. McCallum (Ed.), *Handbook of nonverbal assessment*. Boston: Kluwer/Plenum.

Roid, G. H., Prifitera, A., & Weiss, L.G. (1993). Replication of the WISC-III factor structure in an independent sample. *Journal of Psychoeducational Assessment*, 11, 6–21.

Sattler, J. M. (1988). *Assessment of children* (3rd ed.). San Diego: Author.

Sattler, J. M. (2001). *Assessment of children: Cognitive applications* (4th ed.). La Mesa, CA: Author.

Tellegen, A., & Briggs, P. F. (1967). Old wine in new skins: Grouping Wechsler subtests into new scales. *Journal of Consulting Psychology, 31*, 499–506.

Thorndike, R. L., Hagen, E. P., & Sattler, J. M. (1986). *The Stanford-Binet Intelligence Scale—Fourth Edition Guide for Administering and Scoring*. Itasca, IL: Riverside.

Tsatsanis, K. D., Dartnall, N., Cicchetti, D., Sparrow, S. S., Klin, A., & Volkmar, F. R. (2003). Concurrent validity and classification accuracy of the Leiter and Leiter-R in low-functioning children with autism. *Journal of Autism and Developmental Disorders, 33*(1), 23–30.

Ward, J. (1963). Hierarchical grouping to optimize an objective function. *Journal of the American Statistical Association, 56*, 236–244.

Webster, P. E., Plante, A. S., & Couvillion, L. M. (1997). Phonological impairment and prereading: Update on a longitudinal study. *Journal of Learning Disabilities, 30*(4), 365–375.

Wechsler, D. (1991). *Wechsler Intelligence Scale for Children—Third Edition*. San Antonio, TX: Psychological Corporation.

Wechsler, D. (1992). *Wechsler Individual Achievement Test (WIAT)*. San Antonio, TX: Psychological Corporation.

Wechsler, D. (2003). *Wechsler Intelligence Scale for Children—Fourth Edition*. San Antonio, TX: Psychological Corporation.

Woodcock, R. W. (1999). What can Rasch-based scores convey about a person's test performance? In S. E. Embretson & S. L. Hershberger (Eds.), *The new rules of measurement: What every psychologist and educator should know* (pp. 105–128). Mahwah, NJ: Erlbaum.

Woodcock, R. W., & Dahl, M. N. (1971). A common scale for the measurement of person ability and test item difficulty (AGS Paper No. 10). Circle Pines, MN: American Guidance Service.

Woodcock, R. W., & Johnson, M. B. (1989). *Woodcock-Johnson—Revised, Tests of Achievement*. Itasca, IL: Riverside.

Woodcock, R. W., & Mather, N. (1989). *Woodcock-Johnson—Revised, Tests of Cognitive Abilities*. Itasca, IL: Riverside.

Wright, B. D., & Linacre, J. M. (1999). *WINSTEPS: Rasch analysis for all two-facet models*. Chicago: MESA Press.

Universal Nonverbal Intelligence Test (UNIT)

Bruce A. Bracken, R. Steve McCallum

THEORY UNDERLYING THE UNIVERSAL NONVERBAL INTELLIGENCE TEST

The Universal Nonverbal Intelligence Test (UNIT; Bracken & McCallum, 1998) was published by Riverside Publishing Company as a language-free test of cognitive ability to meet the needs of a diverse U.S. population. Nonverbal assessment is a critical component of psychoeducational assessment, especially given the changing demographics of the United States. According to the 2000 U.S. Census report, 31,844,979 people in the United States spoke a primary language other than English and nearly 2,000,000 U.S. residents spoke no English (U.S. Bureau of the Census, 2000).

According to estimates from the 1997 reauthorization of the Individuals with Disabilities Education Act (IDEA; P.L. 105-17), nearly one of three people in the country was a member of an ethnic or racial minority group, and collectively minorities comprise an even larger percentage of public school children. In some of America's largest cities, minorities comprise an overwhelming percentage of the population: Miami (approximately 84%), Chicago (89%), and

Houston (88%). Not only are there large numbers of people in the United States who speak English as a second language, but there is an incredible number of primary languages spoken. For example, more than 200 languages are spoken in the Greater Chicago public schools alone (Pasko, 1994) and an estimated 140 languages are spoken throughout California schools (Unz, 1997). The trend for increased numbers of linguistic minorities does not exist only in major urban or coastal cities; in 2002, Forester estimated that 61 languages were spoken in the schools of the Appalachian city of Knoxville, Tennessee.

It is important to note that minority children also are commonly overrepresented in special education classes (e.g., although African Americans comprise 16% of the population, they constitute 21% of the enrollment in special education) and underrepresented in classes for the gifted (Ford, 1996; Jensen, 1968; Naglieri & Ford, 2003, 2005; Oakland & Parmelee, 1985). In most school systems throughout the country, intelligence tests are used as part of the referral-to-placement process, and they contribute to the overidentification of ethnic and linguistic minorities. Because it is not feasible to adapt or translate tests to accommodate all linguistically different students or students with special needs, use of nonverbal methods to assess these linguistically and culturally diverse children is a viable approach.

Similar assessment-related challenges exist for children with limited hearing abilities or those students who have receptive and expressive language disabilities. Students with communication difficulties are at an unfair disadvantage when assessed by means that require written, spoken, or receptive language. Best practice requires that educators select and administer technically sound tests that will *not* result in discriminatory practices for examinees who have language-based limitations and/or are culturally different or have speech and language deficits. To meet the needs of children who speak English as a second language or who have communication difficulties, the UNIT addresses the issue of *consequential validity* through an administration that requires no receptive or expressive language from the examiner or the examinee.

Several innovative features characterize the UNIT. First, test administration using examiner demonstrations, nonscored sample items, unique and teachable *checkpoint* items, and a standardized set of eight universal gestures helps ensure that the examinee understands the nature of the task prior to attempting the subtest for credit. Second, the UNIT allows for motoric and motor-reduced (i.e., pointing) responses, which facilitates an equitable administration for students with motor difficulties. Third, UNIT test items include line drawings of people and common objects that are generally recognized within all cultures. Fourth, the UNIT is model-based and assesses both reasoning—a higher-order mental processing activity—as well as complex memory. Additionally, half of the UNIT subtests are symbolically oriented and allow for verbal mediation to facilitate solving the problem; the remaining subtests are nonsymbolic and solved more holistically. UNIT subtest and scale scores are interpreted in light of these theoretical underpinnings. Fifth, the validation of the UNIT included samples of non-English-speaking individuals from within and outside the United States and standardization data were obtained from examinees from diverse cultures and children residing in the United States who have limited English facility and/or special education diagnoses. Sixth, the examiner can control UNIT administration time by using one of three administration formats: a two-subtest battery, a four-subtest "standard" battery, and an extended six-subtest battery. Seventh, reliability estimates were calculated not only for the entire standardization sample, but for two critical cut points (i.e., for students with FSIQs near 70 and those with FSIQs near 130), as well as for students of different genders, races, and ethnicities. Finally, a large array of support resources are available for using the UNIT, including a training video, a university training manual, and a computerized scoring and interpretation software program.

DESCRIPTION OF THE UNIT

UNIT Subtest Background and Structure

Examiners administer three memory and three reasoning subtests as part of the UNIT Extended Battery. This battery, as well as the two briefer batteries, are based on a 2×2 structural/theoretical administration and interpretation scheme (Figure 11.1). As a result of the 2×2 structural scheme, each of the Extended, Standard, and Abbreviated batteries produce several scale scores that can be calculated, including a Full Scale score (FSIQ), Memory Quotient (MQ), Reasoning Quotient (RQ), Symbolic Quotient (SQ), and Nonsymbolic Quotient (NSQ). Individual subtest scores can be derived for each of the six subtests for further analysis of the examinee's performance. The first three subtests described in the following section are designed to assess memory; the second three assess reasoning.

1. *Symbolic Memory (Memory and Symbolic Scales):* The examinee is presented a stimulus for

UNIT Scales and Subtests	Memory Subtests	Reasoning Subtests
Symbolic Subtests	Symbolic Memory Object Memory	Analogic Reasoning
Nonsymbolic Subtests	Spatial Memory	Cube Design Mazes

FIGURE 11.1
Structure of the UNIT Scales and Subtests for the Extended Battery

five seconds and then recalls and recreates sequences of visually presented universal symbols of man, woman, boy, girl, and baby, using two colored chips (e.g., green boy, black woman).

2. *Spatial Memory (Memory and Nonsymbolic Scales):* The examinee is exposed to a matrix with green or black circles of varying number and location to be recalled and recreated on a blank 3 × 3 or 4 × 4 cell grid, using black and/or green plastic chips for placement.

3. *Object Memory (Memory and Symbolic Scales):* The examinee is shown a visual array of common objects (e.g., shoe, telephone, tree) for five seconds, after which the examinee identifies the exposed objects from a larger array of pictured objects.

4. *Cube Design (Reasoning and Nonsymbolic Scales):* Using bi-colored (i.e., green and white) cubes, the examinee completes a three-dimensional block design using one to nine green and white blocks to match a pictured stimulus object.

5. *Analogic Reasoning (Reasoning and Symbolic Scales):* The examinee completes matrix analogies using common objects (e.g., hand/glove, foot/?) and novel geometric/figural analogies.

6. *Mazes (Reasoning and Nonsymbolic Scales):* The examinee completes a series of mazes by tracing a path through each maze from the center starting point to an exit.

UNIT Scales

UNIT subtests combine theoretically to assess functioning in the areas of Memory, Reasoning, Symbolic, and Nonsymbolic processing.

ADMINISTRATION AND SCORING

UNIT administration and scoring is straightforward and follows a highly similar procedure for each of the six subtests, including a description of the materials needed, demonstration of the task, use of sample items and checkpoint items, and common scoring procedures.

UNIT Materials

Materials required to administer the UNIT include a stopwatch, number-2 lead pencils, one red-lead pencil, and two test booklets (one for the Mazes subtest, and one for recording the students' performance on the remaining five subtests). Except for Mazes and Object Memory (optional subtests, to be administered as part of the Extended Battery only), the stimulus plates for all subtests are contained within a single standup easel. Object Memory stimuli are presented on a small separate easel. The comprehensive easel containing the four Standard Battery subtests contains subtest stimuli printed on the front and back of each page for efficiency and economy; colored tabs are provided to inform the examiner as to the direction of administration (i.e., tabs with subtest names in green alert the examiner that the book is oriented in the correct direction for those subtests). Cube Design, Symbolic Memory, and Object Memory all have additional pieces (e.g., cubes, chips, response mats) that are placed on the desktop during administration.

Administration Time

Completion of all six subtests requires approximately 45 minutes; the four-subtest Standard Battery requires about one-half hour; the two-subtest Abbreviated Battery takes about 15 minutes. The Abbreviated Battery is used for screening purposes (Symbolic Memory and Cube Design), the Standard Battery is for most purposes including placement decisions (the Abbreviated Battery subtests, plus Spatial Memory, Matrix Analogies), and the Extended Battery is for diagnostic purposes (the Standard Battery subtests, plus Object Memory and Mazes).

Scoring

Raw scores for each item are summed to provide a subtest total raw score. Raw scores are transformed to standard scores either by using the norm tables provided in the *UNIT Examiner's Manual* (1998) or by using the UNIT Compuscore scoring software (Bracken & McCallum, 2001). Raw scores are converted to standard scores with a traditional standard score metric (i.e., mean = 100, standard deviation = 15); subtests report scaled scores, each with a mean of 10 and standard deviation of 3.

Nonverbal Administration

Although administration of the UNIT is 100% nonverbal, the examiner may establish rapport or communicate with the examinee to whatever extent possible using language (e.g., if they have a common language), and may discuss extra-test issues to establish rapport. The examiner presents the UNIT stimuli nonverbally using demonstrations and eight standardized nonverbal gestures presented in the Manual, on the *Administration at a Glance* guide, and on the UNIT training video. To aid in teaching subtest task demands to the examinee, the examiner may liberally use demonstration items, sample items, and *checkpoint* items to ensure the examinee understands what is expected. Checkpoint items are transitional items

that provide the examinee with feedback for items completed incorrectly; however, unlike Demonstration and Sample Items, Checkpoint Items are scored for credit.

ADMINISTRATION AND SCORING

Memory

Symbolic Memory

Subtest stimulus plates are presented sequentially on an easel. The easel contains plates showing pictures of one or more of the following universal human figures, in series of ever-increasing numbers of objects to be recalled (i.e., a green baby, a black baby, a green girl, a black girl, a green boy, a black boy, a green woman, a black woman, a green man, a black man). The examinee is presented the stimulus plate to examine for five seconds, and then is instructed through gestures to replicate the order shown on the stimulus plate, using 1 1/2"×1 1/2" plastic response chips. Each chip depicts one of the universal human figures, and can be moved by the examinee to reproduce the array depicted on and recalled from the stimulus plate. The task has no completion time limits. Each correct item is assigned one point credit, assuming each chip of correct color, gender, and human figure is arrayed in the proper number and sequence.

Spatial Memory

For this subtest, the examiner briefly presents a series of items depicted on stimulus plates on the administration easel. The stimulus plates include grids showing one or more green or black polka dots placed within cells. Easier items use a 3 × 3 grid with a few polka dots embedded within; the more difficult items require a 4 × 4 grid and incrementally more colored dots. The stimulus plate is shown to the examinee for five seconds and then is removed from view. The examinee places response chips on a blank grid that is placed on the tabletop in front of the child.

Spatial Memory (SM) has no time limits. Each correct response is assigned one point credit.

Object Memory

Object Memory (OM) presents to the examinee pictures of common objects arranged on stimulus plates located on an administration easel. The easel is laid flat on the table and the examinee is shown a plate containing line drawings of one or more objects for five seconds; the examinee is then shown a second plate containing pictures from the first plate *and* drawings of "distractor objects." The examinee identifies only the objects on the second plate that were shown on the first plate. To create a semipermanent response, the examinee places black chips on the pictures selected. This memory task is not timed (other than the five-second exposure). To earn one point credit, the examinee must identify correctly all objects shown on the stimulus plate, but no distractor objects.

Reasoning Scale

Cube Design

Cube Design (CD) requires the examinee to manipulate as many as nine cubes to replicate three-dimensional designs shown on a stimulus plate. Each cube contains six facets: two white sides, two green sides, and two sides that contain diagonals (triangles), one green and one white. The cubes can be arranged to replicate the three-dimensional figures depicted on the stimulus plates. This task is timed to ensure closure is reached for each item, but the time limits are liberal to emphasize the power. Except for the very early items, which are scored either correct or incorrect and yield a maximum of one point per item, examinees may earn up to three points (per item) for a correct response. Each facet of the three-dimensional construction is judged to be either correct or incorrect, and each correct facet is assigned one point credit. Bonus points may also be assigned for fast completion,

but a maximum of two bonus points can be accrued for any three-point item.

Analogic Reasoning

Analogic Reasoning (AR) requires the examinee to solve analogies presented in a matrix format, and is not timed. The examinee is directed to indicate which one of several options best completes a two-cell or a four-cell analogy. Task solution requires the examinee to determine the relationships between objects. For example, in the four-cell matrix the first cell might depict a fish and the second water; the third cell might show a bird, and the fourth cell would be blank. The examinee would select from several options the picture that best completes the matrix. In this case, a picture of the sky would be a correct response, which is assigned one point credit.

Mazes

Mazes requires the examinee to complete a path throughout a maze using a number-2 lead pencil. The examinee is presented a maze showing a mouse in the center and one or more pieces of cheese on the outside of the maze (i.e., real or foil exits). The task is to determine the correct path from the center to the (correct) piece of cheese. The examinee is stopped after committing his or her first error and the item is discontinued. The task is timed, though the time limits are quite liberal. Each decision point is scored and correct decisions are assigned one point credit.

Use of Scoring and Report Writing Software

The *Compuscore* program (Bracken & McCallum, 2001) aids examiners in creating various standard scores and descriptive results (e.g., percentile ranks, ability classifications) for subtests and scales. In addition, the program generates text that qualitatively describes the scores, reflecting strengths and weaknesses and related instructional suggestions. Finally, the program allows the examiner to edit the content to add results from other tests to create a final comprehensive report. Various report options allow the examiner to choose and print reports with relatively more or less detail.

STANDARDIZATION, NORMS, AND PSYCHOMETRICS

Readers are urged to consult the UNIT Manual for a detailed description of the standardization sample and results of numerous special studies conducted to assess UNIT technical adequacy, including reliability, validity, and fairness data for a variety of populations. We summarize some of the most important data from the Manual in the following sections of this chapter. In addition, we describe results of various relevant studies published independently after the UNIT was released in 1998.

Characteristics of the Standardization Sample

The UNIT standardization sample (2,100 children and adolescents) followed a carefully designed, stratified, random sampling plan; consequently, the sample closely represented the U.S. population of children from ages 5 years, 0 months through 17 years, 11 months, 30 days. Data were obtained from 108 sites in 38 states. Strata included: sex, race, Hispanic origin, region, community setting, classroom placement (including proportional representation of those receiving special education services), and socioeconomic status (i.e., parental educational attainment). Numerous tables in the Manual show the close correspondence between the sample and population percentages based on U.S. census data. In addition to the 2,100 children and adolescents in the normative sample, an additional 1,700 students were assessed for UNIT reliability, fairness, or validity studies.

Reliability of the Scales

UNIT reliability data reported in the Manual are strong and meet the field's expectations for tests used for eligibility and placement purposes. Extensive data are reported for a variety of populations and by race, sex, exceptionality, and important decision-making levels in the Manual. The average scale and full scale reliability coefficients range from .86 to .96 for the typical and clinical/exceptional samples across all batteries, with comparable reliabilities for males, females, whites, blacks, and Hispanics. Subsample FSIQ internal consistency coefficients range from .91 to .93; stability coefficients (corrected for restriction in range) range from .79 to .84. The average test–retest practice effects (over an approximately three-week interval) are 7.2, 5.0, and 4.8 IQ points for the Abbreviated Battery, Standard Battery, and Extended Battery, respectively.

USE OF THE TEST

The UNIT can be used for a variety of reasons, as suggested from the various interpretive strategies described below. For example, scores can be used for administrative decision making, to help determine eligibility for special education services, and to aid in pinpointing cognitive strengths and weaknesses. First and foremost, the UNIT is used to provide an equitable cognitive assessment for students who would be unfairly assessed with a language-loaded ability test.

Interpreting the UNIT

Norm-referenced multidimensional test interpretation is complicated, partly because it requires that examiners engage in a number of steps, consult numerous tables, consider a variety of cognitive models, consider carefully the limitations of the instruments they use, and finally and most importantly, make the test results relevant for real-world application. UNIT norm-referenced test interpretation is straightforward and allows the examiner to contrast the examinee's subtest and scale scores with normative data. The goal is to determine whether the student is within or beyond the range of ability that is considered typical (i.e., +/–1 *SD*). If the examinee exceeds the normal range, then the consideration is whether the student is functioning intellectually at levels that are significantly subnormal (e.g., levels of retardation) or above average (e.g., levels of giftedness). Norm-referenced assessment is the basis for most educational classification systems (e.g., giftedness, mental retardation).

In addition to normative interpretation, there are at least three other interpretive models available to interpret the UNIT (i.e., traditional ipsative strategies, subtest profile base-rate analyses, and cross-battery assessment—CBA). Traditional ipsative interpretation is somewhat controversial (Kaufman, 1994; McCallum, Bracken, & Wasserman, 2001; McDermott, Fantuzzo, & Glutting, 1990), but is frequently used by practitioners who want to get more information from the instruments they use than the strong predictive capabilities of an FSIQ. The goal of ipsative interpretation is to uncover intra-child relationships between cognitive strengths and weaknesses and important academic and work-related skills. We first describe traditional ipsative strategies, followed by brief descriptions of subtest base-rate profile analyses, then CBA. Citations are provided for more specific guidelines for the ipsative, base-rate, and CBA methods.

Ipsative Interpretation

Interpretation requires multiple steps and considerations. General steps for interpretation are discussed below, followed by a discussion of three specific interpretative procedures. The following guidelines are based on the psychometric strengths expressed in the UNIT Manual, and detailed guidelines are provided there and within Compuscore scoring and interpretation software (Bracken & McCallum, 2001). Guidelines are presented in brief form here; for a more in-depth approach to test interpretation the reader should consult Bracken (1992).

1. Interpret the UNIT composite or global score within a normative context. First, the FSIQ should be interpreted according to its relative standing in the population using standard scores, percentile ranks, and age equivalents. For multidimensional tests like the UNIT, it is useful to provide some statement regarding the representativeness of the score; that is, does the FSIQ adequately represent the examinee's overall intellectual functioning? Then, consider the next level of global scores—the scale scores (i.e., Reasoning Quotient, Memory Quotient, Symbolic Quotient, or Nonsymbolic Quotient). Are these scores comparable or do they deviate significantly from one another? If these scores show considerable variability, the most global score may not adequately represent the examinee's overall intellectual functioning. Considerable scatter reveals a profile with peaks and valleys and corresponding cognitive strengths and weaknesses. These relative strengths and weaknesses should be determined by examining magnitude of differences using statistical significance and frequency of occurrence data, as discussed below in Step 3.

2. The band of error of the UNIT FSIQ should be communicated next, using the composite score within a band of confidence framed by one or more standard errors of measure (SEMs).

3. Step 3 provides elaboration of Step 1 and transition to the more specific interpretative procedures described below. In Step 3, all UNIT standard scores should be compared *systematically*. As stated in Step 1, if UNIT scale (global) scores are highly variable (i.e., if there are statistically significant differences among them) the composite score cannot be considered to be representative of the examinee's overall intellectual functioning. However, if there is little variability (i.e.,

nonsignificant amounts of variability), the composite score may be considered as a reasonable estimate of the examinee's overall functioning.

Further description of the examinee's performance can be evaluated next. For example, the examiner may provide additional information about the nature of the UNIT and what it is presumed to measure; in addition, the examiner may indicate that the examinee's abilities in particular areas (e.g., short-term memory, reasoning) are uniformly developed (or not, as the case may be). The examinee's overall level of ability should provide implications about the examinee's prognosis for achievement. If qualitative (e.g., intra-subtest scatter) and quantitative (i.e., variable scores) data show variability in the examinee's performance, further analysis may determine unique intra-child (ipsative) strengths and weaknesses.

Subsets of Ipsative Interpretation

More specific interpretation may rely on the following three procedures (see McCallum & Whitaker, 2000), depending on the nature of the score variability. The three interpretative procedures include (1) the pooled procedure, (2) the independent factors procedure, and (3) the rational-intuitive procedure. The *pooled procedure* is the first of the three techniques discussed. It requires that the mean of all six UNIT subtests be computed and each subtest score is individually compared to that mean to identify *outliers* (i.e., scores that differ significantly from the overall subtest mean). The *independent factors procedure* is so named because it relies on interpretation based on the (independent-factor) factor-analytic structure of the UNIT (i.e., it is based on the factor structure obtained by maximizing the independence of the factor). For the UNIT, the best factor-analytic solution from currently available data shows a good two-factor model (i.e., the best factor solution appears to reveal a three-subtest memory factor and a three-subtest reasoning factor). Thus, the examiner should first look for

the pattern of consistently higher memory (over reasoning) subtests, or the reverse, assuming little within-factor variance. The *rational-intuitive procedure* is so named because it relies on the interpretation of a multidimensional test based on the theoretical model that underpins the development of a test, or on other theoretical models of which the examiner is aware. In this case, users of the UNIT may find that some children will perform well on all the symbolic subtests, relative to the nonsymbolic subtests, or vice versa. Examiners should keep in mind that other cognitive models can be applied to ipsative interpretation

Base-Rate Interpretation

In 1997, Glutting, McDermott, and Konold applied a model of interpretation using subtest profile base-rate analysis as a beginning point to interpret WISC-III performance. They described procedures that allow an examiner to determine the extent to which an examinee's profile of subtest scores is rare in the population, using sophisticated statistical techniques to calculate common profiles in the WISC-III standardization data; then, they made those profiles available to test users. Next, they provided examiners with a set of relatively straightforward calculations that allow them to determine the likelihood that a particular profile matches one or more of these common profiles. Glutting, McDermott, and Konold argue that unusual profiles are more likely to have clinical significance than those that occur often in the population.

Using the procedure described by Glutting, McDermott, and Konold (1997), Wilhoit and McCallum (2003) provide the information examiners need to apply the base-rate method to analysis of UNIT scores. Although the base-rate analysis is not particularly complicated to use, deriving the data necessary to obtain common or typical profiles is difficult. Wilhoit and McCallum describe the lengthy cluster analyses procedures used to provide those profiles from the UNIT standardization data. That is, using cluster analyses, six common profiles were identified for the Standard Battery (i.e., Delayed, Low Average, Average, Above Average with High Memory and Symbolic Quotients, Above Average with High Reasoning and Nonsymbolic Quotients, and Superior) and seven for the Extended Battery (i.e., Delayed, Low Average with Higher Memory and Symbolic than Reasoning and Nonsymbolic Quotients, Low Average with Higher Reasoning and Nonsymbolic than Memory and Symbolic Quotient, Average with Higher Memory and Symbolic than Reasoning and Nonsymbolic Quotients, Average, High Average, and Superior). Specific demographics are associated with each of these profiles (e.g., percentage of females, males, blacks, whites, family educational levels). Because these profiles are considered typical, profiles of examinees that fit one of them may not be diagnostic, using the logic from Glutting, McDermott, and Konold.

Examiners can determine the fit by following a few easy steps. First, each of the examinees' subtest scores is subtracted from the like subtest scores provided from the profiles in the relevant table with the closest FSIQ. These scores are squared and summed to produce a score that can be compared to a critical value (e.g., 272 for the Standard Battery and 307 for the Extended Battery). This procedure is repeated for the three profiles with FSIQs closest to the examinees' obtained FSIQs. If the obtained score from any one of these comparisons is equal to or larger than the critical value, the obtained profile is considered rare in the population, and thus, potentially diagnostic. To obtain the FSIQs and subtest scores for the common profiles for both Standard and Extended Batteries, see Tables 2, 3, 5, and 6 in the Wilhoit and McCallum (2003) article in the *School Psychology Review*.

Cross-Battery Assessment (CBA)

The rationale and procedures required to use the cross-battery process were first described by Flanagan & McGrew (1997), and then in considerably more detail by McGrew and Flanagan (1998). One important assumption of CBA is that subtests can be selected from different batteries and used to assess particular cognitive constructs, thereby increasing assessment precision and efficiency. According to Flanagan and McGrew, this technique can be implemented when there is no need to administer and interpret a test in its entirety. More recently, Flanagan and Ortiz (2001) characterized cross-battery assessment as "efficient" and "theoretically defensible." However, as with any new practice, independent research is needed empirically to determine its value in practice.

In their original description of the cross-battery approach, McGrew and Flanagan (1998) provided a cognitive nomenclature, based on the work of several researchers, particularly Cattell (1963), Horn (1968, 1994), and Carroll (1993). This nomenclature is embedded in a system, referred to as the *Cattell-Horn-Carroll (CHC) model*, and uses a three-tier hierarchical arrangement: Stratum I represents *g*, the general cognitive energy presumed to underlie performance across all tasks individuals undertake; Stratum II represents relatively broad abilities that can be operationalized fairly well as "factors" from a factor analysis (e.g., short-term memory, long-term memory, fluid ability, acquired knowledge, visual processing, auditory processing, processing speed); Stratum III represents abilities at a more specific level, and can be assessed relatively purely by many existing subtests; and two or more of these subtests can be used to operationalize Stratum II abilities. McGrew and Flanagan characterized subtests from most existing batteries as measures of Stratum II and III abilities, and provided several caveats about the use of these operationalizations, with worksheets to aid examiners in using CBA.

Application of CBA is somewhat detailed, requiring the use of worksheets containing the names of tests and subtests and the broad Stratum I and II abilities those subtests measure. Using a variation of the worksheets provided by McGrew and Flanagan (1998) and Flanagan and Ortiz (2001) and their guidelines for establishing strengths and weaknesses, Wilhoit and McCallum (2003) extended the McGrew and Flanagan model to assessment of cognitive constructs via the UNIT and other nonverbal tests, based on operationalizations of the CHC model using subtests from various nonverbal measures. Assessment of Stratum II abilities is the primary focus. Typically, each subtest from nonverbal tests assesses a narrow Stratum III ability, and two or more can be used to provide a good assessment of Stratum II. The six Stratum II abilities assessed by nonverbal tests include: fluid intelligence (G*f*), crystallized intelligence (G*c*), visual processing (G*v*), short-term memory (G*sm*), long-term memory (G*lr*), and processing speed (G*s*). The other ability typically included in CBA, auditory processing (G*a*), is not assessed by nonverbal tests and is not included on the worksheets. The examiner calculates the mean performance by averaging scores from all subtests. Each Stratum II ability score (determined by averaging two or more Stratum III measures within that Stratum II ability) can be compared to the overall Stratum II average in an ipsative fashion. Assuming all subtests use a mean of 100 and a standard deviation of 15 (or have been converted accordingly), each average Stratum II ability score that is more than 15 points from the overall mean is considered a strength or weakness, depending on the direction of the difference.

Importantly, the Stratum II abilities have been linked to several important real-world products (e.g., processing speed, auditory processing, and working memory underpins the ability to learn to decode words quickly, according to Bell & McCallum, 2008, Mather & Jaffe, 2002, and Wolf & Bowers, 1999).

The UNIT was developed primarily for equitable assessments of non-English-speaking populations and those with language-based deficits and it eliminates the traditional language demands of conventional intelligence tests and the need for costly translations. The UNIT gestures (e.g., affirmative head nods, pointing) were chosen because they seem to be ubiquitous modes of communication across most cultures. Also, the authors attempted to use universal item content (i.e., objects found in all industrialized cultures). The format is appropriate for children who are deaf or who have hearing problems, and for those who have other types of language deficits (e.g., selective mutism, severe dyslexia, speech articulation difficulties). Additional clinical applications of the UNIT as well as other nonverbal tests can be found in McCallum, Bracken, and Wasserman (2001). For example, they provide information describing how members of various populations compare on the UNIT scores, technical data such as reliability coefficients for those examinees who earn scores close to typical cutoff points of 70 and 130, a case study illustrating use of the test for a child with language delays, and a UNIT Interpretive Worksheet showing step-by-step interpretation guidelines. In addition, McCallum (2003) provides a description of procedures/techniques to help examinees choose technically appropriate and fair(est) tests for assessing a range of nonverbal abilities, including nonverbally functional behaviors, academic skills, personality, cognition, and neurological functioning.

CASE STUDY

Antonio

Background and Reason for Referral

Antonio (age 5:2) was referred for a psychoeducational assessment because of suspected language delay and maternal-reported autistic spectrum–related behaviors. Antonio's mother, Glenda Weaver, voiced concerns that Antonio frequently points, uses echolalic speech patterns, and prefers to play alone rather than interact with other children his age. She believes Antonio comprehends more than he expresses, but that often he seems to be "in a world of his own" and doesn't express himself well.

Antonio is monolingual English speaking and lives with both biological parents in an upper-middle-class community. His parents are both professionals; his father, James, is a chiropractor and Glenda is a Certified Public Accountant. He has one sibling, Marcia, who is 11 years old and is developing normally in all areas, according to her parents.

Test Behavior

Antonio is an attractive young boy with wavy brown hair and a coy smile. He seldom made eye contact with the examiner during the assessment, and frequently appeared fascinated with test materials and objects—feeling the texture and edges of blocks and chips. He attended well to pictured stimuli and interacted with all test materials in an appropriate manner.

The assessment was conducted in two sessions and Antonio was willing and eager to participate throughout the duration of both sessions. He appeared to enjoy the activities and occasionally named pictured objects presented in the test stimuli.

Tests Administered

Bracken Basic Concept Scale—Third Edition Receptive (BBCS-3:R)

Bracken Basic Concept Scale—Expressive (BBCS-E)

Universal Nonverbal Intelligence Test (UNIT)

Parent Form of the Clinical Assessment of Behavior (CAB)

Assessment Results

Antonio's receptive basic concept development is in the Average range with standard scores of 90 on the School Readiness Composite (SRC) and 90 on the Total Test. These measures have a mean of 100 and standard deviation of 15. In contrast to his average receptive concept development, Antonio's expressive concept knowledge is significantly lower and in the Delayed range of functioning (SRC = 75; Total Test = 78). The magnitude of the difference between Antonio's receptive and expressive concept development occurs less than 10% of the time in the general population.

Because of the discrepancy between Antonio's receptive and expressive verbal abilities, the UNIT was administered as a 100% nonverbal measure. The UNIT FSIQ of 91 is commensurate with his receptive language abilities, suggesting that Antonio's overall intelligence and receptive language are both in the Average range, with delayed expressive language abilities. Further support for this determination is the significant difference between the UNIT Symbolic Scale (SS = 82) and Nonsymbolic Scale (SS = 103), which is consistent with a difference between lower verbal processing than nonverbal.

The CAB was completed by Antonio's mother. While the CAB Behavioral Index was slightly elevated (T Score = 60; Mild Clinical Risk), his Critical Behavior Scale (T Score = 70) and Autistic Spectrum Scale (T Score = 78) are both in the Significant Clinical Risk range. Specific critical behaviors endorsed by Antonio's mother include: (Uses bizarre speech; Is preoccupied with unusual thoughts; and makes odd hand and finger movements.) Consistent with Glenda's concerns about Antonio's autistic-related behaviors, she also rated his Social Skills as being significantly delayed.

Conclusions

Given Antonio's significantly lower expressive language skills than receptive, his overall average intelligence, with significantly weaker symbolic than nonsymbolic processing, and his mother's consistent report of autistic-like behaviors and poor social skills and interactions, his assessment performance is consistent with a diagnosis of autistic spectrum disorders.

IDENTIFICATION OF SPECIAL POPULATIONS

Identifying and Helping Individuals with Specific Learning Disabilities: Implications from IDEA 2004

Although the definition of *specific learning disability* is written into law and did not change in the latest version of IDEA (2004), the legislation describing methods for identification changed significantly. In fact, three procedures are now possible. Although criticized as a *wait-to-fail* model, the traditional IQ–Achievement discrepancy model is included in the legislation. This strategy requires that a significant discrepancy between ability and achievement be established, typically taking into account regression to the mean. A second method requires that a student fail to respond adequately to successive and increasingly intensive empirically supported interventions before identification. In this case, traditional measures (e.g., instruments to determine cognitive functioning and adaptive skills) may be administered at the last step to rule out mental retardation (or other competing explanations for the academic deficits). Finally, a third procedure is included, which simply states that the use of other alternative research–based procedures can be used. Any one of these three procedures can be used to operationalize a specific leaning disability, defined still as a disorder in one or more psychological processes involved

in understanding or using language to listen, think, speak, read, write, or compute.

The implications for using the UNIT to identify a specific learning disability are obvious to many educators. For those examiners who continue to use the IQ–Achievement discrepancy model, the UNIT can provide an assessment of ability; for those who use the *response to intervention* method, the UNIT can be used in the later stages of that process to rule out mental retardation or language-related problems. The UNIT can also be used for those who choose an alternative procedure of identification that might require assessment of processing strengths/deficits that might underlie academic limitations and their remediation.

Some data are available illustrating how those already identified as having a specific learning disability may function. For example, data from a sample of 61 children with specific learning disabilities yielded correlation coefficients (corrected for restriction in range) between the FSIQs from the three UNIT batteries and the WISC-III FSIQ from .78 to .84, and their mean scores were generally lower than those from a matched control group; effect size differences ranged from .31 to .74. Importantly, the effect sizes were larger for the Symbolic Quotient than for the Nonsymbolic Quotient, which might be predicted given that many students with specific learning disabilities are presumed to have language-related deficits (Lerner & Johns, 2009). This finding is particularly important given that predictive validity coefficients obtained between the UNIT and various achievement tests are relatively strong, and comparable to those between language-loaded tests and achievement measures (Bracken & McCallum, 1998). Of interest from the studies reported in the UNIT Manual is that the magnitude of the coefficients between the UNIT global Symbolic Quotient and measures of language-based achievement (e.g., reading subtests) is often higher than the magnitude of coefficients between the UNIT Nonsymbolic Quotient and these language-loaded achievement measures. In fact, this pattern is found in 21 out of 36 comparisons (58%). This pattern would be predicted from the nature of the symbolic versus nonsymbolic distinction, and provides some additional evidence of predictive and construct validity of the test model.

Attention Deficit Hyperactivity Disorder

Although no studies have been published investigating use of the UNIT with ADHD students, logically the instrument appears to be a less-than-desirable tool to assess the cognitive functioning of ADHD students. With three memory subtests, which each require concentrated attention, coding, and recall, it would be anticipated that ADHD students would be at a disadvantage on those tasks. One of the reasoning subtests seems similarly problematic; the Mazes subtest is terminated at the occurrence of the examinee's first error (which would put impulsive examinees at a distinct disadvantage). If the examiner, however, wishes to document the extent to which the student's ADHD affects his or her academic/cognitive functioning, the UNIT subtests would likely provide ample evidence for such an effect.

Identifying and Helping Individuals Who Are Gifted

Because the UNIT is a sound measure of multiple cognitive abilities and provides a strong measure of g, it can be used to assess intellectual giftedness. Because it is administered in a nonverbal format, it eliminates the construct-irrelevant variance associated with assessing cognition of those who are intellectually superior but have trouble communicating using traditional language-loaded strategies (Naglieri, 2008). In the UNIT Manual, data show mean differences on the UNIT for a group of children previously identified as gifted using traditional language-loaded tests such as the Wechsler scales versus those from a matched control group. In all cases, the means were higher for the gifted sample, with effect sizes ranging from .23 to .91. Typically, the mean global scores of those in the gifted sample were just above one standard deviation above the population mean (e.g., the Standard Battery FSIQ for this group was 118). These data suggest that the UNIT will identify many of the same highly functioning individuals as would a language-loaded test. But more importantly, it will identify a significant number of different individuals—those with strong cognitive skills, but with more limited language-based abilities.

Identifying and Helping Those with Mental Retardation

As previously indicated, the UNIT can be used to identify those with mental retardation. To illustrate how those previously identified as having mental retardation are likely to perform on the UNIT, mean scores from such a sample were compared to those of a matched control group. In all cases, the scores were significantly lower for those identified as having mental retardation; the effect sizes range from 1.39 to 2.27. The mean FSIQ from the sample with mental retardation is 60.96, and can be compared to the mean from the matched control group of 95.01.

Identifying and Helping Individuals Who Have English as Second Language (ESL)

In a study conducted since the UNIT was published, Borghese and Gronau (2005) compared the UNIT and the WISC-III scores for 30 Mexican-American ESL students. Correlations ranged from .62 to .90 for the WISC-III FSIQ and Unit global scores. Importantly, the correlation coefficient between the UNIT Symbolic Quotient and the WISC-III Verbal Scale IQ was .71, and higher than the coefficient between the UNIT Nonsymbolic Quotient and the Verbal IQ (.59). Similarly, the coefficient between the UNIT Nonsymbolic Quotient and the WISC-III Performance IQ was .89, and quite a bit larger than the coefficient between the UNIT Symbolic Quotient and the WISC-III Performance IQ. This pattern of scores supports the UNIT model and shows the correspondence between the verbal portion of the WISC-III and the symbolically laden (but nonverbal) portion of the UNIT and between the nonverbal portion of the WISC-III and the nonsymbolic (and more visual-spatial) portion of the UNIT. Also, consistent with predictions, the UNIT mean global scores were all larger than the WISC-III scores for the ESL students. For example, the UNIT FSIQ was 90.83 and can be compared to the WISC-III mean FSIQ of 79.60.

Additional data relevant for understanding how the UNIT can be used for students who have limited English-language skills was obtained by Scardapane, Egan, Torres-Gallegos, Levine, and Owens (2002). They investigated the relationship between the UNIT, the Wide Range Intelligence Test (WRIT; Glutting, Adams, & Sheslow, 2000), and the Gifted and Talented Evaluation Scales (GATES; Gilliam, Carpenter, & Christensen, 1996) for English-speaking children and English Language Learners (ELL). The correlation coefficient obtained between the WRIT Visual and the UNIT FSIQ of .59 can be compared to the coefficient between the UNIT FSIQ and the WRIT Verbal scale of

.11. Contrary to the authors' predictions, the coefficients showing the relationship between the GATES scores and the WRIT Verbal IQ were not higher than the coefficients showing relationships between the UNIT FSIQ and the four GATES scores. The coefficients between the UNIT FSIQ and the GATES scales of Intellectual Ability, Academic Skills, Creativity, Leadership, and Artistic Talent range from .50 to .57 ($p < .05$); the coefficients between the WRIT Verbal IQ and these GATES scores range from .004 to .10 ($p > .05$). The authors conclude that their data support the use of the UNIT as a nonverbal measure of intelligence.

Identifying and Helping Individuals Who Have Autism Spectrum Disorders

Burton (2002) compared the performance of 31 children (mean age, 39.95 months) previously identified as having autism spectrum disorders—autism (19), asperger's disorder (7), pervasive developmental disorder (PDD-NOS; 2)—and three others who were identified only as having autism spectrum disorder. The mean scores of these individuals were compared to those of a matched control group; the UNIT FSIQ mean of the autism spectrum group is 81.85, as compared to the mean of the matched control group of 103.89. The mean Nonsymbolic Quotient for the autism spectrum group of 85.42 was larger than the mean of the Symbolic Quotient of 81.74; though this difference did not reach significance and the effect size (.19) is small, the difference is in the predicted direction, given the poor language skills generally associated with those with autism spectrum disorders.

Identifying and Helping Gifted and Talented Students

The UNIT Manual reports a validation study with 160 high-ability students in which the UNIT produced significantly higher mean Full Scale IQ (i.e., 117.64) for previously identified high-ability students than a matched sample from the standardization sample (i.e., 104.14). Based on such promising preliminary analyses, the UNIT was employed as one of two cognitive ability tests in a federally supported curriculum scale-up study, Project Athena (Bracken, VanTassel-Baska, Brown, & Feng, 2007).

The UNIT was employed in Project Athena, a Jacob Javits grant administered through the U.S. Department of Education. The project was implemented in 15 schools in seven school districts across three states (i.e., Maryland, South Carolina, Virginia). One of the primary objectives for Project Athena was to develop and implement instrumentation sensitive to low-socioeconomic learners for the purposes of identification and assessment of learning (i.e., equitable assessment and identification). The ethnic composition of the sample was diverse, with 43% white, 27.5% African-American, 18% Hispanic, and 2.4% Asian-American students participating. The remaining students (9.1%) were identified as Pacific Islander, American Indian, or Other. Ethnic or racial minority students comprised 53.5% of the Project Athena student sample. Gender was approximately evenly divided within and across groups.

The two cognitive ability tests used in Project Athena included the Verbal and Nonverbal scales of the *Cognitive Abilities Test* (CogAT; Lohman & Hagen, 2001) and the Abbreviated Battery of the *Universal Nonverbal Intelligence Test* (UNIT; Bracken & McCallum, 1998). Of interest in the project was the sensitivity of the two instruments for identifying gifted students, especially students from diverse cultural backgrounds.

Not all students were tested on both instruments due to variations in the research protocol across participating districts, student absenteeism, and so on. For those students who were assessed on both instruments, Bracken (2007) found that by using two nonverbal measures of intelligence and one verbal measure we identified nearly twice as many Title One students as gifted as compared to the school districts' identification

procedures. Of 253 students identified as intellectually gifted using an IQ $\geq$ 120, 94 students had been identified by the school districts and an additional 159 were identified by the Project Athena assessments. Using a minimal cut-score of 130, a total of 64 students were identified, with 29 identified by the districts and an additional 35 identified by Project Athena. Importantly, 21% of those students with IQs at 120 or above were African American when identified by the UNIT and 8.8% and 9.8% of those identified were African American when the CogAT Nonverbal and Verbal Scales were used, respectively.

Identifying and Helping Members of Other Groups

Data in the UNIT Manual are available showing performance on the UNIT of a number of other populations, including those with emotional disturbance and those with speech and language impairments. Both of these groups earned scores slightly below the population mean, with global scores typically in the low 90s. Those with speech and language impairments earned mean scores slightly lower than their matched controls, with effect sizes ranging from .18 to .66. Those with emotional disturbance scored very much like their matched counterparts, with effect sizes ranging from .01 to .09.

The UNIT can also help assess the cognitive skills of students with language limitations, as suggested by Farrell and Phelps (2000), who compared scores from the Leiter-R and the UNIT for 43 elementary and middle-school children with severe language disorders. Correlation coefficients between the UNIT quotients and Leiter-R Fluid Reasoning Scale scores range from .65 to .67; the coefficients between UNIT quotients and Leiter-R Visualization Reasoning Full Scale scores range from .73 to .80. For this sample, Leiter-R mean scale scores are 65.07 and 66.33, for the Fluid Reasoning and Visualization/Reasoning FSIQ, respectively. UNIT global scale scores range from 66.71

(FSIQ) to 70 (Symbolic Quotient). The authors conclude that the UNIT shows promise for providing fair and valid assessment of cognitive functioning for children with severe language impairments, and that it should be considered superior to conventional language-loaded tests (e.g., SB-V, WISC-III) for use with this population.

Interventions Based on Test Results

The UNIT authors present educational guidelines and instructional implications in the Manual. For example, those who have stronger Memory than Reasoning skills should receive instruction consistent with that strength (e.g., use of mnemonics, memorization of spelling rules) (see Mastropieri & Scruggs, 2000, Minskoff & Allsopp, 2003, and Naglieri & Pickering, 2003). Similarly, those with stronger symbolic than nonsymbolic abilities should be (more) responsive to instruction that capitalizes on their stronger capability for using concrete symbols, relative to instruction that relies more on abstract ideas and visual-spatial depiction and juxtaposition of concepts. These suggestions should provide researchers with hypotheses for testing, although in our experience such aptitude X treatment studies are difficult to conduct in real-world settings. For example, logistical and ethical obstacles make educators reluctant to allow random assignment to treatments over long enough periods to achieve results. In addition, Bracken and Van Tassel-Baska have found in two large-scale federally funded intervention grants (e.g., Bracken et al., 2007) that good instructional interventions relying only on relevant elements of an intervention (and not on irrelevant elements) are difficult to design and implement without treatment contamination. Finally, treatment fidelity is difficult to achieve (Bracken et al., 2007). Nonetheless, the information obtained from the UNIT can be used to help select interventions that would likely best fit the learner.

Profiles of Abilities and Their Relationship to Diagnosis

As was apparent from the data reported in this section ("Identification of Special Populations") and from studies reported in the Manual (some of which are summarized in this chapter), there are considerable data showing how the UNIT can aid in diagnosing individuals within special populations, including those with mental retardation, learning disabilities, emotional/social limitations, and autism, as well as those who are gifted.

VALIDITY

Various types of validity data are available to support the use of the UNIT. The UNIT Manual reports results supporting the internal structure of the test as well as data from a large number of studies showing empirical relationships between the UNIT and other measures of cognition and achievement. Results from several studies are summarized in the following, as are results from additional independent researchers.

Empirical Support for the Test Structure and Use

Data reported in the UNIT Manual show expected raw score age progressions. For example, for Cube Design, the mean scores are 13, 19, 26, and 33 for the 5–7, 8–10, 11–13, and 14–17 age groups, respectively. Exploratory and confirmatory factor-analytic data provide strong support for the UNIT model. Using the standardization data, exploratory analysis yielded a large first eigenvalue of 2.33; others are below 1.0, suggesting the presence of a strong first factor, commensurate with the interpretation of the FSIQ as a good overall index of global intellectual ability (g); five of the six subtests have strong g loadings (i.e., above .70). The confirmatory factor structure also supports the two-factor memory and reasoning model, showing strong fit statistics for a two-factor Memory and Reasoning model and for the two-factor Symbolic and Non-symbolic dichotomy. Concurrent validity data show strong correlation coefficients between the UNIT and other cognitive measures, including the Wechsler scales, the Stanford-Binet, and the Woodcock-Johnson—Revised Cognitive Battery. Coefficients typically range from .50 to .80.

Since publication of the UNIT, results from several studies have become available showing relevant technical data. For example, Hooper and Bell (2006) explored the relationship between the Leiter International Performance Scale—Revised (Roid & Miller, 1997) and the UNIT for 100 elementary and middle-school students. Correlation coefficients obtained from the comparison of the Leiter-R FSIQ and Fluid Reasoning scale and all UNIT global scales (Memory, Reasoning, Symbolic and Nonsymbolic Quotients) are statistically significant ($p <$ .01) and range from .33 for the UNIT Memory Quotient/Leiter-R Fluid Reasoning comparison to .72 for the UNIT FSIQ and the Leiter-R FSIQ. Importantly, global scale means for the two tests are similar generally, although the UNIT FSIQ is approximately 5 points higher than the Leiter-R FSIQ. The other mean global scores are more similar in magnitude across the two tests; the UNIT means range from 101.5 to 103.7 and the Leiter-R Fluid Reasoning score is 99.1.

Hooper and Bell (2006) also reported correlation coefficients ranging from .49 to .72 between the four UNIT global scores and end-of-year scores from the Total Reading, Total Math, and Total Language scores of the Comprehensive Test of Basic Skills (CTBS/McGraw-Hill, 1996) for 100 elementary and middle-school children. In an additional analysis of these data using stepwise multiple regression analyses, Hooper (2002) reported that the UNIT FSIQ predicted all three academic areas from the CTBS better than the Leiter-R FSIQ; the UNIT FSIQ entered the multiple regression equation first, accounting for from 39% to 55% of the variance in the three

criterion scores and the Leiter-R contributed an additional 1% to 2% for each.

The UNIT Manual contains several studies depicting relationships between the UNIT scores and various measures of real-world achievement (e.g., WJ-R Tests of Achievement, WIAT, PIAT-R). Most of those studies show the magnitude of the correlation coefficients between UNIT scores and measures of achievement to be comparable to the magnitude of those between language-loaded cognitive measures and achievement. Coefficients between the UNIT scores and scores from various tests of the Woodcock-Johnson—Revised, Wechsler Individual Achievement Test (WIAT), and Peabody Individual Achievement Test—Revised (PIAT-R) are typically within the .40–.60 range.

THE UNIT IN PRACTICE: A MODEL OF FAIRNESS

Because the UNIT was conceptualized and developed to serve an increasingly diverse society and to be sensitive to the need to ensure sensitive and equally valid assessment for a wide variety of populations, the authors were motivated to make it as fair as possible. In order to address this goal, the UNIT Manual includes an entire chapter entitled "Fairness," and describes extensive efforts to ensure that the test is appropriate for use for all children in the United States (i.e., that construct-irrelevant variance is minimized for all relevant populations). (Also, see McCallum, 1999, for additional descriptions of efforts to ensure fairness for UNIT.)

Five *fairness assumptions* guided development of the UNIT: (1) A language-free test is less susceptible to bias than a language-loaded test; (2) a multidimensional measure of cognition is fairer than a unidimensional one; (3) a test that minimizes the influence of acquired knowledge (i.e., crystallized ability) is fairer than one that does not; (4) a test that minimizes speeded performance is fairer than one with greater emphasis on speed; and (5) a test that relies on a variety of response modes is more motivating and thereby fairer than those relying on a unidimensional response mode. In addition, several other steps were taken to ensure fairness (e.g., items were submitted to a panel of "bias experts" for review) and unfair items identified by these individuals, and those identified via statistical item bias analyses, were removed.

Finally, a number of statistical procedures were undertaken to help ensure fairness, including calculation of separate reliabilities, factor structure statistics, mean-difference analyses, and so on, for subpopulations. For example, reliabilities for FSIQs for females, males, African Americans, and Hispanic Americans were all greater than .91, uncorrected, and .94, corrected, for the Abbreviated Battery, and greater than .95 for the Standard and Extended Battery. Separate confirmatory factor analyses for these subpopulations provide evidence for "a single general intelligence factor as well as the primary and secondary scales . . . and provides evidence supporting the construct validity of the UNIT across sex, race, and ethnic groups" (p. 182, Bracken & McCallum, 1998).

The UNIT Manual also reports several mean IQ difference analyses using matched groups from the UNIT standardization data as evidence of fairness. For example, mean scores of males and females matched on age, parent educational level, and ethnicity are very similar, with effect sizes ranging from .02 to .03 across all three batteries. Mean differences, estimated via effect sizes, range from .22 to .43 for FSIQs across all batteries for Native Americans matched on age, sex, and parent educational levels; the largest mean difference, 6.50, was obtained from the Standard Battery. Mean differences of FSIQs, reflected via effect sizes, range from .10 to.14 for matched Hispanic Americans across all batteries; the largest difference, 2.13, occurred on the Standard Battery. Effect sizes for matched African Americans range from .51 to .65; a mean FSIQ difference of 8.63 between African Americans and whites was obtained using

the Standard Battery. A mean FSIQ Standard Battery difference of 6.20 was found between deaf and hearing-impaired examinees and a matched nonimpaired sample; a Standard Battery FSIQ mean difference of 5.33 was found between Ecuadorian and matched non-Ecuadorian examinees. Evidence that prediction is not a function of gender and racial membership was provided by using the regression slope as a measure of the strength of the relationships between UNIT and scores and achievement on the Woodcock-Johnson—Revised Achievement Battery subtests in a regression equation; race and sex did not contribute significantly to the prediction ($p > .05$).

Upson (2003) used a matching strategy more refined than the one reported in the Manual for SES and found a further reduction of mean difference scores between Hispanic Americans and whites. Matching on all relevant variables reported in the Manual *and* community size *and* the educational level of both parents, rather than just one, reduced the mean differences between matched Hispanic Americans and whites considerably for the Standard Battery FSIQ, from 2.13 to .47. Although further refinement reduced the African-American and white differences slightly, the reductions were not as pronounced. The Standard Battery FSIQ difference of 8.51 for 168 matched African Americans and whites is only slightly smaller than the 8.63 reported in the Manual.

Data from another study generated after the UNIT was developed has relevance for UNIT fairness as well. Maller (2000) conducted a sophisticated item analysis of using the Mantel-Haenszel (MH) and item response theory (IRT) to detect differential item functioning (DIF) for 104 deaf children and adolescents. Using a group of children from the UNIT standardization sample matched on age, gender, and ethnicity to the 104 deaf and hearing-impaired children, she concluded that no items in the UNIT exhibited DIF using either the MH or IRT; that is, the probability of a correct response on the UNIT items does not seem to be affected by hearing status. Consequently, she notes that the UNIT seems appropriate for this population, and there may be no need to develop special norms for deaf children. Additional evidence for this conclusion is provided by Krivitski (2000), who compared children who are deaf to a matched sample of hearing children from the UNIT standardization sample; children were matched on age, race/ethnicity, SES, and gender. Results of a profile analysis show that children who are deaf display patterns of UNIT subtest performance similar to children who are not. Krivitski concludes that the data support use of the UNIT for children classified as deaf.

The preponderance of data from the literature is supportive of the use of the UNIT for non-English-speaking children; however, not all the studies provide uniformly positive results. Jimenez (2001) in a small sample study reported that the internal consistency reliability for five of the six UNIT subtests "failed to show acceptable internal consistency" and did not reach "the recommended coefficient of .90" for test–retest stability for 60 Puerto Rican children. It should be noted, however, that a criterion of .90 reliability for a cognitive subtest is extremely high (i.e., a criterion expected for Full Scale scores), and very few cognitive ability tests produce subtests with reliability at this level.

The UNIT correlation coefficients with the Bateria-R Reading Cluster were moderate to low for these Puerto Rican children. Finally, they scored almost one-half standard deviation lower than a matched control group of non-Hispanic children. Jimenez concludes that although the UNIT may be a fair instrument to measure cognitive abilities of Puerto Rican children, it may not be optimal used in isolation, and should be part of a multifaceted assessment process.

In a comprehensive review, Athanasiou (2000) compared five nonverbal assessment instruments for psychometric integrity and fairness, including the UNIT. All have unique strengths and weaknesses. For example, although the UNIT fails to meet Bracken's (1987) criterion for test–retest

stability (.90) for different age levels, her assessment of the UNIT is mostly favorable. She noted that the UNIT's reliance on only nonverbal directions likely reduces the potential for cultural bias in administration, the use of checkpoint items allows for periodic assessment of understanding during the administration, presentation of psychometric properties of subpopulations enhances the confidence users can have that the test is appropriate for a variety of examinees, the floors, ceilings, and item gradients for UNIT Standard and Extended batteries exceed minimum recommendations, and so on. But perhaps the most important observation Athanasiou offers regarding the UNIT addresses the extent to which the Manual provides evidence of test fairness. She noted that all five of the tests she reviewed are generally impressive in terms of their technical adequacy, but that the UNIT provides much more statistical evidence of test fairness than the others, commenting that it is the only test "to provide evidence of consistent factor structure across subgroups" (p. 227).

In another independent review, Fives and Flanagan (2002) noted that the test is well constructed, theoretically driven, psychometrically sound, and highly useful, and that its use will permit more effective assessment of some traditionally difficult-to-assess populations. They conclude their review by presenting a case study illustrating use of the UNIT for a 12-year-old Hispanic female. Her UNIT IQ scores were higher than those obtained from more language-loaded tests, even those typically considered to assess nonverbal performance and fluid abilities; the authors conclude that use of the UNIT in this case might have prevented an error in classification and service delivery.

There are additional reviews in the literature (e.g., Bandalos, 2001; Kamphaus, 2001; Sattler, 2001), and all are generally positive, particularly regarding basic technical properties (e.g., reliability, floors, ceilings). Bandalos concluded the review reported in the *Buros Mental Measurement Yearbook* by noting that UNIT provides strong measures for obtaining reliable and valid assessments of intelligence for children with a wide array of disabilities who cannot be tested accurately with existing instruments. All these reviewers note the need for certain types of validity studies, particularly those investigating the construct validity of the Symbolic and Nonsymbolic processing and the ability of the UNIT to predict grades and/or classroom achievement. Borghese and Gronau (2005) demonstrated the convergent validity of the Symbolic Scale with the WISC-III Verbal Scale and the Nonsymbolic Scale with the WISC-III Performance Scale, and the discriminant validity of the Symbolic and Nonsymbolic scales with the WISC-III PIQ and VIQ, respectively.

SUMMARY

In summary, the UNIT provides a strong and fair assessment of cognitive abilities and its use has implications for identifying and serving traditionally underserved populations (e.g., those from diverse and culturally different backgrounds, those who have language deficits, and those who may be hard of hearing or deaf). Data in support of its theoretical model and psychometric integrity are robust. Studies reported in the Manual and now by several independent researchers show evidence of how the UNIT can be used in practice to predict important real-world outcomes and to identify cognitive strengths and weaknesses for planning instruction. Although the model has strong theoretical implications for treatment utility, empirical studies are needed to investigate further the treatment applications of the instrument.

REFERENCES

Athanasiou, M. S. (2000). Current nonverbal assessment instruments: A comparison of psychometric integrity and test fairness. *Journal of Psychoeducational Assessment*, *18*, 211–299.

Bandalos, D. L. (2001). Review of the Universal Nonverbal Intelligence Test. In B. S. Plake & J. C. Impara (Eds.), *Fourteenth mental measurements yearbook* (pp. 1296–1298). Lincoln, NE: Buros Institute.

Bell, S. M., & McCallum, R. S. (2008). *Handbook of reading assessment*. Boston: Pearson, Allyn & Bacon.

Borghese, P., & Gronau, R.C. (2005). Convergent and discriminant validity of the Universal Nonverbal Intelligence Test with limited English proficient Mexican-American elementary students. *Journal of Psychoeducational Assessment*, *23*, 140–145.

Bracken, B. A. (1987). Limitations of preschool instruments and standards for minimal levels of technical adequacy. *Journal of Psychoeducational Assessment*, *5*, 313–326.

Bracken, B. A. (1992). The interpretation of psychological tests. In R. Most and M. Zeidner (Eds.), *Psychological testing: An inside view* (pp. 119–158). Palo Alto, CA: Consulting Psychologists Press.

Bracken, B. A. (2007). Nontraditional strategies for identifying nontraditional gifted and talented students. In J. VanTassel-Bask (Ed.), *Alternative assessment of gifted learners* (pp. 1–23). Washington, DC: National Association of Gifted Children.

Bracken, B. A., & McCallum, R. S. (1998). *The Universal Nonverbal Intelligence Test*. Austin, TX: Pro-Ed.

Bracken, B. A., & McCallum, R. S. (2001). *UNIT Compuscore*. Chicago: Riverside.

Bracken, B. A., VanTassel-Baska, J., Brown, E. F., & Feng, A. (2007). Project Athena: A tale of two studies. In J. VanTassel-Baska and T. Stambaugh (Eds.), *Overlooked gems: A national perspective on low-income promising learners* (pp. 63–67). Washington, DC: National Association of Gifted Children.

Brown, L., Sherbenou, R. J., & Johnson, S. K. (1990). *Test of Nonverbal Intelligence—2*. Austin, TX: Pro-Ed.

Burton, B. (2002). *Assessment of cognitive abilities in children with a pervasive development disorder using the Universal Nonverbal Intelligence Test*. Unpublished doctoral dissertation, University of Tennessee, Knoxville.

Carroll, J. B. (1993). *Human cognitive abilities: A survey of factor-analytic studies*. Cambridge: Cambridge University Press.

Cattell, R. B. (1963). Theory for fluid and crystallized intelligence: A critical experiment. *Journal of Educational Psychology*, *54*, 1–22.

CTBS/McGraw-Hill (1996). *Comprehensive test of basic skills*. Monterey, CA: CTB/McGraw-Hill.

Farrell, M. M., & Phelps, L. (2000). A comparison of the Leiter-R and the Universal Nonverbal Intelligence Test (UNIT) with children classified as language impaired. *Journal of Psychoeducational Assessment, 18*, 268–274.

Fives, C. J., & Flanagan, R. (2002). A review of the Universal Nonverbal Intelligence Test (UNIT): An advance for evaluating youngsters with diverse needs. *School Psychology International, 23*, 425–448.

Flanagan, D. P., & McGrew, K. S. (1997). A cross-battery approach to assessing and interpreting cognitive abilities: Narrowing the gap between practice and cognitive science. In D. P. Flanagan, J. L. Genshaft, & P. L. Harrison (Eds.), *Contemporary intellectual assessment: Theories, tests, and issues*. New York: Guilford Press.

Flanagan, D. P., & Ortiz, S. (2001). *Essentials of cross-battery assessment*. New York: Wiley.

Ford, D. Y. (1996). Multicultural gifted education: A wake up call to the profession. *Roeper Review, 19* (2), 72–78.

Gilliam, J. E., Carpenter, B. O., & Christensen, J. R. (1996). *Gifted and talented evaluation scales: A norm referenced procedure for identifying gifted and talented students*. Austin, TX: Pro-Ed.

Glutting, J., Adams, W., & Sheslow, D. (2000). *WRIT: Wide Range Intelligence Test Manual*. Wilmington, DE: Wide Range.

Glutting, J., McDermott, P. A., & Konold, T. R. (1997). Ontology, structure, and diagnosis benefits of a normative subtest taxonomy from the WISC-III standardization sample. In D. P. Flanagan, J. L. Genshaft, & P. L. Harrison (Eds.), *Contemporary intellectual assessment* (pp. 349–372). New York: Guilford.

Hooper, V. S. (2002). *Concurrent and predictive validity of the Universal Nonverbal Intelligence Test and the Leiter International Performance Scale—Revised*. Unpublished doctoral dissertation, University of Tennessee, Knoxville, TN.

Hooper, V. S., & Bell, S. M. (2006). Concurrent validity of the Universal Nonverbal Intelligence Test and the Leiter International Performance Scale—Revised. *Psychology in the Schools, 43*(2), 143–148.

Horn, J. L. (1968). Organization of abilities and the development of intelligence. *Psychological Review, 75*, 242–259.

Horn, J. L. (1994). Theory of fluid and crystallized intelligence. In R. J. Sternberg (Ed.), *Encyclopedia of human intelligence* (pp. 443–451). New York: Macmillan.

Individuals with Disabilities Education Act (IDEA) Amendments of 1997, Pub. L. No. 105-17, 111 Stat. 37 (1997).

Individuals with Disabilities Education Improvement Act of 2004, 20 U.S.C. 1400-1485 (2004 supp. IV), Pub. L. No. 108th Congress, 2d Sess.

Jensen, A. R. (1968). Social class, race, and genetics: Implications for education. *American Educational Research Journal, 5* (1), 1–42.

Jensen, A. R. (1980). *Bias in mental testing*. New York: Free Press.

Jimenez, S. (2001). An analysis of the reliability and validity of the Universal Nonverbal Intelligence Test (UNIT) with Puerto Rican children. Doctoral dissertation, Texas A&M University, *Dissertation Abstracts International, 62*, 5424.

Kamphaus, R. W. (2001). *Clinical assessment of child and adolescent intelligence* (2nd ed.). Boston: Allyn & Bacon.

Kaufman, A. S. (1994). *Intelligent testing with the WISC-III*. New York: Wiley.

Krivitski, E. C. (2000). Profile analysis of deaf children using the Universal Nonverbal Intelligence Test. Doctoral dissertation, State University of New York at Albany, *Dissertation Abstracts International, 61*, 2593.

Lerner, J., & Johns, B. (2009). *Learning disabilities and related mild disabilities* (11th ed.). Boston: Houghton Mifflin Harcourt.

Lohman, D. F., & Hagen, E. P. (2001). *Cognitive Abilities Test (CogAt), Form 6*. Itasca, IL: Riverside.

Maller, S. J. (2000). Item invariance in four subtests of the Universal Nonverbal Intelligence Test (UNIT) across groups of deaf and hearing children. *Journal of Psychoeducational Assessment, 18*, 240–254.

Markwardt, F. C. (1989). *Peabody Individual Achievement Test—Revised: Manual*. Circle Pines, MN: American Guidance Service.

Mastropieri, M. A., & Scruggs, T. E. (2000). *Inclusive classroom strategies for effective instruction*. Columbus, OH: Merrill.

Mather, N., & Jaffe, L. E. (2002). *Woodcock-Johnson III: Reports, recommendations, and strategies*. New York: Wiley.

McCallum, R. S. (1999). A "baker's dozen" criteria for evaluating fairness in nonverbal testing. *School Psychologist, 53*, 40–43.

McCallum, R. S. (Ed.). (2003). *Handbook of nonverbal assessment*. New York: Kluwer Academic/Plenum Press.

McCallum, R. S., Bracken, B. A., & Wasserman, J. (2001). *Essentials of nonverbal assessment*. New York: Wiley.

McCallum, R. S., & Whitaker, D. A. (1997). Using the Stanford-Binet—FE to assess preschool children. In B. A. Bracken (Ed.), *The psychoeducational assessment of preschool children* (3rd ed.). Boston: Allyn & Bacon.

McCallum, R. S. & Whitaker, D. A. (2000). The assessment of preschool children with the Stanford-Binet Intelligence Scale—Fourth Edition. In B. A. Bracken (Ed.) *The psychoeducational assessment of preschool children* (3rd ed.). Boston: Allyn & Bacon.

McDermott, P. A., Fantuzzo, J. W., & Glutting, J. J. (1990). Just say no to subtest analysis: A critique on Wechsler theory and practice. *Journal of Psychoeducational Assessment, 8*, 290–302.

McGrew. K. S., & Flanagan, D. P. (1998). *The intelligence test desk reference (ITDR): Gf-Gc cross-battery assessment*. Boston: Allyn & Bacon.

Minskoff, E., & Allsopp, D. (2003). *Academic success strategies for adolescents with learning disabilities and ADHD*. Baltimore: Brookes.

Naglieri, J. (1985). *Matrix Analogies Test—Expanded Form: Examiner's manual*. San Antonio, TX: Psychological Corporation.

Naglieri, J. A. (2008). Traditional IQ: 100 years of misconception and its relationship to minority representation in gifted programs. In J. VanTassel-Baska (Ed.), *Critical issues in equity and excellence in gifted education series alternative assessment of gifted learners* (pp. 67–88). Waco, TX: Prufrock Press.

Naglieri, J. A., & Ford, D. Y. (2003). Addressing underrepresentation of gifted minority children using the Naglieri Nonverbal Ability Test (NNAT). *Gifted Child Quarterly, 47*(2), 155–160.

Naglieri, J. A., & Ford, D. (2005). Increasing minority children's participation in gifted classes using the NNAT: A response to Lohman. *Gifted Child Quarterly, 49*, 29–36.

Naglieri, J. A., & Pickering, E. (2003). *Helping children learn: Intervention handouts for use in school and at home*. Baltimore: Brookes.

Oakland, T., & Parmelee, R. (1985). Mental measurement of minority-group children. In B. H. Wolman (Ed.), *Handbook of intelligence: Theories, measurements, and applications* (pp. 699–736).

Pasko, J. R. (1994). Chicago—don't miss it. *Communique, 23*, 2.

Psychological Corporation (1992). *Wechsler Individual Achievement Test: Manual*. San Antonio, TX. Author.

Raven, J. C. (1960). *Guide to standard progressive matrices*. London: Lewis.

Reed, M. T., & McCallum, R. S. (1994). Construct validity of the Universal Nonverbal Intelligence Test (UNIT). Manuscript submitted for publication.

Roid, G. H., & Miller, L. J. (1997). *Leiter International Performance Scale—Revised*. Wooddale, IL: Stoelting.

Sattler, J. M. (2001). *Assessment of children: Cognitive applications* (4th ed.). San Diego: Author.

Scardapane, J. R., Egan, A., Torres-Gallegos, M., Levine, N., & Owens, S. (2002, March). Relationships among WRIT, UNIT, and GATES scores and language proficiency. Paper presented at the *Council for Exceptional Children*, New York.

Thorndike, R. L., Hagen, E. P., & Sattler, J. M. (1986). *The Stanford-Binet Intelligence Scale—Fourth Edition*. Chicago: Riverside.

U.S. Bureau of the Census. (2000). Language use. [Online]. Available at http://www.census.gov/population.www.socdemo/lang_use.html.

Unz, R. (1997). Perspective on education: Bilingual is a damaging myth; a system that ensures failure is kept alive by the flow of federal dollars; a 1998 initiative would bring change. *Los Angeles Times*, Opinion Section, part M, p. 5.

Upson, L. M. (2003). *Effects of an increasingly precise socioeconomic match on mean score differences in nonverbal intelligence test scores*. Unpublished doctoral dissertation, University of Tennessee, Knoxville, TN.

Wechsler, D. (1939). *The measurement of adult intelligence*. Baltimore: Williams & Wilkins.

Wechsler, D. (1991). *Wechsler Intelligence Scale for Children—III*. San Antonio, TX: Psychological Corporation.

Wilhoit, B. E., & McCallum, R. S. (2002). Profile analysis of the Universal Nonverbal Intelligence Test standardized sample. *School Psychology Review*, *31*, 263–281.

Wilhoit, B., & McCallum, R. S. (2003). Cross-battery analysis of the UNIT. In R. S. McCallum (Ed.), *Handbook of nonverbal assessment*. New York: Kluwer Academic/Plenum Press.

Wolf, M., & Bowers, P. G. (1999). The double-deficit hypothesis for the developmental dyslexias. *Journal of Educational Psychology*, *91*, 415–438.

Woodcock, R. W. (1990). Theoretical foundations of the WJ-R measures of cognitive ability. *Journal of Psychoeducational Assessment*, *8*, 231–258.

Woodcock, R. W. (1991). Woodcock Language Proficiency Battery—Revised: English and Spanish forms. *Journal of Psychoeducational Assessment*, *8*, 231–258.

Woodcock, R. W., McGrew, K. S., & Mather, N. (2001). *Woodcock-Johnson III Tests of Cognitive Abilities*. Itasca, IL; Riverside.

Woodcock, R. W., & Muñoz-Sandoval, A. F. (1996). *Bateria Woodcock-Muñoz Pruebas de habilidad cognoscitiva—Revisada*. Chicago: Riverside.

CHAPTER 12

Wechsler Nonverbal Scale of Ability (WNV)

Jack A. Naglieri, Kimberly Brunnert

INTRODUCTION

General ability (*g*) has been the underlying model for IQ tests since the early 1900s. These tests were and continue to be comprised of questions that are verbal (e.g., vocabulary or word analogies), quantitative (e.g., math word problems or math calculation), and spatial (arranging blocks to match a simple design or assembling puzzles to make a common object). The *spatial* tests have been described as *nonverbal* because it is an easier concept to understand, not because of any intention to measure *nonverbal ability*. In fact, Wechsler's view was that "the subtests are different measures of intelligence, not measures of different kinds of intelligence" (1958, p. 64). The *Technical and Interpretive Manual* for the Wechsler Nonverbal Scale of Ability (WNV; Wechsler & Naglieri, 2006a) also cites Boake (2002) as noting that "Wechsler viewed verbal and performance tests as equally valid measures of intelligence" (2006, p. 1). Further, Naglieri (2003b, 2008a) wrote that the term *nonverbal* refers to the content of the test, not a type of ability.

There is considerable experimental support for the concept of general intelligence as measured by tests such as the Wechsler and Binet (see Jensen, 1998, for a review). But the content of these tests sometimes presents a problem for assessment of culturally and linguistically diverse populations. For an individual who has not had the chance to acquire verbal and quantitative skills due to limited opportunity to learn or a disability, verbal and quantitative tests designed to measure general ability may be a good predictor of current academic performance but not a good reflection of their ability. For example, typical Native-American Navajo children living on a reservation in northern Arizona earn low scores on the Verbal scale but average scores on the Performance scale of the Wechsler (Naglieri & Yazzie, 1983) because they speak English as a second language and have had insufficient exposure to the language of a typical American child. Suzuki and Valencia (1997) argued that verbal and quantitative questions found on most traditional IQ tests interfere with accurate assessment of minority children; therefore, a nonverbal test of general ability such as the WNV (Wechsler & Naglieri, 2006b) offers a viable method for evaluating ability for these children.

The essence of a nonverbal test of general ability is that it does not contain verbal and quantitative test questions, although it may

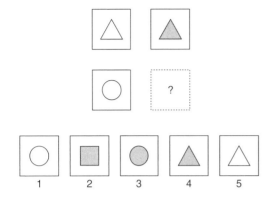

FIGURE 12.1
Simple Test Question from the WNV Matrices Subtest

involve verbal ways to solve the problem and it does require intellectual effort on the part of the examinee. For example, Figure 12.1 shows a simple nonverbal test question like those included in the Matrices subtest of the WNV. The item has shapes that vary across the horizontal and vertical dimensions that the examinee must recognize and understand to answer the analogy expressed using geometric figures (e.g., it is a figural analogy arranged in a matrix). In Figure 12.1, for example, the differences between the top and bottom rows is that the shape inside boxes changes (a triangle appears on the top row and a circle on the bottom row). The difference between the first and second column included in the top row is the addition of shading in the right column. The examinee needs to understand the interrelationships among these variables (shape and shading across the columns and rows) to arrive at the correct answer (option 3). The child may, or may not, use a verbal description (in any language) of the figures contained within the matrix or the child may simply look at the shapes and understand which option is the answer with minimal verbal analysis.

Tests that measure general ability nonverbally may have different formats, but the essential goal of these tests is the same: to measure ability nonverbally. For example, some nonverbal tests are comprised of one type of item, the progressive matrix (e.g., the Naglieri Nonverbal Ability Test—Second Edition [NNAT-2]; Naglieri, 2008b) given in a group format or individual format (Naglieri Nonverbal Ability Test—Individual Form [NNAT-1]; Naglieri, 2003b). Another method is to use several different types of nonverbal subtests as found in the WNV (as well as the Universal Nonverbal Intelligence Test [UNIT; Bracken & McCallum, 1998]; see Bracken and McCallum's chapter in this book). The slight variation in administration format and subtest composition notwithstanding, the goal is the same: to measure general ability nonverbally, and in so doing, provide a way effectively and fairly to assess a wide variety of individuals regardless of their educational or linguistic backgrounds.

DESCRIPTION OF THE WNV

Subtest Background

The WNV is comprised of a variety of subtests that are intended to measure general ability in different ways. For example, although the nonverbal subtests on the WNV are all alike in that they do not require language or arithmetic skills, they are diverse in their specific requirements. For example, some of the subtests have a strong visual-spatial requirement, others demand recall of spatial information or recall of the sequence of information, and others involve paper-and-pencil skills. This multidimensionality of task requirements distinguishes the WNV from tests that use one type of test format, such as the NNAT-2 (Naglieri, 2008b), which uses progressive matrices exclusively.

Most of the WNV subtests have appeared in previous editions of the Wechsler scales (Wechsler Preschool and Primary Scale of Intelligence—Third Edition [WPPSI-III], Wechsler Intelligence Scale for Children—Third Edition [WISC-III], Wechsler Intelligence Scale for Children—Fourth Edition

[WISC-IV], Wechsler Intelligence Scale for Children—Fourth Edition—Integrated [WISC-IV Integrated], Wechsler Adult Intelligence Scale—Fourth Edition [WAIS-III], Wechsler Memory Scale—Third Edition [WMS-III]), and have an established record of reliability and validity for the nonverbal measurement of general ability. Adaptation of the subtests was necessary to accommodate the new pictorial directions format, identify items that were most appropriate for the specific ages, and provide directions in the six languages. Each WNV subtest was included only after careful examination of both the content and form of the items vis-à-vis the goals of this particular instrument. The origins and descriptions of the WNV subtests are referenced in Table 12.1.

Each subtest is further described in the following.

Matrices

The Matrices (MA) subtest requires the examinee to discover how different geometric shapes are spatially or logically interrelated. The multiple-choice options provide potential answers that vary in the degree to which each option completes the relationships among the parts. The items are displayed using basic geometric figures such as squares, circles, and triangles using some combination of the colors black, white, yellow, blue, and green. Items were constructed using shapes and colors that would maintain interest and minimize the likelihood that impaired color

TABLE 12.1   Subtests Origin and Description

Subtest (Abbreviation)	Origin and Description
Matrices (MA)	This subtest was adapted from the NNAT–I. The examinee looks at an incomplete figural matrix and selects which of the four or five response options is the missing piece.
Coding (CD)	This subtest was adapted from the WISC-IV. The examinee follows a key that provides symbols that correspond with shapes (Coding A) or numbers (Coding B).
Object Assembly (OA)	This subtest was adapted from the WPPSI-III and the WISC–III, and has one new item. The child is presented with puzzle pieces that are placed by the examiner in a specified layout. The child completes the puzzle within a specified time limit.
Recognition (RG)	This is a new match-to-stimulus subtest. The child looks at a page with a design with geometric patterns on it for three seconds. The child then chooses which of four or five response options on the next page match the viewed stimulus.
Spatial Span (SSp)	This subtest was adapted from the WMS–III. The examinee mimics the examiner's tapping on a series of blocks either in the same order as the examiner (Spatial Span Forward) or in the reverse order (Spatial Span Backward).
Picture Arrangement (PA)	This subtest is adapted from the WAIS–III and a research version of the WISC–IV Integrated. The examinee uses a set of picture cards, which the examiner has placed on the table in a specified order, to tell a logical story within a specified time limit.

vision would influence the scores. The WNV Matrices items are composed of a variety of formats (e.g., geometric patterns, reasoning by analogy, and spatial visualization) previously used in the NNAT-I. Matrices is always administered (i.e., it is given to examinees in both age bands and is included in both the 4- and 2-subtest batteries).

Coding

The Coding (CD) subtest requires the examinee to copy symbols (e.g., a dash, two vertical lines, an open parenthesis) that are paired with simple geometric shapes or numbers according to a key provided at the top of the page. There are two forms of the Coding subtest: Form A is used in the 4-subtest battery for ages 4:0–7:11 and Form B is used in the 4-subtest battery for ages 8:0–21:11. The Coding subtest is adapted for use in the WNV from the WISC-IV by eliminating reversible shapes (e.g., left and right parentheses) for the younger age group and evenly distributing the use of each code across each row (e.g., for Coding Form B, the stimuli range from 1 to 9).

Object Assembly

The Object Assembly (OA) subtest is comprised of items that require the examinee to complete pieces of a puzzle to form a recognizable object such as a ball or a car. These items vary in the number of pieces (from 2 to 11) and the complexity with which they have been disassembled. Object Assembly is included in the 4-subtest battery of the WNV for examinees ages 4:0–7:11. The Object Assembly subtest was adapted for use in the WNV by using items from WPPSI-III (e.g., bear, apple, dog, star, calf, and tree), the WISC-III (e.g., ball), and one new item (i.e., glasses).

Recognition

The Recognition (RG) subtest was created for use in the WNV and is included in both the 4- and 2-subtest batteries for examinees ages

4:0–7:11. It requires the examinee to examine a stimulus (e.g., a square with a small circle in the center) for three seconds and then choose which option is identical to the stimulus that was just seen. The figures are colored black, white, yellow, blue, and/or green to maintain interest and minimize the likelihood that impaired color vision will influence the scores.

Spatial Span

The Spatial Span (SSp) subtest requires the examinee to touch a group of blocks arranged on an 8-by-11-inch board in a nonsystematic spatial manner in the same and reverse order of that demonstrated by the examiner. Spatial Span is included in both the 4- and 2-subtest batteries for ages 8:0–21:11. The Spatial Span subtest was adapted for use in the WNV from the WMS-III and adapted, like all the subtests, to the pictorial directions format.

Picture Arrangement

The Picture Arrangement (PA) subtest requires the examinee to arrange cartoon-like illustrations into a sequence that is logical and makes sense. Picture Arrangement is included in the 4-subtest battery for examinees ages 8:0–21:11. The Picture Arrangement subtest was adapted for use in the WNV by merging colorized items from the WAIS-III (e.g., choir, speak, and shark) and items from a research edition of the WISC-IV Integrated (e.g., duck, storm, farm, shadow, and broken).

STRUCTURE OF THE TEST

The WNV is structured in four ways, combining subtests selected to best meet the examinee's and examiner's needs. There are 4- and 2-subtest batteries for each age band, 4:0–7:11 and 8:0–21:11. The subtests that are in each are referenced in Figure 12.2.

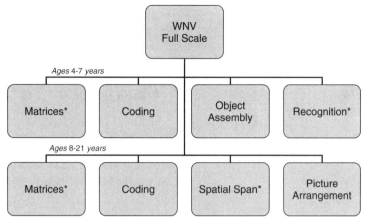

Note: Subtests included in the 2-subtest version have an asterisk.

FIGURE 12.2

Structure of the WNV

The examinee's raw scores are converted to T scores for each subtest, which have a mean of 50 and a standard deviation of 10. Using the T scores for each subtest, analyses can be performed to compare the examinee's performance across the subtests and to identify strengths and weaknesses. There is a Full Scale Score that can be calculated for each battery that has a mean of 100 and a standard deviation of 15. There are separate WNV norms tables based on standardization samples collected in the United States and Canada. For Spatial Span, there are additional analyses that can be performed to examine the difference between Spatial Span Forward and Spatial Span Backward, as well as the longest span in either direction.

ADMINISTRATION AND SCORING

Tips on Administration

Unlike most tests of its kind, the WNV administration begins with a standardized short introduction that tells examinees that they need to look at the pictorial directions and that they can ask the examiner questions if necessary. Like the other spoken text included in the WNV, these sentences are provided in English, French, Spanish, Chinese, German, and Dutch. Actual administration procedures follow carefully scripted directions designed to ensure that the demands of the tasks are completely understood by all examinees. There are three steps to the administration directions:

Step 1 uses the standardized directions, which are always administered and should never be changed. These directions must be administered in every case and include gestures that correspond to the pictorial directions. Pictorial directions are used at Step 1 to provide a standardized method of communicating the demands of the task. These pictorial directions (see Figure 12.3) show a scene like the one the examinee is currently in. The frames of the directions show the progression of an examinee being presented with the question, then thinking about the item, and finally, choosing the correct solution.

Step 1 instructions include actions by the examiner that must be carefully followed to maximize the likelihood that the examinee understands the correspondence between the materials and the task. Gestures are used to direct the examinee's attention to specific portions

Note: The actual WNV Pictorial Directions appear in color.

FIGURE 12.3

WNV Pictorial Direction

of the pictorial directions and to the stimulus materials and sometimes to demonstrate the task itself. Sometimes simple statements are also included because they convey the importance of both time and accuracy to the examinee.

Step 2 directions are used only after the standard directions are provided. These instructions must also be followed exactly and are given only when an examinee is unclear about what he or she is being asked to do. These directions include standardized simple sentences and gestures for communicating the requirements of the task to the examinee. Verbal directions provide another way to ensure that the examinee understands the demands of the tasks and are provided in English as well as Spanish, German, French, Chinese, and Dutch. These translations are to be used only when the following two conditions are both met: (1) the WNV is being administered to an examinee who speaks one of the languages, and (2) the examiner or a professional interpreter speaks the language.

Step 3 gives an opportunity to provide help, but these directions are used only after the previous two steps have been administered. This is the only step of administration that gives the examiner flexibility. For example, the examiner may say or sign additional instructions or questions. In general, examiners are given the opportunity to communicate in whatever manner they think will best explain the demands of the subtest based

on their judgment of the examinee's needs. This could include providing further explanation or demonstration of the task, restating or revising the verbal directions, or using additional words to describe the requirements of the task. At no time, however, is it permissible to teach the examinee how to solve the items. Instead, the goal of Step 3 instructions is to provide additional help to ensure that the examinee understands the demands of the task, not to show how to teach a way to solve the items. The amount of help provided and the determination about when to stop is based on professional judgment.

When using an interpreter to facilitate communication prior to and during administration, it is important that the interpreter have guidelines and training about what is and what is not permitted. This person should translate a general explanation of the testing situation for the examinee, including the introductory paragraph at the beginning of Chapter 3 in the WNV *Administration and Scoring Manual* before administration begins. It is also important that the interpreter recognize the boundaries of his or her role in administration. For example, although it is appropriate for the interpreter to translate the examiner's responses to an examinee's response to a sample item, it is not acceptable for the interpreter to make additional statements unless instructed to do so. Importantly, at no time should the interpreter communicate any information that could influence the examinee's scores. See Brunnert, Naglieri, and Hardy-Braz (2009) for more information about working with translators and especially when testing those who are deaf or hard of hearing.

Administration of the WNV subtests is designed to be simple and easy. The *Administration and Scoring Manual* includes a section prior to actual administration directions that describes the subtest, the materials needed, start, stop, and reverse rules, scoring, as well as general issues unique to each subtest. The Manual also provides considerable discussion of the physical materials, uses and applications for the two versions of the WNV, and general testing, administration, and scoring issues. In this chapter, we will highlight some of the most important points, but the reader is advised to carefully study that Administration and Scoring Manual. What follows is a subtest-by-subtest discussion of specific administration issues.

Matrices

Although the Matrices subtest is a very straightforward subtest to administer, examiners should always be aware of possible responses that may suggest concern. For example, some students who are particularly impulsive might select the option that is mostly but not completely correct because the options were written with varying degrees of accuracy. If an examinee is not looking at the options closely, one of those that is almost correct may be selected. Similarly, if an examinee takes a long time to respond, the examiner may (after about 30 seconds) prompt a response.

Coding

The examinee is allowed to correct mistakes by crossing out the incorrect symbol and writing his or her response next to it, so the pencil without an eraser needs to be used for the Coding subtest. The examiner should ensure that the examinee works from left to right and from top to bottom without skipping any items or row and by providing the appropriate instruction when needed.

The examiner also provides instruction that informs the examinee to work as quickly as possible. For that reason, examinees should not be allowed to spend too much time making corrections.

Object Assembly

The examiner should always set up the puzzle pieces on the same side of the Stimulus Book as the examinee's dominant hand. Then remove the Stimulus Book before administering the Sample Item. The examiner should also ensure that the examinee works as quickly as possible. If the examinee is still completing a puzzle when the time limit expires, the examiner should place his or her hand over the puzzle to stop the examinee's progress, and record the examinee's answer. If the examinee seems upset at that point, the examiner should allow the examinee to finish but not consider any additional work for scoring purposes. It is also important to remember to begin timing after the last word of the instruction is provided. Assembling the pieces for the examinee requires a specific method fully articulated in the WNV *Administration and Scoring Manual* (Wechsler & Naglieri, 2006c). Essentially, the method requires that the puzzle pieces are put before the child in a specific format *face down*. Once all the pieces are before the child, then they are turned over in the order indicated by the number on the back of each piece.

Recognition

Examiners must be sure to expose each stimulus page for exactly 3 seconds. To do so will likely require that the page be exposed at a precise time when the stopwatch strikes an exact second and then being prepared (e.g., having your finger under the page so that you are ready) to turn the page exactly when the 3 seconds have elapsed. Do not allow examinees to turn the pages.

Spatial Span

The Spatial Span Board must be placed so that the examinee can easily reach all cubes on the board and only the examiner can see the numbers on the back of each blue block. Also, always set the Spatial Span Board on the same side of the Stimulus Book as the examinee's dominant hand. Tap the blocks at a rate of one per second and raise the hand approximately one foot above the Spatial Span Board between each tap. If the examinee does not respond after the examiner taps a sequence, the examiner can say, "It's your turn." Always administer both Spatial Span Forward and Spatial Span Backward, regardless of the examinee's performance on Spatial Span Forward and always administer both trials of an item regardless of the examinee's performance on the first trial.

Picture Arrangement

The examiner should always place the Picture Arrangement Cards on the same side of the Stimulus Book as the examinee's dominant hand and remove the Stimulus Book with Pictorial Directions before administering the Sample Item. Having the cards in the box in the order in which they are to be exposed to the examinee is an excellent way to efficiently deliver the item. When the examinee completes the item, record his or her sequence, then resequence the cards in the presentation order for the next administration. If the examinee is going very slowly, it is permissible to ensure that the examinee realizes that he or she should work as quickly as possible. If the examinee orders the cards from right to left instead of left to right, the examiner should ask, "Where does it start?"

If the examinee is in the midst of completing a story when the time limit expires, the examiner should place his or her hand over the story to stop the examinee's progress, and record the examinee's answer. If the examinee seems upset that he or she was stopped while completing the story, the examiner should allow the examinee to finish. However, the examiner should not consider any additional work by the examinee for scoring purposes.

How to Score the Test

Five of the six subtests (i.e., Matrices, Coding, Recognition, Spatial Span, and Picture Arrangement) are scored by summing the number of points earned during administration. The sixth subtest (i.e., Object Assembly) has time bonuses for some items that might be part of the raw score.

The raw scores are converted to T scores. The sum of T scores is converted to a Full Scale Score, which has a corresponding percentile rank and confidence interval.

Information can also be assessed at the subtest level for the 4-subtest battery by comparing the T score an examinee earned on a subtest to the mean T score for all four subtests administered. If the difference between the subtest T score and the mean T score is significant, then that subtest is considered a strength or weakness. Base rates are provided for each difference. Additionally, optional analyses can be performed on the Spatial Span results as described later in this chapter.

Use of Scoring and Report Writing Software

The WNV Scoring Assistant provides an automated way to obtain all standard and derived scores based on the U.S. as well as the Canadian versions of the test. The report writing feature of the software provides reports that are appropriate for clinicians as well as parents. The parent report is available in English, French, and Spanish. The software also provides links between the WNV and the WIAT-II and all the ability comparisons to achievement.

STANDARDIZATION, NORMS, AND PSYCHOMETRICS

Characteristics of the Standardization Sample

There were two samples collected for the creation of the WNV norms: one in the United

States and the other in Canada. There were also samples collected of special groups and of other tests for validity research. The U.S. sample consisted of 1,323 examinees stratified across 5 demographic variables: age (4:0–21:11), sex, race/ethnicity (Black, White, Hispanic, Asian, and Other), education level (8 years or less of school, 9–11 years of school, 12 years of school [high school degree or equivalent], 13–15 years of school [some college or associate's degree], and 16 or more years of school [college or graduate degree]), and geographic region (Northeast, North Central, South, and West). Note that education level was determined by the parent education for examinees ages 4:0–17:11 and by the examinee's own education for ages 18:0–21:11.

The Canadian sample consisted of 875 examinees stratified across five demographic variables: age (4:0–21:11), sex, race/ethnicity (Caucasians, Asians, First Nations, and Other), education level (less than a high school diploma; high school diploma or equivalent; college/vocational diploma or some university, but no degree obtained; and a university degree), and geographic region (West, Central, and East). Additionally, the Canadian sample consisted of 70% English speakers, 18% French speakers, and 12% speakers of other languages.

Reliability of the Scales

The reliability estimates for the WNV were provided by subtest and Full Scale Scores by age and over all ages. There are reliability estimates provided for the U.S. normative sample, for the Canadian normative sample, and for all the special groups that are reported in the WNV *Technical and Interpretive Manual*. The reliability estimates for the U.S. normative sample ranged from .74 to .91 for the subtests and were .91 for both Full Scale Scores across ages. The reliability estimates for the Canadian normative sample ranged from .73 to .90 for the subtests, were .90 for the Full Scale Score: 4-Subtest Battery, and .91 for the Full

TABLE 12.2 Reliability Estimate Ranges by Special Study

Special Group	Reliability Estimate Range
Gifted	.77–.97
MR Mild	.80–.93
MR Moderate	.87–.93
Reading and Written Expression Learning Disorders	.72–.88
Language Disorders	.74–.97
English Language Learners	.70–.96
Deaf	.77–.98
Hard of Hearing	.75–.97

Scale Score: 2-Subtest Battery. The reliability estimates for the studies with examinees that were diagnosed with or classified as being gifted, having mild mental retardation, moderate mental retardation, reading and written expression learning disorders, language disorders, English language learners, Deaf, and Hard of Hearing are shown in Table 12.2.

Other reliability information is provided in the WNV *Technical and Interpretive Manual*. This other information includes the standard error of measurements (SEM), confidence intervals, and test–retest stability estimates. SEMs are provided for both the U.S. and the Canadian normative samples by subtest and Full Scale Scores by age in years, for ages 4:0–15:11, and by age bands, from ages 16:0–21:11. The confidence intervals, which are calculated with the standard error of estimate (SEE), are provided alongside the *T* Score to Full Scale Score conversion tables at both the 90% and 95% levels (see Tables A.2 and A.3 in the WNV *Administration and Scoring Manual*). Test–retest stability estimates were also provided in the WNV *Technical and Interpretive Manual*.

USE OF THE **WNV**

Interpretation Methods

Like any test, WNV test results should always be interpreted with consideration of the many factors that can influence obtained scores. Perhaps the most important are issues such as the behaviors observed during testing, and relevant educational and environmental backgrounds, and physical and emotional status, all within the context of the reason for referral. In order to obtain the greatest amount of information from the WNV, there are some important methods of interpretation that warrant discussion. Some of these methods are the same for the 4- and 2-subtest batteries, and others are unique to each version. In this chapter, the issues that apply to both batteries will be covered first and then the finer points of interpretation relevant to each version will be examined separately.

Interpretation of the Two WNV Versions

Both versions of the WNV are comprised of subtests (set at a mean of 50 and SD of 10) that are combined to yield a Full Scale score (set at a mean of 100 and SD of 15). The WNV subtest scores are set on the T score metric of 50 and 10 (as opposed to a traditional scaled score with a mean of 10 and SD of 3). This format was selected because the individual subtests had sufficient range of raw scores, allowing for the use of T scores, which have a greater range and precision than scaled scores. For example, the WNV subtest T scores range from 10 to 90, yielding 81 possible different scores, whereas a scaled score typically ranges from 3 to 20, yielding only 18 different scores. The use of the T score also provides greater precision on each subtest, allowing for higher reliability coefficients of the Full Scale score.

The WNV Full Scale scores are standard scores with a mean of 100 and SD of 15 based on either the 4- or 2-subtest batteries. This score

provides a nonverbal estimate of general ability that has excellent reliability and validity. Both the Full Scale and subtest T scores are based on the U.S. or Canadian standardization samples and can be used to measure general ability nonverbally. It is important to recognize that the *nonverbal* label refers to the fact that the test items do not contain verbal and quantitative content and does not suggest that a specific type of ability is being assessed. Additionally, even though the WNV subtests have different demands—that is, some are spatial (e.g., Matrices or Object Assembly), others involve sequencing (Picture Arrangement and Spatial Span), require memory (e.g., Recognition and Spatial Span), or use symbol associations (Coding)—they all measure general ability. The WNV measures general ability nonverbally. General ability allows us, for example, to understand spatial as well as verbal and mathematical concepts, remember visual relationships as well as quantitative or verbal facts, and work with sequences of information of all kinds. The content of the questions may be visual or verbal, and require memory or recognition, but general ability (sometimes referred to as g) underlies performance on all these kinds of tasks and the WNV Full Scale is an excellent measure of g.

WNV 4-Subtest Battery Interpretation

Step 1: The first step in interpretation of the 4- and 2-subtest versions of the WNV is to examine the Full Scale score. This score is the most reliable and valid representation of general ability on the scale. The Full Scale score should be reported with its associated percentile score, categorical description (Average, Above Average, etc.), and confidence interval. A statement such as the following illustrates how these concepts might be included in a written document:

Sam obtained a WNV Full Scale score of 91, which is ranked at the 27th percentile and falls within the Average classification. This means that he performed as well as or better than 27% of examinees his age in the normative sample. There is a 90% chance that his true Full Scale score falls within the range 85–99.

Step 2: The second step in interpretation of the 4-subtest version of the WNV is to examine the *T* scores the examinee earned on the subtests. Analysis of this type must take into consideration the lower reliability of these scores and the increased probability that variability will reflect measurement error. Examination of the four WNV subtests should also be conducted with consideration that even though the subtests are all nonverbal measures of general ability they do have unique attributes (i.e., some involve remembering information, others spatial demands, etc.). Additionally, variability across the subtests should be expected and, therefore, statistical guidelines should be followed to ensure that any differences interpreted are beyond those that could be expected by chance. In fact, Wechsler and Naglieri (2006a) reported the cumulative percentages, mean, and *SD* of subtest scatter (e.g., highest–lowest subtest score for each individual in the U.S. standardization group) in Table B.5 in the WNV *Administration and Scoring Manual*. The mean score was 16.5 (*SD* = 7.5), indicating that practitioners can expect differences among the WNV subtests. In fact, approximately 50% of that sample had a range of subtest scores that was between 0 and 16. If *unusual* is defined at 10% of the U.S. standardization sample, then a range of 27 or more would meet that criterion. Scatter is one way to determine whether the WNV subtests vary, but when the goal is to determine whether there is significant variability and to relate the unique contributions of each subtest to other findings,

a different method is recommended. That method requires that the examinee's subtest scores are compared to that examinee's mean.

The values needed for significance when comparing a WNV subtest for an examinee to that examinee's mean *T* score are provided in the WNV *Administration and Scoring Manual* (Table B.1) and in more detail by Brunnert, Naglieri, and Hardy-Braz (2009) and summarized here in Table 12.3. These values were computed utilizing Davis's (1959) formula (and Silverstein's 1982, modification of this procedure) for the difference between the average of several scores obtained by one examinee and each of his or her scores included in the average. For example, when four WNV subtest *T* scores are compared with the mean of the four *T* scores, a *z* value that takes into account the number of comparisons needs to be used. The standard errors of measurement for the WNV subtest *T* scores of the U.S. and Canadian samples were obtained from the WNV *Technical and Interpretive Manual* (Wechsler & Naglieri, 2006a, Tables 4.4 and 4.5) and were used for these calculations. (See Silverstein, 1982, for more information and Naglieri and Paolitto, 2005, for values for the WISC-IV.)

The following steps should be used to compare each of the four WNV subtest *T* scores to the child's mean subtest *T* score:

1. Calculate the mean of the four subtest *T* scores.
2. Calculate the difference between each subtest *T* score and the mean.
3. Subtract the mean from each of the subtest *T* scores (retain the sign).
4. Find the value needed for significance using the examinee's age group and the desired significance level in Table 12.3.
5. If the absolute value of the difference is equal to or greater than the value in the table, the result is statistically significant.

TABLE 12.3   Differences Required for Significance When Comparing Each WNV Subtest for the 4-Subtest Battery *T* Scores to the Examinee's Average Subtest *T* Score for the U.S. and Canadian Standardization Samples by Age Group

Country	Age	*p*-Value	MA	CD	OA	RG
United States	4:0–7:11	.10	7.4	7.9	8.7	8.6
		.05	8.3	8.8	9.7	9.6
			MA	CD	SSp	PA
	8:0–21:11	.10	6.8	8.7	7.5	9.3
		.05	7.6	9.7	8.4	10.4
			MA	CD	OA	RG
Canada	4:0–7:11	.10	8.1	8.0	9.1	8.6
		.05	9.0	8.9	10.1	9.6
			MA	CD	SSp	PA
	8:0–21:11	.10	6.8	8.7	7.4	9.6
		.05	7.6	9.7	8.3	10.7

NOTE: MA = Matrices, CD = Coding, OA = Object Assembly, RG = Recognition, SSp = Spatial Span, and PA = Picture Arrangement.

6. If the subtest difference from the mean is lower than the mean, then the difference is a weakness; if the subtest difference from the mean is greater than the mean, then the difference is a strength.

For example, if an 18-year-old from the United States obtained *T* scores of 65 on Matrices, 42 on Coding, 39 on Spatial Span, and 61 on Picture Arrangement, the mean *T* score would be 51.8. Using the values from Brunnert et al. (2009) and the .05 level of significance, Matrices would be considered a relative strength for this examinee (65 − 51.8 = 13.3, which exceeds the critical value of 7.6 for the .05 level of significance). The *T* score for Spatial Span is significantly lower than the examinee's mean *T* score (39 − 51.8 = −12.8, which exceeds the critical value of 8.4 for the .05 level of confidence), and would be considered a relative weakness. Similarly, the *T* score for Coding is significantly lower than the mean *T* score (42 −

51.8 = −9.8, which exceeds the critical value of 9.7 for the .05 level of confidence), and is also a relative weakness.

When there is significant variability in the WNV subtests, it is also important to determine whether a weakness relative to the examinee's overall mean is also sufficiently below the average range. Determining whether a child has significant variability relative to his or her own average score is a valuable way to determine strengths and weaknesses relative to the child's mean score, but Naglieri (1999) cautioned that a relative weakness could also be significantly below the normative mean. He recommended that any subtest score that is low relative to the child's means should also fall below the average range to be considered a noteworthy weakness (e.g., < 1 *SD* below the mean). In the example above, the Spatial Span *T* score of 39 would be considered a weakness from the ipsative *and* normative perspectives, but the Coding score of 42 would not. This would strengthen the

TABLE 12.4 Differences Required for Significance When Comparing Recognition or Spatial Span to Matrices on the WNV 2-Subtest Battery for U.S. and Canadian Standardization Samples by Age Group

United States		Age Group in Years	
		4:0–7:11	8:0–21:11
$p = .10$	MA vs. RG	9.9	—
	MA vs. SSp	—	5.3
$p = .05$	MA vs. RG	11.8	—
	MA vs. SSp	—	6.3
Canada			
$p = .10$	MA vs. RG	9.2	—
	MA vs. SSp	—	8.1
$p = .05$	MA vs. RG	11.0	—
	MA vs. SSp	—	9.7

level of concern about this finding and more strongly suggest that additional examination using a multidimensional measure of ability such as the Cognitive Assessment System (see Naglieri, 1999) could be appropriate. Subtest differences that are significant (in addition to the Full Scale score) should be described in a manner similar to the following:

> *His scores on the individual WNV subtest scores varied significantly, suggesting a relative strength on Matrices, a subtest that requires understanding the relationships among spatial designs. A relative weakness was found on Coding and his Spatial Span subtest T score was significantly below his overall subtest mean and the normative mean of 50. Both of these subtests require recall of information, and this finding suggests that further examination of immediate memory may be indicated.*

WNV 2-Subtest Battery Interpretation

The differences required for significance when each pair of WNV subtests included in the 2-Subtest battery are compared are provided in Table 12.4. These values are used, for example, to determine whether a T score difference of 11 points between Matrices and Recognition is significant for an examinee who is 7:3 years old. To use this table, simply subtract one subtest T score from the other (ignore the sign) and compare the result to the value in the table that corresponds to the desired level of significance (.10 or .05). If the obtained value is equal to or greater than the value in the table, then the result is significant. Determining how often a difference of a specific magnitude occurred in the U.S. or Canadian samples would further clarify the importance of the finding. For example, Table B.4 of the WNV *Administration and Scoring Manual* provides the base rates of subtest T score differences by the direction of the difference. Using that table, we find that about 11% of examinees aged 8:0–21:11 obtained T scores for Matrices that were 14 or more points higher than their T scores for Spatial Span. This information can be used to augment the interpretation of the significance of the difference between the scales.

WNV Full Scale Score Interpretation

The WNV Full Scale score is a nonverbal measure of general ability that should be reported with the corresponding confidence interval, percentile rank, and classification. The Full Scale and subtest T scores could be described in a manner similar to the following:

> *Gene obtained a WNV Full Scale score of 98, which falls in the Average range and is ranked at the 45th percentile. This means he did as well as or better than 45% of examinees his age in the normative sample on this nonverbal measure of general ability. There is a 90% chance that his true Full Scale score falls within the range of 91 to 105. There was significant variability between the two subtests that comprise the WNV. Gene performed significantly better on a subtest requiring reasoning with geometric designs (Matrices) than he did on a subtest requiring recall of a sequence of movements arranged in a spatial array (Spatial Span).*

This difference is also unusual, with only 4.3% of the population obtaining differences this large or larger, suggesting that further investigation is appropriate.

In-depth Interpretation of Spatial Span

The WNV Spatial Span subtest Forward and Backward scores can be interpreted separately, particularly when this test is embedded within the greater context of a comprehensive assessment. The sizes of the differences required for statistical significance by age and for the U.S. and Canadian samples are 11 and 13 for the .10 and .05 levels for the United States, and 10 and 13 for the Canadian standardization samples for the combined ages 8:0–21:11. This comparison can be accomplished using Table C.1 of the WNV *Administration and Scoring Manual*, which provides a way to convert the raw scores to *T* score equivalents for Spatial Span Forward and Spatial Span Backward. According to Table C.2 of the Manual, a difference of 9 *T* score points is needed at the .15 level (13 at the .05 level) to have a significant difference between these two scores. The frequency with which Forward and Backward score differences occurred in the normative sample are provided in Table C.3 of the test Manual, which presents the bases for the *T* score differences for the U.S. sample. The tables provide the base-rate data by the direction of the difference. For example, about 24% of examinees obtained Spatial Span Forward scores 7 or more points higher than their Spatial Span Backward scores, whereas about 25% obtained Spatial Span Backward scores 7 or more points higher than their Spatial Span Forward scores.

Comparison of the differences between Spatial Span Forward and Backward *T* scores may provide useful information, but it should be integrated within the greater context of a comprehensive assessment. For example, if a Spatial Span Forward *T* score is 14 points higher than the Spatial Span Backward *T* score for a 13-year-old U.S. examinee, the difference would be significant (only 12 points are needed at the .05 level),

and the difference occurs in only 9% of the normative sample (see WNV *Administration and Scoring Manual*, Table C.3). This information would be expected to be similar to other similar test scores, such as WISC-IV Digit Span Forward vs. Digit Span Backward. Both of these tests' Backward scores should be related to the Planning Scale of the Cognitive Assessment System (see Naglieri, 1999) and may suggest that the examinee has difficulty with development and utilization of strategies for reversing the order of serial information.

IDENTIFICATION OF SPECIAL POPULATIONS

Specific Learning Disabilities

The Individuals with Disabilities Education Improvement Act (IDEIA) of 2004 has brought about widespread discussion of policies regarding the identification of children with *Specific Learning Disabilities (SLD)*. The law no longer requires, but does not disallow, the use of an ability–achievement discrepancy for eligibility determination, but the law clearly states that a comprehensive evaluation is required and that evaluation must include tests that are not culturally or linguistically discriminatory. This need for a comprehensive evaluation has also been advocated by the National Association of School Psychologists' "Position Statement on Identification of Children with Specific Learning Disabilities" (2007). Some researchers have argued that SLD is best identified by examining a pattern of strengths and weaknesses in cognitive processing scores (e.g., Hale, Flanagan, & Naglieri, 2008; Naglieri & Kaufman, 2008). How does the WNV fit into the process of evaluating children with SLD?

The WNV provides a nonverbal measure of general ability that can be compared to current achievement test scores to help determine whether a child is demonstrating academic performance that is commensurate with ability.

Unlike other measures of general ability that contain verbal and quantitative tests, the WNV provides an evaluation of ability that is not influenced by achievement-like content (see Naglieri & Bornstein, 2003, or Naglieri, 2008a, for more discussion of the similarity of test questions on ability and achievement tests). The WNV also provides a measure of ability that can be viewed as nondiscriminatory on the basis of race, ethnicity, language, and disability (see the following sections). The WNV is not, however, designed to be a test of basic psychological processes, and other tools should be used for that purpose (e.g., the Cognitive Assessment System; Naglieri & Das, 1997).

Practitioners who wish to compare WNV scores with the Wechsler Individual Achievement Test—Second Edition (WIAT–II; Pearson, 2005) can do so using the predicted-difference and simple-difference methods. The predicted-difference method takes into account the reliabilities and the correlations between the two measures. In this method, the ability score is used to predict an achievement score, and the differences between predicted and observed achievement scores are compared. Tables B.1–B.7 in the WNV *Technical and Interpretive Manual* provide the values needed for significance when conducting this analysis for children in the United States and Tables B.8–B.14 are used for comparing scores using the WNV Canadian normative sample with the WIAT–II (see Wechsler & Naglieri, 2006a for more details).

Simple differences between the WNV 4- and 2-subtest Full Scale standard scores compared with other achievement tests are provided by Brunnert et al. (2009). The achievement tests include the Kaufman Test of Educational Achievement—Second Edition (K–TEA II; Kaufman & Kaufman, 2004), Woodcock-Johnson Tests of Achievement—Third Edition (Woodcock, McGrew, & Mather, 2001), Diagnostic Achievement Battery—Third Edition (Newcomer, 2001), and the Wide Range Achievement Test—Fourth Edition (Wilkinson

& Robertson, 2006). Regardless of which method is used, the examiner can augment those findings with the base rates provided in the WNV *Technical and Interpretive Manual*'s Tables B.1–B.14 for the WIAT–II. Using both the reliability of the difference and the rate at which ability and achievement test score differences occur in the normal population will provide an effective comparison of these two measures.

Attention Deficit Hyperactivity Disorders

The attention deficit hyperactivity disorders (ADHD) are evaluated on the basis of the correspondence of behavioral characteristics described by parents with the DSM-IV-TR criteria. The essential feature of ADHD is currently described as a consistent pattern of inattention and/or hyperactivity-impulsivity found more frequently and more severely than is typical in individuals at a comparable level of development. Although the DSM-IV-TR states that those with ADHD may demonstrate variability in IQ, the diagnostic criteria are based on behavioral rather than cognitive factors even though some have argued that cognitive processing scores *should* play a role in identification (Goldstein & Naglieri, 2006). The WNV, therefore, like any test of general ability, plays a minimal role in the diagnostic process; its only role may be in helping evaluate the child's level of general ability.

Gifted

The underrepresentation of minority children in classes for the gifted has been and continues to be an important educational problem (Ford, 1998; Naglieri & Ford, 2005). In fact, Naglieri and Ford (2003) stressed that Black, Hispanic, and Native-American students are underrepresented by 50% to 70% in gifted education programs. In recent years, addressing this problem has become more focused on the types of tests used when evaluating the ability of children potentially eligible for gifted programming. Some have argued that the verbal and quantitative content of some of the ability tests used and procedures followed are inconsistent with the characteristics of culturally, ethnically, and linguistically diverse populations (Naglieri & Ford, 2005; Naglieri, Brulles, & Lansdowne, 2009). That is, because IQ has traditionally been defined within a verbal/quantitative/nonverbal framework, students with limited English-language and math skills earn lower scores on the Verbal and Quantitative scales these tests include because they do not have sufficient knowledge of the language or training in math, not because of low ability (Bracken & Naglieri, 2003; Naglieri, 2008a). If a student has not had the chance to acquire verbal and quantitative skills due to limited opportunity to learn, or a disability, verbal and quantitative tests designed to measure general ability may be a good predictor of current academic performance but an inaccurate reflection of their ability to learn especially after instruction is provided. One way to address this issue is to include tests that measure general ability nonverbally. Naglieri and Ford (2003) demonstrated the effectiveness of using a group nonverbal measure of general ability (the Naglieri Nonverbal Ability Test—Multilevel Form [NNAT-ML; Naglieri, 1997]) for increasing the identification of Hispanic and Black students. Similarly, the WNV provides an individually administered way to assess general ability nonverbally and increase the participation of minorities in gifted classes. There is evidence that children in gifted education programs earn high scores on the WNV.

The WNV was administered to gifted children who were carefully matched to control subjects included in the standardization sample on the basis of age, race/ethnicity, and education level. The differences between the means were calculated using Cohen's (1996) formula (i.e., the difference between the means of the two groups divided by the square root of the pooled variance). The study included 41 examinees, all of whom had already been identified as gifted using a standardized ability measure where they performed at 2 standard deviations above the mean or more. The students in the gifted programs performed significantly better than their matched counterparts from the normative sample with effect sizes that were large for the Full Scale Score: 4-Subtest Battery and Full Scale Score: 2-Subtest Battery. See Table 12.5 for more details.

Mentally Retarded

Naglieri and Rojahn (2001) suggested that assessment of mental retardation should take into

TABLE 12.5 WNV Means, *SD*s, and Effect Sizes for Special Populations and Matched Control Groups

	Special Population		**Matched Sample**			
	Mean	**SD**	**Mean**	**SD**	*n*	**Effect Size**
Moderate Mental Retardation	45.9	8.9	99.5	14.1	36	−4.5
Mild Mental Retardation	67.3	12.9	97.4	15.3	51	−2.1
Gifted	123.7	13.4	104.2	12.3	41	1.5
English Language Learners	101.7	13.4	102.1	13.4	55	0.0
Hard of Hearing	96.7	15.9	100.5	14.2	48	−0.3
Profoundly Deaf	102.5	9.0	100.8	14.3	37	0.1

consideration the appropriateness of the content of the IQ test used for the individual being evaluated. They found that minority children who were previously identified as having mental retardation earned lower Verbal than Performance IQ scores on the WISC-III, presumably because of the academic content of the verbal tests (Naglieri & Bornstein, 2003). When these same subjects were evaluated using a measure of ability that does not contain verbal and quantitative test questions (the Cognitive Assessment System; Naglieri & Das, 1997), the number of children who would still qualify as having mental retardation was reduced. They concluded, therefore, that measures of ability that do not contain verbal and quantitative questions are more desirable when assessing children for mental retardation, particularly when the children have had limited educational opportunities and have culturally and/or linguistically diverse backgrounds. The WNV is a tool that can evaluate general ability nonverbally, and thereby provide a way to assess ability without undue influence of language and knowledge for individuals suspected of having mental retardation.

There were two special studies of examinees with mental retardation performed with the standardization of the WNV, one for examinees who were diagnosed with Mild Mental Retardation and the other for examinees who were diagnosed with Moderate Mental Retardation. Examinees who were diagnosed with Mild Mental Retardation were included in the study if their cognitive ability was between 55 and 70 on a standardized ability test, if they were not institutionalized, and if they met the general criteria for inclusion in a special study (see Appendix C of the WNV *Technical and Interpretive Manual*). There were 51 examinees included in this study; 43 of these examinees were 8–21 and performed significantly worse than their matched counterparts from the normative sample with effect sizes (Cohen's *d*) large for the Full Scale Score: 4-Subtest Battery and Full Scale Score: 2-Subtest Battery. See Table 12.5 for more details.

Examinees who were diagnosed with Moderate Mental Retardation were accepted in the study if their cognitive ability was between 40 and 55 on a standardized ability test, if they were not institutionalized, and if they met the general criteria for inclusion in a special study (see Appendix C of the WNV *Technical and Interpretive Manual*). There were 31 examinees included in this study; 28 of these examinees were 8–21 and performed significantly worse than their matched counterparts from the normative sample with effect sizes (Cohen's *d*) large for the Full Scale Score: 2-Subtest Battery and Full Scale Score: 4-Subtest Battery. See Table 12.5 for more details.

Deaf and Hard of Hearing

There are numerous issues surrounding the evaluation of ability for individuals who are deaf or hard of hearing. A thorough discussion of these issues and those particularly relevant to the WNV can be found in Brunnert et al. (2009). In general, however, the assessment issues center on (1) content of the test and (2) communicating test requirements to the examinee. The former issue has been covered in the previous sections regarding evaluation of mentally retarded and gifted. The issue of communicating test requirements has also been discussed in the administration portion of this chapter. In essence, because the directions are given pictorially, and can be augmented with additional statements and/or communication using sign language, the WNV offers considerable advantages for appropriate evaluation of individuals who are deaf or hard of hearing as the research studies that follow illustrate.

Profoundly Deaf

Wechsler and Naglieri (2006a) reported a study of profoundly deaf examinees who were compared with cases from the standardization of the WNV who were matched on a number of important demographic variables. This included 37 examinees who "must not have been able to hear tones to interpret spoken language after the age of 18 months, must not lip read, must not be trained in the oral or auditory-verbal approach, and must not use cued speech (i.e., they must have routine discourse by some means of communicating other than spoken language). They must have severe to profound deafness (hearing loss measured with dB, Pure Tone Average greater than or equal to 55)" (Wechsler & Naglieri, 2006a, p. 65). Thirty-one of these examinees were 8–21 and performed minimally differently than their matched counterparts from the normative sample with effect sizes (Cohen's *d*) negligible for Full Scale Score: 4-Subtest Battery and Full Scale Score: 2-Subtest Battery. There is additional information about this sample of examinees from a survey collected with the WNV standardization (Wechsler & Naglieri, 2006a, Appendix D). See Table 12.5 for more details.

Hard of Hearing

The WNV Manual also describes a study of individuals who were hard of hearing and compared their WNV scores to a group from the standardization sample who were matched on a number of important demographic variables. This study included 48 examinees who "could have a unilateral or bilateral hearing loss or deafness, and the age of onset of their inability to hear could be any age and [they] could have cochlear implants" (WNV *Technical and Interpretive M*anual, pp. 65–66). Sixteen of these examinees were 4–7 and performed minimally differently than their matched counterparts from the normative sample with effect sizes (Cohen's *d*) that were negligible for Full Scale Score: 4-Subtest Battery, and Full Scale Score: 2-Subtest Battery. Thirty-two of these examinees were 8–20 and performed minimally differently than their matched counterparts from the normative sample with effect sizes (Cohen's *d*) that were negligible for Full Scale Score: 4-Subtest Battery, and Full Scale Score: 2-Subtest Battery. See Table 12.5 for more details; for more details about the sample, see the WNV *Technical and Interpretive Manual* (Appendix D).

English as a Second Language

It is clear that as the United States continues to become more diverse, the number of individuals whose primary language is not English will continue to increase. The largest of these groups is the Hispanic population, which is approximately 37 million or about 13% of the U.S. population, making it the largest minority group (Ramirez & de la Cruz, 2002). This population of Hispanics is dominated by individuals of Mexican origin (66.9%) who reside in the Western (44.2%) and Southern (34.8%) regions of the country. Hispanics aged 25 and older are less likely to have a high school diploma than non-Hispanic whites (57.0% and 88.7%, respectively). Importantly, 27.0% of Hispanics have less than a ninth-grade education compared with only 4.0% of non-Hispanic whites (Ramirez & de la Cruz, 2002). The large number of immigrants in this country makes clear the need for psychological tests that are appropriate for those who come from these working-class homes with parents who have limited academic and English-language skills. Nonverbal tests of general ability such as the WNV are, therefore, a particularly useful way to assess minority children because they yield smaller race and ethnic differences (which is attributed to the difference in content) while these instruments retain good correlations with achievement, and can help identify minority children for gifted programs (Bracken & McCallum, 1998; Naglieri & Ford, 2003; Naglieri & Ronning, 2000a, 2000b).

Wechsler and Naglieri (2006a) provide evidence of the utility of the WNV for individuals who are learning English. The study involved examinees who speak English as a second language who were compared to a matched sample from the WNV standardization sample. This included 55 examinees aged 8–21 years whose "native language was not English, they spoke a language other than English at home, and the examinee's parents had resided in the United States less than 6 years" (Wechsler & Naglieri, 2006a, p. 63). There were 27 Hispanics and 28 examinees who specified their primary language was Cantonese, Chinese (unspecified), Korean, Russian, Spanish, or Urdu. Additional information about this sample is available in the WNV *Technical and Interpretive Manual* (Appendix D). These examinees performed very similarly to their matched counterparts from the normative sample with negligible effect sizes (Cohen's *d*) for the Full Scale Score: 4-Subtest Battery and Full Scale Score: 2-Subtest Battery, as shown in Table 12.5.

Interventions Based on Test Results

The WNV can be used in at least two ways when a plan for instruction is being developed. At the global level, the Full Scale score provides an indication of general ability that can suggest specific instructional needs based on the characteristics of the child. For example, a child who has limited English-language skills who earns a high WNV Full Scale score as part of an assessment for possible placement in Gifted should receive these special services in an environment that recognizes his or her strengths and needs. Naglieri, Brulles, and Lansdowne (2008) provide explicit suggestions about the manner in which children who are low in academic skills but high on a nonverbal measure of general ability should be taught. Their book includes strategies that are particularly useful for diverse populations of gifted students. Instructional topics for bilingual students include critical and creative thinking, appropriate gifted educational objectives, and student-directed learning in areas such as language arts, social studies, mathematics, and science.

The specific subtest scores of the WNV, like other tests of general ability, could be used to develop hypotheses about characteristics of the student that may have implications for instruction. These hypotheses should be further evaluated by other evidence and, when possible, tested to see whether a desirable response to instruction occurs. Subtest scores on the WNV could suggest hypotheses that could be further

investigated or evaluated on the basis of the child's response to intervention. For instance, a Spatial Span Forward *T* score of 54 and a Spatial Span Backward *T* score of 38 could suggest a weakness with Planning as defined by Naglieri (2008c). These two scores are both significantly different and the difference occurs in only 6.2% of the U.S. standardization sample. If this finding is corroborated by a weakness on the Planning scale of the Cognitive Assessment System (Naglieri & Das, 1997) and academic problems are found, the application of methods described by Naglieri and Pickering (2003) for teaching strategy use should be attempted. There is research that supports the value of teaching children to be strategic and the positive influence this instruction has on math and reading comprehension (see Naglieri, 2008c, for a summary).

Subtest performance on the WNV may also suggest a weakness on tests of general ability that require recall of information. The Recognition subtest requires recall of information, and if the score on that subtest is significantly lower than the child's mean and less than one *SD* from the mean (< 40), the hypothesis should be considered. Once corroborated with other test data and if accompanied by academic problems in tasks that require recall of information, teaching strategies for remembering should be implemented. This would include teaching chunking or other mnemonic methods of recall of information, for which there is considerable evidence of effectiveness (Mastropieri & Scruggs, 2006; Minskoff & Allsopp, 2003). Ways in which these methods can be communicated to teachers and parents in instructional handouts are provided by Naglieri and Pickering (2003). The WNV could, therefore, help develop possible explanations for problems associated with difficulty in the classroom.

Summary

The research studies summarized here suggest that the WNV offers an effective measure of general ability that yields expected results. Individuals identified as having mental retardation earned low scores with those with the most severe retardation earning lower scores than those with mild retardation. In contrast, children identified as being gifted earned very high scores on the nonverbal measure of general ability. Importantly, individuals who were acquiring English-language skills performed very similarly to the normative mean of 100; in fact their score was 101.7, which was very similar to the matched control group, which had a score of 102.1. Additionally, the results for individuals who are hard of hearing, as well as those for the deaf, show that these two groups also earned scores on the WNV that were very similar to the matched control groups. In summary, these data provide strong support for the use of the WNV with diverse populations.

VALIDITY

Relationships between WNV and Other Ability and Achievement Tests

The WNV is strongly related to other nonverbal measures of ability and other measures of ability that contain verbal and nonverbal scales. For example, Wechsler and Naglieri (2006a) reported that the WNV 4-subtest battery Full Scale score correlated .79 with the UNIT and .73 with the NNAT-1. Similarly, the WNV Full Scale score correlated .82 with the WPPSI-III, .82 with the WISC-IV, .84 with the WAIS-III, and .83 with the WISC-IV Spanish. These findings provide evidence that the WNV is a good test of general ability even though it does not contain verbal and quantitative subtests.

The WNV is strongly correlated with achievement (.66) as measured by the WIAT-II. The correlations between the WNV and the WIAT-II are consistent with other studies of the relationship between ability and achievement, which have yielded a correlation of about .6 (Naglieri, 1999). Previous research (e.g., Naglieri

& Ronning, 2000b) with the NNAT-ML has shown a correlation of .5 to .6 for large samples of children in grades K–12. The results illustrate that the 4-subtest battery Full Scale score is effective as a predictor of academic achievement.

Demographic Differences

English Language Learners

There is good evidence that the WNV is an appropriate measure of general ability for those who have limitations in either knowledge or use of the English language. Wechsler and Naglieri (2006a) provide evidence of the utility of the WNV with examinees who have English-language limitations and hearing problems that limit their ability to acquire information. The first study included examinees whose native language was not English, where the primary language they spoke was not English, a language other than English was spoken at home, and their parents resided in the United States less than six years. When compared to a group from the normative sample matched on basic demographics, they found that the examinees learning English earned essentially the same score as the matched control of English-speaking examinees in the normative group (effect sizes for the 4- and 2-subtest batteries were .03 and .04, respectively). While these results suggested that the WNV measures general ability effectively and fairly for those with limited English-language skills when combined with the studies involving students with hearing limitations, the strength of this instrument is more clearly understood.

The findings summarized above for English language learners suggest that the WNV may be useful for addressing the underrepresentation of minority children in classes for the gifted. This has been described as one of the most important problems facing educators of gifted students (Ford, 1998; Naglieri & Ford, 2005). One solution has been to use nonverbal tests of general ability as a part of the identification procedure, particularly for children whose primary language is not English. Support for the use of a nonverbal test in this context is amply documented by Naglieri (2008a). The logic is based on the fact that traditional measures of ability include tests that require knowledge of English words and the use of language even when questions involving mathematics are used, which poses a barrier for English language learners. Suzuki and Valencia (1997) argued that these verbal and quantitative questions interfere with accurate assessment of minority children. Naglieri & Ford (2005) maintained that tests like the WNV provide an effective way to assess these individuals. Because the WNV does not penalize English language learners, it is an effective tool for assessing general ability and, therefore, should be used as part of the process to identify gifted examinees whose primary language is not English.

Deaf and Hard of Hearing

Wechsler and Naglieri (2006a) reported that the WNV Full Scale scores are also very similar for two matched samples of deaf and hearing examinees and a study with hearing-impaired examinees matched with the same demographic characteristics to hearing examinees from the normative sample. Those in the deaf sample had not ever heard spoken language; they had never heard tones after the age of 18 months, could not lip read or use cued speech, and were classified as having severe-to-profound deafness. The hard-of-hearing sample had exposure to spoken language, either through hearing or lip reading, and could have a unilateral or bilateral hearing loss or deafness. Their inability to hear could have occurred at any age and they could have cochlear implants. The results for these two groups, like the sample of examinees with English-language limitations, earned WNV Full Scale scores that were close to average and were very similar to the matched control group. The effect sizes are considered negligible and small. Taken as a whole, these studies suggest that language has a negligible effect on the WNV Full Scale score and illustrate the strength of this instrument for assessment of individuals with hearing as well as language limitations.

Gender Differences

Gender differences in ability has been a topic of considerable interest for some time, resulting in a substantial body of literature on the topic (e.g., Fennema & Sherman, 1977; Geary, 1996; Halpern, 1997). Hyde and Linn (1988) found a small mean effect size (favoring females) of .11 in verbal skills for students aged 5 through 18 years, but the differences between genders were not uniform across tasks. Halpern (1997) concluded that females outperform males on tests of verbal fluency, foreign language, fine motor skills, speech articulation, and reading and writing, but males do better on tasks that involve mental rotation, mechanical reasoning, math and science knowledge, and verbal analogies. Lynn and Irwing (2004) argued that sex differences must be viewed developmentally and with consideration of the role played by biology. Based on his research using Raven's Progressive Matrices, Lynn (2002) argued that females are slightly better than males between the ages of 10 and 13 and that after 14 males catch up and overtake females, ending up with an advantage that reaches about 2 IQ points among adults. The differences between WNV scores by gender were recently studied by Brown (2008).

Table 12.6 provides the effect sizes for WNV Full Scale and subtest scores for 1,300 girls and boys aged 4–21 years (broken into four age groups: 4–7, 8–10, 11–14, and 15–21) who participated in the standardization sample. The results indicate that both the 4- and 2-subtest Full Scale scores showed minimal gender differences. The 4-subtest effect sizes ranged from 0.0–.16 and the 2-subtest Full Scale effect sizes ranged from .01–.10. These are negligible and inconsequential differences. Interestingly, the subtest differences were also small with the exception of the Coding subtest, which showed a female superiority of .31, .33, .17, and .48 across the four age groups. These findings indicate that the WNV Full Scale scores yield values that are very similar by gender and the differences found for Coding have little influence on the total test score.

TABLE 12.6   Male/Female Effect Sizes for the 4- and 2-Subtest Batteries Full Scales and Individual Subtests by Age in Years in the Standardization Sample

	Age (in Years)			
	4–7	8–10	11–14	15–21
Full Scale—4	−.16	−.06	.00	−.05
Full Scale—2	−.09	.05	.01	.10
Matrices	−.04	.08	−.06	.16
Coding	−.31	−.33	−.17	−.48
Object Assembly	−.02	—	—	—
Recognition	−.12	—	—	—
Spatial Span	—	.01	.07	.01
Picture Arrangement	—	.07	.10	.20

NOTES:

$N = 1,300$.

Positive effect sizes indicate male scores were higher than female scores.

Effect Size = $(X_1 − X_2) / \mathrm{SQRT} \left[(n_1 * \mathrm{SD}_1{}^2 + n_2 * \mathrm{SD}_2{}^2)/(n_1 + n_2) \right]$.

Empirical Support for the Test Structure

The WNV offers subtest-level data as well as a Full Scale score. Empirical support for this structure was examined in three ways and reported in the Technical and Interpretive Manual. These three ways are intercorrelations, confirmatory factor analysis: communality, specificity, and error variance, and confirmatory factor analysis: model fit.

The intercorrelations for all comparisons (subtest to subtest, subtest to full-scale score, and full-scale score to full-scale score) matched the patterns reported for other Wechsler scales (e.g., WISC-IV, WPPSI-III, and WAIS-III). Additionally, the intercorrelations for the Full Scale scores were moderate to high for both age bands (4:0–7:11 and 8:0–21:11) for both the U.S. and the Canadian standardization samples.

The next measure of the strength of the test structure is comparison of the specificity and error variance as well as an examination on the loadings of each subtest on g. "For a subtest to provide a unique contribution to the latent variable (g), it is expected that the specificity will exceed the error variance" (Wechsler & Naglieri, 2006a, p. 46). In each way the specificity and error variance were reported (by age band: 4:0–7:11 and 8:0–21:11; and by smaller groupings for the older age band: 8:0–10:11, 11:0–14:11, and 15:0–21:11) the specificity exceeded the error variance, allowing the conclusion that each subtest measures something unique. An additional conclusion from the g loadings is that all of the subtests load on g.

Finally, the model fit for a single factor (g) model was examined. The findings indicate good fit for this model for each of the two age bands (i.e., 4:0–7:11 and 8:0–21:11). However, when the older age band was broken down, the 11:0–14:11 students did not fit as well as all other age bands, but still showed adequate fit.

Overall, the conclusion about the test structure based on empirical support is that the WNV provides useful information both at the subtest level and at a single, general factor level. Subtest scores as well as Full Scale scores are useful and important when reporting the results of the WNV.

SUMMARY

The WNV was explicitly designed to provide a nonverbal measure of general ability that would be appropriate for a wide variety of culturally and linguistically diverse populations. The selection of tests that are described as nonverbal in conjunction with Pictorial Directions and oral directions in five languages provides a unique approach to measuring general ability. The evidence provided in this chapter supports the utility of the test for fair assessment of cognitive ability of those from culturally diverse backgrounds as well as those with language differences or deficiencies as well as those who are deaf or hard of hearing. The research provided in the test manual provides a base to support the use of the instrument but additional research is needed, especially regarding the utility of the instrument within diverse clinical environments.

REFERENCES

Boake, C. (2002). From the Binet-Simon to the Wechsler-Bellevue: Tracing the history of intelligence testing. *Journal of Clinical and Experimental Neuropsychology*, *24*, 383–405.

Bracken, B. A., & McCallum, R. S. (1998). *Universal Nonverbal Intelligence Test*. Austin, TX: Pro-Ed.

Bracken, B. A., & Naglieri, J. A. (2003). Assessing diverse populations with nonverbal tests of general intelligence. In C. R. Reynolds & R. W. Kamphaus (Eds.), *Handbook of psychological and educational assessment of children* (pp. 243–273). New York: Guilford.

Brown, C. (2008). Gender differences on the Wechsler Nonverbal Scale of Ability. Manuscript in preparation.

Brunnert, K., Naglieri, J. A., & Hardy-Braz, S. (2009). *Essentials of WNV Assessment*. New York: Wiley.

Cohen, B. H. (1996). *Explaining psychological statistics*. Pacific Grove, CA: Brooks & Cole.

Davis, F. B. (1959). Interpretation of differences among averages and individual test scores. *Journal of Educational Psychology*, *50*, 162–170.

Fennema, E., & Sherman, J. (1977). Sex-related differences in mathematics achievement, spatial visualization, and affective factors. *American Educational Research Journal*, *14*, 51–71.

Ford, D. Y. (1998). The underrepresentation of minority students in gifted education: Problems and promises in recruitment and retention. *Journal of Special Education*, *32*, 4–14.

Geary, D. C. (1996). Sexual selection and sex differences in mathematical abilities. *Behavioral and Brain Sciences*, *19*, 229–247.

Goldstein, S., & Naglieri, J. A. (2006). The role of intellectual processes in the DSM-V diagnosis of ADHD. *Journal of Attention Disorders*, *10*, 3–8.

Hale, J. N., Flanagan, D. P., & Naglieri, J. A. (2008, June). Alternative research-based methods for IDEA 2004 identification of children with specific learning disabilities. *Communique*, *36*(1), 14–15.

Halpern, D. F. (1997). Sex differences in intelligence. *American Psychologist*, *52*, 1091–1102.

Hyde, J. S., & Linn, M. C. (1988). Gender differences in verbal ability: A meta-analysis. *Psychological Bulletin*, *104*, 53–69.

Jensen, A. R. (1998). *The "g" factor: The science of mental ability*. Westport, CT: Praeger.

Kaufman, A. S., & Kaufman, N. L. (2004). *Kaufman Test of Educational Achievement—Second Edition*. San Antonio: Pearson.

Lynn, R. (2002). Sex differences on the progressive matrices among 15–16 year olds: Some data from South Africa. *Personality and Individual Differences*, *33*, 669–673.

Lynn, R., & Irwing, P. (2004). Sex difference on progressive matrices: A meta-analysis. *Intelligence*, *32*, 481–498.

Mastropieri, M. A., & Scruggs, T. E. (2006). *Inclusive classroom: Strategies for effective instruction* (4th ed.). Upper Saddle River, NJ: Prentice Hall.

Minskoff, E., & Allsopp, D. (2003). *Academic success strategies for adolescents with learning disabilities and ADHD*. Baltimore: Brookes.

Naglieri, J. A. (1997). *Naglieri Nonverbal Ability Test—Multilevel Form*. San Antonio: Psychological Corporation.

Naglieri, J. A. (1999). *Essentials of CAS assessment*. New York: Wiley.

Naglieri, J. A. (2003a). Naglieri nonverbal ability tests: NNAT and MAT-EF. In R. S. McCallum (Ed.), *Handbook of nonverbal assessment* (pp. 175–190). New York: Kluwer.

Naglieri, J. A. (2003b). *Naglieri Nonverbal Ability Test—Individual Form*. San Antonio: Psychological Corporation.

Naglieri, J. A. (2008a). Traditional IQ: 100 years of misconception and its relationship to minority representation in gifted programs. In J. VanTassel-Baska (Ed.), *Critical issues in equity and excellence in gifted education series alternative assessment of gifted learners* (pp. 67–88). Waco, TX: Prufrock Press.

Naglieri, J. A. (2008b). *Naglieri Nonverbal Ability Test—Second Edition*. San Antonio: Pearson.

Naglieri, J. A. (2008c). Best practices in linking cognitive assessment of students with learning disabilities to interventions. In A. Thomas &

J. Grimes (Eds.), *Best practices in school psychology* (5th ed., pp. 679–696). Bethesda: NASP.

Naglieri, J. A., & Bornstein, B. T. (2003). Intelligence and achievement: Just how correlated are they? *Journal of Psychoeducational Assessment*, *21*, 244–260.

Naglieri, J. A., Brulles, D., & Lansdowne, K. (2009). *Helping gifted children learn*. San Antonio, TX: Pearson.

Naglieri, J. A., & Das, J. P. (1997). *Cognitive Assessment System*. Austin, TX: ProEd.

Naglieri, J. A., & Ford, D. Y. (2003). Addressing under-representation of gifted minority children using the Naglieri Nonverbal Ability Test (NNAT). *Gifted Child Quarterly*, *47*, 15–160.

Naglieri, J. A., & Ford, D. Y. (2005). Increasing minority children's participation in gifted classes using the NNAT: A response to Lohman. *Gifted Child Quarterly*, *49*, 29–36.

Naglieri, J. A., & Kaufman, A. S. (2008). IDEIA 2004 and specific learning disabilities: What role does intelligence play? In E. Grigorenko (Ed.), *Educating individuals with disabilities: IDEIA 2004 and beyond* (pp. 165–195). New York: Springer.

Naglieri, J. A., & Paolitto, A. W. (2005). Ipsative comparisons of WISC-IV Index scores. *Applied Neuropsychology*, *12*, 208–211.

Naglieri, J. A., & Pickering, E. B. (2003). *Helping children learn: Intervention handouts for use at school and home*. Baltimore: Brookes.

Naglieri, J. A., & Rojahn, J. (2001). Evaluation of African-American and White children in special education programs for children with mental retardation using the WISC-III and Cognitive Assessment System. *American Journal of Mental Retardation*, *106*, 359–367.

Naglieri, J. A., & Ronning, M. E. (2000a). Comparison of White, African-American, Hispanic, and Asian children on the Naglieri Nonverbal Ability Test. *Psychological Assessment*, *12*, 328–334.

Naglieri, J. A., & Ronning, M. E. (2000b). The relationships between general ability using the NNAT and SAT Reading Achievement. *Journal of Psychoeducational Assessment*, *18*, 230–239.

Naglieri, J. A., & Yazzie, C. (1983). Comparison of the WISC-R and PPVT-R with Navajo children. *Journal of Clinical Psychology*, *39*, 598–600.

Newcomer, P. (2001). *Diagnostic Achievement Battery—Third Edition*. Austin, TX: ProEd.

Pearson. (2005). *Wechsler Individual Achievement Test—Second Edition*. San Antonio, TX: Pearson.

Ramirez, R. R., & de la Cruz, G. (2002). *The Hispanic population in the United States: March 2002*. Current Population Reports, 20-545, U.S. Census Bureau, Washington, DC.

Silverstein, A. B. (1982). Two- and four-subtest short forms of the Wechsler Adult Intelligence Scale—Revised. *Journal of Consulting and Clinical Psychology*, *50*, 415–418.

Suzuki, L. A., & Valencia, R. R. (1997). Race-ethnicity and measured intelligence. *American Psychologist*, *52*, 1103–1114.

Wechsler, D. (1958). *The measurement and appraisal of adult intelligence* (4th ed.). Baltimore: Williams & Wilkins.

Wechsler, D. (1991). *The Wechsler Intelligence Scale for Children—Third Edition*. San Antonio, TX: Pearson.

Wechsler, D. (1997a). *Wechsler Adult Intelligence Scale—Fourth Edition*, San Antonio, TX: Pearson.

Wechsler, D. (1997b). *Wechsler Memory Scale—Third Edition*. San Antonio, TX: Pearson

Wechsler, D. (2002). *Wechsler preschool and primary scale of intelligence—Third Edition*. San Antonio, TX: Pearson.

Wechsler, D. (2003). *Wechsler Intelligence Scale for Children—Fourth Edition*, San Antonio, TX: Pearson.

Wechsler, D., Kaplan, E., Fein, D., Kramer, J., Morris, R., Delis, D.C., & Maerlender, A. (2004). *Wechsler Intelligence Scale for Children—Fourth Edition—Integrated*. San Antonio, TX: Pearson.

Wechsler, D. & Naglieri, J. A. (2006a). *Wechsler Nonverbal Scale of Ability Technical and Interpretive Manual*. San Antonio, TX: Pearson.

Wechsler, D. & Naglieri, J. A. (2006b). *Wechsler Nonverbal Scale of Ability*. San Antonio, TX: Pearson.

Wechsler, D. & Naglieri, J. A. (2006c). *Wechsler Nonverbal Scale of Ability Administration and Scoring Manual*. San Antonio, TX: Pearson.

Wilkinson, G. S., & Robertson, G. J. (2006). *WRAT4 Wide Range Achievement Test professional manual* (4th ed.). Lutz, FL: Psychological Assessment Resources.

Woodcock, R. W., McGrew, K.S., & Mather, N. (2001). *Woodcock-Johnson III Test of Achievement*. Itasca, IL: Riverside Publishing Company.

PART IV

Achievement Tests

CHAPTER 13

Basic Achievement Skills Inventory (BASI)

Achilles N. Bardos, Kathrine M. Koehler-Hak

RATIONALE UNDERLYING THE TEST

Millions of children are attending public and private schools each year. Parents, teachers, and society want to ensure that they are educated properly. Evaluating their progress and growth has a challenge from an educational and a legislative perspective. Federal, state, and local governments require schools to develop mechanisms of evaluating student outcomes with laws such as No Child Left Behind (NCLB, 2001) and the most recently reauthorized Individuals with Disabilities Education Act (IDEA, 2004). Although the tests comprising the Basic Achievement Skills Inventory (BASI; Bardos, 2004a, 2004b) that are presented in this chapter address these legal requirements, the driving force and premise of the BASI is based on the belief that classroom instruction and assessment are intertwined, needing and benefiting from each other with an ultimate goal of nurturing a student's success and learning. The literature has consistently demonstrated that when used properly, classroom assessments can inform teaching methods as well as offer suggestions for curriculum adjustments and improvements (Stiggins, 2004).

Assessment data can provide effective feedback to both students and teachers. Students can recognize areas of strengths and areas in need of improvement. Teachers can use the data to target their efforts in helping students achieve their learning goals (Black & Wiliam, 1998).

HISTORICAL INFORMATION

The Basic Achievement Skills Inventory series includes a screening tool, the Basic Achievement Skills Inventory—Survey (BASI-S; Bardos, 2004b), and a comprehensive version, the Basic Achievement Skills Inventory—Comprehensive (BASI-C; Bardos, 2004a). The BASI-C was designed to provide comprehensive assessment data for all students in a classroom. It was developed to serve as a tool for those who are involved as *helping agents* in a student's learning process: the teachers, the school and its curriculum, and the student's family/parents. Two federal laws were mentioned earlier: NCLB and IDEA. In brief, NCLB requires the assessment of all students in order for schools to demonstrate their students' adequate yearly progress (AYP). IDEA relates to students who need to be identified as those who might be or are eligible for special education services. The two laws appear to be somewhat disconnected; however, proper implementation of the reauthorized IDEA is promising in terms of the process it proposes for the identification of at-risk students. IDEA recommends a process of assessing all regular education students followed by the identification of those who might need possible additional services, including, if deemed eligible, special education services. The BASI-C was conceptualized and was under development during the discussions that led to the reauthorization of IDEA. Despite the confusion, controversies, and sometimes polarized positions on the role of assessment in the implementation of the new IDEA, many states across the country are endorsing and adopting IDEA's philosophy, making this an exciting time for reform for both general and special education.

The multi-tier model described in a typical Response to Intervention (RtI) model involves three levels or tiers. At the *Universal Level*, also referred to in the literature as *Tier I* level, "all students receive research-based, high quality, general education that incorporates ongoing universal screening, progress monitoring, and prescriptive assessment to design instruction" (Colorado Department of Education, 2008). For a classroom teacher, this call translates into two simple, yet very important questions: Do I have enough data about each of my students in class so I can help them individually and as a group? Based on my students' overall performance, do I need to alter or rethink my instructional approach and curriculum? An expected outcome of the Universal Level screening is the identification of some students (about 20%) who might experience difficulties. Assessment data from the Universal Level should guide the interventions that will be provided to students identified as at-risk of academic difficulties and/or those identified as underachieving who might require specific supports to make sufficient progress in general education. At the second level, also referred as the Targeted Level, "interventions are provided to students identified as at-risk of academic challenges and/or students identified as

underachieving who require specific supports to make sufficient progress in general education" (Colorado Department of Education, 2008). The assessment process and data used at the second level should and must be connected to the data obtained in the first level (Tier I) and ideally continue at the third level (Intensive Level or Tier III) if and when decisions are to be reached for special education eligibility services. Tier III assessment data should provide in-depth diagnostic and sensitive information to guide the intensive interventions to the greatest degree possible as the decisions that are considered (i.e., special education) are of the highest importance for the students being evaluated.

The BASI-C is consistent with the philosophical premises of IDEA; thus it can serve as a tool in its implementation. In the next few paragraphs we will describe the BASI-C and demonstrate how the multilevel, multiform features of the test can serve as the basis for an assessment model that offers data for all three tiers of instruction and intervention within the IDEA-proposed assessment model of Response to Intervention (RtI).

Description of the BASI—Comprehensive (BASI-C)

Structure and Organization

The Comprehensive version of the BASI (BASI-C) assesses three major achievement areas—Reading, Written Language, and Mathematics—using six achievement subtests: Vocabulary, Reading Comprehension, Spelling, Language Mechanics, Math Computation, and Math Application. *Reading* is assessed using two subtests, Vocabulary and Reading Comprehension. The *Vocabulary* subtest includes items that measure a student's skills in recognizing the meaning of words presented in isolation, identifying the meaning of words within the context of a sentence, recognizing synonyms and antonyms, and analyzing verbal analogies. The *Reading Comprehension* subtest consists of passages that the examinee reads and is followed by questions that demonstrate their understanding of literal aspects of the passage such as the passage's main idea, sequence of events, setting, as well as inferential comprehension questions to demonstrate his or her comprehension skills, such as identifying cause-and-effect relationships, predicting outcomes, and drawing conclusions. *Written Language* is assessed using two subtests, Spelling and Language Mechanics. The *Spelling* subtest requires the examinee to identify correctly spelled and misspelled words including sight words, commonly misspelled words, and words with affixes. The *Language Mechanics* subtest measures a student's knowledge of grammar and syntax rules such as punctuation, capitalization, verb forms, and tense agreement. Finally, *Math* skills are assessed with two subtests, Math Computation and Math Application. In the *Math Computation* subtest students demonstrate their knowledge that ranges from the four basic arithmetic operations to algebraic equations. The *Math Application* subtest assesses a student's ability to apply his or her basic arithmetic operations skills in solving math problems, such as reading and interpreting graphs, and applying measurement principles as they relate to money, length, weight, volume, and so forth. A detailed description of the content areas covered in each subtest across grades is presented later.

The BASI-C is organized into four levels: Level 1 for grades 3–4, Level 2 for grades 5–6, Level 3 for grades 7–8, and Level 4 for grades 9–12. Each Level includes two forms. Form A was standardized in the fall and Form B was standardized in the spring of the school year. There are eight test booklets, each booklet containing all of the six subtests described earlier.

In addition to the Comprehensive version, the BASI series includes a screening tool, the BASI—Survey (BASI-S; Bardos, 2004). The BASI-S is a set of two brief (25-minute) screening tools that assess an examinee's Verbal and Math skills. Verbal skills are assessed with items that measure vocabulary, language mechanics, and reading comprehension skills, while the Math skills are assessed with items similar to the Math

Computation and Math Application items of the Comprehensive version. The BASI-S was standardized with nationally representative samples of school-age children and adults ranging from 8 to 80 years old. For a detailed description of the BASI-Survey test, the reader is referred to the publisher's website or may contact the test author directly.

Types of Scores Offered by the BASI

The BASI-C offers a variety of scale scores. All subtest and total scores are standard scores organized with a mean of 100 and *SD* of 15, a familiar metric system for individually administered tests. The norms were grade based to accurately reflect the content and curriculum that each student was exposed to. Confidence intervals, percentile scores, and age- and grade-equivalent scores can also be calculated on the self-scoring answer sheet and printed on the computer-generated report (see Figure 13.1). To further facilitate the use of the BASI as a progress-monitoring tool, Growth Scale Value (GVS) scale scores are also presented for each of the six subtests and the three total scores in Reading, Written Language, and Math. While the grade-based standard scores are level (the BASI-C includes four grade-based levels) and form (Forms A and B) dependent, the GSV scores allow the comparison in performance across levels and forms, thus facilitating the use of the BASI-C as a continuous progress-monitoring tool. A detailed description of the approach along with the respective tables needed to calculate the scores manually is included as an addendum to the technical manual on the publisher's website: http://pearsonassessments.com/pdf/basi_addendum.pdf. Using the standardization data, a classification scheme describes a student's performance with three categories: below average, average, and above average for each of the six subtests (see the lower part of the computer-generated report in Figure 13.1). In addition, a percentage correct score is

BASI™
Basic Achievement Skills Inventory

Student Summary Report: BASI Level 4
Achilles N. Bardos, PhD

Student: Sample, Matt A.	**Teacher:** Teacher, Christine B.
Student ID: 61	**Class/Group:** 23231
Birth Date: 08/25/1989	**School:** Aces High
Grade: 12	**District Code:** 12345

Timed: Yes	
ESL Student: No	
Accommodations: No	
Test Date: 09/25/2007	
Report Date: 09/25/2007	
Form: A	
Norms: Fall / 12th Grade	

Composite or Subtest	SS	Confidence Interval	%ile	GSV	GE	AE
Reading Total	119	111-125	90	119		
Vocabulary	118	108-125	88	121	12.9	18-0
Reading Comprehension	121	109-128	92	120	12.9	18-0
Written Language Total	105	97-112	63	114		
Spelling	104	93-113	60	118	12.2	17-4
Language Mechanics	108	100-115	70	111	12.9	18-0
Math Total	107	97-116	68	109		
Math Computation	109	98-118	73	112	12.9	18-0
Math Application	106	93-117	66	107	12.2	17-4

Matt's BASI results are presented in the tables on this page. *Standard scores* compare Matt's performance with that of other 12th grade students in a national sample. *Confidence intervals* indicate the range of standard scores that is likely to include Matt's true score. *Percentile (%ile) scores* indicate what percentage of the norm group Matt scored as well as or better than. The *GSV score* is a measure of raw performance on a particular subtest or composite. The GSV scale for a subtest or composite is consistent across BASI forms and levels, making GSV scores useful for measuring change over time. GSV scores from different subtests or composites cannot be compared.

The tables below present Matt's results for the various achievement areas included in each of the six BASI subtests. The results shown are percentage correct (PC) and a rating of his performance relative to that of other examinees. These results identify the areas in which he excels and those in which he might need help. They can also help track Matt's progress if he takes the BASI test again.

SS = Standard Score **(mean = 100, SD = 15)**   **%ile** = Percentile Rank   **GSV** = Growth Scale Value   **GE** = Grade Equivalent   **AE** = Age Equivalent   **PC** = Percentage Correct

Achievement Area	PC	Performance
Vocabulary	**75**	**Above Average**
Similar words, synonyms, antonyms	79	Above Average
Prefixes, suffixes, roots	94	Above Average
Verbal analogies	50	Average
Reading Comprehension	**78**	**Above Average**
Plot, main idea, topic sentence	75	Average
INFERENTIAL COMPREHENSION	78	Above Average
Theme, plot elements	50	Average
Cause, effect	75	Average
Compare, contrast	100	Above Average
Inferences, conclusions	100	Above Average
Purpose, technique, tone	50	Average
Fact, opinion, persuasion, bias	86	Above Average
Figurative language	100	Above Average
Setting	100	Above Average

Achievement Area	PC	Performance
Spelling	**63**	**Average**
Prefixes and suffixes	78	Above Average
Commonly misspelled words	47	Average
Spelling rules	67	Average
Language Mechanics	**68**	**Average**
GRAMMAR	86	Above Average
Nouns, pronouns, articles	67	Average
Subject/verb agreement	91	Average
Adjectives, adverbs	100	Average
SYNTAX	44	Average
Capitalization	40	Average
Internal punctuation	46	Average

Achievement Area	PC	Performance
Math Computation	**56**	**Average**
Whole numbers	50	Average
Fractions	60	Average
Decimals, order of operations, percents	60	Average
Integers, absolute value	60	Average
Algebra	50	Average
Math Application	**47**	**Average**
Word problems, exponents	44	Average
Geometry	17	Below Average
Algebra	100	Above Average
Statistics, probability	29	Average

Copyright © 2004, 2007 NCS Pearson, Inc. All rights reserved. **BASI** is a trademark of NCS Pearson, Inc.
[1.4 / 1 / 2.1.11]

Source: With permission from the BASI—Comprehensive technical manual.

FIGURE 13.1
Report Sample for a 12th-Grade Student Using Form A of the BASI-C

presented for each subtest and for each of the content/curriculum subareas that comprise every subtest to facilitate the use of the subtest scores in a criterion-referenced interpretation approach. The percentage correct scores are available only through the computer scoring option. A graph with a student's performance using the three-level classification description, a graphical representation of the percentile scores, and a narrative describing the test performance is also available for the parents (see Figure 13.2).

Administration and Scoring

The BASI-C can be administered in various ways with self-administration being the main feature of the test. Being a self-administered test, the BASI-C can be given to a small group of students or to an entire classroom, or be administered individually. Both forms of the BASI series, the Survey and the Comprehensive versions, can be administered either using the paper-and-pencil version of the test or through a personal computer. The materials needed for the chosen administration format also vary. For

Source: With permission from the BASI—Comprehensive technical manual.

FIGURE 13.2

BASI-C Parent Summary Report

example, if the paper-and-pencil version of the BASI–C is selected, the user must determine which of the four test booklets (according to the student's grade level) and which test form (Form A—Fall norms or Form B—Spring norms) will be used. Each of the BASI testing booklets contains all six subtests. They can be administered in the order presented in the test booklet, but if needed, they can be administered in any order to accommodate scheduling needs. The examinees record their answers using either a scannable answer sheet or a self-scoring answer sheet.

The BASI can also be administered on an individual computer or a network. The test is available as one of many instruments included in Pearson's QLocal test administration and scoring software program. The user selects the appropriate level of the test for the examinee. The examinee follows and responds to the various test items presented on the screen. Upon completion of the administration, the software creates a database with the examinee's background and testing data. Next, the test can be scored and a report is generated with normative as well as criterion-referenced test data for each student along with an optional one-page report for the parents.

The BASI-C was standardized with specific time limits for each subtest (Vocabulary = 10 min; Spelling = 10 min; Reading Comprehension = 30 min; Language Mechanics = 10 min; Math Computation = 20 min; Math Application = 35 min); therefore, all standard scores, confidence intervals, percentile ranks, grade-equivalent scores, and age-equivalent scores are interpretable only for timed administrations. However, the BASI-C can be administered in alternative ways with some necessary changes in how the obtained scores can be used and what reports will be generated by the scoring program when these options are exercised. For example, there might be a situation where the examiner is not interested in the normative information under the timed conditions but rather is interested in knowing what specific content the examinee has and has not mastered within each of the areas tested from a criterion-referenced-only perspective. In this case, only the percentage correct scores for subtests and for specific achievement areas should be interpreted. In another scenario using the paper-and-paper version, the examiner may administer the BASI-C in a standardized manner with the specific time limits, obtain the standardized report, and then return to each subtest and allow the examinee to complete all items. In both scenarios described above, the reports and relevant information can be obtained only when using the QLocal scoring software.

Scoring Options

The variety of administration options leads to a variety of scoring options. When using the paper-and-pencil administration, the test can be scored using the self-scoring answer sheets or responses can be entered in the scoring software program manually or with an optical scanner. When using the self-scoring answer sheet, the student responses can be recorded on the carbonless multipage answer sheets. Each level-specific answer sheet can be used to administer either Form A or Form B. Following the test administration, the examiner removes the form's perforating seal, which reveals the key for both Form A and Form B, scores each test item, and determines the total raw score for each of the six subtests. The total number of correct responses are summarized and can be transformed to a variety of scores (i.e., standard scores, classification of performance, percentiles, confidence intervals, GSV, etc.), as discussed earlier.

The self-scoring form offers a quick way to score the test but it does not offer the option for a detailed breakdown of the various subareas or learning objectives that make up each of the six subtests. In order to obtain the detailed scoring report, one must use the QLocal scoring program. The examiner can manually enter a student's response on the QLocal software program and then score the test. This might be appropriate when a small number of students take the BASI-C, such as students who are assessed as part of a Tier II or Tier III assessment process. When administering the BASI-C as part of the Tier I assessment process, however, using an optical scannable answer sheet is the most beneficial and efficient option to follow. Scoring using the optical scannable answer sheets could be accomplished using the publisher's mail-in scoring services or the answer sheets can be scanned and scored locally with the assistance of an optical scanner available from the publisher (http://pearsonassessments.com/scoring/scanning.htm).

When the test is administered on a personal computer, it can be scored immediately after the administration. This option offers the advantage of complete local control of the entire administration, scoring, and reporting options. The most important feature of using QLocal to administer and score the BASI-C is the availability of individual reports for each student and his or her parents, all test score data from the student's actual responses to scored responses, summative standard scores, and criterion-referenced scores. Figure 13.2 presents a sample report for a 12th-grade student who was administered Form A of the BASI-C. Additional sample reports with timed and untimed administrations and other administration options can be found on the publisher's website. All data presented in the two-page report are stored by the software and can be exported to create further administrative and instructional reports (see later discussion).

Of special interest to school counselors and school psychologists and to students in the upper grades is the extra report generated for those planning to attend college. In addition to the standard two-page summary report offered for all BASI-C test levels, a third optional page is included that describes a student's performance on the BASI-C and compares his or her performance to a sample of college freshmen who were attending either a two- or four-year college and who were administered the BASI-C Level 4 during the test standardization (see Figure 13.3).

Composite or Subtest	%tile	GSV	Community College Sample		College/University Sample	
			Avg	Middle 50%	Avg	Middle 50%
Reading Total	90	119	110	104-117	118	114-123
Vocabulary	88	121	112	107-121	124	118-130
Reading Comprehension	92	120	111	102-117	118	113-122
Written Language Total	63	114	111	107-117	119	115-124
Spelling	60	118	118	112-124	125	120-133
Language Mechanics	70	111	109	102-112	116	111-121
Math Total	68	109	103	100-106	112	109-117
Math Computation	73	112	106	100-109	118	112-127
Math Application	66	107	102	98-105	109	104-113

%tile = Percentile Rank   GSV = Growth Scale Value

College Report: BASI Level 4
Achilles N. Bardos, PhD

Student: Sample, Matt A.
Student ID: 61
Birth Date: 08/25/1989
Grade: 12

Teacher: Teacher, Christine B.
Class/Group: 23231
School: Aces High
District Code: 12345

Timed: Yes
ESL Student: No
Accommodations: No
Test Date: 09/25/2007
Report Date: 09/25/2007
Form: A
Norms: Fall / 12th Grade

Basic Achievement Skills Inventory

This report shows how the student's BASI scores compare to the scores of a census-matched national sample at the student's grade level and to two samples of college students: those in their first year at a two-year community college, and those in their first year at a four-year college or university.

The *percentile (%tile) ranks*, shown in the table at the left, indicate what percentage of the national sample the student scored as well as or better than. The table also shows the student's *GSV (Growth Scale Value)* scores for the BASI composites and subtests and the corresponding GSV scores for first-year community college students and first-year college/university students. In addition to the college students' average GSV score, the range of the middle 50% of scores is shown.

The box plot below illustrates these scores. The box represents the range of the middle 50% of scores for college students. The horizontal line to the right of the box shows the range of the upper 25% of scores, and the horizontal line to the left of the box shows the range of the lower 25% of scores. The diamond in each plot depicts the student's GSV score in comparison to the college students' scores.

The GSV is a yardstick that represents levels of performance on a particular BASI subtest or composite. It enables comparison of a subtest score from one BASI level to another to accurately measure growth or--as in this report--to compare an individual's score to others' scores. It's important to remember that, unlike a percentile rank, the GSV score does not have any meaning in and of itself; it is a tool for comparison.

	Reading Total	Written Language Total	Math Total
Community College			
College/University			

◆ = Student's GSV Score

Source: With permission from the BASI—Comprehensive technical manual.

FIGURE 13.3
Comparing the Performance of a High School Student to That of a College Freshman Student

PSYCHOMETRIC PROPERTIES

Standardization

The BASI-C was standardized using a stratified random sampling plan that closely matched the 2000 U.S. Census population by gender, race/ethnicity, parental educational level, and region. The sample included a total of 2,439 students in grades 3 through 12 in the standardization of Form A and 2,130 students who participated in the standardization of Form B. An additional sample of approximately 800 college students were also administered Level 4 of the BASI-C, creating the ability to generate an additional report for high school graduates and to compare their performance on the BASI-C to that of freshmen college-age students. Following the appropriate permissions granted by each institution, the BASI-C was administered by the classroom teachers, who returned the testing materials to the publisher for scoring and other quality control checks.

The BASI—Survey was standardized concurrently with the BASI-C using a sample of 2,518 school-age children ages 8–18 and a sample of 2,452 adults ages 19–80.

Reliability

The reliability of the BASI-C was determined with a variety of methods and examined the internal consistency of items within the test, across different forms of the test, or across repeat administrations of the test. Cronbach's alpha coefficients were calculated to estimate the test's internal consistency reliability and to determine standard errors of measurement. The stability of scores over time was examined with test–retest studies, while studies were conducted to investigate the alternate-forms reliability.

Internal consistency reliability coefficients were calculated for each grade level for the six subtests and the three total scores using data collected during the standardization of the test. The coefficients obtained were high (.80 or

greater) for the majority of the subtests across the two forms of the test and very high (most at or above .90) for the three total scores of Reading, Written Language, and Math. As is typical, the reliability coefficients were somewhat lower for the subtest scores than those for the total scores because the subtests have fewer items. These internal consistency reliability coefficients were used for the calculation of the error of measurement and the confidence intervals for the standard scores.

Three studies were conducted to examine the test—retest stability of the BASI-C at Level 1 ($N = 70$), Level 2 ($N = 74$), and Level 3 ($N = 53$) using a retest interval of two weeks. A trend of small gains in means scores was observed as expected due to practice, while test–retest stability coefficients were statistically significant ($p < .001$). Of the 27 total test–retest coefficients, 24 were .70 or greater and 20 were .80 or greater, suggesting that the BASI-C scores were stable over time.

The BASI-C alternative form reliability was also established with three studies at Level 1 ($n = 94$), Level 2 ($n = 88$), and Level 3 ($n = 78$) that examined the relationship between Forms A and B. In all studies, Form A was administered first followed by the administration of Form B within the same week. In all studies, the coefficients obtained were statistically significant at $p < .001$ with values that ranged from .57 to .87, demonstrating a high level of reliability between the two BASI-C test forms.

Internal consistency reliability coefficients were also calculated for the Survey form (BASI-S) for the Verbal and Math skills total score. Internal consistency was .75 and .73 for the 8-year-olds in the Verbal and Math skill areas. When used as a screening tool of academic skills for 8-year-old students, the examiner should consider these somewhat lower reliability estimates and consider the somewhat greater error of measurement. Reliability coefficients for all of the remaining age groups (9–90) were in the upper .80s to mid-.90s, thus suggesting that the BASI-S is a highly reliable instrument.

Validity

The BASI-C was developed to evaluate students' achievement across three broad academic areas—reading, written language, and math—using a variety of grade-appropriate academic tasks in the subject areas of vocabulary, spelling, language mechanics, reading comprehension, math computation, and math application. Therefore, the validity of the BASI-C as an achievement test refers to the quality of inferences that can be made from its test score(s) and the evidence that is presented to support these inferences. In this respect, validity is a continuing process of evidence building and includes both the process used to build the BASI-C to assess its constructs (content validity) as well as empirical evidence with studies including relationships with other tests and performance of clinical or special populations.

Relationships between Test Scores and State Curriculum

Perhaps the most important evidence of validity in an achievement test is the degree to which the test represents the curriculum or content areas taught at various grade levels in schools. The content of the BASI-C was developed in consultation with content experts. First, a test specification matrix representing each content area was proposed by the author using state and national standards. Next, content experts in each area were consulted, who used the Model Curriculum and Assessment Database (MCAD) to refine the content of each domain area. The MCAD is a proprietary database of NCS Pearson California and represents a collection of local, state, and national educational standards from U.S. schools for grades 3–12. Figures 13.4 to 13.6 illustrate the depth of content coverage of the BASI-C within each of the six achievement areas across the four levels of the BASI-C.

A student's performance across each of these areas is also presented in the report generated by the scoring software (see Figure 13.1). A total of 2,665 items were written by the author, a team of teachers, and professionals with extensive background in each respective content area. Further, a team of four or five Pearson education professionals with content expertise reviewed each item before it was submitted as a potential question for the item selection pilot studies. In addition to content representation, this review included an examination of possible race, gender, and region bias. Following the pilot studies, the BASI-C was standardized with numerous items within each of the content areas. For example, within each form and across the four levels of the test (see Figure 13.7), there were 164 items for the Vocabulary test, 166 items for the Spelling subtest, 155 items for the Language Mechanics subtest, 172 items for the Reading Comprehension subtest, 128 items for the Math Computation subtest, and 132 items for the Math Application subtest. The number of items included within each subtest and form of the BASI-C allow a comprehensive coverage of content in each area that is grade specific and targeted. Thus, a student's score within a subtest area and test level represents skills that are more comprehensive and grade specific than individually administered tests that by the nature of their design cover a particular domain area with items ranging from Kindergarten through 12th grade. In addition, the existence of an equivalent form enhances the content validity of the BASI-C and makes it an appropriate and sensitive tool to monitor student progress.

Other Evidence of Validity

In addition to the content validity evidence presented earlier, numerous studies were conducted to establish the BASI-C concurrent validity through its relationship with other group self-administered and individually administered tests. A summary of these studies is presented next.

Achievement Area	Level 1	Level 2	Level 3	Level 4
Meaning, context, idioms	x	x	x	
Similar words, synonyms, antonyms	x	x	x	x
Prefixes, suffixes, roots	x	x	x	x
Verbal analogies		x	x	x
Literal Comprehension				
Plot, main idea, topic sentence	x		x	x
Order of events, steps in process	x	x		
Relevant details	x	x		
Written directions	x	x		
Inferential Comprehension				
Theme, plot elements	x	x	x	x
Cause, effect	x	x	x	x
Compare, contrast			x	x
Probable outcome	x	x		
Inferences, conclusions	x	x	x	x
Purpose, technique, tone		x	x	x
Fact, opinion, persuasion, bias		x	x	x
Figurative language			x	x
Setting			x	x

SOURCE : With permission from the BASI—Comprehensive technical manual (Table 5.10 and Table 5.13).

FIGURE 13.4

BASI-C Content Coverage in Reading

Relationship to Group Administered Tests

The BASI and the Iowa Achievement Tests (ITBS and ITED). A sample of 285 students in grades 3 through 10 participated in the study. Data for the ITBS and ITED were provided by the schools who administered the BASI and the IOWA tests within a 6-week period. Students who were administered Levels 1 and 3 scored above average on all BASI measures while those who were administered Level 4 received mostly below-average scores. Statistically significant correlations were observed between subtests and total scores between the two measures of similar constructs. Unfortunately, scores on the Iowa test were reported on an IRT scale, thus not allowing mean comparisons across subtests and total scores.

The BASI Level 4 (Form A) and the Tests of Adult Basic Education (TABE). The BASI-C Level 4 (Form A) was administered to 40 high school students who attended grades 9 through 12. All students but three attended regular education classes and one student was receiving services for the gifted. Overall, the sample performed in the lower end of the average range across the majority of the BASI subtests, earning the lowest scores on Reading Comprehension and Math Computation. Despite the somewhat restricted range of many of the BASI scores, the majority of the moderate correlations obtained

Achievement Area	Level 1	Level 2	Level 3	Level 4
Prefixes and suffixes	x	x	x	x
Commonly misspelled words	x	x	x	x
Spelling rules	x	x	x	x
Grammar				
Nouns, pronouns, articles	x	x	x	x
Subject/verb agreement	x	x	x	x
Adjectives, adverbs	x	x	x	x
Double negatives		x	x	
Syntax				
Capitalization	x			x
Internal punctuation	x	x	x	x
Ending punctuation	x			

SOURCE: With permission from the BASI—Comprehensive technical manual (Table 5.11 and Table 5.12).

FIGURE 13.5

BASI-C Content Coverage in Written Language

between the two tests were statistically significant, as expected between measures of similar constructs. Once again, the reporting of IRT scaled scores of the TABE prohibited the direct comparison of means between the two achievement measures. In a second study with 161 students who were administered Form B of the BASI-C and the TABE, the sample earned BASI-C standard scores that were in the average range, yet still with some restriction in the sample's overall performance. Correlations between the BASI-C and TABE were statistically significant in the areas expected and of moderate values.

Relationships with Individually Administered Achievement Tests

Group administered achievement tests have traditionally been used in regular education as program evaluation and progress-monitoring tools, while individually administered achievement tests have traditionally been used when a student is referred for a comprehensive psychoeducational evaluation due to academic difficulties. A comprehensive psychoeducational evaluation typically includes the administration of an individually administered test in order to gain an objective picture of a child's academic skills and to assist with diagnostic and placement decisions. A student's performance on an individually administered achievement test is typically described with a standard score that compares his or her performance to other students of similar age or grade. Until the most recent reauthorization of IDEA in 2004, these standard scores were compared to intelligence test scores to determine whether a significant discrepancy occurs. The new regulations do not encourage the use of a discrepancy formula for the identification of a learning disability but still require a comprehensive evaluation of academic skills when determining the presence of a learning disability. The BASI-C can be administered both in a group setting, and as an individually administered test. The findings of the following studies

Achievement Area	Level 1	Level 2	Level 3	Level 4
Whole numbers	x	x	x	x
Fractions	x	x	x	x
Decimals, order of operations, percents	x	x	x	x
Integers, absolute value		x	x	x
Algebra		x	x	x
Whole numbers, money	x	x	x	
Fractions, proportions	x	x	x	
Decimals, percents	x	x	x	
Word problems	x			
Measurement[a]	x	x	x	
Algebra, graphs, tables	x			
Algebra		x	x	x
Statistics, probability		x	x	x
Geometry			x	x
Word problems, exponents				x

[a]For Level 1 only, this achievement area is divided into three categories: Length, Weight, and Perimeter.
SOURCE: With permission from the BASI—Comprehensive technical manual (Table 5.14 and Table 5.15).

FIGURE 13.6

BASI-C Content Coverage in Math

Subtest	Level 1		Level 2		Level 3		Level 4	
	Form A	Form B	Form A	Form B	Form A	Form B	Form A	Form B
Vocabulary	40	40	40	40	40	40	44	44
Spelling	46	46	40	40	40	40	40	40
Language Mechanics	38	38	39	39	38	38	40	40
Reading Comprehension	44	44	44	44	43	43	41	41
Math Computation	36	36	30	30	30	30	32	32
Math Application	30	30	30	30	36	36	36	36

SOURCE: With permission from the BASI—Comprehensive technical manual (Table 5.17).

FIGURE 13.7
Content Coverage across All Subjects, Levels, and Forms of the BASI-C

provide support for its use as a tool either to complement individually administered tests or to be used for the identification of learning disabilities. Two concurrent validity studies were conducted using two of the most frequently used achievement tests: the Wechsler Individual Achievement Test—Second Edition (WIAT-II; Wechsler, 2001), and the Woodcock-Johnson Psychoeducational Battery—III (WJ III; Woodcock, McGrew, & Maher, 2001).

In the BASI-C with the Wechsler Individual Achievement Test—Second Edition (WIAT-II; Wechsler, 2001) study, 41 students in grades 3 through 8 were administered the BASI-C Form A and the WIAT-II and another 30 in grades 3 through 8 were administered the BASI-C Form B and the WIAT-II in a counterbalanced order. As shown in Figure 13.8, the samples performed similarly across subtests and areas measuring similar constructs. Statistically significant correlations were obtained between the subtest scores and total scores of the two tests that measure similar achievement areas, providing further concurrent validity evidence of the BASI-C (see Figure 13.9).

The BASI-C and the Woodcock-Johnson Achievement—Third Edition (WJ-III; Woodcock, McGrew, & Maher, 2001). Similar findings were also observed in another study with the BASI-C and the WJ-III, with a sample of 40 students in grades 3 through 8 who completed the BASI-C Form A and were also administered

the WJ-III battery by trained examiners in a counterbalanced order. Similarly to the WIAT-II, the means and standard deviations on the BASI and WJ-III were similar across the two tests (see Figure 13.10) and the correlations observed were statistically significant (see Figure 13.11). The results of these studies with two individually administered achievement tests provide further evidence that the BASI test can be used to complement these individually administered tests or in some cases replace them as the measure of choice.

The choice of which instrument to use in a comprehensive evaluation should always rest with the examiner, who has to weight a number of variables in his or her decision, with psychometric qualities with content coverage being the most important, as well as resources needed for the number of evaluations to be completed considering issues of efficiency, administration time, and other logistics, including cost. The evidence presented in this chapter

BASI Test	Form A Sample N = 41		Form B Sample N = 30	
	Mean	*SD*	Mean	*SD*
Vocabulary	110.8	12.3	112.0	12.0
Spelling	113.5	14.2	110.1	12.6
Language Mechanics	112.1	10.6	114.6	12.0
Reading Comprehension	111.8	10.8	111.4	13.7
Math Computation	108.3	11.4	114.8	14.3
Math Application	108.0	15.5	112.4	9.6
Reading Total	110.8	10.1	110.9	11.2
Written Language Total	113.1	12.2	112.7	11.4
Math Total	108.3	13.8	113.8	9.6
WIAT-II				
Word Reading	109.4	10.2	107.9	10.2
Reading Comprehension	103.9	9.9	105.2	9.9
Numerical Operations	112.1	10.9	113.7	10.6
Math Reasoning	109.3	13.1	110.3	13.4
Math Composite	112.2	13.0	113.8	13.1
Spelling	112.6	11.9	112.6	12.1
Written Expression	106.0	10.0	106.4	8.7
Written Language Composite	110.4	12.2	110.6	11.9

NOTE: WIAT-II = Wechsler Individual Achievement Test—Second Edition.
SOURCE: With permission from the BASI—Comprehensive technical manual (Table 5.39).

FIGURE 13.8

Performance on the BASI-C and the WIAT-II

WIAT-II	BASI Test								
	VO	SP	LM	RC	MC	MA	Read	Writ	Math
Word Reading	.57**	.53**	.46**	.57**	.28	.25	.69**	.55**	.29
Reading Comprehension	.50**	.38*	.55**	.56**	.27	.40**	.63**	.48**	.39*
Numerical Operations	.15	.23	.39*	.44**	.40*	.41**	.37*	.33*	.47**
Math Reasoning	.35*	.28	.61**	.49**	.49**	.52**	.50**	.47**	.58**
Math Composite	.29	.30	.58**	.52**	.52**	.52**	.49**	.47**	.60**
Spelling	.46**	.69**	.53**	.57**	.26	.25	.61**	.70**	.28
Written Expression	.42**	.52**	.53**	.53**	.38*	.34*	.52**	.60**	.39*
Written Language Composite	.49**	.69**	.59**	.61**	.34*	.32*	.64**	.73**	.36*

NOTE: $N = 41$, VO = Vocabulary, SP = Spelling, LM = Language Mechanics, RC = Reading Comprehension, MC = Math Computation, MA = Math Application, Read = Reading Total, Writ = Written Language Total, Math = Math Total, WIAT-II = Wechsler Individual Achievement Test—Second Edition.

$^*p < .05.$ $^{**}p < .01.$

WIAT-II	BASI Test								
	VO	SP	LM	RC	MC	MA	Read	Writ	Math
Word Reading	.63**	.44*	.64**	.54**	.28	.42*	.69**	.61**	.43*
Reading Comprehension	.71**	.34	.59**	.45*	.15	.71**	.66**	.50**	.48**
Numerical Operations	.09	.19	.29	.00	.43*	.20	.07	.28	.45*
Math Reasoning	.41*	.26	.49**	.20	.39*	.44*	.35	.42*	.53**
Math Composite	.30	.26	.47**	.13	.49**	.37*	.26	.42*	.57**
Spelling	.52**	.46**	.48**	.36*	.11	.36	.51**	.53**	.26
Written Expression	.48**	.40*	.50**	.54**	.10	.27	.55**	.48**	.20
Written Language Composite	.54**	.47**	.53**	.46*	.11	.33	.55**	.56**	.25

NOTE: $N = 30$, VO = Vocabulary, SP = Spelling, LM = Language Mechanics, RC = Reading Comprehension, MC = Math Computation, MA = Math Application, Read = Reading Total, Writ = Written Language Total, Math = Math Total, WIAT-II = Wechsler Individual Achievement Test—Second Edition.
$^*p < .05.$ $^{**}p < .01.$
SOURCE: With permission from the BASI—Comprehensive technical manual (Table 5.40 and Table 5.41).

FIGURE 13.9

Correlations between the BASI-C and WIAT-II

demonstrates that the BASI-C is a viable tool as it can serve multiple roles, particularly within the assessment framework and requirements of IDEIA, serving student needs at the Tier I–Tier III levels.

INTERPRETATION METHODS OF THE BASI-C

The driving force behind the development of the BASI-C is the belief/philosophy that assessment data can inform instruction in order for instruction to be targeted for all students,

at the school/classroom level (Tier I) and at the individual student level (Tiers II and III). Thus, interpretation of the BASI-C test results spans all levels, and it relates to either groups of students or individual students. In the following, we will first present a scenario where a school is using the BASI-C as a progress-monitoring tool within the three-tier system, followed by a case study for an individual student.

Using and Interpreting the BASI-C for a Group of Students

Figure 13.12 outlines a scenario of how the BASI-C should be used throughout the school

BASI Test	Mean	SD
Vocabulary	106.4	14.3
Spelling	107.8	14.9
Language Mechanics	108.1	13.1
Reading Comprehension	108.0	15.6
Math Computation	106.1	12.0
Math Application	104.9	15.1
Reading Total	106.8	14.2
Written Language Total	107.3	14.0
Math Total	105.3	13.8
WJ III		
Letter-Word Identification	104.0	10.5
Reading Vocabulary	112.7	13.6
Passage Comprehension	101.4	10.7
Reading Comprehension	108.3	13.6
Spelling	107.5	14.5
Punctuation & Capitals	108.5	14.9
Writing Samples	104.6	11.5
Editing	106.8	10.2
Basic Writing Skills	107.8	11.7
Calculation	112.5	9.0
Quantitative Concepts	102.6	13.1
Math Reasoning	102.8	10.2
Applied Problems	103.8	10.6
Academic Skills	109.8	12.7
Academic Applications	103.3	9.1

NOTE: $N = 40$. WJ III = Woodcock-Johnson Psychoeducational Battery-III.
SOURCE: With permission from the BASI—Comprehensive technical manual (Table 5.42).

FIGURE 13.10

Performance on the BASI-C and WJ-III

year within a school system. In this scenario, the BASI-C (Form A) is administered at the beginning of the academic year. The classroom teacher receives data for the entire class and for each individual student; thus, the BASI-C serves as a screening yet comprehensive tool of academic performance (IDEIA; Tier I). The assessment data obtained at this point can answer a number of questions that could be posed by a teacher at the beginning of a school year or a new instructional period. These questions include:

- What do I know about my entire student body as a group?
- What curriculum adjustments, if any, do I need to introduce and how do I need to alter my teaching?

- What curriculum areas are mastered by the students and must be celebrated?
- What curriculum areas need attention for the entire class? Are any of the skills represented by these areas prerequisite skills that might affect subsequent content areas?
- Who are the students that need special attention and in which areas? Individual students experiencing difficulties in certain areas can be identified and both teachers and parents are informed of each student's present skills and needs.

Armed with this information about his or her classroom, a teacher designs his or her instruction for all students and conducts additional, frequent,

WJ III	BASI Test								
	VO	SP	LM	RC	MC	MA	Read	Writ	Math
Letter-Word Identification	.47**	.50**	.41**	.36*	.41**	.52**	.48**	.50**	.56**
Reading Vocabulary	.44**	.43**	.31	.36*	.53**	.54**	.48**	.40*	.63**
Passage Comprehension	.47**	.53**	.42**	.53**	.46**	.64**	.57**	.52**	.66**
Reading Comprehension	.51**	.54**	.41**	.49**	.56**	.64**	.58**	.51**	.71**
Spelling	.40*	.66**	.40*	.32*	.60**	.44**	.43**	.58**	.59**
Punctuation & Capitals	.39*	.50**	.39*	.37*	.66**	.53**	.47**	.48**	.69**
Writing Samples	.18	.32*	.33*	.45**	.11	.29	.38*	.35*	.25
Editing	.47**	.71**	.31	.41**	.43**	.25	.51**	.57**	.37*
Basic Writing Skills	.51**	.77**	.43**	.41**	.63**	.42**	.54**	.66**	.60**
Calculation	.08	.10	−.02	−.03	.60**	.29	.04	.03	.53**
Quantitative Concepts	.32*	.25	.09	.14	.57**	.37*	.28	.17	.55**
Math Reasoning	.33*	.22	.03	.24	.52**	.44**	.33*	.11	.56**
Applied Problems	.25	.14	−.03	.30	.33*	.39*	.31	.04	.42**
Academic Skills	.40*	.55**	.34*	.27	.64**	.51**	.40*	.49**	.67**
Academic Applications	.45**	.44**	.28	.56**	.52**	.67**	.58**	.38*	.71**

NOTE: $N = 40$. VO = Vocabulary, SP = Spelling, LM = Language Mechanics, RC = Reading Comprehension, MC = Math Computation, MA = Math Application, Read = Reading Total, Writ = Written Language Total, Math = Math Total. WJ III = Woodcock-Johnson Psychoeducational Battery-III.
*$p < .05$. **$p < .01$.
SOURCE: With permission from the BASI—Comprehensive technical manual (Table 5.43).

FIGURE 13.11
Correlations between the BASI-C and the WJ-III

and targeted assessments using curriculum-based measurements.

In about three to four months, perhaps close to December or the beginning of January, another administration of the BASI-C should obtain midyear benchmark data. Information from this midyear evaluation provides normative data and feedback for all students' progress. The consistency of use of the same measurement tool facilitates the progress-monitoring needs for the entire group and for individual students. Once again, informed decisions can be made for all students, including those who were identified as having specific needs and perhaps were receiving additional assistance in certain areas (IDEIA; Tier II) or might need to be referred for additional help (Tier III). Data points become available from both a normative and a criterion-referenced perspective and appropriate instructional decisions can be targeted. Finally,

this step is repeated toward the end of the school year and, once again, decisions can be made regarding curriculum issues and instructional needs for an entire grade level or school and for individual students. Throughout this process, student background data are gathered that allow the generation of reports required by the NCLB to supplement school data for Adequate Yearly Progress (AYP) reports while individual student performance can address student needs as required by IDEA.

In order to accomplish all of the above data management efficiently, the school and classroom teacher must use the scoring options offered through the QLocal scoring program of the BASI-C. All student data from the QLocal scoring software can be exported to any commercially available database management program and be manipulated to create school, grade, and classroom reports. The author of the BASI-C has created a Microsoft Excel program

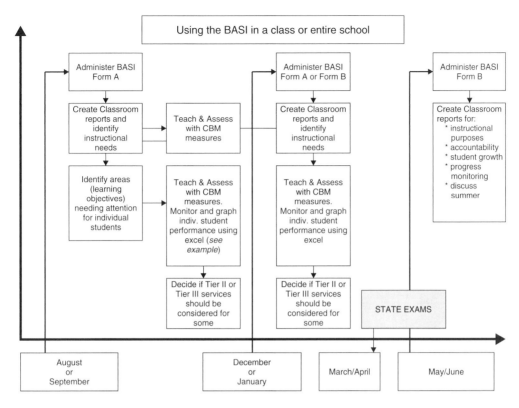

FIGURE 13.12

Using the BASI in a School or Classroom

that imports the data generated by QLocal and utilizes Excel's worksheets to summarize the data and create classroom reports (see Figures 13.13 and 13.14).

Once the data are exported from QLocal and imported into Excel, separate Excel worksheets automatically generate a variety of reports. Figure 13.14 shows a summary performance from a third-grade class. A color-coded scheme is used to facilitate interpretation and the calculation of percentages to determine the level of mastery. The teacher of this classroom can answer a number of questions about his or her students:

1. *What do I know about my entire class as a group?*
   Overall, the group is performing well in the areas of Reading and Written Language.

Eighty percent of the students in the class are in the average to above-average range as compared to a national sample of students of the same grade level. However, there are noted difficulties in Math, with about half of the class experiencing difficulties with their performance in the areas of Math Computation and Math Application.

2. *What curriculum adjustments, if any, do I need to introduce and how do I need to alter my teaching?*
   There is no apparent need to alter the instructional plan in the literacy area (Reading and Written Language) as the majority of the students are performing as expected. However, both of the Math areas need to be further examined. Figure 13.14 presents a summary of the class performance that is

WELD ELEMENTARY SCHOOL

Teacher's Name:	Ms. Jane Brown				BASI-C	Administration	9/12/2008
Grade:	3rd					Level	One
Academic Year:	2008-2009					Form	A

Student Name	Vocabulary	Reading Comprehension	Reading Total		Spelling	Language Mechanics	Written Language Total	Math Computation	Math Application	Math Total
Nicolette Johnston	AVG	AVG	AVG		AVG	AVG	AVG	AVG	AVG	AVG
Katerina Border	AVG	AVG	AVG		B_AVG	B_AVG	B_AVG	B_AVG	B_AVG	B_AVG
Austin Brown	AVG	AVG	AVG		AVG	AVG	AVG	B_AVG	B_AVG	B_AVG
David Barista	AVG	AVG	AVG		AVG	AVG	AVG	AVG	AVG	AVG
Tim Querry	AVG	AVG	AVG		AVG	AVG	AVG	AVG	A_AVG	AVG
Alex Wonder	A_AVG	AVG	A_AVG		A_AVG	A_AVG	A_AVG	A_AVG	A_AVG	A_AVG
John Darwin	B_AVG	B_AVG	B_AVG		B_AVG	B_AVG	B_AVG	B_AVG	B_AVG	B_AVG
Lia Latters	B_AVG	B_AVG	B_AVG		B_AVG	B_AVG	B_AVG	B_AVG	B_AVG	B_AVG
Michael Lefont	A_AVG	A_AVG	A_AVG		A_AVG	A_AVG	A_AVG	A_AVG	A_AVG	A_AVG
William Earnesto	B_AVG	B_AVG	B_AVG		B_AVG	B_AVG	B_AVG	B_AVG	B_AVG	B_AVG
Bob Founder	A_AVG	AVG	A_AVG		A_AVG	A_AVG	A_AVG	A_AVG	A_AVG	A_AVG
Mary Mapple	AVG	AVG	AVG		AVG	AVG	AVG	B_AVG	B_AVG	B_AVG
Kate Neverland	AVG	AVG	AVG		AVG	AVG	AVG	AVG	AVG	AVG
Danny Oppitz	AVG	AVG	AVG		AVG	AVG	AVG	B_AVG	B_AVG	B_AVG
Kim Papas	AVG	AVG	AVG		AVG	AVG	AVG	AVG	B_AVG	B_AVG
B_AVG n =	3	3	3		4	4	4	7	8	8
%	20	20	20		27	27	27	47	53	53
AV n =	9	11	9		8	8	8	5	3	4
%	60	73	60		53	53	53	33	20	27
A_AVG n =	3	1	3		3	3	3	3	4	3
%	20	7	20		20	20	20	20	27	20
Total %	100	100	100		100	100	100	100	100	100

FIGURE 13.13

A Classroom Report Generated from BASI-C Imported Data

generated automatically by one of the Excel worksheets for the Math Computation skill area. The classroom performance in the overall Math Computation is presented once again in the first column, followed by a breakdown of the overall score into the three content areas that make up the Math Computation skills area. This further subcomponent analysis demonstrates that the group has mastered the first learning objective that relates to whole numbers, place value, and so on, but is experiencing serious difficulties in the areas relevant to fractions, decimals, and calculation of percentage scores. Informed follow-up instruction should be targeted to those areas.

3. *Who are the students who need special attention and in which areas?*

A visual inspection of Figure 13.13 suggests that three students are experiencing difficulties across all subject areas. An additional student is also experiencing difficulties in the Written Language area. In addition to these four students, eight students (53% of the entire class) are experiencing difficulties in Math. The teacher consults with each student individually and creates a learning and progress-monitoring plan.

4. *How do I address each student's unique learning and assessment needs?*

The classroom teacher presents each student and his or her parent with the individual report generated by the QLocal scoring program (see Figure 13.1). Normative scores (standard scores, percentiles, confidence intervals, etc.) are presented and explained.

Classroom report on Math performance					BASI-C		
Teacher's Name:	Ms. Jane Brown				Administration		9/12/2008
Grade:	3rd				Level		One
Academic Year:	2008-2009				Form		A

Student Name	Math Computation	MC_LO1	MC_LO2	MC_LO3
Nicolette Johnston	AVG	AVG	AVG	AVG
Katerina Border	B_AVG	AVG	B_AVG	B_AVG
Austin Brown	B_AVG	AVG	B_AVG	B_AVG
David Barista	AVG	AVG	AVG	AVG
Tim Querry	AVG	AVG	AVG	B_AVG
Alex Wonder	A_AVG	A_AVG	A_AVG	A_AVG
John Darwin	B_AVG	B_AVG	B_AVG	B_AVG
Lia Latters	B_AVG	B_AVG	B_AVG	B_AVG
Michael Lefont	A_AVG	A_AVG	A_AVG	A_AVG
William Earnesto	B_AVG	AVG	B_AVG	B_AVG
Bob Founder	A_AVG	A_AVG	A_AVG	AVG
Mary Mapple	B_AVG	AVG	B_AVG	B_AVG
Kate Neverland	AVG	AVG	B_AVG	B_AVG
Danny Oppitz	B_AVG	AVG	B_AVG	B_AVG
Kim Papas	AVG	AVG	AVG	AVG
Below Average	7	2	8	9
(B_AVG) %	47	13	53	60
Average	5	10	4	4
(AVG) %	33	67	27	27
Above Average	3	3	3	2
(A_AVG) %	20	20	20	13
Total %	100	100	100	100

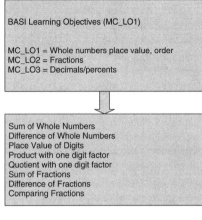

BASI Learning Objectives (MC_LO1)

MC_LO1 = Whole numbers place value, order
MC_LO2 = Fractions
MC_LO3 = Decimals/percents

Sum of Whole Numbers
Difference of Whole Numbers
Place Value of Digits
Product with one digit factor
Quotient with one digit factor
Sum of Fractions
Difference of Fractions
Comparing Fractions

FIGURE 13.14

Classroom Report on Math Computation

Next, a learning and progress-monitoring plan is designed for each student in the areas needing attention (see the case study, below). The teacher explains the concept of *mastery learning*, the expectations of the student, and the resources available in order to reach each of the learning objectives. Finally, the teacher presents the student with the means he or she will be using to monitor his or her performance using another Excel program (see the case study) that allows the recording and graphing of performance in the targeted areas.

CASE STUDY

Overview of Steps

The BASI-C technical manual presents the steps that need to be followed for the test results interpretation. These steps are familiar to those involved with the interpretation of standardized tests and include the following for each achievement area:

1. Interpret the overall performance in each area using the standard scores and their corresponding confidence intervals.

2. Compare composite areas to determine statistically significant strengths and weaknesses (i.e., comparing the Reading Total score and the Written Language Total score).

3. Compare subtest score areas within each domain area (i.e., comparing Math Computation and Math Application standard scores to determine whether there is a statistically significant difference).

4. Compare differences between the BASI-C specific areas and test scores available from other assessment tools.

5. Determine the amount of discrepancy between the BASI-C test scores with the score of a cognitive assessment test. This last step remains an option for some educational agencies who wish to utilize the discrepancy approach (IQ vs. Achievement) for the determination of learning disabilities and for those psychologists in private practice who follow the DSM-IV diagnostic manual for the identification of learning disabilities.

Case Study Background Information

Katerina is a fourth-grade student who was administered the BASI-C Form A in late August of her school year as part of the school assessment plan. Katerina has been attending the same school since first grade with an excellent attendance record. She is a physically healthy child with no reported issues or concerns about her behavior and interactions with others at school. Katerina has been performing well academically throughout her academic career across all subjects. Reading, writing, and art (drawing, dance) have been her strong academic areas, but she has always had difficulties with math. Throughout her schooling, her performance in math has been somewhat lower in comparison to other areas but she has successfully met all grade-level requirements. Katerina was administered the BASI-C as part of the school annual assessment program. Tables 13.1 and 13.2 are selected data extracted from Katerina's individual student report generated by the BASI-C scoring program.

Katerina's performance in the areas of Reading and Written Language was consistent with her performance in previous years. She earned scores in the average (Reading) to above-average

TABLE 13.1   Individual Student Performance on the BASI-C

| **Student Name: Katerina** | | **Grade: Fourth** | |
Composite or Subtest	**Standard Score**	**Confidence Interval**	**Percentile**
Reading Total	101	95–107	53
Vocabulary	99	92–106	47
Reading Comprehension	107	98–115	68
Written Language Total	111	104–117	77
Spelling	107	99–114	68
Language Mechanics	116	106–123	86
Math Total	78	71–89	7
Math Computation	84	77–93	14
Math Application	82	73–97	12

TABLE 13.2   Detailed Student Performance on Math Computation and Math Application

Achievement Area	Percentage Correct	Performance
Math Computation		Below Average
Whole numbers	75	Average
Fractions	48	Below Average
Decimals, order of operations, percents	47	Below Average
Math Application	56	Below Average
Whole numbers, money	72	Average
Fractions, proportions	60	Below Average
Decimals, percents	54	Below Average
Word problems	51	Below Average
Algebra, graphs, tables	48	Below Average
Measurement	32	Below Average
Length	30	Below Average
Weight	49	Below Average
Perimeter	72	Average

range (Written Language) but earned scores in the below-average range in Math when compared to students in the same grade in the general student population (see Table 13.1).

Katerina's teacher identified her as a student at risk for failure in this area (Tier II). She further analyzed her performance in the mathematics content areas and identified areas that she has mastered and others that need further instruction and monitoring (see Table 13.2). In a one-on-one meeting with Katerina and her parents, the teacher presented the overall BASI-C assessment data and created a remedial mathematics plan of action. Figure 13.15 represents the learning objectives set by the teacher in the area of Math Computation. Out of the seven identified areas for her grade level, Katerina has mastered two areas, Sum of whole numbers and Product with one digit. She needs to demonstrate mastery on the rest. The scheme presented in Figure 13.16 is a hypothetical scenario of how and what Katerina has been doing in the months that followed. She has improved in three areas (Difference of whole numbers; Place value of digits; and Sum of fractions) and in fact met the mastery criterion (80% accuracy in teacher-prepared quizzes). Finally, Katerina is showing progress in two areas (Quotient with one digit factor; Difference of fractions) but she has yet to meet the mastery criterion. The classroom teacher recorded her performance across the various classroom assessments in an Excel program that managed the test scores and provided a graphic representation of her performance (see Figure 13.16).

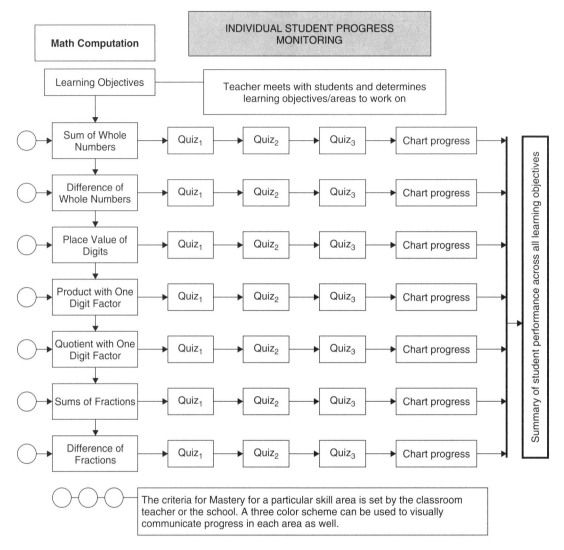

FIGURE 13.15
Individual Student Instructional and Progress Monitoring Plan

TEST SCORES FOR SPECIAL POPULATIONS

The consent form completed by parents during the BASI-C standardization requested the identification of special education services that their children might be receiving. Parents were offered among 10 categories of possible services, a general category for the gifted programs and one labeled "Other." The accuracy of parental reports of services and diagnoses was not verified with school records.

As the data in Figure 13.17 describe, a total of eight categories, three specific to learning disabilities in reading, writing, and math, were

PROGRESS MONITORING DATA SHEET

Student's name:		Katerina				
Grade:		4th				
Teacher		Nicolette B.				

			test date	test date	test date	
MATH COMPUTATION LEARNING OBJECTIVES	BASI pretest	questions per quiz	raw score quiz 1	raw score quiz 2	raw score quiz 3	BASI posttest
Sum of Whole Numbers	Average		N/A	N/A	N/A	
Difference of Whole Numbers	Blw Avrg	12	5	7	11	
Place Value of Digits	Blw Avrg	12	6	8	12	
Product with one digit factor	Average					
Quotient with one digit factor	Blw Avrg	12	5	7	10	
Difference of Fractions	Blw Avrg	12	6	8	9	
Comparing Fractions	Blw Avrg	12	7	9	8	
Sum of Fractions	Blw Avrg	12	10	9	12	
LEARNING OBJECTIVES	BASI pretest	questions per quiz	% correct quiz 1	% correct quiz 2	% correct quiz 3	BASI posttest
Sum of Whole Numbers	Average		N/A	N/A	N/A	
Difference of Whole Numbers	Blw Avrg	12	42	58	92	
Place Value of Digits	Blw Avrg	12	50	67	100	
Product with one digit factor	Average		N/A	N/A	N/A	
Quotient with one digit factor	Blw Avrg	12	42	58	83	
Difference of Fractions	Blw Avrg	12	50	67	75	
Comparing Fractions	Blw Avrg	12	58	75	67	
Sum of Fractions	Blw Avrg	12	83	75	100	

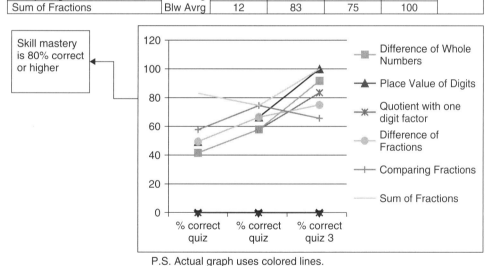

Skill mastery is 80% correct or higher

- Difference of Whole Numbers
- Place Value of Digits
- Quotient with one digit factor
- Difference of Fractions
- Comparing Fractions
- Sum of Fractions

P.S. Actual graph uses colored lines.

FIGURE 13.16
An Excel Program That Monitors Student Performance

formed, along with five other categories such as students identified with attention deficit disorders, hearing impairments, emotional disabilities, and speech and language disabilities, and 57 who identified the services as "other" but did not offer specific descriptions of the services or diagnoses.

BASI Subtest or Total Score	Learning Disability: Reading N = 135		Learning Disability: Writing N = 76		Learning Disability: Math N = 88		Attention Deficit Disorder N = 142		Hearing Impairment N = 24		Emotional Disability N = 20		Speech or Language Disability N = 97		Other N = 57	
	M	SD	M	SD	M	SD	M	SD	M	SD	M	SD	M	SD	M	SD
Vocabulary	83.5	12.5	82.2	12.5	82.5	12.6	98.1	16.6	96.5	18.1	86.7	14.0	90.3	15.5	97.8	15.7
Spelling	84.5	14.0	82.5	12.0	84.3	13.3	96.4	15.9	98.7	17.2	87.6	15.6	95.4	16.4	94.5	15.5
Language Mechanics	83.6	12.2	81.9	12.2	81.2	11.1	95.9	15.3	93.5	15.8	87.1	15.6	88.3	14.5	95.9	15.7
Reading Comprehension	84.8	12.1	84.1	12.9	85.1	12.5	94.1	16.5	95.3	19.7	88.2	13.8	91.7	17.1	97.0	16.4
Math Computation	93.1	14.0	92.7	12.9	88.4	11.5	98.2	14.5	97.5	16.0	89.7	11.5	98.5	13.0	98.5	14.5
Math Application	88.6	12.5	87.4	13.0	85.8	9.9	96.9	14.0	97.6	15.2	88.2	11.3	94.0	14.6	98.6	15.9
Reading Total	83.0	11.1	82.2	11.5	82.9	11.2	95.5	15.0	95.5	18.0	87.2	11.5	89.8	15.2	96.7	15.0
Written Language Total	81.1	13.0	79.4	11.8	79.7	12.1	94.7	15.6	95.1	16.2	85.7	14.7	90.1	15.7	94.0	15.7
Math Total	88.2	13.4	87.6	12.9	83.9	10.2	96.3	14.6	96.0	16.1	87.4	11.3	94.5	14.3	97.6	15.4

SOURCE: With permission from the BASI—Comprehensive technical manual (Table 5.45).

FIGURE 13.17

Performance of Special Populations on the BASI-C

Specific Learning Disabilities

Students who were receiving special education services in any of the three learning disabilities categories performed about one standard deviation below the mean across all academic subjects. These data could suggest that perhaps the BASI-C is not sensitive in differentiating students with reading disabilities from those with written expression disabilities. Parental self-report aside, it is known that a primary disability in one area does not exclude impairment or difficulties in another area. Students with reading problems also tend to have trouble with their written expression skills and by grade 3 or 4 those reading difficulties affect all subject areas—including math, as math cannot be completely independent from reading at this grade level. The performance of students with learning disabilities on the BASI-C supports that position.

Samples with Other Disabilities

Figure 13.17 also describes the performance of additional special samples. Although the mean scores of the groups identified with a specific learning disability were the lowest across all disability categories as expected, the mean scores for the attention deficit disorder, hearing impaired, and other impairment groups were all between 93.5 and 98.7. Overall, these results suggest that the BASI test can be used effectively to identify students with learning difficulties, as part of a screening process or during a comprehensive psychoeducational evaluation.

Performance of Bilingual Students

A total of 402 students, 194 males (48.3%) and 208 females (51.7%), in grades 3 through 12 were reported as bilingual by their parents, who were asked during the standardization process if their child spoke another language

BASI Subtest or Total Score	Mean	Standard Deviation
Vocabulary	95.8	14.8
Spelling	100.5	15.2
Language Mechanics	96.3	14.5
Reading Comprehension	97.2	15.1
Math Computation	102.1	14.3
Math Application	98.9	13.7
Reading Total	95.6	13.7
Written Language Total	97.1	14.7
Math Total	99.7	13.6

SOURCE: With permission from the BASI—Comprehensive technical manual (Table 5.46).

FIGURE 13.18

Performance of Bilingual Students on the BASI-C

in addition to English. Unfortunately, the nature and process of data collection did not allow the cross-validation of this parental information with school records or the degree or level to which the students spoke the other language. Of these 402 students, BASI Level 1 was administered to 130 (32.3%), Level 2 to 95 (23.6%), Level 3 to 71 (17.7%), and Level 4 to 106 (26.4%). Of these students, three were identified as receiving special education services, and nine were identified as gifted. The majority of the students (246; 61.2%) were Hispanic/Latino, 83 (20.6%) were white, 9 (2.2%) were African American, 5 (1.2%) were American Indian, 44 (10.9%) were Asian American, 2 (0.5%), were Pacific Islanders, 8 (2.0%) were "other," and 5 (1.2%) were missing data on race/ethnicity. The parents of these students reported their own educational background as follows: 97 (24.1%) less than 12th grade, 80 (19.9%) high school graduate or GED, 108 (26.9%) 1–3 years of college, and 102 (25.4%) 4 or more years of college, while 15 (3.7%) did not report their educational level. Figure 13.18 presents the means and standard deviations of the sample's performance on Form A of the BASI-C. Overall, the sample earned scores in the average range.

Interventions Based on Test Results

As discussed earlier in the case study interpretation, the BASI-C can guide interventions at the group (Tier I and Tier II) or at the individual (Tier II and Tier III) level. Academic interventions including curriculum changes and identification of students with learning disabilities, when needed, should be entertained with multiple sources of data including other achievement and psychological test data (personality, ability). The BASI-C offers the specificity and sensitivity of test data that an individual teacher or team of teachers can utilize to inform their instruction.

SUMMARY

The reauthorization of IDEA (2004) recommends that local educational agencies assess all students in a classroom (Tier I), identify those that are at risk for academic difficulties (Tier II), and identify those who might benefit from special education services (Tier III). The BASI-C with its comprehensive content coverage and variety of administration and scoring options offers an assessment of academic skills that connects and addresses regular and special education student needs. In conjunction with other educational and cognitive assessment data, the BASI-C can be used to guide classroom instruction and assist in the development of appropriate educational plans for a group or an individual student as well as offer a mechanism to monitor the progress of students' academic performance.

REFERENCES

Bardos, A. N. (2004a). *Basic Achievement Skills Inventory—Comprehensive*. Minneapolis: Pearson.

Bardos, A. N. (2004b). *Basic Achievement Skills Inventory—Survey*. Minneapolis: Pearson.

Black, P., & Wiliam, D. (1998). Inside the black box: Raising standards through classroom assessment. *Phi Delta Kappa, 80*(2), 139–148.

Colorado Department of Education (2008). Response to Intervention (RtI): A practitioner's guide to implementation (www.cde.state.co.us).

Stiggins, R. (2004). New assessment beliefs for a new school mission. *Phi Delta Kappa, 86*(1), 24.

Wechsler, D. (2001). *Wechsler Individual Achievement Test—II (WIAT-II)*. San Antonio, TX: Harcourt Assessment.

Woodcock, R. W., McGrew, K. S., & Maher, N. (2001). *Woodcock-Johnson Psychoeducational Battery—III (WJ-III)*. Itasca, IL: Riverside.

CHAPTER 14

Using the Comprehensive Test of Phonological Processing (CTOPP) to Assess Reading-Related Phonological Processes

Richard K. Wagner, Joseph K. Torgesen

Reading is an example of an important skill that results from the coordinated execution of almost all perceptual, linguistic, and cognitive processes that have been identified by cognitive psychologists and other researchers. Although normal reading requires sophisticated eye movements and visual information processing, the reading performance of most readers, including individuals with dyslexia or reading disability, does not appear to be limited by their visual system unless significant impairments exist, as in blindness. Rather, the typical development of reading and the atypical development of dyslexia both appear to be related more to language than vision for nearly all individuals (Wagner, Piasta, & Torgesen, 2006). A key player in the early development of reading and an important factor that interferes with reading growth in students with dyslexia appears to be the area of language referred to as phonological processing (Liberman, Shankweiler, & Liberman, 1989; Piasta & Wagner, 2007; Torgesen, 1999; Wagner, 2005;

Wagner & Muse, 2006; Wagner & Torgesen, 1987). Compared to reading-level matched controls, most individuals with dyslexia perform poorly on measures of phonological awareness and phonological decoding, and have fewer words that can be decoded by sight (Ehri, 1998; Fox, 1994; Rack, Snowling, & Olson, 1992; Siegel & Faux, 1989). Traces of problems in phonological processing persist into adulthood (Bruck, 1990, 1992, 1993).

The Comprehensive Test of Phonological Processing (CTOPP) (Wagner, Torgesen, & Rashotte, 1999) was developed to assess reading-related phonological processing. In this chapter, we begin by reviewing the rationale underlying the CTOPP, including a brief discussion of levels of phonological representation, kinds of phonological processing, and the model of phonological processing that underlies the test. A detailed description of the CTOPP is then presented, followed by directions for administration and scoring. The normative sample is described and the psychometric properties of the test are reviewed. A case study is presented as an example of how to score and interpret CTOPP performance.

RATIONALE UNDERLYING THE CTOPP

Phonological processing refers to the use of phonological information in processing written and oral language (Jorm & Share, 1983; Wagner & Torgesen, 1987). The term *phonological* derives from the Greek root *phone*, which means "voice" or "sound." Phonological processing can be thought of as using speech-sound-based codes for processing both oral and written language. Phonological processing can be categorized on the basis of levels of phonological representation and the specific kind of processing that a task requires.

Four Levels of Phonological Representation

Language can be represented at multiple levels (Crowder & Wagner, 1992; Piasta & Wagner, 2007). From the lowest to highest, these levels are the acoustic, phonetic, phonological, and morphophonemic.

At the most basic *acoustic* level, a spoken word such as *thoughtful* is represented by continuously varying waves of acoustic energy that physically induce the ear drum and other structures associated with the ear to vibrate. This energy can be observed in a spectrogram, which represents the magnitude of acoustic energy present by frequency. One of the most interesting things you will observe if you examine a spectrogram is that the separation of words into component parts, or even of sentences into words, is largely a cognitive-perceptual phenomenon rather than something inherent in the acoustic signal itself. The acoustic signal that arrives at your ear is largely continuous. This fact is sometimes more apparent when you happen to listen to a speaker of a language that is foreign to you. The

speech seems to be much more rapid than that of your native language. However, observers of you speaking will experience the same phenomenon if they are not fluent speakers of your language.

At the *phonetic* level, speech is represented by strings of *phones*. Phones refer to the universal set of speech sounds found in languages. Any given language will use only a subset of possible phones. Each phone is produced by a combination of articulatory gestures that involve placement of the tongue in the mouth, how the lips are formed, and whether the vocal cords vibrate. Examples of different phones include the sounds of the letter *t* in the words *pat*, *tap*, and *stop*. To confirm that these indeed are different phones, try this little test. Put your hand just in front of your mouth. Now, say the three words *pat*, *tap*, and *stop*. You will notice a pronounced burst of air associated with the sound of the *t* in *pat*, somewhat less of a burst associated with the sound of the *t* in *tap*, and the least amount of air associated with the sound of the *t* in *stop*.

At the *phonological* level, speech is represented by *phonemes*. Phonemes refer to speech sounds that make a difference in meaning. Phonemes correspond roughly to the letters of the alphabet. The three phones associated with the sound of the *t* in *pat*, *tap*, and *stop* are referred to as *allophones* of the single phoneme /t/. The words *pat* and *bat* have different meanings, and this difference is signaled by the fact that they begin with different phonemes, /p/ and /b/.

Finally, the highest level is called the *morphophonemic* level. At this level, aspects of meaning as well as pronunciation are represented. For example, the fact that the meanings of the words *receipt* and *receive* are related is represented in their similar spellings.

Three Kinds of Phonological Processing

Three kinds of phonological processing appear to be related to normal development in the domains of reading, writing, and mathematics, and also are suspected origins of learning disabilities in these domains. The three kinds of phonological processing are *phonological awareness, phonological memory*, and *rapid naming*.

Phonological Awareness

Phonological awareness refers to an awareness of and access to the sound structure of one's oral language (Mattingly, 1972). Spoken words are comprised of phonemes, and these phonemes often correspond to the written representations of the words in alphabetic writing systems such as English. For example, the words *dog*, *log*, and *fog* are related phonologically: They have different initial phonemes (/d/, /l/, and /f/) but identical medial and final phonemes (/o/ and /g/). This fact is reflected in the spellings, as they have different first letters but identical second and third letters. Children with well-developed phonological awareness are aware of these similarities and differences. Consequently, the words' spellings are sensible. Phonological awareness shows a developmental trajectory related to the levels of phonological representation described previously. Initially, awareness is limited to word-length phonological units, and this level of awareness can be demonstrated on tasks that require blending of *cow* and *boy* to make *cowboy*, or segmenting *cowboy* into *cow* and *boy*. Next, awareness of syllable-length phonological units is demonstrated when children are able to blend or segment the two syllables that comprise the word *monkey*. Later, children become aware of phonological units within a syllable. This first occurs for onsets and rimes, which refer to the initial sound and the remaining sounds respectively. For example, the onset of the first syllable in the word *rattle* is the phoneme /r/, and the rime is the remaining vowel and consonant (*at*). Finally, full-blown phonological awareness is demonstrated when individuals are able to isolate and manipulate individual phonemes, including individual phonemes from combinations such as consonant clusters. Examples include segmenting the word *cat* into its three constituent phonemes, or blending the phonemes associated with the letters *s*, *t*, and *r* to produce the initial part of the word *string*. Based on this developmental progression, the items

on the phonological awareness subtests of the CTOPP typically begin with compound words, then switch to syllables, then to onset and rime, and finally to individual phonemes.

Children who are impaired in phonological awareness commonly have difficulty in reading and writing, and knowing this has clear implications for recommended intervention. First, interventions exist that have been shown to improve phonological awareness, and many children show not only improved phonological awareness but also improved reading as a result of such interventions (National Reading Panel, 2000). Second, approaches to teaching reading that feature systematic, explicit instruction in phonetic decoding skills result in better reading outcomes for children who are poor in phonological awareness compared to reading approaches that do not teach these skills explicitly (National Reading Panel, 2000).

Phonological Memory

Phonological memory refers to the use of phonological codes for short-term storage of language-based information. An everyday example of phonological memory is remembering a phone number that you have looked up in a directory while you key the numbers into your phone. Most people do this task by keeping the names of the digits active in short-term memory using phonological codes (i.e., the pronunciations of the names of the digits), rather than trying to visualize the string of numbers. Phonological memory is believed to consist of two components that work together (Baddeley, 1986, 1992). The first component is a phonological store than can be thought of as a tape recording loop that continuously records the most recent two seconds' worth of auditory information that has been processed. The second component is an articulatory control process that can provide input to the phonological store and can refresh its content so that information can be stored for longer than two seconds.

A deficit in phonological memory is commonly observed in children with specific language impairment and dyslexia (Torgesen, 1996), and measures of phonological memory such as nonword repetition serve as important markers of the phenotype of specific language impairment in recent molecular genetic studies of language impairment (Bishop, 2006).

Rapid Naming

Reading requires efficient retrieval of phonological codes from long-term storage. Examples include retrieving letter sounds and pronunciations associated with larger strings of letters. Efficiency of retrieval of phonological codes from long-term storage is commonly assessed by rapid naming tasks in which an individual is asked to rapidly name common stimuli such as pictures of objects, colors, letters, or digits. The efficiency with which the retrieval occurs presumably affects the degree to which phonological information can be used to decode printed words. Poor performance on measures of retrieval of phonological codes from long-term storage is associated with poor reading performance independently of poor phonological awareness (Wagner et al., 1997).

A Model of Phonological Processing that Underlies the CTOPP

The basic model of phonological processing that underlies the CTOPP is presented in Figure 14.1. Three kinds of phonological processing are represented: phonological awareness, phonological memory, and rapid naming. The connecting arrows indicate that the three kinds of phonological processing are related rather than completely independent. Most studies have found that phonological awareness and phonological memory are more closely related to one another than to rapid naming.

DESCRIPTION OF THE CTOPP

The CTOPP assesses phonological awareness, phonological memory, and rapid naming. A deficit in one or more of these kinds of

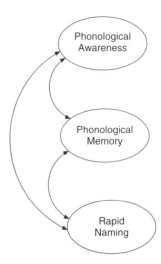

FIGURE 14.1
The Model of Phonological Processing that Underlies the CTOPP

phonological processing is viewed as a common cause of reading disabilities, which is a special case within the larger category of learning disabilities. The CTOPP was developed to assess phonological processing abilities for individuals ranging in age from 5 to 24. Because of this wide range in age and the considerable development of phonological processing that occurs during these years, two versions of the CTOPP were developed. The first version is for individuals who are 5 or 6 years old and consists of seven core subtests and one supplemental subtest. The second version, for ages 7 through 24, consists of six core subtests and six supplemental subtests. The supplemental subtests are provided to permit more in-depth assessment of strengths and weaknesses in phonological processing. Both versions are individually administered and the core subtests take roughly 30 minutes to administer.

Subtest Background and Structure

Experimental studies of phonological processing over the years by the authors of the CTOPP (Torgesen & Houck, 1980; Torgesen, Wagner,

Simmons, & Laughon, 1990: Wagner, Torgesen, & Rashotte, 1994; Wagner et al., 1997) resulted in the development of a number of tasks used to measure phonological awareness, phonological memory, and rapid naming. These experimental tasks were then refined to form the subtests of the CTOPP. The CTOPP has multiple subtests that assess each of the three kinds of phonological processing described in the model.

The 13 subtests that are included on one or both versions of the CTOPP as either a core or supplemental subtest are listed in Table 14.1. The phonological awareness subtests have items that represent different levels of linguistic complexity ranging from compound words, syllables, onset-rime units, and individual phonemes. The phonological awareness subtests assess skills that are relevant to reading instruction. Elision requires segmenting spoken words into smaller parts that correspond to spellings. Segmenting Words assesses a skill that is prerequisite to letter-sound mapping in that letter-sound mapping requires that words be segmented into letter-size parts. Blending Words requires combining sounds together, and is required when decoding words letter-by-letter or by larger phonological units and then combining the decoded parts to identify the target word. Sound Matching requires identification of the first sound in a word, and this is one of the first reading skills taught.

Blending and Segmenting Nonwords are included for clinicians and researchers who prefer nonword items. Some authorities believe that nonword items provide purer measures of phonological processing because the influence of vocabulary is reduced. However, nonword items are more difficult for examiners to administer and score. In addition to presenting problems for some examiners, some examinees, especially younger children, have difficulty working with or pronouncing nonwords. Based on these concerns, nonword items were included only on supplemental subtests. Also, to reduce error attributable to individual differences in the

accuracy with which examiners are able to pronounce nonwords, items for subtests involving nonwords are presented via a digital recording.

Turning to phonological memory, a number of digit span tasks are available on various tests. Digit Span on the CTOPP was constructed to be a purer measure of phonological memory than is provided by the typical digit span task. To maximize the extent to which this subtest assesses phonological memory rather than rehearsal or memory strategies, the digits are presented at a rate of 2 per second. This rate of presentation minimizes the opportunity for rehearsal or use of other memory strategies to affect performance. All items require forward recall of digits only because backward recall of digits introduces cognitive complexity and strategic processing, and may be a better measure of working memory than of phonological memory per se. Two strategies were used to improve reliability. First, the Digit Span items are presented using a digitally recorded format. This ensures that the digits are presented at a rate of 2 per second and that rate of presentation does not vary across examiners. Second, three items are presented at each string length, and the score is the number of items recalled correctly as opposed to a span length. The items for the Nonword Repetition task were created in a way that minimizes their similarity to actual words. The items were constructed by randomly combining phonemes and then retaining for possible inclusion resultant strings that were pronounceable. Other nonword repetition tasks have items that are more word-like, which encourages lexical processing using knowledge of real words as opposed to phonological processing.

Turning to rapid naming, 5- and 6-year-olds are asked to name only common objects and colors. Although rapid naming of digits and letters is more predictive of reading, younger children are asked to name only objects and colors because rapid naming tasks ought to measure differences in rates for naming familiar items as opposed to differences in familiarity

TABLE 14.1   The 13 Subtests of the CTOPP

Core Phonological Awareness Subtests

1. *Elision*. This is a 20-item subtest that measures the ability to drop a phonological segment from a word and pronounce the remaining portion. For example, an examinee might be asked to say the word *cat* without saying /c/. The correct answer is *at*.

2. *Blending Words*. This is a 20-item subtest that measures the ability to combine phonological segments into words. For examine, an examinee might be asked, "What word do these sounds make: /c/ /a/ /k/? The correct answer is *cake*.

3. *Sound Matching*. This 20-item subtest measures the ability to match sounds. The examiner pronounces a word and then three responses. All words are represented by pictures. For the first half of the subtest, the task is to match initial sounds. For example, the examinee might be asked, "Which word begins with the same sound as *pan*: *hat*, *pig*, or *cone*?" The correct answer is *pig* because it begins with the same sound as *pan*. For the second half of the subtest, the task is to match final sounds, so for the same items, *cone* would now be the correct answer because it ends in the same sound as *pan*.

Core Phonological Memory Subtests

4. *Memory for Digits*. This 21-item subtest measures forward digit span for strings varying in length from 2 to 8 digits in length.

5. *Nonword Repetition*. This is an 18-item subtest that assesses phonological memory by asking individuals to repeat nonwords ranging in length from 3 to 15 phonemes. For example, the examinee might listen to and then pronounce the nonword *jatsiz*.

Core Rapid Naming Subtests

6. *Rapid Color Naming*. This 72-item subtest measures the speed at which a series of pictured colored blocks can be named. It is administered in two trials, each of which requires the individual to name 36 items as quickly and accurately as possible. The colors to be named are blue, red, green, black, yellow, and brown. This is a core subtest for the 5- and 6-year-old version of the CTOPP, and a supplemental subtest for the 7- through 24-year-old version.

7. *Rapid Object Naming*. This subtest is identical to Rapid Color Naming except that the stimuli to be named are the objects pencil, star, fish, chair, boat, and key. This also is a core subtest for the 5- and 6-year-old version of the CTOPP, and a supplemental subtest for the 7- through 24-year-old version.

8. *Rapid Digit Naming*. This subtest is identical to Rapid Color Naming except that the stimuli to be named are the digits 2, 3, 4, 5, 7, and 8. This is a core subtest for the 7- through 24-year-old version only.

9. *Rapid Letter Naming*. This subtest is identical to Rapid Color Naming except that the stimuli to be named are the letters *a*, *c*, *k*, *n*, *s*, and *t*. This is a core subtest for the 7- through 24-year-old version only.

Supplemental Subtests

10. *Phoneme Reversal*. This 18-item subtest requires reversing the order of sounds in a speech segment and pronouncing the resultant word. For example, the examinee might be asked to say *ood* backwards. The correct answer is *do*.

11. *Blending Nonwords*. This 18-item subtest is identical to the Blending Words subtest except that the stimuli are nonwords rather than words.

12. *Segmenting Words*. This 20-item subtest requires an individual to separate a word into its constituent parts and pronounce the parts individually. For example, the examinee might be asked to say the word *cat* one sound at a time.

13. *Segmenting Nonwords*. This 20-item subtest is identical to the Segmenting Words subtest except that the stimuli are nonwords.

---

with the items to be named. When young children are asked to name digits and letters, their performance can be affected by their limited knowledge of the digits and letters to be named. Rapid naming of letters and of digits form the core subtests for older children. However, rapid naming of colors and of objects are available as supplemental subtests for those interested in a measure of rapid naming that is less affected by letter or digit knowledge.

Composite Scores

Composite scores are available on the CTOPP that correspond to the three kinds of phonological processing being measured. In addition to the three primary composite scores, there are two alternate composite scores available for the 7- through 24-year-old version. The composite scores are formed by adding together the standard scores of the subtests that comprise the composite.

Phonological Awareness Composite Score

For the 5- and 6-year-old version of the CTOPP, this composite score is a combination of Elision, Blending Words, and Sound Matching. For the 7- through 24-year-old version, Elision and Blending Words make up the composite.

Phonological Memory Composite Score

This composite score is made up of the Memory for Digits and Nonword Repetition subtests for both versions of the CTOPP.

Rapid Naming Composite Score

For the 5- and 6-year-old version, this composite score is made up of the Rapid Color Naming and Rapid Object Naming subtests. For the 7- through 24-year-old version, Rapid Digit Naming and Rapid Letter Naming make up the composite.

Alternate Phonological Awareness Composite Score

This alternate composite score, available only for the 7- through 24-year-old version, is made up of the Blending Nonwords and Segmenting Nonwords subtests. This alternate composite provides an estimate of phonological awareness based on nonword stimuli.

Alternate Rapid Naming Score

This alternate composite score, also available only for the 7- through 24-year-old version, is made up of the Rapid Color Naming and Rapid Object Naming subtests. It provides an estimate of rapid naming for stimuli that are not part of the alphabetic script.

ADMINISTRATION AND SCORING

Chapter 3 of the CTOPP Examiner's Manual provides detailed instructions for administration and scoring and it is important to read and review this chapter before administering the CTOPP. However, abbreviated instructions are also included in the Profile/Examiner Record Booklet so that the test can be administered without using the Manual. It is important to use the correct Profile/Examiner Record Booklet, as there are different Record Booklets for the 5- and 6-year-old and 7- through 24-year-old versions of the test.

The Profile/Examiner Record Booklets consist of four sections. Section I is for recording identifying information and calculating the examinee's age. If it routinely is completed before the CTOPP is administered, it will be possible to verify that the appropriate Profile/Examiner Record Booklet is being used given the examinee's age. Date tested and date of birth are recorded in this section and age is calculated by subtracting date of birth from date tested in a manner similar to that done for many other standardized tests. It may be necessary to borrow a year to add 12 months, or borrow a month to add 30 days to the date tested to be able to subtract a date of birth that has a month or day that is greater than that of the date tested. An example of how to do this is presented in the Examiner's Manual. Sections II and III, used for recording and displaying scores, are filled out after the test has been administered.

Section IV consists of the subtests presented in order of administration. The core subtests are presented first, followed by the supplemental subtests. As noted previously, administration of several of the subtests is done by playing a digitally recorded file. A device to present the recorded subtests is required. The recorded subtests come in the CTOPP kit on a CD, but the files can be played on any device that is capable of presenting them at normal volume levels over speakers.

Specific scoring instructions are provided by subtest in the CTOPP Examiner's Manual. Once this information has been reviewed, the Profile/Examiner Record Booklets provide sufficient prompts so that raw scores can be generated without reference to the Examiner's Manual. Scores are recorded in Section II of the Profile/Examiner Record Booklet, although tables in the Examiner's Manual must be referenced for converting raw score totals into age equivalent, grade equivalent, and standard scores. Beginning with the left side of Section II, the raw score totals for the administered subtests are entered. Then, age and grade equivalents are obtained from Appendix C of the Examiner's Manual and recorded in the appropriate locations of Section II. Percentiles and standard scores are obtained from Appendix A and recorded in a similar manner. For individual subtests, the standard scores have a mean of 10 and a standard deviation of 3.

The right side of Section II is devoted to calculating and recording the composite scores. The subtests that make up the composites are listed in a row at the top. For each composite, the relevant subtests to include are indicated by the presence of a blank under a subtest. The standard scores are entered in the blanks, and the sum of the standard scores that make up a composite is entered in a box. Table B.1 of the Examiner's Manual is used to convert the sum of standard scores into a Composite Score and a corresponding percentile rank. The composite standard scores have a mean of 100 and a standard deviation of 15. Finally, at the bottom of Section II, room is provided for including other test data.

Section III provides a way to graphically represent standard scores for composites and individual subtests. This makes it possible to note the pattern of strengths and weaknesses in a single glance. Other test data can be included on the graph as well. The CTOPP Examiner's Manual contains a table and a formula that can be used to convert other tests with standard scores that have different means and standard deviations from those on the CTOPP to a standard score with a mean of 100 and a standard deviation of 15. By doing so, the results of the other tests can be included on the profile for comparison purposes.

In all, six types of scores can be generated from the CTOPP subtests and/or composites:

1. *Raw scores*. Raw scores on the CTOPP subtests are the number of correct items. Because the subtests have differing numbers of items and the items are not matched in difficulty, use of raw scores is limited to their role in generating the remaining score types and for some research purposes.

2. *Age equivalents*. Age equivalents refer to the age at which an examinee's score would be the average value. They are derived by calculating the average normative group scores at six-month intervals, then using interpolation and smoothing to generate age equivalents associated with each raw score. Age equivalents have limited value and are misleading and prone to misinterpretation. If, for example, an examinee who is 7 years old obtains an age equivalent of 10:0, it is not the case that the examinee has phonological

processing skills identical to those of the typical 10-year-old. Some school districts or other agencies require their use and that is the only reason they are provided for the CTOPP.

3. *Grade equivalents*. Grade equivalents refer to the grade at which an examinee's score would be an average value. They are calculated in a manner similar to that for age equivalents and suffer from the same limitations.

4. *Percentiles*. Percentiles represent the percentage of individuals expected to score equal to or below an examinee's score. They are also known as *percentile ranks*. Percentiles are provided for individual subtest performance and for the composite scores on the CTOPP. An advantage of percentiles is that they are easy to understand. A minor disadvantage is that the difference between percentiles varies depending on how far the percentiles are from the center of their distribution (i.e., the 50th percentile). For example, the difference in performance represented by the difference between the 96th and 99th percentiles is substantially greater than the difference represented by the difference between the 56th and 59th percentiles.

5. *Subtest standard scores*. Subtest standard scores are the best scores to use for interpreting performance on the CTOPP at the subtest level. All CTOPP subtests have standard scores with means of 10 and standard deviations of 3. For that reason, they are useful for comparing performance across subtests in a way that is not possible using raw scores. When comparing performance across subtests, it is important to determine whether an observed difference between standard scores is large enough to be statistically significant. Otherwise, one might be interpreting differences that actually represent chance differences in performance. The Examiner's Manual presents a table (Table 4.4) to be used for determining whether a difference in standard scores for any pair of subtests

on the CTOPP is statistically significant. For all possible pairs of subtests, the size of the difference required to be statistically significant is either 3 or 4. Differences between subtest standard scores indicative of a severe discrepancy between subtest performances are provided in Table 4.6 of the Examiner's Manual. These values range from 4 to 8 depending on the particular pair of subtests being compared.

6. *Standard scores for composites*. The composite standard scores represent the best scores to use for evaluating phonological processing abilities. They are more reliable than individual subtest standard scores by virtue of the fact that they are formed by combining either two or three subtests. The standard scores for composites have a mean of 100 and a standard deviation of 15. Table 4.5 in the Examiner's Manual can be used to determine whether a difference between composite standard scores is statistically significant. Depending on the composites being compared, the required difference ranges from 12 to 16. Differences indicative of severe discrepancies between composite scores are presented in Table 4.7 of the Examiner's Manual. These differences range from 23 to 37 depending on the composites being compared.

STANDARDIZATION, NORMS, AND PSYCHOMETRICS

Norms were obtained for the CTOPP by administering the test to a sample of 1,656 individuals selected to be nationally representative based on census data updated to 1997. Representativeness was achieved by matching census data on geographic region, gender, race, rural or urban residence, ethnicity, family income, parent education, and disability status. A table in the Examiner's Manual (Table 5.1) presents data comparing the demographic characteristics of the normative sample with census data. This comparison reveals that the standardization sample is representative of census data with the exception of demographic region of the country for the adult sample.

Reliability of the Scores

Reliability refers to consistency of measurement. Reliability is evaluated by estimating sources of error variance. Three sources of error variance are relevant to evaluating the reliability of CTOPP scores: content sampling, time sampling, and interscorer differences.

Content Sampling

Content sampling error refers to unreliability associated with the specific content of the subtests and composite. To estimate content sampling error, Cronbach's coefficient Alpha was calculated for all subtests and composites except those involving rapid naming. Alpha is not appropriate for speeded tests. For the rapid naming subtests, alternate-form reliability was used to investigate content sampling error. The average reliabilities were in the 80s or 90s for all subtests except Memory for Digits, Nonword Repetition, and Rapid Object Naming, which were in the high 70s. The reliabilities for all composite scores were in the 80s or 90s and were typically higher than were those of the individual subtests as would be expected.

Time Sampling

Time sampling error refers to unreliability associated with measurement occasion. Scores can vary if a test is administered on different occasions because of changes within individuals or changes in the testing environment. For example, an examinee could be well rested on one testing occasion but not on another. Or, perhaps the room where the test was administered was noisy on one occasion and quiet on another. Time sampling error was investigated for the CTOPP by administering the test on two occasions separated by a two-week interval. For the total sample of examinees who participated in the study of test–retest reliability, all test–retest reliability coefficients were equal to or greater than .70.

Interscorer Differences

Interscorer differences refer to test error attributable to variability in scoring the test. Interscorer differences were examined by having two examiners independently score 60 CTOPP protocols and correlating the two sets of scores. The error attributable to interscorer differences was minimal, with reliability coefficients equal to or greater than .96.

USE OF THE TEST

Interpretation of performance on the CTOPP is relatively straightforward. The test assesses the three phonological processing constructs of phonological awareness, phonological memory, and rapid naming. The best score to use for evaluating an individual's level of performance on the three constructs is the corresponding core composite score. Because the composite scores are made up of either two or three subtests, composite scores are more reliable than are scores of the individual subtests that comprise them.

If a deficit is suspected on the basis of poor performance on a core composite, several follow-up assessment strategies can be considered. For the 7- through 24-year-old version, poor performance on the Phonological Awareness Composite can be followed up with administering the subtests for the Alternate Phonological Awareness Composite. The Alternate Phonological Awareness Composite provides two additional subtests (Blending Nonwords and Segmenting Nonwords) that assess phonological awareness using nonword stimuli. Poor performance on the Rapid Naming Composite can be followed up by administering the Alternate Rapid Naming Composite. This Composite consists of the Rapid Color Naming and Rapid Object Naming subtests. Because these two subtests do not involve letters or digits, comparing the Rapid Naming and Alternate Rapid Naming Composites can be useful in determining the nature of the deficit in rapid naming. For example, poor performance on the Rapid Naming Composite combined with adequate performance on the Alternate Rapid Naming Composite is suggestive of a deficit in automaticity of grapheme-phoneme correspondences. Poor performance on both Composites is suggestive of either a more general phonological problem or a problem in general perceptual-motor speed.

CASE STUDY

The summary sheet from the Profile/Examiner Record Book of the case of Joshua is presented in the CTOPP Examiner's Manual. This summary sheet is presented in Figure 14.2.

Beginning with Section I, Identifying Information, we see routine identifying information including date of birth and date tested. By subtracting date of birth from date tested, we calculate an age of 8 years, 4 months. This age will be required for entering tables to convert raw scores to standard scores. Note that age is recorded in years and months only, and there is no blank to record days of age. Days of age are ignored for the purposes of determining age used to enter the normative tables. Do not round up age in months. For example, an age of 8 years, 11 months, and 28 days is counted as 8 years, 11 months, not 9 years, 0 months.

Moving to Section II, Record of Scores, subtest performance is recorded in the left half of the section and composite performance is recorded in the right half of the section. Beginning with the subtests, raw scores are entered in the first column. These raw scores are transferred from the Total Raw Score line at the bottom of each subtest page of the Profile/Examiner Record Book.

Given Joshua's age of 8 years, 4 months, Table A.7 from the Examiner's Manual is entered to obtain standard scores and percentiles. This table is used for ages 8:0 through 8:11. Taking Elision, for example, Joshua obtained a total raw score of 9. Looking up a raw score of 9 in Table A.7 yields a standard score of 8 and a percentile of 25. These values are entered in the appropriate columns of the row for entering Elision scores. Table C.1 is used to obtain Age and Grade Equivalents. Using this table, a raw score of 9 on Elision corresponds to an Age Equivalent of 7:6 and a Grade Equivalent of 2.4. These values are entered in the same row. This procedure is followed for the remaining subtests.

Turning to the Composites, the first step is to enter the Standard Scores for subtests administered that are included in the composites. It is important to remember to enter standard scores rather than raw scores. For the 7- through 24-year-old Profile/Examiner Record Book, five composites are listed. The Phonological Awareness Composite has blanks to be filled in under the columns headed EL for the Elision subtest and BW for the Blending Words subtest. The Phonological Memory Composite has blanks to be filled in under the columns headed MD for the Memory for Digits subtest and NR for the Nonword Repetition subtest. The Rapid Naming Composite has blanks for be filled in under the columns headed RD for the Rapid Digit Naming subtest and RL to the Rapid Letter Naming subtest. The Alternate Phonological Awareness Composite has blanks to be filled in under the columns headed BN for the Blending Nonwords subtest and SN for the Segmenting Nonwords subtest. Finally, the Alternate Rapid Naming Composite has blanks to be filled in under the columns headed RC for the Rapid Color Naming subtest and RO for the Rapid Object Naming subtest.

For each Composite, the sums of the subtest standard scores are entered into the boxes under the Sum of SS column. Then, Table B.1 in the Examiner's Manual, titled Converting Sums of Standard Scores to Percentiles and Composite Scores, is used to obtain Composite Scores and Percentile Ranks. Returning to the example of Joshua's Profile/Examiner Record Book, he obtained standard scores of 8 on the Elision subtest and 6 on the Blending Words subtest, the two subtests that comprise the Phonological Awareness Composite. The sum of these standard scores is 14, and this value is entered in the appropriate box. Turning to Table B.1 in the Examiner's Manual, you will see columns for Sum of 3 Subtests and Sum of 2 Subtests. The Sum of 2 Subtests column is used for the Phonological Awareness Composite for the 7- through 24-year-old version of the CTOPP, because the composite consists of the two subtests of Elision and Blending Words. A Sum of 2 standard scores of 14 corresponds to a Composite Score of 82 and a Percentile Rank of 12. Because all Composite Scores have a mean of 100 and a standard deviation of 15, a Composite Score of 82 is little more than one standard deviation below the mean. The corresponding Percentile Rank of 12 indicates that this level of performance exceeded that of only 12% of examinees who are comparable in age. This same procedure is used for determining Composite Scores and Percentile Ranks for the remaining Composites. The only time the column in Table B.1 titled Sum of 3 Subtests is used is for the Phonological Awareness Composite for the 5- and 6-year-old version of the CTOPP. The subtests that make up the Phonological Awareness Composite for the younger version are Elision, Blending Words, and Sound Matching. All other Composites for both versions of the CTOPP are made up of only two subtests.

Test Scores for Special Populations

Reliabilities are reported by subgroup in Table 6.3 of the Examiner's Manual. The subgroups included are male, female, European American, African American, Hispanic American, Asian American, individuals with learning disabilities, and individuals with speech/language disabilities. Examination of the reliabilities in this table shows that reliabilities are comparable for these subgroups.

VALIDITY

Three kinds of validity evidence are available for the CTOPP: content-description or content validity; criterion-prediction or criterion-related validity, and construct identification or construct validity.

Content-Description Validity

Content-description validity refers to an examination of the content of a test to determine whether it is representative of the domain being assessed. Evaluation of procedures used for item selection and evaluation is relevant to examining content-description validity.

Item and Subtest Development

The original impetus for developing the CTOPP came from an article published in *Psychological Bulletin* (Wagner & Torgesen, 1987) that summarized the literature on reading-related phonological processes and proposed the framework consisting of phonological awareness, phonological memory, and rapid naming. Experimental tasks were created to measure reading-related phonological processes over the years. Revised versions of these tasks became the preliminary version of the CTOPP. Experts were then asked to review the preliminary tasks and their feedback was used to make minor revisions.

The subtests were next administered to 603 public school students in kindergarten through fifth grade. Extensive item and subtest analyses were done using classical item statistics, item-response theory modeling, and

Profile/Examiner Record Booklet

Comprehensive Test of Phonological Processing
for Ages 7 through 24

Section I.   Identifying Information

Name _Joshua Jones_   Female ☐   Male ☒

School _Covert Avenue School_   Grade _3_

Examiner's Name _Dr. Aimee Summers_

Examiner's Title _Psychologist_

	Year	Month	Day
Date Tested	98	11	16
Date of Birth	90	7	8
Age	8	4	

Section II.   Record of Scores

Subtests

Core	Raw Score	Age Equiv.	Grade Equiv.	%ile	Std. Score
I. Elision (EL)	9	7-6	2.2	25	8
II. Blending Words (BW)	7	6-6	1.4	9	6
III. Memory for Digits (MD)	9	5-9	<2	9	6
IV. Rapid Digit Naming (RD)	64	6-6	1.4	9	6
V. Nonword Repetition (NR)	9	6-6	1.4	25	8
VI. Rapid Letter Naming (RL)	58	7-2	2.0	16	7
Supplemental					
VII. Rapid Color Naming (RC)	76	6-9	1.7	16	7
VIII. Phoneme Reversal (PR)	1	5-9	k.7	9	6
IX. Rapid Object Naming (RO)	90	6-6	1.4	9	6
X. Blending Nonwords (BN)	5	6-3	1.7	25	8
XI. Segmenting Words (SW)	6	<7.0	<2.0	25	8
XII. Segmenting Nonwords (SN)	3	<7.0	<2.0	9	6

Composites

	EL	BW	MD	RD	NR	RL	Sums of SS	%ile	Composite Scores
Phonological Awareness	8	6					14	12	82
Phonological Memory			6		8		14	12	82
Rapid Naming				6		7	13	8	79
	RC	RO	BN	SN					
Alternate Phonological Awareness			8	6			14	12	82
Alternate Rapid Naming	7	6					13	8	79

Other Test Data

Test Name	Date	Std Score	CTOPP Equiv.
1. CTONI	9/98	105	105
2.			
3.			

Section III.   Profile of Scores

[profile chart plotting composite scores, quotients, and subtest standard scores with X marks]

FIGURE 14.2

Summary Sheet from the CTOPP Profile/Examiner Record Booklet for the Case of Joshua confirmatory factor analysis. Minor changes were made on the basis of these results, and the subtests then were administered to a sample of (1) 25 students each from Kindergarten, second grade, fifth grade, and seventh grade, (2) 40 high school students, and (3) 22 college students. Analyses of these data confirmed that the items and subtests were operating as desired and national norming of the CTOPP was begun.

Several issues that had to be addressed in developing the CTOPP were related to the use of nonword items on the test. We were concerned that some examiners would have difficulty presenting nonword items or individual phonemes, and also that nonword items would be more difficult to score reliably than word-based items. We addressed these concerns by using words rather than nonwords as items where possible, and by providing a recorded administration format for nonword items when it was necessary to use them. We addressed the scoring concern by providing explicit scoring instructions and testing to be sure the nonword items could be scored with acceptable reliability. Another issue that had to be addressed was how to generate the nonword items that would be used on the test. A common practice has been to create nonwords by taking real words and swapping out a single phoneme. Thus, the nonword *danana* is creating by swapping out the first phoneme of the word *banana*. The problem with creating nonwords in this manner is that it encourages lexical processing in which knowledge of real words is used in processing nonwords. To minimize lexical processing of nonword items, we developed the following procedure for creating nonwords. A list of potential nonwords was created by combining phonemes randomly. Many of these candidate items were not pronounceable and were struck from the list. The remaining pronounceable items became the source of nonword items for the CTOPP.

Once the data from national norming were available, classical item analyses, item-response theory–based analyses, and confirmatory factor analyses were again carried out. Based on these analyses, a handful of items were deleted and

several items were reordered on the basis of their difficulty.

Identification of potential item bias was carried out by using two approaches for evaluating differential item functioning. As the name suggests, *differential item functioning* refers to the case of an item functioning differently for different subgroups. The first procedure used was a two-step logistic regression approach in which the first step is to predict item performance on the basis of ability (i.e., total score, typically with the item being evaluated removed). In a second step, subgroup membership and the interaction of ability and subgroup membership are added as additional predictors. If no significant additional variance is accounted for by adding the predictors in the second step, differential item functioning can be rejected. If significant additional variance is accounted for at the second step, differential item functioning is suspected because group membership or the interaction of group membership and ability make a contribution to prediction that is independent of ability. Note that the desirable feature of this approach is that it does not assume that the subgroups are necessarily equivalent in ability. The second approach used to evaluate differential item functioning was a Delta score approach. Delta scores are transformations of z-scores that are obtained by standardizing the scores within subgroups. This eliminates subgroup differences in ability from the data, and any substantial differences in Delta scores across subgroups, as determined by correlating the Delta scores across subgroups, suggest differential item functioning. Both approaches were applied to four subgroup comparisons: male versus female; European American versus non–European American; African American versus non–African American; and Hispanic American versus non–Hispanic American. Based on these analyses, 25 items were eliminated from the CTOPP.

Criterion-Prediction Validity

Criterion-prediction validity refers to an examination of evidence about whether a test predicts performance in situations where it should. Given that the CTOPP is a measure of reading-related phonological processing, relevant criterion variables include outcome measures of reading and other measures of phonological processing. A variety of criterion-prediction validity evidence is available for the CTOPP. A number of studies are reported in the test manual and a relatively large number of studies have been carried out since its publication that have administered subtests from the CTOPP for measures of phonological processing and also included outcome measures of reading.

Perhaps the most substantial criterion-prediction validity evidence is provided by validity coefficients between CTOPP subtests and the Test of Word Reading Efficiency (TOWRE) (Torgesen, Wagner, & Rashotte, 1999). Because the CTOPP and TOWRE were co-normed, the data provided by the entire normative sample are available for examining validity coefficients. The TOWRE is a brief measure of word-level decoding that provides three scores. A Sight Word Efficiency score is a measure of the speed and accuracy with which sight words can be decoded. A Phonetic Decoding Efficiency score is a measure of the speed and accuracy with which nonwords can be decoded. The third score is a Total Word Reading Efficiency score that combines the sight word and phonetic decoding efficiency scores. Validity coefficients for the 5- and 6-year-old normative sample are presented in Table 14.2 and those for the 7- through 24-year-old version are presented in Table 14.3. The pattern of results supports the criterion-prediction validity of both versions of the CTOPP given the substantial number of moderate correlations between CTOPP and TOWRE scores.

Other evidence of criterion-prediction validity comes from comparing the CTOPP performance of identified subgroups. Means of CTOPP subtests and composites are presented by age in Table 7.12 in the Examiner's Manual for two gender subgroups (females, males), four ethnic subgroups (European American, African American, Hispanic American, Asian American), and two disability subgroups (individuals with learning disabilities; individuals with speech/language disabilities). Examining the pattern of CTOPP performance by subgroup can provide evidence about the validity of the test because differences in performance would be expected for some subgroup comparisons but not others. For example, there is no reason to expect subgroup differences for males and females. Conversely, because they include a disproportionate number of individuals who are economically disadvantaged, educationally disadvantaged, or who have language experience that differs from standard English usage, African Americans tend to score somewhat lower on a variety of language measures and might be expected to score lower on the CTOPP. Finally, it would be expected that individuals with learning disabilities or speech/language disabilities would score lower on at least some parts of the CTOPP.

The results presented in Table 7.12 support these predictions. There are no substantial differences in subtest or composite performance across gender. African Americans scored lower on the phonological awareness subtests and composites but were comparable for the most part on the other subtests and composites. Hispanic Americans performed at a level comparable to the majority sample with the exception of a Phonological Memory Composite score that was one-half standard deviation below average for the 5- and 6-year-old sample only. For the age 7- through 24-year-old sample, the modest deficit observed in the Phonological Memory Composite for 5- and 6-year-old Hispanic Americans had disappeared. Supporting the criterion-prediction validity of the CTOPP, the individuals with learning disabilities subgroup performed below average on all composite scores. The performance of the individuals with speech/language disabilities subgroup fell in between that of the individuals with learning disabilities subgroup and the majority group.

Turning to training effects, a training study is reported in the Examiner's Manual (p. 106) in which 73 children with reading disabilities were given a phonological awareness intervention

TABLE 14.2   Validity Coefficients between the CTOPP and Subtest and Composite Scores and the TOWRE Subtests for the 5- and 6-Year-Old Normative Sample

CTOPP Score	TOWRE Efficiency Score		
	Sight Word	Phonetic Decoding	Total Word Reading
Subtest Scores			
Elision	.67	.63	.67
Blending Words	.53	.48	.51
Sound Matching	.49	.48	.49
Memory for Digits	.28	.19	.23
Nonword Repetition	.37	.30	.34
Blending Nonwords	.70	.65	.70
Rapid Color Naming	.30	.35	.34
Rapid Object Naming	.36	.36	.37
Composite Scores			
Phonological Awareness	.70	.65	.70
Phonological Memory	.41	.30	.36
Rapid Naming	.38	.40	.40

program. Of the three primary constructs assessed by the CTOPP, phonological awareness is believed to be more responsive to intervention than is phonological memory or rapid naming. The results of the training study supported this view. Effect sizes based on pretest–posttest gains were .82 for phonological awareness, .41 for phonological memory, and an identical .41 for rapid naming. Support for the effect of the phonological awareness intervention on CTOPP performance is provided by a significant interaction in the training study between type of phonological processing (i.e., phonological awareness, phonological memory, rapid naming) and effect size.

Construct-Identification Validity

Construct-identification or construct validity refers to evidence that the test is measuring the intended construct. Construct-identification validity subsumes much of the validity evidence

already discussed. However, some additional evidence can be evaluated that is unique to construct-identification validity.

The CTOPP is based on a clearly specified model of reading-related phonological processing. This model posits three distinct, yet related phonological processing abilities of phonological awareness, phonological memory, and rapid naming. Because the CTOPP contains multiple subtests for each of the three proposed phonological processing abilities, a strong test of construct-identification validity is provided by confirmatory factor analysis of the data provided by the normative sample. The goal is to see whether the factor structure of the CTOPP accurately reflects the proposed underlying model of reading-related phonological processing abilities.

Results for the confirmatory factor analysis of the 5- and 6-year-old version are presented in Figure 14.3. The ovals on the left side of the figure are latent variables representing

TABLE 14.3 Validity Coefficients between the CTOPP and Subtest and Composite Scores and the TOWRE Subtests for the 7- through 24-Year-Old Normative Sample

CTOPP Score	TOWRE Efficiency Score		
	Sight Word	**Phonetic Decoding**	**Total Word Reading**
Subtest Scores			
Elision	.57	.47	.53
Blending Words	.34	.27	.31
Memory for Digits	.30	.30	.45
Nonword Repetition	.38	.36	.39
Blending Nonwords	.39	.31	.37
Rapid Digit Naming	.50	.58	.57
Rapid Letter Naming	.50	.55	.56
Composite Scores			
Phonological Awareness	.51	.40	.40
Phonological Memory	.44	.38	.43
Rapid Naming	.55	.61	.61
Alt. Phonological Awareness	.47	.38	.45
Alt. Rapid Naming	.48	.51	.53

the three constructs of Phonological Awareness, Phonological Memory, and Rapid Naming. The double-headed arrows connecting the ovals represent covariances among the three constructs, and the values on the arrows are standardized covariances that can be interpreted as correlation coefficients. The rectangles to the right represent the CTOPP subtests, with single-headed arrows linking the constructs to the subtests that represent them. The values on the single-headed arrows from the constructs to the subtests can be interpreted as standardized factor loadings. The E's to the far right represent variance in the subtests that is not accounted for by the constructs. This variance includes task-specific systematic variance and unsystematic error variance.

To determine whether the results from confirmatory factor analyses support the underlying model of the CTOPP, it is important to inspect model fit indices and the obtained parameter estimates. The model fit indices are used to determine how well the model fits the data. If the model fits the data poorly, it must be rejected. For present purposes, a good model fit statistic to evaluate is the Comparative Fit Index (CFI). This value ranges from a 0 for the most poorly fitting model possible to 1.0 for a perfectly fitting model. For the confirmatory factor analysis of the 5- and 6-year-old version of the CTOPP presented in Figure 14.3, the CFI was .99, which approaches its maximum possible value. This indicates that the model fits the data well. Turning to the parameter estimates, the loadings or values on the single-headed arrows from the constructs to the subtests are reasonable and indicate that all subtests are contributing to the constructs represented in the model. The values on the double-headed arrows connecting the constructs indicate that they are related, with Phonological Awareness and Phonological Memory being more closely related to one another than to Rapid

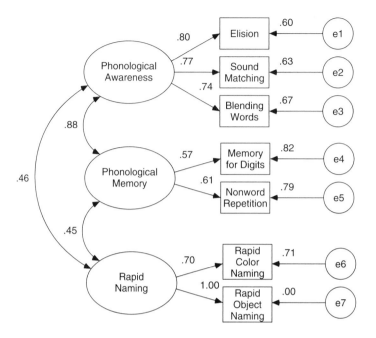

FIGURE 14.3
Confirmatory Factor Analysis of the 5- and 6-Year-Old Version of the
CTOPP

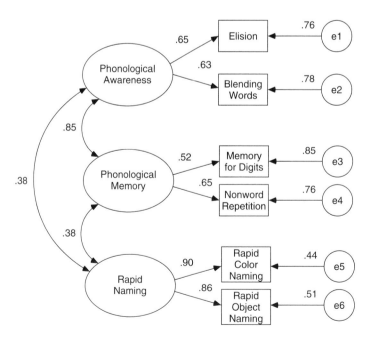

FIGURE 14.4
Confirmatory Factor Analysis of the 7- through 24-Year-Old Version
of the CTOPP

Naming. None of the values are either 0, which would indicate that the constructs were independent, or 1, which would indicate that two constructs were really the same thing.

Results for the confirmatory factor analysis of the 7- through 24-year-old version are presented in Figure 14.4. The model fit was excellent with a CFI of .99, identical to that obtained for the 5- and 6-year-old version. The parameter estimates were very comparable to those obtained for the 5- and 6-year-old version as well.

In summary, the confirmatory factor analyses of both the 5- and 6-year-old and 7- through 24-year-old versions of the CTOPP support the construct-identification validity of the test.

SUMMARY

We began by reviewing aspects of phonological processing that were relevant to the development of the CTOPP. We noted that different levels of phonological representation exist, and that a developmental progression exists in which children become able to isolate (1) individual words within compound words, (2) syllables within single words, (3) onset-rime units within a syllable, and finally (4) individual phonemes. The items on the phonological awareness subtests of the CTOPP sample the different levels of representation. We also noted that three major kinds of reading-related phonological processing have been identified: phonological awareness, phonological memory, and rapid naming. The CTOPP contains multiple subtests that assess each of the three kinds of reading-related phonological processing.

We reviewed administration and scoring issues. One issue that had to be dealt with in developing the CTOPP was the difficulty some examiners have in administering nonword items. We implemented a recorded administration procedure for subtests that contain nonword items. We also implemented a recorded administration

procedure for the Memory for Digits subtest to reduce variability in rates of presentation of digits. The recorded administration for Memory for Digits was also thought to be helpful because we adopted a rate of two digits per second to maximize the phonological demands of the subtest and to minimize the role of memory strategies.

We reviewed the psychometric properties of the CTOPP. Because the CTOPP was based on an explicit, underlying model of phonological processing, it was possible to use confirmatory factor analysis to test whether performance on the CTOPP was consistent with the underlying model. The results of confirmatory factor analyses of the entire normative sample supported the validity of both the 5- and 6-year-old and 7- through 24-year-old versions of the CTOPP.

CTOPP-2

One concern about the CTOPP is that reading instruction has changed since the test was published in 1999 in ways that might affect performance and thereby render the norms out of date. For example, the major reading series now explicitly teach aspects of phonological awareness, something that was less common when the CTOPP normative sample was collected. For this reason, as this chapter was being written, national norming has been completed on the CTOPP-2 (Wagner, Torgesen, & Rashotte, in press). In addition to providing updated norms, a new phonological awareness subtest has been added that is based on a phoneme isolation task. An effort to lower the performance floor of the CTOPP subtests also resulted in being able to include 4-year-olds in the CTOPP-2 normative sample. Finally, minor changes were made in item content to improve the performance of the subtests where possible. Our hope is that the CTOPP-2 proves to be as useful as the CTOPP has been in evaluating individuals who appear to have reading or language problems.

REFERENCES

Baddeley, A. (1986). *Working memory*. New York: Oxford University Press.

Baddeley, A. (1992). Working memory. *Science, 255,* 556–559.

Bishop, D. V. M. (2006). What causes specific language impairment in children? *Current Directions in Psychological Science, 15,* 217–221.

Bruck, M. (1990). Word-recognition skills of adults with childhood diagnoses of dyslexia. *Developmental Psychology, 26,* 439–454.

Bruck, M. (1992). Persistence of dyslexics' phonological awareness deficits. *Developmental Psychology, 28,* 874–886.

Bruck, M. (1993). Word recognition and component phonological processing skills of adults with childhood diagnosis of dyslexia. *Developmental Review, 13,* 258–268.

Crowder, R. G., & Wagner, R. K. (1992). *The psychology of reading: An introduction* (2nd ed.). London: Oxford University Press.

Ehri, L. C. (1998). Grapheme-phoneme knowledge is essential to learning to read words in English. In J. L. Metsala & L. C. Ehri (Eds.), *Word recognition in beginning literacy* (pp. 3–40). Mahwah, NJ: Lawrence Erlbaum.

Fox, E. (1994). Grapheme-phoneme correspondence in dyslexic and matched control readers. *British Journal of Psychology, 85,* 41–53.

Jorm, A., & Share, D. L. (1983). Phonological recoding and reading acquisition. *Applied Psycholinguistics, 4,* 103–147.

Liberman, I. Y., Shankweiler, D., & Liberman, A. M. (1989). The alphabetic principle and learning to read. In D. Shankweiler & I. Y. Liberman (Eds.), *Phonology and reading disability: Solving the reading puzzle* (pp. 1–33). Ann Arbor, MI: U. of Michigan Press.

Mattingly, I. G. (1972). Reading, the linguistic process and linguistic awareness. In J. Kavanagh & I. Mattingly (Eds.), *Language by ear and by eye* (pp. 133–147). Cambridge, MA: MIT Press.

National Reading Panel (2000). *Teaching children to read: An evidence-based assessment of the scientific research literature on reading and its implications for reading instruction.* National Institute of Child Health and Human Development, Washington, D.C.

Piasta, S. B., & Wagner, R. K. (2007). Dyslexia: Identification and classification. In E. Grigorenko & A. Napes (Eds.), *Single word reading: Behavioral and biological perspectives* (pp. 309–326). Mahwah, NJ: Erlbaum.

Rack, J. P., Snowling, M. J., & Olson, R. K. (1992). The nonword reading deficit in developmental dyslexia: A review. *Reading Research Quarterly, 27,* 28–53.

Siegel, L. S., & Faux, D. (1989). Acquisition of certain grapheme-phoneme correspondences in normally achieving and disabled readers. *Reading & Writing, 1,* 37–52.

Torgesen, J. K. (1996). A model of memory from an information processing perspective: The special case of phonological memory. In G. Reid Lyon (Ed.), *Attention, memory, and executive function: Issues in conceptualization and measurement* (pp. 157–184). Baltimore: Brookes.

Torgesen, J. K. (1999). Phonologically based reading disabilities: Toward a coherent theory of one kind of learning disability. In R. J. Sternberg & L. Spear-Swerling (Eds.), *Perspectives on learning disabilities* (pp. 231–262). New Haven: Westview Press.

Torgesen, J. K., & Houck, G. (1980). Processing deficiencies in learning disabled children who perform poorly on the digit span task. *Journal of Educational Psychology, 72,* 141–160.

Torgesen, J. K., Wagner, R. K., & Rashotte, C. A. (1999). *Test of Word Reading Efficiency (TOWRE).* Austin, TX: Pro-Ed.

Torgesen, J. K., Wagner, R. K., Simmons, K., & Laughon, P. (1990). Identifying phonological coding problems in disabled readers: Naming, counting, or span measures? *Learning Disability Quarterly, 13,* 236–244.

Wagner, R. K. (2005). Reading impairment. In P. Strazny (Ed.), *Encyclopedia of psycholinguistics*. New York: Routledge, Taylor, and Francis.

Wagner, R. K., & Muse, A. (2006). Phonological memory and reading disability. In T. Alloway & S. Gathercole (Eds.), *Working memory in neurodevelopmental conditions* (pp. 41–57). East Sussex, England: Psychology Press.

Wagner, R. K., Piasta, S. B., & Torgesen, J. K. (2006). Learning to read. In M. A. Gernsbacher & M. J. Traxler (Eds.), *Handbook of psycholinguistics* (pp. 1111–1142). San Diego: Academic Press.

Wagner, R. K., & Torgesen, J. K. (1987). The nature of phonological processing and its causal role in the acquisition of reading skills. *Psychological Bulletin, 101,* 192–212.

Wagner, R. K., Torgesen, J. K., & Rashotte, C. A. (1994). The development of reading-related phonological processing abilities: New evidence of bi-directional causality from a latent variable longitudinal study. *Developmental Psychology, 30,* 73–87.

Wagner, R. K., Torgesen, J. K., & Rashotte, C. A. (1999). *The Comprehensive Test of Phonological Processing.* Austin, TX: Pro-Ed.

Wagner, R. K., Torgesen, J. K., & Rashotte, C. A. (in press). *The Comprehensive Test of Phonological Processing—2.* Austin, TX: Pro-Ed.

Wagner, R. K., Torgesen, J. K., Rashotte, C. A., Hecht, S. A., Barker, T. A., Burgess, S. R., Donahue, J., & Garon, T. (1997). Changing causal relations between phonological processing abilities and word-level reading as children develop from beginning to fluent readers: A five-year longitudinal study. *Developmental Psychology, 33,* 468–479.

CHAPTER 15

Dynamic Indicators of Basic Early Literacy Skills (DIBELS)

General Outcomes Measurement for Prevention and Remediation of Early Reading Problems

Kathrine M. Koehler-Hak, Achilles N. Bardos

Dynamic Indicators of Basic Early Literacy Skills (DIBELS) are a set of measures developed to assess early literacy and reading skills for Kindergarten through sixth-grade students. The DIBELS were developed by a team of researchers and graduate students at the University of Oregon. Led by Drs. Roland Good III and Ruth Kaminski, the researchers identified those essential early literacy skills most predictive of later reading success and devised standardized methods of directly and efficiently measuring those skills. DIBELS data may be utilized to make screening, progress monitoring, and outcomes decisions about individuals or groups of children. This chapter presents a rationale for DIBELS as part of an effective early literacy model. It includes an overview of administration and scoring, reliability, and validity data for each of the measures, and a discussion of how DIBELS may be utilized to make a variety of educational decisions for individuals and groups of children.

HISTORICAL PERSPECTIVE AND RATIONALE

Reading is perhaps one of the most essential skills for success within our schools and society. A compelling body of evidence links skilled readers with positive school performance (Adams, 1990). Children who struggle with reading in school are at greater risk of dropping out of school, poverty, substance abuse, and incarceration (Barwick & Siegel, 1996; Lyon, 2000; McBride & Siegel, 1997). Certainly, the need for accountability and the assurance that all children learn to read is substantially warranted. Over the past decade, directed and focused national attention has been given both to the need for improved reading skills for all children and to evidence-based teaching practices for meeting those needs (Good, Simmons, & Kame'enui, 2001; Shaywitz, 2003). Yet, Lyon (1996) reports that 20% of students will experience a significant reading disability and another 20% will experience difficulties significant enough to negatively impact reading enjoyment and motivation. Students who experience difficulty in reading fall further and further behind their peers as they progress through schooling (Francis, Shaywitz, Stuebing, Shaywitz, & Fletcher, 1996; Stanovich, 1986; Juel, 1988). Differentiation between good and poor readers is well established by the middle to end of first-grade (Good, Simmons, & Smith, 1998; Torgesen, 2004). According to the authors, DIBELS are based on the assumptions that (1) students who experience difficulty with reading must be identified early, (2) early literacy assessment and intervention must focus on the "big ideas" of reading, and (3) assessment of early literacy must focus on indicators of general outcomes in reading (Kaminski, Good, & Knutson, 2006).

Assumption 1: Students Who Experience Difficulty with Reading Must Be Identified Early

The DIBELS measures assess essential preskills necessary and most predictive of later reading success and are intended for use prior to a child's ability to read connected text. Extensive research in the area of literacy preskills has identified five skills positively related to success in learning to read (Coyne, Kame'enui, & Carnine, 2007; Gunn, Simmons & Kame'enui, 1998). Known as the *big ideas of reading*, phonological awareness, alphabetic principle, vocabulary, comprehension, and fluency provide a basis for understanding early reading development and are the focus of the DIBELS measures. Use of DIBELS begins at the start of Kindergarten before children are able to read. This allows educators to identify children who may be at risk for reading failure and provide intervention before the gap between good and poor readers is evident (Good, Gruba, & Kaminski, 2001; Roehrig, Petscher, Nettles, Hudson, & Torgesen, 2008; Schilling, Carlisle, Scott, & Zeng, 2007).

Assumption 2: Early Literacy Assessment and Intervention Must Focus on the Big Ideas of Reading

There is compelling evidence that children who develop proficiency with several big ideas in reading are more likely to be successful when learning to read (Shaywitz, 2003; Coyne et al., 2007). A *big idea* is defined as a skill that (1) is predictive of later reading achievement, (2) can be taught, and (3) when taught, results in improved reading scores. Current research supports five big ideas in reading:

1. Phonological awareness refers to a child's ability to discriminate and manipulate individual sounds in words. For example, the word *cat* is comprised of the individual sounds /c/ /a/ /t/. Phonological awareness is different from alphabetic principle in that it is completely an auditory skill.

2. Alphabetic principle is comprised of two parts, including the understanding that letters represent sounds (alphabetic understanding) and that letters can be blended together to represent words (phonological recoding).

3. Accuracy and fluency is the automaticity with which a child applies the fundamental skills of reading to quickly and effortlessly read connected text.

4. Comprehension is the child's ability to gain meaning and understanding from spoken language or connected text.

5. Vocabulary is the child's ability to produce specific words for a given meaning and the ability to understand spoken and written words.

Each of the five big ideas in reading works together to provide a foundation on which children successfully progress through reading instruction. Six of the seven DIBELS measures are designed to assess each of the big ideas in early literacy. DIBELS measures do not assess all skills related to reading but sample those skills most predictive of later reading success

(Kaminski, Cummings, Powell-Smith, & Good, 2008). For example, a child's skills in phonological awareness may be evidenced by progressively more sophisticated skills in rhyming, blending, segmenting, and phoneme manipulation. The DIBELS address the critical indicator of Phonemic Segmentation Fluency (PSF) as a measure of a child's overall progression in phonemic awareness. Another DIBELS measure, Letter Naming Fluency (LNF), is included for Kindergarten and beginning first-grade students as an additional indicator of risk as it is highly predictive of later reading success (Stage, Sheppard, Davidson, & Browning, 2001). However, when taught, facility with letter names does not positively affect reading outcomes (Adams, 1990). Therefore, Letter Naming Fluency does not link to a big idea and is intended to be used only as an indicator of risk. Table 15.1 outlines each of the seven DIBELS measures and the corresponding early literacy skill.

Assumption 3: Focus Assessment of Early Literacy on Essential and Measurable Outcomes

The magnitude of reading problems present within our educational system has heightened the attention reading instruction receives from researchers, educators, and legislation. Federal legislation (e.g., No Child Left Behind and the Individuals with Disabilities Act) mandates that schools document the benefits of curriculum and instruction in reading for students with and without disabilities. Current goals are for all children to read at a proficient level by the third grade (National Research Council, 1998). Educators are held accountable for student achievement and as such are required to document the effectiveness of evidence-based interventions for children behind in reading.

One method of documenting the benefits of reading instruction is to focus on statewide assessment and other high-stakes testing. These assessments measure student achievement in reading based on grade-level expectations and

document skills in categories such as "proficient," "partially proficient," or "insufficient." Data can be utilized to compare school- and district-wide performance and to document individual student achievement levels. However, due to the extensive resources necessary, high-stakes testing is summative in nature and does not easily provide formative information regarding student progress and intervention effectiveness.

An alternative method of assessment of student performance is *formative evaluation*. Formative evaluation data are sensitive to change over time and can be used in a proactive manner to differentiate instruction and support student learning. An example of formative evaluation is Curriculum-Based Measurement (CBM). CBM was developed by Deno and colleagues at the Institute for Research on Learning Disabilities at the University of Minnesota in the 1970s and 1980s. CBM is a method of formatively assessing basic academic skills (Deno, 1985; Deno & Fuchs, 1987; Deno, Fuchs, Marston, & Shinn, 2001). Evidence of alternative-form reliability and concurrent criterion-related validity (Shapiro, 2004; Shinn, 1989) supports the use of CBM in identifying children in need of support and in monitoring the progress of reading skills. DIBELS were developed by applying the assessment methodology of CBM to essential early literacy skills. Each measure includes 20 alternative forms, is short in duration (approximately one minute), and is scored in a manner that is sensitive to small change. DIBELS provide standardized procedures for administration, scoring, and interpretation of student progress toward the long-term goal of reading connected text.

General Outcomes Measurement (GOM) is a unique type of formative evaluation that focuses assessment on progress toward a long-term goal (Kaminski & Cummings, 2007). Within GOM, skills and progress are sampled over time by use of short-duration skills probes. Much like the medical field measures height, weight, and temperature as an indicator of general wellness, educators can measure *indicators* (basic early literacy skills) of reading development.

TABLE 15.1   DIBELS Measures and Essential Early Literacy Skills

Early Literacy Skill	DIBELS Measure	Administered
Phonological awareness	Initial Sound Fluency	Kindergarten: F, W
	Phonemic Segmentation Fluency	Kindergarten: W, S
		1st: F, W, S
Alphabetic principle	Nonsense Word Fluency	1st: F, W, S
		2nd: F
Accuracy and fluency reading connected text	DIBELS Oral Reading	1st: W, S
	Fluency	2nd–6th: F, W, S
Comprehension	Retell Fluency	1st: W, S
		2nd–6th: F, W, S
Vocabulary	Word Use Fluency	K–3rd: F, W, S

NOTE: F = fall; W = winter; S = spring.

When using GOM for reading, the evaluator is concerned with the progress or development a child is demonstrating toward fluent reading. Although these indicators do not measure all aspects of a given skill, they are important because they are routine and can be used in an ongoing manner to inform educational decisions.

DESCRIPTION OF THE TEST

Subtest Background and Structure

DIBELS stands for Dynamic Indicators of Basic Early Literacy Skills. Each of the measures shares the common characteristics inherent in the name.

Dynamic

DIBELS are sensitive to small change, which allows educators to measure the progression of reading development over time.

Indicators

Each of the DIBELS measures provides a quick and efficient indication of a child's performance on an essential early literacy measure. For example, number of phonemes segmented in a minute on Phonemic Segmentation Fluency is an indicator of a child's overall phonological awareness.

Basic Early Literacy Skills

The DIBELS measures address those skills that are considered big ideas in early reading and that are most predictive of later reading success.

All DIBELS measures are sensitive to change over time and assess a child's fluency with the early literacy preskills. It is the scoring of the DIBELS that provides the sensitivity to small change necessary for formative evaluation. DIBELS are scored by the smallest unit of skill answered. For example, when asked, "What are the sounds in /CAT/?" a child is able to attain one point for each of the three sounds possible (/c/ /a/ /t/). However, the child need not answer the full three sounds to receive points. If the child answers simply /c/ or /c/ /a/, he or she receives points for the sounds named (one point for /c/ or two points for /c/ /a/). Similarly, each DIBELS measure is scored in a manner that detects small change and can be used to formatively measure the progression of reading development.

Successful readers are those children who perform basic and fundamental preskills quickly and effortlessly. This allows the child's attention to be allocated to understanding the meaning of text (Joseph, 2008; Simmons & Kame'enui, 1998). It is imperative, therefore, to evaluate not only the accuracy but the *speed* with which a child demonstrates early reading skills. All DIBELS measures are timed tasks and utilize fluency of basic early literacy skills as a measure of risk. Finally, DIBELS are short-duration measures (1 minute) and have many alternative forms of equal difficulty (Good et al., 2004). Children who are considered at risk for reading failure due to low DIBELS scores may have ongoing administration of alternative forms of the measures (once to several times a week). Table 15.2 provides a summarization of reliability of DIBELS for both single and multi-administered probes.

Benchmark Scales

DIBELS are intended to identify children who have or have not attained established benchmarks of skill fluency. A benchmark is a critical and minimal level of skills that is demonstrated to be most predictive of later reading success (Kaminski et al., 2008). Therefore, students who score below an established benchmark on a given DIBELS measure are at risk for later reading difficulty and should be provided with early intervention to remediate the discrepancy before substantial difficulty is experienced. Each DIBELS measure has established benchmarks for differing grades (corresponding to which measures are administered at different grades) and times of year (fall, winter, spring). The benchmarks themselves represent a *minimal* progression of skill level and proficiency necessary for later reading success. Therefore, the goal is for all children to attain established benchmarks. Benchmarks for DIBELS were established using data derived from the DIBELS Data System for the academic years 2000/2001 and 2001/2002. As detailed by Good and colleagues (2002), decision rules regarding benchmarks were developed by identifying cutoff scores at which the odds were in favor or not in favor of a child attaining subsequent reading goals. For each measure, multiple Receiver Operator Curves (ROCs) were considered and evaluated. Complete information regarding the development of established benchmarks is detailed through DIBELS Technical Reports 1–11 available on the website.

TABLE 15.2 Technical Adequacy of DIBELS Measures; Technical Adequacy of Dynamic Indicators of Basic Early Literacy Skills

DIBELS Measure	Grade	Reliability		Validity		
		Single Probe	Multi-Probe	Concurrent		Predictive
ISF	K	.61	.91	.36	.37,	.36
PSF	K	.74	.99	.54,	.65,	.60
LNF	K	.89	.99	.70,	.77	.66
NWF	1st	.83	.94	—	—	.67
WUF	1st	.65	.90	.55,	.71	—
RTF	3rd	—	—	.45,	.50	—

NOTE : ISF = Initial Sound Fluency; PSF = Phoneme Segmentation Fluency; NWF = Nonsense Word Fluency; ORF = Oral Reading Fluency; WUF = Word Use Fluency; RTF = Retell Fluency; K = Kindergarten.

The authors of DIBELS do note caution in interpreting and using benchmarks since the sample utilized in determining benchmarks consisted of schools participating in the DIBELS Data System and is not necessarily representative of a national sample. One caution to consider is that schools participating in the DIBELS Data System are more likely to be focused on assessing, teaching, and monitoring the progress of the core areas of early literacy (phonological awareness, alphabetic principle, vocabulary, comprehension, fluency). There was also substantial variability in number of students participating per grade in each school. Although the median number of students participating per grade in each school was 50, participating students ranged from 1 to 700 per grade (Good et al., 2002).

DIBELS benchmarks represent progressive goals toward long-term outcomes in each of the early literacy skills. Based on scores attained at designated times of the year (fall, winter, spring), children are individually identified in one of three proficiency levels including Benchmark (at or above identified benchmark level), Strategic (below established benchmark), or Intensive (well below established benchmark). Benchmark, Strategic, and Intensive correspond to a recommended level of intervention. Students at Benchmark are considered on track toward long-term reading goals, whereas students designated as Strategic are considered at *moderate* risk and may benefit from targeted intervention in one or more early literacy skills. Students designated as Intensive are considered at *high* risk for later reading success and are in need of targeted, direct, and intensive intervention in one or more early literacy skills.

The DIBELS descriptors (Benchmark, Strategic, Intensive) describe the probability of achieving later reading goals. Cutoff scores for each descriptor are based on predictive utility and were determined to be scores at which 80%, 50%, and 20% of students achieved later reading goals, respectively. For example, a student who has attained Benchmark level on specified DIBELS measures for her designated grade has 80% probability that she will attain later reading goals and success and is placed at low risk and need for additional support. However, a child who has not attained Benchmark but rather scores within the Intensive range has only 20% likelihood of achieving later reading goals and success. This child is considered at high risk and it is recommended that she receive intensive support in early literacy. It is important for educators to gather a convergence of data to support and validate decisions based on DIBELS benchmarks. DIBELS, as with any type of assessment, should not be used in isolation to make important educational decisions. Table 15.3 details established benchmarks for each DIBELS measure and the grade for which that benchmark is to be attained.

Organization and Structure of DIBELS

DIBELS are criterion referenced and intended as progressive indicators of reading development. As children become readers, the DIBELS measures utilized represent increasingly sophisticated skills of early literacy and beginning reading. Not all DIBELS are administered at each grade level. DIBELS that measure the most basic of early literacy skills (Initial Sound Fluency, Phonemic Segmentation Fluency) are administered in Kindergarten and beginning first grade while DIBELS that measure more sophisticated early literacy skills of decoding and beginning reading are administered in first and second grades. In this respect, DIBELS function much like steppingstones (Kaminski et al., 2008) toward reading in that success in attaining Benchmark on one skill most likely leads to attaining Benchmark on later and more sophisticated beginning reading skills. Table 15.3 delineates the progressive administration of DIBELS measures. The shaded areas noted on Table 15.3 indicate both the grade and times of year each measure is administered.

TABLE 15.3 Recommended Administration Times and Established Benchmarks for DIBELS Measures

DIBELS	Kindergarten			First			Second			Third		
Measure	Fall	Winter	Spring	Fall	Winter	Spring	Fall	Winter	Spring	Fall	Winter	Spring
ISF		25 initial sounds per minute										
LNF												
PSF			35 phone mes per minute									
NWF					50 letter sounds per minute							
DORF						40 words per minute			90 words per minute			110 words per minute
RTF												
WUF												

NOTE : Shaded areas represent the grade and times of year the authors recommend administration of specific DIBELS measures. Benchmarks are included if they are provided by the authors.

DIBELS data may be utilized in a criterion-referenced manner through use of established benchmarks. Data also may be utilized in a norm-referenced manner through use of national percentiles (available from the DIBELS website) and by developing local norms. As with established benchmarks, percentile scores were derived from the aggregated data DIBELS Data System (academic years 200/2001 and 2001/2002). Although participating schools were distributed throughout the country, it is not verified that the sample utilized is representative of a national population. Best practices in use of DIBELS recommend that all children in a school are administered the appropriate DIBELS measures three times a year (fall, winter, spring). This practice is known as *benchmark testing*. Schools and districts that utilize benchmark testing and data analysis have the added benefit of local norms for reading achievement. Local norms may be used to inform systems-level decisions such as effectiveness of core curriculum and intervention programs, for identifying needs for teachers in-service, for evaluating the progress of all children over time, and to examine the effects of interventions in closing the gap between good and poor readers. Local norms are also very useful in the implementation of response to intervention (RTI) and data-based decision making for special education eligibility (Brown-Chidsey & Steege, 2007).

The uses and application of local norms will be addressed in more detail for both individual children and systems-level decisions later in this chapter.

DIBELS data may be used to make a variety of educational decisions including screening, progress monitoring, and outcomes. Screening decisions are addressed through benchmark assessment for all children. Benchmark assessment is completed three times a year (fall, winter, spring). Individual student scores are then compared to established benchmarks for each measure (Table 15.2) and local norms. Progress-monitoring decisions are addressed through ongoing assessment of one or more specific DIBELS measures for children who are receiving intervention. Data are graphed over time and utilized in a formative manner to make decisions regarding need and type of continued support. Outcomes decisions at an individual level are made by comparing individual student DIBELS scores after intervention to established benchmarks. At a group level, aggregated data are compared to benchmark (Table 15.2) data and inform decisions regarding curriculum, instruction, and allocation of resources.

ADMINISTRATION AND SCORING

Complete directions for standardized administration and scoring and all necessary materials are available through the DIBELS website (http://dibels.uoregon.edu). Materials include benchmark booklets for each grade (to be used for each child three times a year during benchmark assessment) and progress-monitoring booklets for individual measures (to be used ongoing for individual children). Benchmark booklets include a summary table for individual scores while progress monitoring booklets provide graphs for ease in documenting the progress for individual children. DIBELS materials are available to download free of charge from the DIBELS website, may be purchased from the publisher, or may be purchased for use on palm pilots. The DIBELS website also provides a data management system for a nominal cost per year. Schools may elect to use the Web-based data management system or develop an individualized system for organizing and displaying data.

DIBELS are comprised of seven measures: Initial Sound Fluency (ISF), Letter Naming Fluency (LNF), Phonemic Segmentation Fluency (PSF), Nonsense Word Fluency (NWF), Oral Reading Fluency (DORF), Retell Fluency (RTF), and Word Use Fluency (WUF). Each of the measures is standardized in administration and scoring procedures. All measures are timed and therefore provide an indication of the child's fluency with the specific early literacy skill assessed. Materials needed include administration and scoring directions, scoring booklet, student stimulus packet (picture prompts, reading samples, etc.), pencil, and stopwatch. It is recommended that measures be administered in a quiet location free of unusual distractions. Measures may be administered by school psychologists, teachers, specialists, or other school staff who have received the necessary training in the standardized administration and scoring of DIBELS.

This section details the administration and scoring procedures for each DIBELS measure and provides recommendations and tips for reliability of administration. A complete account of all possible scoring scenarios is not possible within the context of this chapter. The reader is referred to the DIBELS website for a complete and detailed description of all scoring rules.

Initial Sound Fluency

Administration

Initial Sound Fluency (ISF) is a measure of early phonological awareness that requires the child to discriminate the beginning sound or sounds of a picture. Initial Sound Fluency is administered in the fall and winter of Kindergarten. Benchmarks goals are available for middle of Kindergarten. The administrator shows the child the picture prompts and follows standardized directions. One sample item is provided:

1. "This is *mouse*, *flowers*, *pillow*, and *letters* (point to each picture while saying the name). *Mouse* (point to mouse) begins with the sound /m/. Listen, /m/, *mouse*. Which one begins with the sound /fl/?"

2. The child may answer by pointing to the flowers, by saying "flowers," or by saying another word that begins with the sound /fl/. Upon receiving a correct response, the administrator says, "Good. *Flowers* begins with the sound /fl/." *Pillow* (point to pillow) begins with the sound /p/. Listen, /p/, *pillow*. What sounds does *letters* (point to the picture of letters) begin with?"

3. The child may answer by verbally producing the beginning sound or sounds of the word (/l/, /le/, /let/). Upon receiving a correct response, the administrator says, "Here are some more pictures. Listen carefully to the words."

Correction Procedure for Practice Item

If the child gives an incorrect answer for the practice items only, the administrator follows a standardized incorrect response procedure. Each incorrect response procedure allows the administrator to model the correct response one time and repeat the question. For example, the administrator would respond, *"Flowers* begins with the sound /fl/. Listen /fl/, *flowers*. Let's try again. Which one begins with the sound /fl/?" If the child again provides an incorrect response, the administrator continues with the next item.

Scoring and Timing

The Initial Sound Fluency measure consists of four pages of four pictures each, for 16 total possible points. The child receives 1 point for each correct response and zero for each incorrect response. For each four-picture prompt, the child is asked to provide three selection-type responses ("Which one begins with . . . ?") and

one production-type response ("What sound does_____begin with?"). If the child does not respond to an individual item within 5 seconds, the item is scored as zero and the next item is presented. Correct responses include:

- Points to the correct picture.
- Says the correct name of the correct picture. For example, when shown a picture of "dog" and asked to identify which one begins with the sound /d/, a correct response is *dog* while a response of *puppy* is incorrect.
- Says another word or sound that begins with the correct sound. For example, in the above scenario of a picture of a dog, the child may receive a correct response for answering *door* to the question, "Which one begins with *d*?"

For production-type responses, a response is considered correct if a child provides any part of the word that has the first sound but not the whole word. For example, when provided with a picture of a brick, a correct response could include /b/, /br/, or /bri/.

Initial Sound Fluency is timed by attaining a total cumulative time for the measure. However, only the time that the child utilizes to answer is counted. The stopwatch is not running while the administrator is presenting pictures or asking specific items. Upon completion of the 16 items, a formula is used to attain a total number of initial sounds per minute:

60 – Total Correct Number of Seconds

= _____ Correct Initial Sounds per Minute

Discontinuation Rule

The measure is discontinued and scored as zero if a child does not provide a correct response within the first five questions.

Benchmark

The Initial Sound Fluency benchmark is 25 initial sounds correct per minute by middle of Kindergarten.

Special Considerations

- Children are not penalized for articulation or dialect. If necessary, have a familiar person or specialist (SLP) complete the testing.
- If a student is identified as English language learner (ELL), provide directions in the student's native language. A Spanish version of DIBELS is available from the website.
- Administrators may have a child repeat back directions or provide one additional practice example.
- Approved accommodations include enlarged pictures, repeating words, and having a child repeat words back. Accommodations should be used only as necessary.

Phonemic Segmentation Fluency

Administration

Phonemic Segmentation Fluency (PSF) is a measure of phonological awareness that requires a child to rapidly discriminate and produce specific phonemes (smallest unit of speech) of words. For example, when presented with the word /cat/, the child would attain full points for responding with the sounds /c/ /a/ /t/. Phonemic Segmentation Fluency is an auditory measure and does not require visual student stimulus materials. Phonemic Segmentation Fluency is administered in the winter and spring of Kindergarten as well as fall, winter, and spring of first grade. Benchmark goals are provided for end of Kindergarten. The administrator presents the child with an auditory word and asks the child to say the sounds in the words. Directions are provided verbatim:

> "I'm going to tell you a word. After I say it, you tell me the sounds in the word. So, if I say *Sam*, you would say '/s/ /a/ /m/.' Let's try one (pause). Tell me the sounds in *mop*."

The child answers by providing as many phonemes as she is able to discriminate. In the practice example, a complete and correct answer is all three phonemes including /m/ /o/ /p/. Upon receiving a correct answer, the administrator continues with the task.

> "Very good; the sounds in *mop* are /m/ /o/ /p/. Okay. Here is your first word."

The administrator then proceeds to orally present each word on the Phonemic Segmentation Fluency probe clearly and with precise pronunciation.

Correction Procedure for Practice Item

Should the child provide an incorrect or partial (fewer than three phonemes) answer on the practice item only, the administrator follows a standardized incorrect response format including a model and additional opportunity to respond. An incorrect response is any answer that does not include a complete and correct response (/m/ /o/ /p/). Incomplete responses are those that omit or combine phonemes (e.g., /m/ /op/, /mo/ /p/, /mop/, /m/, /p/). If after the correction procedure the child gives another incorrect response, the administrator continues with the task. No additional practice items are given.

Scoring and Timing

Phonemic Segmentation Fluency is timed for a total of 1 minute and begins immediately after the first test word is presented. If a child does not respond with a sound segment within 3 seconds, the word is scored based on the segments already provided and the next word is presented. The stopwatch is set to run continuously and is not stopped until 1 minute has been reached. After 1 minute, the task is stopped and the total number of correct phonemes is counted and recorded. A correct response includes any portion of a word segmented. If a child repeats the word back without segmenting, the item is scored as zero.

Discontinuation Rule

The task is discontinued and scored as zero if the child does not get any correct phonemes within the first five words.

Benchmark

The benchmark for Phonemic Segmentation Fluency is 35 correct phonemes per minute at the end of Kindergarten.

Special Considerations

- Students are not penalized for articulation or dialect. If necessary, have a familiar person or specialist (SLP) administer the task.
- Testing in a quiet location is preferred.
- The administrator should familiarize herself with the correct pronunciation of the responses prior to giving the measure.
- *R*-controlled vowels (/ar/, /ir/, /or/) are counted as 1 phoneme (1 point).
- /air, /ear/, /oor/ are considered 2 phonemes.
- /ng/ is considered 1 phoneme.
- Administrators may have the child repeat back directions or repeat the practice example to check for understanding of directions.
- Although the established benchmark for Phonemic Segmentation Fluency is 35 by the end of Kindergarten, PSF can be used to screen and monitor progress for children of any age who are in need of support in phonological awareness.

Nonsense Word Fluency

Administration

Nonsense Word Fluency (NWF) is a measure of a child's facility with the alphabetic principle including decoding and recoding (blending). The task asks the child to read (as well as possible) a page of phonetically regular (CVC and VC) nonsense words and assess whether a child has and consistently uses an efficient decoding strategy for approaching unknown words. The child attains points for both decoding (saying sounds of each letter) and recoding (reading the whole word). Nonsense Word Fluency is administered in the fall, winter, and spring of first grade and in the fall of second grade. Benchmark goals are provided for middle of first grade. The administrator provides the child with an 8.5-by-11-inch sheet of paper with randomly ordered nonsense words and follows standardized procedures for administration and scoring:

> "Look at this word (point to the first word on the practice probe). It's a make-believe word. Watch me read the word: /s/ /i/ /m/, *sim* (point to each letter as you read and then run your finger under the whole word fast). I can say the sounds of the letters /s/ /i/ /m/ (point to each letter), or I can read the whole word, *sim* (run your finger under the whole word). Your turn to read a make-believe word. Read this word as best you can (point to the word *lut* on the practice probe). Make sure to say any sounds you know."

The child answers by reading the word or by sounding out the whole word or parts of the word. In the practice example, a complete and correct example is when the whole word is read or is sounded out and then read. Upon receiving a correct response, the administrator responds by saying, "That's right. The sounds are /l/ /u/ /t/ or *lut*. Here are some more make-believe words (point to student stimulus probe). When I say 'begin,' read the words as best you can. Point to each letter and tell me the sound or read the whole word. Read the words as best you can. Put your finger on the first word. Ready, begin."

Correction Procedure for Practice Item

If on the practice probe only the child provides an incorrect response or no response, the administrator follows a standardized procedure that includes a model and an additional opportunity to respond. "Remember you can say the sounds or you can say the whole word. Watch me: The sounds are /l/ /u/ /t/ (point to each letter) or *lut* (run your finger under the word). Let's try again. Read this word as best you can (point to the word *lut*)."

Scoring and Timing

A response is correct if a child correctly sounds out the word, correctly reads the word, or does both. An item is considered partially correct if the child correctly sounds out or correctly reads a portion of the word. For example, when provided with the nonsense word *fim*, a child would receive full points for reading /f/ /i/ /m/ or *fim* and would receive partial points for reading or sounding out the *fem*. In this case, the child would receive 2 points for correctly sounding out the /f/ and /m/ but would not receive the point for the incorrect response of the medial sound /e/.

Nonsense Word Fluency is timed for a total of 1 minute. The stopwatch is started after the administrator presents the standardized directions (after she says "begin") and is stopped at the completion of 1 minute. If the child does not produce the next letter sound within 3 seconds, the administrator tells the student the correct sound or word and prompts her to the next item. At the completion of 1 minute, two scores are attained. First, the administrator calculates the total number of letter sounds the student provided correctly. Second, the administrator calculates the total number of whole words the child read. When a child reads a nonsense word correctly (blends together), she also receives the full points for sounding out each letter sound.

Discontinuation Rule

If a student does not provide any correct sound or word responses within the first five nonsense words, the task is discontinued and scored as zero.

Benchmark

The benchmark for Nonsense Word Fluency is 50 letter-sounds per minute with at least 15 words read as a whole by the middle of first grade. Interim goals are 13 letter-sounds per minute by middle of Kindergarten and 25 letter-sounds per minute by the start of first grade.

Special Considerations

- The administrator should familiarize herself with the correct pronunciation of the nonsense words prior to administering the task.
- Children are not penalized for articulation or dialect. If necessary, have a familiar person or specialist administer the task.
- General accommodations include checking for understanding of directions, repeating the practice example 1 time, and directions in a student primary language.
- Specific accommodations include use of large print, color overlays, a marker or ruler to keep place, or Braille (upon request from Dynamic Measurement Group).
- *x* and *q* are not used in Nonsense Word Fluency task.
- *h*, *w*, *y*, and *r* are used only in the initial position (first sound).
- *c* and *g* are used only in the final position (last sound).
- If a child is sounding out a word (answering individual letter-sounds), she receives points for correct letter-sounds *regardless of the order*. However, when answering by reading whole words, the child receives points for correct letter-sounds *only if* the letter sounds are in the correct order.
- Although the established benchmark for Nonsense Word Fluency is winter of first-grade, the task may be used with any child, regardless of grade, to monitor her progress in decoding and recoding.

Letter Naming Fluency

Administration

Letter Naming Fluency (LNF) is a measure of a child's facility with letter names. Letter Naming Fluency is included within DIBELS as an additional indicator of risk. However, teaching facility with letter names has not proven to improve later reading achievement and is not considered a big idea in reading. There are no established benchmarks for Letter Naming Fluency. However, it is recommended that the measure be given in the fall, winter, and spring of Kindergarten as well as the fall of first grade. To determine Letter Naming Fluency, scores should always be considered in conjunction with other DIBELS measures.

The child is presented with an 8.5-by-11-inch paper with randomly ordered upper- and lower-case letters. Standardized directions are provided by the administrator:

> "Here are some letters (point). Tell me the names of as many letters as you can. When I say 'begin,' start here (point to first letter), and go across the page (point). Point to each letter and tell me the name of that letter. If you come to a letter you don't know, I'll tell it to you. Put your finger on the first letter. Ready, begin."

If the student provides letter-sounds rather than letter names, the administrator says:

> "Remember to tell me the letter name, not the sound it makes."

Scoring and Timing

Students receive 1 point for each letter *named* correctly. Substitutions and omissions are scored as incorrect and do not receive a point. If a child self-corrects within 3 seconds, the item is scored as correct. The maximum time for each letter is 3 seconds. If a child does not respond to a letter in 3 seconds, the administrator tells the child the letter name and prompts them to the next letter. At the end of 1 minute, the administrator tells the child to stop and the total number of letters named correct is calculated.

Discontinuation Rule

If a child does not name any letters correct within the first 10 letters, the task is discontinued and scored as zero.

Benchmark

There is no established benchmark for Letter Naming Fluency.

Special Considerations

- Students are not penalized for articulation or dialect. If necessary, have a familiar person or specialist administer the task.
- If a student skips an entire row, draw a line through it and do not count the row in the scoring.
- Similar letters such as uppercase *I* and lowercase *l* are scored correct with either response. However, if a child provides the answer "one," the item is scored as incorrect.
- General accommodations include clarifying directions, checking for understanding, and providing directions in the child's primary language.
- Specific accommodations include large print, colored overlay, Braille, and use of a marker to keep place.

Oral Reading Fluency

Administration

DIBELS Oral Reading Fluency (DORF) is a measure of a child's accuracy and fluency with connected text. The task requires the child to read for 1 minute from a leveled reading passage. During benchmark assessment times (fall, winter, and spring), each child is administered three passages and the median score is recorded. DIBELS Oral Reading Fluency is administered in the winter and spring of first grade and in the fall, winter, and spring of second through sixth grades. Benchmarks are established for the end of each grade. The administrator provides the child with an 8.5-by-11-inch paper with a specific reading passage. Standardized directions are provided:

> "Please read this (point) out loud. If you get stuck, I will tell you the word so you can keep reading. When I say 'stop,' I may ask you to tell me about what you read, so do your best reading. Start here (point to the first word of the passage). Begin."

The administrator starts the stopwatch and times for 1 minute.

Scoring and Timing

The child receives 1 point for each correct word read in the 1 minute. If a child does not give the next word within 3 seconds, the administrator tells the child the word and prompts her to the next word. A word is considered "read correctly" if it is correctly pronounced within the context of the sentence. Omissions and substitutions are scored as an error. Inserted words are counted neither as an error nor as correct. If a child self-corrects an error within 3 seconds, the word is scored as correct. At the completion of 1 minute, the stopwatch is stopped and the total number of words read correctly is calculated.

Discontinuation Rule

If a child does not read any words correctly in the first row of the passage, the passage is discontinued and scored as zero. If the child reads less than 10 words correct on the first passage of the three, that score is recorded and the other two passages are not administered.

Benchmark

Benchmarks are established for first through sixth grade. Each benchmark refers to the number of words read correctly within that given grade-level text. Therefore, the first-grade benchmark is established using first-grade-level text and the second-grade benchmark is established using second-grade text, and so forth. Established benchmarks include:

- 40 words correct per minute by end of first grade
- 90 words correct per minute by end of second grade
- 110 words correct per minute by end of third grade
- 118 words correct per minute by end of fourth grade
- 124 words correct per minute by end of fifth grade
- 125 words correct per minute by end of sixth grade

Special Considerations

- Giving all three passages and using the median score increases the reliability of the score attained. It is recommended that schools give all three DIBELS Oral Reading Fluency passages.
- Students are not penalized for articulation or dialect.
- Do not prompt the child to "read as fast as she can." The purpose of the DIBELS Oral Reading Fluency measure is to attain a reliable measure of the child's current reading skills. If she attempts to "race read," this may increase error, reduce comprehension, and limit the utility of that specific score.

- General accommodations include repeating and verifying directions, giving directions in native language, and use of a marker to keep place.
- If a child skips an entire row, these items are not counted in the score. Draw a line through the row.
- The title of the passage is not included in the scoring. The child is not expected to read the title. The examiner points to the first word of the passage and instructs the child to begin reading at that place.

Retell Fluency

Administration

Retell Fluency (RTF) is a measure of a child's ability to comprehend what was read. It is intended to identify children who can accurately and fluently read text but who have difficulty with comprehension. The task requires the child to orally retell as much as possible about a selected DIBELS Oral Reading Fluency passage that has just been read. The scoring section is located at the bottom of each scoring sheet for DIBELS Oral Reading Fluency. Retell Fluency is administered at the winter and spring of first grade and in the fall, winter, and spring of second grade and beyond. Retell Fluency is an optional measure. Benchmarks are determined based on total number of words a child has read on the DIBELS Oral Reading Fluency (at least 25%). If a child has read at least 10 words correctly on the DIBELS Oral Reading Fluency, Retell Fluency is administered following standardized directions. After the child completes the 1-minute DIBELS Oral Reading Fluency passage, the administrator says:

> "Please tell me about what you have just read. Try to tell me everything you can."

Start the stopwatch and time for 1 minute.

Count the number of words the child retells by moving your pen through the numbers listed in the Retell Fluency scoring section on each DIBELS Oral Reading Fluency scoring page.

Scoring and Timing

Retell Fluency is timed for 1 minute. At the end of 1 minute, the administrator stops the stopwatch, instructs the child to stop, and records the total number of words orally retold that relate to the passage. The first time a child does not say anything for 3 seconds, the administrator uses standardized directions to prompt the child.

Discontinuation Rule

If the child does not say anything for 5 seconds (after the first prompt given), the task is stopped and the number of words retold is calculated. If the child gets off track of the passage topic for 5 seconds, the task is stopped and the total number of words retold is calculated. The median score (one Retell score from each DIBELS Oral Reading Fluency passage) is recorded.

Benchmark

Based on the child's individual DIBELS Oral Reading Fluency score, it is recommended that a child retell at least 25% of words read.

Special Considerations

- Administer Retell Fluency only if a child has attained at least 10 words correct on DIBELS Oral Reading Fluency.
- Only actual words are counted. Fillers such as *ummm* or *uh* are not counted.
- If a child repeats what she has retold, it is counted only once.
- Contractions are counted as one word.
- Only words that are relevant to the passage are counted. The administrator must use professional judgment in determining

whether the child is giving a retell or has gotten off track.

Word Use Fluency

Administration

Word Use Fluency (WUF) is a measure of a child's vocabulary and expressive language. The task requires the child to use specific words in a sentence with correct context or by giving a definition. Word Use Fluency is an optional measure. The task is auditory and does not require any visual student stimulus materials. Word Use Fluency is administered in the fall, winter, and spring of Kindergarten through third grade. There are no established benchmarks. Use of local norms is recommended in determining risk. When making educational decisions, scores on Word Use Fluency must be analyzed in conjunction with other DIBELS measures. The administrator follows standardized directions for Word Use Fluency.

The administrator says:

> "Listen to me use this word: *green* (pause). 'The grass is green.' Here is another word: *jump* (pause). 'I like to jump rope.' Your turn to use a word (pause): *rabbit*."

Upon receiving a correct response, the administrator says:

> "Very good; okay, here is your first word."

Start the stopwatch and time for 1 minute.

Present one word at a time to the child. Give each word immediately after the child has finished the response for the preceding word.

Correction Procedure for Practice Item

If a child answers incorrectly on the practice item, the administrator follows standardized directions: "Listen to me use the word *rabbit* (pause). 'The rabbit is eating a carrot.' Your turn: *rabbit*."

Scoring and Timing

Word Use Fluency is timed for a total of 1 minute. For each word given, the administrator calculates the total number of words in the sentence or definition given and determines whether the word was used in correct context/correct word meaning. At the completion of 1 minute, the task is stopped and the total number of words used in correct context is calculated. A word is considered used correctly if (1) it conveys accurate meaning in a phrase, expression, sentence, or utterance, (2) the student provides a correct definition, or (3) the student provides a correct synonym. The child does not need to use the target word in the definition or in synonyms provided.

Discontinuation Rule

If a child does not respond to a word within 5 seconds, that item is scored as zero and the next word is presented. If a child has given no responses within the first five words, the task is discontinued and scored as zero.

Benchmark

There are no established benchmarks for Word Use Fluency. Use of local norms is recommended. Districts may consider children at risk if their score falls at or below the 20th percentile, at moderate risk if their score falls between the 20th percentile and 40th percentile, and at low risk if their score falls at or above the 40th percentile (Good et al., 2000).

Special Considerations

- Students are not penalized for articulation and dialect. If necessary, have a specialist (SLP) administer the task.
- Words do not need to be used in a grammatically correct manner to be scored as correct. Word Use Fluency is a measure of vocabulary, not grammar.

- Vague responses or any response that raises doubt as to the child's understanding of the word are scored as incorrect.

- Present words clearly. The only correct responses are those that demonstrate meaning of the target word. The child does not receive points if she has misheard the target word.

- If a student repeats the target word as her definition or sentence, the item is scored as incorrect.

- If a child gives a long response, count only those words in the most *complete* utterance given. Direct the child back to task by providing the next word.

STANDARDIZATION, NORMS, AND PSYCHOMETRICS

Characteristics of the Standardization Sample

There is a substantial and ongoing body of research available on the reliability of DIBELS measures (Good, Gruba, & Kaminski, 2001). The DIBELS website provides a series of technical reports on the reliability and sensitivity of DIBELS measures. According to Good and colleagues (Technical Report #9), more than 37,000 children were used to determine benchmarks for Kindergarten and first-grade students. Children utilized in the standardized sample were those who participated in the DIBELS data management system. The authors make no guarantee regarding the correspondence of the sample to the U.S. population.

Reliability of the Scales

Alternative-form reliabilities for DIBELS are considered adequate (Salvia & Ysseldyke, 2001) ranging from .72 to .94. Reliability for each measure increases with repeated measurement using alternative forms. Because DIBELS are short in duration, it is easy to attain repeated measures.

Table 15.2 provides alternative reliabilities for single and multiuse probes.

USE OF THE TEST

Interpretation of DIBELS

DIBELS measures are validated for use in making screening, progress-monitoring, and outcomes-based educational decisions. Because they function as a General Outcomes Measurement and provide formative evaluation, DIBELS function within an outcomes-driven model of educational decision making. The outcomes-driven model includes (1) problem identification, (2) problem validation, (3) planning and implementing support, (4) evaluating support, and (5) reviewing outcomes. The outcomes-driven model is an integral part of RTI both for identifying children in need of Tier 2 or Tier 3 intervention and in documenting the effectiveness of evidence-based interventions implemented at each tier. The following section will provide a detailed case study of how DIBELS data are used at each step of the outcomes-driven model for individual and systems-level educational decisions.

Problem Identification

The purpose of problem identification is to identify those children who may benefit from additional reading support. DIBELS are administered to all children in a school during the fall, winter, and spring and individual student scores are compared to established benchmarks. Children scoring below an established benchmark are identified and further data are collected. At a systems level, aggregated data are utilized to develop local norms. Norms for a district, school, grade, or class may be compared against benchmarks to identify systems-level need for support.

Validate Need for Support

The second step of the outcomes-driven model is to validate the need for support identified in the problem ID phase. The primary focus is to examine alternative hypotheses for low scores, rule out hypotheses, and gather a convergence of evidence supporting the need for additional support. Error in standardized testing is not uncommon and is more likely with younger children. Alternative hypotheses for low scores may fall into areas of evaluator error, situational error, or child error (Salvia & Ysseldyke, 2001). For example, it is important to determine that the test was administered in a standardized manner and scores were recorded correctly. Additionally, it is important to determine whether the testing situation or conditions were conducive to optimal performance (was the room too cold or loud, was the test given during recess, etc.) and that the child was able to demonstrate her best skill (was she sick, did she have breakfast, etc.).

One method of verifying a need for support is to readminister DIBELS. A strength of DIBELS lies within repeated measurement. As seen in Table 15.2, the reliability of each measure increases with use of multi-probes. Even so, DIBELS are one source of data in a literacy model and must be evaluated in context of additional data, including teacher observation, parent information, records, and additional informal information gathered regarding the children's early reading achievement. As with individual student decisions, it is important to be reasonably certain of the needs at a systems level and DIBELS data must be analyzed in context of a convergence of alternative data and information gathering.

Plan and Implement Support

A third step in the outcomes-driven model is to set measurable goals and plan and implement support based on a convergence of data. First, goals are set for individual children based on the author's established benchmarks. A child who is below benchmark on Phonemic Segmentation Fluency could have a goal based on the benchmark of 35 phonemes named per minute. In setting a goal, it is important to consider the author's recommended benchmark, the age of the child, and the severity of need. A goal of 35 on Phonemic Segmentation Fluency may require a rate of progress that is not reasonable for a child who is younger with more severe need. A child in first grade with strategic need may be able to attain the goal of 35 phonemes per minute in fewer weeks than a child with intensive need for support. Therefore, goals set will be individual for each student but will consider the current level of the specific early literacy skill and the rate of progress necessary to meet the author's established benchmarks.

DIBELS correspond to the big ideas in literacy and directly inform intervention decisions. For example, a student who scores below benchmark on Nonsense Word Fluency but at benchmark on Phonemic Segmentation Fluency could benefit from additional support in decoding and encoding. However, a child who scores below benchmark on both measures could benefit from support in phonemic awareness as well as beginning skills in decoding and encoding. With regard to implementation, both the outcomes-driven model and RTI stress the importance of evidence-based interventions and intervention integrity.

Evaluate Support

An essential and fourth step in the outcomes-driven model is to evaluate the support provided for individuals and groups of children. At an individual level, children who receive support in one or more early literacy skills may have their progress monitored using specified DIBELS measures several times a month to document response to the intervention and to plan for continued support. Individual scores on progress-monitoring probes are plotted on a graph and compared to the individual aimline. An *aimline* is determined by the rate of progress between a child's individual baseline score and the goals set for that student. Specific student goals are set based on an analysis of the student's current skill in relation to the author's established benchmarks and the rate of progress necessary to meet the benchmark. Specific examples of DIBELS-based aimlines are given in a later section in the chapter. Should three consecutive points fall at any point below the aimline (Kaminski et al., 2007), instructional modifications are recommended. Three or more consecutive progress-monitoring points at or above the aimline indicate effectiveness of the current interventions. Thus, by evaluating progress in a formative way, educators may make data-based decisions regarding the effectiveness of support for children receiving intervention and make changes to that support at a point early enough to impact outcomes.

Review Outcomes

The final step is to review outcomes and inform the ultimate question of sufficient early literacy development both at an individual and systems level. For individual students, the question arises as to whether the child has attained benchmark and is therefore considered on track to successful reading development. To answer this question, educators compare the child's scores on the fall benchmark assessment of DIBELS to the winter and spring benchmark assessments. At a systems level, school-, grade-, or district-level data are analyzed to determine overall effectiveness of the literacy program. DIBELS data may be analyzed according to how many children attain benchmark when provided with the core reading curriculum, how many children were in need of additional support, and of those children receiving support, how many made sufficient progress to close the gap and attain benchmark. The goal for any literacy program is to ensure successful reading achievement for all children. DIBELS and established benchmarks provide an objective tool through which districts may formatively evaluate their progress toward this goal.

CASE OF SOPHIE

Sophie is a first-grade student in Mrs. Evans's class at Pleasantville Elementary School. She enrolled at PES at the start of her first-grade year. Records review indicates that she attended Kindergarten in a neighboring community with good attendance. Schoolwide data were collected in the fall of her first-grade year. Sophie's scores fell within the Intensive range with the following individual scores: Phonemic Segmentation Fluency = 10, Letter Naming Fluency = 42, and Nonsense Word Fluency = 6. Because of her very low score on the Phonemic Segmentation Fluency measure, the data collection team decided to administer Initial Sound Fluency as an additional indicator of phonological awareness skill. Sophie attained a score of 31 on Initial Sound Fluency. At the end of data collection, the team met to review data for individual children. Sophie was identified as a student who may need additional support in the areas of phonological awareness (Phonemic Segmentation Fluency) and decoding (Nonsense Word Fluency). Her score on Letter Naming Fluency demonstrates facility with upper- and lowercase letter names and her score on Initial Sound Fluency demonstrates facility with the basic phonological awareness skill of discriminating beginning sounds of words.

To validate a need for support, the team determined that all measures were administered and scored following standardized procedures. However, notes written on Sophie's individual probes indicated that she was not feeling well that day. Furthermore, review of Kindergarten records (though lacking DIBELS data) indicated average performance in beginning reading. Sophie was retested by her classroom teacher using alternative forms of the DIBELS on two separate days. The additional DIBELS data validated previous scores. Also, classroom performance reported by her current teacher indicated that Sophie struggled with classroom tasks including daily phonological awareness activities and beginning decoding. Upon reviewing additional data, the team was reasonably confident that Sophie would benefit from additional support in early literacy skills.

Sophie's level of need was determined to be Intensive. Goals were set in Phonemic Segmentation Fluency and Nonsense Word Fluency. Phonemic Segmentation Fluency was determined to be the priority because of the positive impact increased phonemic awareness has on beginning reading and decoding. However, Sophie is in first grade and she is at high risk for meeting her mid-second-grade Nonsense Word Fluency benchmark (50 letter-sounds per minute with 15 words recoded). Goals in Phonemic Segmentation Fluency and Nonsense Word Fluency were set and individual aimlines were calculated for Sophie on each skill (Figure 15.1). The goal for Phonemic Segmentation Fluency was set at the author's established benchmark of 35 phonemes per minute. The goal for Nonsense Word Fluency was set at 20 letter-sounds per minute. This goal is derived from the rate of progress necessary for Sophie to reach the benchmark of 50 letter-sounds per minute by winter of second grade. Thus, an interim goal for Nonsense Word Fluency was set.

Sophie was placed in small-group instruction in phonological awareness using an evidence-based intervention five days a week provided by the reading specialist. She was further placed in a small group in the classroom and received daily direct instruction in letter-sound correspondence and decoding from the regular classroom teacher. Sophie's progress

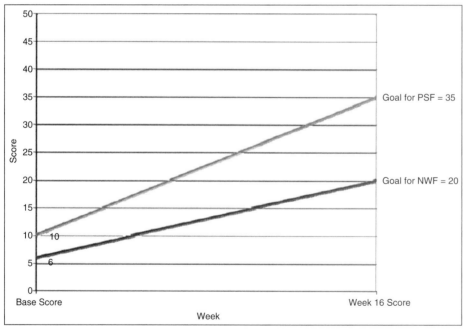

Note: PSF = Phonemic Segmentation Fluency; NWF = Nonsense Word Fluency.

FIGURE 15.1

Sophie's Aimlines for Phonemic Segmentation Fluency and Nonsense Word Fluency

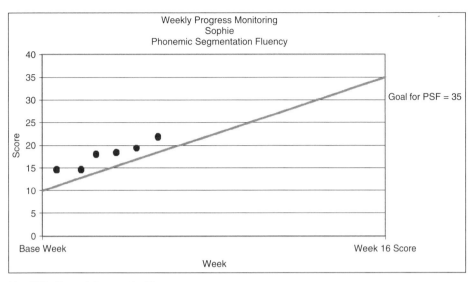

Note: PSF = Phonemic Segmentation Fluency.

FIGURE 15.2

Sophie's Weekly Progress Monitoring on Phonemic Segmentation Fluency

on Phonemic Segmentation Fluency and Nonsense Word Fluency was monitored and graphed each week by the reading specialist. Data were reviewed on a weekly basis. As seen in Figure 15.2, weekly data points on Phonemic Segmentation Fluency fell at or above the aimline. Therefore, Sophie's progress in Phonemic Segmentation Fluency was considered sufficient to meet her goal and the intervention was continued.

Progress monitoring data were reviewed. As seen in Figure 15.2, weekly data points on Phonemic Segmentation Fluency fell at or above Sophie's individual aimline necessary to meet her goal. Therefore, Sophie's progress in Phonemic Segmentation Fluency was considered sufficient to meet her goal and the intervention was continued. However, she continued to struggle with decoding skills. Weekly data points gathered for Nonsense Word Fluency after the first intervention was implemented reveal three consecutive points below the aimline (Figure 15.3), indicating that it was unlikely that Sophie would meet her goal on Nonsense Word Fluency given the current intervention. Modification of support for decoding was warranted. Sophie continued to receive the small-group support direct instruction in the classroom. She was additionally provided with daily in-class small-group direct instruction from the reading specialist. The reading specialist focused on preteaching skills that would be later covered by the classroom teacher. Progress-monitoring data after the second intervention demonstrated effectiveness of the modified intervention (Figure 15.3).

The final step in addressing Sophie's early literacy needs is to review the outcomes of the interventions implemented. At the start of the year, Sophie's scores indicated intensive need for support in Phonemic Segmentation Fluency and Nonsense Word Fluency. However, after 16 weeks of implementing the interventions, winter benchmark data were collected. At this time, Sophie attained a score of 39 on Phonemic Segmentation Fluency and 22 on Nonsense Word

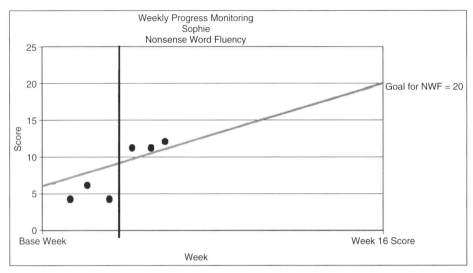

Note: NWF = Nonsense Word Fluency.

FIGURE 15.3

Sophie's Weekly Progress Monitoring on Nonsense Word Fluency

Fluency. Her winter scores for both measures fell at or above the author's established benchmark. Based on current scores, interventions were gradually faded while progress monitoring verified retention and continued development of skills.

SYSTEMS-LEVEL CASE STUDY

When reviewing schoolwide data collection at Pleasantville Elementary, the literacy team addressed systems-level concerns regarding the effectiveness of the school's current literacy model. As this was the second year of the schoolwide use of DIBELS, it was possible to compare scores from one year to the next. During the preceding year, the team identified and prioritized building-level needs based on DIBELS benchmark testing three times a year. For the purpose of this discussion, data from first grade will be highlighted. Figure 15.4 displays the aggregated data for first-grade Phonemic Segmentation Fluency measures in the fall. In reviewing local normative data from the first year, the literacy team noted that 75% or more of first-graders started the year below the author's established benchmark on Phonemic Segmentation Fluency and Nonsense Word Fluency. However, once in first grade, 80% of those children who started below benchmark improved when given intervention. The team concluded that (1) the first-grade curriculum and intervention was successful in addressing identified early literacy concerns for most children, (2) the Kindergarten curriculum did not successfully address early literacy skills of phonological awareness and alphabetic principle, (3) additional support for

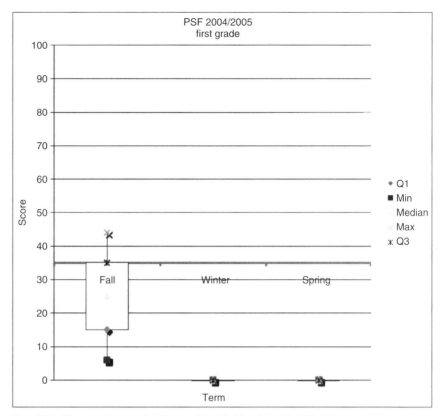

Note: PSF = Phonemic Segmentation Fluency. Established benchmark for PSF = 35.

FIGURE 15.4

Schoolwide Data for Phonemic Segmentation Fluency (PSF) Fall 2004

first-graders who did not respond to the adopted intervention was necessary, and (4) targeted staff development in the big ideas of early literacy and specific interventions was warranted for Kindergarten and first-grade teachers.

The literacy team targeted Kindergarten and first-grade curriculum. Supplemental curriculum in phonological awareness was purchased for Kindergarten teachers, and continued staff development and support was provided throughout the year. Emphasis in the core curriculum included daily phonological awareness and direct instruction in letter-sound knowledge. In addition to the emphasis placed on phonological awareness and decoding, the school continued to support enriched vocabulary, expressive language, and comprehension skills.

At the start of the second year of DIBELS data collection, systems-level data were again reviewed and compared to the previous year and to benchmarks. The current year data indicated that 82% of first-graders started the year at or above benchmark on Phonemic Segmentation Fluency (Figure 15.5). The data suggest that the supplemental Kindergarten curriculum and staff development were successful in meeting the needs for improving the phonological awareness skills of most children. However, continued need for supplemental

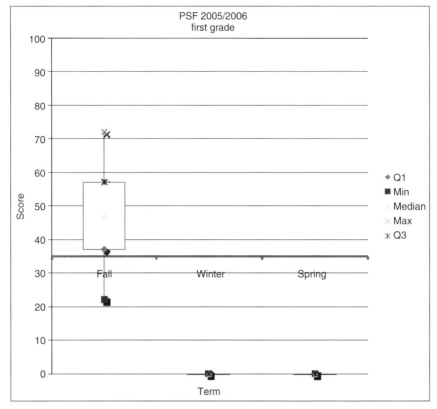

Note: PSF = Phonemic Segmentation Fluency. Established benchmark for PSF = 35.

FIGURE 15.5
Schoolwide Data for Phonemic Segmentation Fluency (PSF) Fall 2005

support for those children not responding to the adopted curriculum and interventions was necessary. Though some children continued to show Strategic or Intensive needs in early literacy, Pleasantville Elementary School was successful in addressing phonological awareness within the core reading program for most children.

Use of DIBELS with Special Populations

DIBELS can generally be used with all children in a school. The DIBELS measures are appropriate for children who are making sufficient progress as well as for children who struggle with developing beginning reading skills or are identified with specific learning disabilities. However, it is essential for literacy teams and teachers to consider the appropriateness of measuring some early literacy skills for some children. For example, it would not be appropriate to measure phonological awareness for a child who is deaf or hard of hearing. Some children with specific disabilities such as autism spectrum disorder or significant and multiple disabilities also may not benefit from use of DIBELS. The essential question to ask when determining whether DIBELS are appropriate for a given child is, "Does the information inform relevant goals and instruction for this child?"

A Spanish version of DIBELS (*Indicadores Dinamicos del Exito en la Lectura*—IDEL) is available through the DIBELS website and through the publisher. Administration and scoring for the Spanish version is essentially the same. However, administrators must consider articulation, Spanish language conventions, and dialects. There are no established benchmarks available for IDEL.

Interventions Based on DIBELS

DIBELS link directly to the big ideas in early literacy. Therefore, DIBELS data directly inform specific areas of interventions. At an individual level, each child's scores on the administered DIBELS measures along with alternative sources of data are used to target areas of need, set goals, and monitor progress. Although DIBELS inform the intervention, it is both essential and recommended that the interventions themselves do not teach the specific skill measured on the DIBELS task. For example, Nonsense Word Fluency is an *indicator* of a child's ability and fluency with decoding and encoding. An appropriate intervention would focus on directly teaching the skills of letter-sound correspondence, decoding, and blending. Interventions should not teach children to decode, blend, or read nonsense words. When selecting evidence-based interventions, educators must distinguish between those interventions that address skills toward the general outcome of reading and those that teach to the test.

VALIDITY

Kaminski and colleagues (2008) present evidence of concurrent validity of DIBELS measures with other measures of reading and reading readiness, including the Woodcock-Johnson Psycho-Educational Battery Readiness Cluster score (Initial Sound Fluency = .36, Phonemic Segmentation Fluency = .54, Letter Naming Fluency = .70), Metropolitan Test of Reading (Phonemic Segmentation Fluency =.65, Letter Naming Fluency = .77), and language samples (Word Use Fluency = .71). Validity coefficients range from .36 for Initial Sound Fluency to .77 for Letter Naming Fluency (Table 15.2). Data supports the predictive validity of DIBELS with the Woodcock-Johnson Psycho-Educational Battery Total Reading score. Validity coefficients range from .37 (Initial Sound Fluency) to .67 (Nonsense Word Fluency). Good and colleagues (2004) reported the concurrent related validity of Initial Sound Fluency with Phonemic Segmentation Fluency to be .47 and the predictive validity of Phonemic Segmentation Fluency with winter first-grade Nonsense Word Fluency to be .58. Predictive validity coefficients for Kindergarten scores on Phonemic Segmentation Fluency and Letter Naming Fluency as well as first-grade scores on Nonsense Word Fluency range from .52 to .75 (Good et al., 2004).

Additional studies examining the diagnostic accuracy of DIBELS have been conducted (Hintze, Ryan, & Stoner, 2003; Schilling, Carlisle, Scott, & Zeng, 2007). Hintze and colleagues (2003) found moderate to strong correlations between DIBELS and the Comprehensive Test of Phonological Processing. Furthermore, the researchers found that utilizing the author's established benchmarks for Initial Sound Fluency and Phonemic Segmentation Fluency resulted in high rates of correctly identifying children in need of phonological awareness intervention. However, while DIBELS resulted in high positive identification, the authors also noted a high rate of false identification.

The predictive validity of DIBELS was evaluated using data derived from the first Reading First school cohort in Michigan (Schilling et al., 2007). Data for the study were gathered from 44 participating schools within nine districts.

Pearson correlations of DIBELS with the Iowa Test of Basic Skills (ITBS) indicated significant correlations with each testing time (benchmark assessment) and grade level. However, the magnitude of the correlation varied greatly by subtest (range of .32–.75) with Nonsense Word Fluency, Phonemic Segmentation Fluency, and DIBELS Oral Reading Fluency, resulting in the strongest correlations. Word Use Fluency was found to have low correlations with each of the ITBS subtests. The authors further found that the DIBELS tests administered for each grade in the fall and winter significantly predicted the ITBS reading total with the highest portion of variability (57%) accounted for in the winter of second grade. Both Letter Naming Fluency and Nonsense Word Fluency accounted for most variability in year-end reading scores.

SUMMARY

DIBELS are a set of fluency measures intended to assess prereading skills and assist in identifying children who may be in need of early reading intervention. The DIBELS are administered and scored following standardized procedures. Data are interpreted in relation to the author's recommended benchmarks, local norms, and individual progress. Best practices recommend use of DIBELS within an outcomes-driven model and as one part of an effective literacy program. The structure of DIBELS allows educators to (1) identify children early, (2) directly assess the big ideas in early literacy, and (3) monitor progress for individual children. The use of DIBELS as formative data enables educators to make ongoing decisions about continued need for intervention and to modify interventions as necessary. In addition, aggregated DIBELS data may be used at a systems level to develop local norms and inform decisions about curriculum, instruction, and resource allocation. In using DIBELS, districts have the ability to evaluate the effects of core curriculum and interventions, and to improve outcomes for individual students and groups of children. A growing body of evidence supports the use of DIBELS for screening, progress monitoring, and outcomes-based educational decisions. However, continued research in reliability, validity, and the use of benchmark cutoff scores of DIBELS is warranted.

REFERENCES

Adams, M. J., (1990). *Beginning to read: Thinking and learning about print*. Cambridge, MA: MIT Press.

Barwick, M., & Siegel, L. S. (1996). Learning difficulties in adolescent clients of a shelter for runaway and homeless street youth. *Journal of Research on Adolescence, 6,* 649–670.

Brown-Chidsey, R., & Steege, M. W. (2007). *Response to intervention: Principles and strategies for effective instruction*. New York: Guilford Press.

Coyne, M. D., Kame'enui, E. J., & Carnine, D. W. (2007). *Effective teaching strategies that accommodate diverse learners* (3rd ed.). Upper Saddle River, NJ: Prentice Hall.

Deno, S. L., (1985). Curriculum-based measurement: The emerging alternative. *Exceptional Children, 52,* 219–232.

Deno, S. L., & Fuchs, L. S. (1987). Developing curriculum-based measurement systems for data-based special education problem solving. *Focus on Exceptional Children, 19*(8), 1–15.

Deno, S. L., Fuchs, L. S., Marston, D., & Shin, J. (2001). Using curriculum based measurement to establish growth standards for students with learning disabilities. *School Psychology Review, 30,* 507–524.

Francis, D. J., Shaywitz, S. F., Stuebing, K. K., Shaywitz, B. A., & Fletcher, J. M. (1996). Developmental lag versus deficit models of reading disability: A longitudinal, individual growth curves analysis. *Journal of Educational Psychology, 88,* 3–17.

Good, R. H., Gruba, J., & Kaminski, R. A. (2001). Best practices in using dynamic indicators of basic early literacy skills (DIBELS) in an outcomes driven model. In A. Thomas & J. Grimes (Eds.) *Best practices in school psychology* (4th ed., pp. 699–720). Bethesda, MD: National Association of School Psychologists.

Good, R. H., III, Kaminski, R. A. (2002). *DIBELS administration and scoring guide*. Longmont, CO: Sopris West Educational Services.

Good, R. H., Kaminski, R. A., Bratten, J., & Smith, S. (2000). Reliability, validity and sensitivity of DIBELS. Unpublished raw data.

Good, R. H., III, Kaminski, R. A., Shinn, M., Bratten, J., Shinn, M., & Laimon, D. (2004). *Technical adequacy and decision making utility of DIBELS*. Eugene: University of Oregon.

Good, R. H., III, Simmons, D. C., & Kame'enui, E. J. (2001). The importance and decision-making utility of a continuum of fluency-based indicators of foundational reading skills for third-grade high-stakes outcomes. *Scientific Studies of Reading*, *5*, 257–288.

Good, R. H., III, Simmons, D. C., Kame'enui, E. J., Kaminski, R. A., & Wallin, J. (2002). *Summary of decision rules for intensive, strategic, and benchmark instructional recommendations in Kindergarten through third grade* (Technical Report No. 11). Eugene: University of Oregon Press.

Good, R. H., Simmons, D. C., & Smith, S. B. (1998). Effective academic interventions in the United States: Evaluating and enhancing acquisition. *School Psychology Review*, *27*(1), 45–57.

Gunn, B. K., Simmons, D. C., & Kame'enui, E. J. (1998). Emergent literacy: Instructional and curricular basics and implications. In D. C. Simmons & E. J. Kame'enui, *What reading research tells us about children with diverse learning needs: Bases and basics* (pp. 51–59). Mahwah, NJ: Lawrence Erlbaum Associates.

Hall, S. L. (2006). *I've DIBEL'd: Now what?* Longmont, CO: Sopris West.

Hintze, J. M., Ryan, A. L., & Stoner, G. (2003). Concurrent validity and diagnostic accuracy of the dynamic indicators of basic early literacy skills and the comprehensive test of phonological processing. *School Psychology Review*, *32*(4), 541–556.

Hosp, M. K., Hosp, J. L., & Howell, K. W. (2007). *The ABCs of CBM: A practical guide to curriculum based measurement*. New York: Guilford Press.

Joseph, L. M. (2008). Best practices on interventions for students with reading problems. In A. Thomas & J. Grimes, *Best practices in school psychology* (5th ed., pp. 1163–1180). Bethesda, MD: National Association of School Psychologists.

Juel, C. (1998). Learning to read and write: A longitudinal study of fifty-four children from first through fourth grade. *Journal of Educational Psychology*, *80*(4), 437–447.

Kaminski, R. A., & Cummings, K. D. (2007, winter). Assessment for learning using general outcomes measures. *Threshold*, 26–28.

Kaminski, R. A., Cummings, K., Powell-Smith, K., & Good, R. H. (2008). Best practices in using dynamic indicators of basic early literacy skills for formative assessment and evaluation. In A. Thomas & J. Grimes, *Best practices in school psychology* (5th ed., pp. 1181–1203). Bethesda, MD: National Association of School Psychologists.

Kaminski, R. A., & Good, R. H. (1996). Toward a technology of assessing basic early literacy skills. *School Psychology Review*, *25*(2), 215–227.

Kaminski, R. A., Good, R. H., III, & Knutson, N. (2006). *DIBELS mentoring workshop*. Eugene: OR: Dynamic Measurement Group.

Kaminski, R. A., Good, R. H., III, Shinn, M. R., Smith, S., Laimon, D., Shinn, M., et al. (2004). *Development and research on DIBELS Word Use Fluency measure for first through third grades* (Technical Report No. 13). Eugene: University of Oregon.

Lyon, G. R. (1996). Toward a definition of dyslexia. *Annals of Dyslexia*, *45*, 3–27.

Lyon, G. R. (2000). Why reading is not a natural process. In L. Abbeduto (Ed.), *Taking sides: Clashing views on controversial issues in educational psychology* (pp. 250–255). Guilford, CT: Dushkin/McGraw Hill.

McBride, H., & Siegel, L. S. (1997). Learning disabilities and adolescent suicide. *Journal of Learning Disabilities*, *30*, 652–659.

McKenna, M. K. (2003). *Assessing reading comprehension: The relation between DIBELS Oral Reading Fluency and Oregon State Assessment scores*. Eugene: University of Oregon.

National Research Council. (1998). *Preventing reading difficulty in young children*. Washington, DC: National Academic Press.

Roehrig, A. D., Petscher, Y., Nettles, S. M., Hudson, R. F., & Torgesen, J. K. (2008). Accuracy of the DIBELS oral reading fluency measure for predicting third grade reading comprehension outcomes. *Journal of School Psychology*, *46*, 343–366.

Salvia, J., & Ysseldyke, J. E. (2001). *Assessment* (8th ed.). Boston: Houghton Mifflin.

Schilling, S. G., Carlisle, J. F., Scott, S. E., & Zeng, J. (2007). Are fluency measures accurate predictors of reading achievement? *Elementary School Journal, 107*(5), 429–448.

Shapiro, E. S. (2004). *Academic skills problems: Direct assessment and intervention*. New York: Guilford Press.

Shaywitz, S. (2003). *Overcoming dyslexia: A new and complete science-based program for reading problems at any level*. New York: Alfred A. Knopf.

Shinn, M. R. (Ed.). (1989). *Curriculum based measurement: Assessing special children*. New York: Guilford Press.

Simmons, D. C., & Kame'enui, E. J. (Eds.). (1998). *What reading research tells us about children with diverse learning needs: Bases and basics*. Mahwah, NJ: Erlbaum.

Stage, S., Sheppard, J., Davidson, M. M., & Browning, M. M. (2001). Prediction of first-graders' growth in oral reading fluency using Kindergarten letter fluency. *Journal of School Psychology, 39*(3), 225–237.

Stanovich, K. E. (1986). Matthew effects in reading: Some consequences of individual difference in the acquisition of literacy. *Reading Research Quarterly, 21*(4), 360–406.

Torgesen, J. K. (2004). Lessons learned from the last 20 years of research on interventions for students who experience difficulty learning to read. In P. McCardle & V. Chhabra (Eds.), *The voice of evidence in reading research*. Baltimore: Brookes.

The Gray Oral Reading Test—Fourth Edition (GORT-4)

Brian R. Bryant, Minyi Shih, and Diane Pedrotty Bryant

RATIONALE UNDERLYING THE TEST

To best understand the historical significance of William S. Gray's *Gray Oral Reading Tests* (GORT; Gray & Robinson, 1963, 1967), we must recognize that the scholar's *Studies of Elementary-School Reading through Standardized Tests* was one of the first doctoral dissertations to examine reading (Smith, 2002). Gray's work helped contribute to a growing body of achievement and aptitude tests that were being developed at a furious pace in the early 1900s (Bryant, Bryant, & Kethley, 2004). Gray and many of his counterparts, notably Arthur Gates, who along with Gray was called by Smith one of the two "'giants' in the field of reading instruction" (p. 209), not only influenced reading assessment but instruction as well. Gray and Gates, with numerous colleagues, helped write many of the basal readers used in instruction from the early 1920s through the 1950s. The classic *Fun with Dick and Jane* in the Scott Foresman basal reading series was but one of many of Gray's contributions.

Two years before his dissertation was completed, Gray published his first edition of the *Standardized Oral Reading Paragraphs* (Gray,

1915), which was the most popular oral reading test of its time and remained widely used until the GORT was published in 1963. Both tests, the original *Standardized Oral Reading Paragraphs* and the 1963 version of the GORT, were consistent with Gray's (1940) line of thinking about the act of reading and can be inferred to be the rationale behind his tests—"reading assumes not only the fluent, accurate recognition of words, but in addition, a clear grasp of the meanings implied by the symbols used" (p. 21). The rationale behind the 1963 GORT subtests can be inferred from this last quote.

The original GORT had four alternate, equivalent forms, each composed of 13 stories of increasing difficulty. Examiners read aloud each passage, and the examiner recorded the amount of time (in seconds) it took to read a passage and also noted the number of errors made during reading. After each passage was read, four comprehension questions were asked of the examinee, and the examiner awarded 1 point for each correct answer in each story. Half-credit was given for some answers. Results were transferred to the coversheet of the Examiner Record Booklet. For each story, a Passage Score was derived using a scoring matrix, with number of errors on one axis and the time in seconds on the other. Their intersecting point provided the Passage Score, which ranged from 0 to 9 points. At the end of testing, Passage Scores were summed and converted to a grade equivalent. No derived scores were provided for number of errors, time in seconds, or comprehension. Interestingly, Gray and Robinson (1963) noted, "The Gray Oral Reading Test questions are not designed to measure comprehension; they are designed to determine the extent of understanding at the simplest level" (p. 3). Space in the Examiner Record Booklet was provided to note the types of reading errors (e.g., gross mispronunciation, omission) and make observations (e.g., word-by-word reading, monotonous tone).

The GORT was one of the most widely used tests of oral reading rate, accuracy, and comprehension in the United States from the 1960s to the 1980s and was cited regularly in the professional literature. In 1981, Pro-Ed, Inc. purchased the rights to the GORT from the Bobbs Merrill Publishing Company and commissioned the revision of the venerable instrument. Drs. J. Lee Wiederholt and Brian R. Bryant revised the test and it was published as the *Gray Oral Reading Tests—Revised* (GORT-R; Wiederholt & Bryant, 1986) in 1986. The GORT-R had two alternate forms that included 13 new or modified (from the original GORT) stories. For each passage, the examiner recorded the number of reading errors and the time required for the student to read each passage. At the end of each passage, five multiple-choice questions were read aloud to the examinee. Like its predecessor, the GORT-R provided a passage score (a combination of rate and accuracy), but instead of one matrix for all stories, the authors provided four matrices, one for use in Stories 1 and 2, one for Stories 3 through 6, another for Stories 7 and 8, and a final matrix for Stories 9 through 13. The new test also provided scores for comprehension and overall performance. All new national norms, reliability information, and validity data were collected and presented in the Examiner's Manual. In addition, the authors

provided a *miscue analysis system* to classify the types of oral reading substitution errors.

The test was revised twice more, as the authors examined reviewers' and users' concerns in 1992 and 2001. Improvements to the test included separate rate and accuracy scores, scoring simplification, an increased size of a stratified normative sample, and additional reliability and validity analyses. The latest version, the 2001 edition of the GORT-4, also renamed the Passage Score to *Fluency* to better relate to contemporary terminology. It is the 2001 edition of the GORT that is the focus of the remainder of this chapter.

DESCRIPTION OF THE TEST

The GORT-4 is a norm-referenced, reliable test that yields valid scores of oral reading rate, accuracy, fluency, comprehension, and total reading. Individually administered, the test is appropriate for students ages 6 years, 0 months (6:0) through 18 years, 11 months (18:11). The GORT-4 has two alternate, equivalent forms, Form A and Form B, each containing 14 stories. Five multiple-choice comprehension questions follow each story. Performance on the GORT-4 yields five scores. *Rate* (from 0 to 5 points per passage) is based on the time in seconds that it takes a student to read a passage. *Accuracy* (also 0–5 points per passage) is based on the number of words read incorrectly (i.e., errors made) in a passage. *Fluency* (0–10 points per story) is the sum of the Rate and Accuracy scores. *Comprehension* (0–5 points) is the number of questions correctly answered following each passage. The final GORT-4 score, *Overall Reading Ability*, is a composite score based on the student's Fluency and Comprehension scores across all of the stories read.

Rate, Accuracy, Fluency, and Comprehension results are reported as subtest standard scores having a mean of 10 and a standard deviation of 3. The overall oral reading composite score is reported as an ability score, based on a standard score distribution having a mean of 100 and a standard deviation of 15. Age equivalents, grade equivalents, and percentiles are also available.

The original GORT also provided a system for evaluating specific types of reading errors made (e.g., gross mispronunciation, repetition). In the 1986 revision of the GORT, Wiederholt and Bryant borrowed from the work of Cohen (1974–1975), Goodman (1969), Goodman and Burke (1972), and others and provided miscue classification systems to analyze readers' ability to use graphic/phonemic, syntactic, and semantic cues while reading, and also self-corrections where appropriate.

The GORT-4 provides for miscue analyses that can be used to assign reading substitutions (i.e., a word that is incorrectly substituted for a text word) into one or more of five categories. A word is classified as a *Meaning Similarity* miscue if the substituted word means the same as the text word (e.g., *house* is misread as *home*). *Function Similarity* is assigned to miscues that fit grammatically within the sentence ("the man *ran* to the store" for "the man *walked* to the store"). A miscue is categorized as *Graphic/Phonemic Similarity* if any part of the word is similar to the look and sound of the printed word (e.g., *painted* for *prince*—the /p/ sound begins both the text word and the substitution). *Multiple Sources* is selected if the student's miscue is assigned to more than one previous category. For example, consider that the sentence, "The man ran to the store" is read as "The man *raced* to the store." In this case, the substitution *raced* fits multiple categories (i.e., meaning, function, and graphic/phonemic similarity); thus, *Multiple Sources* is also selected. Finally, a word is assigned to *Self-Correction* if the student misreads a word but, within 3 seconds, rereads the misread word correctly. The occurrence of each of the reading miscue categories across all of the stories is reported as a percentage.

The GORT-4 complete kit contains an Examiner's Manual, a Student Book, Form A Profile/Examiner Record Booklets, and Form B Profile/Examiner Record Booklets. The Examiner's Manual contains a description of the GORT-4 and its purposes, directions for test administration and scoring, a means to interpret test scores, and information concerning the test's technical characteristics (i.e., normative data, reliability, and validity). Tables in the manual's appendices are used to convert raw scores to subtest standard scores, age equivalents, grade equivalents, and percentiles. A table is also available for converting the sum of the Fluency and Comprehension standard scores to an ability score (i.e., the total score). The Student Book contains the stories and comprehension questions for both Form A and Form B. Consumable Profile/Examiner Record Booklets are provided for Forms A and B. Examiners use the booklets to record the student oral responses to the stories read, note the types of oral reading errors made, and record the rate, accuracy, and comprehension scores. The front cover of the Profile/Examiner Record Booklet provides space to note student identifying information and his or her test performance in the GORT-4 and any other measures administered that are considered diagnostically relevant.

Subtest Background and Structure

Story and Comprehension Questions Construction

The GORT uses the story passage format to test oral reading proficiency. Students orally read passages and answer questions that pertain to what they read. This format lends itself well to testing because children and adolescents read passages as part of their daily school regimen and in daily living.

In composing the stories for the first revision of the test in 1986, Wiederholt and Bryant commissioned a professional writer to write the stories and the comprehension questions. She was instructed to select interesting topics that would not become quickly dated, to control for the syntactic complexity of each story in line with increasing reader levels, and control vocabulary appropriately with respect to grade level text. Finally, the writer was directed to avoid stereotypic language and concepts.

The authors report in the Manual that the GORT-4 stories (the same stories on the original GORT-R are on the GORT-4, with the exception of a single story that was added at the lowest level to help decrease floor effects) "are of general interest and timeless in nature. Each story has a logical connection among ideas and sentences. In addition, the vocabulary level of each story is controlled by graded word lists. These three factors help ensure content validity of the GORT-4" (Wiederholt & Bryant, 2001, p. 74).

To assess comprehension in the original GORT, Gray used open-ended questions. In this format, a question was asked and a student provided the answer based on his or her recollection of the story. The authors of the current GORT changed to a multiple-choice format in their revisions. In writing the questions, the professional writer was presented with the comprehension research that focused on a variety of comprehension question types, passage dependence, text features, and vocabulary levels. The writer was asked to create literal, inferential, critical, and affective questions. Six questions were created for each passage. The four strongest questions were retained after an item analysis procedure was conducted that eliminated empirically weak items (i.e., items that did not contribute to the validity of the scale).

Rate, Accuracy, and Fluency

One of the key uses of the GORT over the years has been to determine a student's oral reading fluency. Adams (1990) observed, "the most salient characteristic of skillful readers is the speed and effortlessness with which they seem able to breeze through text" (p. 409). Lyon (l994) noted that poor fluent word recognition is the most frequently cited factor in reading disorders.

Fluency on the GORT-4 is assessed by combining the rate and accuracy scores, because fluent readers demonstrate a combination of the two skills (National Institute of Child Health and Human Development, 2000). In the original GORT, Gray and Robinson (1963, 1967) assessed fluency by providing a passage score. As described earlier, the examiner (1) counted the number of errors in word reading accuracy, (2) noted the time in seconds it took to read the story, and (3) used a single matrix to derive a passage score for each story (a score based on a combination of rate and accuracy). In the GORT-R, Wiederholt and Bryant (1986) generated a matrix for each story to retain the Passage Score that Gray had developed, with time in seconds on one axis of each matrix and Deviations from Print (the authors' words for *errors*) on the other axis.

In their second revision, the GORT-3 (Wiederholt & Bryant, 1992), the authors changed their procedure. They created a chart by which time in seconds was converted to a 0–5 rate score and number of Deviations from Print was converted to a 0–5 accuracy score. The two scores were summed to create the 0–10 Passage Score for each story.

Scales the Test Yields

The GORT-4 yields six types of scores: Total Scores, Subtest Standard Scores, an Oral Reading Quotient, Percentile Ranks, Age Equivalents, and Grade Equivalents. *Total Scores* for the comprehension subtest is the total number of questions answered correctly across all of the stories. For Rate, Accuracy, and Fluency, the Total Scores are the sum of all related scores across the passages read. Each of the Total Scores is converted to a *Standard Score* that is based on a distribution having a mean of 10 and a standard deviation of 3. Standard Scores allow the examiner to compare scores for intraindividual oral reading differences. For example, if Owen's Standard Score was 14 on Rate and 6 on Comprehension, he would be considered Above Average on the first score and Below Average on the second. Such a difference in performance is usually considered a cause for concern and should lead to further evaluation to find out why Owen reads quickly yet fails to understand what he reads.

The *Oral Reading Quotient (ORQ)*, a composite based on performance on Comprehension and Fluency, is another type of Standard Score and serves as the best measure of a student's overall oral reading ability. This Standard Score is based on a distribution having a mean of 100 and a standard deviation of 15. If Owen's ORQ is 100, his performance would be considered Average; a quotient of 125 would be considered Superior.

Percentile Ranks represent values on a scale from 1 to 99 that indicate the percentage of the distribution that is equal to or below each value. Owen's percentile of 75 for Comprehension indicates that 75% of the standardization sample at his age scored at or below his Total Score on that subtest.

Age and *Grade Equivalents* are also reported on the GORT-4, but the authors note that the use of these equivalents has come under close scrutiny and criticism over the past few decades. Organizations such as the American Psychological Association (APA, 1985) have advocated discontinuing these scores because they have inadequate statistical properties and are often misleading. But many agencies and school systems mandate these equivalents, so the GORT-4 authors decided to retain them.

Structure of the Test

The GORT-4 is individually administered and uses basals and ceilings to shorten administration time. The GORT-4 incorporates separate basals and ceilings for Fluency and Comprehension. It is important that testing continue until both basals and ceilings are achieved across the passages. Examiners administer passages one at a time, record Rate and Deviations from Print, ask comprehension questions, and note the accuracy of student responses. Testing continues until ceilings are established for Fluency and Comprehension. Following testing, the examiner computes the Total Test scores, and converts those scores into derived scores. A miscue

analysis may also be conducted based on the student's substitution Deviations from Print.

Administration and Scoring

Testing Tips

For each story, the examiner reads aloud a story prompt, presents the Student Book to the reader, points to the start of the story, and says "Begin." At that point, the examiner starts the timer, follows along as the student reads the story, and marks any errors (i.e., Deviations from Print) on the Profile/Examiner Record Form. When the reader stops reading the passage, the examiner stops the timer and notes the number of seconds the student took to read the story. The "Time" is then converted to a Rate score.

Like most oral reading tests, it takes practice to administer and score the GORT-4 accurately. Having taught many reading classes at the undergraduate and graduate levels, we have found that it is not easy for beginners to listen to a reader and record errors that are made as the person continues to read aloud. Nor is it easy to classify reading miscues into specific categories (see below). Thus, examiners are encouraged to practice administering the test by tape recording oral reading performance, listening intently for Deviations from Print, and recording and classifying substitution miscues.

Examiners can choose to mark deviations using one of two procedures: a *slash marking* system or *miscue marking* procedure. With the slash marking system, a slash mark is made (/) using the criteria that follow:

1. Place a slash on each word that is not read correctly. For example, if the sentence *Jon is a good boy* is read *Jon is a great boy* or *Jon is a goob boy*, a slash is placed on *good*: *Jon is a go/od boy*.

2. Place a slash on the word if the student pauses for word providing. That is, if a student pauses for 5 seconds without making an audible attempt to read a word, say (i.e., provide) the word, mark the deviation, and

proceed. If over 20% of the words have to be said aloud to the student in any one story, the comprehension questions should not be administered. A Comprehension Score of 0 is awarded for that story. For convenience, the maximum number of words that can be provided to the reader appears under each story prompt in Section VIII of the Examiner Record Booklet.

3. If the student attempts to sound out the word, give him or her 10 seconds to decode; then say the word, mark the deviation, and continue.

4. For self-corrections, place a slash on the gap before the word corrected. For example, if the student reads *Jon is a bad … good boy*, place a slash on the gap between *a* and *good*: *Jon is a/good boy*.

5. If the student reads *Jon is a really neat and good boy*, place a slash between the words where the addition is made: *Jon is a/good boy*. Note that a single slash is used even if several words are added.

6. For repetitions, such as *Jon is a … a good boy*, place a slash after the word repeated: *Jon is a/good boy*.

7. Regional pronunciations, provided the pronunciations are correct, are not marked as deviations.

8. If the reader skips a line, stop the timer, direct the student's attention to the correct line, and commence timing when the first word is said. This is scored as one deviation (Wiederholt & Bryant, 2001, p. 17).

After a student reads a passage, the slashes are summed to compute a Deviations from Print score. This score is converted to an Accuracy score.

The miscue marking system is a bit more challenging to conduct, because examiners must recognize substitution miscues and record them above the text word as the student continues to read. For the GORT-4, the authors consider nonwords or pseudowords as substitutions; for example, *sandwich* misread as *sawhich*. Obviously,

sawhich is not a word, but it was substituted for *sandwich*, so it would be recorded above the text word as a substitution.

We described earlier the miscue categories: Meaning Similarity, Function Similarity, Graphic/Phonemic Similarity, Self-Corrections, and Multiple Sources. In the case of nonword substitutions, they should never be marked as Meaning Similarity or Function Similarity, but the pseudoword should be checked for Graphic/Phonemic Similarity. Some immature readers have not grasped that reading should be a meaningful activity that uses real words to convey meaning. Instead, they focus on the sound-symbol correspondences and constitute a word they have never heard of and read it as they think it sounds (e.g., *sawhich*). However, even some mature readers sound out words and treat them as nonwords. For instance, a student may correctly use phonetic analysis to decode *catastrophic*, read it aloud correctly, yet have no idea whether *catastrophic* is a word, because it is not in their speaking, listening, or meaning vocabularies. The point is that many students may not realize they have read aloud a pseudoword; they are simply reading aloud what they are seeing.

When conducting miscue analyses, a minimum of 25 substitutions across at least two stories must be available for inspection. If 25 substitutions have not been made, or if they have been made in only one story (unlikely), the examiner must have the student read aloud the next story (or stories) until 25 substitutions are made.

We offer several test administration tips. First, examiners should memorize the passages if they plan on administering the test as a regular part of reading assessments. Although this may seem a bit cumbersome, it makes checking for Deviations from Print much easier. For examiners who memorize the passages, any deviations jump out and make for quick recording. Also, when examiners read unfamiliar passages as students read aloud, it is somewhat difficult to concentrate on what the student is saying while they (the examiners) are also concentrating on what they are seeing (the text words) for the first time.

Second, examiners should make sure that students read loud enough and clearly enough to be heard and understood. For students with articulation difficulties, examiners may wish to solicit the help of speech-language pathologists, either for training in hearing sound substitutions, omissions, distortions, and additions, or to actually ask them to administer the test under the examiner's watchful eye. Tape recording passages may be helpful during administration, but because basals and ceilings are obtained during administration, going back and marking deviations after the fact may result in improper testing (i.e., misapplying basals and ceilings).

Finally, move briskly through the comprehension questions. Some examiners take too long reading the stem and response choices, so that students lose concentration and forget what has been read to them or lose track of the question being asked. Examiners should give students their best chance at answering correctly. The Examiner's Manual does not prohibit repeating the questions and/or stems, but do so judiciously. Constant repetition just extends testing time and may lead to examinee fatigue.

How to Score the Test

Once the time in seconds and the number of Deviations from Print are noted, Rate, Accuracy, and Fluency scores are computed. For each story in the Profile/Examiner Record Booklet, there is a conversion table (see Figure 16.1). The first row of each table is a 0- to 5-point conversion scale for Rate/Accuracy Scores, each number having its own column. The second row contains the Time values (shown in seconds). To convert Time to a Rate Score, the examiner notes the number of seconds taken to read the passage in the Time row. As shown in Figure 16.1, Owen's 57 seconds that it took him to read Story 5 converts to his Rate Score (found immediately above the 57-second location) of 3 points.

The third row of the table contains the Deviations from Print values. The examiner finds the reader's number of deviations (i.e., the slash marks or combination of slash marks, substitutions, and self-corrections) and matches that number to its related score (0–5) in the top row. In our example, Owen made 21 deviations, which converts to an Accuracy Score of 0.

The Fluency Score is derived by simply adding the Rate and Accuracy scores for each story. Owen's Rate (3) and Accuracy (0) sum to a Fluency Score of 3 points.

For comprehension, the examiner reads aloud the questions and notes the student's response. Each answer is scored as correct or incorrect, and the number of correctly answered questions is summed to derive a passage's Comprehension Score (in Owen's case, 4).

Once Fluency and Comprehension scores are tabulated, the Oral Reading Quotient (ORQ) is computed by summing the two contributing standard scores (Fluency and Comprehension)

Rate/Accuracy Scores	Converting Time and Deviations from Print to Rate and Accuracy					
	0	1	2	3	4	5
Time	>119	76–119	65–75	50–64	41–49	<41
Deviations from Print	>10	8–10	6–7	5	3–4	0–2

FIGURE 16.1
Table for Converting GORT-4 Time and Deviations from Print Scores to Rate and Accuracy Scores

and converting the sum to the ORQ using a table in the manual's appendix. When the test has been scored, data are transferred to the front page of the Profile/Examiner Record Form, where derived scores are also recorded (see Figure 16.2). Additional information is also recorded about the student's performance.

To help in discussing scoring miscues, we borrow from Wiederholt and Bryant (2001) (see Figures 16.3 and 16.4). In Figure 16.3, we see a story that has been marked using the combination of the slash and miscue marking systems. Note that in the first line the student read *perched* as *sitting*, *a* as *the*, *for* as *at the*, and *flown* as *field*. These and the remaining miscues are "scored" using the Worksheet for Recording GORT-4 Miscues on the second page of the Profile/Examiner Record Booklet (see Figure 16.4). From left to right on the worksheet, the examiner records the line of text where the miscue occurred, the text word, and the Deviation from Print (i.e., substitution miscue). Next, the classification occurs by writing a 1 or 0 in the space for each category (the 1 signifies that the miscue fits the category). This is done for all 25 or more substitution miscues, even though the authors only provide 14 miscues in their example, which we reproduce in Figure 16.4. The Total and Percentage of miscues for each category are then calculated and recorded.

The authors do not provide extensive information about how to interpret the miscue analysis. However, GORT-4 users should assume that the higher the percentage of meaning, function, and graphic/phonemic similarity miscues that are made, the more the reader is adhering to meaning, function, and graphic/phonemic cues that are present in text, which is a good thing, especially if the Multiple Sources percentage is high. Mature readers tend to self-correct their errors, so a high percentage of self-corrections can also be perceived as a positive indication (although, of course, it would be better if students read the words accurately in the first place).

STANDARDIZATION, NORMS, AND PSYCHOMETRICS

Characteristics of the Standardization Sample

According to the GORT-4 manual, the test was normed on a sample of 1,677 students in 28 states from fall 1999 through fall 2000. The authors state that standardization sites were selected in each of the four major geographic regions as designated by the U.S. Bureau of the Census (i.e., Rochester, New York—Northeast; Mandan, North Dakota—Midwest; Brownsville, Texas, and Austin, Texas—South; and Brookings, Oregon—West).

In addition to securing "major" sites in each of the geographic regions, the authors also invited individuals from all 50 states to test students with the GORT-4. People from 20 states agreed to test between 10 and 20 students in their area whose demographic makeup matched that of their community.

The normative sample's characteristics with regard to geographic region, gender, race, rural or urban residence, ethnicity, family income, educational attainment of parents, and disability are provided in Table 16.1. The characteristics were compared to those reported in the 1997 edition of the *Statistical Abstract of the United States* (U.S. Bureau of the Census, 1997) for children ages 6:0 through 18:11. The authors claim that the comparison of the percentages found in the table demonstrates that the sample is representative of the nation as a whole. This claim has been supported by test reviewers (e.g., Crumpton, 2003), although Rathvon (2004) pointed out that the numbers of students in the sample at ages 6 and 18 are somewhat low (i.e., 87 and 72, respectively).

Reliability of the Scales

The authors explore reliability by reporting data on content sampling, time sampling, and interscorer differences. The authors note that

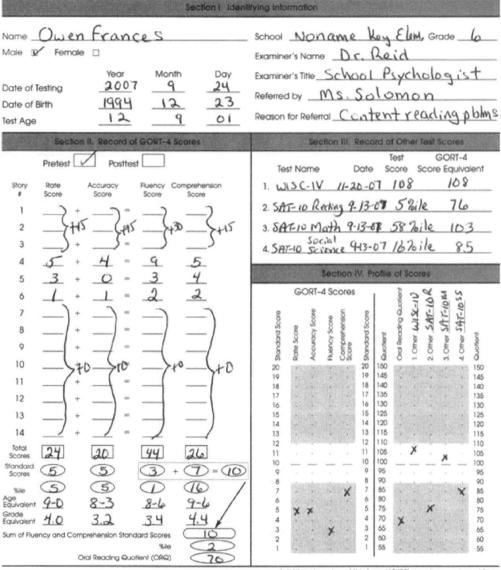

Story 5

Prompt: Say, "This story is about a bird having a problem. Read the story to find out what the problem is and how it is solved."

Maximum words examiner may provide: 21

                  sitting   *the*   *at the*   *field*

1   A blue jay was perched on a limb looking for water. Having just flown

                                          the *minute*

2   a great distance, she was (very) thirsty. At that moment she happened to

         big   *flied*   *of water*

3   spot a water jar on the ground, so she flew down and tried to get a drink

                                                        able

4   from the jar. But there was (so) little water in the jar that she was unable to

           fell   *hit,*

5   drink. Just as she felt that she would (surely) die of thirst, an idea struck her.

        gained   *dripping*

6   The jay gathered a pile of stones and began dropping them in the jar. Little

                             least   *full*

7   by little the water rose and at last the jay (could) drink her fill.

Time (in seconds): ___57___   Deviations from Print: ___21___

Comprehension Questions

__1__ 1. Why couldn't the jay drink the water?
    A. The water was too low in the jar.
    B. The jar had a leak.
    C. The water tasted bad.
    D. The water was too dirty.

__1__ 2. The jay in this story is _____.
    A. clever
    B. tired
    C. hungry
    D. silly

__1__ 3. What is the main idea in this story?
    A. A bad situation never lasts a long time.
    B. Hope is better than anger.
    C. Brains are often the key to survival.
    D. Everyone likes a good joke.

__0__ 4. How do you think the jay felt when she was unable to drink?
    A. surprised
    B. puzzled
    C. worried
    D. hopeful

__1__ 5. When the jay was finally able to reach the water, she was probably _____.
    A. tired from all her hard work
    B. proud of her idea
    C. rested from her journey
    D. angry about wasting so much time

      | 4 | Comprehension Score

Converting Time and Deviations from Print to Rate and Accuracy

Rate/Accuracy Scores	0	1	2	3	4	5
Time	>119	76–119	65–75	50–64	41–49	<41
Deviations from Print	>10	8–10	6–7	5	3–4	0–2

Rate Score | 3 | + Accuracy Score | 0 | = Fluency Score | 3 |

FIGURE 16.3
Sample Depicting Owen's Oral Reading Performance for Story 5

Section V. Worksheet for Recording GORT-4 Miscues

Categorized Miscues

Story Numbers: _____ _____ _____ _____

Miscue No.	Line	Text Word	Deviations from Print	Meaning Similarity	Function Similarity	Graphic/ Phonemic Similarity	Multiple Sources	Self- Correction
1	1	perched	sitting	1	1	0	1	0
2	1	a	the	1	1	0	1	0
3	1	for	at the	0	1	0	0	0
4	2	flown	field	1	1	1	1	0
5	2	that	the/ ✓	1	1	1	1	1
6	2	moment	minute	1	1	1	1	0
7	3	flew	flied	1	1	1	1	0
8	5	unable	able	0	1	1	1	0
9	5	felt	fell	0	0	1	0	0
10	6	struck	hit	1	1	0	1	0
11	6	gathered	gained	0	1	1	1	0
12	7	dropping	dripping	0	1	1	1	0
13	8	last	least	0	1	1	1	0
14	8	fill	full	1	1	1	1	0
15								
16								
17								
18								
19								
20								
21								
22								
23								
24								
25								
			Total	8	13	10	12	1
			Percentage	57	93	71	86	7

Section VI. Summary of Other Reading Behaviors

Other Miscues

Type		Number
Omissions	◯	4
Additions	∧	2
Dialect	∨	0
Reversals	∼	0

Other Observations

Type	Check	Type	Check
Posture		Disregard of punctuation	
Word-by-word reading	✓	Head movement	
Poor phrasing		Finger pointing	✓
Lack of expression	✓	Loss of place	
Pitch (too high) or low	✓	Nervousness	✓
Voice too soft or strained		Poor attitude	
Poor enunciation		Other _____	

Section VII. Interpretation and Recommendations

_____

_____

_____

FIGURE 16.4

Sample of Completed Profile/Examiner Record Form, Section V. Worksheet and Summary for GORT-4 Miscues

TABLE 16.1   Demographic Characteristics of the GORT-4 Normative Sample

Characteristics	Percentage of School-Age Sample	Percentage of School-Age Population[a]	Characteristics	Percentage of School-Age Sample	Percentage of School-Age Population[a]
Geographic Area			*Educational Attainment of Parents*		
Northeast	21	18	Less than Bachelor's degree	72	74
Midwest	24	24	Bachelor's degree	21	18
South	34	35	Master's, Professional, Doctoral degrees	7	8
West	22	23			
Gender			*Disability Status*		
Male	47	51	No Disability	92	89
Female	53	49	Learning Disability	2	5
Race			Speech-Language Disorder	<1	3
White	85	79	Attention-Deficit Disorder	2	<1
Black	12	16	Other Handicap	2	1
Other	3	5			
Residence			*Age*		
Urban	83	75	6(N = 87)	5	NA
Rural	17	25	7(N = 171)	10	NA
Ethnicity			8(N = 177)	11	NA
Native American	1	1	9(N = 189)	11	NA
Hispanic	12	13	10(N = 182)	11	NA
Asian	2	4	11(N = 158)	9	NA
African American	12	15	12(N = 120)	7	NA
European American	72	67	13(N = 93)	6	NA
Other	1	<1	14(N = 111)	7	NA
Family Income (in dollars)			15(N = 113)	7	NA
Under 15,000	17	14	16(N = 111)	7	NA
15,000-24,999	17	14	17(N = 93)	6	NA
25,000-34,999	18	14	18(N = 72)	4	NA
35,000-49,999	22	19			
50,000-74,999	18	20			
75,000 and over	9	19			

"content sampling reflects the degree of homogeneity among items within a test" (Wiederholt & Bryant, 2001, p. 60) and is estimated using the coefficient Alpha and alternate forms procedures.

Coefficient Alphas for Rate, Accuracy, Fluency, and Comprehension were computed at each age interval (6 though 18) using data from the entire normative sample. The coefficients for both Forms A and B of the subtests range from .87 to .98. Average coefficients across ages for all subtests exceed .90. Coefficient Alphas for the Oral Reading Quotient (ORQ) composite were derived using a formula provided by Guilford (1954, p. 393). All coefficients meet or exceed .94, with the average coefficient across ages being .96 and .97 for Forms A and B, respectively. Standard errors of measurement based on the Alphas are consistently small.

To investigate immediate alternate forms reliability for Rate, Accuracy, Fluency, and Comprehension Scores, scores on Forms A and B were correlated at 13 different age intervals using

the test performance of the normative sample. The raw score means and standard deviations for Form A and Form B and the correlations between the two forms at various ages are found in Table 16.2.

The authors report that the raw score means and standard deviations for Forms A and B are similar at every age interval. Correlation coefficients depicting the relationship between Form A and Form B exceed .80 for Rate, Accuracy, and Fluency. Coefficients are lower for Comprehension, ranging from .71 to .86 (median = .76). No immediate alternate forms reliability data are reported for the Oral Reading Quotient. The authors state that the data provide evidence that the GORT-4 scales have little content sampling error.

The GORT-4 authors report the findings of a test–retest study that was collected on a mixed sample of students. The sample was composed of 30 elementary school children attending school in Ohio, 10 middle school

TABLE 16.2   Alternate Forms Reliability of the GORT-4

Age	Rate			Accuracy			Fluency			Comprehension		
	Form A	Form B	r_{ab}	Form A	Form B	r_{ab}	Form A	Form B	r_{ab}	Form A	Form B	r_{ab}
6	11(8)	9(8)	.93	11(8)	10(9)	.91	22(16)	20(17)	.93	12(9)	10(8)	.76
7	16(9)	14(10)	.96	16(9)	14(9)	.91	32(18)	28(19)	.95	16(9)	14(10)	.77
8	22(8)	20(9)	.95	22(8)	21(10)	.88	43(16)	41(18)	.93	21(8)	20(11)	.71
9	27(8)	27(10)	.94	27(9)	26(9)	.90	54(16)	53(18)	.94	26(9)	26(11)	.75
10	31(7)	32(9)	.93	31(9)	31(10)	.90	62(15)	63(18)	.92	29(10)	30(13)	.75
11	33(8)	33(10)	.94	33(9)	33(10)	.89	65(15)	66(19)	.93	32(11)	35(12)	.77
12	36(9)	38(11)	.87	38(11)	39(12)	.82	74(17)	76(21)	.87	38(15)	41(14)	.85
13	39(10)	40(11)	.91	41(12)	41(12)	.88	80(20)	82(20)	.93	41(13)	43(12)	.73
14	45(14)	47(13)	.86	46(16)	47(14)	.89	92(27)	94(26)	.90	50(13)	47(12)	.86
15	50(14)	51(13)	.82	51(14)	51(13)	.81	102(26)	102(24)	.84	51(13)	47(13)	.80
16	50(18)	51(17)	.85	50(18)	51(17)	.85	103(36)	104(30)	.84	51(14)	47(14)	.73
17	50(21)	50(19)	.91	50(21)	50(20)	.91	102(40)	105(32)	.93	52(12)	49(15)	.83
18	54(18)	54(19)	.97	55(18)	55(19)	.97	110(33)	110(35)	.97	55(12)	50(13)	.76
M(SD)	34(17)	34(18)	.94	34(18)	34(18)	.94	68(34)	63(35)	.95	34(17)	33(18)	.85

students living in Tennessee, and 9 high school students attending various public high schools in Texas. The combined sample ranged in age from 6 through 18 years. Both forms of the test were administered twice to the sample, with an intervening time span of about two weeks.

Total scores for the sample were changed to Standard Scores and the Standard Scores were correlated. The authors report two test–retest correlations, one for Form A and another for Form B. The resulting coefficients were .95, .92, .93, .96, and .98, respectively, for Form A Rate, Accuracy, Fluency, Comprehension, and the Oral Reading Quotient. For Form B, coefficients for Rate, Accuracy, Fluency, Comprehension, and Oral Reading Quotient were .95, .92, .93, .96, and .98, respectively. Although the authors claim that these data demonstrate that the GORT-4 has acceptable test–retest reliability, reviewers of the GORT-4 (e.g., Rathvon, 2004) criticized the procedure used by the authors and recommended that the study be rerun and reported at each age in the normative sample (6–18) rather than combining all ages and reporting a single coefficient.

In another reliability analysis, Form A was given to a group of students, followed later (the time between administrations was not identified in the manual) by Form B administration. The authors report that the delayed alternate-form coefficients were .91 for Rate, .91 for Accuracy, .91 for Fluency, .78 for Comprehension, and .95 for Oral Reading Quotient. Wiederholt and Bryant (2001) claim that the magnitude of the coefficients further suggest that GORT-4 users can have confidence in the test scores' stability over time.

To examine interscorer error, two individuals scored a set of 30 tests that had been selected at random from the normative sample. The sample was composed of students ranging from 12 to 18. All scores were computed and derived, and Standard Scores of the scorings were correlated. Resulting coefficients ranged from .94 to .99, with the median coefficients across all scores (e.g., Rate, ORQ) for both forms being .99.

The authors conclude their section on reliability by noting that the data strongly suggests that the GORT-4 possesses little test error and that test users can have confidence in its results. Test reviewers by and large have agreed with the authors (e.g., Bradley-Johnson, 2004).

USE OF THE TEST

Interpretation Methods: A Case Study

To describe how the test can be used and how test scores can be interpreted, we provide a case study for Owen, who was introduced earlier in the discussion of performance on the GORT-4. By taking a closer look at Owen's scores, we can provide an analysis of how GORT-4 scores can be best used as part of a comprehensive reading assessment.

Owen is an outgoing 12-year-old who has struggled in reading for the past two years, according to his sixth-grade teacher. All previous testing has shown no emotional or social maladjustments, nor have any of his teachers previously reported any behavioral difficulties. Owen is popular with his peers, gets along with his teachers, and excels in mathematics. His teacher, Ms. Jenna Solomon, reports that Owen's mother is a teacher who helps Owen with his daily homework, and Owen's father is also an interested and involved parent. Owen has one older sister who is consistently on the honor roll. Owen's academic history shows no problems in developing early reading skills, but for the past two years, Owen has struggled reading content area material.

After informed consent was obtained from his parents, a diagnostic workup was conducted to identify possible explanations for Owen's current academic deficiencies. As part of his diagnostic workup, Owen was administered the *Wechsler Intelligence Scale for Children—Fourth Edition* (WISC-IV; Wechsler, 2003) and showed above-average intelligence. His Full Scale was 108. The school psychologist noted that Owen was cooperative and mannerly during testing and that he thoughtfully responded to scale items.

The psychologist decided to administer the GORT-4 because he wanted to assess Owen's oral reading skills and check for specific miscues that Owen might exhibit during oral reading. Because Owen is in the sixth grade, the examiner began testing with Story 5. Owen's Comprehension score of 4 (see Figure 16.3) resulted in the establishment of a basal for that score, but his fluency score of 3 did not establish a basal. Therefore, Owen read aloud Story 4, where he made 1 Deviation from Print in 33 seconds. He answered all five comprehension questions correctly. Because Owen reached a basal for Fluency with a score of 9, the examiner had him read Story 6. During the 130 seconds it took Owen to read the passage (resulting in a Rate Score of 1), he made 16 reading deviations, which translated to an Accuracy score of 1 point. Owen missed three of the five comprehension questions, meaning that he reached a ceiling on that score as well.

Reexamining Figure 16.2, we see a completed front cover of the Profile/Examiner Record Form, which depicts Owen's GORT-4 performance. As can be seen in Section I, Owen's date of birth is listed, along with the date of testing, which shows that his age at the time of testing was 12 years, 9 months. Additional information is provided concerning Owen's school, examiner (and his title), the person who referred Owen for testing (Ms. Solomon, Owen's teacher), and the reason Owen was referred for testing. Section II provides Owen's GORT-4 performance, which will be discussed in detail shortly. In Section III, we see that Owen was administered the WISC-IV and the *Stanford Achievement Test* (10th ed.) (SAT-10; Psychological Corporation), a group-administered achievement test administered to all students at Owen's school. Owen's SAT-10 Reading, Mathematics, and Social Science scores are recorded.

Turning to Section II in Figure 16.2, Owen is given full credit for all scores below the basal (Stories 1, 2, and 3) and no credit for scores above the ceiling (Story 6). Total Scores are summed for each column of data, and standard scores, percentiles, age equivalents, and grade equivalents are derived using the normative tables in the appendix of the test manual. Note how the standard scores for Fluency and Comprehension are added together to yield a sum of 10, which is transferred by following the arrow to the ellipse. This number is converted to a Percentile (2) and Oral Reading Quotient (70).

At the parent conference convened to discuss Owen's performance, Ms. Solomon thanks Owen's parents for being present and explains that Owen is a bright student who works hard and gets along with his classmates and all of the adults on staff. She also reminds Owen's parents that she referred Owen for testing because she was concerned that Owen was struggling reading the content area textbooks. Owen's mother and father acknowledge his struggles and explain what they have done at home to help Owen with his homework.

Ms. Solomon then introduces Dr. Reid, the school psychologist, who explains his role at the school and the tests that he administered to Owen. Dr. Reid presents the SAT-10 scores and discusses how the Reading and Social Science scores are much lower than Owen's Math score. Dr. Reid also explains that the reading scores may explain why Owen's Social Science score (85) is also low—the format of the test requires reading, which presents difficulties in answering the test questions. Ms. Solomon explains that Owen does very well in science and social studies and is able to answer all questions posed to him verbally, but when asked to respond to written questions he struggles selecting the right answer on a multiple-choice test or writing answers to open-ended questions.

Dr. Reid then introduces the GORT-4 as a popular oral reading test that assesses oral reading skills such as rate accuracy and reading comprehension. Dr. Reid discusses the test booklet with those present and discusses how he used the test to look at Owen's reading rate, the accuracy with which he reads words in continuous text, and Owen's ability to answer a variety of questions based on the passage that he read.

While discussing Owen's test scores, Dr. Reid points out that subtest Standard Scores between 8 and 12 are indicative of average performance. Owen's Standard Scores of 5 and 5 for Rate and Accuracy fall in the Poor range, showing that he struggles to read words and, as a result, reads slowly. Slow reading, Ms. Solomon explains, is a hardship when having to read large quantities of content area text, a reality that will create even greater demands for Owen in coming years.

Dr. Reid then points out that oral reading fluency is a combination of rate and accuracy, and that Owen's Fluency standard score of 3 reflects his low performance on the contributing subtests. Owen's Comprehension Standard Score of 7 also reflects Below-Average understanding of what he read. The combination of scores yields a Total Score, called the Oral Reading Quotient, of 70, which reflects poor performance.

As a teacher, Ms. Solomon understands that Owen's low reading score is unexpected, based on his average intellect. That is, Owen's WISC-III Full Scale Quotient of 108 is 38 points greater than his GORT-4 Oral Reading Quotient, connoting an aptitude–achievement discrepancy.

Next, Dr. Reid discusses the miscue analysis that was conducted based on Owen's oral reading substitution errors (see Figure 16.5). Because of the percentage of Meaning, Function, and Graphic/Phonemic Similarity miscues (all categories approaching or exceeding 50%), Dr Reid expresses his opinion that Owen is demonstrating strategic reading skills, in that he understands that reading should make semantic and syntactic sense, and he demonstrates an ability to make sound-symbol associations. He further posits that the existing aptitude–achievement discrepancy often indicates the presence of a learning disability (LD), but Dr. Reid is reluctant to offer such a diagnosis at this time because up until last year, Owen's test scores have always been average or above; and nothing in his educational or medical history would explain such a dramatic dropoff in achievement.

Owen's parents are told that, currently, LD is being diagnosed after intervention is conducted to see whether students respond to intensive intervention. After a lengthy discussion among Owen's parents, Ms. Solomon, and Dr. Reid, it is decided that Owen may benefit from one-on-one remedial assistance to help improve his reading problems. Ms. Solomon suggests that Owen can benefit from explicit instruction in syllable patterns and their applications in decoding multisyllabic words that are commonly found in content area textbooks. There is a staff member in place who specializes in reading interventions, particularly those geared to help students access content material; and she and Ms. Solomon have collaborated successfully in the past. Further, Ms. Solomon and Dr. Reid offer that Owen can also benefit from learning to use graphic organizers before, during, and after reading to activate prior knowledge of the topic being read, predict what will occur in the text, and check to see whether the prediction is accurate. Owen's mother asks that she and her husband be able to observe the instruction taking place so that they might be able to assist Owen as he applies his new learning to his homework. After the discussion, it is decided to place Owen in an intensive intervention program for six weeks and then to readminister the GORT-4 using the alternate form. Before the intervention, Owen will be administered the *Gray Diagnostic Reading Test—2* (Bryant et al., 2006) to identify specific strengths and weaknesses across reading and related areas. The group will then reconvene to discuss the results of Owen's intervention and any additional test results that are gathered.

Test Scores for Special Populations

The GORT has a long history of use in identifying students as having reading problems and as part of progress monitoring during reading disability interventions. To demonstrate that the test is technically sound and that examiners can use the test with confidence with students who have disabilities and with students

Section V. Worksheet for Recording GORT-4 Miscues

Categorized Miscues

Story Numbers: 5   6   _____   _____

Miscue No.	Line	Text Word	Deviations from Print	Meaning Similarity	Function Similarity	Graphic/Phonemic Similarity	Multiple Sources	Self-Correction
1	1	perched	sitting	1	1	0	1	0
2	1	a	the	1	1	0	1	0
3	1	for	at the	0	1	0	0	0
4	2	flown	field	1	1	1	1	0
5	2	that	the/?	1	1	1	1	1
6	2	moment	minute	1	1	1	1	0
7	3	flew	flied	1	1	1	1	0
8	5	unable	able	0	1	1	1	0
9	5	felt	fell	0	0	1	0	0
10	6	struck	hit	1	1	0	1	0
11	6	gathered	gained	0	1	1	1	0
12	7	dropping	dripping	0	1	1	1	0
13	8	last	least	0	1	1	1	0
14	8	fill	full	1	1	1	1	0
15	1	lot	loot	0	1	1	1	0
16	1	people	person	0	0	1	0	0
17	1	work	walk	0	0	1	0	0
18	2	several	some	1	1	1	1	0
19	2	cleaning	clean	1	0	1	1	0
20	3	weeds	trees	0	1	1	1	0
21	3	swings	wings	0	1	1	1	0
22	6	built	but	0	0	1	0	0
23	7	children	kids	1	1	1	1	0
24	7	everyone	everybody	1	1	1	1	0
25	8	neighborhood	neighbor/?	0	0	1	0	1
			Total	12	19	21	19	2
			Percentage	48	76	84	76	8

Section VI. Summary of Other Reading Behaviors

Other Miscues

Type	Number
Omissions	4
Additions	2
Dialect	0
Reversals	0

Other Observations

Type	Check	Type	Check
Posture		Disregard of punctuation	
Word-by-word reading	✓	Head movement	
Poor phrasing		Finger pointing	✓
Lack of expression	✓	Loss of place	
Pitch too high or low	✓	Nervousness	✓
Voice too soft or strained		Poor attitude	
Poor enunciation		Other_____	

Section VII. Interpretation and Recommendations

FIGURE 16.5

Sample of Owen's Completed Profile/Examiner Record Form, Section V. Worksheet and Summary for GORT-4 Miscues for Stories 5 and 6 of different backgrounds, Wiederholt and Bryant (2001) provide evidence that the GORT-4 yields consistent scores. They noted (p. 62),

One cannot always assume that because a test is reliable for a general population, it will be equally reliable for every subgroup within that population. Therefore, those persons who build tests should demonstrate that their tests are indeed reliable for subgroups, especially those subgroups that are likely to be tested or that might experience test bias because of ethnic, racial, disability, or linguistic differences.

As shown in Table 16.3, the GORT-4 is reliable for both males and females, students in different ethnic categories, and students with LD and attentional problems.

Evidence in the GORT-4 manual also demonstrates that the GORT-4 differentiates among students with varying reading abilities. As would be expected, students with LD scored lower than typical students, and students who are gifted scored higher than typical students.

Interventions Based on Test Results

Wiederholt and Bryant (2001, p. 47) note in their manual that:

In this manual, we do not provide a comprehensive overview of reading programs and interventions. Most professionals who administer the GORT-4 will be familiar with the reading programs and interventions used in their schools or clinics. However, those individuals who are unfamiliar with reading programs or interventions can learn about them by reading books on the topic, attending workshops, or enrolling in courses on reading. Reading organizations . . . keep professionals abreast of new and rapid developments in reading instruction.

The GORT has been used extensively in research to help identify reading interventions that may be helpful in ameliorating reading

TABLE 16.3   Internal Consistency Reliability of the GORT-4 for Various Subgroups in the Normative Sample

GORT-4 Score	Male	Female	European American	African American	Hispanic American	Asian American	Learning Disability	Attention-Deficit/ Hyperactivity Disorder
Form A								
Rate	94	94	94	94	94	95	92	93
Accuracy	94	94	94	94	94	95	90	93
Fluency	95	95	95	95	95	95	92	94
Comprehension	98	98	98	98	98	98	98	98
Oral Reading Quotient	98	98	98	98	98	98	96	97
Form B								
Rate	94	95	94	94	95	96	94	93
Accuracy	94	94	94	94	94	94	93	94
Fluency	98	98	98	98	98	98	98	98
Comprehension	98	98	98	98	98	98	98	98
Oral Reading Quotient	99	99	99	99	99	99	99	99

The header row spans: Male, Female, European American, African American, Hispanic American, Asian American, Learning Disability, Attention-Deficit/Hyperactivity Disorder are all under the **Subgroup** heading.

problems at the elementary and secondary levels. The GORT has been used to determine a student's reading speed, accuracy, and fluency; researchers have included the comprehension component of GORT to determine the efficacy of their reading program. In this section, we overview several research studies that have been conducted using the GORT-3 and GORT-4 as pre-/post-measures to determine the programs' effectiveness.

Elementary

Vaughn, Chard, Bryant, Coleman, Tyler, Linan-Thompson, and Kouzekanani (2000) used the GORT-3 and the *Testing of Reading Fluency* (TORF; Children's Educational Services, 1987) to evaluate the differential effects of two fluency and comprehension instructional programs: partner reading (PR) instruction, which is designed to enhance fluency; and collaborative strategic reading (CSR) instruction, which is focused on fostering comprehension of text. One hundred and eleven students with reading problems from eight classrooms were given the GORT-3 and TORF during pre- and post-testing. A repeated measures analysis of variance (ANOVA) was conducted to compare the performance in CSR and PR groups on Rate, Accuracy, and Comprehension, as measured by the GORT-3, and the number of words read correctly per minute on the TORF. No significant group or *group-by-time* effect was found for all the measures, which indicated that students either did not perform differently with respect to different treatment, or students in different groups did not perform differently at different rates over time. However, the Time effect was statistically significant for Rate, which indicated that both interventions had positive effects on students' reading rate performance over time.

Torgesen, Alexander, Wagner, Rashotte, Voeller, and Conway (2001) also used the GORT-3, along with the *Comprehensive Test of Phonological Processes* (CTOPP; Wagner, Torgesen, & Rashotte, 1999), the *Lindamood Auditory Conceptualization Test* (LAC; Lindamood & Lindamood, 1998), the *Woodcock Reading Mastery Tests—Revised* (WRMT-R; Woodcock, 1987), the *Test of Word Reading Efficiency* (TOWRE; Torgeson et al., 1999), the *Kaufman Test of Educational Achievement* (Kaufman & Kaufman, 1985), the *Woodcock-Johnson Psychoeducational Battery—Revised* (Woodcock, & Johnson, 1989), and the *Clinical Evaluation of Language Fundamentals—Third Edition* (Semel, Wiig, & Secord, 1995), as pre-, post-, and follow-up measures to evaluate the different effects of the two intervention programs: *Auditory Discrimination in Depth Program* (ADD; Lindamood & Lindamood, 1984) and an *Embedded Phonics* (EP) program.

Fifty children with severe reading disabilities that were randomly assigned into two conditions received the pre-, post-, and follow-up measures. The pre- versus post-test effects were examined using a repeated measures analysis of variance (2 × 2 ANOVA). The Rate, Accuracy, and Comprehension scores of the GORT-3, 5 scores from other reading measures, and 12 scores from nonreading measures were reported. The results showed that students in both conditions improved significantly from pretest to post-test for all the reading measures. The effect for treatment showed that the rates of growth from pre- to post-test were significantly different between the two treatment groups in the Word Attack scores, and the Rate and Accuracy scores of GORT-3. The time and treatment interaction showed that children in the ADD condition progressed more than those in the EP condition, even though there was no significant difference in growth rates on GORT-3 Comprehension scores. A 2 × 3 ANOVA was carried out to examine the growth during the follow-up period. The results showed that students in both groups did not keep pace with normal growth on the Word Attack test. Students had significant growth in phonemic decoding, sight word vocabulary, word identification, sight word efficiency, and passage comprehension during the follow-up period; however, no significant growth was found on the GORT-3 Accuracy, Rate, and Comprehension measures. No significant time × treatment nor treatment effects were found during the follow-up period.

In another study, Rashotte, MacPhee, and Torgesen (2001) evaluated the effects of a phonologically based reading program, *Spell Read PAT Program* (Macphee, 1990a), that focused on auditory processing on 115 struggling readers from first through sixth grade. Students were paired by matching phonetic decoding and word-level reading skills at each grade level. Students in each pair then were randomly assigned into Group 1 or Group 2. Students in Group 1 received the first wave, 8-week intervention daily, while Group 2 students acted as no-treatment controls. Following the completion of the first 8-week intervention given to Group 1 students, the same intervention was provided to students in Group 2 for seven weeks, while students in Group 1 received no further intervention. The GORT-3, CTOPP (Wagner et al., 1999), *Woodcock Diagnostic Reading Battery* (WDRB; Woodcock, 1998a), TOWRE (Torgeson et al., 1999), *Spell Read* test battery (MacPhee, 1990b), *Schonell Spelling Tests* (Schonell & Schonell, 1982), and the Vocabulary subtest of the *Stanford-Binet Intelligence Scale—Fourth Edition* (SB4; Thorndike, Hagen, & Sattler, 1986) were used as pre- and post-test batteries. Three waves of testing were given: (1) pretest for all students before intervention began; (2) post-test-1 for all students upon completion of the first wave of intervention for students in Group 1; and (3) post-test-2 for all students following the completion of the second wave of intervention for students in Group 2.

GORT-3 Rate, Accuracy, and Comprehension scores, along with 10 other scores from pre- and post-tests were reported. A series of analyses of covariance (ANCOVA) were conducted to compare the treatment-versus-control effects during the first wave of intervention (pretest to post-test-1), the second wave of intervention (pretest to post-test-2), and a 2-month follow-up for Group 1 students (post-test-1 to post-test-2).

The post-test-1 comparison between the intervention (Group 1) and control (Group 2) group with pretest scores as covariates showed that students in Group 1 had more significant growth than those in Group 2 on all measures except the Word Efficiency measure. No significant effects for grade or group × grade interactions were found. Level of reading deficiency, based on students' pretest phonetic decoding scores, was then added to the ANCOVA analyses as an additional between-subject factor within group. The results showed no significant group × deficiency level of interaction effects for any of the measures. The post-test-2 comparison between the intervention (Group 2) and control group (Group 1) showed no significant difference between the treatment and control group. No significant grade nor grade × grade interactions were found except for grade effects for GORT-3 Rate and the TOWRE Phonetic Decoding Efficiency subtests. A group × grade effect on the WDRB comprehension subtest was noted.

A repeated measures analysis of variance (ANOVA) was used to determine whether the effects of the Spell Read PAT Program for Group 1 students maintained after two months of intervention. The results showed no significant decline for all measures. In addition, significant growth was found for all the phonological measures, and for all the reading measures except the GORT-3 measures and the TOWRE Phonetic Decoding Efficiency. Grade effects and time × grade interaction effects were found only for GORT-3 Comprehension. When deficiency level was added as the between-subject factor, the repeated measures ANOVA showed significant interaction for the CTOPP Elision subtest only.

Denton, Fletcher, Anthony, and Francis (2006) also used the GORT-4 and the TOWRE (Torgeson et al., 1999) plus the *Woodcock-Johnson Tests of Achievement—Third Edition* (WJ-III; Woodcock, McGrew, & Mather, 2001) to examine the effects of an intensive reading intervention on 27 students (5 in grade 1, 11 in grade 2, and 11 in grade 2) with persistent reading difficulties. All students received 8 weeks of the *Phono-Graphix program* (McGuiness et al., 1996), which focused on decoding strategies, and 8 weeks of the *Read Naturally program* (Ihnot, Mastoff, Gavin, & Hendrickson, 2001), which is designed to enhance oral reading fluency.

The Fluency and Comprehension scores of GORT-4 and 8 other scores were reported and a repeated ANOVA was carried out at each 8-week phase to evaluate the separate effects for each intervention. Analyses across all 16 weeks were also carried to examine the specific effects of both interventions as a package. The results of the analyses that focused on the effects of *Phono-Graphix* intervention indicated that students significantly improved in their decoding and spelling abilities as well as their reading fluency and comprehension performance on all measures. The results of the effects on *Read Naturally* demonstrated significant improvement on all measures except for the GORT-4 Comprehension. The effects of the two interventions as a package also showed significant changes from pretest to post-test on all measures.

Kuhn, Schwanenflugel, Morris, Morrow, Woo, Meisinger, Sevcik, Bradley, and Stahl (2006) used the GORT-4, the TOWRE (Torgesen, Wagner, & Rashotte, 1999), and the *Wechsler Individual Achievement Test* (WIAT; Wechsler, 1992) to compare the effects of two instructional approaches on second graders' reading fluency: fluency-oriented reading instruction (FORI), and wide-reading approach. Twenty-four second-grade classrooms from eight schools in New Jersey and Georgia, with a total of 349 students, were given the GORT-4 and TOWRE during pretest (fall), midyear test (winter), and post-test (spring). The GORT-4 fluency scores, TOWRE Sight Word Efficiency scores, and the WIAT Reading Comprehension scores were reported. The results of the analyses showed that both interventions had long- and short-term effects on the sight word reading as measured by the TOWRE. Only the wide-reading intervention showed short- and long-term effects on Fluency as measured by the GORT-4. The benefits of long-term use of the two interventions on reading comprehension

were examined by evaluating the spring reading comprehension scores of the WIAT Reading Comprehension subtest. The results showed significant improvements in students' reading comprehension scores for both interventions.

Other researchers reported on the GORT-4's Oral Reading Quotient, which is a composite score based on performance on Comprehension and Fluency. For example, Blachman, Schatschneider, Fletcher, Clonan, Shaywitz, and Shaywitz (2004) evaluated the effects of an explicit and intensive reading intervention for second- and third-graders who have poor word-level reading skills. Two cohorts of 69 students were assigned to a treatment or control group based on random assignment. Students in the treatment received an intervention focusing on understanding the phonologic and orthographic connections, and text-based reading. The GORT-3, WRMT-R (Woodcock, 1987), WJ-III (Woodcock et al., 2001), and *Wide Range Achievement Test—3* (WRAT3; Wilkinson, 1993) were used as pre- and post-test measures to evaluate the effects of the treatment and the maintenance at a one-year follow-up. The GORT-3 Oral Reading Quotient, WRMT Basic Skills Cluster, and WRAT Spelling scores were reported. An analysis of covariance (ANCOVA) was conducted to examine the treatment effects. The results showed significant differences between the treatment group and the control group at post-test on all measures, while the post-test means were covaried by each measure's respective pretest score. The results of the follow-up analysis also showed significant difference between control and treatment groups on all measures except for the Accuracy and Comprehension of the GORT-3.

The differential treatment effects based on initial student ability levels in each group were also estimated. Students in both groups were divided into two ability groups: a higher- and a lower-skilled group. A series of 2×2 ANCOVAs were conducted to examine the treatment and initial skill interaction on all measures. The results showed that students in the higher initial skill treatment group significantly outperformed those in the higher initial skill control group on the WRMT-R Basic Skills Cluster and WRAT3 Spelling at pretest and at the end of the follow-up year but not on the GORT-3 Oral Reading Quotient. A similar pattern was also observed between the lower initial skill control and treatment groups. The results of the analyses showed that there were significant differences between students in the lower initial skill treatment group and those in the lower initial skill control group on the WRMT-R Basic Skills Cluster, WRAT3 Spelling, and GORT-3 Oral Reading Quotient in favor of the lower initial skill students in the treatment group at pretest and at the end of the follow-up year.

Burns, Senesac, and Symington (2004) evaluated the *Helping One Student to Succeed* (HOSTS, 1998) program on 129 students from six elementary schools in Michigan using the GORT-4, the *Test of Early Reading Abilities—Second Edition* (TERA-2; Reid, Hresko, & Hammill, 1989), and the *Dynamic Indicators of Basic Early Literacy Skills* (DIBELS; Kaminski & Good, 1998). The HOSTS program is a structured and comprehensive literacy program. Students who were identified as at risk for reading failure received this supplemental instruction by volunteer tutors. Elementary schools in Michigan that participated in the HOSTS program were randomly selected as the experimental group. The control group included four schools not participating in the HOSTS program. Control schools were matched to schools in the experimental group. GORT-4 Fluency and Oral Reading Quotient, TERA-2 Reading Quotient, and DIBELS scores from pre- and post-test were reported. An analysis of covariance (ANCOVA) was used to evaluate the effects of the 5-month treatment. The results showed significant difference for the DIBELS Fluency measure, GORT- 4 and TERA-2 Quotients, and GORT-4 Comprehension in favor of students in the HOSTS program but no significant difference was found for the GORT-4 Fluency measure.

O'Connor, White, and Swanson (2007) evaluated different effects of two reading fluency interventions on 37 struggling readers who were either in second or fourth grade. Students from eight classes were placed in groups of 3 based on their Fluency scores on the GORT-4. Students in each group then were randomly assigned into three conditions: repeated reading (RR), continuous reading (CR), or control. In both treatment conditions, each student was provided with opportunities to read aloud to a trained adult listener for a total of 15 minutes a day, three days a week, for 14 weeks. Students in RR condition repeatedly read each predetermined passage three times for 15 minutes, whereas students in CR read aloud pages from the same book for 15 minutes but without repeating passages. In the control condition, students received existing interventions or services from each class. The reading materials were selected based on students' instructional reading level.

The GORT-4, the *Peabody Picture Vocabulary Test—Third Edition* (TTPT-III; Dunn & Dunn, 1997), and the *Woodcock Reading Mastery Tests—Normative Update* (WRMT-NU; Woodcock, 1998b) were used as pretests, midway tests, and post-tests to assess student performance in reading rate, word identification, and passage reading comprehension. The GORT-4 Fluency, Comprehension, and Oral Reading Quotient, along with six other reading scores, were reported. A hierarchical linear modeling with repeated measures was used to determine the different effects across conditions. The results showed that students in the two treatment conditions had significantly faster growth rates in reading fluency as measured by GORT-4 and ARI than those of students in the control condition. Students in the treatment conditions also had significantly faster growth rate in word identification and passage comprehension; however, students across conditions performed similarly in vocabulary growth. There were no significant differences between RR and CR conditions across all measures. Additional analyses were conducted to evaluate the effects of treatment by grade level. No significant interaction effect was found, which indicated that students in grades 2 and 4 had similar growth rates.

Secondary

In addition to reporting separate scores for Rate and Accuracy, some researchers chose to combine the two scores and report the Fluency score as an additional indicator. For example, in their study, Shippen, Houchins, and Sartor (2005) used the GORT-4 and two subtests of the TOWRE (Torgeson et al., 1999) to examine the effects of two direct instruction reading programs on 55 seventh-graders. Treatments used in this study included: *Corrective Reading Decoding B2* (Engelmann, Johnson, Carnine, Meyer, Becker, & Eisele, 1999), which focuses on basic word-attack skills, including letter-sound correspondences, digraphs, and blends; *Corrective Reading Decoding C* (Engelmann, Meyer, Johnson, & Carnine, 1998), which emphasizes decoding more sophisticated, multisyllabic words; and *Reading Excellence: Word Attack and Rate Development Strategies* (REWARDS; Archer, Gleason, & Vachon, 2000), which teaches an explicit decoding strategy that is faded during the final eight lessons. Among the 55 students, 29 were placed in *Corrective Reading Decoding B2* level and 26 students were in *Corrective Reading Decoding C* level, based on the *Corrective Reading Decoding* (Engelmann, Johnson, Meyer, Becker, & Eisele, 1999) placement test. Students in each level then were randomly assigned into Corrective Reading Decoding group or REWARDS group. Students in each treatment group received a 55-minute daily lesson for 30 instructional sessions.

The GORT-4 and two subtests of the TOWRE (Torgesen et al., 1999) were used as pre- and post-test measures to evaluate student progress. The authors reported the GORT-4 Rate, Accuracy, and Fluency scores, along with the TOWRE Word Reading Efficiency scores. A repeated measures multivariate analysis of variance (MANOVA) was used to investigate the effects of both treatments. The results, which

showed a significant main effect for time, indicated that students, regardless of which type of intervention they received, made significant gain from pretest to post-test on all measures. No significant interaction effect was found for time × level or time × treatment group.

Shippen, Houchins, Calhoon, Furlow, and Sartor (2006) evaluated the effects of two theoretically different comprehensive school reform models for urban middle school students with disabilities using the GORT-4 and the WRMT-R (Woodcock, 1998b). The school that adopted the *Success for All* model (SFA; Slavin, Madden, Karweit, Dolan, Wasik, & Ross, 1996) followed a constructivist approach to design the instructional program. The school that implemented Direct Instruction (DI) used explicit instruction that emphasized fast-paced, scripted, well-sequenced, rule-based lessons. The participants in this study were 44 urban middle school students with mild disabilities. Twenty-one students were in the school that employed the SFA model, whereas 23 students were receiving instruction using the DI model. The GORT-4 and the WRMT-R (Woodcock, 1998b) were given as pre- and post-test measures at the beginning of the second semester of the school year and during the last month of the same school term, respectively. Biweekly curriculum-based measures were also given during the study to monitor student progress. The GORT-4 Oral Reading Quotient, WRMT-R Basic Skills Cluster, and WRMT-R Total Reading Short Scale were reported. A repeated measures multivariate analysis of variance (MANOVA) was used to investigate the different effects of the models. No significant main effects for time, treatment, or interaction between time and treatment were found. The results suggested that urban middle school students with disabilities made little or no progress in their reading abilities using either school reform model.

In summary, the GORT has been used extensively to help demonstrate the effectiveness, or ineffectiveness, of reading programs used with elementary- and secondary-level struggling students. Such studies provide evidence that the GORT-4 can be used with confidence to examine the effects of classroom- or clinic-based remedial interventions for students with a variety of reading-based conditions.

VALIDITY

A test is presumed to be valid if the authors demonstrate empirically that the test measures what it is supposed to measure. Obviously, a reading test must assess meaningful components of reading. The National Reading Panel (National Institute of Child Health and Human Development, 2000) designated five core areas of reading: Phonemic Awareness, Phonics (Word Study/Recognition), Fluency, Vocabulary, and Comprehension. The GORT-4 assesses three of the five core areas. The GORT-4 Accuracy score assesses word recognition skills, Fluency assesses oral reading fluency (a combination of Rate and Accuracy), and Comprehension provides a measure of passage comprehension. In the remainder of this section, we describe information that the GORT-4 authors present in the Examiner's Manual in their discussion of validity. We also present reviewers' comments that support the validity of the GORT-4 scores. (*Note:* The Interventions Based on Test Results section on the use of the GORT-3 and GORT-4 in intervention studies provides additional evidence of the validity of the GORT-4 scores.)

The GORT-4 manual provides evidence of what Anastasi and Urbina (1997) call content description, criterion prediction, and construct identification validity. For content description validation, the authors provide rationales underlying the GORT-4's story format and content (which we presented earlier in this chapter), results of conventional item analyses, and results of differential item functioning analysis that are used to show the absence of bias in tests.

To examine the test's item characteristics, the authors undertook an item analysis using the entire GORT-4 normative sample. The resulting item discrimination coefficients reported in the manual's tables "for the most part, provide evidence of content validity" (Wiederholt & Bryant, 2001, p. 80).

The authors also followed the suggestion of Camilli and Shepard (1994), who recommend that test developers perform statistical tests for item bias. The authors employed Swaminathan and Rogers's (1990) logistic regression procedure, which was developed to detect Differential Item Functioning (DIF), to examine items bias for the Comprehension items. No examination for bias was made for Rate, Accuracy, or Fluency.

This procedure compares the adequacy of two different logistic regression models to account for ability being measured. The first model used ability (i.e., subtest score) alone to predict item performance (restricted model), whereas the second model used ability and group membership to predict item performance (full model). The strategy used in this technique is to compare the full model with the restricted model to determine whether the full model provides a significantly better solution. If the full model does not provide a significantly better solution than the restricted model, then the differences between groups on the item are best explained by ability alone. In other words, if the full model is not significantly better at predicting item performance than the restricted model, then the item is measuring differences in ability and does not appear to be influenced by group membership (i.e., the item is not biased). Stated another way, if the full model is significantly better at predicting item performance than the restricted model, then the item is said to exhibit uniform DIF. Uniform DIF occurs when one group consistently performs better on the item than the other group, at all levels of ability (Wiederholt & Bryant, 2001, pp. 80–81).

Using the GORT-4 normative sample as subjects, the logistic regression procedure was applied to all 140 Comprehension items for Forms A and B for four dichotomous group comparisons: male/female, African American/ Non–African American, European American/ Non–European American, and Hispanic

American/Non–Hispanic American. Only 9 of 560 comparisons were found to be statistically significant ($p < .001$), and none of the 9 statistically significant comparisons had moderate or large effect sizes (Jodoin & Gierl, 2000). The authors concluded that the comprehension items were nonbiased in regard to gender, race, and ethnicity.

To examine criterion-prediction validity, the authors reported analyses conducted using earlier versions of the GORT (i.e., the GORT-R and the GORT-3) and also included the results of more recent GORT-4 studies. The authors state that the use of these earlier studies is acceptable because the administration instructions, response format, and items of the GORT-4 were the same as those of the GORT–R and GORT-3 "with two exceptions, story order and the addition of new first stories on each form" (p. 84).

The GORT scores were correlated with scores from two other tests of reading in what the authors called the "GORT family": the *Gray Diagnostic Reading Tests—Second Edition* (GDRT-2; Bryant, Wiederholt, & Bryant, 2006) and the *Gray Silent Reading Tests* (GSRT; Wiederholt & Blalock, 2000). In addition, GORT scores were correlated with other tests of reading (i.e., WRMT-R—Word Attack; *Wide Range Achievement Test—Revised*—Reading) (Wilkinson, 1993). In all of the studies, GORT Form A Standard Scores were used in the analyses. Results reported in the manual provide evidence of the GORT's validity. Specifically, Wiederholt and Bryant (2001) reported that the median coefficients for Rate, Accuracy, and Fluency, are "High" using MacEachron's (1982) criteria for evaluating the magnitude of correlation coefficients. Correlation coefficients between the criterion measures and the GORT Comprehension subtest were in the "Moderate" range. The size of the coefficients is what would be expected to support the criterion-prediction validity of the GORT-4.

Anastasi and Urbina (1997) note: "The construct-identification validity of a test is the extent to which the test may be said to measure a theoretical construct or trait" (p. 126). The authors follow Linn and Gronlund's (1995) three-step procedure for demonstrating this kind of validity.

First, several constructs presumed to account for test performance are identified. Second, hypotheses are generated that are based on the identified constructs. Third, the hypotheses are verified by logical or empirical methods. Nine basic constructs thought to underlie the GORT-4 and nine related testable questions are discussed in the remainder of this chapter (Wiederholt & Bryant, 2001, p. 86).

Using the procedure, Wiederholt and Bryant (2001) hypothesized that the GORT-4 scores (1) should be strongly correlated to chronological age, (2) should correlate significantly with each other, (3) should correlate significantly with spoken language abilities, (4) should correlate with tests that measure expressive written language, (5) should correlate with measures of intelligence or aptitude, (6) should correlate with measures of rapid automatized naming (RAN), (7) should differentiate between groups of people known to be average and those known to be low average or below average in reading ability, (8) should improve over time as a result of reading instruction, and (9) should possess items that are highly correlated with the total score of the subtest they form.

To examine the GORT relation to age, the authors demonstrated that the raw score means and standard deviations for the GORT subtests at 13 age intervals become larger as the subjects grow older. In addition, coefficients demonstrating the relationship of age to performance on the GORT-4 subtests were calculated to be .74 for Rate, .73 for Accuracy, .66 for Fluency, and .74 for Comprehension. All coefficients are high enough to support the test's construct-identification validity.

The GORT-4's subtests should be significantly intercorrelated if they measure some aspects of oral reading ability. A correlation matrix in the test manual demonstrates that inter-correlations are statistically significant ($p < .01$) and range from "Moderate" to "Very High," providing what the authors call "convincing evidence for the GORT-4's construct-identification validity" (p. 87).

When they examine the relationship between the GORT and measures of spoken language, Wiederholt and Bryant (2001) first present correlations depicting the relationship between reading and spoken language that are reported in a number of spoken-language test manuals ranging from .36 to .81, averaging about .51. They also cite findings from *Correlates of Reading: The Consensus of Thirty Years of Correlational Research* (Hammill & McNutt, 1981) that found the average correlation between reading and spoken language to be .51.

The authors then cite studies by Cornwall (1992) and Catts (1993), who investigated the GORT-R's relationship to spoken language. These researchers reported median coefficients of .49 for Fluency and .57 for Comprehension, which the GORT authors state "are well within the moderate range and provide clear evidence of the GORT-4's construct-identification validity" (p. 88).

Wiederholt and Bryant (2001) report the results of four studies that investigated the GORT's relationship to written language. The first three studies were conducted by the authors using the GORT-3. The fourth study was conducted by Cornwall (1992). The median coefficient between the GORT's ORQ and writing measures of .59 is offered as further evidence for the GORT-4's construct-identification validity.

In providing evidence of the relationship between aptitude/intelligence and the GORT, the authors first cite evidence (i.e., correlational data among reading and intelligence tests) depicting the relationship between reading and verbal, nonverbal, and general intelligence to be .65, .41, and .61, respectively. The authors then provided correlational data between the GORT-R, GORT-3, and GORT-4 and four tests of intelligence using separate samples of children. Five median coefficients in the manual's tables range from "Moderate" to "High" and are consistent with what would be expected based on the typical correlation coefficients between reading and intellect. Again, the authors report that "these findings provide convincing evidence of the GORT-4's construct-identification validity" (p. 92).

The relationship of RAN and reading has been studied by many researchers, (e.g., Manis, Doi, & Bhadah, 2000; Manis, Seidenberg, & Doi, 1999; Meyer, Wood, Hart, & Felton, 1998; Scarborough, 1998; Wagner, Torgesen, & Rashotte, 1999). When combined, the median coefficient from these researchers' studies was found to be .41, depicting a low-moderate relationship between reading and RAN.

Three studies (Catts, 1993; Cornwall, 1992; Wagner et al., 1999) are reported in the GORT manual that investigate the relationship between the GORT and RAN. The median coefficients for GORT-4 Fluency are reported as .49 and for Comprehension as .48, which are slightly higher than the .41 reported above. No data were reported for the Total Score of the GORT, the ORQ. Although the authors can cite those data as providing evidence of the GORT's construct-identification for two GORT subscales, the same cannot be said for the test's Total Score.

Wiederholt and Bryant (2001) make the logical argument that students diagnosed as having specific learning disabilities in reading should do more poorly on the GORT than typical readers. They also argue that members of minority groups should score near members of majority groups because they paid special attention to controlling for test bias during the item-selection process. They then report data on three typical subgroups (males, females, European Americans), two "minority" subgroups (African Americans, Hispanic Americans), and three "disability" subgroups (learning disability, serious emotional disturbance, and attention-deficit/ hyperactivity disorder). They also provide data on gifted children.

For the typical and minority groups, all score in the average range (8–12 on the GORT subtests and 90–110 for the ORQ). The authors then cite three studies using the GORT that showed group differentiation. Two studies, one conducted by Ackerman, Dykman, Oglesby, and Newton (1995) and the other by Branch, Cohen, and Hynd (1995), compared two groups of students who had LD in reading. In both cases, significant differences in favor of typical readers were found between the groups.

To document GORT changes over time based on reading interventions, Wiederholt and Bryant (2001) cite studies by independent researchers (Burns & Kondrick, 1998; Dryer, Beale, & Lambert, 1999; Torgesen et al., 2001). All of the studies provide support of the GORT's ability to detect treatment-induced changes in reading performance over time and provide additional evidence of the GORT-4's construct-identification validity.

Finally, the authors cite Guilford and Fruchter (1978) and hypothesize that evidence of a test's content-descriptive and construct-identification validity can be found by correlating item performance with the Total Score to which it contributes. The authors note that the magnitude of the coefficients provided in the content-descriptive section of their manual provides evidence of the GORT construct-identification validity.

In summary, Wiederholt and Bryant (2001) provide convincing evidence in support that the GORT-4 scores have validity. Several GORT reviewers, including Pierangelo and Guiliana (2006), agree, claiming, for example, that the validity is extensive and includes studies that illustrate that the GORT-4 can be used with confidence to measure change in oral reading over time (p. 128).

RELATIONSHIPS BETWEEN TEST SCORES AND STATE CURRICULUM

There is no "national reading curriculum" per se, but most states include Word Recognition, Fluency, and Comprehension in their early grade (e.g., Kindergarten through 5) reading standards. Many states have adjusted their standards to include the five areas of reading (i.e., Phonemic Awareness, Phonics [and word study], Fluency, Vocabulary, and Comprehension) recommended by the National Reading Panel (National Institute of Child Health and Human Development, 2000) and that form the foundation of Reading First interventions across the United States. As discussed in the "Validity" section of this chapter, the GORT-4 measures three of the five reading areas.

SUMMARY

The GORT-4 has a long and distinguished history in reading assessment. Originally devised by William S. Gray in the early 1900s, oral reading passages allowed examiners to compare reading performance to the students' peers represented by a standardization sample, and also provided an informal analysis of types of errors that students made while reading aloud. Various iterations of Gray's work appeared until the *Gray Oral Reading Tests* were published in 1963. Wiederholt and Bryant revised the GORT in 1986 and continued to revise the test until 2001, when they published their fourth edition of the GORT.

The GORT-4 remains a popular test of oral reading to this day. The authors of the GORT-4, in their previous revisions, relied heavily on test reviewers and test users to identify ways to improve the GORT, and each edition has been an improvement on previous editions (Rathvon, 2004). In this chapter, we provided a historical overview of the GORT that provides the rationale underlying the test, a description of the GORT-4, a discussion of how the test is administered and scored, and a description of the test's psychometric properties. We also provided a case study showing how the test can be used to identify struggling readers and help teachers examine student performance for intervention clues.

REFERENCES

Ackerman, P. T., Dykman, R. A., Oglesby, M., & Newton, J. E. O. (1995). EEG power spectra of dysphonetic and non-dysphonetic poor readers. *Brain and Language*, *49*, 140–152.

Adams, M. J. (1990). *Beginning to read: Thinking and learning about print*. Cambridge, MA: MIT.

American Psychological Association (1985). *Standards for educational and psychological testing*. Washington, DC: Author.

Anastasi, A., & Urbina, S. (1997). *Psychological testing* (7th ed.). Upper Saddle River, NJ: Prentice-Hall.

Archer, A. L., Gleason, M. M., & Vachon, V. (2000). *REWARDS: Reading excellence: Word attack and rate development strategies*. Longmont, CO: Sopris West.

Blachman, B. A., Schatschneider, C., Fletcher, J. M., Clonan, S. M., Shaywitz, B. A., & Shaywitz, S. E. (2004). Effects of intensive reading remediation for second and third graders and a 1-year follow-up. *Journal of Educational Psychology*, *96*(3), 444–461.

Bradley-Johnson, S. (2004). Gray Oral Reading Tests—Fourth Edition: A test review. Unpublished manuscript, Central Michigan University.

Branch, W., Cohen, M.J., & Hynd, G.W. (1995). Academic achievement and ADHD in children with left or right hemisphere dysfunction. *Journal of Learning Disabilities*, *28*(1), 35–43.

Bryant, B. R., Bryant, D. P., & Kethley, C. (Winter, 2004). Reading assessment: Introduction to the special series. *Assessment for Effective Intervention*, *29*, 3–12.

Bryant, B. R., Wiederholt, J. L., & Bryant, D. (2006). *Gray Diagnostic Reading Tests—Second Edition*. Austin, TX: Pro-Ed.

Burns, G. L., & Kondrick, P. A. (1998). Psychological behaviorism's reading therapy program: Parents as reading therapists for their children's reading disability. *Journal of Learning Disabilities*, *31*(3), 278–285.

Burns, M. K., Senesac, T. V., & Symington, T. (2004). The effectiveness of the HOSTS program in improving the reading achievement of children at-risk for reading failure. *Reading Research and Instruction*, *43*(2), 87–104.

Camilli, G., & Shepard, L. (1994). *Methods for identifying biased test items*. Thousand Oaks, CA: Sage.

Catts, H. (1993). The relationship between speech–language impairments and reading disabilities. *Journal of Speech and Hearing Research*, *36*, 948–958.

Children's Educational Services. (1987). *Testing of reading fluency*. Minneapolis: Author.

Cohen, A. S. (1974–1975). Oral reading errors of first-grade children taught by a code emphasis approach. *Reading Research Quarterly*, *10*(4), 616–650.

Cornwall, A. (1992). The relationship of phonological awareness, rapid naming, and verbal memory to severe reading and spelling disability. *Journal of Learning Disabilities*, *25*(8), 532–538.

Crumpton, N. L. (2003). Gray Oral Reading Tests—Fourth Edition. In B. S. Plake, J. C. Impara, & R. A. Spies (Eds.), *Fifteenth annual mental measurements yearbook* (pp. 417–419). Lincoln, NE: University of Nebraska Press.

Denton, A. C., Fletcher, J. M., Anthony, J. L., & Francis, D. J. (2006). An evaluation of intensive intervention for students with persistent reading difficulties. *Journal of Learning Disabilities*, *39*(5), 447–466.

Dryer, R., Beale, I. L., & Lambert, A. J. (1999). The balance model of dyslexia and remedial training: An evaluative study. *Journal of Learning Disabilities*, *32*(2), 174–186.

Dunn, L. M., & Dunn, D. M. (1997). *The Peabody Picture Vocabulary Test—Third Edition*. Circle Pines, MN: American Guidance Services.

Engelmann, S., Johnson, G., & Carnine, L. (1999). *Corrective reading skill applications C*. Columbus, OH: SRA.

Engelmann, S., Johnson, G., Carnine, L., Meyer, L., Becker, W., & Eisele, J. (1999). *Corrective reading decoding strategies B2*. Columbus, OH: SRA.

Engelmann, S., Johnson, G. Meyer, L. Becker, W., & Eisele, J. (1999). *Corrective Reading Decoding Placement Tests*. Columbus, OH: SRA.

Engelmann, S., Meyer, L., Johnson, G., & Carnine, L. (1988). *Skills application: Student's book decoding C*. New York: Macmillan/McGraw-Hill.

Goodman, K. S. (1969). What we know about reading. In P. D. Allen & J. W. Watson (Eds.), *Findings of research in miscue analysis: Classroom implications* (pp. 57–69). Urbana, IL: ERIC Clearinghouse on Reading and Communication Skills & the National Council of Teachers of English.

Goodman, Y. M., & Burke, C. L. (1972). *Reading miscue inventory*. New York: Macmillan.

Gray, W. S. (1915). *Standardized oral reading paragraphs*. Bloomington, IL: Public School Publishing.

Gray, W. S. (1940). Reading and factors influencing reading efficiency. In W. S. Gray (Ed.), *Reading in general education* (pp. 18–44). Washington, DC: American Council on Education.

Gray, W. S., & Robinson, H. (1963). *Gray Oral Reading Tests*. Austin, TX: Pro-Ed.

Gray, W. S., & Robinson, H. (1967). *Gray Oral Reading Tests*. Austin, TX: Pro-Ed.

Guilford, J. P. (1954). *Psychometric methods* (2nd ed.). New York: McGraw-Hill.

Guilford, J. P. (1956). *Fundamental statistics in psychology and education* (3rd ed.). New York: McGraw-Hill.

Guilford, J. P., & Fruchter, B. (1978). *Fundamental statistics in psychology and education*. New York: McGraw-Hill.

Hammill, D. D., & McNutt, G. (1981). *The correlates of reading: The consensus of thirty years of correlational research*. Austin, TX: Pro-Ed.

HOSTS Corporation. (1998). *HOSTS language arts program*. Vancouver, WA: Author.

HOSTS Corporation. (2002). *HOSTS puts reading first*. Vancouver, WA: Author.

Ihnot, C., Mastoff, J., Gavin, J., & Hendrickson, L. (2001). *Read naturally*. St. Paul, MN: Read Naturally.

Jodoin, M. G., & Gierl, M. J. (2000, April). *Evaluating Type I error rates using an effect size measure with the logistic regression procedure for DIF detection*. Paper presented at the meeting of the American Educational Research Association, New Orleans.

Kaminski, R. A., & Good, R. H. (1998). Assessing early literacy skills in a problem-solving model: Dynamic indicators of basic early literacy skills. In M. R. Shinn (Ed.), *Advanced applications of curriculum-based measurement* (pp. 113–142). New York: Guilford.

Kaufman, A. S., & Kaufman, N. I. (1985). *Kaufman Test of Educational Achievement*. Circle Pines, MN: American Guidance Service.

Kuhn, M. R., Schwanenflugel, P. J., Morris, R. D., Morrow, L. M., Woo, D. G., Meisinger, E. et al. (2006). Teaching children to become fluent and automatic readers. *Journal of Literacy Research*, *38*(4), 357–387.

Lindamood, C., & Lindamood, P. (1984). *Auditory discrimination in depth program*. Austin, TX: Pro-Ed.

Lindamood, C., & Lindamood, P. (1998). *Lindamood auditory conceptualization test*. Austin, TX: Pro-Ed.

Linn, R. L., & Gronlund, N. E. (1995). *Measurement and evaluation in teaching* (7th ed.). Upper Saddle River, NJ: Merrill.

Lyon, G. R. (l994). Critical issues in the measurement of learning disabilities. In G.R. Lyon (Ed.), *Frames of reference for the assessment of learning disabilities: New views on measurement issues* (pp. 1–13). Baltimore, MD: Paul H. Brookes.

MacEachron, A. E. (1982). *Basic statistics in the human services: An applied approach*. Austin, TX: Pro-Ed.

MacPhee, K. (1990a). *Spell Read Phonological Auditory Training (P.A.T.)*. P.A.T. Learning Systems. Rockville: MD.

MacPhee, K. (1990b). Phonological auditory assessments. Unpublished tests, Spell Read P.A.T. Charlottetown, Prince Edward Island.

Manis, F. R., Doi, L. M., & Bhadah, B. (2000). Naming speed, phonological awareness, and orthographic knowledge in second graders. *Journal of Learning Disabilities*, *33*, 325–333.

Manis, F. R., Seidenberg, M. S., & Doi, L. M. (1999). See Dick RAN: Rapid naming and longitudinal prediction of reading subskills in first and second grades. *Scientific Studies of Reading*, *3*(2), 129–157.

McGuiness, C., McGuiness, D., & McGuiness, G. (1996). Phono-Graphix: A new method for remediating reading difficulties. *Annals of Dyslexia*, *46*, 73–96.

Meyer, M. S., Wood, F. B., Hart, L. A., & Felton, R. H. (1998). Selective predictive value of rapid automatized naming in poor readers. *Journal of Learning Disabilities*, *31*, 106–117.

National Institute of Child Health and Human Development. (2000). Report of the National Reading Panel. *Teaching children to read: An evidence-based assessment of the scientific research literature on reading and its implications for reading instruction* (NIH Publication No. 00-4769). Washington, DC: U.S. Government Printing Office.

O'Connor, R. E., White, A., & Swanson, H. L. (2007). Repeated reading versus continuous reading: Influences on reading fluency and comprehension. *Exceptional Children, 74*(1), 31–46.

Pierangelo, R., & Guiliana, G. A. (2006). *Assessment in special education: A practical approach*. Boston: Allyn & Bacon.

Rashotte, C. A., MacPhee, K., & Torgesen, J. K. (2001). The effectiveness of a group reading instruction program with poor readers in multiple grades. *Learning Disability Quarterly, 24*, 119–134.

Rathvon, N. (2004). *Early reading assessment: A practitioner's handbook*. New York: Guilford Press.

Reid, K. D., Hresko, W. P., & Hammill, D. D. (1989). *Test of Early Reading Abilities—Second Edition*. Austin, TX: Pro-Ed.

Scarborough, H. S. (1998). Predicting the future achievement of second graders with reading disabilities. *Annals of Dyslexia, 48*, 115–136.

Schonell, F. J., & Schonell, F. E. (1950). *Diagnostic and attainment testing*. London, Edinburgh: Oliver and Boyd. Reproduced in: Newton, M. J., & Thomson, M. E. (Eds.), *Aston index: A classroom test for screening and diagnosis of language difficulties* (pp. 55–60). Cambridge: Learning Development Aids, 1982.

Semel, E., Wiig, E. H., & Secord, W. (1995). *Clinical evaluation of language fundamentals—3*. San Antonio, TX: Psychological Corp.

Shippen, M. W., Houchins, C. S., Calhoon, M. B., Furlow, C. F., & Sartor, D. (2006). The effects of comprehensive school reform models in reading for urban middle school students with disabilities. *Remedial and Special Education, 27*(6), 322–328.

Shippen, M. W., Houchins, C. S., & Sartor, D. (2005). A comparison of two direct instruction reading programs for urban middle school students. *Remedial and Special Education, 26*(3), 175–182.

Slavin, R. E., Madden, N. A., Karweit, N. L., Dolan, L., & Wasik, B. A., (1996). *Every child,* *every school: Success for all*. Newbury Park, CA: Corwin.

Slavin, R. E., Madden, N. A., Dolan, L. J., Wasik, B. A., & Ross, B. A. (1996). Success for all: A summary of research. *Journal of Education for Students Placed at Risk, 1*, 41–76.

Smith, N. B. (2002). *American reading instruction: Special edition*. Newark, DE: International Reading Association.

Swaminathan, H., & Rogers, H. J. (1990). Detecting differential item functioning using logistic regressions procedures. *Journal of Educational Measurement, 26*, 55–66.

Thorndike, R. L., Hagen, E. P., & Sattler, J. M. (1986). *Stanford-Binet Intelligence Scale—Fourth Edition*. Chicago: Riverside.

Torgesen, J., Alexander, A., Wagner, R., Rashotte, C., Voeller, K., & Conway, T. (2001). Intensive remedial instruction for children with severe reading disabilities: Immediate and long-term outcomes from two instructional approaches. *Journal of Learning Disabilities, 34*(1).

Torgeson, J., Wagner, R., & Rashotte, C. (1999). *Test of Word Reading Efficiency*. Austin, TX: Pro-Ed.

Vaughn, S., Chard, D. J., Bryant, D. P., Coleman, M., Tyler, B, Linan-Thompson, S., & Kouzekanani, K. (2000). Fluency and comprehension interventions for third-grade students. *Remedial and Special Education, 21*(6), 325–335.

Wagner, R., Torgesen, J., & Rashotte, C. (1999). *Comprehensive test of phonological processes*. Austin, TX: Pro-Ed.

Wechsler D. (1992). *Wechsler individual achievement test*. San Antonio, TX: Psychological Corporation.

Wechsler, D. (2003). *Wechsler Intelligence Scale for Children—4th Edition*. San Antonio, TX: Harcourt Assessment.

Wiederholt, J. L., & Blalock, G. (2000). *Gray Silent Reading Tests*. Austin, TX: Pro-Ed.

Wiederholt, J. L., & Bryant, B. (1986). *Gray Oral Reading Tests—Revised*. Austin, TX: Pro-Ed.

Wiederholt, J. L., & Bryant, B. (1992). *Gray Oral Reading Tests—Third Edition*. Austin, TX: Pro-Ed.

Wiederholt, J. L., & Bryant, B. (2001). *Gray Oral Reading Tests—Fourth Edition*. Austin, TX: Pro-Ed.

Wilkinson, G. S. (1993). *The Wide Range Achievement Test—3*. Wilmington, DE: Wide Range.

Woodcock, R. W. (1987). *Woodcock Reading Mastery Tests—Revised*. Circle Pines, MN: American Guidance Services.

Woodcock, R. W. (1998a). *Woodcock Diagnostic Reading Battery*. Itasca, IL: Riverside.

Woodcock, R. W. (1998b). *The Woodcock Reading Mastery Tests—NU*. Circle Pines, MN: American Guidance Services.

Woodcock, R. W., & Johnson, M. B. (1989). *Woodcock-Johnson Psychoeducational Battery—Revised*. Allen, TX: DLM Teaching Resources.

Woodcock, R. W., McGrew, K., & Mather, N. (2001). *Woodcock-Johnson Tests of Achievement* (3rd ed.). Itasca, IL: Riverside.

Kaufman Test of Educational Achievement—Second Edition

Elizabeth O. Lichtenberger, Marlene Sotelo-Dynega

RATIONALE UNDERLYING THE TEST

Tests of achievement are typically used by clinicians to gauge an individual's level of academic competence in comparison to their same-age or grade-level peers. Lichtenberger and Smith (2005) outline the major uses of achievement tests, which include: "diagnosing achievement, identifying processes, analyzing errors, program planning, measuring academic progress, evaluating interventions and programs, making placement decisions, research, and screening" (pp. 2–4). The design and structure of the Kaufman Test of Educational Achievement—Second Edition (KTEA-II; Kaufman & Kaufman, 2004a) allows the clinician to use the test for all of these various activities.

The KTEA-II has both a Brief and a Comprehensive form. The *KTEA-II Brief Form* (Kaufman & Kaufman, 2005) provides a screening of the academic abilities of adolescents and adults spanning the age range from 4:6 to 90. The KTEA-II Comprehensive form provides an in-depth assessment of academic achievement for children, adolescents, and adults ages 4:6 to 25 (the

Comprehensive Form will be the focus of this chapter). The KTEA-II Comprehensive Form assesses the eight areas in which a specific learning disability may be identified according to the Individual with Disabilities Education Improvement Act (IDEA, 2004): basic reading skills, reading comprehension, reading fluency, mathematics calculation, mathematics reasoning, oral expression, listening comprehension, and written expression. The KTEA-II is advantageous in that it allows for a comprehensive analysis of academic achievement, a targeted assessment of a specific skill, and the ability qualitatively to analyze performance.

HISTORICAL INFORMATION

Drs. Alan and Nadeen Kaufman developed the first edition of the Kaufman Test of Educational Achievement (K-TEA) over a four-year period that began in 1981. Originally published in 1985, the K-TEA was restandardized in the mid-1990s to match the 1994 U.S. Bureau of the Census estimates of the population. The renorming of the K-TEA was finalized with the publication of the K-TEA/Normative Update (K-TEA/NU; Kaufman & Kaufman, 1997).

Studies of test usage have shown that both the K-TEA and K-TEA/NU were used frequently in educational and clinical settings (Archer et al., 1991; Hammill et al., 1992; Hutton et al., 1992; Laurent & Swerdlik, 1992; Stinnett et al., 1994; Wilson & Reschley, 1996). As a result, in 1995, the authors decided to revise the test based on current research and practice, with the intention of revising the test so that it would provide the most useful and practical information to clinicians. The Kaufmans identified four main goals for the revision of the K-TEA: Improve the measurement of achievement domains; add content that is appropriate for preschool and college-age students; add subtests to assess written and oral expression, listening comprehension, and reading-related skills; make error-analysis more informative through the systematic representation of skills: and, on some subtests, take a more fine-grained approach to classifying errors.

The *KTEA-II Comprehensive Form Manual* (Kaufman & Kaufman, 2004a, Chapter 5) discusses the content development for each subtest in depth. Generally, the first step in the development of each subtest was to define at a conceptual level which skills should be measured. The authors conducted extensive literature reviews and obtained the opinion of experts to make this determination. Then, the original K-TEA items were reviewed to determine which item formats should be retained and which should be modified. The content and structure of the four new achievement areas (Written Expression, Oral Expression, Listening Comprehension, and Reading-Related Skills) that were added to the KTEA-II were based on expert recommendations. To fortify the error-analysis procedures, the test authors assured that key academic skills were included within the subtests.

DESCRIPTION OF THE KTEA-II

Structure and Organization

The KTEA-II Comprehensive Form assesses four domains (reading, math, written expression, and oral language), and is comprised of two independent, parallel forms (A and B). Eight of the 14 KTEA-II Comprehensive Form subtests are grouped into four domain composites: Reading, Mathematics, Written Language, and Oral Language. As shown in Figure 17.1, the Comprehensive Achievement Composite comprises six of the subtests that contribute to the domain composites from grade 1 through age 25, and four subtests from age 4:6 through Kindergarten. At all grades and ages, each of the four domains is represented in the Comprehensive Achievement Composite. The other six KTEA-II subtests measure skills related to reading that contribute to four additional composites, as shown in Figure 17.2.

The clinician may choose to administer a single subtest or any combination of subtests to assess a student's academic achievement in one or more domains, or to obtain the desired composite score(s). The subtests that are described briefly in the following section are organized by content area. Regardless of whether grade or age norms are used, selection of subtests is guided by the student's grade level.

Pairs of KTEA-II Comprehensive Form subtests—Reading Comprehension and Listening Comprehension, and Written Expression and Oral Expression—were developed with similar formats to enable useful comparisons to be made between each pair of subtests. These comparisons help the clinician distinguish specific problems in reading or writing from more general language problems.

The KTEA-II allows for the assessment of pre-Kindergarten children (those who have not yet begun Kindergarten). A total of seven subtests can be administered to children at

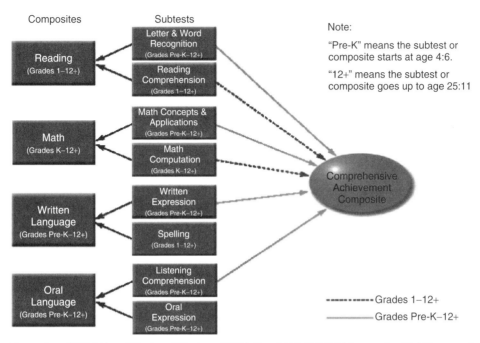

Composites   Subtests

Reading (Grades 1–12+)

Letter & Word Recognition (Grades Pre-K–12+)

Reading Comprehension (Grades 1–12+)

Math (Grades K–12+)

Math Concepts & Applications (Grades Pre-K–12+)

Math Computation (Grades K–12+)

Written Language (Grades Pre-K–12+)

Written Expression (Grades Pre-K–12+)

Spelling (Grades 1–12+)

Oral Language (Grades Pre-K–12+)

Listening Comprehension (Grades Pre-K–12+)

Oral Expression (Grades Pre-K–12+)

Comprehensive Achievement Composite

Note:

"Pre-K" means the subtest or composite starts at age 4:6.

"12+" means the subtest or composite goes up to age 25:11

- - - - - - Grades 1–12+

———— Grades Pre-K–12+

Source: From KTEA-II Manual (Kaufman & Kaufman, 2004b). Copyright © 2004 NCS Pearson, Inc. All rights reserved. This material is used by permission of NCS Pearson, Inc.

FIGURE 17.1

Composite Structure of the KTEA-II Comprehensive Form: Four Domain Composites and the Comprehensive Achievement Composite

this level. The KTEA-II Comprehensive yields two domain composites: Written Language and Oral Language. Although no math domain composite is calculated at the pre-K level, Math Concepts and Applications (a math subtest) is administered to these children. In addition, three reading-related subtests are administered: Letter and Word Recognition, Associational Fluency, and Naming Facility. Oral Fluency, a Reading-Related composite, may be calculated for pre-K children.

For Kindergarteners, the KTEA-II Comprehensive yields three domain composites based on the administration of eight subtests: Math, Written Language, and Oral Language. No Reading domain composite is obtained for Kindergarteners, but three

reading-related subtests are administered: Letter and Word Recognition, Associational Fluency, and Naming Facility. Similar to pre-K children, only one Reading-Related composite may be calculated for Kindergarteners: Oral Fluency.

For children and adolescents in grades 1 through 12 and above, the four aforementioned domain composites are calculated based on scores yielded from eight KTEA-II Comprehensive subtests. From grade 1 to 12+, two of the Reading-Related composites are calculated for the entire age range: Decoding and Oral Fluency. However, Sound-Symbol is calculated only from grades 1 through 6, and Reading Fluency is calculated only from grades 3 through 12 and above. Figure 17.2 displays the reading-related subtests

Composites   Subtests

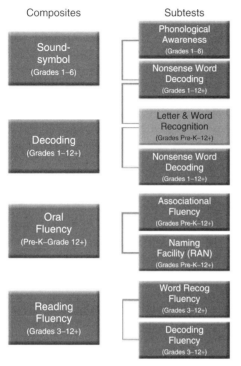

FIGURE 17.2
Composite Structure of the KTEA-II Comprehensive Form: Composites Formed by the Reading-Related Subtests

contributing to the four Reading-Related composites.

DESCRIPTIONS OF THE KTEA-II COMPREHENSIVE FORM SUBTESTS

Reading Subtests

Letter and Word Recognition (Ages 4:6 through 25:11)

The student identifies letters and pronounces words of gradually increasing difficulty. Most words are irregular to ensure that the subtest measures word recognition (reading vocabulary) rather than decoding ability. This subtest measures the ability to recognize words and letters, which is central to the ability of reading with understanding and reading vocabulary. The initial items begin with the assessment of letter names and letter sounds. Words selected from the Dolch lists of high-frequency words are then introduced that include phonetically regular words that can be sounded out by grapheme-phoneme correspondence rules, in addition to highly familiar irregular *sight words*. In this way, the subtest provides an easy transition from letter-word recognition to word reading. As the items become more difficult, the proportion of words with unpredictable pronunciations increases.

Reading Comprehension (Grade 1 through Age 25:11)

For the easiest items, the student reads a word and points to its corresponding picture. In following items, the student reads a simple instruction and responds by performing the action. In later items, the student reads passages of increasing difficulty and answers literal or inferential questions about them. Finally, the student rearranges five sentences into a coherent paragraph, and then answers questions about the paragraph. The Reading Comprehension passage items emphasize the ability to extract meaning from a set of related sentences, and deemphasize the measurement of vocabulary level. The passages rely on the structure and sequence of ideas, their phrasing, and their sentence syntax to challenge the reader.

Phonological Awareness (Grades 1 through 6)

The student responds orally to items that require manipulation of sounds. Tasks include rhyming, matching sounds, blending sounds, segmenting sounds, and deleting sounds. Phonological awareness, the ability to hear and manipulate the sounds that make up words, combines with understanding that words are composed of individual letters to form the "alphabetic principle" that supports decoding. The content of this subtest was developed to correspond with the five levels of phonemic awareness, described by Adams (1990).

Nonsense Word Decoding (Grade 1 through Age 25:11)

The student applies phonics and structural analysis skills to decode invented words of increasing difficulty. The processing of printed letters and letter patterns into sounds, or phonological decoding, appears to be characteristic of the reading process at all levels of skill (Adams, 1990). The Nonsense Word Decoding subtest is designed to assess the student's ability to transform printed letters and letter patterns into sounds and integrate those sounds into an oral expression that conforms to standard pronunciation rules of English. It is built from commonly occurring letter patterns, including units such as suffix and inflections, in combinations that have predictable pronunciations. Measures of phonological decoding such as pseudoword decoding tests are highly sensitive to reading problems (Chard, Simmons, & Kameenui, 1998).

Word Reading Fluency (Grade 3 through Age 25:11)

The student reads isolated words (grades 3 and up read words from the Letter and Word Recognition subtest) as quickly as possible for one minute. The number of words they read correctly in one minute is the basis of their score. Automaticity is critical for competent reading. Speed of response to printed words provides information about word recognition ability that is not given by accuracy data alone. Some poor readers can recognize words accurately, but do so at a rate of speed that adversely affects comprehension.

Decoding Fluency (Grade 3 through Age 25:11)

The student applies decoding skills to pronounce as many nonsense words (grades 3 and up read words from the Nonsense Word Decoding subtest) as possible in one minute. The same rationale for assessing Word Reading Fluency applies to the Decoding Fluency subtest: the automaticity with which a student reads nonsense words is determined based on the number of words he or she reads correctly in one minute.

Associational Fluency (Ages 4:6 through 25:11)

The student says as many words as possible in 30 seconds that belong to a semantic category or have a specified beginning sound. The ability to retrieve words fluently is important for effective speaking and writing. Associational fluency tasks are one commonly used means of assessing retrieval ability. The KTEA-II Associational Fluency subtest includes two trials each for semantic and phonological fluency.

Naming Facility (Ages 4:6 through 25:11)

The student names objects, colors, and letters as quickly as possible. *Rapid automatized naming (RAN)* is the skill referred to as Naming Facility in the KTEA-II. The automaticity with which a student can retrieve the names of things (objects, colors, letters) from his or her lexical store has been found to be related to reading ability among early readers (Moats, 1993; Neuhaus & Swank, 2002; Stahl & Murray, 1994). Naming facility and phonological awareness are the components of the *double-deficit hypothesis*, which proposes that a deficit in either of these areas interferes with learning to read, and deficits in both produce an additive effect (Wolf, 1997).

Math Subtests

Math Concepts and Applications (Ages 4:6 through 25:11)

The student responds orally to test items that focus on the application of mathematical principles to real-life situations. Skill categories include number concepts, operation concepts, rational numbers, measurement, shape and space, data investigations, and higher math concepts. The development of the item blueprint for Math Concepts and Applications began with a review of current textbooks and the curricula of several large school districts, the learning standards developed by several states, and the standards of the National Council of Teachers of Mathematics. The Math Concepts and Applications subtest focuses on reasoning and mathematical concepts and their application to meaningful problem solving.

Math Computation (Kindergarten through Age 25:11)

The student computes solutions to math problems printed in a student response booklet. Skills assessed include addition, subtraction, multiplication, and division operations; fractions and decimals; square roots, exponents, signed numbers, and algebra.

Written Language Subtests

Written Expression (Ages 4:6 through 25:11)

Kindergarten and pre-Kindergarten children trace and copy letters and write letters from dictation. At grades 1 and higher, the student completes writing tasks in the context of an age-appropriate storybook format. Tasks at those levels include writing sentences from dictation, adding punctuation and capitalization, filling in missing words, completing sentences, combining sentences, writing compound and complex sentences, and, starting at spring of grade 1, writing an essay based on the story the student helped complete. The development of this subtest was based on several factors that included Berninger's (1994) observation that the most common reason for referral for writing problems is an inability to get ideas down on paper. Based on this observation, the Kaufmans set out to create a subtest that assessed the functional or pragmatic aspect of writing.

Spelling (Grade 1 through Age 25:11)

The student writes words dictated by the clinician from a steeply graded word list. Words were selected to match acquired spelling skills at each grade level, and for their potential for error analysis. Early items require students to write single letters that represent sounds. The remaining items require students to spell orthographically regular and irregular words of increasing complexity. The design of this subtest is based on the consideration of the developmental sequence of spelling skills (Ganske, 1999; Moats, 1994). The subtest begins with the assessment of how well the student can apply phonetic principles, and how sensitive the student is to the relation of letter patterns to sounds, and ends with commonly misspelled words to help achieve a sufficient ceiling.

Oral Language Subtests

Listening Comprehension (Ages 4:6 through 25:11)

The student listens to passages played on a CD and then responds orally to questions asked by the clinician. Questions measure literal and inferential comprehension. The KTEA-II authors developed the Listening Comprehension subtest to reflect the sort of listening comprehension that is required in school—that is, comprehension of relatively formal speech rather than casual speech—as well as to parallel the passage items of the Reading Comprehension subtest so that a comparison can be made to determine whether a reading problem versus a more general deficit in language development exists.

Oral Expression (Ages 4:6 through 25:11)

The student performs specific speaking tasks in the context of a real-life scenario. Tasks assess pragmatics, syntax, semantics, and grammar. The Oral Expression subtest was developed to assess the student's ability to communicate ideas in speech just as the Written Expression subtest was designed to assess how well a student can convey ideas on paper. In addition, the similarities in the design and content of the Oral and Written Expression subtests allow for the comparison of the student's performance to highlight a problem that may be specific to writing or a broad language deficit that may affect performance on both subtests.

ADMINISTRATION AND SCORING

The *KTEA-II Comprehensive Form Manual* (Kaufman & Kaufman, 2004a, Chapter 2) reviews the general administration procedures and the test easels list specific administration directions. The KTEA-II Comprehensive Form allows examiners to tailor the administration of the test based on the assessment needs. For instance, an examiner may choose to administer the entire battery of subtests, or a specific composite or subtest. Although the easels and record form provide the suggested administration order, standardization procedures are not affected if an alternative administration order is followed.

Starting and Discontinuing Subtests

The KTEA-II's record form and each respective subtest's direction page, located in the testing easels, lists the grade-based starting points, and basal and ceiling criteria. Although the test authors encourage examiners to begin subtest administration based on the child's particular grade level, examiners can use their clinical judgment to determine the need to begin testing at a lower or higher starting point. As with the administration of the majority of standardized tests, the examiner must be certain that basal and ceiling criteria are met. Some subtests on the KTEA-II do not have traditional basal rules because the items are grouped into item sets (Reading Comprehension, Listening Comprehension, Oral Expression, and the Writing subtest).

Sample and Teaching Items

Three KTEA-II Comprehensive form subtests include either sample or teaching items (indicated by an apple icon in the record form) that allow the examiner to provide the child with additional information: Phonological Awareness, Nonsense Word Decoding, and Oral Expression.

Recording Responses

Accurately recording responses during administration of KTEA-II subtests is a key factor if you intend on conducting an error analysis upon scoring completion. Three subtests (i.e., Written Expression, Spelling, and Math Computation) require the examinees to write their own responses, requiring no recording on the examiner's part until scoring is conducted. Phonological Awareness and Math Concepts and Applications require simple recording of either a 0 for incorrect or a 1 for correct, or recording a one-word response. Reading Comprehension and Listening Comprehension require the essence of the examinee's responses to be recorded, whereas the Oral Expression and Associational Fluency subtests require that an examinee's responses are recorded verbatim. Letter and Word Recognition and Nonsense Word Decoding require careful listening to correctly record the child's responses. Mispronunciations on these two subtests should be recorded using the phoneme key provided on the record form or by writing the student's response phonetically. Recording responses either by the phonetic key or by phonetically spelling the child's response takes some practice. The *KTEA-II Comprehensive Form Manual* (Kaufman & Kaufman, 2004a, Chapter 4) describes how to record responses for use with the error-analysis system in detail.

Timing

Four out of the six Reading-Related subtests require timing. The scoring for Word Recognition Fluency, Decoding Fluency, and Associational

Fluency subtests are based on the student's performance within a given timeframe. The Naming Facility (RAN) subtest entails that the task completion time be converted to a point score.

Querying

In the event that an examinee's response is presented without the precision needed to be considered as correct, the examiner is required to query the examinee to clarify his or her response. The easel specifies queries for the relevant subtests. It is important to note that if a query is made, the examiner must make a notation of the query on the record form (e.g., "Q").

SCORING

Standard Scores and Scaled Scores

Before an examiner can convert raw scores to standard scores, a decision must be made based on the examinee's background information and details of the referral to determine whether age- or grade-based norms will be used. When grade-norms are selected, the examiner must use either fall or spring sets of norms, depending on the time of year the student is being tested.

Norm-based standard scores allow the student's performance to be compared to that of others. The KTEA-II standard scores have a mean of 100 and an *SD* of 15. The range of standard scores for the subtests and composites is 40 to 160. Because scores have error associated with them, it is wise to report standard scores with a band of error or within a confidence interval. The KTEA-II allows you to choose from 85%, 90%, or 95% confidence levels (the record form directs you to circle which level of confidence you are reporting). Tables N.6 and N.7 in the *KTEA-II Comprehensive Form Norms Book* provide the bands of error for age-based standard scores and grade-based standard scores.

Grade and Age Equivalents

Grade and age equivalents represent the level at which the average student performs the same as the student being assessed. However, grade and age equivalents are not as precise as standard scores, and often suggest large differences in performance, when the differences are actually insignificant. For example, a raw score of 71 on Reading Comprehension yields an age equivalent of 14 years, 8 months, and earning just 2 more points for a raw score of 73 corresponds to an age equivalent of 16 years, 6 months. On the same subtest, an examinee age 15:5 would earn an age-based standard score of 99 (for a raw score of 71) and an age-based standard score of 101 (for a raw score of 73). Thus, this 2-point standard score difference appears much smaller than the nearly two-year difference in age equivalents, when comparing scores based on the same raw scores.

Percentile Ranks

Percentile ranks are the simplest means of communicating a child's performance to parents and teachers. The percentile rank represents the number of individuals that the student outperformed at his or her age (age norms) or grade level (grade norms). For example, a 12-year-old who scored at the 60th percentile on the Letter and Word Recognition subtest performed better than 60 percent of 12-year-olds on that subtest.

Descriptive Categories

The KTEA-II system differs from the system used for the original KTEA and from many other classification systems, such as Wechsler's (2002, 2003), because it depends on the standard deviation of 15 to define its categories, with the Average range of 85–115 corresponding to ± 1 standard deviation (*SD*) from the mean (100 ± 15); Below Average defined as 1 to 2 *SD*s below the mean (70–84); and so forth.

USE OF SCORING AND REPORT WRITING SOFTWARE

KTEA-II ASSIST™

The authors of the KTEA-II have created a computer software program, the KTEA-II ASSIST™, to facilitate the scoring process by eliminating hand scoring. Relevant demographic information and raw scores are inputted and converted into standardized scores by the program. The software contains both Macintosh and Windows programs on one CD-ROM. The printout from the KTEA-II ASSIST™ includes a summary of student performance by composite or subtest, comparisons of skill areas or subtests for easy interpretation of results, achievement/ability comparisons, and error analysis for all standard subtests. It also offers additional information, including best practices instructional suggestions for designing IEP goals that match students' score information with remediation strategies, and lists of math problems or reading or spelling words similar to those that were difficult for the student. The KTEA-II ASSIST™ works on the same platform as the KABC-II ASSIST™, so examinee information (e.g., name, date of birth, dates of testing) will be saved and can transfer from one program to the next.

PSYCHOMETRIC PROPERTIES

Standardization

The KTEA-II Comprehensive Form was standardized with an age-norm sample of 3,000 examinees ages 4.5 through 25, and a grade-norm sample of 2,400 students in Kindergarten through grade 12. Sample sizes for each grade level ranged from 140 to 220 students, and the sample sizes for each age level ranged from 100 to 220 students (with the exception of age 19, which had a sample of only 18 examinees). Standardization of the two parallel forms of the KTEA-II Comprehensive Form required that half of the norm sample be administered Form A and the other half administered Form B. The standardization sample was chosen to closely match the U.S. population based on data obtained from the 2001 Current Population Survey of the Bureau of the Census.

The KTEA-II Brief Form was standardized on a large representative sample that also closely corresponded to the 2001 Current Population Survey of the Bureau of the Census. The grade-norm sample consisted of 1,645 students from Kindergarten through grade 12. The number of students sampled from each grade ranged from 75 to 90 for grades 9–12 to 110 to 125 for grades 3–8, and 210 students were sampled for grades 1 and 2. The size of the Brief Form total age sample ($N = 2,495$) was larger than that of the grade sample. At each age, for children under age 15, the samples included 100–210 children. For ages 15–25, the samples included 75–150 children, and the adult samples over age 25 (to age 90) included 50–60 individuals for each age group.

Reliability

The KTEA-II Comprehensive internal-consistency reliability values are strong for both Forms A and B. The average internal-consistency reliability value across grades and forms for the Comprehensive Achievement Composite was .97. The averages for the Reading, Math, and Decoding composites were .96, .96, and .97, respectively. The average reliability values for the Written Language Composite and Sound-Symbol Composite were .93. For Oral Language and Oral Fluency composites, the average reliabilities were .87 and .85, respectively. Reliability values based on age groups were very similar to what was reported for the reliability values found with the grade-level samples.

The KTEA-II Brief Form also had strong average internal-reliability values. For the individual subtests scored via *grade* norms (grades K–12), the average reliability values were .94,

.90, and .86 for the Reading, Math, and Writing subtests, respectively. For the individual subtests scored via *age* norms (ages 4:6–90), the values were .95, .91, and .90 for the Reading, Math, and Writing subtests, respectively. The split-half reliability values for the Brief Achievement Composite were .96 for both the grade and the age norms.

Forms A and B of the KTEA-II Comprehensive were administered approximately 3 1/2 to 4 weeks apart, on average, to a sample of 221 children in order to calculate alternate-form reliability values. The Comprehensive Achievement Composites showed very high consistency across time and forms (low to mid-.90s). The Reading, Math, Written Language, Decoding, and Reading Fluency composites have alternate-form reliabilities in the high .80s to mid-.90s. These strong values indicate that the alternate forms of the KTEA-II will be useful for reducing practice effects when the test is administered more than once.

For the KTEA-II Brief Form, test–retest reliability was examined by administering the test twice within a 2-to-8-week period (mean interval 3.7 weeks) to 327 students. Across the grade-norm and age-norm samples, the average adjusted test–retest reliabilities were as follows: Reading = .93, Math = .90, Writing = .81, and Brief Achievement Composite = .94.

VALIDITY

The validity of the KTEA-II was demonstrated via multiple methods. Intercorrelations between the subtests and composites were calculated to show the relationships between the academic domains. Factor analyses were conducted to show that the structure of the test was empirically grounded. Correlations with other instruments were also conducted to evaluate the construct validity of the test. Finally, special population studies were conducted to show the efficacy of applying the KTEA-II to the assessment of children with learning disabilities, mental

retardation, and attention-deficit/hyperactivity disorder, and of children with other special qualities such as deafness or giftedness. The results of these special studies are summarized in the "Identification of Special Populations" section in this chapter.

Confirmatory factor analysis was conducted to investigate the relationships between the KTEA-II Comprehensive Form subtests and composites in a systematic manner. The factor analysis proceeded in a stepwise fashion with the eight primary subtests yielding a final model comprised of four factors. The final model had good fit statistics and all subtests had high loadings on their factors. The results of the factor analysis are shown in Figure 17.3.

The KTEA-II Comprehensive and Brief Forms were administered along with other tests of achievement and cognitive ability during standardization. Correlations were calculated between the KTEA-II Comprehensive and Brief Forms. In a sample of 1,318 students administered both the Comprehensive and Brief Forms, the correlations were .85, .86, .78, and .89 for Reading, Math, Writing, and Achievement Composite. Further correlations were calculated between the KTEA-II Comprehensive Form and the following achievement tests: WIAT-II, Woodcock-Johnson Tests of Achievement—Third Edition (WJ-III ACH; Woodcock, McGrew, & Mather, 2001), the Peabody Individual Achievement Test—Revised—Normative Update (PIAT-R/NU; Markwardt, 1989, 1998), and the Oral and Written Language Scales (OWLS; Carrow-Woolfolk, 1996). A summary of the KTEA-II Comprehensive Form correlational studies with the WIAT-II and WJ-III are provided in Table 17.1 (for grades 1–5 and 6–11). The results of the studies with the WIAT-II and WJ-III are very similar to those found with the original K-TEA. That is, most correlations between like-named composites were in the mid-to-high .80s, and correlations between most of the total achievement scores hovered around .90. The correlations with the PIAT-R/NU overall composite score

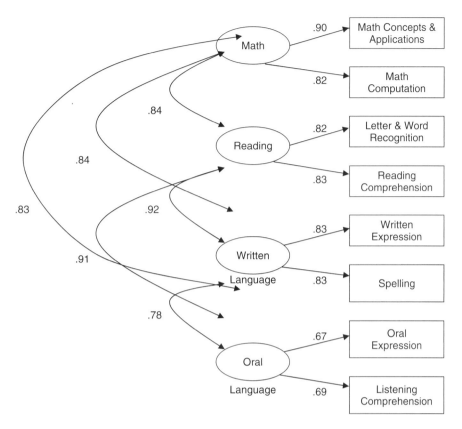

Note: Figure is adapted from Figure 7.1 of the *KTEA-II Comprehensive Form Manual* (Kaufman & Kaufman, 2004a, p.101). Result are based on the complete norm sample (age norms) at grade 1 and above (n = 2,560). Factors are shown in the ovals on the left, and subtests are in rectangles on the right. The numbers represent factor intercorrelations or factor loadings

FIGURE 17.3
Results of Confirmatory Factor Analysis of Eight KTEA-II Comprehensive Form Subtests

were .86 for both grades K–5 and 6–9. For domain composites, the PIAT-R/NU's highest correlations were for reading (ranging from .89 to .78), and lower correlations were found for mathematics and spelling (ranging from .67 to .70). The OWLS has three subtests, and the highest correlation with the KTEA-II was between the tests of Written Expression (.75); the instruments' measures of Oral Expression and Listening Comprehension correlated at only a modest level (in the .40s).

In addition to the correlational data showing the relationships between the KTEA-II

and other tests of academic achievement, the *KTEA-II Comprehensive Form Manual* provides data showing the correlations between the KTEA-II and three tests of cognitive ability: the KABC-II, Wechsler Intelligence Scale for Children—Third Edition (WISC-III; Wechsler, 1991), and the Woodcock-Johnson Tests of Cognitive Abilities—Third Edition (WJ-III COG; Woodcock, McGrew, & Mather, 2001). A very large sample ($N = 2,520$) was used in the study with the KABC-II, as this test was co-normed with the KTEA-II. Sample sizes were 97 and 51

TABLE 17.1 Correlations of KTEA-II Composites with Like-Named Composites of Other Achievement Tests

KTEA-II Composite	WIAT-II		WJ III	
	Grades 1-5	Grades 6-11	Grades 1-5	Grades 6-11
Reading Composite	.85	.85	.82	.76
Mathematics Composite	.82	.87	.87	.87
Written Language Composite	.87	.87	.92	.84
Oral Language Composite	.52	.70	.71	.74
Comprehensive Achievement Composite	.89	.90	.84	.89

NOTE . Data are from Tables 7.17, 7.18, 7.19, and 7.20 of the *KTEA-II Comprehensive Form Manual* (Kaufman & Kaufman, 2004a). All correlations were corrected for the variability of the norm group, based on the standard deviation obtained on the KTEA-II using the variability correction of Cohen et al. (2003, p. 58). Sample sizes for Grades 1-5 were $N = 82$ for the WIAT-II study and $N = 33$ for the WJ III study. Sample sizes for Grades 6-11 were $N = 89$ for the WIAT-II study and $N = 47$ for the WJ III study.

for the studies with the WISC-III and WJ-III COG, respectively.

The KTEA-II Comprehensive Achievement Composite correlates .79 with the KABC-II Fluid Crystallized Index (FCI), .74 with the KABC-II Mental Processing Index (MPI), and .69 with the KABC-II Nonverbal Index (NVI) for the total sample. Very similar correlations were found between the Comprehensive Achievement Composite and global cognitive scores on the WISC-III and WJ-III COG. The Comprehensive Achievement Composite correlated .79 with the WISC-III Full Scale IQ (FS-IQ) and .82 with the WJ-III COG General Intellectual Ability (GIA). For all three tests of cognitive ability, the KTEA-II's Reading Composite and Mathematics Composite had the strongest relationship to overall cognitive ability. Correlations with the Reading Composite were .74, .69, and .72 for the KABC-II FCI, WISC-III FS-IQ, and WJ-III GIA, respectively. Correlations with the Mathematics Composite were .71, .65, and .76 for the KABC-II FCI, WISC-III FS-IQ, and WJ-III GIA, respectively. The other academic domains measured by the KTEA-II did not correlate as strongly with overall cognitive ability.

For example, Written Language and Oral Language correlated .66 and .67, respectively, with the KABC-II FCI.

RELATIONSHIPS BETWEEN TEST SCORES AND STATE CURRICULUM

Extensive reviews of the literature and written recommendations from a panel of experts in various curricular areas shaped the development of the KTEA-II subtests. The well-designed content of the KTEA-II provides clinicians with the necessary tools to comprehensively assess the four key achievement domains (Reading, Math, and Written and Oral Language), and also allows for the assessment of the eight specific learning disability areas identified by IDEA (2004): basic reading skills, reading comprehension, reading fluency, mathematics calculation, mathematics reasoning, oral expression, listening comprehension, and written expression. Table 17.2 exhibits the KTEA-II subtests categorized by their respective academic achievement domain as delineated by IDEA (2004).

TABLE 17.2   KTEA-II's Coverage of the Eight IDEA Academic Achievement Domains

Basic Reading Skills	Reading Compre- hension	Reading Fluency	Mathematics Calculation	Mathematics Reasoning	Oral Expression	Listening Compre- hension	Written Expression
Letter and Word Recogni- tion; Nonsense Word Decoding	Reading Compre- hension	Word Recognition Fluency; Decoding Fluency	Math Concepts and Applications; Math Computation	Math Concepts and Applications	Oral Expression	Listening Compre- hension	Written Expression; Spelling

USE OF THE TEST

Interpretation Methods

The interpretive system, discussed in this chapter, includes the five steps described in the KTEA-II manual (Kaufman & Kaufman, 2004a, Chapter 3), which are clarified in *Essentials of WIAT-II and KTEA-II Assessment* (Lichtenberger & Smith, 2005). To best describe the KTEA-II's interpretive system, the five steps are presented and illustrated with data obtained from an administration of the KTEA-II to a child with a possible learning disability. The reader is encouraged to refer to *Essentials of WIAT-II and KTEA-II Assessment* as it provides easy-to-follow interpretive steps and examples that facilitate the interpretive process of the KTEA-II (Lichtenberger & Smith, 2005).

The interpretive approaches advocated by the authors of this chapter begin at the global level and domain composites and then move to subtests and finally to specific patterns of errors. The KTEA-II's interpretive methods allow the clinician to gain a better understanding of a student's strong and weak areas of academic functioning, from both *normative* (age-based or grade-based) and *ipsative* (person-based) perspectives. The authors urge clinicians not to interpret test scores in isolation; rather, clinicians must seek multiple pieces of data to support interpretive hypotheses.

Such supportive data may be in the form of multiple test scores, behavioral observations, teacher reports, school records, or parent reports.

Interpretation of the complete KTEA-II Comprehensive Form involves five steps:

1. Interpret the Comprehensive Achievement Composite.
2. Interpret domain composite scores and subtest scores.
3. Identify domain composite strengths and weaknesses.
4. Identify subtest strengths and weaknesses.
5. Determine the significance and unusualness of planned comparisons.

An abbreviated interpretation method can be used when administering domain-specific portions of the KTEA-II Comprehensive Form that require only two of the steps listed earlier:

1. Interpret domain composite scores and subtest scores.
2. Determine the significance and unusualness of planned comparisons.

The KTEA-II Brief Form was designed to be a screening instrument to be used to determine when further assessment is necessary; therefore, the level of interpretation is not as in-depth as it is with the Comprehensive Form. Interpretation of the KTEA-II Brief Form is analogous to what we describe for interpreting a partial KTEA-II Comprehensive Form battery. There are two steps to interpreting the Brief Form: (1) Interpret the Brief Achievement Composite, and (2) Compare subtest standard scores. Readers are directed to Step 1 in the case study that follows for interpreting the Achievement Composite for both the Brief and Comprehensive Forms. For information on how to conduct a comparison of subtest scores in the Brief Form, readers are directed to Step 5 in the case study.

The data and calculations needed to conduct each of the interpretive steps outlined in this chapter are recorded on the KTEA-II record form. For the Comprehensive Form, the data for Steps 1 and 2 are recorded on pages 1 and 3 of the record form. The data for Steps 3 and 4 are recorded on page 3 of the record form, and the data for Step 5 are recorded on the back page of the record form. All data for the Brief Form are recorded on the front cover of the Record Form.

Clinical Analysis of Errors

By following the interpretive steps listed earlier, a clinician is able to obtain information about *how* a student performs in relation to his or her same-age or grade-level counterparts, as well as to ascertain whether any academic strengths and weaknesses exist. The KTEA-II provides an additional step of interpretation that allows clinicians to assess *why* students perform the way they do. The details about a student's skills come from a system for analyzing specific errors made on 10 of the KTEA-II's 14 subtests. The system of error analysis determines both strong and weak skill areas across global skills (such as Reading and Math) and more specific skills (such as Math Computation and Math Concepts and Applications).

KTEA-II Illustrative Case Study

Name:	Luis S.
Age:	7 years, 8 months
Grade in school:	Second Grade
Evaluator:	Marlene Sotelo-Dynega, PsyD

Reason for Referral

Despite psychopharmacological treatment for attention-deficit/hyperactivity disorder (ADHD), combined with an intensive, specialized program targeted at improving Luis's reading and writing skills, his writing continues to fall far below grade expectation. As a result, the elementary school's Child Study Team referred the student for a formal evaluation of his academic strengths and weaknesses to better understand his difficulties in the area of written expression.

Tests Administered

Kaufman Test of Educational Achievement—Second Edition (KTEA-II): Comprehensive Form.

Background Information

Ms. S., Luis's biological mother, reported that due to complications that arose during the pregnancy as a result of gestational diabetes, Luis was delivered via emergency cesarean section at 38 weeks' gestation. At birth, Luis was said to have an enlarged heart with a murmur, and, as a result, he had to remain in the Neonatal Intensive Care Unit for approximately 3 weeks after his birth. Ms. S. reported that Luis's cardiovascular issues were monitored by a cardiologist until he was 1 year old, and he was given a clean bill of health as his heart issues had resolved on their own.

Luis currently resides with his biological mother, Ms. S. (33 years old), and his maternal grandmother, Ms. S.S. (58 years old). All of his family members were born and raised in the United States and speak English. Ms. S. reported that all developmental milestones were achieved within the expected timeframe, but she noticed that Luis reversed sounds, numbers, and letters before he began attending school. She added that when Luis began reading books, he read words from right to left. Although Luis attended preschool, Ms. S. stated that behavioral issues (i.e., inattentiveness and distractibility) were not evident until her son began attending Kindergarten at the local elementary school.

Luis's behavioral and academic difficulties have increased since Kindergarten, despite the strong core curriculum instruction that he received in Kindergarten and first grade. Therefore, immediately upon beginning second grade, a Child Study Team meeting was held with Luis's mother, his second-grade teacher, the special-education teacher, the reading specialist, and the principal. Luis's classroom teacher was concerned that his reading and writing levels were below that of his fellow classmates, and that his inattentiveness and distractibility continued to be a major obstacle to his learning. Because of his difficulties at school, Ms. S. obtained a referral to Dr. David of the Children's Neurological Group to rule out an attention-deficit/hyperactivity disorder (ADHD) diagnosis for Luis. According to Ms. S., Dr. David diagnosed Luis with ADHD, and began him on a trial of medication immediately following the diagnosis. Since the inception of this pharmacological treatment, his ADHD symptomology has decreased significantly in school.

In addition to the pharmacological treatment of his ADHD, academic interventions have been implemented at school to address his reading and writing difficulties. Specifically, the Child Study Team recommended more intensive interventions targeted at improving Luis's phonological awareness. He began working with the special education teacher in a program entitled Lindamood Phonemic Sequencing® (LiPS®) for Reading, Spelling and Speech. Eight weeks later, another Child Study Team meeting was held to review Luis's progress. The team found that his progress in reading had gone from a mid-first-grade level to a second-grade level. The special-education teacher stated that Luis's response to the Lindamood Bell LiPS program was noticeably better after he began his treatment for ADHD. The special-education teacher recommended that Luis continue using visual guides (part of the LiPS program) in the regular education classroom and at home when doing his homework in order to help address Luis's letter reversals. However, despite good progress in reading, Luis's progress in writing was minimal. The Child Study Team agreed to refer him for further testing to determine the cause of his difficulties in writing.

Behavioral Observations

Luis is a 7-year, 8-month-old boy of above-average height and weight. He was neatly and appropriately dressed, and appeared to be in overall good health. Immediately upon being introduced to this examiner, he stated, "I know I have to go with you to get tested," and readily accompanied the examiner to the testing office. Luis seemed immediately at ease in the presence of the examiner. Rapport was easily established with Luis as he spoke freely and openly during the evaluation. He was an articulate, friendly, and socially outgoing youngster who seemed at ease interacting with adults. Luis used appropriate eye contact and affect when he communicated. His speech was clear with no articulation difficulties.

He stated that even though he doesn't like school, he is happy when he is there. When asked what he likes about school, Luis stated, "I like specials (gym, music, computer, etc.) and going to Ms. J.'s class (special-education teacher)." Luis added that he is not happy when he has to write or do homework.

Occasionally, Luis stared blankly when task directions were being given. Twice, Luis could not even attempt the tasks because he had not heard any of the directions, although it appeared as though he had been listening. According to his doctor, this difficulty maintaining consistently focused attention is a common side-effect of the medication he is taking for ADHD. His teacher commented that she has also noticed that he sometimes "zones out" during class.

Despite these occasional lapses in attention, after being refocused, Luis was able to attend to the directions and successfully complete all tasks presented to him. While on task, Luis was persistent. Even on the more challenging items, Luis did not give up and attempted every item presented to him. He did not complain about the amount of work that he had to do (although such complaints are common among students of Luis's age, especially when working on a task that assesses an area of weakness).

Due to Luis's high level of effort, motivation, and ability to understand and complete the tasks presented to him, the results of this evaluation are thought to be an accurate assessment of Luis's current academic functioning.

Test Results and Interpretation

Luis was administered the KTEA-II, a test of standardized academic achievement, to obtain information about his strengths and weaknesses that relate to his performance at school. The specific results of his performance on the KTEA-II are summarized in Table 17.3.

Luis's academic abilities vary widely. He earned Written Expression and Spelling standard scores of 73 (3rd percentile) and 85 (16th percentile), respectively, but also earned much higher Math Concepts and Applications and

> **Step 1: Interpret the Comprehensive Achievement Composite (CAC).**
>
> Compare the student's overall achievement score, the CAC, to the normative group by presenting the standard score, confidence interval, percentile rank, and descriptive category. Interpret the CAC with an appropriate explanation of a highly variable profile.

Math Computation standard scores of 130 (98th percentile) and 123 (93rd percentile), respectively. His Comprehensive Achievement Composite (CAC) standard score of 105 (65th percentile) represents the midpoint of very diverse abilities. Because of the variability in the scores that comprise Luis's CAC score, a more meaningful understanding of his diverse academic abilities can be obtained by examining his performance on the separate academic domain composites.

Reading
Luis's Average Reading Composite performance (standard score 98; 45th percentile), along with the two subtests that compose it (Letter and Word Recognition, 99; Reading Comprehension, 98) were labeled as Personal Weaknesses when compared to his CAC standard score of 105 (65th percentile) as they were significantly lower than his academic average. However, his performance in this domain is not problematic because Luis's reading skills were consistently Average, whether he was reading words (standard score 99; 48th percentile on Letter and Word Recognition), sounding out nonsense words using phonics skills (standard score 104; 57th percentile on Nonsense Word Reading), responding orally to items that require manipulation of sounds (standard score 99; 48th percentile on Phonological Awareness), and demonstrating an understanding of what he reads (standard score 98, 45th percentile on Reading Comprehension). Thus, it appears that the intervention he has received through the Lindamood Bell LiPS program at school has been successful in improving his reading ability.

TABLE 17.3 Luis's KTEA-II Comprehensive Form A

Composite/Subtest	Standard Score (Grade-Based)	90% Confidence Interval	Percentile Rank
Reading Composite	*99*	*95-101*	*45*
Letter and Word Recognition	*98*	*95-103*	*47*
Reading Comprehension	*99*	*93-101*	*45*
Reading-Related Composites			
Decoding Composite	**102**	**98-106**	**55**
Nonsense Word Decoding	103	96-110	58
Sound-Symbol Composite	**102**	**95-109**	55
Phonological Awareness	99	90-108	47
Math Composite	*129*	*123-135*	*97*
Math Concepts and Applications	130	122-138	98
Math Computation	123	115-131	94
Written Language Composite	77	*70-84*	*6*
Written Expression	73	61-85	4
Spelling	85	79-91	16
Oral Language Composite	*104*	*96-112*	*61*
Listening Comprehension	103	93-113	58
Oral Expression	105	95-115	63
Comprehensive Achievement Composite	*105*	*101-109*	*63*

Math

Luis's performance in mathematics reveals Above Average functioning in the basic skills of computation (standard score 123; 94th percentile) and the application of mathematical principles to solve word problems (standard score 130; 98th percentile). Luis's consistency on the two subtests indicates that his Math Composite of 129 provides a good overview of his skills in mathematics. When compared to his CAC, Luis's performance on the Math Composite and both subtests that comprise it revealed both normative and

Clinical Analysis of Errors

The KTEA-II Comprehensive Form error analysis uses norm-referenced methodology to determine a child's relative mastery of specific skills that can then lead to effective remediation of skill deficiencies. Each student's performance on certain skills is labeled: "strong," "average," or "weak," compared to other students in the same grade level.

There are two basic types of error classification methods: item-level error classification and within-item classification. In the item-level error classification, each item is classified according to the process, concept, or skill that it assesses. The within-item classification requires judgment on the part of the examiner to determine the error type. That is, the specific details of the student's response will lead examiners to select which of many types of errors that the examinee made. To facilitate this level of interpretation, the KTEA-II test authors included all of the relevant information needed for the analysis of subtests using item-level error classification, and a separate booklet for the analysis of subtests using within-item error classifications.

personal strengths that are not commonly seen in the normal population. In comparison to his peers, Luis exhibited strong areas of skill in subtraction, multiplication, solving problems involving time and money, and solving multistep mathematical problems.

Written Language

Luis's Below Average Written Language Composite performance (standard score 77; 6th percentile) was labeled as both a Normative and a Personal Weakness when compared to his CAC standard score of 105 (65th percentile), as it was a significant difference that occurs infrequently in the population. Luis's written language skills were consistently Below Average, whether he was expressing his ideas in writing (standard score 73; 3rd percentile on Written Expression) or spelling words (standard score 85; 16th percentile on Spelling). Considering the confidence interval associated with his Spelling standard score, there is a 90% chance that his true score lies between 71 and 91. Thus, his spelling ability is also a Personal Weakness and his performance is weaker than expected compared to his peers (a Normative Weakness).

Luis exhibited specific weak skills in written tasks that required him to capitalize letters and properly place punctuation in a sentence. When spelling words, Luis frequently omitted syllables from the stimulus words, misspelled words that had unpredictable letter-sound relationships, and spelled words in a way that did not correspond to the sound of the word. Overall, Luis's performance in the Written Language domain demonstrates the area of greatest concern for both diagnostic and academic skills that require educational intervention.

Oral Language

Luis's oral language skills were consistently Average, whether he was required to demonstrate his ability to understand passages that were presented via a CD recording (standard score 103; 57th percentile on Listening Comprehension) or to express his ideas in words (105; 65th percentile on Oral Expression). Luis's consistency on the two subtests indicates that his Oral Language Composite of 104 (62nd percentile, Average) provides a good overview of his oral language skills.

Summary and Recommendations

Luis, a 7-year-old male in the second grade, has been receiving treatment for ADHD and interventions for his reading difficulties

---

Step 2: Interpret domain composite scores and subtest scores.

Compare the student's domain composite scores to the normative group to determine Normative Strengths (SS > 115) and Weaknesses (SS < 85).

Step 3: Identify domain composite strengths and weaknesses.

Compare the student's domain composite scores to his or her own average level of academic performance. The CAC standard score is used as the value that represents a student's average level of performance, which is compared to the student's performance on the separate domain composites. The difference scores between the student's CAC and the domain composites are considered to be significantly different at the $p < .05$ level if the difference score is equal to or greater than the value indicated in the table (see KTEA-II Comprehensive Form Manual, Table I.1 for grade norms or Table I.3 for age norms). After determining which composites are Personal Strengths and Weaknesses, determine how usual the difference is in the norm sample. If the value of the difference is unusually large (occurring in fewer than 10% of the norm sample cases), then it is considered "Infrequent." To determine whether a discrepancy is unusually large, refer to the "Frequency" column of Table I.1 or Table I.3 of the KTEA-II Comprehensive Form Manual.

and written expression problems. Although the interventions have been successful in improving Luis's reading, he has not shown a positive response to the interventions in the domain of writing. He was referred for a comprehensive evaluation of his academic strengths and weaknesses to help determine the nature of his written expression difficulties. Results of the administration of the KTEA-II revealed that Luis has highly variable academic skills with Above Average mathematical skills (97th percentile), Average-level reading (55th percentile) and oral language skills (61st percentile), but Below Average abilities in Written Language (6th percentile).

Luis's performance in the Written Language domain revealed that his abilities were both significantly below those of his peers and below his own average level of performance. In particular, his weak skill areas in writing included capitalization, punctuation, and spelling. Luis's deficits in Written Language are consistent with the difficulties reported at school and should be considered to help develop appropriate academic interventions to improve his skills.

The results of this evaluation, coupled with Luis's academic and developmental histories, and his school records documenting his lack of response to

Step 4: Identify subtest strengths and weaknesses.

Compare students' performance to their own average level of performance for subtest scores. To identify subtest strengths and weaknesses, follow the same procedure outlined in Step 3: subtract each subtest standard score from the CAC standard score. Then refer to Table I.2 (grade norms) or I.4 (age norms) in Appendix I of the KTEA-II Comprehensive Form Manual to determine whether each difference is statistically significant at the .05 level. If a difference is large enough to be considered significant and the subtest score is higher than the CAC score, then that subtest is a Personal Strength. If a difference is large enough to be considered significant and the subtest score is lower than the CAC score, then that subtest is a Personal Weakness.

If a difference in a subtest is a Personal Strength or Personal Weakness, then determine how unusual it is in the norm sample. Refer to the columns labeled "Frequency" in Table I.2 (grade norms) or Table I.4 (age norms) in Appendix I of the KTEA-II Comprehensive Form Manual. The subtests that are both a Personal Strength or Weakness and are labeled "Infrequent" are worthy of further investigation, as they may provide useful diagnostic information or information related to educational considerations.

Luis's composite and subtest comparisons reveal that his Math skills are significantly better developed than his Reading, Written Language, and Oral Language composites. Luis's Reading ability and Oral Language are both significantly better developed that his Written Language skills. These comparisons between Luis's academic domains continue to support the teacher-noted deficits in his ability to express himself in writing.

Step 5: Determine the significance and unusualness of planned comparisons.

Evaluate hypotheses about specific strong and weak areas of achievement and compare performance between particular academic or reading-related skills. Specific planned comparisons of composites or subtests may provide useful information for diagnosis or instructional planning.

On the Comprehensive Form, there are numerous planned comparisons that can be made depending on the examiner's needs. However, the test authors recommend routinely making at least two comparisons in the Comprehensive Form: (1) Oral Expression Subtest with Written Expression subtest, and (2) Reading Comprehension subtest with Listening Comprehension subtest.

Once you have determined which comparisons you would like to make, then calculate the difference between the interventions aimed at developing his written language abilities, establish that there is a significant and uncommon weakness in his ability to express himself in writing. Additional assess-

> scores, and determine the significance and frequency of that difference. The back page of the KTEA-II Comprehensive Form Record Form and the front page of the KTEA-II Brief Form have places to record the data for these planned comparisons.

ment of his cognitive abilities will help to uncover any processing disorders affecting his areas of deficit, and will help determine whether Luis has a specific learning disability in written expression.

Recommendations

Luis requires a comprehensive assessment of his cognitive abilities to rule out a weakness in one or more of the basic psychological processes that are related to a learning disability in written expression.

Pending the results of the cognitive assessment, consideration must be given to Luis's unique learning characteristics, which include ADHD symptomology. Interventions to develop Luis's writing skills should be provided in a small-group setting where there are minimal distractions.

In the general education setting, Luis should be seated in the front of the classroom, where his teacher can monitor his attention as well as his progress during in-class activities.

Luis will benefit from extended time on tests that require writing.

IDENTIFICATION OF SPECIAL POPULATIONS

Specific Learning Disabilities

The culmination of years of research and practice (Berninger, Dunn, & Alper, 2005; Flanagan et al., 2002; Siegel, 1999; Stanovich, 1999; Vellutino et al., 2000), along with recent changes in the federal legislation (i.e., PL 108-446) has led to many debates regarding how specific learning disabilities (SLD) should be diagnosed (Kaufman & Kaufman, 2001). According to IDEA (2004), state and local agencies are no longer required to use the ability–achievement discrepancy method to determine SLD, which required the comparison of scores obtained from achievement and intelligence tests. Instead, clinicians are now able to use results yielded from achievement tests to determine interindividual academic abilities, and to evaluate how academic deficits are related to or caused by deficits in basic cognitive processes.

The reader is directed to the following publications for additional information regarding the diagnosis of SLD (Berninger, Dunn, & Alper, 2005; Berninger & O'Donnell, 2005; Flanagan, Kaufman, Kaufman, & Lichtenberger, 2008; Flanagan, Ortiz, Alfonso, & Mascolo, 2006).

The following section includes a description of the research conducted on specific learning disabilities in the areas of reading, mathematics, and written expression using the KTEA-II. For the research described below, the subjects were diagnosed with learning disabilities based on a severe discrepancy between performance on an achievement measure and a measure of intellectual ability (the most prevalent definition of a learning disability at the time that the research took place).

Reading Disability Study

A sample of 134 students ages 6–18 with learning disabilities in reading were administered the KTEA-II Comprehensive Form (mean age 13:1) (Kaufman & Kaufman, 2004a). The scores of these students were compared to those of a nonclinical reference group that was matched on gender, ethnicity, and parent education. Compared to the nonclinical reference group, scores on all KTEA-II subtests and composites were significantly lower ($p < .001$) for the sample with *reading disabilities*. The KTEA-II domain composite scores ranged from highs of 87.1 and 85.0 on the Oral Fluency Composite and Oral Language Composite, respectively, to lows of 76.7 and 76.9 on the Decoding Composite and the Reading Composite, respectively. The mean scores for Written Language, Sound-Symbol, and Reading Fluency composites were at a level comparable (i.e., about 1 point different) to the low scores on the Reading Composite and Decoding Composite. Thus, predictably, scores directly measuring reading skill and those related to the fluency of reading as well as phonological awareness (e.g., Sound-Symbol) show the most impairment in the Reading Disability sample. In contrast, scores in the Average range of academic ability on the Oral Language and Oral Fluency Composite (albeit in the lower end of Average) indicate that oral language skills were an area of relative integrity for the Reading Disability sample. Table 17.4 shows the scores for this sample on all KTEA-II subtests and composites (as well as other SLD samples).

Math Disability Study

A sample of 93 students ages 6–18 with learning disabilities in reading were administered the KTEA-II Comprehensive Form (mean age 13:6) (Kaufman & Kaufman, 2004a). Similar to the KTEA-II studies on other SLD, the scores of these students were compared to those of a nonclinical reference group that was controlled for gender, ethnicity, and parent education. Compared to the nonclinical reference group, scores on all KTEA-II subtests and composites were significantly lower ($p < .001$) for the sample with *math disabilities*. An important characteristic to note about this Math Disability sample was that 81% had co-morbid reading disabilities, which contributed to deficits in achievement domains

such as reading and writing. Thus, the overall pattern of KTEA-II scores for the Math Disability sample was similar to that of the Reading Disability sample, with a notably lower score on the Mathematics Composite for the Math Disability sample (see Table 17.4). The lowest average KTEA-II domain composite scores for the Math Disability sample were on the Decoding and Reading Composites (both 76.8), and the Mathematics and Written Language composites (both 77.2). These low scores were closely followed by standard scores for the Reading Fluency (77.7) and Sound-Symbol (77.9) composites. In the Average range of academic ability was the Oral Fluency Composite (85.7). Table 17.4 lists the Math Disability sample's average KTEA-II scores.

Writing Disability Study

A sample of 119 students ages 6–18 (mean age 13:3) with *written expression disabilities* were administered the KTEA-II along with a matched-sample of students with no noted disability. All KTEA-II scores for the sample with written expression disabilities were significantly lower ($p < .001$) than the nonclinical reference group. Most scores were in the Below Average range, with the lowest scores for the Written Expression Disability sample on the Written Language, Decoding, Reading, Reading Fluency, and Sound-Symbol Composites (all standard scores between 77 and 78). Though slightly higher, the Mathematics Composite was also in the Below Average range (81.1). Similar to the Reading Disability and Math Disability samples, the oral language skills of this sample with written expression disabilities appeared to be the least affected of all the domains, with average standard scores ranging from 84.7 on the Oral Language Composite to 88.2 on the Oral Fluency Composite.

Attention Deficit Disorders

Children diagnosed with attention-deficit/ hyperactivity disorder (ADHD) typically have tremendous difficulty in their academic

TABLE 17.4 KTEA-II Scores for Students with Specific Learning Disabilities

KTEA-II Subtest or Composite	Reading Disability Mean (N = 134)	Math Disability Mean (N = 93)	Writing Disability Mean (N = 119)
Letter & Word Recognition	76.8	76.8	77.2
Reading Comprehension	80.4	79.7	80.8
Reading Composite	76.9	76.8	77.4
Math Concepts & Applications	82.3	78.1	82.5
Math Computation	82.9	79.1	82.3
Mathematics Composite	81.2	77.2	81.1
Written Expression	80.2	78.8	80.0
Spelling	76.9	77.4	76.9
Written Language Composite	77.5	77.2	77.5
Listening Comprehension	89.1	86.4	88.7
Oral Expression	85.2	83.5	85.0
Oral Language Composite	85.0	82.6	84.7
Phonological Awareness	82.8	81.7	82.4
Nonsense Word Decoding	78.9	78.8	79.3
Sound-Symbol Composite	77.9	77.9	78.5
Word Recognition Fluency	77.1	77.1	77.2
Decoding Fluency	78.0	78.5	78.1
Reading Fluency Composite	77.4	77.7	77.5
Decoding Composite	76.7	76.8	77.3
Associational Fluency	90.3	88.0	91.0
Naming Facility (RAN)	88.3	87.8	89.4
Oral Fluency Composite	87.1	85.7	88.2
Comprehensive Achievement	78.4	76.1	78.3

NOTE . All KTEA-II data on Specific Learning Disabilities (SLD) are from the *KTEA-II Comprehensive Form Manual* (Kaufman & Kaufman, 2004a): Reading Disability data are from Table 7.29, Math Disability Data are from Table 7.30, and Writing Disability Data are from Table 7.31. All scores from the groups with SLD are significantly lower ($p<.001$) than those of the nonclinical reference comparison groups.

performance and achievement and represent one of the most common referrals to school psychologists and mental health providers (Demaray, Schaefer, & Delong, 2003). Children with ADHD typically do poorly in school as a result of their inattentive, impulsive, and restless behavior in the classroom, which is not conducive to learning, and not because of depressed intellectual capabilities. On standardized tests of academic achievement, children with ADHD typically score 10–30 standard score points lower than their peers in reading, spelling, math, and reading comprehension (Barkley, DuPaul, & McMurray, 1990; Brock & Knapp, 1996; Casey, Rourke, & Del Dotto, 1996).

A sample of 51 students ages 5–18 (mean age 12:11) with ADHD were administered the KTEA-II along with a matched sample of students with no noted disability. All KTEA-II Composite scores for the ADHD sample were significantly lower at the $p < .001$ level than for the nonclinical reference group, except for the Oral Fluency Composite ($p < .05$). Unlike the SLD samples, whose composite scores were frequently more than 1 SD below the normative mean, the ADHD sample's KTEA-II Composite scores ranged from 3 to 12 points below the normative mean of 100. The mean Composite scores for Reading (89.5), Mathematics (88.1), and Written Language (87.7) were not highly variable as they differed by only about 2 points. The mean Oral Language Composite was higher at 94.5, and is clearly an area of integrity within the academic profile. The strongest performance for the ADHD group was on the Oral Fluency Composite (97.0), lending further support to the strength of this sample's oral communication skills. Thus, the overall findings from the ADHD sample tested on the KTEA-II do support previous research that found depressed academic functioning for such children. However, this sample was not as impaired as samples of children with SLD, with most of the ADHD sample's mean scores being classified within the Average range of ability. Future research administering the KTEA-II together with the KABC-II to samples of children with ADHD and samples of children with co-morbid ADHD and SLD will provide useful information to clinicians who work with such children.

Mental Retardation

A sample of 43 students aged 4–17 that were identified with mild mental retardation were given the KTEA-II Comprehensive Form along with a matched sample of students with no noted disability. Criteria for participation included a full-scale score on an intelligence test that ranged between 50 and 70, and concurrent deficits in adaptive behavior. All KTEA-II Composite scores for the MR sample were significantly lower at the $p < .001$ level than the nonclinical reference group. The Comprehensive Achievement (67), Reading (70.4), Math (64.6), Written Language (67.4), Oral Language (69.6), and Sound-Symbol (70.2) composites have mean scores that are approximately 30 points lower than the nonclinical reference group. Although the samples' performance on the Reading Fluency (76.4) and Oral Fluency (84.6) composites were slightly higher, these performances were significantly lower than the nonclinical reference group. Overall, the group performed within the average range on the subtests that make up the Oral Fluency Composite (Associational Fluency [88.1], Naming Facility [85.8]), and their lowest performance was on the subtests that comprise the Mathematics Composite (Math Concepts and Application [65.3], Math Computation [66.5]).

Emotional/Behavioral Disturbance

A sample of 37 students aged 5–18 that were identified as having an emotional or behavioral disturbance (ED) were given the KTEA-II Comprehensive Form along with a matched sample of students with no noted disability. Criteria for participation in this clinical group required that the individual had an emotional condition that, over a long period of time and to a marked degree, had been found to interfere with learning. Overall, the ED group's performance on the Comprehensive Achievement (89.8), Mathematics (89.8), and Written Language (88.3) composites was significantly different from the nonclinical reference group at the $p < .001$ level. The Reading Fluency (93.2) and the Reading (93.5) composites were also found to be significantly different from the nonclinical reference group at the $p < .01$ and $p < .05$ levels, respectively. Overall, all of the subtests that required a written response or reading decoding ability have relatively low scores, with the Math Computation subtest showing the biggest difference of –12.5 points, followed closely by the group's performance on the Written Expression subtest, with –12.1 points lower than the nonclinical reference group. The group's performance on subtests that are more conceptual in nature such as Oral Expression (98.2), Listening Comprehension (95.8), and Reading Comprehension (95.5) was relatively similar across tasks and did not differ significantly from the nonclinical reference group's performance.

Deaf and Hard of Hearing

A sample of 28 students who are deaf or hard of hearing were given portions of the KTEA-II Comprehensive Form by examiners who were experienced in assessing students with this disability. Due to the variability of the group's hearing ability, examiners exercised judgment on a case-by-case basis to determine which subtests to administer due to the nature of American Sign Language (ASL), which conflicts with ability to administer and interpret some of the KTEA-II subtests meaningfully. These subtests include: Listening Comprehension, Nonsense Word Decoding, Word Recognition Fluency, Decoding Fluency, and Phonological Awareness. Based on the subtests that were administered and the respective composites that were yielded, the group's performance differs significantly at the $p < .001$ level from the nonclinical reference group's performance on the Reading (83.8), Mathematics (84.0), and Written Language (85.6) composites and on the Oral Expression (76.8) subtest, which was their lowest mean subtest score.

Gifted and Talented

The KTEA-II Comprehensive Form was administered to 95 students aged 6–18 who had been identified by their respective schools as high performing or talented in one or more academic, artistic, or leadership categories. The mean group performances on the Comprehensive Achievement (119.2), Reading (116.7), Mathematics (118.3), Written Language (116.1), and Sound-Symbol (116.7) composites were all

within the above-average range. Overall, all composite and subtest score differences were significantly different from the nonclinical reference group at the $p < .001$ level, except for Oral Expression, Phonological Awareness, and Associational Fluency, which were significantly different at the $p < .05$ level.

INTERVENTIONS BASED ON TEST RESULTS

Mather and Jaffe (2002) and Naglieri and Pickering (2003) provide valuable references to guide the clinician in the development and selection of interventions based on the unique needs of the individual being assessed. Table 17.5 illustrates some of the interventions that are listed in the Mather and Jaffe and the Naglieri and Pickering publications. The reader is urged to use this table as a first step in intervention selection and development for academic strengths and weaknesses that are identified during the administration of the KTEA-II.

SUMMARY

The KTEA-II provides comprehensive assessment of a broad range of academic achievement domains and their related skills. At the same time, the KTEA-II is a versatile instrument in that it allows the clinician either to administer the test in its entirety, or to simply administer a particular achievement domain or individual subtest. The test's interpretive procedures provide the examiner with a clinical method of analyzing a student's academic achievement that begins with interpretation at a global level and ends with a clinical analysis of errors, which in turn provides the clinician, teachers, and specialists with detailed information about what areas to focus on when developing interventions. Data obtained from the KTEA-II can be more clearly understood when considered

TABLE 17.5 Accommodations, Modifications, and Interventions Based on the KTEA-II Assessment Domains

KTEA-II Subtest	Accommodations, Modifications and Interventions
Letter and Word Recognition/ Nonsense Word Decoding	• Provide multisensory instruction to facilitate letter learning[a] • Teach the students the difference between letter names and letter sounds[a] • Help develop phonological awareness to print through the adapted version of the Elkonin Procedure (Elkonin, 1973, see Mather & Jaffe, 2002, pp. 441-442)[a] • Look-Spell-See-Write strategy to teach sight words (see Mather & Jaffe, 2002, p. 458)[a] • Recording for the Blind & Dyslexic provide audio-taped books for qualified individuals[a] • Teach chunking for reading decoding (see Naglieri & Pickering, 2003, pp. 73-74)[b] • Teach word families (see Naglieri & Pickering, 2003, pp. 75-76)[b] • Teach reading decoding rules (see Naglieri & Pickering, 2003, pp. 79-80)[b]
Reading Comprehension	• Teach the student how to color-code, or highlight specific types of information when reading that will facilitate the review process[a] • Teach the student how to use context clues to facilitate understanding (see Mather & Jaffe, 2002, pp. 439-440)[a] • Provide explicit instruction in paraphrasing, summarizing, and formulating questions and subtitles and answering them after reading the passage[a] • Teach how to make predictions and inferences from text: Directed Reading Thinking Activity (see Mather & Jaffe, 2002, pp. 440-441)[a] • Teach students extended and self-questioning techniques that help students analyze what they are reading at a deeper level[b] • Teach students to underline important parts of the text that they are reading[b] • Teach plans for comprehension (see Naglieri, & Pickering, 2003, pp. 71-72)[b]
Phonological Awareness	• Program: Road to the Code (Blachman, Ball, Black, & Tangel, 2000)[a] • Program: Phonemic Awareness in Young Children: A Classroom Curriculum (Adams, Foorman, Lundberg, & Beeler, 1998)[a] • Program: Lindamood® Phoneme Sequencing Program for Reading, Spelling, and Speech (LiPS®), www.lindamoodbell.com/gander[a] • Program: Earobics, Cognitive Concepts, Inc., www.cogcon.com[a] • Play the chained words game (see Naglieri & Pickering, 2003, pp. 83-84)[b]
Associational Fluency/ Naming Facility	• Teach retrieval strategies: visualizing the object or spelling of the word, think of a category for the target word, talk around the word (e.g., describing its appearance, function, and/or category), using synonyms[a]

(Continues)

TABLE 17.5 (Continued)

KTEA-II Subtest	Accommodations, Modifications, and Interventions
Word Recognition and Decoding Fluency	• Provide extended time on tests involving reading[a] • Rather than specifying a certain number of pages to read for homework, specify the amount of time the student should spend reading[a] • Repeated Reading, Neurological Impress Method, Great Leaps Reading, Speed Drills for Reading Fluency and Basic Skills (see Mather & Jaffe, 2002, Strategies Section)[a]
Math Concepts and Applications	• Teach the student how to use a number line[a] • Use concrete materials to teach new concepts and extensions of known concepts[a] • Provide the study with puzzles and patterns that will allow for the discovery of relationships based on quantity, order, size, and shape.[a] • Use number squares to teach math concepts (see Naglieri & Pickering, 2003, pp. 111-112)[b] • Teach the 7-step strategy for math word problems (see Naglieri & Pickering, 2003, pp. 121-122)[b]
Math Computation	• Teach the student to color-code math computation problems based on the operation required prior to beginning their work[a] • Explain and demonstrate the relationships between addition and multiplication and between subtraction and division[a] • Focus on how the student solved the problem rather than the accuracy of the response[a] • Program: Use a multisensory approach for students struggling to learn basic math facts and the steps of basic operations: Touch Math (Innovative Learning Concepts, www.touchmath.com)[a] • Use the part-whole strategy for math calculation (see Naglieri & Pickering, 2003, pp. 119-120)[b]
Written Expression	• Use sentence starters to give the student practice in different ways to expand sentences[a] • The student uses graphic organizers to classify ideas prior to writing[a] • Teach story plans, and story grammar for writing (see Naglieri & Pickering, 2003, pp. 97-98, 101-102)[b]

TABLE 17.5   (Continued)

KTEA-II Subtest	Accommodations, Modifications, and Interventions
Spelling	• Use word lists to facilitate reading and spelling tasks[a] • Have the student develop his own spelling dictionary that includes words he frequently misspells • Teach spelling strategies that involve visual, auditory, and kinesthetic modalities[a] • Teach the student how to use the Fernald method (Fernald, 143) (see Mather & Jaffe, 2002, pp. 446-447)[a] • Program: Spelling through Morphographs and Spelling Mastery (Dixon & Engelmann, 2000; www.sra4kids.com)[a] • Program: WORDS (Henry, 1990; www.proedinc.com)[a] • Teach chunking. letter ordering, mnemonics, and strategies for spelling (see Naglieri & Pickering, 2003, pp. 89-96)[b]
Listening Comprehension	• Seat the student near the teacher and away from environmental noises[a] • When speaking, face the student, speak slowly, pause between phrases and limit sentence length and complexity[a] • Encourage the student to request clarification and the restating of directions[a] • Provide multimodal instruction[a] • Check with students frequently to confirm that they understand what they are listening to[b]
Oral Expression	• Provide sufficient time for the student to generate an answer[a] • Teach the student how to sequence his ideas either mentally or on paper so he can state them in an organized fashion[a] • Teach the student a strategy for understanding, retelling, and generating narratives[a]

[a]From: Mather, N., & Jaffe, L. (2002). *Woodcock-Johnson III: Reports, Recommendations, and Strategies*. New York: John Wiley & Sons.
[b]From: Naglieri, J.A., & Pickering, E.B. (2003). *Helping Children Learn: Intervention Handouts for Use in School and at Home*. Maryland: Paul H. Brookes Publishing Co.

in the context of a comprehensive evaluation. When the KTEA-II is used in conjunction with cognitive measures like the KABC-II, and information about the child's classroom performance, background information, and other formal and informal assessment data, a more comprehensive picture of the student as a learner is made available. This comprehensive information can then be used to develop the appropriate individualized educational programs and interventions that will in turn maximize the student's success.

REFERENCES

Adams, M. J. (1990). *Beginning to read: Thinking and learning about print*. Cambridge, MA: MIT Press.

Archer, R. P., Maruish, M., Imhof, E. A., & Piotrowski, C. (1991). Psychological test usage with adolescent clients: 1990 findings. *Professional Psychology: Research & Practice, 22,* 247–252.

Barkley, R. A., DuPaul, G. J., & McMurray, M. B. (1990). A comprehensive evaluation of attention deficit disorder with and without hyperactivity. *Journal of Consulting and Clinical Psychology, 58,* 775–789.

Berninger, V. W. (1994). Future directions for research on writing disabilities: Integrating endogenous and exogenous variables. In G. R. Lyon (Ed.), *Frames of reference for the assessment of learning disabilities: New views on measurement issues.* (pp. 419–439). Baltimore: Brookes.

Berninger, V., Dunn, A., & Alper, T. (2005). Integrated multilevel model of branching assessment, instructional assessment, and profile assessment. In A. Prifitera, D. Saklofske, L. Weiss, & E. Rolfhus (Eds.), *WISC—IV: Clinical use and interpretation* (pp. 151–185). San Diego: Academic Press.

Berninger, V., & O'Donnell, L. (2005). Research-supported differential diagnosis of specific learning disabilities. In A. Prifitera, D. Saklofske, L. Weiss, & E. Rolfhus (Eds.), *WISC—IV: Clinical use and interpretation* (pp. 189–233). San Diego: Academic Press.

Brock, S. W., & Knapp, P. K. (1996). Reading comprehension abilities of children with attention-deficit/hyperactivity disorder. *Journal of Attention Disorders, 1,* 173–186.

Carrow-Woolfolk, E. (1996). *Oral and Written Language Scales.* Circle Pines, MN: AGS.

Casey, J. E., Rourke, B. P., & Del Dotto, J. E. (1996). Learning disabilities in children with attention deficit disorder with and without hyperactivity. *Child Neuropsychology, 2,* 83–98.

Chard, D. J., Simmons, D. C., & Kame'enui, E. J. (1998). Word recognition: Research bases. In D. C. Simmons & E. J. Kame'enui (Eds.), *What reading research tells us about children with diverse learning needs: Bases and basics* (pp. 141–167). Mahwah, NJ: Lawrence Erlbaum Associates.

Demaray, M. K., Schaefer, K., & Delong, K. (2003). Attention-deficit/hyperactivity disorder (ADHD): A national survey of training and current assessment practices in the schools. *Psychology in the Schools, 40*(6), 583–597.

Flanagan, D. P., & Kaufman, A. S. (2004). *Essentials of WISC-IV assessment.* New York: Wiley.

Flanagan, D. P., Kaufman, A. S., Kaufman, N. L., & Lichtenberger, E. O. (2008). Agora: The marketplace of ideas. Best practices: Applying response to intervention (RTI) and comprehensive assessment for the identification of specific learning disabilities. [DVD]. Available from NCS Pearson, Inc., PO Box 1416, Minneapolis, MN 55440; PearsonAssessments.com.

Flanagan, D. P., Ortiz, S. O., Alfonso, V. C., & Mascolo, J. T. (2002). *The achievement test desk reference (ATDR): Comprehensive assessment and learning disabilities.* Boston: Allyn & Bacon.

Flanagan, D. P., Ortiz, S. O., Alfonso, V. C., & Mascolo, J. T. (2006). *The achievement test desk reference (ATDR): Comprehensive assessment and learning disabilities* (2nd ed.). Boston: Allyn & Bacon.

Ganske, K. (1999). The developmental spelling analysis: A measure of orthographic knowledge. *Educational Assessment, 6,* 41–70.

Hammill, D. D., Fowler, L., Bryant, B., & Dunn, C. (1992). A survey of test usage among speech/language pathologists. Unpublished manuscript.

Hutton, J. B., Dubes, R., & Muir, S. (1992). Assessment practices of school psychologists: Ten years later. *School Psychologist Review, 21,* 271–284.

Individuals with Disabilities Education Improvement Act (IDEA) of 2004, 20 U.S.C. § 1400 (2004).

Kaufman, A. S., & Kaufman, N. L. (1997). *Kaufman Test of Educational Achievement—Normative Update.* Circle Pines, MN: AGS.

Kaufman, A. S., & Kaufman, N. L. (2001). *Specific learning disabilities and difficulties in children and adolescents.* New York: Cambridge University Press.

Kaufman, A. S., & Kaufman, N. L. (2004a). *Kaufman Test of Educational Achievement—Second Edition Comprehensive Form Manual.* Circle Pines, MN: AGS.

Kaufman, A. S., & Kaufman, N. L. (2004b). *Kaufman Assessment Battery for Children—Second Edition Manual.* Circle Pines, MN: AGS.

Kaufman, A. S., & Kaufman, N. L. (2004c). *Kaufman Brief Intelligence Test—Second Edition Manual.* Circle Pines, MN: AGS.

Kaufman, A. S., & Kaufman, N. L. (2005). *Kaufman Test of Educational Achievement—Second Edition Brief Form Manual.* Circle Pines, MN: AGS.

Kaufman, A. S., Lichtenberger, E. O., Fletcher-Janzen, E., & Kaufman, N. (2005). *Essentials of KABC-II assessment*. Hoboken, NJ: Wiley.

Laurent, J., & Swerdlik, M. (1992). *Psychological test usage: A survey of internship supervisors*. Paper presented at the annual meeting of the National Association of School Psychologists, Nashville, TN.

Lichtenberger, E. O., & Smith, D. R. (2005). *Essentials of WIAT-II and KTEA-II assessment*. Hoboken, NJ: Wiley.

Markwardt, F. C., Jr. (1989, 1998). *Peabody Individual Achievement Test—Revised*. Circle Pines, MN: AGS.

Mather, N., & Jaffe, L. E. (2002). *Woodcock-Johnson III: Reports, recommendations and strategies*. New York: Wiley.

Mather, N., & Woodcock, R. W. (2001). *Woodcock-Johnson III Tests of Achievement—Examiner's Manual*. Itasca, IL: Riverside.

Moats, L. C. (1993). Honing the concepts of listening and speaking: A prerequisite to the valid measurement of language behavior in children. In G. R. Lyon (Ed.), *Frames of reference for the assessment of learning disabilities: New views on measurement issues* (pp. 229–241). Baltimore: Brookes.

Moats, L. C. (1994). Spelling: A window on linguistic development. In S. Brody (Ed.), *Teaching reading: Language, letters, and thought* (pp. 109–236). Milford, NH: LARC.

Naglieri, J. A., & Pickering, E. B. (2003). *Helping children learn: Handouts for use in school and at home*. Baltimore: Brookes.

Neuhaus, G. F., & Swank, P. R. (2002). Understanding the relations between RAN letter subtest components and word reading in first grade students. *Journal of Learning Disabilities*, 35(2), 158–174.

Psychological Corporation. (1999). *Wechsler Abbreviated Test of Intelligence*. San Antonio, TX: Author.

Siegel, L. S. (1999). Issues in the definition and diagnosis of learning disabilities: A perspective on *Guckenberger v. Boston University*. *Journal of Learning Disabilities*, 32, 304–319.

Stahl, S. A., & Murray, B. A. (1994). Defining phonological awareness and its relationship to early reading. *Journal of Educational Psychology*, 86(2), 221–234.

Stanovich, K. E. (1999). The sociopsychometrics of learning disabilities. *Journal of Learning Disabilities*, 32, 350–361.

Stinnett, T. A., Havey, J. M., & Oehler-Stinnett, J. (1994). Current test usage by practicing school psychologists: A national survey. *Journal of Psychoeducational Assessment*, 12, 331–350.

Vellutino, F. R., Scanlon, D. M., & Lyon, G. R. (2000). Differentiating between difficult-to-remediate and readily remediated poor readers: More evidence against the IQ-achievement discrepancy definition of reading disability. *Journal of Learning Disabilities*, 33, 223–238.

Wechsler, D. (1991). *Wechsler Intelligence Scale for Children—Third Edition*. San Antonio, TX: Psychological Corporation.

Wechsler, D. (1997). *Wechsler Adult Intelligence Scale—Third Edition*. San Antonio, TX: Psychological Corporation.

Wechsler, D. (2001). *Wechsler Individual Achievement Test—Second Edition*. San Antonio, TX: Psychological Corporation.

Wechsler, D. (2002). *Wechsler Individual Achievement Test—Second Edition Supplement for Adults and College Students*. San Antonio, TX: Psychological Corporation.

Wechsler, D. (2003). *Wechsler Intelligence Scale for Children—Fourth Edition*. San Antonio, TX: Psychological Corporation.

Wilkinson, G. S. (1993). *Wide Range Achievement Test—Third Edition Administration Manual*. Wilmington, DE: Wide Range.

Wilson, M. S., & Reschley, D. J. (1996). Assessment in school psychology training and practice. *School Psychology Review*, 21, 9–23.

Wolf, M. (1997). A provisional, integrative account of phonological and naming-speed deficits in dyslexia: Implications for diagnosis and intervention. In B.A. Blachman (Ed.), *Foundations of reading acquisition and dyslexia: Implications for early intervention* (pp. 67–92). Mahwah, NJ: Lawrence Erlbaum Associates.

Woodcock, R. W., McGrew, K. S., & Mather, N. (2001). *Woodcock-Johnson III*. Itasca, IL: Riverside.

Wechsler Individual Achievement Test—Second Edition

Kurt T. Choate

RATIONALE UNDERLYING THE TEST

The *Wechsler Individual Achievement Test—Second Edition: Update 2005* (WIAT-II; Psychological Corporation, 2005) is a revision of the *Wechsler Individual Achievement Test* (WIAT; Wechsler, 1992). There were three goals followed in the creation of the original WIAT. The changes in national and state educational trends during the development of the original WIAT heavily influenced the objectives and decisions made in its creation. In addition, a statistical link was needed between the Wechsler Intelligence Scales (e.g., *Wechsler Intelligence Scale for Children—Third Edition*; Wechsler, 1991) and a comprehensive achievement test due to the heavy influence of the ability–achievement discrepancy analyses used for diagnostic considerations at the time. Finally, in conjunction with the mandates of Public Law 94-142 from 1975, the WIAT subtests were developed to assess the seven areas of achievement outlined in the federal law: reading comprehension, basic reading skill, mathematics calculation, mathematical reasoning, oral expression, written expression, and listening comprehension. The basic content domains reflected in the WIAT

included reading, writing, mathematics, and oral expression. The original WIAT was intended for individuals between the ages of 5 years, 0 months and 19 years, 11 months. In addition, it contained grade-based norms ranging from Kindergarten to grade 12.

The revision of the instrument began in the late 1990s, updating the content to reflect current federal curriculum standards (i.e., Individuals with Disabilities Education Act Amendments of 1997) in addition to retaining the basic content domains of the original WIAT. Several changes to the original WIAT in the revision improved the test's overall utility as a diagnostic instrument. The revision of the WIAT remained an individually administered achievement test; however, the age range was extended to include individuals between the ages of 4 and 85 years. Grade-based norms were also extended to include pre-Kindergarten individuals as well as college students from two- and four-year colleges. There were six objectives that the test developers utilized to modify and improve the test revision (Psychological Corporation, 2005).

First, due to the changes in federal standards and classroom practices, the WIAT-II subtests were improved to strengthen the theoretical base of the instrument. Second, the WIAT-II revision strengthened the link between assessment and intervention by expanding the skill analysis features coinciding with the associated subtest and by evaluating both the product (e.g., writing sample) and the process (e.g., word fluency) that contribute to the acquisition of the particular skill. Third, the age range was extended from 5–19 years in the WIAT to 4–85 years in the WIAT-II, with the intention of improving early diagnosis and intervention for younger children at risk for future academic failure as well as to assess college students and adults needing an evaluation of academic skills. Fourth, the scoring system for certain subtests was improved by introducing scoring rubrics consistent with instructional practice (providing increased face validity) and by providing the examiner with additional annotated scoring examples. Fifth, the WIAT-II includes ability–achievement (predicted and simple) discrepancy information based on the IQ and index scores from the *Wechsler Preschool and Primary Scale of Intelligence—Revised* (WPPSI-R; Wechsler, 1989), the *Wechsler Intelligence Scale for Children—Third Edition* (WISC-III; Wechsler, 1991), and the *Wechsler Adult Intelligence Scale—Third Edition* (WAIS-III; Wechsler, 1999). Finally, the WIAT-II was linked to the *Process Assessment of the Learner—Test Battery for Reading and Writing* (PAL-RW; Berninger, 2001), an instrument utilized for diagnosing underlying processes believed to be associated with the successful attainment of reading and writing skills.

DESCRIPTION OF THE TEST

The WIAT-II is comprised of nine individually administered subtests that yield four domain composites and one overall composite. Each of these subtests and each composite, including the overall Total Composite, yield a standard score with a mean of 100 and a standard deviation of 15. In addition, confidence intervals, percentile ranks, Normal Curve Equivalents (NCEs), stanines, age equivalents, and grade equivalents

can be determined. Supplemental scores utilizing quartiles and deciles can also be derived from the Reading Comprehension, Written Expression, and Oral Expression subtests. Table 18.1 lists, by domain, each of the subtests used to obtain the various composite scores. In addition, the table describes the types of abilities measured by each subtest. Each domain and subtest is described in more detail in the following.

Reading Subtests

The reading subtests included in the WIAT-II utilized the work of Virginia Berninger (e.g., Berninger, 1989; Berninger, Cartwright, Yates, Swanson, & Abbott, 1994) as well as recommendations by the National Reading Panel (2000). The preponderance of Berninger's work indicates that instruction and assessment of reading skills be aimed at low-level (i.e., word recognition) and high-level (i.e., comprehension) skills, and all levels of language (subword, word, and text). In addition, literature suggests that early assessment of letter identification and phonological awareness seems to be a reliable predictor of later reading achievement (Torgesen, Wagner, & Rashotte, 1994). Therefore, the reading subtests on the WIAT-II were designed and revised in an attempt to assess low-level and high-level skills, as well as providing early assessment data for delays in the reading process.

Word Reading

The Word Reading subtest measures early reading (i.e., phonological awareness), sight word recognition, and decoding skills. For the younger examinee, he or she is asked to demonstrate the ability to name letters of the alphabet, identify and generate rhyming words, identify beginning and ending sounds of words, blend sounds into words, and match sounds with letters and letter blends. Older examinees are asked to read aloud from a word list. Accuracy is scored (correct, incorrect) and automaticity and self-corrections can be noted as part of a qualitative analysis.

TABLE 18.1   Structure of the *Wechsler Individual Achievement Test–Second Edition* Subtests by Domain

Domain	Subtest	Abilities Measured
Reading	Word Reading	• Phonological awareness • Word attack • Automaticity of word
	Reading Comprehension	• Literal and inferential comprehension • Vocabulary • Reading accuracy and fluency • Word recognition in context
	Pseudoword Decoding	• Phonological decoding
Mathematics	Numerical Operations	• One-to-one correspondence • Calculation (addition, subtraction, multiplication, division) • Simple equations
	Math Reasoning	• Counting • Single- and Multi-step problem solving • Money, time, and measurement • Geometry • Interpret graphs • Statistics and probability • Estimation • Identifying patterns
Written Language	Spelling	• Sound-letter awareness • Regular and irregular words • Integration of spelling and lexical comprehension (homonyms)
	Written expression	• Alphabet writing • Written word fluency • Sentence combining • Sentence generation • Descriptive writing organization, vocabulary, and mechanics • Persuasive writing organization, vocabulary, theme development, and mechanics

(Continues)

TABLE 18.1   (Continued)

Domain	Subtest	Abilities Measured
Oral Expression	Listening Comprehension	• Receptive vocabulary • Expressive vocabulary • Inferential comprehension • Oral expression • Oral word fluency • Auditory short-term recall • Story generation • Giving directions

Reading Comprehension

The Reading Comprehension subtest measures several comprehension skills that are taught in the classroom and used in everyday life. Younger examinees are asked to match a written word with its representative picture. Older examinees read different types of passages (e.g., narrative vs. informational) and answer questions involving the content comprehension, including identifying the main idea, making inferences, and defining vocabulary through context cues. In addition, examinees will read short sentences aloud and respond to the comprehension questions. For examinees that remain within their grade-appropriate item set, Reading Speed can be calculated by totaling the time required to read all the passages within the item set. The relation between Reading Speed and Reading Comprehension scores then can be used to describe Reading Rate using the Reading Rate graph on the record form.

Pseudoword Decoding

The Pseudoword Decoding subtest was designed to measure a different skill set than that required for the Word Reading subtest. The Pseudoword Decoding subtest assesses the ability to apply phonetic decoding skills. The examinee reads aloud from a list of nonsense words designed to be representative of the phonetic structure

of words in the English language. The examinee cannot rely on sight-word knowledge to decode the nonwords and must utilize phonological abilities to do so. The pseudowords are decoded on the basis of spelling–phoneme relationships and word-structure knowledge, not by retrieval of word-specific representations. Pseudoword decoding is used to evaluate whether the examinee's phonological decoding mechanism is in line with developmental expectations.

Mathematics Subtests

The updates in the mathematics subtests from WIAT to WIAT-II were developed in response to issues raised by the National Council of Teachers of Mathematics (2000). Many states have utilized these standards when developing their curricula. The mathematical standards include the domains of number and operations, algebra, measurement, geometry, probability, problem solving, connections and representation, and reasoning and proof.

Numerical Operations

The Numerical Operations subtest assesses the ability to recognize, recall, and write numbers, count using one-to-one correspondence, and solve written calculation problems and simple equations. Although it is important to assess examinees' ability to calculate, it is also important to assess their procedural skills as well. Because individuals can solve problems using multiple approaches, asking the examinee to work additional problems after standard test administration and to "think aloud" can provide more qualitative information concerning the procedures employed to solve problems.

Math Reasoning

The Math Reasoning subtest presents mathematics problems with both verbal and visual prompts. The tasks include counting, identifying geometric shapes, solving problems involving whole numbers, fractions, or decimals, interpreting graphs, solving statistics and probability problems, identifying patterns, and solving single- and multistep word problems, with item content related to time, money, and measurement. It is important to note that most items in this subtest are read aloud to the examinee.

Written Language Subtests

The written language subtests were developed and revised to evaluate an individual's strengths and weaknesses in spelling and handwriting (i.e., low-level skills), as well as composition of sentences within a paragraph or essay (i.e., high-level skills). These different levels of language (e.g., subword, word, and sentence) affect the text-generation process and the ability of an individual to express himself or herself effectively. The WIAT-II evaluates writing at the subword, word, sentence, and text levels.

Spelling

The Spelling subtest assesses the examinee's ability to spell dictated letters, letter blends, and words. Homonyms require the examinee to use context clues from the dictated sentences to determine the appropriate word to spell. Early spelling concepts such as sound-to-letter correspondence for vowels, consonants, and

consonant blends are assessed in younger examinees. Other items within the subtest include words that vary in spelling-phoneme predictability, high-frequency homonyms, and contractions.

Written Expression

The Written Expression subtest contains five sections: Alphabet Writing, Word Fluency, Sentences, Paragraph, and Essay. Alphabet Writing is a timed measure of automaticity in writing the letters of the alphabet in order from memory. Word Fluency requires writing a list of words that match a prescribed category. Sentences assess the examinee's ability to combine multiple sentences into a single meaningful sentence as well as generate sentences from visual or verbal cues. Paragraph assesses written text based on mechanics, organization, and vocabulary. Essay assesses written text based on mechanics, organization, theme development, and vocabulary. These various sections within the Written Expression subtest reflect the writing requirements typically encountered in a classroom setting.

Oral Language Subtests

The Oral Language subtests measure a broad range of oral language activities, similar in kind to the types of activities typically found in a classroom setting. The subtests were developed to identify individuals who may require a referral for a comprehensive speech and language evaluation and to provide a link between language and reading activities.

Listening Comprehension

The Listening Comprehension subtest assesses the ability to listen for detail and is composed of three sections: Receptive Vocabulary, Sentence Comprehension, and Expressive Vocabulary. Receptive Vocabulary requires the examinee to select the picture that matches a word. Sentence Comprehension requires the examinee to select the picture that matches a sentence. Expressive

Vocabulary requires the examinee to generate a word that matches a picture and an oral description.

Oral Expression

The Oral Expression subtest assesses the examinee's general ability to use oral language effectively and is composed of four sections: Sentence Repetition, Word Fluency, Visual Passage Retell, and Giving Directions. Sentence Repetition requires a younger examinee to repeat a sentence back to the examiner *exactly* as spoken. Word Fluency requires the examinee to provide specific examples from general categories and prompts. Visual Passage Retell requires the examinee to make up stories based on visual cartoon stimuli, and Giving Directions requires the examinee to provide directions in a verbal format to both verbal and visual stimuli.

ADMINISTRATION AND SCORING

General Procedures

The normative sample of the WIAT-II was collected with individuals aged 4 through 85 years. The test measures academic skills in reading, writing, oral language, and mathematics in children, adolescents, and adults. It is important to examine the school curriculum of the potential examinee. This ensures that the content contained in the WIAT-II provides the most information concerning his or her achievement. Furthermore, the WIAT-II was not designed to test the upper limits of achievement for older individuals; thus, this assessment would not be appropriate in measuring academic giftedness for these examinees.

The purpose of providing normative information is to compare an examinee's performance on a test with a representative sample from the population. This information is gathered using standard procedures for administering and scoring the test. To compare an examinee's performance to this national normative sample in

the WIAT-II, the administration and scoring procedures provided in the *Examiner's Manual: Update 2005* (Psychological Corporation, 2005) should be closely followed. Any time changes in administration and scoring procedures occur for any assessment instrument, these changes can potentially alter the test results and introduce unwanted error into the examinee's scores (*Standards for Educational and Psychological Testing*, 1999). However, it is also important to provide an environment in which the examinee can give his or her best performance. Therefore, do not use an unnatural volume or use a monotone voice in reading the verbatim instructions from the stimulus booklet. Try to maintain rapport, have a genuine interest in what the examinee is doing, and encourage and reinforce the examinee's attempts at the various items.

The *Examiner's Manual* (Psychological Corporation, 2005) provides approximate testing times for complete administration of the WIAT-II. For grades pre-K–Kindergarten, it will take approximately 45 minutes to complete the entire test. As the age of the examinee increases, more subtests are administered and more items are given; therefore, for grades 1–6, it should take approximately 90 minutes, and for grades 7–16 and adults, it should take approximately 1 1/2 to 2 hours.

The administration time for the WIAT-II can also vary depending on the referral question(s), the age/grade of the examinee, the examinee's academic skill strengths and weaknesses, and which subtests are administered. It is important to practice administration prior to a real testing with a client. This will allow the examiner to become more familiar with subtest order and what materials are needed to move through the test in a smooth and natural manner. In addition, the examiner should make note on the front of the record form concerning test-session behavior that had an impact on the examinee's test scores. For example, if the examinee frequently asks for instruction clarification on subtests or is easily distracted by outside noises, this may reduce his or her optimum performance on the WIAT-II and increase the testing time needed.

Try to complete the WIAT-II in one test session. If breaks are needed to reduce fatigue or restlessness, only allow such breaks *after* the completion of a subtest, not in the middle of a subtest.

An important consideration for optimum test performance is the physical setting in which testing occurs. Choose the testing room in a quiet area to prevent the examinee from being distracted and to avoid interruptions in the testing session. Make sure that the examinee has a smooth writing surface on which to write and that the room in which testing occurs is well ventilated. In addition, lighting should be adequate for the examinee to see the items in the response booklets and stimulus booklets. If the examinee utilizes corrective lenses or hearing aids, make sure that the examinee uses them during testing. Remember that the goal of assessment is to give the examinee every opportunity to do his or her best.

Do not choose a room that has the alphabet displayed. One subtest in the WIAT-II asks the younger examinee to write the alphabet. For younger examinees, sometimes it is difficult for the examinee to separate from the accompanying adult and go to the assessment area. It is important to assess the examinee without other adults in the room; however, it is permissible to allow an adult in the room as long as that adult sits out of sight from the examinee and remains silent throughout the testing session.

The physical placement of the examiner and examinee is also important to allow smooth and efficient administration of the WIAT-II. Make sure the chairs and tables are at a comfortable height for both the examiner and examinee. Try to arrange the chairs so that the examiner and examinee are sitting at one corner. This arrangement is best so the examiner and examinee can point to items in the stimulus book without undue straining. In addition, the examiner can lean to one side and easily see the answer choice to which the examinee is pointing.

Prior to testing the individual, have the materials within easy reach during the assessment, but out-of-sight from the examinee. One way to do this is to keep the materials on another chair beside or behind the examiner.

Most of the materials necessary for a complete administration are available in the WIAT-II test kit (Psychological Corporation, 2005). However, there are some items that should be provided by the examiner. The examiner should provide blank, white paper for several subtests, several pencils without erasers, eight pennies for the younger grades, a stopwatch or clock with a second hand, and a clipboard. The testing manual recommends using a tape recorder when the examinee provides long verbal answers to questions. This allows the examiner to be more accurate with scoring after the testing with the examinee is over.

There are several pieces in the WIAT-II kit available from the publisher. To provide smooth, uninterrupted testing, it is important to understand the use of each component. There are two stimulus booklets (1 and 2) provided in the test kit. These books have easel backs, which allows them to be freestanding. These stimulus booklets contain the subtest items, which face the examinee. The back page, which faces the examiner, contains the verbatim instructions to be read to the examinee as well as the correct responses for many of the test items. It is important to keep the examinee from seeing the examiner's page in the stimulus book and from seeing the record form. A clipboard can provide concealment and a firm surface on which to write, but do not be obvious about keeping the material from the examinee. This may cause the examinee to become apprehensive, which might make him or her self-conscious of giving answers. In addition, since all the instructions and responses are provided in the stimulus booklets and in the record form, it is not necessary to use the *Examiner's Manual* (Psychological Corporation, 2005) to administer the test.

One subtest, Pseudoword Decoding, requires the examinee to pronounce nonsense words that follow standard phonemic decoding skills. However, to quickly score this subtest as the examinee is reading the words from a list, the examiner must know what the correct pronunciations are for each word. The test kit provides a tape that contains all the correct pronunciations for this subtest. It is meant to be listened to prior to administering this subtest. It is *not* used during actual testing. In addition, it is also important for the examiner to know the correct pronunciations for the list of words for the Word Reading subtest.

Rapport is the relationship developed between the examinee and examiner to help elicit the best results in an assessment situation (Sattler, 2001). Before beginning the assessment, engage the examinee in light conversation surrounding his or her interests or current activities. Use clinical judgment to determine how much time is needed to ensure enough rapport has been built to support the therapeutic relationship. If the examinee is concerned about the purpose of testing or what the test results will be used for, be sure to answer him or her in a truthful and caring manner.

Once rapport has been established, provide an introduction to the assessment process in language that is appropriate for the individual's ability level and age. Specifically, for the WIAT-II, be sure to state that many of the tasks on this test are similar in content to the academic tasks many individuals do in school. Also, let the examinee know that some people find some of the tasks easy, while some of the other tasks are more difficult. Reinforce the expectation that the examinee is not expected to get all the questions correct, but encourage the examinee to try his or her best.

It is important to keep the rapport with the examinee through the testing process. At various times through the assessment, state your interest in the performance of the examinee. Reinforce the examinee for his or her attempts at the items. However, when giving reinforcement or encouragement, do not let the examinee know whether he or she gave correct or incorrect

responses. An example of appropriate feedback would be, "I really like how hard you are working." Do not say, "Good" or "Nice job." If the examinee begins to demonstrate agitation concerning the difficulty of the test items, let the examinee know that he or she is not expected to get all the correct answers. For example, say, "Remember, some tasks are easy and some are hard. Just do the best you can." For more examples of feedback to provide to examinees to maintain rapport, see the *Examiner's Manual: Update 2005* (Psychological Corporation, 2005) found in the WIAT-II test kit.

Many examinees are referred for evaluations who have physical and/or language impairments. Sometimes it is necessary to modify the standardized procedures to allow the examinee to take full advantage of the content within the WIAT-II. The type and extent of the impairment as well as the demands of the subtest administered will indicate whether the instructions need to be modified or whether the individual needs accommodations to complete the subtest. For example, an individual with vision impairment may have difficulty seeing the list of words on the Word Card. It might be necessary to enlarge the words prior to administration to compensate for the vision impairment.

It is important to determine the extent of the examinee's strengths and weaknesses and determine what will impact the validity of the assessment. For example, for someone who prefers sign language as her mode of communication, it may be necessary to deviate from the standardized procedures and instructions. However, try to maintain as many standard procedures as possible while still taking the examinee's needs into account. Remember that data on the WIAT-II were not collected with modifications made to the instructions. Any deviations from these standard instructions will have an effect on the test scores obtained, and if the deviations are significant enough, the standard scores in the norm tables will not be valid for the modified subtest. However, qualitative information gleaned from the modifications used provides possibilities for future recommendations and interventions.

Subtest Administration

Because the WIAT-II subtests were standardized in a specific order, the sequence of administration should be the same. This sequence is indicated in the stimulus booklets and on the record form. If only certain subtests are being administered, the same sequence of administration should be followed.

Start points, reverse rules, discontinue rule, and stop points for each subtest are indicated in the record form and in the stimulus booklets. The grade of the individual being tested will determine the specific administration rules.

Start Points

The grade level for examinees still in school will determine where to start for each subtest. When testing adults, the start point for each subtest is determined by the last grade completed by the individual.

Reverse Rules

The *basal level* of a test indicates the point at which an examinee is assumed to get all previous items correct. *Reverse rules* are used to obtain these basal levels for each subtest. Word Reading, Numerical Operations, Spelling, Math Reasoning, Listening Comprehension, and Oral Expression require the examinee to receive three consecutive correct answers. Once this basal level has been established, the examiner automatically scores all previous items on the subtest 1 point. If the examinee receives 0 points on any of the first three items administered from the grade-appropriate start point, the examiner reverses administration of items until three consecutive 1-point answers have been achieved. Once the basal has been established, the examiner awards 1 point to all previous items and continues administration of the subtest in a normal manner until the discontinue criterion has been met.

A second type of reverse rule exists for the Reading Comprehension subtest. This routing task requires that the examinee receives at least 1 point within the first grade-appropriate item set to continue. If the examinee receives all incorrect responses within the first grade-appropriate item set, do not reverse-administer items. Instead, reverse item sets. You may do reverse items only *one* time during this subtest regardless of how the individual performs in the new item set. Administer all the items in the new grade-based item set. Do not discontinue, but administer all of the items in the new grade level and stop at that grade level's stop point if the reverse rule has been applied. Grades 4–8 reverse 3 start points below the original start point (i.e., grade 8 reverses to the grade 4 start point, grade 7 reverses to the grade 4 start point, etc.); grades 2–3 reverse to the grade 1 start point. For grades 9–12, if the examinee scores 0 on all grade-appropriate items, administer items 75–114. Finally, if individuals in grades 13–16 score 0 on all grade-appropriate items, administer items 94–127.

Discontinue Rule

Stop administering the subtest when the *discontinue rule* is achieved. The discontinue rule is similar to the basal rules, except this criterion is applied at the end of a subtest. It refers to the number of consecutive 0-point responses the examinee must give to stop administration of the subtest. The discontinue rules apply to any items on a subtest that are administered in forward order. On some subtests you must keep reversing until you get a certain number of items correct, which establishes the basal level. If the examiner is unsure whether the discontinue rule has been met because of uncertainty of scoring, the examiner should administer further items (i.e., testing the limits) until he or she is certain of achieving the discontinue criteria. There are no discontinue rules for the Reading Comprehension and Written Expression subtests. All items for the particular grade level must be administered. Each section on the Listening Comprehension subtest (Receptive Vocabulary, Sentence

Comprehension, and Expressive Vocabulary) has its own set of discontinue rules. Only the Sentence Repetition on the Oral Expression subtest has a discontinue rule.

Stop Points

Another method of stopping administration of a subtest is to utilize *stop points* instead of using the discontinue rule. Stop points can be determined by specific items or when time limits have been reached. The Reading Comprehension and Written Expression are the only two subtests on the WIAT-II that have item-specific stop points. The examiner should stop administering the subtest when all items are administered within the particular grade level and the stop point is reached. Alphabet Writing, Word Fluency, Paragraph, and Essay use time limits to determine the examinee's stop point. Stop administration of the section within the Written Expression and Word Fluency subtests when the time limit is reached.

Time Limits

Two subtests have strict time limits: Written Expression and Oral Expression. Timing is also necessary on the Reading Comprehension subtest. Using a stopwatch or a clock with a second hand, the examiner records the amount of time required to read passages. This time should be recorded on the record form in seconds. Do not be obvious with the timing; use a stopwatch without noise.

Strict timing with a stopwatch should not be used on the Word Reading subtest. More informal counting is permitted to determine whether it takes the examinee more than 3 seconds to read the word. This helps with qualitative interpretations and enables the calculation of accuracy and automaticity. On the other subtests, use the timing information only as a guideline. Never stop an examinee who is actively working on a task because the suggested time limit expires.

Teaching Tasks

Teaching tasks or modeling is included in several of the WIAT-II subtests. Most of these tasks are found in sample items. These tasks allow examinees to ask questions and to get clarification on the tasks required by the subtest. It allows examinees the opportunity to perform as well as they can. Since most of the teaching tasks are sample items, they are not included in the examinee's final score on a subtest. Teaching task directions are found in the stimulus booklets for those subtests that contain such items. Ensure that only the teaching items are modeled and be sure to follow the directions found in the stimulus booklets. Utilizing other items for additional teaching would not follow the standardization procedures used in collecting the representative sample. In addition, the scores gathered from an administration containing additional teaching or modeling would not be accurate and would be misleading.

Repeating Items and Querying Responses

When requested by the examinee, it is permissible to repeat items or paraphrase instruction except for those subtests where repeating items is prohibited (i.e., Sentence Comprehension, Listening Comprehension). It is important that the examinee understand the tasks presented to him or her to obtain accurate scores. Note frequent requests for repeating instructions or items and provide that information beside Behavioral Observations on the record form.

It is permissible to prompt the examinee if the examiner thinks the examinee can improve his or her score, if the examinee hesitates in responding to a question, or if the examinee provides an ambiguous answer. If prompting is permitted on the particular subtest, provide a general prompt to the examinee, such as "Tell me more about that."

When you ask an examinee to provide you with more information (i.e., "Tell me more about that"), place a *Q* for "query" and record the examinee's response verbatim in the record form. Award the higher score if the examinee is able to improve his or her answer after querying. Even a 0-point response can get a higher score following a query.

Out-of-Level Testing

Most of the time, examinees who are assessed by the WIAT-II will be in the typical age and grade placements. However, some examinees are older than typical for grade due to retention(s). For example, examinees who are 9 years old and in the second grade would be considered older than typical for that grade and out-of-level. The academic skills of those examinees that are old for grade should be measured against those examinees that have been exposed to the same type of curriculum. The psychometric properties of most of the subtests on the WIAT-II take this into account. However, the Written Expression and Oral Expression subtests have different psychometric properties than the other subtests in the battery. The Update 2005 edition includes age-based norms from the test publisher to address those examinees that are old for grade. When testing examinees who are tested out-of-level and where age-based norms are desired, examiners should ensure that they use the correct norms tables to convert raw scores to standard scores on the Written Expression and Oral Expression subtests.

General Scoring Instructions

It is important to record the responses given by an examinee verbatim since some of the scoring procedures are more subjective. Scoring rules given in the WIAT-II *Examiner's Manual* (2005) provide guidelines to grade the responses and the supplemental manuals provide more detailed information and examples of scoring. The subtests requiring verbatim recordings are the Expressive Vocabulary group of items in the Listening Comprehension subtest, and the Sentence Repetition, Oral Expression Word Fluency, Visual Passage Retell, and Giving Directions group of items in the Oral Expression subtest.

The other subtests (i.e., Numerical Operations, Spelling, and Written Expression) require the examinee to write responses in a response booklet. Examinees should mark through answers with an *X* if they want to change a response. As an examiner, it is important to watch the responses given by the examinee on the Numerical Operations and Spelling subtests to determine when the basal rule and discontinue rule have been met.

Qualitative Observations

Behaviors should be noted on the record form as the test is being administered. This could provide important information as to the processes the examinee goes through to solve problems in the various achievement areas. Behaviors that extend through various subtests, such as fidgeting or frequent impulsive responses, should also be recorded. At the end of various subtests, such as Word Reading, Reading Comprehension, and Spelling, the record form provides a section to rate the frequency of certain behaviors using a Likert-type scale (Never, Seldom, Often, Always, or Not Observed). These qualitative ratings will not give a standardized score; however, they can be useful for understanding the examinee's standardized performance on the WIAT-II and can be helpful in providing interventions or modifications in the classroom.

Scoring Rubrics

Depending on the grade- or age-range to be tested, either the *WIAT-II Scoring and Normative Supplement for Grades Pre-K–12: Update 2005* (Psychological Corporation, 2005) or the *WIAT-II Supplement for College Students and Adults* (Psychological Corporation, 2002) can provide the information needed to score the WIAT-II.

Other than the Written Expression, Reading Comprehension, and Oral Expression subtest, which have stop points, all other subtests will have a discontinue rule, a reverse rule, or both.

These subtests need to be scored during administration of the test. If you are not sure how a response should be scored at the time of administration, write it down verbatim so you can come back later to score it. During test administration, ignore this problematic item when calculating the discontinue rule. However, if this item is later judged to be an incorrect response, include it when calculating the discontinue rule.

The scoring rules for the Word Reading, Numerical Operations, Spelling, Pseudoword Decoding, Math Reasoning, and Listening Comprehension subtests are 0 points for incorrect responses and 1 point for correct responses. The correct answers for the items on each of these subtests are located on the examiner's pages in the stimulus booklet or in the record form.

In relation to these objective subtests, the procedures used in parts of the Reading Comprehension, Written Expression, and Oral Expression subtests are scored subjectively. Many of the items in these subtests require the examiner to use clinical judgment for providing a score. Appendix A of either the *WIAT-II Scoring and Normative Supplement for Grades Pre-K–12: Update 2005* (Psychological Corporation, 2005) or the *WIAT-II Supplement for College Students and Adults* (Psychological Corporation, 2002) provides the specific criteria utilized during the standardization process to judge an examinee's answer as correct or incorrect.

Specifically, the Reading Comprehension is scored using a 0-, 1-, or 2-point scale. The most frequent correct and incorrect answers given during the standardization process are listed in the stimulus booklet. The supplemental manuals, however, provide a more extensive list of answers as well. Higher quality answers are scored more points than lower quality answers.

The Written Expression subtest is divided into several subsections, which are or are not administered depending on the grade-level of the examinee being tested. Each item on the Written Expression—Sentence subsection has three possible point values: 0, 1, or 2 points. The Written Expression—Paragraph subsection

and the Written Expression—Essay subsection can be scored using a quantitative process or a more holistic, qualitative process. To quantitatively score these particular subsections, specific scoring rules and rubrics are found in the *Examiner's Manual* (2005) or in Appendix A of the supplements. These scoring rules look at the way an examinee organizes his or her thoughts in writing, whether the examinee can utilize the mechanics of grammar, and whether he or she has used appropriate vocabulary. However, a more holistic scoring method is also provided to give an overall score on these subsections. It is important to remember, though, that a Written Expression subtest standard score and a Written Language Composite score cannot be obtained if the holistic scoring method has been used.

The Oral Expression subtest is also divided into several subsections. Similar to the Written Expression subtest, scoring rules and examples found in the *Examiner's Manual* (2005) and in Appendix A of the supplements provide a quantitative way of grading the oral responses of the examinee. Oral Expression—Visual Passage Retell and Oral Expression—Giving Directions are scored using the procedure found on the record form.

Using Weighted Raw Scores and Other Supplemental Scores

Because of the statistical procedure involved with the items within certain subtests, some raw scores from the WIAT-II require *weighting* before looking up the standard scores. The tables required to weight raw scores can be found in the supplements (Appendix B for grade-based weighting and Appendix E for age-based weighting). Because item sets are used, the Reading Comprehension subtest requires conversion to a weighted raw score prior to looking up a standard score. Also, portions of the Reading Comprehension subtest, portions of the Written Expression subtest, and the Word Fluency subsection of the Oral Expression subtest require conversions to quartile- or decile-based scores before interpretation. These supplemental scores provide further evaluation of an examinee's performance within each of these subtests. It is important to note that if an examinee has had to reverse on the Reading Comprehension subtest, the quartile scores obtained for the subtest's supplemental scores cannot be interpreted.

General Guidelines

During the scoring of the standardization sample, the test developers gave credit to responses even if the examinee used cultural variations in pronunciation of words or informal language. Therefore, it is important to understand the regional variations of word pronunciation before testing individuals. Also, if an examinee has some form of an articulation disorder, give him or her credit for verbal mispronunciations of words that stem directly from the disorder. Because the Pseudoword Decoding subtest requires correct verbal pronunciations of nonsense words, the examiner should use his or her clinical judgment to determine whether this subtest should be administered to an individual with an articulation disorder.

Credit should also be given to examinees' responses that are correct, regardless of the way the response is given. Most of the time, the way the examinee should respond to a question is provided in the verbal instructions given by the examiner or in the stimulus booklet (e.g., "Point to the second cat from the dog"). However, if the examinee uses another method of response that is otherwise correct, credit for the response should be given.

Spontaneous responses or changes to answers given earlier in a subtest should be allowed only if the examiner is still administering the subtest. If the change in answer requires a change in score, then the examiner should rescore the item. However, if the examinee changes an answer from a subtest that has already been completed, do not change answer responses or point values of scores.

Sometimes an examinee will provide more information concerning an otherwise correct answer that provides insight into the examinee's misconception of a question. This is known as *spoiling* a response. For example, in an item similar to one in the Reading Comprehension subtest, look at a sample response given by an examinee:

> What will happen if Susie has the best horse for Animal Day?
>
> She will win first place . . . because all the kids win.

In the response to this item, the examinee describes the correct answer; however, when elaborating, the examinee provides a misconception of the end result. This response would be scored as incorrect. Sometimes, though, a response is vague rather than spoiled and requires a query to clarify the examinee's answer. Once a query is made, a score should be given to the resulting response.

In addition, some examinees will give several different answers to items. Score only the last response if the examinee gives three or more responses to an item. If only two responses are given, ask which answer the examinee is intending to be the response and score only that particular response.

STANDARDIZATION, NORMS, AND PSYCHOMETRICS

Standardization Sample

Two separate samples were used in the standardization process for the WIAT-II. In the school-age sample, data were gathered from individuals aged 4–19 years. In addition, these individuals were currently enrolled in grades pre-K–12 during the 1999–2000 and 2000–2001 school years. For the college sample, the standardization sample was collected from individuals in grades 13–16 from 2- and 4-year colleges nationwide. The adult standardization sample was collected from individuals aged 17–85 years who were no longer enrolled in secondary school.

Using the October 1998 U.S. Census data, the standardization data in each of these groups was stratified by grade, age, sex, race/ethnicity, U.S. geographic region, and parent/guardian education level (PEL)/self-education level (SEL). The proportions of these particular subgroups were representative of the standardization data collected for the WIAT-II.

The school-age sample was divided into two groups: grade-based normative data and age-based normative data. The grade-based data consisted of 3,600 individuals; half of the data were collected in the fall semester while the other half were collected in the spring semester. There were 1,806 females and 1,794 males in this data set, with an approximately equal number in each grade. The age-based data consisted of 2,950 examinees aged 4 years, 0 months to 19 years, 11 months, with individuals between 15 and 19 years of age who were attending college being excluded from this sample. Of the 2,950 examinees in the age-based normative sample, 2,171 of these individuals were also included in the grade-based normative data set.

The college sample was divided into two groups: students in 2-year colleges and students in 4-year colleges. There were 259 examinees in the 2-year college standardization group and 448 examinees in the 4-year college standardization group. The total college normative group consisted of 393 females and 314 males. For the adult standardization group, examinees were drawn from five age groups: 17–20, 21–25, 26–35, 36–50, and 51–85. The 21–25 age band, the 26–35 age band, and the 51–85 age band were weighted to produce results more representative of the U.S. Census. This weighted adult standardization group consisted of 275 females and 240 males.

Reliability

Reliability measures the underlying construct of a test (Anastasi & Urbina, 1997). The degree of accuracy is measured by a variety of reliability coefficients. For the WIAT-II, two types of reliability coefficients were calculated: *split-half reliability* and *test–retest stability*. However, no matter which type of reliability is used, the interpretation will be the same: the higher the reliability coefficient, the greater the confidence one can place in the consistency, precision, and stability of scores. Reliability coefficients range in value from 0 to 1.

In the school-age standardization sample, the reliability coefficients demonstrated good evidence of inter-item reliability, with coefficients on the WIAT-II subtests ranging from .80 to .98. The overall total composite reliability in this sample is .98. A separate test-retest study was conducted with 297 examinees in this sample that was tested twice. The interval between testing was between 7 and 45 days. The average number of days between testing was 10 days. The results of this study indicate a high degree of stability across time, age, and grade. The mean scores between the first and second testing on the subtests were relatively small, with only about 1 to 4 standard-score points separating the two scores.

The reliability of the college student standardization sample was more variable, with subtest coefficients ranging from .60 to .91. These lower coefficients were explained as "ceiling effects," meaning that many of the examinees achieved close to the maximum score on some of the subtests, which reduced the variability within the particular subtests. The overall total composite reliability in the college sample is .94. The adult standardization sample demonstrated good evidence of inter-item reliability, with coefficients on the subtests ranging from .75 to .96. The overall total composite reliability in the adult sample is .98. A test–retest study was also conducted with 76 examinees from both the adult and college samples. The interval between testing ranged from 6 to 28 days, with an average interval of 11 days between testing. The results of this study with adults and college students indicate an adequate degree of stability across time, age, and grade. The mean scores between the first and second testing on the subtests were relatively small, with only about 1 to 4 standard-score points separating the two scores.

Validity

The lines of validity evidence concerning the interpretation of the WIAT-II show how the scores on various subtests relate to different criteria apart from the WIAT-II, as outlined in the *Standards for Educational and Psychological Testing* (1999). The WIAT-II development team determined the various objectives relating to curriculum in the different domains of the Individuals with Disabilities Education Act Amendments of 1997. This in turn led to the content of the WIAT-II subtests. In order to establish that the content of each of the subtests represented the curriculum standards, expert reviewers examined items throughout the developmental phases of test development. Also, items were examined through various other methods including comparisons to other achievement tests, a review of textbooks, comparisons of state standards, national item tryouts, and surveys of teachers. In addition, item analyses using pilot and tryout data were conducted on each subtest to determine the interrelationship between the items. If an item was judged as not being consistent with other items, it was noted for revision or deletion. In addition to establishing the validity of test content, evidence of validity concerning the construct-related and criterion-related evidence is provided in the following sections.

STUDIES WITH OTHER TESTS

Another method of validating a test for interpretation is to provide appropriate correlations between similar and nonsimilar measures from other tests or criteria. The WIAT-II was correlated with ability tests, namely the *Wechsler Preschool and Primary Scale of Intelligence—Revised* (WPPSI-R; Wechsler, 1989), the *Wechsler Intelligence Scale for Children—Third Edition* (WISC-III;

Wechsler, 1991), the *Wechsler Adult Intelligence Scale—Third Edition* (WAIS-III; Wechsler, 1999), and the *Differential Ability Scales* (DAS; Elliott, 1990). As expected, the data from these studies revealed moderate correlations between the various index scores on the ability tests and the composite scores on the WIAT-II. Upon their revisions, the *Wechsler Intelligence Scale for Children—Fourth Edition* (WISC-IV; Wechsler, 2003) and the *Wechsler Preschool and Primary Scale of Intelligence—Third Edition* (WPPSI-III; Wechsler, 2002) provided data in their respective manuals concerning the correlation between ability and achievement. As with their predecessors, the newer ability tests also demonstrated moderate correlations between their index scores and the composite scores on the WIAT-II.

In addition to the findings with tests of ability, subgroups were tested with the WIAT-II and various individually and group administered achievement tests. Overall, the correlations between other achievement tests that purport to measure similar constructs to the WIAT-II were very consistent with expectations. For example, the matching subtests (i.e., Reading, Math, and Spelling) between the WIAT-II and the *Wide Range Achievement Test—Third Edition* (WRAT3; Wilkinson, 1993) demonstrate moderately high correlations, which indicate similar content measured by both tests. Furthermore, the means and standard deviations between similar subtests on other achievement tests and subtests on the WIAT-II were approximately equal.

STUDIES WITH SPECIAL GROUPS

During the standardization process for the WIAT-II, several special groups were tested to determine how they will perform. Using a matched-control test, the individuals in the special groups were matched with members of the standardization sample on characteristics such as age, grade, sex, race/ethnicity, and parent education level. After computation of the means on each of the subtests for both the special group and the matched control group, the difference between the means was computed and a t-test was utilized to determine whether the difference was statistically significant.

Several special groups were tested during the standardization process of the WIAT-II. A group of 123 individuals in academically gifted programs scored between 9.79 and 15.33 standard score points above the matched control group on the WIAT-II subtests. The composite scores fell between 12.59 and 18.33 standard score points and were 19.15 standard score points above the matched control group on the Total Composite score. A group of 39 individuals diagnosed with an intellectual disability (formerly known as mental retardation) scored between 24.92 and 45.81 standard score points below the matched control group on the WIAT-II subtests and between 31.86 and 45.89 standard score points below on the WIAT-II composite scores.

A group of 85 individuals diagnosed with an emotional disorder scored between 3.42 and 12.97 standard score points below the matched control group on the WIAT-II subtests and between 4.67 and 13.04 standard score points below on the WIAT-II composite scores. A group of 162 individuals diagnosed with a learning disability in reading scored between 6.55 and 25.06 standard score points below the matched control group on the WIAT-II subtests and between 10.77 and 24.05 standard score points below on the WIAT-II composite scores.

A group of 81 individuals diagnosed with a learning disability not specific to reading (i.e., learning disability in mathematics) scored between 7.79 and 22.13 standard score points below the matched control group on the WIAT-II subtests and between 10.49 and 23.94 standard score points below on the WIAT-II composite scores. A group of 178 individuals diagnosed with attention-deficit/hyperactivity disorder (ADHD) scored between 2.05 and 8.17 standard score points below the matched control group on the WIAT-II subtests and between 3.42 and 8.37 standard score points below on the WIAT-II composite scores. It should be noted in this group

that many of the individuals were receiving stimulant medication, which could have impacted the scores on the WIAT-II.

A group of 51 individuals dually diagnosed with ADHD and a learning disability scored between 8.78 and 25.67 standard score points below the matched control group on the WIAT-II subtests and between 12.52 and 25.81 standard score points below on the WIAT-II composite scores. A group of 31 individuals diagnosed with a hearing impairment scored between 12.07 and 20.13 standard score points below on the WIAT-II subtests and between 16.08 and 19.38 standard score points below on the WIAT-II composite scores. A group of 49 individuals diagnosed with a speech and/or language impairment scored between 0.77 and 16.29 standard score points below on the WIAT-II subtests and between 7.28 and 18.84 standard score points below on the WIAT-II composite scores.

The scores across the various special groups tested with the WIAT-II indicate a predicted pattern of performance based on diagnostic category. This indicates that the WIAT-II can separate individuals in tested special groups from those in the matched control group. In general, the WIAT-II can be used to identify large percentages of individuals with these types of disabilities.

USE OF THE TEST

Interpretation

There are eight broad steps in the basic interpretation of WIAT-II performance. The first step in test interpretation always addresses the adequacy of the test instrument to answer the referral questions and be representative of examinee functioning. Once this adequacy of the test instrument has been established, interpretation begins after subtest raw scores and composite scores have been calculated and converted into standard scores. After a conversion to standard scores, the actual composite score is compared to the predicted total achievement score from an ability (i.e., IQ) score. The examiner should also check to see whether significant variability of skills (i.e., subtest scores) occurred or whether the subtest scores were similar.

After examining these differences, the next step is to examine the differences between the composite standard scores. In Appendix K of the supplements obtained in the WIAT-II test kit, it is possible to determine whether the differences between composite scores are statistically significant and how rarely this particular difference occurred in the standardization sample. After determining differences between composite test scores, it is possible to interpret differences between subtest standard test scores as well as determine relative strengths and weaknesses of the examinee based on his or her average subtest standard score. Using Appendix K of the supplements obtained in the WIAT-II test kit, tables are provided to determine how rare these differences were in the standardization sample. After examining the differences between subtest scores, it is necessary to interpret the subtest scatter of the subtest scores. This is completed by subtracting the lowest subtest score from the highest subtest score and comparing the frequency of occurrence in the standardization sample. This table can be found in Appendix K of the supplements obtained in the WIAT-II test kit.

After examining the subtest scatter, the ability–achievement discrepancy can be performed to determine which subtest skills are significantly below that predicted by the ability score. Appendix I and Appendix J in the supplements obtained in the WIAT-II test kit provide tables that help determine statistical significance in discrepancies between ability scores and achievement scores. After determining the ability–achievement discrepancy, an examination of the qualitative observations should be conducted to determine learning or problem-solving abilities utilized by the examinee. Finally, a subtest error analysis should be conducted to determine specific strength and deficit skills necessary for intervention. The following case study provides a possible report writeup that has taken into account the above interpretation guidelines.

CASE STUDY

The Case of John

Name:	John S.
Age:	9 years, 0 months
Grade:	3

Referral Concerns and Background Information

John was referred for an educational evaluation by the pre-referral team at his elementary school due to difficulties in his reading class. Specifically, his classroom teacher stated that he is unable to read grade-level words and is unable to comprehend reading passages appropriate for his grade. Examples of reading comprehension difficulties given by his teacher indicate concerns in understanding the main points given in passages, as well as a failure to distinguish important details given. Although these difficulties seem to affect his ability to read effectively, his teacher stated that his writing and verbal skills tend to be better, with few spelling errors and a good ability to express himself verbally and in writing. In addition, his performance in math computation has been above average when compared to others in his grade; however, his teacher stated that he is beginning to have difficulties in understanding word problems as demonstrated by his inability to associate certain wording in the problem with mathematical functions.

Parent information obtained indicates normal prenatal and postnatal development, with John obtaining all developmental milestones within normal limits. At the age of 5, John had his tonsils removed. All other health history is nonsignificant for major medical difficulties and his parents report that he is currently in good health. They also stated that John's temperament is "happy and well-behaved." John has had a good record of attendance throughout school. His educational history reveals a trend of difficulties in reading, with a remedial focus on phonetic and decoding skills beginning early in the first grade and continuing until the present time. He currently receives a remedial reading class three times a week. His parents have also noted that John's homework is beginning to take longer than expected, especially when focusing on reading assignments. He also receives tutoring at home with a reading tutor twice a week. His parents fear that this significant focus on reading and academic skills may affect his "attitude toward school." These parental observations coincide with teacher observations of difficulties in decoding words and comprehending assignments that require reading passages.

An interview with John reveals a child with age-appropriate interests. During the interview, he stated that he is becoming frustrated with always having "someone bug me about my schoolwork." He stated that he has a hard time getting work done in time, both at home and at school. He reported this difficulty occurs most frequently when completing reading assignments. He stated that his favorite subjects are science and math. He reported that he is able to finish the assignments in these areas in a reasonable amount of time. However, reading and writing are his least favorite subjects. He does not like to read books and stated that he will avoid having to read whenever possible. He did state that school is becoming more stressful, but he will go to his parents when frustrated with tasks to ask for their support. In addition, he has a good support system at school with "lots of friends." He stated that he feels most of the children at school are nice to him and that he gets along well with others. His school has noted no behavioral problems or disciplinary concerns. His teacher reported no concerns with classroom behavior and stated that John asks questions when appropriate and has a good rapport with others.

Assessment Procedures:

Wechsler Individual Achievement Test—Second Edition (WIAT-II)

Classroom Observation

Teacher Interview

Parent Interview

Child Interview

Behavioral Observations:

An observation was conducted in John's classroom during reading instruction at 1:00 P.M. There are approximately 20 students in his class. All desks face the front of the classroom so students' eyes are focused on the teacher and the chalkboard. John sits in the middle of the class, third desk from the front. When the examiner entered the classroom to begin observation, John was seen to be doodling on a piece of paper while other students were reading from a book. When the teacher requested the class's attention, John continued to doodle and the teacher called him by name, at which point he looked up and made eye contact with the teacher. The teacher then called upon students, including John, to read passages from the book. Most students were able to read relatively fluently, each taking approximately 2–3 minutes to read; however, John's reading was stilted and halting, requiring 5–7 minutes to read approximately the same amount as the other students. In addition, during his reading, he required frequent assistance and correction in decoding words. For example, he would say *them* when the word was *they*. He would also skip lines and need to be redirected back to the appropriate line by the teacher.

During the assessment, John was appropriately groomed and dressed for the evaluation. Rapport was slow to build, but was well established as the testing progressed. He was motivated throughout the assessment and asked appropriate questions about the examination process. Good eye contact was made throughout the examination process. His verbal communication was at a normal rate, rhythm, and tone. Between subtests, he discussed riding his bicycle, playing video games, and watching movies. On reading subtests, John was very slow at reading passages and decoding words. He gave up easily when he encountered a word that was unknown to him. As with his classroom observation, he tended to skip lines in reading passages and would start over in reading the passage. In comparison, his ability to solve math computation problems was much faster and less labor intensive.

Achievement Assessment

The WIAT-II is a test that assesses the broad domains of Reading, Writing, Mathematics, and Oral Language. John was administered all subtests from the WIAT-II during this evaluation. In addition to providing results for these broad domains, the WIAT-II also provides a Total Achievement Score. This score is based on all the subtests that make up each domain score. John obtained an age-based standard score of 84 (95% Confidence Interval = 80–88), which places him at the 14th percentile when compared to his same-age peers in the standardization sample. This score falls within the Low Average range. John's performance on each of the broad domains of Mathematics, Written Language, and Oral Expression all fall between the Low Average and Average range when compared to his same-age peers in the standardization sample. However, his performance in the broad domain of Reading indicates a relative weakness in his reading skills. Table 18.2 presents an overview of scores John received during this administration of the WIAT-II.

Reading Domain

The Reading Domain measures John's ability to read words in isolation, utilize phonetic skills to decode nonsense words, and read and answer questions based on passages of text. Overall, John received a standard score of 76 (95% Confidence Interval = 73–79) on the Reading Composite, which is classified in the Borderline range and is a normative weakness for John. This score falls at the 5th percentile rank, meaning that John scored at or above 5% of the standardization sample. Specifically, on a subtest that measures phonological awareness and sight word skills (Word Reading standard score = 74), John demonstrated a significant weakness with these skills. He had difficulty with the phonetic process needed to decode these words, which is supported by his below-average score on a subtest that measures this process (Pseudoword Decoding standard score = 80). In addition, his performance on a subtest that measures his ability to comprehend and understand reading passages was also below average (Reading Comprehension standard score = 79). These reading scores are consistent with the referral concerns of John's teacher and parents.

TABLE 18.2   Academic Skills Summary for the Case of John on the *Wechsler Individual Achievement Test–2nd Edition*

Subtest/Composite	Standard Score (95% C.I.[a])	Percentile Rank
Word Reading	74 (70–78)	4th
Numerical Operations	103 (93–113)	58th
Reading Comprehension	79 (73–85)	8th
Spelling	92 (85–99)	30th
Pseudoword Decoding	80 (75–85)	9th
Math Reasoning	96 (88–104)	39th
Written Expression	84 (73–95)	14th
Listening Comprehension	93 (80–106)	32nd
Oral Expression	99 (89–109)	47th
Reading Composite	76 (73–79)	5th
Mathematics Composite	98 (91–105)	45th
Written Language Composite	86 (79–93)	18th
Oral Language Composite	94 (85–103)	34th
Total Composite	**84 (80–88)**	**14th**

NOTE . Standard Scores are derived from age-based norms.
[a]C.I. = Confidence Interval

Mathematics Domain

The Mathematics Domain measures John's ability to solve problems using operations (i.e., addition, subtraction, multiplication, division) and solve math problems utilizing other aspects necessary in mathematics (i.e., measurement, geometry). John's score on the math domain indicates functioning within the Average range/Within Normal Limits (Mathematics Composite standard score = 98 [95% Confidence Interval = 91–105]). This score falls at the 45th percentile, meaning that John scored at or above 45% of the standardization sample. The subtests that make up this composite include a subtest that involves math computation (Numerical Operations standard score = 103) and math problem solving (Math Reasoning standard score = 96), which both fall within the Average range/Within Normal Limits. It is important to note that the Math Reasoning subtest involves many problems that are read to the examinee. Therefore, this subtest may not reflect the actual curriculum demands John is exposed to in school. This also indicates that John is able to understand the process of solving math problems when given verbally.

Written Language Domain

The Written Language Domain measures John's ability to spell words based on the context of the sentence and express himself in essay form. John's overall score in the Written Language

Domain indicates functioning in the Low Average range (Written Language Composite standard score = 86 [95% Confidence Interval = 79–93]), which falls at the 18th percentile. This means that John scored at or above 18% of the examinees in the standardization sample. The subtests that make up this composite include a subtest that measures John's ability to spell words (Spelling standard score = 92) and a subtest that measures John's ability to express himself in writing (Written Expression standard score = 84). The scores on these subtests fall within the Low Average to Average range. It is also important to note the slow writing speed John demonstrated when writing his essay, which could impact his ability to express himself effectively when writing.

Oral Language Domain

The Oral Language Domain measures John's ability to verbally name objects, verbally tell stories, and verbally give directions based on verbal or visual cues. John's overall score in the Oral Language Domain indicates functioning in the Average range/Within Normal Limits (Oral Language Composite standard score = 94 [95% Confidence Interval = 85–103]). This score falls at the 34th percentile, meaning that John scored at or above 34% of the examinees in the standardization sample. The subtests that make up this composite include a subtest that measures John's ability to comprehend spoken words (Listening Comprehension standard score = 93) and a subtest that measures John's ability to express himself verbally (Oral Expression standard score = 99). The scores on these subtests fall within the Average range/Within Normal Limits.

Summary and Recommendations

John was referred for an evaluation of academic skills due to concerns with his inability to decode words and comprehend meaning from passages of text. Behavior observations and interviews with John and his caregivers reveal a child with no apparent difficulties in his social and emotional development. However, some frustration has been noted surrounding John's ability to complete homework in a timely manner and read passages for meaning. Results of academic assessment support the conclusion that reading is a weakness and that math and oral expression skills are strengths for John. Based on these results, the following recommendations are provided:

1. Further evaluation to determine the underlying processes involved with these weaknesses, as well as overall cognitive functioning, would provide better, more precise diagnosis recommendations and interventions.
2. Recommendations for the school include providing a support system in place for John when he becomes frustrated with tasks, such as taking frequent breaks or seeing a counselor for a few minutes.
3. Reading tasks should be broken down into smaller components so that John can pronounce the frontal, medial, and final sounds of a word. In addition, reading tasks should involve a focus on sight word identification as well as basic phonetic skills necessary for decoding words.
4. Frequent breaks should be given during homework time to decrease the amount of frustration with tasks.

INTERVENTIONS

Intervention after testing with the WIAT-II requires an overview of the skills involved with each of the subtests and composites. An examination of the scores and observations made of the examinee during the assessment process should provide a necessary foundation to develop and adapt academic interventions. The WIAT-II is divided into four broad domains consisting of specific skills (i.e., subtests) that make up each of these domains.

Reading

The goal of the reading composite score is to provide an overview of reading proficiency. This reading proficiency is defined on the WIAT-II by the subtests of Word Reading, Pseudoword Decoding, and Reading Comprehension. In addition, these subtests also measure a younger examinee's ability to identify letters and letter-sounds and an older examinee's ability to decode words phonologically.

Examination of the profile of the WIAT-II subtests should provide a clarification of specific weaknesses in the examinee's reading repertoire. If the Word Reading subtest is low, it may indicate that the examinee has difficulty with sight words and/or phonological awareness. In addition, if the examinee is slow at decoding words, this may indicate a difficulty with word reading automaticity. The Pseudoword Decoding subtest may indicate a need for the examinee to increase his or her awareness of phonemic decoding skills with words. A low Pseudoword Decoding subtest standard score and an average Word Reading subtest standard score may indicate that the examinee is utilizing his or her knowledge of sight words, but cannot decode the nonsense words simply by their lexical structure. Furthermore, low scores on the Reading Comprehension indicate a need for improved reading strategies, modeling, and guided practice. An examination of the specific skills measured by each item on the WIAT-II Reading subtests found in the *Examiner's Manual* (2005) can help guide intervention development.

Mathematics

The Mathematics Composite was designed to assess the examinee's ability to reason and perform mathematical operations. The Mathematics Composite on the WIAT-II is measured by the Numerical Operations subtest and the Math Reasoning subtest.

Examination of each of the subtests represented in the Mathematics Composite should provide a better understanding of how the examinee solves math problems. Low scores on the Numerical Operations subtest indicate difficulties with operations surrounding computational math problems. The Math Reasoning subtest assesses math problem solving utilizing various techniques besides simple math operations to determine the correct answer. Therefore, if a low score is apparent on the Math Reasoning subtest, it may indicate that the examinee may have difficulty solving problems involving quantity, proportions, time, and/or money. Tables provided in the *Examiner's Manual* (2005) provide specific details about each item found on the math subtests.

Writing

The Writing Composite on the WIAT-II was designed to test various aspects of the writing process involved in the basic production of written material. The Writing Composite is measured by the Spelling and Written Expression subtests.

The subtests that compose the Writing Composite should be examined to determine strengths and weaknesses in each of the measured areas. A low score on the Spelling subtest may indicate an examinee's misunderstanding of sound-symbol relationships. In addition, an analysis of the pattern of errors may provide an indication of how to intervene with this examinee through interventions. The Written Expression subtest measures a variety of constructs that all need to be addressed before defining the interventions necessary for improvement. The vocabulary level used in the writing sample provided by the examinee, the way the examinee organizes his or her essay into a cohesive whole, how he or she develops the themes within the writing sample, and the basic mechanics and grammar used by the examinee can all be helpful guidelines to intervention.

Oral Language

The Oral Language Composite consists of subtests deemed necessary for successful understanding and production of spoken language. The Listening Comprehension subtest and the Oral Expression subtest make up the Oral Language Composite.

The Listening Comprehension subtest consists of three major types of listening: Receptive Vocabulary, Sentence Comprehension, and Expressive Vocabulary. A low score on this subtest may indicate a weakness in one or more of the areas measured by this subtest. An item analysis of the examinee's responses will clarify which listening activities are causing a difficulty. The Oral Expression subtest measures several constructs believed to be necessary for how an examinee uses language to communicate with his or her environment. A specific skills analysis of the various types of errors on the items will reveal which are the weaker aspects of the examinee's oral expression repertoire.

SUMMARY

The WIAT-II is an individually administered achievement test that was developed in conjunction with federal and state education laws and regulations. It was developed to measure the skills described in the Individuals with Disabilities Education Act of 1997. The reading, math, writing, and oral language broad skills are broken down into various components that have been developed into various subtests. To administer and score each of the subtests requires patience and practice to flow through the test with an examinee in an easy manner and use the scoring rubrics to determine the examinee's scores on each of the subtests. The standardization and norms developed on the WIAT-II are appropriate for a national comparison of an examinee's peers as well as attempting to distinguish the examinee's performance on the WIAT-II as significantly different from the normative sample. Finally, the WIAT-II is appropriate for determining interventions by a thorough quantitative interpretation as well as a qualitative interpretation and skills analysis of the examinee's performance on the assessment.

REFERENCES

Anastasi, A., & Urbina, S. (1997). *Psychological testing* (7th ed.). Upper Saddle River, NJ: Prentice Hall.

Berninger, V. (1989). Orchestration of multiple codes in developing readers: An alternative model of lexical access. *International Journal of Neuroscience*, *48*, 85–104.

Berninger, V. (2001). *Process assessment of the learner: Test battery for reading and writing*. San Antonio, TX: Psychological Corporation.

Berninger, V., Cartwright, A., Yates, C., Swanson, H., & Abbott, R. (1994). Developmental skills related to writing and reading acquisition in the intermediate grades: Shared and unique variance. *Reading and Writing: An Interdisciplinary Journal*, *6*, 161–196.

Berninger, V., Yates, C., Cartwright, A., Rutberg, J., Remy, E., & Abbott, R. (1992). Lower-level developmental skills in beginning writing. *Reading and Writing: An Interdisciplinary Journal*, *4*, 257–280.

Elliott, C. D. (1990). *Differential Ability Scales*. San Antonio, TX: Psychological Corporation.

Individuals with Disabilities Education Act Amendments of 1997, 20 U.S.C. 1400 *et seq.* (Fed. Reg. 64, 1999).

National Council of Teachers of Mathematics. (2000). *Principles and standards for school mathematics*. Reston, VA: Author.

National Reading Panel. (2000). *Teaching children to read: An evidence-based assessment of the scientific research literature on reading and its implications for reading instruction* (NIH Publication No. 00-4754). Washington, DC: National Institute of Child Health and Human Development.

Psychological Corporation. (2002). *WIAT-II Supplement for College Students and Adults*. San Antonio, TX: Author.

Psychological Corporation. (2005). *Wechsler Individual Achievement Test—Second Edition: Update 2005*. San Antonio, TX: Author.

Sattler, J. (2001). *Assessment of children: Cognitive applications* (4th ed.). San Diego: Author.

Standards for educational and psychological testing. (1999). Washington, DC: American Psychological Association.

Torgesen, J. K., Wagner, R. K., & Rashotte, C. A. (1994). Longitudinal studies of phonological processing and reading. *Journal of Learning Disabilities*, *27*(5), 276–286.

Wechsler, D. (1989). *Wechsler Preschool and Primary Scale of Intelligence—Revised*. San Antonio, TX: Psychological Corporation.

Wechsler, D. (1991). *Wechsler Intelligence Scale for Children—Third Edition*. San Antonio, TX: Psychological Corporation.

Wechsler, D. (1992). *Wechsler Individual Achievement Test*. San Antonio, TX: Psychological Corporation.

Wechsler, D. (1999). *Wechsler Adult Intelligence Scale—Third Edition*. San Antonio, TX: Psychological Corporation.

Wechsler, D. (2002). *Wechsler Preschool and Primary Scale of Intelligence—Third Edition*. San Antonio, TX: Psychological Corporation.

Wechsler, D. (2003). *Wechsler Intelligence Scale for Children—Fourth Edition*. San Antonio, TX: Psychological Corporation.

Wilkinson, G. (1993). *Wide Range Achievement Test—Third Edition*. Wilmington, DE: Wide Range.

CHAPTER 19

Woodcock-Johnson III Tests of Achievement*

Nancy Mather, Barbara J. Wendling

RATIONALE

The *Woodcock-Johnson III Tests of Achievement* (WJ III ACH) is a widely used, individually administered, norm-referenced test covering five important academic domains: reading, written language, mathematics, oral language, and academic knowledge (Woodcock, McGrew, & Mather, 2001). The first edition of the WJ III ACH was published in 1977; it was subsequently revised in 1989 and the third edition was published in 2001. A normative update to the WJ III ACH was made available in 2007 (Woodcock, McGrew, Schrank, & Mather, 2007). This battery of tests is appropriate for use with individuals between the ages of 2 to 90+ years. In addition, the WJ III ACH was co-normed with the WJ III Tests of Cognitive Abilities (WJ III COG) and is part of a family of related assessments that includes the parallel Spanish version, the *Batería III Woodcock-Muñoz Pruebas de aprovechamiento* (Muñoz-Sandoval, Woodcock, McGrew, & Mather, 2005). When used together, the co-normed WJ III COG and WJ III ACH are powerful tools for evaluating and exploring the relationships and interactions among cognitive abilities and academic performance.

DESCRIPTION

The WJ III ACH has 22 tests that are organized into the academic domains of reading, written language, mathematics, oral language, and knowledge. Two parallel forms, Forms A and B, include all 22 tests. The Form C/Brief Battery provides a third parallel set of achievement tests for nine of the most commonly used measures (Woodcock, Schrank, Mather, & McGrew, 2007). Table 19.1 illustrates the organization of the comprehensive and brief forms of the WJ III ACH. Typically, each test contributes to one or more of the clusters, which are composites representing both specific (e.g., Basic Reading Skills) as well as broad academic areas (e.g., Broad Reading). The Selective Testing Table in Figure 19.1 depicts the tests that comprise each of the WJ III clusters.

*Thanks to Dr. Fredrick Schrank for his helpful comments on the initial draft of this chapter.

TABLE 19.1 Organization of the WJ III Tests of Achievement, Forms A, B, and C

Academic Area	Forms A and B Standard Battery	Forms A and B Extended Battery	Form C Brief Battery
Reading			
Basic Skills	1. Letter-Word Identification	13. Word Attack	1. Letter-Word Identification
Fluency	2. Reading Fluency		7. Reading Fluency
Comprehension	9. Passage Comprehension	17. Reading Vocabulary	4. Passage Comprehension
Written Language			
Basic Skills	7. Spelling	16. Editing	3. Spelling
Fluency	8. Writing Fluency		9. Writing Fluency
Expression	11. Writing Samples		6. Writing Samples
Mathematics			
Basic Skills	5. Calculation		5. Calculation
Fluency	6. Math Fluency		8. Math Fluency
Reasoning	10. Applied Problems	18. Quantitative Concepts	2. Applied Problems
Oral Language			
Oral Expression	3. Story Recall	14. Picture Vocabulary	
Listening Comprehension	4. Understanding Directions	15. Oral Comprehension	
Knowledge		19. Academic Knowledge	
Supplemental	12. Story Recall-Delayed	20. Spelling of Sounds	
	H. Handwriting Legibility Scale	21. Sound Awareness	
		22. Punctuation and Capitalization	

Reading

The WJ III ACH includes the following six achievement tests that measure various aspects of pre-reading and reading performance: Test 1: Letter-Word Identification (identification of letters and words); Test 2: Reading Fluency (silent reading rate); Test 9: Passage Comprehension (understanding of short passages); Test 13: Word Attack (application of phonic skills); Test 17: Reading Vocabulary (understanding of word meanings); and Test 21: Sound Awareness (phonological awareness skills). Various combinations of these tests are used to create the following clusters, or composites, for interpretation: Broad Reading, Brief Reading, Basic Reading Skills, Reading Comprehension, Phoneme-Grapheme Knowledge (requires one supplemental test), and Phonemic Awareness 3 (requires two WJ III COG tests). Table 19.2 provides a description of each of the reading-related tests and clusters.

Tests of Achievement	Broad Reading	Basic Reading Skills	Reading Comprehension	Oral Language-Standard	Oral Language-Extended	Listening Comprehension	Oral Expression	Broad Math	Math Calculation Skills	Math Reasoning	Broad Written Language	Basic Writing Skills	Written Expression	Academic Knowledge	Phoneme/Grapheme Knowledge	Academic Skills	Academic Fluency	Academic Applications	Total Achievement
Standard Battery																			
1. Letter-Word Identification	■	■														■			■
2. Reading Fluency	■																■		■
3. Story Recall				■	■		■												
4. Understanding Directions				■	■	■													
5. Calculation								■	■							■			■
6. Math Fluency								■	■								■		■
7. Spelling											■	■				■			■
8. Writing Fluency											■		■				■		■
9. Passage Comprehension	■		■															■	■
10. Applied Problems								■		■								■	■
11. Writing Samples											■		■					■	■
12. Story Recall-Delayed																			
Extended Battery																			
13. Word Attack		■													■				
14. Picture Vocabulary				■			■												
15. Oral Comprehension				■		■													
16. Editing												■							
17. Reading Vocabulary			■																
18. Quantitative Concepts										■									
19. Academic Knowledge														■					
20. Spelling of Sounds															■				
21. Sounds Awareness																			
22. Punctuation and Capitalization																			

Source: From the WJ III Tests of Achievement by R.W. Woodcock, K.S. McGrew, and N. Mather, 2001, Rolling Meadows, IL: Riverside Publishing. Copyright © 2001 by the Riverside Publishing Company. Used with permission

FIGURE 19.1
Selective Testing Table for the WJ III Tests of Achievement

Written Language

The WJ III ACH has the following five tests that measure different aspects of writing ability: Test 7: Spelling (spelling of real words); Test 8: Writing Fluency (speed of sentence formulation); Test 11: Writing Samples (expression of ideas); Test 16: Editing (proofreading); and Test 22: Punctuation and Capitalization (knowledge of conventions). The following five clusters may be derived: Broad Written Language, Brief Writing, Basic Writing Skills, Written Expression, and Phoneme-Grapheme Knowledge (requires one reading test). Table 19.3 provides a description of each test and cluster in the written language domain.

Mathematics

The following four tests measure aspects of math performance: Test 5: Calculation (computation); Test 6: Math Fluency (automaticity with basic facts); Test 10: Applied Problems (mathematical reasoning and problem-solving); and

TABLE 19.2   Description of Tests and Clusters in the Reading Domain

TESTS	DESCRIPTION
Letter-Word Identification	Oral word reading task that requires identifying or reading isolated letters and words.
Reading Fluency	Timed reading task that requires quick comprehension of simple sentences.
Passage Comprehension	Comprehension task that requires reading a short passage and supplying a key missing word.
Word Attack	Oral reading task that requires pronouncing phonically regular nonsense words.
Reading Vocabulary	Vocabulary task that requires reading and providing synonyms, antonyms, and analogies.
Sound Awareness	Phonological awareness tasks that require rhyming, deletion, substitution, and reversal.

CLUSTERS	DESCRIPTION
Broad Reading	Provides the broadest view of overall reading achievement including measures of decoding, fluency, and comprehension. Requires Letter-Word Identification, Reading Fluency, and Passage Comprehension.
Brief Reading	Includes the same measures of decoding and comprehension in Broad Reading, but without the timed test, Reading Fluency.
Basic Reading Skills	Measures decoding skills using both real and phonically regular nonsense words. Requires Letter-Word Identification and Word Attack.
Reading Comprehension	Measures comprehension at both the single-word and connected discourse levels. Requires Passage Comprehension and Reading Vocabulary.
Phoneme-Grapheme Knowledge	Combines decoding and encoding tasks that use nonsense words requiring the examinee to apply phonological and orthographic knowledge. Requires Word Attack and one supplemental test, Spelling of Sounds.
Phonemic Awareness 3	Provides information about phonological awareness, an oral language ability which is a prerequisite skill for reading. Requires Sound Awareness and 2 WJ III COG tests, Sound Blending and Incomplete Words.

Test 18: Quantitative Concepts (knowledge and concepts). Four clusters are available for interpretation: Broad Math, Brief Math, Math Calculation Skills, and Math Reasoning. Table 19.4 provides a description of each test and cluster in the mathematics domain.

Oral Language

The following five tests measure aspects of oral language: Test 3: Story Recall (meaningful memory) and Test 12: Story Recall—Delayed; Test 4: Understanding Directions (memory and listening comprehension); Test 14: Picture Vocabulary (knowledge of word meanings); and Test 15: Oral Comprehension (comprehension of short passages). The following five clusters are available for interpretation: Oral Language—Extended, Oral Language—Standard, Listening Comprehension, Oral Expression, and Delayed Recall (requires one WJ III COG test). Table 19.5 provides a description of each test and cluster in the oral language domain.

TABLE 19.3   Description of Tests and Clusters in the Written Language Domain

TESTS	DESCRIPTION
Spelling	Encoding task that requires writing real words presented orally.
Writing Fluency	Timed task that requires formulating and writing simple, short sentences incorporating 3 stimulus words.
Writing Samples	Expressive writing task that requires writing sentences in response to a series of demands.
Editing	Proofreading task that requires identifying and correcting errors in short written passages.
Spelling of Sounds	Encoding task that requires writing nonsense words presented orally.
Punctuation/Capitalization	Basic writing skills task that requires use of punctuation and capitalization marks.
Writing Evaluation Scale	An analytic evaluation that can be used to evaluate an essay or composition.
Handwriting	Measures writing legibility using a sample of writing from another source (e.g., Writing Samples).

CLUSTERS	DESCRIPTION
Broad Written Language	Provides the broadest view of overall writing achievement including measures of spelling, fluency, and expression. Requires Spelling, Writing Fluency, and Writing Samples.
Brief Writing	Includes the same measures of spelling and expression in Broad cluster, but eliminates the timed test, Writing Fluency.
Basic Writing Skills	Measures encoding and editing skills. Requires Spelling and Editing.
Written Expression	Measures written expression skills including rapid sentence formulation and quality of ideation. Requires Writing Fluency and Writing Samples.

Academic Knowledge

The Academic Knowledge test measures general information, including knowledge of science, humanities, and social studies. This test does not require any reading, and responses require either pointing or one-word answers. The test may be combined with one WJ III COG (General Information) to create a Knowledge cluster.

ADMINISTRATION AND SCORING

The WJ III ACH uses an easel-style test book for the administration of all tests. The easel contains the examiner directions, administration instructions, and for many of the tests, the

actual test items. In addition, eight tests require the use of a Subject Response Booklet (SRB) where the examinee writes his or her responses. The SRB also has a worksheet, if needed by the examinee, on the Applied Problems and Quantitative Concepts tests. Five of the tests require use of an audio recording to administer items and three of the tests are timed. With the exception of the timed tests, all of the other tests use estimated starting points with basal and ceiling rules.

Order of Administration

Many examiners administer tests in the order they appear in the easel. This numeric order varies the tasks and areas being measured,

TABLE 19.4   Description of Tests and Clusters in the Mathematics Domain

TESTS	DESCRIPTION
Calculation	Computation task that requires calculation of simple to complex facts and equations.
Math Fluency	Timed task requiring rapid calculation of single digit addition, subtraction, and multiplication facts.
Applied Problems	Problem-solving task that requires analyzing and solving practical math problems.
Quantitative Concepts	Math knowledge and reasoning task that measures aspects of math knowledge and quantitative reasoning.

CLUSTERS	DESCRIPTION
Broad Math	Provides the broadest view of overall math achievement including measures of calculation, fluency, and reasoning. Requires Calculation, Math Fluency, and Applied Problems.
Brief Math	Includes the same measures of calculation and reasoning in Broad cluster, but eliminates the timed test, Math Fluency.
Math Calculation Skills	Provides a measure of basic math skills including computation and automaticity of facts. Requires Calculation and Math Fluency.
Math Reasoning	Provides a measure of math knowledge and problem-solving skills. Requires Applied Problems and Quantitative Concepts.

TABLE 19.5   Description of Tests and Clusters in Oral Language Domain

TESTS	DESCRIPTION
Story Recall	Story retelling task that requires listening to passages and recalling orally story elements.
Understanding Directions	Language task that requires pointing to objects in a picture after listening to a series of instructions.
Picture Vocabulary	Word knowledge task that requires naming familiar to less familiar pictured objects.
Oral Comprehension	Listening task that requires providing a missing final word to a passage just heard.
Story Recall-Delayed	Requires recalling elements of stories presented earlier (30 minutes to 8 days earlier).

CLUSTERS	DESCRIPTION
Oral Language-Extended	Provides the broadest overall view of oral language abilities including measures of receptive and expressive language. Requires Story Recall, Understanding Directions, Picture Vocabulary, and Oral Comprehension.
Oral Language-Standard	Provides a broad measure of oral language abilities including both receptive and expressive language. Requires Story Recall and Understanding Directions.
Oral Expression	Provides a measure of expressive language abilities. Requires Story Recall and Picture Vocabulary.
Listening Comprehension	Provides a measure of receptive language abilities. Requires Understanding Directions and Oral Comprehension.

which can help keep the examinee motivated and interested. The tests, however, may be administered in any order. Because the WJ III encourages practitioners to use the principle of selective testing, examiners may just select the tests that are relevant to the referral question and purpose of testing. In these situations, the examiner must use professional judgment in determining the administration order. One sequence is to maintain the numeric order, but skip the tests that will not be administered to the examinee. For example, if the referral question centered only on performance in mathematics, the evaluator may want to administer only Tests 5, 6, 10, and 18. Order may also be altered based on the examinee's characteristics. For example, a student may enjoy taking math tests, but dislike taking the tests involving writing. The examiner may then decide to alternate between these types of tasks, rather than administer one writing test, followed by another.

Administration Tips

All of the necessary information for learning how to administer the WJ III ACH is located in the Examiner's Manual and test easels. Another helpful resource for using and interpreting the WJ III ACH is the *Essentials of WJ III Tests of Achievement Assessment* (Mather, Wendling, & Woodcock, 2001); Chapter 2 reviews key administration points for each test and Appendix A provides a compilation of fine points of administration.

Good Testing Practices

Clearly, all examiners for all administrations should use good testing practices that are common to norm-referenced tests. These practices include such factors as ensuring a quiet, distraction-free test environment; establishing rapport with the person; having all necessary materials; and striving for a brisk but accurate administration. Examiners are expected to follow the standardized procedures for all tests they are using and must guard against applying their own

rules or the rules that have been learned from another test. Table 19.6 lists common administration errors that may be made by beginning, as well as more experienced, examiners.

Basals, Ceilings, and Complete Page Rule

The basal and ceiling rules are stated at the top of each test in the Test Record. Because the criteria are not the same for each test, it is important to review the rules before testing. The basal and ceiling rules on the WJ III differ from many other widely used tests, so particular care must be taken to understand and apply these rules correctly. In the WJ III, when a stimulus is visible to the examinee, administration is conducted by complete pages. By completing the page, it seems as though the test has been completed, which then creates a natural transition to another test. This complete-page rule may, however, impact the determination of the ceiling, as well as the calculation of the raw score. For example, if the ceiling rule is six consecutive items incorrect and the examinee has six consecutive errors before the page is completed, the examiner still needs to complete the page. If in the process of completing the page, the examinee gets an additional item correct, then credit would be awarded for that response and testing would continue until a new ceiling has been reached. If a pattern of two apparent basals or ceilings appears, the lowest-numbered set is used as the basal, and the highest-numbered set is the ceiling. The WJ III procedures do not use what is referred to in other instruments as *false basals* or *false ceilings*, where the examiner is told to ignore incorrect responses below a second, higher-numbered basal, as well as any correct responses that would occur after the first ceiling has been reached.

For example, on the WJ III ACH Letter-Word Identification test, the basal is the 6 lowest correct and the ceiling is the 6 highest correct. If a child passed the first 6 items and then missed Item 7 and then passed another 6 items, Item 7 would still be scored as incorrect. As another example, if a child missed Items 11–16 and then got Item 17 right, and then missed Items 18–24,

TABLE 19.6   Common Examiner Errors

Failing to provide the materials needed for the test (e.g., a pencil with an eraser, a stopwatch).

Failing to have necessary equipment, including a CD player or tape recorder and a stopwatch.

Failing to record the birth date correctly.

Failing to keep the test record behind the easel when recording responses.

Failing to write down responses.

Failing to administer all of the queries.

Failing to observe the time limits on the timed tests.

Attempting to paraphrase test instructions to make them easier to understand.

Attempting to translate test instructions into another language.

Providing more practice or explanation than the test instructions provide.

Informing examinees of correct and incorrect answers.

Mispronouncing or not knowing the correct pronunciations of the more difficult test items.

Adding scores from sample or practice items into the raw score.

Making errors in counting up the total number of correct items.

Failing to add in the correct items below the basal level.

Failing to follow the basal and ceiling rules.

the examiner would give credit for Item 17. The examiner did not stop testing when the child had missed six items in a row because of the rule of testing in complete pages. As a general principle, correct responses are always scored as correct and incorrect responses are always scored as incorrect. The reason for this rule is that taking into account all items passed and all items missed provides the most accurate estimate of a person's ability.

Essentially, credit is given for all administered items that were answered correctly and for all items that were not given but fall below the basal. If an examiner begins testing at a place where no basal is established (e.g., the child does not give six consecutive correct responses on the Letter-Word Identification test), then the examiner must continue testing backward (by complete pages starting from the top of the page) until a basal is established or Item 1 has been administered. Item 1 serves as the basal in these cases. If no ceiling is established, then administration continues until the last item is administered; the last item is then considered to be the ceiling.

Queries, Error Boxes, and No Response Boxes

On many of the tests, the WJ III ACH provides additional queries and Error or No Response boxes on the examiner's page in the test easels. The queries and boxes provide additional procedures for examiners to follow when an examinee's response or lack of response requires clarification or additional instruction. Some of the boxes also provide additional guidance and/or practice trials for the examinee or procedures for clarifying ambiguous responses. Adherence to the instructions in these boxes and queries is essential for accurate, valid administrations.

Suggested Starting Points

Many of the WJ III ACH tests provide Suggested Starting Points so that all examinees do not have to start with Item 1. Examiners select the starting point based on the examinee's estimated level of achievement rather than on the person's actual grade placement or chronological age. In cases where the examinee is experiencing academic difficulties, the examiner would select a starting point below the examinee's age or grade level. In cases where the examinee is more advanced than his or her grade peers, the examiner would select a starting point above the examinee's age or grade.

Scoring the Test

The WJ III ACH requires the examiner to record the item-level scores (usually 1 or 0) and to calculate raw scores, or the total number correct. Once the raw score has been obtained, examiners may consult the scoring tables that appear in the test record to determine estimated age and grade equivalents. This immediate information can be helpful in cases where little is known about the examinee's achievement levels. After testing is completed, the raw scores are then entered into the computer-scoring software program, Compuscore, which comes with the test kit. All derived scores and profiles are generated by Compuscore. Because of the complexity of the WJ III and the numerous scoring options, no hand-scoring scoring option exists. Examiners who wish to use software that generates reports as well as the scores and profiles may obtain the Woodcock Interpretation and Instructional Interventions Program (WIIIP) (Schrank, Wendling, & Woodcock, 2008).

In many instances, examiners should also write down the person's actual responses for incorrect items so that these errors can be reviewed and analyzed after testing is completed. This type of qualitative analysis often provides important information for more in-depth assessment, as well as instructional planning.

INTERPRETING THE SCORES

The WJ III ACH provides a wide array of derived scores that includes raw scores, W scores, age equivalents, grade equivalents, standard scores, percentile ranks, relative proficiency indexes, standard score/percentile rank profiles, age/grade profiles, instructional zones, and CALP levels. Many of these scores are familiar to practitioners (e.g., percentile ranks and standard scores). Some scores, however, such as the W score, relative proficiency index (RPI), instructional ranges, age/grade profiles, and CALP levels are uncommon or unique to the Woodcock family of tests, and thus require additional explanation.

Hierarchy of Scores

The WJ III scores can be grouped into an interpretive framework with four hierarchical levels of information. Each level provides different types of information about the examinee's performance. Information from one level is not interchangeable with information from another. Information from the following four levels is useful for describing an individual's performance:

1. *Qualitative level*: includes error analysis, behavioral observations, and informal data. This level of information is helpful for instructional planning.
2. *Development/instruction level*: includes age equivalents and grade equivalents. This level is helpful in determining level of development or instruction.
3. *Criterion-referenced level*: includes RPIs, CALP levels, and instructional zones. This level is helpful in identifying levels of proficiency and instructional levels (easy-to-difficult ranges).
4. *Peer comparison level*: includes standard scores and percentile ranks. This level is helpful for comparing the person's performance to peers by showing relative standing within a group (age- or grade-mates).

The following extract from Mather and Jaffe (2002, p. 35) illustrates the various types of quantitative and qualitative information that may be used to describe an individual's test performance. The example begins with peer comparison scores, progresses to RPIs and instructional zones, explains any significant differences among the tests, and then adds in pertinent qualitative information obtained from error analysis:

> *On the WJ III ACH Broad Reading cluster, Kasey obtained a standard score of 66 (± 1SEM = 63-69). When Kasey's actual standard score in Broad Reading is compared to his predicted score (based on the average of the other three areas of achievement), only 1 out of 1,000 people would obtain a score the same or lower. His Relative Proficiency Index of 4/90 indicates that when average grade-mates are having 90% success, Kasey will have approximately 4% success, performance well below the frustration level. His grade scores on the Instructional Zone indicate that an easy level of reading for Kasey is mid-first grade, whereas a frustration level is beginning second grade. Although all reading scores were in the Low to Low Average range, Kasey's score on the Reading Fluency test, which requires rapid reading of simple sentences, was significantly lower than his scores on the Letter-Word Identification and Passage Comprehension tests. In general, many of Kasey's reading errors involved medial vowel sounds, such as pronouncing* must *as "mist." Even when accurate, his word recognition was slow. Kasey appeared to lack confidence in his reading ability, and he remarked during testing that reading has been difficult for him since first grade.*

W Score and W Difference Score

The *W score* and the *W difference score* are available because an equal interval scale, the W scale, underlies the WJ III. The *W scale* is a special transformation of the Rasch ability scale (Rasch, 1960; Wright & Stone, 1979). Essentially, the W scale is like an equal interval ruler that underlies each test. Each item in the test is then ordered by its difficulty level along this ruler. Each norm group's performance as well as each person's performance falls at some point along this same ruler. The point at which a reference group's median performance falls is called the *Reference W* (REF W). The point at which an individual's performance falls represents the obtained raw score or W score. In the WJ III, the W score for each test and cluster is displayed in the Table

of Scores generated by Compuscore (version 3.1 and higher). Because the W score is an equal interval score, it is preferred over the raw score when various statistical analyses are performed.

The W difference score (W DIFF) describes how far the examinee's performance falls from the average performance (REF W) of the reference group (age- or grade-mates). The examinee's performance may be better than average, resulting in a positive difference score, or the examinee's performance may be lower than average, resulting in a negative difference score. Other tests have begun to reference the concept of *absolute distance from average* and are using terms such as *change sensitive scores*, or *growth scale values*. The W DIFF describes this absolute distance from average using equal interval units from the W scale. Table 19.7 illustrates two practical applications of the W DIFF: defining an individual's proficiency on a task and identifying the instructional implication for that individual on similar tasks. For example, an individual with a W DIFF of –40 has very limited proficiency on the task and will find similar tasks extremely difficult. Practitioners have the option to include the W DIFF as an additional score in the Table of Scores when using either the Compuscore (version 3.1) or the WIIIP.

Relative Proficiency Index

The *relative proficiency index (RPI)* is a criterion-referenced indicator of performance. The RPI allows statements to be made about an individual's quality of performance, or functionality, on a task. This score also predicts how successful the individual will be on similar tasks. The RPI uses the W difference score to create a functional description expressed as a fraction. The criterion, the reference group's average performance, is reflected as the denominator in the fraction and is fixed at 90. The examinee's performance is expressed in the numerator and can range from 0 to 100. For example, an RPI of 10/90 indicates the examinee had about 10% proficiency, whereas average age- or grade-mates had about 90%

TABLE 19.7 Practical Applications of the W DIFF Score

W Diff	Proficiency	Implications (Will find similar tasks to be ...)
+31 and above	Very advanced	Extremely easy
+14 to +30	Advanced	Very easy
+7 to +13	Average to advanced	Easy
−6 to +6	Average	Manageable
−13 to −7	Limited to average	Difficult
−30 to −14	Limited	Very difficult
−50 to −31	Very limited	Extremely difficult
−51 and below	Negligible	Impossible

proficiency on the same task. An RPI of 10/90 describes very limited proficiency and indicates that the examinee will find grade-level tasks to be extremely difficult or impossible.

Instructional Zones

One of the main goals of many evaluations is to create appropriate instructional recommendations. The WJ III ACH provides not only the RPI, but also *instructional zones* (or developmental zones in the WJ III COG) that identify the individual's present level of functioning from an easy or independent level to a difficult or frustration level. Most practitioners are familiar with the concept of independent, instructional, and frustration levels as they are used on informal reading inventories. The RPIs (described previously) help identify and quantify these levels. RPIs between 76/90 and 95/90 are considered indicative of instructional levels. RPIs 75/90 or lower indicate frustration or failure levels and RPIs 96/90 or higher indicate independent levels.

Age/Grade Profiles

Age or *grade profiles* provide graphic representations of the examinee's performance created by plotting the developmental or instructional zones for each test or cluster administered. Grade profiles are more commonly used with the WJ

III ACH to illustrate the examinee's level of instructional performance. Age profiles are more commonly used with the WJ III COG to indicate developmental levels of performance. The individual's grade placement (or chronological age) is shown as a vertical line on the profile and serves as a reference for interpreting the zones. For example, if an entire zone (easy-to-difficult) is below the examinee's age or grade placement, the examinee will find age- or grade-appropriate tasks frustrating. To be most effective, instruction must be adjusted to the fall within the individual's instructional zone. The profile is a good way to illustrate the examinee's variable needs in instruction and to communicate that information to teachers or parents. Profiles are generated by the Compuscore program if they are selected as an option. The profiles can be printed and appended to a report.

CALP Levels

Cognitive Academic Language Proficiency (CALP) is a well-known concept in bilingual education and assessment. CALP is defined as language proficiency in academic situations and includes those aspects of language that emerge with formal schooling. Cummins (1984) formalized a distinction between CALP and Basic Interpersonal Communication Skills (BICS), the type of language proficiency that is acquired naturally without formal schooling. The five CALP levels are indicated by the numerals 1–5. A CALP level of 1 indicates negligible proficiency, whereas a CALP level of 5 indicates advanced proficiency. When evaluating individuals that are English Language Learners (ELL), knowledge of their CALP levels can be valuable in planning an appropriate educational program. CALP levels are available for 8 clusters relevant to language performance: Oral Language—Extended, Oral Language—Standard, Listening Comprehension, Broad Reading, Reading Comprehension, Broad Written Language, Written Expression, and Academic Knowledge. To display CALP levels, practitioners must select the additional score option in the software scoring program.

Discrepancy Scores

The WJ III ACH provides two different procedures that use discrepancy scores: the intra-ability variation procedure and the oral language ability–achievement discrepancy procedure. See the "Standardization, Norms, and Psychometrics" section of this chapter for an explanation of these scores and the "Step-by-Step Guide to Interpretation of the WJ III ACH" section for examples of these procedures.

STANDARDIZATION, NORMS, AND PSYCHOMETRICS

The WJ III ACH, WJ III COG, and the Diagnostic Supplement were nationally normed on 8,818 individuals between the ages of 24 months and over 90 years. The original sample (using the 2000 Census projections) was designed to represent the U.S. population from ages 24 months to 90+ years. Normative data for the test were gathered in more than 100 geographically diverse communities. Individuals were randomly selected within a stratified sampling design that controlled for 10 specific community and individual variables and

13 socioeconomic status variables. The final sample consisted of 1,143 preschool subjects; 4,784 Kindergarten-through-twelfth-grade subjects; 1,165 college and university subjects; and 1,843 adult subjects.

Normative Update

In 2007, a normative update (WJ III NU) was completed using the original WJ III sample of 8,782 individuals ranging in age from 2 to 90+ years. Using innovative statistical advancements, the update was developed through a recalculation of the normative data so that the norms would reflect the most current and accurate comparisons to the U.S. population (McGrew, Dailey, & Schrank, in press). The original WJ III norms were based on the U.S. Census Bureau's 2000 Census projections, which were issued in 1996, whereas the normative update is based on the final 2000 Census statistics that were released in 2005. From the Census projections to the final Census statistics, changes were apparent in population size, age, sex, race, Hispanic origin, and residence. For the update, both the demographic and community characteristics were adjusted so that WJ III NU norms are more reflective of the final 2000 Census statistics for the general population. As of the writing of this chapter, the most current software to score the WJ III is the Woodcock-Johnson III Normative Update Compuscore and Profiles Program (version 3.1) (Schrank & Woodcock, 2008). Additional information about development, standardization, norms construction, normative update, reliability, and validity is available in the *Technical Manual for the Woodcock-Johnson III Normative Update* (McGrew, Schrank, & Woodcock, 2007).

Age and Grade Norms

Unlike some tests, the WJ III provides both age and grade norms for the achievement and cognitive batteries. Age norms are reported for each month from ages 2:0 through 18:11 and then by one-year intervals from 19 through

95+ years of age. Grade norms are reported for each tenth of a year from grades K.0 through 18.0. A continuous-year procedure was used to gather these data, rather than sampling only at 2 points in the year, such as fall and spring. These month-by-month norms increase the precision of the scores and meet reporting requirements for educational programs such as Title I.

Discrepancy Norms

The co-norming of the WJ III ACH and the WJ III COG made it possible to compute discrepancy scores for each individual in the norming sample and then to prepare discrepancy norms using that information. For both the variation and discrepancy procedures, norms are used to determine the significance and frequency of any variations or discrepancies. These discrepancy norms offer several advantages to practitioners. First, both the cognitive and achievement batteries were normed on the same large, nationally representative sample, eliminating errors from unknown differences that exist when using tests based on different norm samples. Second, the correlation coefficients are known between ability and achievement at all ages so it is not necessary to estimate and make a correction for the amount of regression based on a few correlations and a limited sample. Third, practitioners can evaluate the significance of a discrepancy by using either the percentile rank of the discrepancy (Discrepancy PR) or the difference between the achievement score and the predicted achievement score in standard error of estimate units (Discrepancy SD).

Discrepancy Percentile Rank

This score defines the percent of the population that has a particular size discrepancy between the actual and predicted scores. The Discrepancy PR is a norm-based estimate of the base rate of a particular discrepancy in the population. Unlike base rates offered by other tests, which are typically based on cross-sectional data, the WJ III provides more precision by reporting the information by subgroups (same age or grade) within the norm sample.

Discrepancy Standard Deviation

This score reflects the distance that the examinee's score is above or below the average score for age or grade mates. The Discrepancy SD allows the criterion of significance to be defined in terms of the standard error of the estimate. Commonly, a Discrepancy SD of +/−1.5 or greater is selected as being significant. A discrepancy of this magnitude would occur approximately 6 out of 100 times. Practitioners may, however, select a different level of significance ranging from +/−1.0 to +/−2.3 when using the various WJ III software scoring programs.

Reliability

The WJ III ACH tests and clusters meet or exceed the benchmarks typically used for reliability. During development of the WJ III ACH, the goal for reliability was .80 or higher for the tests and .90 or higher for the clusters. Twenty of the 22 tests meet or exceed reliabilities of .80 and nine are at or above .90. Two tests, Spelling of Sounds and Punctuation and Capitalization, had median reliabilities of .76 and .79, respectively. All but three clusters meet or exceed the goal of .90. The three clusters that had median reliabilities below .90 are Oral Language—Standard (.87), Oral Expression (.85), and Listening Comprehension (.89). Additional information on reliability can be found in the chapter in this text on the WJ III COG. Complete technical information can be found in the WJ III Technical Manual (McGrew & Woodcock, 2001) and the Woodcock-Johnson III Normative Update (NU) Technical Manual (McGrew, et al., 2007).

Validity

The validity of a test is determined by the degree that the available empirical evidence supports the test's use and interpretation. Extensive information relevant to the validity of the WJ III ACH is provided in the WJ III Technical Manual (McGrew & Woodcock, 2001) and the WJ III NU Technical Manual (McGrew et al., 2007).

Content and Concurrent Validity

Content or *substantive* validity refers to the extent to which the test content represents the abilities that it is designed to measure. The WJ III ACH was designed to cover oral language competency as well as the core academic areas that are emphasized in school. The items for the various tests were selected using the results from item validity studies as well as expert opinion. Items that appeared to be biased for certain groups were discarded from the item pool. The WJ III ACH tests were selected to provide a sampling of academic skills from early readiness skills to advanced, complex tasks. Each test measures a specific narrow ability and the tests are combined into various clusters that are designed to measure broader abilities, such as basic reading skills or math reasoning.

Concurrent validity or criterion-prediction validity is designed to demonstrate the extent to which the test scores are related to scores on criterion measures, such as other tests with similar content. The technical manual provides descriptions of several studies that demonstrate that WJ III ACH is highly related to other measures of school achievement. The patterns and magnitudes of the correlations indicate that the WJ III ACH is measuring similar academic abilities to other widely used achievement tests.

Special Populations

Tests like the WJ III ACH are frequently used for the assessment of individuals with suspected or confirmed disabilities. Therefore, an important aspect of validity is whether the test distinguishes between individuals with differing special needs. To determine this, the performance of various clinical groups has been evaluated using selected tests and clusters from the WJ III ACH.

Table 19.8 summarizes the results of these studies for children and adolescents younger than 19 years of age. Table 19.9 summarizes the results for adults older than 19 years of age.

These studies provide evidence that the WJ III is sensitive to differences in the population. For example, Table 19.8 indicates that individuals identified as having mental retardation had the lowest median scores, whereas the individuals who were identified as gifted had the highest median scores. Furthermore, the lowest median score for individuals with math disabilities was on the Brief Math cluster and the lowest median score for individuals with written language disabilities was on the Brief Writing cluster. In other words, the clinical groups' performances on the WJ III ACH are what would be predicted by the varied diagnoses, further demonstrating the sensitivity and validity of the test.

USE OF THE TEST

The comprehensive nature of the WJ III ACH makes it appropriate for a variety of purposes, including determining an individual's present performance levels in achievement, identifying an individual's academic strengths and weaknesses, comparing an individual's performance to age or grade peers, investigating need for special services, monitoring educational progress across the school years, and assisting with instructional planning.

Historically, within schools, the WJ III ACH has been used primarily for determining eligibility for special education services. With the changes in the Individuals with Disabilities Education Improvement Act of 2004 (IDEA, 2004), the diagnostic capabilities of the WJ III ACH may be better used by practitioners. Instead of focusing primarily on establishing a discrepancy between ability and achievement, practitioners may now focus more on understanding an individual's learning strengths and weaknesses and using the evaluation data to help develop instructional plans.

TABLE 19.8   Performance of Special Populations Younger than 19 Years of Age on Selected WJ III ACH Tests and Clusters

	Brief Reading	Brief Writing	Brief Math	Listening Comp	Oral Expression
REFERENCE SAMPLE					
WJ III Norm Group					
n	5054	4483	4527	1364	4850
Median (SS)	101	101	101	101	100
CLINICAL SAMPLES					
ADHD					
n	757	476	728	81	119
Median (SS)	93	90	92	99	100
Autism Spectrum					
n	80	34	78	--	--
Median (SS)	87	86	83	--	--
Gifted					
n	87	85	87	--	--
Median (SS)	118	117	121	--	--
Language Disorders					
n	132	85	132	72	62
Median (SS)	90	96	89	79	89
Math Disorder					
n	165	155	159	92	90
Median (SS)	95	91	78	96	95
Mental Retardation					
n	111	93	109	26	--
Median (SS)	54	54	48	63	--
Reading Disorders					
n	445	413	434	133	120
Median (SS)	83	83	92	97	98
Writing Disorders					
n	364	340	351	148	142
Median (SS)	90	85	97	101	104

In cases where the referral question involves exploring the presence of a specific learning disability, all eight academic areas that are mandated in IDEA 2004 are available in the WJ III ACH: basic reading skills, reading comprehension, reading fluency, written expression, math calculation, math problem solving, oral expression, and listening comprehension. Reading fluency is the only area that has just one test, suggesting that in some cases, the examiner

TABLE 19.9   Performance of Special Populations Older than 19 Years of Age on Selected WJ III ACH Tests and Clusters

	Brief Reading	Brief Writing	Brief Math	Listening Comp	Oral Expression
REFERENCE SAMPLE					
WJ III Norm Group					
n	2602	2412	2495	309	2469
Median (SS)	103	104	102	94	101
CLINICAL SAMPLES					
ADHD					
n	112	81	98	30	34
Median (SS)	96	96	94	94	93
Head Injury					
n	357	273	309	144	143
Median (SS)	98	97	96	96	93
Math Disorder					
n	105	83	83	68	71
Median (SS)	100	105	88	104	106
Reading Disorders					
n	180	101	102	44	64
Median (SS)	87	90	96	106	101
Writing Disorders					
n	169	117	119	80	97
Median (SS)	90	92	104	108	10

will want to supplement the WJ III ACH with additional measures of reading rate and fluency. Additional testing is common practice because IDEA 2004 specifically prohibits the use of any single assessment instrument as the sole criterion for identification of a disability.

INTERPRETATION METHODS

As mentioned previously in the score interpretation section of this chapter, the WJ III ACH provides information at four different interpretive levels. The skilled clinician must integrate information from these levels as well as from a variety of other sources to develop a more complete understanding of the examinee. When making high-stakes decisions, like special education eligibility, practitioners often use cluster-level information because of higher reliabilities and broader coverage of the construct. The examiner should, however, also consider performance on the narrow abilities so that the person's strengths and weaknesses are clearly understood. If an examiner looks at performance only on the broad clusters, which are composed of numerous abilities, he or she may not fully grasp the specific nature of the problem, such as a problem only in spelling. When planning an appropriate instructional program, information from the clusters, the individual tests, and even item-level information can be useful in interpreting and explaining performance.

In addition to the more traditional interpretive frameworks, the WJ III ACH also provides two unique discrepancy procedures for determining an individual's intraindividual strengths and weaknesses in performance. Under IDEA (2004), documentation of the pattern of strengths and weaknesses is an essential consideration in determining whether the person has a specific learning disability.

Intra-achievement Variation Procedure

The *intra-achievement variation procedure* allows practitioners to analyze intraindividual differences, identifying strengths and weaknesses that may exist within academic performance. Discrepancy norms are used in determining the significance and frequency of the individual's variations in performance. Four different options are available when using this procedure, depending on which tests and clusters are administered:

1. *Brief*: requires administration of the six tests that create the Brief Reading, Brief Writing, and Brief Math clusters. The three cluster scores are used in the procedure.
2. *Broad*: requires administration of the nine tests that create the Broad Reading, Broad Written Language, and Broad Math clusters. The three cluster scores are used in the procedure.
3. *Standard*: requires administration of the 11 tests that create the Oral Language-Standard, Broad Reading, Broad Written Language, and Broad Math clusters. The four cluster scores are used in the procedure.
4. *Extended*: requires administration of the 17 tests that create the Basic Reading, Reading Comprehension, Basic Writing Skills, Written Expression, Math Calculation Skills, Math Reasoning, Oral Expression, Listening Comprehension, and Academic Knowledge

clusters. The eight cluster scores are used in the procedure.

Oral Language Ability–Achievement Discrepancy Procedure

The *oral language ability–achievement discrepancy procedure* allows evaluators to use the examinee's oral language ability, based on the Oral Language—Extended cluster, as the predictor of achievement, much as an ability score or intelligence test score is used. Comparisons are then made between the examinee's oral language ability and his or her achievement in reading, writing, and math. Discrepancy norms are used to determine the significance and frequency of any discrepancies present in the individual's performance. This procedure is helpful in clarifying the presence of a specific learning disability, especially in the area of reading. The number of tests administered will vary depending on which achievement clusters the practitioner wishes to include.

STEP-BY-STEP GUIDE TO INTERPRETING THE WJ III ACH

An understanding of the WJ III ACH results can be facilitated by considering information from the following five sources: (1) the clusters and tests; (2) the intra-achievement variation procedure; (3) the oral language ability–achievement discrepancy procedure; (4) the criterion-referenced information; and (5) the qualitative information. The evaluator can review this data in a step-by-step fashion. Each step is described in detail and illustrated using Bart's case study data, which appear at the end of this section of the chapter.

Step 1: Interpretation of Clusters and Tests
  Step 1A: Interpretation of clusters. The first step is interpreting the clusters, which are

composites created by administering two or more tests. Clusters are more reliable than individual tests and, therefore, are recommended when making important decisions. They provide comprehensive, norm-referenced measures of the academic domains. When performance is consistent on the tests that comprise the cluster, interpretation may be focused at the cluster level.

Step 1B: Interpretation of tests. At times, significant differences may exist, however, between the tests that comprise each cluster. When these differences exist, the reasons for the differences should be clarified, which may require further testing. Significant differences can be determined by examining the confidence bands for the tests within each cluster. The Standard Score/Percentile Rank Profile (SS/PR Profile) provides a graphic representation of these bands, making it easy to see whether significant differences exist among the clusters and the tests. Three basic rules exist for interpreting these bands: If the bands overlap, there is no significant difference; if a separation exists between the two bands but it is not as wide as either band, a probable difference exists; if the separation between the two bands is wider than either band, it is likely that a real difference exists. Figure 19.2 illustrates Bart's SS/PR Profile for the six reading tests.

No significant differences exist among the three tests that form the Broad Reading cluster (Letter-Word Identification, Reading Fluency, and Passage Comprehension). The confidence bands of all three tests overlap. All three aspects of reading (decoding, fluency, and comprehension) are limited for Bart and represent normative weaknesses (< 85). It is probable that performance on the Word Attack test is higher than on the other four reading tests, whereas performance on the phonological awareness test, Sound

Awareness, is significantly higher than on all of the five reading tests.

When one examines the two Basic Reading Skills tests, Letter-Word Identification and Word Attack, the bands do not overlap, and Word Attack is significantly higher than Letter-Word Identification. Presently, Bart's phonic skills are significantly higher than his word identification skills. In this case, the practitioner would explain the reasons for the differences. Bart does better on phonically regular nonsense words than he does on real words, many of which have irregular spelling patterns. Because of extensive tutoring in school and over the summer, his phonics skills have improved. However, he is still having difficulty recognizing common spelling units (e.g., *ight*) or what are referred to as *orthographic patterns*.

Interpretation at the test level may also provide a useful link to instructional planning. Each WJ III ACH test measures a narrow aspect of a broad achievement domain, facilitating the identification of the individual's specific academic limitations. As an aid to practitioners, each WJ III test is linked to a bank of instructional interventions and accommodations in the software program, WIIIP. When an individual's performance is below average, appropriate interventions are made available for consideration by the examiner. Table 19.10 contains a selection of some of the possible instructional interventions and accommodations from the WIIIP that are related to Bart's limitations on the reading tests.

Step 2: Interpretation of the Intra-achievement Variation Procedure

The second step helps determines whether any significant strengths or weaknesses exist in the individual's performance. Bart's Intra-achievement Variation (shown in Table 19.11) uses the extended clusters. Using Reading Comprehension as the example, Bart obtained an actual standard score of 70. Based on the average of all the other clusters, it was predicted that he would have a score of 96. His actual score was 26 points lower

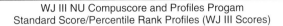

WJ III NU Compuscore and Profiles Progam
Standard Score/Percentile Rank Profiles (WJ III Scores)

Name: K.Bart   Grade: 3.2
Date of Birth: 01/14/1999
Age: 8 years, 10 months
Sex: Male
Date of Testing: 11/07/2007

Peer Comparisons   ← 68% →   Confidence   Norms based on: Grade (K 0-12.9)
                                             Band

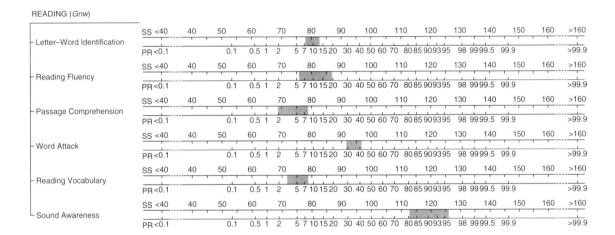

Note: Profiles generated by the Woodcock–Johnson III Normative Update Compuscore and
Profiles Program (Version 3.1), 2008, Riverside Publishing

FIGURE 19.2

Bart's SS/PR Profile for Selected Clusters/Tests

than predicted, resulting in a difference score of –26. This size difference is unusual, resulting in a PR of 0.2. This percentile rank means that less than 1% of the population, or two out of 1,000 people, would have that large of a difference between their actual and their predicted scores. Bart's actual score is significantly low, almost three standard deviations (–2.93) below his predicted score. Therefore, reading comprehension is both a significant intrapersonal and normative weakness. In addition, Bart has significant intrapersonal and normative weaknesses (< 85) in Basic Writing Skills and Written Expression.

He has significant intrapersonal and normative strengths (> 115) in Oral Expression, Listening Comprehension, and Academic Knowledge.

Step 3: Interpretation of the Oral Language Ability–Achievement Discrepancy Procedure

The third step involves determining whether a significant discrepancy exists between the individual's oral language ability and academic performance. This procedure helps document whether the individual's achievement is commensurate with oral language ability and helps

TABLE 19.10   Sample of Selected Reading Interventions for Bart Generated by the Woodcock Interpretation and Instructional Intervention Program (WIIIP)

Use of an explicit, systematic, synthetic phonics program may be beneficial for Bart. These programs begin instruction at the phoneme level and then introduce graphemes. Bart would be taught explicitly the relationship between sounds (phonemes) and letters (graphemes) and then how to blend the sounds to make words.

Increased time spent reading may increase Bart's exposure to printed words and may result in an increase in the number of words that he can recognize orthographically.

Word recognition strategies may help Bart build automatic sight-word recognition. These strategies include word walls, flow lists, word banks, flash cards, and games. It is beneficial to use high-frequency words when implementing these strategies, as this will enhance Bart's ability to read independently. For example, a word wall might present five high-frequency words that Bart needs to learn. The teacher engages him in activities, both planned and unplanned, which use the words on the wall. Word walls help build word recognition and analysis skills, vocabulary, and serve as a spelling reference.

The phrase drill error correction procedure may be helpful for developing Bart's reading fluency. In this procedure, immediate corrective feedback is combined with rehearsal of the corrected error. When Bart makes an error on a word, the teacher or partner models the correct word immediately. Then the teacher or partner would ask Bart to reread the phrase where the error occurred three times.

Incorporating self-monitoring strategies may help Bart to recognize and resolve his comprehension errors as they arise. Click or Clunk is one example of a self-monitoring strategy that teaches students to monitor their performance while reading. For example, if Bart understands a word, a point, a sentence, etc., he says "click." If he doesn't understand, he says "clunk." Once students can recognize the "clunks," they are taught strategies to address them, including use of a glossary, a dictionary, a reading checklist, or discussion with a peer.

Bart also may benefit from a simple reading accommodation. If Bart listens to a tutor read text while he reads the text silently, or just listens while text is read, more information may be acquired in that fixed amount of time compared to what Bart would accomplish if reading silently and answering comprehension questions.

clarify the role of language in the individual's learning difficulties. Table 19.12 illustrates Bart's Oral Language Ability–Achievement discrepancy procedure. Bart has significant discrepancies between his oral language ability and all reading and writing clusters as well as Math Calculation Skills. His performances in Broad Math, Math Reasoning, Academic Knowledge, and Brief Math are not significantly above or below his oral language ability. In other words, Bart's oral language abilities do not appear to be the reason for his difficulties in reading and writing development.

Step 4: Interpretation of Criterion-Referenced Information

Step 4 helps practitioners make appropriate instructional recommendations. The Relative Proficiency Index (RPI) and the Age/Grade Profile, described in the "Hierarchy of Scores" section of this chapter, provide valuable information. The RPI is especially helpful in describing functionality on a task and sometimes provides insights not available from peer-comparison scores. For example, Bart obtained a standard score of 93 on Word Attack, which indicates average standing relative to age-mates (see Table 19.13). However, his RPI of 66/90 indicates he has limited proficiency on this task compared to age-mates with average proficiency and that he is at a frustration level. Bart's performance was really further from average than indicated by his standard score. The RPI provided a more accurate description of Bart's actual performance in the classroom.

Figure 19.3 illustrates several of the cluster scores of Bart's Grade Profile. Bart is a

TABLE 19.11   Bart's Intra-Achievement Variation Procedure

VARIATIONS	STANDARD SCORES			VARIATION		Significant at
	Actual	Predicted	Difference	PR	SD	+ or − 1.50 SD
Intra-Achievement (Ext)						
BASIC READING SKILLS	84	94	−10	15	−1.02	No
READING COMP	70	95	−25	0.2	−2.93	Yes
MATH CALC SKILLS	81	95	−14	13	−1.14	No
MATH REASONING	99	91	8	78	+0.78	No
BASIC WRITING SKILLS	68	96	−28	0.2	−2.91	Yes
WRITTEN EXPRESSION	69	96	−27	0.3	−2.73	Yes
ORAL EXPRESSION	116	91	25	98	+2.09	Yes
LISTENING COMP	122	90	32	99.7	+2.75	Yes
ACADEMIC KNOWLEDGE	120	90	30	99.8	+2.87	Yes

TABLE 19.12   Bart's Oral Language Ability/Achievement Discrepancy

DISCREPANCIES	STANDARD SCORES			DISCREPANCY		Significant at
	Actual	Predicted	Difference	PR	SD	− 1.50 SD (SEE)
*Oral Language/Achievement Discrepancies**						
BROAD READING	73	113	−40	<0.1	−3.32	Yes
BASIC READING SKILLS	84	111	−27	1	−2.18	Yes
READING COMP	70	114	−44	<0.1	−3.85	Yes
BROAD MATH	93	111	−18	9	−1.32	No
MATH CALC SKILLS	81	108	−27	3	−1.83	Yes
MATH REASONING	99	113	−14	14	−1.09	No
BROAD WRITTEN LANG	58	111	−53	<0.1	−3.96	Yes
BASIC WRITING SKILLS	68	112	−44	<0.1	−3.40	Yes
WRITTEN EXPRESSION	69	110	−41	0.1	−3.05	Yes
ACADEMIC KNOWLEDGE	120	116	4	66	+0.42	No
BRIEF READING	74	112	−38	<0.1	−3.11	Yes
BRIEF MATH	97	111	−14	15	−1.06	No
BRIEF WRITING	67	110	−43	<0.1	−3.29	Yes

*These discrepancies compare Oral Language (Ext) with Broad, Basic, Brief, and Applied ACH clusters

TABLE 19.13 Computer-Generated Results for Bart's WJ III ACH Clusters and Tests

TABLE OF SCORES

Woodcock-Johnson III Normative Update Tests of Achievement (Form A)

Woodcock Interpretation and Instructional Interventions Program, Version 1.0

Norms based on ages 8–10

CLUSTER/Test	W	AE	Proficiency	RPI	SS (68% Band)	PR
ORAL LANGUAGE (Ext)	508	12–8	advanced	98/90	122 (118–126)	93
ORAL EXPRESSION	507	12–3	avg to adv	97/90	116 (111–121)	86
LISTENING COMP	510	13–3	advanced	98/90	122 (117–127)	93
BRIEF ACHIEVEMENT	455	7–4	v limited	20/90	78 (75–80)	7
BROAD READING	456	7–1	v limited	19/90	73 (70–75)	3
BROAD MATH	485	8–4	average	82/90	93 (89–96)	31
BROAD WRITTEN LANG	456	6–8	v limited	15/90	58 (54–63)	0.3
BRIEF READING	446	7–1	v limited	8/90	74 (72–77)	4
BASIC READING SKILLS	457	7–6	v limited	23/90	84 (82–86)	15
READING COMP	462	6–10	v limited	18/90	70 (67–73)	2
BRIEF MATH	485	8–7	average	86/90	97 (93–101)	41
MATH CALC SKILLS	480	7–8	lmtd to avg	71/90	81 (75–86)	10
MATH REASONING	490	8–9	average	89/90	99 (96–103)	49
BRIEF WRITING	452	6–9	v limited	9/90	67 (63–70)	1
BASIC WRITING SKILLS	452	6–11	v limited	11/90	68 (64–72)	2
WRITTEN EXPRESSION	466	6–10	limited	34/90	69 (63–75)	2
ACADEMIC SKILLS	449	7–1	v limited	11/90	73 (70–75)	3
ACADEMIC FLUENCY	474	6–10	limited	58/90	66 (59–72)	1
ACADEMIC APPS	473	7–6	limited	53/90	82 (79–85)	12
ACADEMIC KNOWLEDGE	509	11–4	advanced	98/90	120 (115–126)	91
PHON/GRAPH KNOW	484	7–8	lmtd to avg	71/90	91 (89–94)	28
Letter-Word Identification	434	7–3	v limited	4/90	79 (77–82)	8
Reading Fluency	475	7–2	limited	64/90	80 (74–85)	9

TABLE 19.13 (Continued)

CLUSTER/Test	W	AE	Proficiency	RPI	SS (68% Band)	PR
Story Recall	500	10–6	average	93/90	107 (100–115)	69
Understanding Directions	507	13–10	advanced	98/90	119 (112–126)	90
Calculation	477	7–11	lmtd to avg	69/90	87 (80–94)	19
Math Fluency	483	6–9	lmtd to avg	73/90	70 (66–75)	2
Spelling	437	6–5	negligible	2/90	64 (59–68)	1
Writing Fluency	465	6–5	limited	34/90	67 (55–79)	1
Passage Comprehension	458	6–11	v limited	15/90	75 (71–79)	5
Applied Problems	494	9–2	average	94/90	104 (99–109)	61
Writing Samples	466	7–0	limited	34/90	76 (71–81)	5
Word Attack	480	7–10	limited	66/90	93 (91–95)	32
Picture Vocabulary	513	12–9	advanced	99/90	116 (111–121)	86
Oral Comprehension	513	12–11	advanced	99/90	119 (114–124)	90
Editing	466	7–6	limited	41/90	83 (78–88)	13
Reading Vocabulary	465	6–9	v limited	21/90	78 (75–81)	7
Quantitative Concepts	486	8–4	average	82/90	94 (89–99)	35
Academic Knowledge	509	11–4	advanced	98/90	120 (115–126)	91
Spelling of Sounds	488	7–5	lmtd to avg	75/90	86 (80–92)	18
Sound Awareness	502	12–1	avg to adv	97/90	118 (111–124)	88

	STANDARD SCORES			VARIATION		Significant at
VARIATIONS	Actual	Predicted	Difference	PR	SD	+ or – 1.50 SD
Intra-Achievement (Ext)						
BASIC READING SKILLS	84	94	−10	15	−1.02	No
READING COMP	70	95	−25	0.2	−2.93	Yes
MATH CALC SKILLS	81	95	−14	13	−1.14	No
MATH REASONING	99	91	8	78	+0.78	No
BASIC WRITING SKILLS	68	96	−28	0.2	−2.91	Yes
WRITTEN EXPRESSION	69	96	−27	0.3	−2.73	Yes
ORAL EXPRESSION	116	91	25	98	+2.09	Yes
LISTENING COMP	122	90	32	99.7	+2.75	Yes
ACADEMIC KNOWLEDGE	120	90	30	99.8	+2.87	Yes

(Continues)

TABLE 19.13   (Continued)

DISCREPANCIES	STANDARD SCORES			DISCREPANCY		Significant at
	Actual	Predicted	Difference	PR	SD	−1.50 SD
Oral Language/Achievement Discrepancies*						
BROAD READING	73	113	−40	<0.1	−3.32	Yes
BASIC READING SKILLS	84	111	−27	1	−2.18	Yes
READING COMP	70	114	−44	<0.1	−3.85	Yes
BROAD MATH	93	111	−18	9	−1.32	No
MATH CALC SKILLS	81	108	−27	3	−1.83	Yes
MATH REASONING	99	113	−14	14	−1.09	No
BROAD WRITTEN LANG	58	111	−53	<0.1	−3.96	Yes
BASIC WRITING SKILLS	68	112	−44	<0.1	−3.40	Yes
WRITTEN EXPRESSION	69	110	−41	0.1	−3.05	Yes
ACADEMIC KNOWLEDGE	120	116	4	66	+0.42	No
BRIEF READING	74	112	−38	<0.1	−3.11	Yes
BRIEF MATH	97	111	−14	15	−1.06	No
BRIEF WRITING	67	110	−43	<0.1	−3.29	Yes

*These discrepancies compare Oral Language (Ext) with Broad, Basic, Brief, and Applied ACH clusters

third-grade student whose greatest instructional needs are in the areas of reading and written language. The instructional zones for all of the reading and writing clusters are below his current grade placement. The implication of this is clear. Instruction in these areas must be provided below the third-grade level. For example, Bart's instruction in basic reading skills should occur at about the beginning-to-mid-second-grade level. In contrast, Bart's math abilities are right at his current grade placement, and his oral language abilities are above his grade placement. These findings suggest that Bart will profit from grade-level instruction in mathematics, and accelerated instruction in oral language.

Communicating this important information to parents is facilitated by the Parent Report option in the WJ III NU Compuscore. This report (see Figure 19.4) translates the RPI information into an easy-to-understand grid representing the individual's performance. The proficiency levels associated with the RPI, ranging from negligible to very advanced, are listed across the top of the grid. The clusters and tests administered are listed along the left side. An *X* is placed in the grid corresponding to the individual's level of proficiency on each task. For example, Bart has limited proficiency in Broad Reading, but average proficiency in Broad Math. National percentile ranks are also included in the column at the far right of the Parent Report.

Step 5: Interpretation of Qualitative Information

Step 5 focuses on integrating informal and observational information that was gathered during the evaluation process. The WJ III ACH provides a framework for recording behavioral

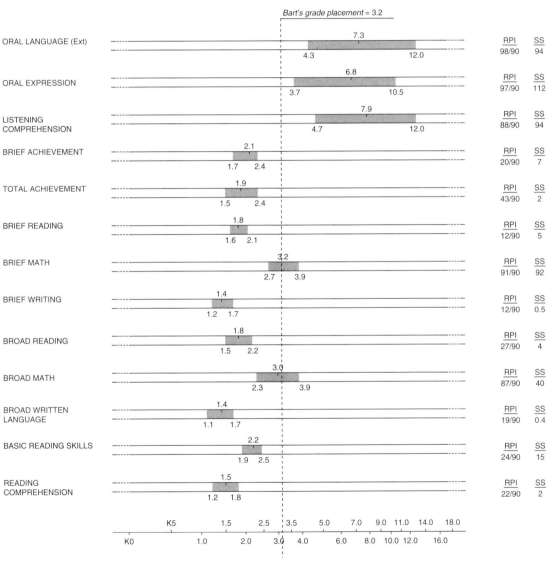

FIGURE 19.3

Bart's Grade Profile for Selected Clusters/Tests

W J⁹⁹ **Woodcock-Johnson III Normative Update Tests of Achievement, Form A**
III   Parent Report for Bart K

Date of Birth: 01/14/1999   Grade: 3.2
Age: 8 years, 10 months
Sex: Male
Date of Testing: 11/07/2007

Bart was administered a set of tests from the Woodcock-Johnson III Normative Update Tests of Achievement, Form A. His performance in each area is shown below. Based on a comparison to others in his grade, Bart's Total achievement national percentile rank of 3 means that he scored in the lowest 3 percent of third-grade students nationally.

TASK	Negligible	Very Limited	Limited	Limited to Average	Average	Average to Advanced	Advanced	Very Advanced	National Percentile Rank
TOTAL ACHIEVEMENT			X						3
BROAD READING			X						4
BROAD MATH					X				40
BROAD WRITTEN LANGUAGE		X							0.4
ACADEMIC SKILLS		X							3
ACADEMIC APPLICATIONS			X						15
ACADEMIC FLUENCY			X						1
MATH CALCULATION SKILLS				X					14
WRITTEN EXPRESSION			X						2
Letter-Word Identification		X							10
Reading Fluency				X					11
Calculation				X					28
Math Fluency				X					3
Spelling	X								1
Writing Fluency			X						1
Passage Comprehension		X							4
Appllied Problems						X			71
Writing Samples			X						4

Note: Parent Report generated by the Woodcock–Johnson III Normative Update Compuscore and Profiles Program (Version 3.1), 2008, Riverside Publishing.

FIGURE 19.4

Bart's Parent Report

observations by including a Test Sessions Observation Checklist on the first page of each Test Record. The categories on the checklist include level of conversational proficiency, level of cooperation, level of activity, attention and concentration, self-confidence, care in responding, and response to difficult tasks. In addition, practitioners should note how the examinee approaches each task, observing things such as speed of response and strategies employed. To facilitate the recording of observations, the WJ III ACH Form C includes Qualitative Observations for the nine tests in the battery. For example, the Qualitative Observations for Test 1, Letter-Word Identification, asks the examiner to choose one of six statements that best describes the ease with which the examinee identified the words: (1) Identified words rapidly and accurately with little effort (automatic word identification skills); (2) Identified initial items rapidly and accurately and

identified more difficult items through increased application of phoneme-grapheme relationships (typical); (3) Identified initial items rapidly and accurately but did not apply phoneme-grapheme relationships to incorrectly answered letter items; (4) Required increased time and greater attention to phoneme-grapheme relationships to determine the correct response (nonautomatic word identification skills); (5) Was not able to apply phoneme-grapheme relationships; or (6) None of the above, not observed, or does not apply.

Finally, practitioners should record examinee errors and then analyze those errors for patterns and instructional implications. More than any score, the types of errors an individual makes inform the instructional planning process. Bart's errors on the Letter-Word Identification test suggest that he does not pay careful attention to the sequence of letters in words (e.g., pronouncing *could* as *cloud* and *own* as *now*).

CASE STUDY

This case study example is provided to illustrate several of the WJ III ACH interpretive features and scores. Because of space limitations, only the results on the WJ III ACH reading tests are discussed, as well as results from the intra-achievement and oral language ability–achievement discrepancies. In addition, diagnostic impressions and examples of a few recommendations to address the referral concerns are provided. Bart's complete set of obtained scores on the WJ III ACH are included in Table 19.13. See Chapter 8 of this book for a discussion of Bart's results from the WJ III Tests of Cognitive Abilities as well as an integration of some of his cognitive and achievement results.

Reason for Referral

Bart was referred for an evaluation by his mother, Ms. Maria Urso. Ms. Urso wished to obtain a better understanding of her son's educational needs, as well as any factors that were interfering with his educational development. Ms. Urso expressed concerns regarding Bart's ongoing difficulties acquiring basic reading, spelling, and writing skills despite advanced verbal abilities. Ms Urso also requested recommendations regarding specific reading programs that could be used by his tutor. She noted that she sometimes wonders whether Bart's problems are caused by a lack of interest in reading and low motivation.

Background Information

Bart was adopted as a baby. He currently lives with his mother and his 11-year-old sister, who is also adopted. Ms. Urso described all of his developmental milestones as being within normal limits. Although Bart has received special-education services at school for reading since the first grade, his mother feels that his progress has been unsatisfactory.

For Kindergarten, Bart attended Desert Vista. At the end of the year, his teachers felt that he was not ready for first grade. His mother concurred with their recommendation and he repeated Kindergarten. In first grade, Bart was referred for an evaluation for poor reading. He qualified for additional reading support in the resource room. Bart completed first and second grade at Desert Vista, and then transferred to Redwood Elementary School, a local charter school, where he has just started third grade. This summer Bart received individualized reading tutoring four times a week from a certified special-education teacher, Ms. Sammons. Ms. Sammons provided Bart with intensive instruction in a synthetic phonics approach, teaching him the associations between sounds and letters in a systematic, sequential way. Although Ms. Sammons reported that Bart's ability to apply phonics skills when reading and spelling had improved, she also commented that his progress had been much slower than her other students. Ms. Sammons was hoping that the present evaluation would provide specific recommendations for additional methods or materials that she could implement in their tutoring sessions.

Assessments

Woodcock-Johnson III: Tests of Achievement (WJ III ACH)

Passage from a classroom textbook

Woodcock-Johnson III: Tests of Cognitive Abilities[1](WJ III COG)

Behavioral observations

Bart was cooperative and attentive throughout all testing sessions, and generally appeared at ease and comfortable. During the evaluation, his ability to express himself orally was clearly advanced for his age. Although Bart was willing to attempt all of the tasks, on several tests when he perceived that the questions or problems were becoming too difficult, he made statements such as "These are getting way too hard for me" or "I don't think I can do any more of these." When encouraged to continue, Bart would generally persist.

Reading

Bart's score on the WJ III Broad Reading Score exceeded only 3% of his age peers (percentile rank of 3). His RPI of 19/90 indicates that on similar classroom reading tasks, he would have about 19% success when his average age peers would have about 90% success. Overall, his performance was low in all aspects of reading.

Bart's proficiency level on the WJ III Letter-Word Identification test was very limited. When attempting to pronounce words on this test, Bart tended to confuse and misread words that have a similar visual appearance, such as reading the word *could* as *cloud* and the word *since* as *science*. Bart's proficiency was also very limited on the Passage Comprehension test. Given Bart's advanced use and comprehension of spoken language, his low performance on this test can be attributed primarily to poor word identification, rather than limited ability to understand the meanings of the words and sentences.

On the Reading Fluency test, Bart's proficiency was limited. Upon completion of the test, Bart commented that he was much better at reading aloud than silently. Although Bart's highest

---

[1]See Chapter 8 for Bart's cognitive testing results.

performance was on the Word Attack test, he self-corrected numerous times before coming up with a response. On many of the items, he read the words very slowly, attempting to pronounce each of the sounds of the letters in the nonsense word before producing a response. Bart did not recognize common spelling patterns, such as *ight*, and made several errors pronouncing medial vowel sounds, such as saying *hig* for *heg*.

When asked to read a page from his classroom science textbook, Bart's rate was very slow. He sounded out common words and repeated words and phrases. Even when not having any apparent difficulty with the particular words, he read slowly. Bart demonstrated considerable difficulty reading grade-level text although he clearly tried to use the phonics skills that he has learned from the resource room and his summer tutoring. At one point, Bart stopped reading the passage and asked: "Why is reading so hard for me?"

Variations and Discrepancies

On the WJ III ACH, the intra-individual variation procedure illustrates a person's significant strengths and weaknesses. This variation procedure shows the likelihood of a person obtaining a particular score, given the average of their other achievement cluster scores. When Bart's Reading Comprehension cluster score (SS = 70) was compared to his other areas of achievement, it was significantly lower than predicted (SS = 96). Only 2 out of 1,000 people (variation percentile rank of .2) would have a difference of this size. (Note that similar results were obtained for the Basic Writing Skills and Written Expression clusters.)

The Oral Language Ability–Achievement Discrepancy Procedure compares the person's performance on the Oral Language—Extended cluster to his or her performance in reading, writing, and mathematics. When Bart's Oral Language—Extended score was compared to his scores in reading, all areas of reading were significantly lower than predicted. For Broad Reading, Reading Comprehension, and Brief Reading, less than 1 out of 1,000 students would have discrepancies of this size. On Basic Reading Skills, Bart's actual standard score was 84, whereas his predicted standard score was 111. Only 1 out of 100 students would have a difference of this size. These findings indicate that Bart's reading abilities are significantly lower than would be predicted by his oral language ability.

Summary

It is important to understand that Bart's difficulties with reading are not caused by a lack of motivation or effort. He wants to improve his reading and does not understand why reading is so difficult for him. Bart's oral language abilities predict that his reading skills should be more advanced than they presently are. He has normative strengths (standard scores > 115) in oral language, oral expression, listening comprehension, academic knowledge, and sound awareness, all of which provide a solid foundation for reading and suggest that his reading difficulties are unexpected. Bart has normative weaknesses (standard scores < 85) in all of the reading and writing tests, except Word Attack (SS = 93) and Spelling of Sounds (SS = 86). Both of these tasks have no time limits and use phonically regular nonsense words, capitalizing on Bart's intact phonemic awareness and his increased knowledge of phonic elements. His difficulties in reading appear to stem from his lack of automaticity with word decoding, indicating possible weaknesses in orthographic processing and perceptual speed. Further support of this possibility is Bart's very limited proficiency in spelling real words and his slow performance on all timed tasks. Bart has trouble recalling how words look and his decoding and encoding skills are not automatic. His limited basic skills are affecting his higher-level skills in reading comprehension and written expression. Bart's learning difficulties primarily affect his performance on tasks requiring reading and writing. With the exception of his performance on the speeded math facts test, Math Fluency, Bart's performance in math falls within the average range.

Bart appears to exhibit a pattern of strengths and weaknesses that indicates a specific learning disability. To further explore Bart's difficulties, a comprehensive cognitive evaluation is recommended. Of particular interest would be his performance on tasks requiring associative memory, rapid automatized naming, processing speed, working memory, and cognitive fluency, as these areas may help further explain his academic difficulties.

Instructional Recommendations

Bart will benefit from continued tutoring that is directed toward helping him improve his basic reading and writing skills. In spite of increased instruction both in school and at home, Bart still has difficulty recognizing words with ease and has not fully mastered basic phonics skills. His difficulty reading both isolated words and text indicates that he requires further reading instruction in phonics skills, recognition of common letter patterns, and strategies for pronouncing longer words. The following recommendations are provided to help Bart improve his reading skills:

Continue to teach Bart phonic skills by using a highly structured synthetic phonics approach, such as the *Phonic Reading Lessons: Skills and Practice* (available from www.AcademicTherapy.com). Provide instruction for 10 to 15 minutes with this program daily. Alternate between pronouncing rows of words and then dictating words for spelling.

To help Bart improve his ability to sequence letters and sounds, use the activities provided in the *Making Words* books (available from www.schoolspecialtypublishing.com). Provide Bart with 6 to 8 letters that he will use to make 12 to 15 words. The activities begin with short, easy words and end with one big word that uses all of the letters.

As Bart's accuracy improves, use a program specifically designed to improve reading rate and fluency, such as Great Leaps Reading (available from www.greatleaps.com). This program increases reading speed and fluency while reinforcing phonics skills. One-minute timings are done that employ three stimuli: phonics, sight phrases, and short stories. Use the program designed for grade 3. Chart performance on graphs so that Bart can see his progress. This activity will take approximately 10 minutes a day.

Provide daily reading practice in decodable text (text based on a controlled vocabulary with many presentations of the reading/spelling patterns taught and in the same sequence). Bart needs practice with decodable text so that he can integrate skills and develop automaticity in word identification. Try to set aside at least 15 minutes each day for reading.

For independent reading practice, provide Bart with high-interest/low-vocabulary books that he will enjoy. These types of books are available from Scholastic, Inc. (www.scholastic.com) and High Noon, a subsidiary of Academic Therapy Publishing Company (www.AcademicTherapy.com).

SELECTION OF INTERVENTIONS BASED ON TEST RESULTS

As with the results from any test, an examiner must consider a variety of factors when determining appropriate educational interventions for a person—other than just the test scores. Examples of pertinent information would include the person's age, prior history of interventions, the success of previous interventions, the type of educational environment, the training of the personnel, the motivation and persistence of the person, and the severity of the problem, as well as the available resources in the setting. As long as test results are viewed along with consideration of these additional factors, the WJ III ACH can provide valuable information for selecting appropriate academic interventions. Table 19.14 provides a summary of educational interventions related to the academic domains measured by the WJ III ACH. Additional information on interventions can be found in *Educational Interventions Related to the Woodcock-Johnson III Tests of Achievement* (Wendling, Schrank, & Schmitt, 2007), as well as *Woodcock-Johnson III: Recommendations, Reports, and Strategies* (Mather & Jaffe, 2002). In addition, a bank of targeted instructional interventions, related to an individual's performance

on the WJ III tests and clusters, is available in the Woodcock Interpretation and Instructional Interventions Program (Schrank et al., 2008).

The instructional implications that can be derived from some patterns of scores are clearer than others. For example, if Ralph, a fourth-grade student, has a low score on the Phoneme-Grapheme Knowledge cluster (which would indicate poor phonics skills) but has average scores on measures of oral language (which would indicate adequate verbal ability), the evaluator would likely recommend that Ralph receive instruction in a systematic synthetic phonics approach. This approach would be designed to teach him a planned

TABLE 19.14 Examples of Educational Interventions for Academic Domains Based on WJ III ACH Results

Clusters	Related Interventions
Basic Reading Skills	Explicit, systematic, synthetic phonics instruction; Word recognition strategies; high frequency words; instruction in pronouncing multi-syllabic words.
Reading Comprehension	Vocabulary enrichment; activation of prior knowledge; use of graphic organizers; strategies for monitoring comprehension
Reading Fluency	Repeated readings; passage previewing; timed readings
Basic Writing Skills	Multi-sensory techniques; instruction in common irregular words; direct instruction in spelling and editing; strategies for proofreading
Written Expression	Explicit instruction in planning and revising; instruction with sentence combining
Math Calculation Skills	Manipulatives; direct instruction; mnemonic strategies; concrete-representational-abstract teaching sequence; speed drills
Math Reasoning	Strategy instruction; use of visual representations; direct instruction; manipulatives
Oral Expression	Direct instruction in vocabulary and sentence structure; modeling and feedback
Listening Comprehension	Read aloud; practice listening and following directions (e.g., barrier games)

SOURCE : Adapted from *Educational Interventions Related to the Woodcock-Johnson III Tests of Achievement*, by B. J. Wendling, F. A. Schrank, & A. J. Schmitt, 2007 (Assessment Service Bulletin No. 8). Rolling Meadows, IL: Riverside Publishing. Copyright © 2007 by the Riverside Publishing Company. Adapted with permission.

sequence of phoneme-grapheme relationships directly and provide him with considerable practice and review of these phonics elements. If Martha has a low score on the Calculation test, the examiner can identify the types of errors that Martha makes and then make recommendations regarding instruction in how to perform certain types of problems, such as adding and subtracting with fractions.

In other cases, more information is needed before one can develop specific instructional recommendations. For example, an evaluator may also note that Ralph had a low score on the Sound Awareness test, indicating poor phonological awareness. Before recommending additional training in phonological awareness, the evaluator may first want to determine exactly what Ralph can and cannot do on a variety of different types of phonological awareness tasks, such as tasks involving blending and segmentation at both the syllable and phoneme levels. For Martha, who made many computational errors, the evaluator may want to conduct a more detailed evaluation of her computation abilities, attempting to determine her conceptual level of understanding of various arithmetic operations. Results from a more in-depth exploration of performance often help the evaluator to develop more precise instructional recommendations.

For some academic areas, the evaluator has to consider the influence of other areas of performance before making recommendations. For example, if a student has difficulty on tasks involving math reasoning, the evaluator would first want to identify the reason or reasons for the difficulty. In one case, low oral language abilities may be a contributing factor, whereas in another case, poor computational skill may be the cause of the errors.

SUMMARY

The WJ III ACH is a useful diagnostic tool for exploring an individual's present performance levels in oral language, reading, writing, mathematics, and academic knowledge. In addition, WJ III ACH is helpful to practitioners who need to determine whether an individual has a specific learning disability. IDEA 2004 addresses the need to document a pattern of strengths and weaknesses and to identify a deficit in one or more of eight areas. The WJ III ACH measures all eight areas and provides unique variation and discrepancy procedures helpful in quantifying a pattern of strengths and weaknesses.

This battery of academic tests is often used in conjunction with the *Woodcock-Johnson III Tests of Cognitive Ability* (WJ III COG), which is described in Chapter 8. Because the WJ III COG and the WJ III ACH were co-normed using a single sample, together they provide an accurate, valid diagnostic system for identifying an individual's strengths and weaknesses among specific cognitive, linguistic, and academic abilities. The discrepancy procedures provide additional ways to demonstrate varied patterns of performance. Once the specific areas of concern have been identified, the evaluator can then create the most appropriate instructional recommendations for an individual.

REFERENCES

Cummins, J. (1984). *Bilingualism and special education: Issues in assessment and pedagogy*. Austin, TX: Pro-Ed.

Individuals with Disabilities Education Improvement Act of 2004. (PL No. 108-446, 20 USC 1400).

Mather, N., & Jaffe, L. (2002). *Woodcock-Johnson III: Recommendations, reports, and strategies*. New York: Wiley.

Mather, N., Wendling, B. J., & Woodcock, R. W. (2001). *Essentials of WJ III Tests of Achievement assessment*. New York: Wiley.

McGrew, K. S., Dailey, D., & Schrank, F. A. (in press). *WJ III/NU score differences; What the user can expect and why*. (Assessment Service Bulletin). Rolling Meadows, IL: Riverside.

McGrew, K. S., Schrank, F. A., & Woodcock, R. W. (2007). *Technical Manual: Woodcock-Johnson III Normative Update*. Rolling Meadows, IL: Riverside.

McGrew, K. & Woodcock, R. (2001). *Technical Manual: Woodcock-Johnson III*. Rolling Meadows, IL: Riverside.

Muñoz-Sandoval, A. F., Woodcock, R. W., McGrew, K. S., & Mather, N. (2005). *Batería III Woodcock-Muñoz: Pruebas de aprovechamiento*. Rolling Meadows, IL: Riverside.

Rasch, G. (1960). *Probabilistic models for some intelligence and attainment tests*. Copenhagen, Denmark: Danish Institute for Educational Research.

Schrank, F. A., Wendling, B. J., & Woodcock, R. W. (2008). *Woodcock Interpretation and Instructional Interventions Program (WIIIP)*. Rolling Meadows, IL: Riverside.

Schrank, F. A., & Woodcock, R. W. (2008). Woodcock-Johnson III Normative Update Compuscore and Profiles Program (Version 3.1) (Computer software). *Woodcock-Johnson III Normative Update*. Rolling Meadows, IL: Riverside.

Wendling, B. J., Schrank, F. A., & Schmitt, A. J. (2007). *Educational interventions related to the Woodcock-Johnson III Tests of Achievement* (Assessment Service Bulletin No. 8). Rolling Meadows, IL: Riverside.

Woodcock, R. W., McGrew, K., & Mather, N. (2001). *Woodcock-Johnson Tests of Cognitive Abilities and Tests of Achievement* (3rd ed.). Rolling Meadows, IL: Riverside.

Woodcock, R. W., McGrew, K. S., Schrank. F. A., & Mather, N. (2007). *Woodcock-Johnson III Normative Update*. Rolling Meadows, IL: Riverside.

Woodcock, R. W., Schrank, F. A., Mather, N., & McGrew, K. S. (2007). *Woodcock-Johnson III Tests of Achievement Form C/Brief Battery*. Rolling Meadows, IL: Riverside.

Wright, B. D., & Stone, M. H. (1979). *Best test design*. Chicago: MESA Press.

CHAPTER 20

Achievement Assessment and Progress Monitoring with the Wide Range Achievement Test—Fourth Edition

Gale H. Roid, Jon Bos

INTRODUCTION

Clinicians and educators often need to assess the skills of individuals in basic reading and mathematics quickly and easily. Psychologists working in settings with disabled adults or educators working with newly immigrating students require a rapid assessment of basic academic skills. Because of the wide age range and diverse background of individuals, basic skills instruments need to be wide-ranging in scope and age appropriateness. One of the brief achievement tests that has an established history of usefulness is the *Wide Range Achievement Test* (WRAT). The WRAT has been in continuous use as an achievement measure for more than 70 years. The first unpublished version of the test was developed to add an achievement measure to test batteries such as the *Wechsler-Bellevue Scales* (Wechsler, 1939). The test has been revised four times since the first edition (Jastak, 1946) but has continued to measure basic reading, spelling, and mathematics using convenient administration and objective scoring methods. Various editions of the WRAT are frequently used in medical research (e.g.,

Bass, Wilson, & Griffith, 2003), neuropsychology (e.g., O'Bryant, Schrimsher, & Jile, 2005), education (e.g., Friend & Olson, 2008), and other research areas because of their wide range and ease of use. This chapter describes the recent fourth edition (WRAT4; Wilkinson & Robertson, 2006) and a series of brief tests derived from WRAT4. This series of brief (15-item) tests, called the *Progress Monitoring Version* (WRAT4-PMV; Roid & Ledbetter, 2006), was designed for monitoring the progress of students as part of evaluations that require repeated testing during treatment or instruction (Fuchs & Vaughn, 2006). Both the original, longer version of the WRAT4 and the progress-monitoring version provide the same convenience of administration and scoring, as well as coverage of reading, spelling, and mathematics.

Rationale and Theoretical Basis of the Tests

The WRAT4 was constructed initially on the practical rationale that literacy and numeracy—basic skills in reading, mathematics, and spelling—are important to the functioning of every individual. Thus, basic academic skills have been measured by assessment professionals in a wide variety of settings, including schools and clinics, and medical, vocational, and rehabilitation settings. For example, an inspection of the national and state standards for learning in U.S. public schools (Education World, 2008) shows clearly that the curriculum content of the WRAT4 aligns with many of the literacy (and numeracy) standards for student learning assessment, particularly at the early grade levels. The measurement of basic reading (word reading and sentence comprehension) and mathematics (computation) has traditionally been included in comprehensive evaluations of adults with stroke or neurological difficulties (e.g., Lezak, Howieson, & Loring, 2004). The WRAT4 academic areas have been measured for decades as important dimensions by special educators, occupational therapists, clinical and school psychologists, neuropsychologists, vocational counselors, and examiners who conduct evaluations in forensic, worker-compensation, and social security settings.

On a conceptual level, verbal knowledge (e.g., vocabulary, word-reading) and quantitative reasoning (e.g., mathematics problem solving) have been included as factors in theories of human abilities. Carroll (1993) included specific factors such as language comprehension (e.g., vocabulary, reading comprehension), quantitative reasoning (mathematics skills and applications), reading speed, and spelling within the hierarchical factors of crystallized ability and fluid reasoning. The widely employed model of human ability called *CHC theory* also includes similar factors, due to the work of Cattell (1943), Horn (1985, 1994), Horn and Cattell (1966), and Carroll (1993). CHC theory includes factors for quantitative knowledge, such as mathematics calculation in WRAT4, and reading-writing ability, such as word reading, sentence comprehension, and spelling (Carroll, 1993; Mather & Woodcock, 2001a). The traditional distinctions between cognitive ability and achievement are somewhat blurred by these theories. Perhaps the

cognitive aspects of crystallized and fluid abilities are processes such as planning, problem-solving strategies, and similar "thinking processes" that generalize across academic disciplines. Achievement measures such as WRAT4 emphasize the "content" of academic skills that are affected by school learning. Thus, achievement measures, as compared to ability measures, require grade-level norms for sensitivity to the changes in reading, spelling, and mathematics due to specific curriculum, teaching, and learning effects.

Additionally, the rationale for the related version—WRAT4-PMV—is the extensive new literature on educational assessment of students within the model of special-education reform called *response-to-intervention (RTI)* (Fuchs & Vaughn, 2006; Gresham, 2002; Hale, Kaufman, Naglieri, & Kavale, 2006; Vaughn, Linan-Thompson, & Hickman, 2003). RTI has grown to include a wide range of innovative systems for frequent assessment and tailoring of instruction to meet the needs of low-performing students whether they are in general- or special-education classrooms throughout a school district (Barnes & Harlacher, 2008). RTI emerged from the need to fulfill the requirements of new federal laws such as the *No Child Left Behind Act* (2002) and the encouragement of national educational associations (e.g., National Association of State Directors of Special Education, 2006). The testing element in these models includes frequent testing and monitoring of student achievement (in reading especially) at multiple levels or "tiers," including the regular classroom, various tutoring or compensatory programs, and special education (Fuchs & Fuchs, 2005). The *Individuals with Disabilities Education Improvement Act* (IDEIA, 2004), labeled *IDEA 2004* in this chapter, specifically suggests the use of RTI-style and progress-monitoring approaches as a part of the identification of specific learning disabilities (Hale et al., 2006; Posny, 2007; U.S. Department of Education, 2004). This progress-monitoring approach was suggested as an alternative to the frequently employed method of contrasting achievement and intellectual ability and calculating a *discrepancy* between the two that was included in the original IDEA (1997). The limitations of the discrepancy method have been questioned in terms of validity (Stuebing, Fletcher, LeDoux, Lyon, Shaywitz, & Shaywitz, 2002). The IDEA 2004 legislation implementation (Naglieri, 2007; Posny, 2007; U.S. Department of Education, 2004) included both the progress-monitoring approach and comprehensive assessment approaches that have traditionally included cognitive, ability, achievement, and behavioral measures. The new recognition of progress monitoring that appeared in IDEA 2004 was based on published studies of special education models and learning-disability identification such as the work of the Deno (1985, 2003), Fuchs (e.g., Fuchs & Fuchs, 1998, 2005), Good (e.g., Good & Kaminski, 2002), Gresham (2002), Shinn (1998), Tindal (e.g., Alonzo, Ketterlin-Geller, & Tindal, 2007), Vaughn (e.g., Vaughn, Linan-Thompson, & Hickman, 2003), and others. These researchers argued for the use of repeated testing over a period of weeks to test the hypothesis that students with learning difficulties may not be responding to classroom or scientifically based instructional interventions.

Although the WRAT4-PMV does not address all the complexities of RTI, it does provide one simple approach to the frequent testing required in some RTI educational implementations. Also, the WRAT4-PMV was designed to fill the need for nationally normed and psychometrically equivalent sets of test forms that will allow precise comparison of student achievement across repeated occasions. When the WRAT4-PMV was published (Roid & Ledbetter, 2006), it filled a gap in availability of progress-monitoring achievement measures for the secondary grades (middle-school and high school) as well as college level. Thus, the WRAT4-PMV may have a role in identifying failure to respond to instruction and indicate the need for further comprehensive evaluation of students with learning difficulties (Hale et al., 2006; Naglieri, 2007; Naglieri &

Crockett, 2005; National Association of School Psychologists, 2007).

Description of the Tests

The WRAT4 measures the four basic academic skills of word reading, sentence comprehension, spelling, and mathematics computation for individuals 5–94 years of age. The four academic areas can be assessed individually in 8–10 minutes (a ceiling of 15 minutes for Mathematics Computation), or in 30–45 minutes as a total battery. Each area has two test forms, Blue and Green, for use in individual administration or as parallel forms for pre- and post-testing. The spelling and mathematics computation subtests can be administered to small groups (2–5 participants) because examinees write their answers on response sheets. The tests were nationally standardized on a representative sample of more than 3,000 individuals, providing age- and grade-based norms. WRAT4 produces standard scores, percentiles, stanines, normal curve equivalents, grade equivalents, and item-response theory (IRT; Rasch, 1980) scaled scores. The interpretation of the tests is straightforward and the tests can be administered by a wide array of professionals in education, psychology, health care, and other human-service and research professions.

The WRAT4-PMV is a system of brief test forms that includes four parallel forms for each of six levels (from Kindergarten to Adult) for each of the four academic areas measured by the WRAT4. Each of these brief tests has 15 items (administered in 5 minutes or less) and total 24 test forms across the six levels. The levels and test forms for both versions of the WRAT4 are listed in Table 20.1.

The six levels cover grade groupings equivalent to elementary, middle, and high school as well as college or adult level. All test forms have been composed from the total item bank represented by all the items in the Blue and Green forms of the WRAT4—carefully selected to match grade levels and item difficulty across each set of four forms at each of the

TABLE 20.1   Levels and Number of Test Forms for WRAT4 and WRAT4-PMV

Version	Age and Grade	Levels	Number of Test Forms			
			WR	SC	SP	MC
WRAT4	5-94	K-12	2	2	2	2
WRAT4-PMV	5-6[a]	K-1	4	4	4	4
	7-8[a]	2-3	4	4	4	4
	9-10[a]	4-5	4	4	4	4
	11-13[a]	6-8	4	4	4	4
	14-18[a]	9-12	4	4	4	4
	19-24[a]	13-16	4	4	4	4
Total for PMV	5-24	K-16	24	24	24	24

NOTE : [a]= Age range may vary within grade levels, WR = Word Reading, SC = Sentence Comprehension, SP = Spelling, and MC = Math Computation

six levels. The statistical equivalence of the set of four forms at each level allows educators and all assessment professionals to implement progress monitoring as required in the new IDEA 2004. The WRAT4-PMV tests are similar to curriculum-based measurement (Deno, 1985; Shinn, 1998) and the approach used by Good and Kaminski (2002) in the *Dynamic Indicators of Basic Early Literacy Skills* (DIBELS), a widely used system of progress-monitoring reading tests. However, unlike other curriculum-based measures, the WRAT4-PMV test forms are strictly parallel tests. Each set of four test forms was designed to be statistically equivalent based on extensive item analysis and IRT scaling. Statistical equivalence allows assessment professionals to accurately compare performance levels from one test to the next, even using raw scores within each set of four tests at each level.

ADMINISTRATION AND SCORING

Administration Guidelines and Tips

The longer WRAT4 versions and the WRAT4-PMV brief tests have many similarities in administration given that they were constructed from the same item pool. However, the length of the tests determines some particular guidelines and rules that differ between the two versions. Administration aspects of each version will be described within the topics included below.

Standard Order of Administration

Both the WRAT4 and the WRAT4-PMV contain four subtests that may be given separately or in any combination of two or more. The recommended order of testing is as follows: Word Reading, Sentence Comprehension, Spelling, and Math Computation. This is the order in which the subtests were administered in the standardization program. The most important order is that the Word Reading subtest should be administered before the Sentence Comprehension subtest because scores obtained from Part 2 of the Word Reading subtest can be used as a routing test. The routing test can help to determine the appropriate starting item on Sentence Comprehension and thereby shorten the testing time required. If the Word Reading subtest is not administered before Sentence Comprehension, then the examinee must begin with Item 1 of the Sentence Comprehension subtest. Also, if a raw score of 4 or less is obtained on the Word Reading section, then Sentence Comprehension should *not* be administered because of the apparent lack of skill in reading the words within the sentences.

Physical Arrangements for Testing

Choose a location for testing that is quiet, free from distractions or interruptions, well ventilated, adequately lighted, and large enough to hold a table and two chairs. The best arrangements are for the examiner to be across a table with the table top narrow enough for the examiner to reach the materials in front of the examinee. In some cases, examiners prefer a 90-degree angle from the examinee so that the examiner can see the examinee's responses more clearly. For small-group administration, allowed for math calculation and spelling, provide room for each examinee. For small groups, especially with younger children, the examiner should check each examinee for attention and progress using direct eye contact. The test forms and any test material that provides clues to correct answers should be kept out of view.

Test Materials

Both versions of the WRAT4 have forms for the examiner as well as examinee response forms and stimulus-display cards as shown in Table 20.2.

Rapport

It is important for the examiner to establish rapport with the examinee before beginning the tests. Attempting to create a positive, relaxed atmosphere is important if the examinee's best effort is to occur. Avoid rushing into the test. Give the examinee a brief explanation of the purpose of testing, couched in language the examinee can understand. Administer the test in a pleasant, conversational manner. Under no circumstances should an actual test item be explained to the examinee. If the examinee asks whether a response is correct, the examiner

should give a neutral response, such as, "That's fine." If it is obvious that the examinee cannot answer a difficult item, the examiner should give a response such as, "That was a hard one. Let's try another."

Start, Basal, and Discontinue Rules

Both the WRAT4 and the WRAT4-PMV have rules for starting, establishing basal performance, and stopping or "discontinuing" testing. These rules are printed clearly on each of the Test Forms and Record Sheet/Booklets.

The longer tests in the regular WRAT4 have the "5/7/10 Rules" to establish basal performance levels and stopping (discontinue) rules. This notation on the test forms pertains to all four subtests in slightly different ways. The "5 Rule" for Word Reading, Spelling, and Math Computation refers to the minimum number of items—5—that must be answered correctly in order to waive administration of the 15 preliminary items in each subtest. For example, an examinee who answered only three items correctly on the Word Reading section would need to have the 15 preliminary Letter Reading items administered.

For Sentence Comprehension, the 5 Rule actually consists of two parts: (1) a minimum of five words must be read correctly on Part 2 (Word Reading) of the Word Reading subtest in order to meet the minimum criterion for administration of Sentence Comprehension, and (2) an examinee who begins Sentence Comprehension at a starting item other than item 1 must answer *five consecutive items correctly* in order to establish a starting point, or basal level. If the first five items are not answered correctly, the examiner must test backwards, or in reverse order, from the starting item until the examinee answers five consecutive items correctly. This is designated the "basal" level. If the examinee is unable to do this, discontinue the administration of the Sentence Comprehension subtest.

The "7 Rule" is the discontinue rule for the Sentence Comprehension test. Testing should be discontinued when an examinee answers *seven*

TABLE 20.2   Forms and Materials for the Subtests of the WRAT4 and WRAT4-PMV

Version	Materials	Forms	Subtests:	WR	SC	SP	MC
WRAT4	Professional Manual						
	Test Form	Blue, Green		+	−	+	+
	SC Test Form	Blue, Green		−	+	−	−
	Response Form	Blue, Green		−	−	+	+
	Cards	Blue, Green		Read/ Spell[a]	Sample & Test[b]	Spell/ Read[a]	−
WRAT4-PMV	Professional Manual						
	Record Sheet	6 Levels		+	−	−	−
	Record Booklet	6 Levels		−	+	+	+
	Cards	6 Levels		+	Sample	+	Written & Oral[c]
	Response Booklet	6 Levels		−	+	+	+
	Place Marker	1 only		−	+	−	−
Other materials							
	Pen/pencil for examiner or examinee (Spelling and Math Computation)						
	Clock, stop-watch, or wrist watch for timing						

NOTE : In the Table, + means the material is provided and − means that the material is not needed for this subtest.
[a]Two-sided card: Letters/words for WR and the other side letters/words for SP.
[b]Two different cards: One for sample sentences, the other for test sentences.
[c]Two different cards per form: One for Oral Math (Levels 1-3), one for written problem solving. WR = Word Reading, SC = Sentence Comprehension, SP = Spelling, and MC = Math Computation.

consecutive items incorrectly. This point is also referred to as a *ceiling* level.

The "10 Rule" is the discontinue rule for the Word Reading and Spelling subtests. It is unnecessary to administer items beyond an examinee's ceiling level because it is highly unlikely that the examinee can give a correct response to items of that difficulty. So after 10 consecutive errors on the Word Reading or Spelling subtest, the examiner should discontinue administration. The 5/7/10 Rules are printed on the test forms and cards to remind the examiner of these rules, which were in effect for the standardization testing and should be followed in test administration.

For the WRAT4-PMV brief tests, the Record Sheet or Record Booklets have tables for deciding whether raw scores obtained on a given 15-item form are sufficient (e.g., not too low, such as 0 or 1, and not too high, such as 14 or 15) to prevent moving down one level or up one level. Otherwise, the start points are always at the examinee's grade level (13–16 for ages 19–24 not in college). The discontinue rule for each subtest on the WRAT4-PMV is usually four consecutive incorrect responses, except for Word Reading, which goes quickly enough and makes a stopping point unnecessary. Time limits on responses are 10 seconds per item for Word Reading and 15 seconds for Spelling words. Zero item scores are given for attempts that exceed the item time limits. Math Computation has a total time limit of 5 minutes (Level 1), 8 minutes (Levels 2–3), or 10 minutes (Levels 4–6).

Subtest Suggestions for Examiners

Brief tips on test administration are described below for each of the four subtests in each version—WRAT4 and WRAT4-PMV. Additional details of administration, examiner statements (in quotes), and other directions are provided both on the Test Forms (and Record Sheets/Booklets) and in the Professional Manuals.

WORD READING   Basically, the examinee is shown the Reading List Card and asked, "Read to me the letters/words one-by-one across the line aloud so I can hear you … " for each test form. Ask the examinee to read slowly and clearly, but if you do not understand the word, ask the examinee to repeat it. For the WRAT4-PMV, be sure to fold the Sample Card so that only the specific test form page (Forms 1–4) is shown.

SENTENCE COMPLETION   The sentences to be read have one or two missing words at (or near) the end of the sentence and the examinee is to speak the correct fill-in word(s). You explain the task by showing the specific sample sentences (using the Sample card) and saying, "Look at this sample. Read the sentences to yourself [pause]. What word goes in the blank at the end of the sentence?" You can remind the examinee one time to provide just one (or two, depending on item) words if he or she provides three or more words.

SPELLING   Lists of letters (Levels 1–3 for WRAT4-PMV) or words are presented by the examiner, saying the letter or word, and, for words, using the word in the sentences provided. Thus, the task is to "spell words in context" so that the examinee can recognize variations in the use of words. Pronunciation guides are provided for the examiner. For the spelling words, the examiner's basic instructions are, "Listen carefully, so that you hear each word I say. Then try to spell the word correctly. I will say the word, then read a sentence with the word in it, and then say the words again. Please

write … " If you choose to use a small-group administration format, be sure that all examinees keep up with the rate of dictation. If the examinee cannot spell the word, have him or her draw a line in the space provided on the Response Form/Booklet.

MATH COMPUTATION   The test forms include both Oral Math (computation problems spoken by the examiner, with printed pictures provided on the Response Form or Card) and sets of printed computation problems. For the brief WRAT4-PMV forms, Levels 1–3 must be administered individually. Hand calculators or computers cannot be used. Time limits are given for each form (and by level for WRAT4-PMV). The printed math problems can be administered to small groups using the Response Form/Booklets, with the spoken instructions, "Look at the problems printed on this page [point]. I want to see how many of these problems you can work. Look carefully to see what you're supposed to do—add, subtract, multiply, or divide—then put your answer on or below the lines given [point]." After the time limits are reached, ask the examinee to stop.

OTHER TIPS   The younger the examinees (especially ages 5–6), the more likely they will want to "chit-chat" and need breaks between subtests. Consider the unique characteristics of each child (e.g., whether boisterous, quiet, calm, or active) and adjust your speaking volume, enthusiasm, and motivational techniques. Give play breaks, tokens for a reward at the end of the evaluation, stickers, toys, or other items as motivators or rewards if appropriate to the child and parent/guardian. Be sure to establish eye contact and ask "Ready?" before starting each subtest.

When using tests in clinical practice, the individual's performance often warrants returning to easier items to establish a basal level. Returning to items with lower number levels or items that are easier, or turning back in a response booklet, can often elicit from the patient/student questions about their performance, anxiety, and/or a negative cognitive set regarding the evaluation process or examiner. One way to avoid these hurdles to effective assessment is to begin one level lower than the basal level indicated in the examiner's manual and test record form. This strategy often results in establishing the proper basal level without having to turn back in a booklet or return back to items that are clearly easier to the examinee, and helps the individual avoid developing a negative cognitive set regarding the evaluation process.

Specific Scoring Instructions

Word Reading

Careful attention should be given to the pronunciation guide (provided in this manual and on the Test Form/Record Booklet) during test administration in order to score an examinee's responses correctly. One point is given for each letter and/or word read correctly. Circle the letter items or the first letter of the word items if the response is correct. Cross out the letter or first letter of the word if the response is incorrect. If the examinee changes his or her response, score the last attempt.

To score the Word Reading subtest, first record the number of items answered correctly for the Letter Reading section in the space provided for the Letter Reading Raw Score. Then, add the number of items answered correctly for the Word Reading section.

For the WRAT4, note that the number of words read correctly on the Word Reading section is used to determine the starting item for the Sentence Comprehension subtest. If the Sentence Comprehension test is to be administered next, circle the corresponding score range in the box provided on the Sentence Comprehension Test Form.

Sentence Comprehension

Examiners may use any preferred system to score an examinee's responses. A recommended procedure is to record the examinee's response in the blank space within each sentence under the column labeled Item/Response. Then, if a correct response is given, record a "1" under the Score column, and if an incorrect response is given, record a "0" under the Score column. The main criterion for evaluating the correctness of a response is whether the response shows that the examinee understands the meaning of the sentence. Ungrammatical responses, unconventional word choice, and irregularities in usage are scored correct *if their intended meaning is clear*. Failure to use correct grammar and accepted usage, or exactly the right word, does not automatically result in the response being scored incorrect. If the intended meaning of the response is clear and appropriate for completing the meaning of the sentence, then the mistakes of the types cited would *not* result in scoring such responses as incorrect. Special care was taken to prepare a comprehensive list of correct responses obtained during standardization so that these could be listed to guide users in scoring the final subtest. Incorrect responses questioned by examiners were also evaluated to determine their correctness and recorded for use in the final edition to assist users in scoring such responses. These correct and incorrect responses are the basis for the responses listed on the Test Form and in the Appendix of the manual. If the examiner is unsure of scoring, provisional correct designation is recommended, followed by review after the testing session is completed.

To score the Sentence Comprehension subtest, simply sum the Score column located on the Sentence Comprehension Test Form, and record the total.

Spelling

To score the Spelling subtest, first circle the item number of each correctly written letter in the Letter Writing section and circle the item number for each correctly spelled word in the Spelling section. Cross out the item number if the response is incorrect. Then, count the number of circled items and record the total points. Read carefully the specific directions for crediting the writing of the examinee's name, and the specific scoring directions on WRAT4 for giving full credit for Letter Writing. To obtain the raw score for the Spelling section, count the number of circled items and record the total in the space provided for the Spelling Raw Score.

Math Computation

The scoring keys for both the Blue and Green Oral Math and Math Computation are provided in the Appendix of the WRAT4 test manual, and provide quick and accurate scoring. Correct answers for WRAT4-PMV are found in the Response Booklet or Computation Card. Examiners should circle the item number of each correct answer given by the examinee and cross out the item number for each incorrect response. Give one point for each correct answer on Oral Math and Math Computation. Sum the Oral Math points and add any Math Computation points. On the WRAT4 (only), check to see whether an examinee aged 8 and older has answered at least five of the Math Computation items correctly. If so, then the full credit of 15 points for the Oral Math section should be given and recorded for the Oral Math Raw Score.

Use of the Scoring Software

As an added convenience, both the WRAT4 and the WRAT4-PMV have computer scoring software. Both software programs allow an unlimited number of scorings and generate a report with graphic profile displays, file handling, and report editing. Users enter raw subtest scores that are converted to a wide array of derived scores (age based and grade based for WRAT4), including optional item-response theory (Rasch, 1980; Wright & Linacre, 1999) scores. Reports, based on standard-score profile interpretations, can be exported to common word processing programs.

Derived Scores Offered

Several types of scores are available to aid interpretation of the WRAT4 and WRAT4-PMV. For the WRAT4, raw scores can be converted to norm-referenced scores based on both age and grade. Derived scores include standard scores with confidence intervals, percentiles, stanines, normal curve equivalents, grade equivalents, and Rasch ability scaled scores. For the WRAT4-PMV, raw scores for each test form are plotted on graphs showing the normative range for the grade levels covered by that form. Because the test forms within each level of the WRAT4-PMV are statistically equivalent, raw scores are directly comparable across the four forms in that level. For cross-level comparisons, raw scores can be converted to Rasch-based Level Equivalence (LE) scores. Each of these types of scores is briefly described below.

Standard Scores

For the WRAT4 subtests, normalized standard scores have a mean of 100 and a standard deviation of 15 for each of the norm groups—age or grade—on which they are based. About two-thirds of the individuals in an age or grade norm group earn standard scores between 85 and 115 and about 95 percent earn standard scores between 70 and 130. A standard score of 85 is one standard deviation below the mean, a standard score of 115 is one standard deviation above the mean, a standard score of 70 is two standard deviations below the mean, and so forth. This metric of standard score allows direct comparison to a wide variety of ability, cognitive, and neuropsychological scales, and has desirable equal-interval properties for statistical research.

Percentiles

Although not desirable for statistical analysis, percentiles can be easily explained to most examinees, parents, and others. Percentiles show the percent of individuals scoring below a particular standard score in the norm group.

Percentile ranks range from a low of 1 to a high of 99, with 50 representing the median or "typical" performance.

Confidence Intervals

To take account of measurement error, confidence intervals (bands or ranges) can be constructed, based on standard error of measurement, to show the range of scores within which an individual's true score can be expected to occur a specified percentage of the time. Confidence intervals for each of the WRAT4 subtests and composite standard scores have been calculated and are presented for each of the forms (Blue, Green, Combined) in appendices of the Professional Manual (and programmed into the scoring software) for the age-based and grade-based norms, respectively. Three levels of confidence intervals are provided: 85%, 90%, and 95%. These confidence-level intervals are commonly reported in psychological and educational test manuals and allow the user a degree of flexibility in choosing the desired level of measurement precision.

For the WRAT4-PMV, error of measurement is addressed in three ways: (1) with conventional standard errors of measurement for each test form for user-constructed confidence intervals, (2) built into the graphs of the examiner's Record Sheet/Booklet for each subtest via a shaded area showing a range around the grade-level mean score, and (3) in all comparisons between raw scores within levels of the test or between levels with Level Equivalence (LE) scores. Tables of statistical significance for raw-score differences are provided on each examiner's Record Sheet/Booklet, and difference score tables are provided in the Professional Manual. The scoring software automatically evaluates the significance of differences among raw scores and LE scores.

Normal Curve Equivalents

Normal Curve Equivalents (NCEs) are provided because they are required in many states to report test results for special government-sponsored programs such as Title I. NCEs are a type of standard score with a mean of 50 and a standard deviation of 21.06, and range from a low of 1 to a high of 99. NCEs were developed to provide equal-interval scores for statistical analysis and they cover the same range as percentile ranks, with percentile ranks of 1, 50, and 99 corresponding to similar NCEs. Other values of the two scales, however, are not comparable.

Stanines

These single-digit standard scores range from a low of 1 to a high of 9, with a mean of 5 and a standard deviation of about 2. Stanines are often used for reporting test scores when broader score ranges are appropriate, such as reporting test results to students and parents.

Grade Equivalents

Grade Equivalents (GEs) are presented in the WRAT4 manual to show the month of the grade for which a particular test score was the average score obtained by students in the standardization program. Grade equivalents are reported in decimals to conform to the 10-month school year and usually range from K.0 or 1.0 to 12.9. While grade equivalents appear to be easily understood and seem to convey an obvious meaning, they are easily (and frequently) misinterpreted. Perhaps the most frequent misinterpretation of grade equivalents is that they indicate the student's actual functional grade level. For example, suppose a third-grade student received a grade equivalent of 5.2 on the Math Computation subtest. This result does not mean that the student's mathematics performance is similar to that of students in the second month of fifth grade and that the student could successfully perform fifth-grade mathematics. It simply means that the student performed very well on the content in the mathematics test administered to third-grade students.

Grade equivalents for the WRAT4-PMV are available separately from the test manual by contacting the publisher, but play a lesser role in the interpretation of these repeated brief tests. Direct comparison of raw scores to grade-level performance is shown on the graphs printed on the examiner's Record Sheet/Booklet. These graphs provide a shaded area in which the mean score occurs (with a confidence interval) at each grade level, providing a pictorial view to the user of the distance between the examinee's score and the grade-level average.

Rasch Ability Scale Scores

Users of the WRAT4 interested in assessing growth from one time to another will find the Rasch Ability Scale Scores (RASS) provided in an appendix of the Professional Manual. The use of the one-parameter IRT latent-trait (Rasch) model facilitated the development of these scores, which are sensitive to changes occurring over time. For each of the WRAT4 subtests, the RASS were derived from the W-Ability scores for scaling and norming purposes by setting the mean RASS for the grade 5 fall semester norm group at 500 (Woodcock & Dahl, 1971). By establishing the value of 500 as the average, or typical, performance of grade 5 students in the fall of the school year, the RASS scale values benefit from having a clear reference point and are similar to the W-scores provided in the Woodcock series of tests (McGrew & Woodcock, 2001; Woodcock, 1999), the Change Sensitive Scores (CSS) of the *Stanford-Binet* (Roid, 2003; Roid & Barram, 2004), and other tests. Caution must be used in interpreting the RASS because values other than 500 are not comparable across the four WRAT subtests due to the differential growth rates of the skills assessed in the WRAT4 content areas. On the WRAT4-PMV, these Rasch-based scores are called Level Equivalence (LE) scores as mentioned previously.

STANDARDIZATION, NORMS, DEVELOPMENT, AND PSYCHOMETRICS

Standardization and Norms

The WRAT4 was standardized on a sample of 3,021 individuals from 5 to 94 years of age, selected to match the percentages of the March 2001 U.S. Census (U.S. Bureau of Census, 2001). The stratified quota sampling plan was designed to represent the demographic variables of gender, race/ethnicity, educational attainment, and geographic region. For purposes of grade-based norms, a subset of 1,800 students enrolled in U.S. schools, grades K–12, was selected from the total sample. Qualified examiners were recruited and trained throughout the nation to administer two parallel test forms, labeled the Green and Blue forms. Full details of the sample, the selection of participants, recruitment and training of examiners, test-form equating, and quality control of standardization data are contained in the comprehensive test manual by Wilkinson and Robertson (2006). Some of the essential information about these details is described in the following sections.

Description of the Sample

Females and males were selected in proportion to the U.S. Census data in each of 19 age groups: 8 whole-year age groups of children from 5 to 12, 4 groups of teens and young adults, including 13–14, 15–16, 17–18, and 19–24, and 7 ten-year groups of adults from 25–34 to 85–94. Approximately 120–200 individuals per age group were tested through age 64 and approximately 100–125 participants per frame for ages 55–84. There were 48 elderly adults tested in the 85–94 age group.

Demographic Variables Used for Standardization

Four classifications were used for race/ethnicity: (1) African American, (2) Caucasian—

Non-Hispanic, (3) Hispanic (including Latino, Spanish equivalents), and (4) Other (including Asian, American Indian, Hawaiian/Pacific Islander, among others). To control for socioeconomic status (SES), parent educational attainment was obtained for participants aged 5–18 years; for participants aged 19 years and above, the number of years of school completed by the participant was obtained and classified by the four Census categories: (1) College Graduate and Above, (2) Some College (no degree), (3) High School Graduate (no further education beyond high school), and (4) Less than High School (no high school diploma). A parent educational attainment index was developed from the information reported for either or both parents. For geographic region, the U.S. was divided into the typical four U.S. Census geographic regions—Northeast, South, North Central, and West—with proportionate sampling in each region. A slight degree of case weighting was used to adjust the percentages for gender, race/ethnicity, and educational attainment to match the targeted Census percentages. However, geographic region did not require case weighting. The weighting brought the percentages of the entire standardization sample into adequate match with Census percentages (e.g., the median difference was 1.4%, such as that between weighted percentage of 14.0% for individuals with African-American ethnicity and Census percentage target of 12.6%). Differences ranged from 0.1% to 3.6% across all the levels of the three adjusted demographic variables (education, ethnicity/race, and gender). This magnitude of difference in percentages is similar to many widely used nationally standardized tests. The percentages for geographic region were slightly larger, within 2.2–5.4% of Census targets. For more extensive tables, see Wilkinson and Robertson (2006).

Inclusion of Special Education Cases

Efforts were made to include individuals with various types of educational disabilities in proportion to their occurrence in the U.S. school population. Both special-education placement as well as the incidence of attention-deficit/hyperactivity disorder (ADHD) were monitored and coded on their response forms for students enrolled in grades K–12, ages 5–18. A total of 93 special-needs students (5.2% of the grade-norming sample of 1,800) were included, representing specific learning disabilities (SLD, 2.7%), speech or language impairments (0.7%), mental retardation (0.3%), emotional disturbance (0.7%), physical impairments (0.2%), and ADHD (0.6%). These percentages are smaller than the estimated percentages compiled by the National Center for Education Statistics (2002), which shows a total of 15.6% for these categories, including 6.0% for SLD and 4.0% for ADHD.

Derivation of Normative Standard Scores

An innovative method of calculating norms has been applied to an expanding number of tests in recent years (Roid, 2006). The method called *continuous norming* (Gorsuch, 1983, 2005; Roid, 1983, 1986, 1989, 1992, 2006; Roid, Gorsuch, Pomplun, & Reynolds, 2003; Zachary & Gorsuch, 1985) was used to develop normalized standard scores for both the WRAT4 and the WRAT4-PMV. Continuous norming calculates the trends in score statistics (mean, standard deviation, skew, and kurtosis) across age or grade groups in the entire normative sample (e.g., 3,021) rather than calculating norms based on score distributions for each of the smaller age groups (approximate $N = 150$). The following steps were employed in the development of age-based standard scores with a mean of 100 and a standard deviation of 15 for each of the four WRAT4 subtests.

Total scores for each subtest (the item-response theory, Rasch-model estimates of achievement level that transformed each number-correct raw score) were used to form frequency distributions for each of the 19 age groups, ages 5–94. The same case-weighting procedure described earlier in the section on "Demographic Variables used for Standardization" was employed for these statistical analyses of these scores (e.g., weights for gender, race/ethnicity, and educational attainment). Means, standard deviations (*SD*s), skewness, and kurtosis estimates were obtained for each of the four WRAT4 subtests separately for each of the 19 age groups and plotted on graphs across age groups.

Second- and third-degree polynomial functions, as required, were fitted to the plotted data points of means, *SD*s, skewness, and kurtosis across age groups. These polynomial functions were subsequently used to derive the smoothed mean, standard deviation, skewness, and kurtosis for the midpoint of each age interval for each of the 19 age groups.

Once the smoothed polynomial functions were computed, the method of continuous norming was used to develop normalized standard scores with a mean of 100 and a standard deviation of 15. Continuous norming used the trends in mean, *SD*, skew, and kurtosis across the entire normative sample. The WRAT4 calculations were based on the sample of 3,021 and WRAT4-PMV on the age range of 5–24 ($N = 1,929$) rather than score distributions for the smaller age groups (approximate $N = 150$) only. For each age group, initial frequency percentiles were derived, using an algorithm developed by Hill (1976) and his associates (Hill, Hill, & Holder, 1976) and adapted to norming by Roid (1989). The algorithm is based on a family of frequency curves described by Johnson (1949). The four moments of each distribution derived from the polynomial functions for each age were used to select one of three possible Johnson curves as the appropriate estimate of the WRAT4 score distributions. Standard normal deviates (z) corresponding to the estimated percentiles of each total score were then derived from the Johnson curve transformation selected and transformed to standard scores by applying the linear transformation $15 (z) + 100$.

Summary tables showing the resulting subtest standard scores were then developed for each of the subtests by using the subtest standard scores for each age group. Standard score entries were smoothed vertically and horizontally, as required, to remove slight inconsistencies in the progression of the standard scores. Next, the smoothed Rasch-based scores were converted back to their corresponding raw scores in order to develop the final raw score–to–standard score conversion tables.

Grade-Based Standard Scores

The grade-based standard scores were quite similar to the method described previously for age-based standard scores. For purposes of norms development, the school year was divided into tenths, starting with September (.0) and ending with June (.9). Thus, in grade 2, for example, September testing in grade 2 would be 2.0 while June testing would be 2.9; in grade 3, testing in September would be 3.0. Standard scores were derived for two seasons of the school year: fall (August–January) and spring (February–July). In order to accommodate year-round testing, July was included with the spring norms, and August with the fall norms. Grade-based standard scores were developed for the midpoint of each testing period: fall (.2) and spring (.7).

Equating Forms

A major goal of the standardization program was the concurrent norming of the two WRAT4 parallel forms, designated the Blue Form and the Green Form. To meet this goal, individuals in the standardization were randomly assigned to 8 subsamples of approximately 275 subjects who were administered the complete (four-subtest) Blue Form or Green Form, plus one additional subtest from the alternate form (e.g., Blue Form plus Word Reading of the Green Form). This common-person equating design (Wright & Stone, 1979) was selected along with counterbalanced random order of administration (Blue or Green administered first in one-half of the sample). This design had the advantages of (1) ease of assembling test forms in proper order prior to shipment to examiners, and (2) more realistic administration time compared to the use of two complete test forms. A total of 2,341 individuals were tested in the common-person sample, with 1,164 receiving the Blue Form (or its single subtest) first, and 1,177 receiving the Green form (or its single subtest) first. The standardization and equating program research design was carried out for all participants aged 8 years and older because there is only one form of the test available for the Letter Reading, Letter Writing, and Oral Math sections, the tests typically administered to participants aged 5, 6, and 7.

Development of the Test Versions

The longer test forms of the WRAT4 were developed first through field-testing, revision, and standardization cycles, and the brief test forms of WRAT4-PMV derived from the final standardization version of WRAT4. In the WRAT4, 77% of the items overall were drawn from the WRAT3 (Wilkinson, 1993) and 23% were new. As for the subtests, Spelling was the least changed (11.9% were new), followed by Word Reading (26.4% new item content), and Math Computation (30% new item content). Each of the WRAT3 items were extensively studied and carefully selected on the basis of the performance of the WRAT3 standardization sample, and their inclusion in the WRAT4 ensures continuity with the achievement content domains measured by the WRAT3.

In the development of the WRAT4 item pool, items were eliminated from the WRAT3, only after extensive content review by outside experts who evaluated the WRAT3 items in terms of their current relevance and freedom from apparent gender or ethnic bias. For the Word Reading Subtest, only three items were eliminated on the basis of reviewers' comments. The purpose of adding 29 items to the subtest was to extend the length of each of the test forms from 42 items to 55 items. New items were selected from standard word-list reference sources such as the Educational Development Laboratories

(EDL) vocabulary collection (Taylor, Frackenpohl, White, Nieroroda, Browning, & Birsner, 1989).

For the Spelling Subtest, six items were eliminated, three from each form. Ten items were needed to replace the six eliminated items and to extend the length of the subtest by two items in each form. The replacement items were selected from standard reference sources such as Hillerich (1978) and current web-based sources.

The Math Computation Subtest required the addition of 24 new items. Edward Manfre, a nationally recognized mathematics textbook author and curriculum expert, identified items for elimination and prepared the new items to replace them. The content blueprint for WRAT4 Math Computation included approximately 50% items for whole-number arithmetic (addition, subtraction, multiplication, division, and counting/rounding), 20% arithmetic operations with fractions, 10% decimals, and 20% percentages and algebra/statistics (Wilkinson & Robertson, 2006). Items were added to the subtest so that the domains measured conform to the current mathematics content emphasis and appropriate assessment item format.

The procedures used to develop the Sentence Comprehension Subtest followed all the recommended steps in content-valid test development. Items were prepared in accordance with detailed content specifications, and the items were submitted to an extensive, data-based item analysis and expert review. Content specifications included guidelines such as avoiding overly specific topics that would give advantage to specific student groups, wide coverage of natural and social sciences, humanities, hobbies, sports, entertainment, weather, food, and travel. Parts of speech for the target words (those deleted from the sentences) were systematically varied. Sentences were purposely assigned a word-count cap/ceiling of fewer than 50 words. Correct responses had to be as few in number as possible. Answers were not to be totally dependent on vocabulary acquisition, but also on syntax and sentence-context factors. In addition to classical and IRT-based item statistics, item validities were obtained by administering the *WRAT—Expanded* (Robertson, 2001) Reading Comprehension subtest to all participants. These data added important information to the final item-selection and subtest-assembly processes. A panel of experts reviewed the Sentence Comprehension items to identify items judged inappropriate for reasons of gender, racial, or ethnic bias, negative stereotypes, incorrect response options, and understandability to children.

In summary, the WRAT4 content-development process drew heavily on the WRAT3 items, which were studied in detail earlier in the development of the WRAT3. These items were subjected to extensive review by outside experts, who assessed their suitability for use in the WRAT4. Although these items typically show universal applicability and relatively little aging, or change in their suitability for use over time, nevertheless about one-fourth of the WRAT3 items were replaced in the WRAT4. The procedures of expert review (for content and bias-elimination) and data-based item analysis were designed to ensure that the WRAT4 test content is universally appropriate, up-to-date, and free from various forms of gender and racial/ethnic bias.

For the brief forms of the WRAT4-PMV, extensive item selection methods were employed using multiple cycles of tentative item selection followed by analysis of seven statistical attributes:

1. Conventional percentage correct (*p*-value) for each item, using the appropriate grade ranges (all students in one of the six levels previously specified)

2. Range of *p*-values, mean, and standard deviation (*SD*) of *p*-values for each test form

3. Rasch item difficulty estimates, placed on the Woodcock-Dahl (1971) "W-scale" (used in nearly all the Woodcock series of tests; McGrew & Woodcock, 2001), with a center of 500 at the beginning of grade 5 (age 10 years, 0 months), analyzed for each of the four content areas separately (i.e., word reading,

sentence comprehension, math computation, spelling)

4. Range of Rasch item difficulty estimates and their means for each test form

5. Mean, median, *SD*, and range of the raw scores (number of correct items) for each test form

6. Internal consistency reliability—Alpha (Cronbach, 1951)—for each test form

7. Intercorrelations among the items within each form (required for the study of form equivalence)

The above statistics and indexes were examined across the six major levels to ensure an even progression of increase in Rasch mean and range across levels (e.g., 10–20 points), and a steady pattern of mean *p*-values and mean raw scores providing sufficient variability at each level. All statistics and indexes were stored on computer files in such a way that dynamic changes and adjustments could be made, followed by recalculation of the statistics and indexes. The final goal was to provide parallel and equivalent test forms at each level on which the examiner could identify authentic changes in raw scores across testing occasions.

Reliability of the Scales

The design and uses of the WRAT4 and the WRAT4-PMV are different in several ways that require somewhat different perspectives on the evaluation of test reliability. The longer WRAT4 subtests are intended for less frequent and more summative assessment as compared to the more frequent and more formative nature (suggesting changes in instruction) of the WRAT4-PMV test forms. The WRAT4 has two test forms (Blue and Green) for each curriculum area, whereas WRAT4-PMV has four test forms per level (24 forms across all 6 levels) for each subtest area. The WRAT4 is designed to be included in a comprehensive battery of tests or for initial evaluations, comparison to cognitive and behavioral measures, formation of diagnostic hypotheses, and identification of strengths and weaknesses in a comprehensive array of measures for an individual. The WRAT4-PMV test forms were designed for brief and frequent assessments to evaluate the effects of instruction or intervention on the examinee's progress across time. For these reasons, the WRAT4 test forms were designed to be longer and more comprehensive in coverage than the brief WRAT4-PMV test forms. Thus, we would expect and require a somewhat higher level of reliability for the WRAT4 test forms as compared to the PMV forms. The three primary types of reliability estimates for these tests would be test–retest, alternative forms, and internal consistency. Also, the test forms for both tests can be combined in various ways—the two forms of WRAT4 combined, and the test forms of WRAT4-PMV evaluated as a combination (e.g., four test forms given across time and the pattern of all four evaluated).

Test–Retest Reliability

For the WRAT4, test–retest studies of the identical test forms were not conducted because of the common practice of giving the alternative form (Blue vs. Green) upon retest. However, alternative forms of WRAT4 were given to individuals using an immediate retest on a sample of 329 subjects, ages 7–74, and also a delayed retest (average 30 days) on 115 individuals ages 7–18. In each case, the retest design employed random counterbalancing of the order of administration of the Blue or Green forms. Table 20.3 presents the results of the immediate alternative-form retest for the WRAT4 under the Alternative Form portion of the table, showing estimates ranging from .86 to .90. Greater details of all the reliability studies for WRAT4 are presented in Wilkinson and Robertson (2006).

For the WRAT4-PMV, a true test–retest study was conducted on a sample of 67 students (mean age = 11:3) using counterbalanced administration order and an average 31-day delay between first and second testing. The results of the study are shown in the top section of Table 20.3. More details of all the reliability studies for WRAT4-PMV are presented in Roid and Ledbetter (2006). The test–retest estimates shown in Table 20.3 are medians of each content area test form across the six levels of forms. Results show an excellent level of test–retest reliability for 15-item test forms—median estimates of .83–.90. In nearly all the reliability studies of WRAT4 and WRAT4-PMV, the Mathematics Computation subtests have the lower estimates and the other subtests alternate in having the highest estimates. These compare favorably to other progress-monitoring tests such as DIBELS (Good & Kaminski, 2002).

Alternative Form Reliability

For WRAT4, as mentioned in the test–retest section, Table 20.3 shows resulting reliabilities ranging from .86 to .90 for the immediate-retest alternative form study. Wilkinson and Robertson (2006) reported reliabilities of .75 to .89 (corrected for differences in sample variance) for the delayed retest (mean = 30 days delay between testings) alternative form study.

For the WRAT4-PMV, alternative forms correlations were computed for each level of the test. Median alternative form estimates of reliability ranged from .76 to .86 for Levels 1–3, covering elementary school levels of the test. Estimates ranged from .74 to .84 for the secondary grade levels of the test.

Internal Consistency Reliability

Finally, Table 20.3 shows the estimates of internal consistency reliability using Cronbach's (1951) Alpha coefficient. WRAT4 Alpha coefficients are medians across all age groups (5–94) as presented in Wilkinson and Robertson (2006). WRAT4-PMV coefficients are medians across the four forms at each level (Roid & Ledbetter, 2006) and are based on students with achievement levels similar to the grade range of each level. For the longer WRAT4 forms, the internal consistency estimates of reliability tend to be slightly higher than the alternative form

TABLE 20.3 Median Reliability Estimates (Test-Retest, Alternative Form, Internal Consistency, and Multiple Forms Composite) of Subtests by Type of Estimate, Form, and Level for WRAT4 and WRAT4-PMV

Estimate Type & Test	Test Form or Level (Grades)	WR	SC	SP	MC
Test-Retest					
WRAT4-PMV	Levels 1 to 6 (K-16)	.90	.89	.93	.83
Alternative Form					
WRAT4[a]	Blue and Green	.90	.86	.89	.87
WRAT4-PMV	Levels 1 to 3 (K-5)	.86	.84	.83	.76
	Levels 4 to 5 (6-16)	.84	.84	.83	.74
Internal Consistency					
WRAT4	Blue Form	.92	.93	.91	.89
	Green Form	.92	.93	.90	.87
	Combined forms[b]	.96	.96	.95	.94
WRAT4-PMV	Levels 1 to 3 (K-5)	.80	.81	.78	.74
	Levels 4 to 6 (6-16)	.80	.83	.79	.74
	Combination of 4 forms[b]	.95	.95	.95	.94

NOTE : [a]Only the WRAT4-PMV had a conventional test-retest study. The WRAT4 used a retest-design employing alternative forms with both immediate and delayed retesting, and the immediate retest results are shown as estimates of Alternative Form reliability.
[b]Estimates of composite reliability assuming 4 forms are given to the same student. WR = Word Reading, SC = Sentence Comprehension, SP = Spelling, and MC = Math Computation.

estimates. For the WRAT4-PMV, the opposite pattern is true, with median internal consistencies of .74–.83 and the highest reliabilities obtained for the test–retest estimates of test form reliability (.83–.93). Such a pattern would be expected for brief tests of only 15 items each, especially for mathematics, where the mixture of arithmetic tasks is characteristic.

Thus, as mentioned in the introduction to this section, the reliability estimates for the longer WRAT4 forms (e.g., 70 items in the Word Reading subtest) are higher, as expected, than the brief (15-item) WRAT4-PMV test forms. Reliability coefficients above the .90 range are considered excellent for assessments intended for individual diagnosis and important decision making (Reynolds, Livingston, & Willson, 2006). Many of the reliability levels of the WRAT4-PMV—14

out of 20 entries in Table 20.3—are above .80 and considered acceptable for individually administered subtests within widely used test batteries (Reynolds et al., 2006). And, all the coefficients in Table 20.3 for the PMV are above .70, considered the expected level for brief classroom-oriented tests and for research-based scales (Nunnally, 1967; Reynolds et al., 2006). The primary use of the WRAT4-PMV is to use a series of brief tests to monitor student achievement across several occasions while instruction is being adjusted to match student needs (Gresham, 2002). Once the results of each repeated test are plotted on a progress graph (on the Record Forms of the WRAT4-PMV), it is the pattern of test scores across time that determines "response to instruction," not each individual observation. Therefore, an overall appraisal of the reliability of the WRAT4-PMV test forms (the "combination of four forms" shown at the bottom of Table 20.3) shows that the combination of four forms provides a very high level of reliability—estimates of .94 to .95. This combined reliability is estimated from the formula for composite reliability (Tellegen & Briggs, 1967).

TEST USES AND INTERPRETIVE STRATEGIES

Uses of WRAT4 and WRAT4-PMV

The two versions of the WRAT vary in their intended purposes and uses. The WRAT4 is designed and most often used as an initial assessment of basic academic skills as part of a larger, comprehensive battery of tests at Tier 3 as recommended by the NASP SLD position paper. The WRAT4 is particularly valuable for individuals who need a rapid screening evaluation. The results of a WRAT assessment may aid in determining whether a more extensive battery of testing is indicated. Clinical cases that may warrant further testing may include the assessment of specific learning disorders, medical conditions impacting academic and cognitive functions, or the need for educational or vocational screening. The WRAT4 is also designed for pre- and post-testing of basic skills in a research project or program evaluation, because of the availability of the Blue and Green alternative forms. WRAT4 subtests are widely used in special-education assessments, for annual performance reviews, in global skill level evaluations, or in reevaluations for specific learning disorders. The WRAT4 may play a role as an alternative basic skills assessment for examinees who have already taken several achievement tests and need a reevaluation or confirmation from another instrument. The WRAT4 has traditionally been used as part of the evaluation of ability–achievement discrepancies. The new IDEA legislation (IDEA, 2004) still allows the discrepancy approach in learning

disability identification, but also encourages use of frequently repeated progress-monitoring and comprehensive batteries of tests. Thus, the WRAT4-PMV has emerged as an alternative in monitoring and evaluating specific learning disorders (e.g., by showing lack of responsiveness to effective reading instruction or identifying the need for more comprehensive assessment).

The Interpretive Process

Ultimately, the purpose of most assessments in education and psychology is to assist the person being tested either to understand herself or himself, improve skills, feelings, or behaviors, or obtain services, accommodations, or access to other needed assistance. For these reasons, the assessment professional is always cautious to study the background characteristics of the person (language, environment, history, health, quality of life, etc.). Interpretations of tests can only be done fairly and accurately if the examiner understands some basics of the background, test sophistication, language competence, and condition of that person at the time of testing. Taking some time to obtain background information (from examinee or others) is certainly a starting point for professional interpretation. One of the prominent concerns of examiners currently is recognizing and adapting to the diversity of the examinee. With an increasingly diverse society and significant immigration rates in most developed countries, examiners need to be aware of different expectations for the testing experience from examinees with ethnic or nonmajority-language background. One of the best beginning primers for these issues is the helpful book by Paniagua (2005), who points to the importance of understanding the acculturation status of the examinee. *Acculturation* is the quality and rate of integration of a new member of a culture into the mores, attitudes, and behaviors of the majority culture. People vary in their acceptance or integration into various domains (academics, community, entertainment, sports, home life, work settings), and thus may not be fully ready to take tests or instructions from an examiner in expected ways. And, the examinee and his or her family may or may not understand or accept different types of greetings, interactions, or feedback from the examiner. Thus, the building of rapport and the presentation and explanation of test interpretations and scores must be done with sensitivity to these differences. The reader is referred to the work of Paniagua (2005) and Dana (2005) for more perspectives on testing in the context of diversity.

Interpretive Strategies

The WRAT4 and the WRAT4-PMV differ fundamentally in the strategies used to interpret results. The best way to discuss these strategies is to use case studies for each test version and explain the rationale and steps in interpretation for each version.

Strategies for WRAT4

Interpretation of the WRAT4 begins by scoring the test and plotting the standard scores on a profile so that the general skill level of the individual can be evaluated. Various differences between scores are explored for statistical significance and the rarity in the general population. Rarity of differences is evaluated by examining the frequency with which differences of a given magnitude occur in the normative sample. Performance on the WRAT4 is also compared to other assessments (e.g., cognitive, achievement, or behavioral). The case study of an 18-year-old adolescent is presented to demonstrate the interpretive process and strategies.

CASE STUDY #1: THE CASE OF "GRACE"

Background

Grace is 18 years, 9 months of age and was referred to assess neuropsychological strengths and weaknesses that seemed to suggest a learning disability. Her personal history included some complications at birth that might be relevant to the evaluation. Grace was carried to term and born weighing 7 lb, 6 oz following six hours of labor. However, the delivery was complicated, with Grace aspirating some fluid. Grace remained in the hospital for five days following her delivery. Grace attained her early infancy and childhood developmental milestones within expected timeframes, and her early childhood proceeded in a nonremarkable manner. When she was three years old, she had tubes placed in her ears for chronic ear infections. When she was 15 years old, Grace had a tonsillectomy. She also wears glasses, which she used for both testing sessions. Approximately one year ago, a car in which she was a passenger drove into a ditch. Grace was a belted passenger in the rear seat. She was taken to the emergency room and later released. She has never been tested, or placed in a special-education classroom, reportedly dislikes going to school, and has been absent from high school frequently. She maintained a 2.2 GPA in high school.

Assessment Results for Case #1

In order to provide a screening of her academic skills, Grace was administered the *Wide Range Achievement Test—Fourth Edition*. Grace's performance on the WRAT4 is summarized in Table 20.4.

1. *Interpretive Step 1*: An initial review of Grace's WRAT4 profile indicates the concerns about learning appear to be justified. Three of the five WRAT4 indices are below the 15th percentile, which serves as the statistical marker for the low end of the average range.

TABLE 20.4   WRAT4, WJ III Cognitive, and WJ III Achievement Scores for Subtests and Composites for "Grace," an 18-year old Female Adolescent

Test/Academic Domain	Standard Score	% Rank	90% Confidence Interval
WRAT4			
Wording Reading	76	5th	70-83
Sentence Comprehension	94	34th	88-101
Spelling	86	18th	79-95
Math Computation	79	8th	72-89
Reading Composite	83	13th	78-89
WJ III Cognitive			
Comprehension Knowledge	88	22nd	82-94
Auditory Processing	89	22nd	80-98
Short-Term Memory	79	8th	72-86
Visual-Spatial Thinking	97	43rd	90-105
Fluid Reasoning	104	60th	96-111
Phonemic Awareness	89	24th	81-97
Working Memory	81	10th	74-97
Broad Attention	89	22nd	83-95
Cognitive Fluency	85	16th	80-90
WJ III Achievement			
Broad Reading	76	6th	72-80
Broad Math	77	6th	72-82
Broad Written Language	82	12th	76-88
Math Calculation	71	3rd	72-82
Written Expression	86	17th	78-93

2. *Interpretive Step 2*: Extended Interpretation: An analysis of Grace's WRAT4 results revealed nonoverlapping confidence intervals for her Word Reading and Sentence Comprehension subtests. Using the standard score worksheet on the bottom of the record form, the 18-point difference was entered in the score-difference column. Next, Wilkinson and Robertson (2006, Table G1, p. 488) was consulted to determine whether the difference was statistically significant, and if so, at what level. Table G1 indicates the 18-point difference between Word Reading and Sentence Comprehension is significant at the .01 level. Next, Table H1 (p. 490) was consulted to identify the base rate occurrence of an 18-point difference in the standardization population. Table H1 indicates an 18-point difference between Word Reading and Sentence Comprehension subtests occurred in 10–15% of the standardization sample. Clinically, the large difference between the Word Reading and Sentence Comprehension subtests suggests Grace benefits from the context

of the passage in order to derive meaning from the sentence, but when words are shown individually, she has difficulties decoding words.

Grace's performance (see Table 20.4) on the *Wide Range Achievement Test—Fourth Edition* indicated she was a good candidate for administration of a comprehensive evaluation, including full intellectual and achievement batteries, to determine strength and weaknesses in cognitive processes and academic skills (Naglieri, 2007; Posny, 2007). The data derived from the WRAT4 indicated Grace could be expected to have difficulties with reading decoding and reading comprehension, as well as mathematics. As a result, Grace was administered the *Woodcock-Johnson Tests of Cognitive Ability—Third Edition* (WJ-III—Cognitive; Mather & Woodcock, 2001), as well as the *Woodcock-Johnson Tests of Academic Achievement—Third Edition* (WJ-III—Achievement; Mather & Woodcock, 2001). Selected scores that align with the WRAT4 and provide additional interpretive information are included in Table 20.4.

Cognitive/Intellectual

The WJ-III—Cognitive battery showed that Grace's profile showed some weaknesses evidenced by standard scores in Comprehension Knowledge (88), Auditory Processing (89), and Short-Term Memory (79) ranging from the 22nd to 8th percentiles (%ile). Strengths in the profile included Fluid Reasoning (104, 60th %ile) and Visual-Spatial Thinking (97, 43rd %ile). The clinical-cluster scores of the WJ-III—Cognitive showed weaknesses in Working Memory (81, 10th %ile) and Cognitive Fluency (85, 16th %ile). The pattern of weaknesses ranged from 11 to 21 standard score points below the normative average (100) and equally below the average of her Fluid and Visual-Spatial scores (97 and 104). This pattern of weaknesses suggests difficulties in Grace's attention and memory processes, often associated with ADHD, deficits in word analysis in reading, and learning disorders (Friend & Olson, 2008; Kamphaus, 2001; Lezak et al., 2004).

Academic Achievement

Grace was administered the WJ-III Achievement tests, the academic companion to the cognitive battery described above. Her performance on the WJ-III Achievement can be summarized as follows: (1) all scores were below the 17th percentile, including reading, math, and writing; (2) Math Calculation was the lowest at the 3rd percentile (standard scores of 71); (3) her highest score (86) was in Written Expression (17th percentile), showing some area of relative strength; but (4) both Broad Reading and Broad Math were at the 6th percentile (standard scores of 76 and 77). The percentile levels of the WRAT4 (5th–34th) were generally similar to the somewhat lower WJ-III achievement performance, with the exception of Sentence Comprehension in the WRAT4, which apparently provides her with contexts for word selection and sentence understanding.

Her Broad Reading index score was 14 points lower than predicted achievement (based on GAI score of 86), a finding that occurs in only 7% of the general population. Her Math Calculation score was 21 points lower than predicted, a finding that occurs in 5% of the general population.

Summary

Grace is an 18-year-old adolescent Caucasian female presenting with concerns regarding attention and learning. The test findings in Table 20.4 indicate that Grace is probably eligible for academic accommodations (e.g., more time on exams) and that she should consult with the office of student academic services at the local university.

The clinical picture is of a college-bound young adult who has hypothesized symptoms associated with ADHD—Inattentive Type, as well as Reading and Mathematics Disorders. Grace has never been treated for her ADHD symptoms, and reportedly has never received special-education services. Grace is referred to the Student Academic Services Office at the local university for assistance and accommodations, as these possible clinical diagnoses clearly have educational relevance for her.

WRAT4-PMV Interpretation

The brief tests of the WRAT4-PMV require a different approach to interpretation. The process begins with repeated testing over a period of time (e.g., 4 weeks to 4 months, with one test per time period). Raw scores are plotted on an interpretive graph showing whether the scores are in the vicinity of the mean scores (plus or minus a confidence-interval amount) for comparable grade levels. If instruction is started (or changed significantly in method), the date of instruction is marked on the graph so that "response to instruction" can be evaluated. The four test forms can be repeated if the time period for evaluation is longer (e.g., 8 tests across 8 months). If the brief tests span more than one level (e.g., a young child moves from one grade level to another—grades 3–4), raw scores are converted to Level Equivalence (LE) scores for comparison. Differences between each pair of scores and between initial testing and post-instruction or final testing can also be contrasted, using tables of statistical significance. If the examinee does not show any significant change or growth in reading, math, spelling, and so on, based on the brief tests, a multidisciplinary team should conduct a comprehensive evaluation of the child's functioning, including observations in the classroom and home (e.g., from parent reports).

CASE STUDY #2: ADOLESCENT WITH AUTISM SPECTRUM DISORDER (ASD)

ASD was included as an official category of special-education services in recent years (Salvia & Ysseldyke, 2007). As part of these special-education services, teachable targets for intervention in ASD could include basic academic skills (vocabulary; word reading and comprehension), basic social perceptions and skills (knowledge of pragmatic conversational language; identification of emotions in others; understanding social interactions between people), and behavioral flexibility (ability to shift focus as instructional topics or problems change; shifting topics in conversation).

One case study (Roid, 2008) shows the promise of using the WRAT4-PMV in the academic portion of a comprehensive ASD evaluation. The case study included a single-case design, with alternating testing and treatment, with an adolescent diagnosed ASD. For confidentiality, we call the student "Tim." Tim participated in a cooperative work project between an urban high school and a local university, and permission was given to test him on a variety of the tests between January and May of a spring semester. Tim presented himself as a friendly young man who is prone to ask questions about the same topics (e.g., people's work or personal life) repeatedly, week to week. He was currently attending a public high school, and had a part-time job in a printing shop. His schedule and activities were supervised by his parents and by the special-education coordinator of the high school.

Extensive indicators of deficits in complex information processing (Minshew & Golstein, 1998) were found in this case study (e.g., poor understanding of sequential or repeated visual patterns, inflexibility in expressive language topics, deficits in visual and verbal working memory). Tim was functioning in the borderline levels of cognitive functioning on the *Stanford-Binet—Fifth Edition* (SB5; Roid, 2003) fluid reasoning subtests (approximately 80 IQ), and was more than two grade levels below national norms on the *Wide Range Achievement Test—PMV*, *Word Reading Tests* (WRAT4-PMV; Roid & Ledbetter, 2006). This case study showed the potential usefulness of the WRAT4-PMV in progress monitoring, in response to intervention, and in assessing cases with ASD.

To measure outcomes of two simultaneous ASD interventions, the single-case experimental design employed successive alternations between baseline and treatment (A-B-A-B). The study was implemented over a period of four months. The purpose of the study was to verify the usefulness of cognitive and academic measures in ASD assessment. The two treatment targets selected to demonstrate the usefulness of measures were cognitive and achievement skills of (1) sequential pattern comprehension, and (2) breadth of word-reading vocabulary. The outcome assessments consisted of the *Leiter International Performance Scale—Revised* (Leiter-R; Roid & Miller, 1997) Repeated Patterns subtest and the WRAT4-PMV Word Reading subtest. The Leiter-R subtest was scored for the number of objects or pictures correctly placed in sequence, as the model for the assessment of sequential pattern-identification tasks. The Leiter-R is widely used as a cognitive assessment for individuals with ASD (e.g., Tsatsanis et al., 2003). The brief tests (15 graded words each) of the WRAT4-PMV (Roid & Ledbetter, 2006) were employed to measure number of words correctly read aloud.

The case study included the experimental use of an academic intervention (the "B" phase of the experiment) employing the twin objectives of increasing skill and motivation in sequential reasoning and word reading enhancement. The reasoning component included direct teaching of sequences of objects and color patterns employing colored poker chips and prompting to test Tim's perception of patterns. Patterns included plastic and pictured objects in sequences (e.g., blue square, yellow circle, red triangle . . . repeated). For word reading enhancement, a trained interventionist met with Tim weekly and used games such as Scrabble, going to libraries, reading books of interest to the subject (e.g., machinery, animals), and conversations directed at word reading topics.

Table 20.5 shows the results and the effect of the reasoning training on the number of correctly sequenced objects or pictures (baseline involved assessment but no instruction or intervention).

During the baseline periods, Tim showed a strong tendency to use "matching" (where the same object, shape, or color is used to match the last element in a pattern) instead of paying attention to the repeated pattern. For example, if the pattern presented showed a sequence of shapes: circle, square, triangle; circle, square, _____, Tim would select the square instead of the triangle as the next object. Thus, qualitative evidence of *cognitive rigidity* (Minshew & Williams, 2007) was observed.

The treatment effects, shown in Table 20.5, were able to overcome some of Tim's rigidity tendency (at Treatment 2). Differences in IRT scores were highly significant statistically according to guidelines in the Leiter-R manual (Roid & Miller, 1997), wherein IRT gains of 22 or more are significant at $p < .01$. The gain from Baseline 2 to Treatment 2 exceeded this critical value (43 points).

This example also shows the promise of the IRT-type *growth score*, which is more sensitive to the up-and-down trends of the A-B-A-B design than the raw scores or the scaled scores.

TABLE 20.5   Raw and IRT Scores for Leiter-R and WRAT4-PMV for the Case of Tim

	A₁ Baseline 1	B₁ Treatment 1	A₂ Baseline 2	B₂ Treatment 2
Leiter-R Scores				
# of Sequenced Objects	10	14	8	22
Scaled Score	1	1	1	7
IRT (Leiter-R) Score	463	475	457	500
WRAT4-PMV Scores				
Raw Score Vocabulary	10 8	10 12	8 9	9 9
IRT (PMV "LE") Scores*	508 494	507 523	514 521	519 520
	Level 3 Tests**		Level 4 Tests	

NOTE : *WRAT4-PMV tests have 4 separate forms at each level, thus the IRT scores vary somewhat even with the same raw score on two brief tests.
**Level 3 (Grades 4-5) tests were given during Baseline 1 and Treatment 1, and Level 4 (Grades 6-8) tests were given during Baseline 2 and Treatment 2.

Data for word reading showed a statistically significant increase across eight test administrations (each with a different parallel form of the WRAT4-PMV). Tim began reading 8 words out of 15 (Level 3 of WRAT4-PMV—approximately grade 5 level) during Baseline 1, with an IRT low score of 494 to a final level of 520 at Level 4 (grade 8 level) during Treatment 2. The findings of this single-case study provide evidence that the overall value of using the WRAT4-PMV tests is sound in the following ways:

- WRAT4-PMV Word Reading brief tests (15 items) were sensitive to intervention effects in an adolescent with ASD.
- The single-case controlled study replicates the findings of Minshew & Williams (2007), where cognitive rigidity was found in ASD cases.
- The metric of IRT growth scales (Rasch model on both the Leiter-R and the WRAT4-PMV, both scores similar to those used on the Woodcock-Johnson tests) proved to be sensitive to changes across sessions.
- The concept of using strictly parallel (psychometrically equivalent) test forms on the WRAT4-PMV to assess pre- and post-treatment effects was verified.
- The skills of sequential-pattern recognition and word-reading vocabulary were found to be sensitive to intervention in ASD and measurable with the tests employed.

TEST SCORES IN SPECIAL POPULATIONS

Both test manuals—the WRAT4 (Wilkinson & Robertson, 2006) and the WRAT4-PMV (Roid & Ledbetter, 2006)—present specific studies of scores for children with learning disabilities. Traditionally, *specific learning disabilities* (IDEA, 1997) are defined as "imperfect ability to listen, think, speak, read, write, spell, or do mathematical calculations" (Salvia & Ysseldyke, 2007, p. 617). Thus, the WRAT4 scores of Word

Reading and Sentence Comprehension (specific disability in reading), Spelling, or Math Computation can be used to evaluate students with potential specific learning disabilities. There were 49 students (ages 6–18) with official assignment to learning disability (LD) classrooms that were tested with all four subtests of the WRAT4. The sample was composed of 49% female students, 31% of students with Hispanic background (43% Anglo, 18% African American), and 49% of students with parental education levels of high school graduate. The LD sample showed means ranging from 86.9 to 87.0 with standard deviations of 13–14 on the four subtests (standardization mean 100, SD 15). This was significantly lower ($p < .01$) than a matched normative control sample of 49 students with similar ethnicity and parental education background (means of 97.5–99.0; SDs of 12.4–15.4). The differences between the two samples showed large effect sizes (Cohen's 1988 d statistic, the standardized mean difference, of .74–.80).

A study of students with learning disabilities was also conducted for the WRAT4-PMV. A subset of 30 students in the WRAT4 LD sample had complete data on the 24 multiple forms of the WRAT4-PMV Word Reading subtest, across all grade levels. Roid and Ledbetter (2006) report the detailed data on this sample of LD students for the Word Reading and show, again, that the LD sample has significantly lower scores on the brief WRAT4-PMV tests as compared to matched normative students. The effect sizes of these differences, based on the shorter 15-item tests of WRAT4-PMV, were more varied than those obtained by the WRAT4 study—ranging from .37 to .98 (Cohen's d) with the tendency for lower effect sizes above grade 9.

EVIDENCE OF VALIDITY

Numerous studies providing evidence related to test content, relationship to other variables, consequences of test usage, and general construct-related findings (AERA/APA/NCME, 1999) were included in the test manuals for WRAT4 (Wilkinson & Robertson, 2006) and Roid and Ledbetter (2006). Prior to the recent release of the fourth edition, an extensive literature on previous editions of the WRAT can be found in medical research (e.g., Bass, Wilson, & Griffith, 2003; O'Callaghan, O'Callaghan, Najman, Williams, & Bor, 2007), neuropsychology (e.g., O'Bryant, Schrimsher, & Jile, 2005), education (e.g., Friend & Olson, 2008; Saint-Aubin & Klein, 2008), and other research areas.

Evidence Related to Test Content

For the WRAT4, three of the subtests—Word Reading, Spelling, and Math Computation—appeared in WRAT3 and earlier editions of the test, and the items in these tests had received extensive statistical analysis at the time of the WRAT3 standardization conducted in the early 1990s. Items for these subtests in WRAT4 were drawn largely from the proven WRAT3 items, with deletions and additions based on an extensive content review by the development staff and outside experts. The WRAT4 drew 77% of its items, overall, from WRAT3, whereas 23% were new. Extensive studies were conducted on all items in both the WRAT3 and WRAT4, examining item characteristics (difficulty, discrimination, guessing), various bias statistics, and fit of each item to one of the four subtest scales (e.g., Word Reading) based on IRT analysis (Wright & Linacre, 1999; Rasch, 1980). This empirical evidence provides, as described by Kamphaus (2001), content-related evidence of validity.

As for the subtests, Spelling was least changed (11.9% were new), Math Computation was most changed (30% were new), and Word Reading had 26.4% new items. Thus, the items retained from WRAT3 constitute a substantial portion of the items in WRAT4, and this brings consistency across editions and allows the content-related validity of WRAT4 to build on the previous edition. In assembling the WRAT4 item pool, items were eliminated from WRAT3, as stated previously, only after extensive content review by outside experts who evaluated the WRAT3 items in terms of their current relevance and freedom from apparent gender or ethnic bias. Several indirect measures were used to control item difficulty at the item-preparation stage. Item writers were assigned specified numbers of items at five target grade levels: pre-K–1; 2–3; 4–5; 6–8; 9–13 and above. The *EDL Core Vocabularies in Reading, Mathematics, Science, and Social Science* (Taylor et al., 1989) was used as the source for estimating the difficulty of words used in an item. Item writers were instructed to draw about half of the words in an item from the core list for the target grades, with no more than about 25% of the words *above* the target grade level and no more than about 25% of the words *below* the target grade level.

The procedures used to develop the Sentence Comprehension subtest contributed to evidence of its validity. Items were prepared in accordance with detailed content specifications, and data were collected on all items in a field-testing sample during the fall of 2002, with 1,989 students in grades 3–12 completing the draft test items. In addition to classical and IRT-based item statistics, item validities were obtained by administering the *WRAT—Expanded* Reading Comprehension subtest (Robertson, 2001) to all participants. These data added important information to the final item selection and test assembly processes. The Sentence Comprehension items were also reviewed by the panel of outside experts:

- To ensure that the items were free from gender, racial/ethnic bias
- To avoid items that might suggest unfavorable or negative stereotypes
- To ensure the accuracy of all possible correct responses
- To ensure that the sentences used in the spelling test were concise and accurate, using the fewest possible words to illustrate the meaning of the word

Item analysis data obtained from the national standardization program were used to review the item characteristics one final time before the final editions of the Blue and Green forms were prepared for publication. Both classical item statistics and IRT one-parameter item calibration data were obtained based on the entire standardization sample. After reviewing these data, very few deletions or changes were made in the items for the Word Reading, Spelling, and Math Computation subtests. For the Sentence Comprehension subtest, 20 items were deleted, 10 from the Blue Form and 10 from the Green Form.

The addition of Sentence Comprehension also addresses one of the major concerns and criticisms of the earlier editions of WRAT—that reading consists of much more than word recognition and should include comprehension (Lezak et al., 2004). Clearly, even with the addition of sentence comprehension items, the WRAT4 does not address all the dimensions of reading achievement that would be assessed by a comprehensive, diagnostic reading test. The chief advantage of the WRAT4 approach is a rapid and easy test administration, but this comes at the sacrifice of breadth of coverage—a common dilemma in educational and psychological assessment (Salvia & Ysseldyke, 2007).

WRAT4-PMV Validity

Much of the evidence for validity based on test content for the WRAT4-PMV comes from the evidence described above for the WRAT4. WRAT4-PMV employed only items from WRAT4 and did not have any new items of its own. Similar steps in development and standardization were followed for the two versions, including extensive planning of item coverage (e.g., each WRAT4-PMV test form was balanced with similar types of words, sentences, or math problems within each grade level), classical and IRT-based item analysis (Hambleton, Swaminathan, & Rogers, 1991), and rigorous development of equivalent forms. Clearly, given the brevity of the WRAT4-PMV scales, it was not possible to have the breadth of content coverage found in the WRAT4 full-length scales (e.g., 15-item PMV Word Reading forms versus 70-item Blue or Green forms).

Evidence Based on Relations with Other Variables (Criterion Related)

Evidence of validity is based in part on the relationships of the WRAT4 subtests with scores from other tests including measures of academic achievement and cognitive ability. Strong construct validity is suggested whenever there is an appropriate pattern of convergent (measures of the same construct) and divergent associations (measures of other constructs) between an instrument and external tests or variables (Gregory, 2007). The test manuals for the WRAT4 (Wilkinson & Robertson, 2006) and WRAT4-PMV (Roid & Ledbetter, 2006) provide demographic characteristics of the participants in each concurrent study. In addition, summary tables across different measures are provided to facilitate the understanding of the evidence collected. Highlights of this information are provided below.

Correlations with Other Achievement Tests

In separate studies, the WRAT4 was compared with the *Wechsler Individual Achievement Test—Second Edition* (WIAT-II; Psychological Corporation, 2002; [n = 33]), *Woodcock-Johnson III Tests of Achievement* (WJ-III; Mather & Woodcock, 2001; [n = 31]), and the *Kaufman Test of Educational Achievement—Second Edition—Comprehensive* (KTEA-II—Comprehensive; Kaufman, & Kaufman, 2004b; [n = 28]). Convergent validity evidence for the WRAT4 reading subtests is presented in Table 20.6, showing like-subtest-by-subtest comparison between the WRAT4 subtests and each of the other individual achievement tests. Presented in Table 20.6 are all correlations that are similar in broad categorical terms for all reading scores, whether or not they are word reading, comprehension, or composite. In

addition, the bolded correlations in Table 20.6 are the matched subtest scores from both instruments (i.e., KTEA-II Word Recognition versus WRAT4 Word Reading). The medians of the bolded correlations are given to represent the central tendency of the matched comparisons. These median matched correlations ranged from .71 for Word Reading to .73 for the Reading Composite and .60 for Sentence Comprehension. Given that these comparative achievement tests have differing content, test-item formats, standardizations, and authors, the correlations are expected, particularly those above .70.

Correlations with the Spelling and Math Computation subtests of WRAT4 are detailed in Wilkinson and Robertson (2006), but are summarized as follows: Spelling showed a range of matching-variable correlations between .64 and .89, with a median of .75. Math Computation showed a range of .64–.92, with a median of .75.

WRAT4-PMV Correlations with Achievement Tests

Roid and Ledbetter (2006) report studies of similar correlates with the brief tests of WRAT4-PMV using the same samples employed by the WRAT4 validity studies. Examples include the following correlations corrected for variability in the samples: (1) correlation of .68 between the Word Reading and the KTEA-II Brief Form (Kaufman & Kaufman, 2005) Letter/Word Recognition subtest, (2) correlation of .69 between the Word Reading and the Word Reading subtest of WIAT-II, (3) correlation of .65 between the Spelling subtests on WRAT4-PMV and WIAT-II, and (4) correlation of .48 between Math Computation and the Number Operations subtest of WIAT-II and the Mathematics subtest of KTEA-II Brief Form.

Correlations with Cognitive Tests

The degrees of relationship between tests of achievement and cognitive ability are also important data to be included in the supportive

TABLE 20.6   Corrected Correlations of WRAT4 Scores vs Like Subtest Scores from Other Achievement Measures

	WRAT4		
	Word Reading	Sentence Comprehension	Reading Composite
WIAT II			
Word Reading	**.71**	.49	.73
Reading Comprehension	.82	**.61**	.79
Decoding	**.71**	.60	.76
Reading Composite	.80	.54	**.78**
W-J III			
Basic Reading	**.66**	.56	.73
Broad Reading	.70	.54	**.73**
Reading Comprehension	.85	**.60**	.83
KTEA-II Comprehensive			
Letter/Word Recognition	**.76**	.56	.74
Reading Comprehension	.54	**.42**	.53
Reading Composite	.61	.45	**.58**
Median of Bolded Correlations	**.71**	**.60**	**.73**

NOTE : Correlations in bold represent the closest match between subtests.
WIAT-II= Wechsler Individual Achievement Test: Second Edition.
(The Psychological Corporation, 2002). WJ-III= Woodcock-Johnson III Tests of Achievement
(Mather & Woodcock, 2001).
KTEA-II Comprehensive form= Kaufman Test of Educational Achievement:
Second Edition (Kaufman, & Kaufman, 2004).
Sample sizes were 33, 28, 33, 28, and 30 for WIAT-II, WJ III, and KTEA-II respectively.
All correlations are corrected for restriction of range (variability) in the samples.
For uncorrected correlations, see the source of this table—Wilkinson & Robertson, 2006, Reprinted by permission of PAR, Inc.

evidence because cognitive tests are often used to predict student learning and achievement. In separate studies, the WRAT4 was compared with the *Wechsler Intelligence Scale for Children—Fourth Edition* (WISC-IV; Wechsler, 2003), *Stanford-Binet Intelligence Scales—Fifth Edition* (SB-5; Roid, 2003), *Wechsler Adult Intelligence Scale—Third Edition* (WAIS-III; Wechsler, 1997), *Wechsler Abbreviated Scale of Intelligence* (WASI; Psychological Corporation, 1999),

and *Kaufman Brief Intelligence Test—Second Edition* (KBIT-2; Kaufman, & Kaufman, 2004a).

The detailed demographic characteristics of the participants who comprised these various external validity studies are provided in Wilkinson and Robertson (2006). The sample sizes and correlations for selected variables (e.g., verbal and full-scale IQ) for these studies are presented in Table 20.7.

TABLE 20.7   Corrected Correlations between WRAT4 Scores and Cognitive Ability Scores

Cognitive Ability Scores	WRAT4 Subtests				
	Word Reading	Sentence Comprehension	Reading Composite	Spelling	Math Computation
Verbal Ability Scores					
WISC-IV Verbal Comprehension (ages 5-9)	.65	.48	.66	.54	.59
WISC-IV Verbal Comprehension (ages 10-15)	.69	.62	.70	.48	.49
SB-5 Verbal IQ	.65	.75	.71	.57	.60
WAIS-III Verbal IQ	.64	.63	.72	.61	.70
WASI Verbal Scale	.55	.65	.66	.36	.46
KBIT-II Verbal IQ (ages 5-18)	.61	.51	.65	.59	.56
KBIT-II Verbal IQ (ages 19-55)	.59	.67	.70	.46	.55
Median	.64	.65	.70	.54	.56
Full Scale Ability Scores					
WISC-IV Full Scale (5-9)	.79	.50	.71	.68	.75
WISC-IV Full Scale (10-15)	.74	.77	.81	.57	.66
SB-5 Full Scale IQ (5-18)	.74	.77	.78	.67	.76
WAIS-III Full Scale IQ	.64	.75	.79	.61	.72
WASI Full Scale IQ	.65	.71	.73	.46	.60
KBIT-II Composite IQ (5-18)	.60	.44	.60	.57	.59
KBIT-II Composite IQ (19-55)	.60	.70	.72	.47	.57
Median	..65	.70	.73	.57	.66

NOTE : WISC-IV (Wechsler, 2003), SB-5 (Roid, 2003), WAIS-III (Wechsler, 1997), WASI (The Psychological Corporation, 1999), KBIT-II (Kaufman & Kaufman, 2004).
Sample sizes were 24 and 35 for the two WISC-IV samples, 70 for SB-5, 58 for WAIS-III, 90 for WASI, and 52 and 54 for the two KBIT samples. Correlations are corrected for variability (Guilford & Fruchter, 1978). Uncorrected correlations are in Wilkinson and Robertson (2006).

The median correlations between WRAT4 subtests and Full Scale ability scores ranged from .59 (Spelling) to .73 (Reading Composite) with median-of-medians .64. Median correlations with Verbal cognitive measures ranged from .54 (Spelling) to .70 (Reading Composite), with median-of-medians .66. These correlations are as expected and similar to other studies of achievement and IQ relationships (Sattler, 2008).

It would be anticipated that the verbal indices would be more highly correlated with the academic achievement skills on the WRAT4 than the nonverbal indices. A further inspection of the tables in Wilkinson and Robertson (2006) confirms that this is true. Each WRAT4 subtest median correlation with the verbal indices is higher (.64, .65, .70, .54, and .56 in Table 20.7) than the corresponding correlations with the nonverbal indices (.53, .55, .64, .47, and .54 in the WRAT4 test manual), and similar to the correlations for Full Scale indices (in Table 20.7).

WRAT4-PMV Correlations with Cognitive Measures

Two cognitive batteries, the SB5 (Roid, 2003) and the *Reynolds Intellectual Assessment Scales* (RIAS; Reynolds & Kamphaus, 2003), were correlated with the brief test forms of the WRAT4-PMV. Details of the studies can be found in Roid and Ledbetter (2006), but a few highlights will show the general magnitude of these correlations. With a sample of 67 students (mean age 12.4), median correlations of .32 were found between Word Reading and the SB5 scores, with the Knowledge factor index (which includes the Vocabulary subtest of SB5) correlated highest at .53. The Quantitative Reasoning factor of SB5 correlated .41 (uncorrected) with the Math Computation brief tests. With a sample of 114 students (mean age = 11.7), the RIAS composite (Index) scores had a median correlation of .44 with Word Reading, with the Nonverbal Intelligence Index most highly correlated at .56. These moderate to moderately low correlations are expected when the achievement measures are brief 15-item test forms. What will be more important for the WRAT4-PMV is true longitudinal data from actual school-based application of progress monitoring (e.g., for a special-education student across several months) showing the relationship between the plotted *pattern* of scores and external measures of achievement and cognition.

Construct-Related Evidence of Validity

The category of construct-related evidence is now considered much broader in the 1999 technical standards for tests (AERA/APA/NCME, 1999) than in previous editions of the standards. Hence, the evidence for relations with other

tests, discussed in the section above, also pertains to construct validity, especially convergent versus divergent evidence (Campbell & Fiske, 1959). Another type of construct-related evidence is from developmental trends (e.g., across age groups), and this evidence is discussed next.

Evidence of Developmental Trends

One important characteristic of the achievement content domains measured by WRAT4 is that acquisition of these skills increases with an individual's age or grade in school, suggesting a strong developmental component underlying these basic skills. This finding leads to an expectation that the mean raw scores on the various WRAT4 subtests will increase monotonically at successive age and grade levels, at least until a point when the skills eventually level off and subsequently show a decline beginning in late middle age. Results obtained for the WRAT4 standardization sample generally agree with these expectations. Mean raw scores by age for the WRAT4 scores of the Blue and Green Forms are shown in several detailed tables in Wilkinson and Robertson (2006). These data generally support the stated expectations, with raw scores generally increasing until ages 45–54, at which point they undergo a gradual decline throughout the remaining ages (55–94). For Word Reading, for example, raw score means (of number-correct score on 70 items) ranged from 14.8 to 45.0 between the age groups of 5 years and 12 years of age for the Blue Form, and 13.9–44.3 for the same age range on the Green Form. Both of these Forms show an approximate peak of 62 and 59 in the 45–54 age group. The other WRAT4 subtests show similar trends (given the smaller number of items in these scales), with age 5 scores in the 11–12 range (about 7 points for age 6, where Sentence Comprehension begins) to peak scores of approximately 43–46 in the age range 45–54. These developmental trends are very consistent with those reported by Wilkinson (1993, p. 177) for age-related changes in mean score with age on WRAT3, in which the mean subtest scores increased until ages 45–54, after which age the average raw scores began to decline.

Mean raw scores on WRAT4 by grade generally increase throughout the grade range, with a slight reversal at grade 12 on both the Blue and Green forms. The age data discussed previously, however, suggest that raw scores continue to increase at ages 17–18, the ages that typically consist mainly of grade 12 students, so the slight reversal observed in WRAT4 may be due to a minor sampling fluctuation in the grade 12 data.

WRAT4-PMV Evidence for Developmental Trends

Roid and Ledbetter (2006) present data showing that the scores for each of the WRAT4-PMV subtests have progressively greater means across Levels 1 (grades K–1) to 6 (grades 13–16). Also, a graph showing the developmental curve was drawn by taking IRT-based Level Equivalence scores for Word Reading (used so that across-grade brief tests can be compared across age levels of students) and plotting them by age group in the WRAT4-PMV standardization sample. The curve clearly follows the developmental trend found in other IRT-scaled reading achievement scores such as those in the *WJ III Tests of Achievement* (Mather & Woodcock, 2001).

Evidence of Consequential Validity

Messick (1980) introduced the idea of examining the societal consequences of using various test scores for important decisions about the lives of individuals. This type of consequential-validity research is complex because individuals have to be followed longitudinally for an indefinite time period to track delayed effects of various test-usage decisions. However, some types of evidence can be collected at the time of test publication, and one of these would be evidence of test fairness (non-bias) among various ethnic, gender, and socioeconomic groups. Differential item functioning (DIF; Holland & Wainer, 1993)

was investigated for the WRAT4 subtests by the *comparison of item parameters* method as described by Hambleton et al. (1991). As applied to the Rasch model, this amounts to a comparison of independently calibrated item-difficulty parameters for the subgroups of interest. As Camilli and Shepard (1994) caution, DIF analyses per se do not automatically provide an indication that items are biased. Such a determination can be made only by combining logical analysis with the DIF results to arrive at a judgmental decision about the presence or absence of bias in a test item. Independent item calibrations were conducted for the four WRAT4 Blue and Green form subtests, using data from the national standardization program for the following contrast groups: Male versus Female, African American versus Caucasian, and Hispanic versus Caucasian. The resulting correlations between the two sets of item-difficulty parameters for each comparison group show extremely high correlational results. For the comparison of males and females, the correlations ranged from .992 to .998 across the four subtests. For African American versus Caucasian, the correlations ranged from .982 to .995, and the range was .984 to .995 for the Hispanic–Anglo comparison. For each comparison, the Sentence Comprehension subtest had the lowest correlations and Spelling had the highest.

Thus, the data indicate generally very high agreement, meaning that very minimal DIF (or apparent bias) appeared in these data for the four WRAT4 subtests. The correlations between the two sets of Rasch item-difficulty parameters are all .98 or higher, with 21 of the 24 values .991 or higher. Graphs of the scatter-plots of each pair of difficulty values (in Wilkinson & Robertson, 2006) show that pairs of items cluster very close to the identity line (1.00). When data such as these are considered along with the comments made by expert reviewers, the conclusion is that any potential bias would be a rare consequence of using the WRAT4.

SUMMARY

The current edition and the progress-monitoring versions add features to the widely used WRAT achievement test. In response to expert concerns that the Word Reading subtest is not sufficient in the assessment of general reading ability (Lezak et al., 2004), the Sentence Comprehension subtest was added. This provides the quick-and-easy administration and scoring that is characteristic of WRAT tests, providing a good starting point for possible comprehensive evaluations.

The WRAT editions have continued to be popular in special education, in some types of reading research (e.g., Friend & Olson, 2008; Saint-Aubin & Klein, 2008), in neuropsychology (O'Bryant et al., 2005), in medical research (e.g., O'Callaghan et al., 2007), and in other settings that demand a quick-and-easy assessment of basic achievement levels. Also, the WRAT4 scores often provide a quick and objective method of estimating reading level (O'Bryant et al., 2005). And, both test manuals (Roid & Ledbetter, 2006; Wilkinson & Robertson, 2006) present a good deal of reliability and validity evidence.

The WRAT4-Progress Monitoring Version brings the WRAT series into a new realm of application, spurred by new legislation (e.g., IDEA 2004; U.S. Department of Education, 2004), as discussed previously. The brief 15-item tests of WRAT4-PMV were carefully equated within grade-range levels (e.g., the four test forms for grades 2–3) so that assessment professionals can record the progression of repeated test results on graphs that show the grade-level norms in a straightforward way using a shaded band across the graph. Thus, two patterns of repeated test performance can be distinguished: (1) a "flat" pattern of nonsignificant differences in repeated test performance, and (2) a changing, significant increase in test performance, perhaps attributable to the effects of instruction (Vaughn & Fuchs, 2003; Vaughn, Linan-Thompson, & Hickman, 2003). The WRAT4-PMV provides tables of significant differences printed near the test-record graph to facilitate the differentiation of such patterns. Clearly, this method of identifying "lack of response to instruction" by patterns of repeated test results requires future research to measure the degree of accuracy in the identification of significant student progress or learning difficulties. These research questions are some of the many questions remaining about the implementation of RTI systems and its impact on student learning.

In summary, the WRAT4 and the WRAT4-PMV provide relatively brief and easily administered tests of basic achievement skills that show acceptable levels of reliability and validity. The major uses of WRAT4 appear to be in rapid evaluations, in research, and for supplementing a comprehensive battery of other instruments. The tests were not necessarily developed as standalone assessments, nor intended to replace diagnostic batteries in reading, spelling, and mathematics. Their practical utility cannot be denied, however, given the 70-year record of continued use in education and psychology.

REFERENCES

AERA/APA/NCME: American Educational Research Association, American Psychological Association & National Council on Measurement in Education (1999). *Standards for educational and psychological testing*. Washington, DC: Author.

Alonzo, J., Ketterlin-Geller, L. R., & Tindal, G. (2007). Curriculum based assessment. In L. Florian (Ed.), *Handbook of special education*. Thousand Oaks, CA: Sage Publications.

Barnes, A. C., & Harlacher, J. E. (2008). Clearing the confusion: Response-to-intervention as a set of principles. *Education and Treatment of Children*, *31*, 417–431.

Bass III, P. F., Wilson, J. F., & Griffith, C. H. (2003). A shortened instrument for literacy screening. *Journal of General Internal Medicine*, *18*, 1036–1038.

Camilli, G., & Shepard, L. (1994). *Methods for identifying biased test items*. Thousand Oaks, CA: Sage Publications.

Campbell, D. P., & Fiske, D. W. (1959). Convergent and discriminant validation by the multitrait-multimethod matrix. *Psychological Bulletin, 56,* 81–105.

Carroll, J. B. (1993). *Human cognitive abilities: A survey of factor-analytic studies.* Cambridge; New York: Cambridge University Press.

Cattell, R. B. (1943). The measurement of intelligence. *Psychological Bulletin, 40,* 153–193.

Cohen, J. (1988). *Statistical power analysis for the behavioral sciences* (2nd ed.). Mahwah, NJ: Erlbaum.

Cronbach, L. J. (1951). Coefficient Alpha and the structure of tests. *Psychometrika, 16,* 297–334.

Dana, R. H. (2005). *Multicultural assessment* (2nd ed.). Mahwah, NJ: Erlbaum.

Deno, S. L. (1985). Curriculum-based measurement: The emerging alternative. *Exceptional Children, 52,* 219–232.

Deno, S. L. (2003). Developments in curriculum-based measurement. *Journal of Special Education, 37,* 184–192.

Education World. (2008, July 9). National and state standards. Retrieved from http://www.education-world.com/standards/.

Friend, A., & Olson, R. K. (2008). Phonological spelling and reading deficits in children with spelling disabilities. *Scientific Studies of Reading, 12,* 90–105.

Fuchs, L.S., & Fuchs, D. (1998). Treatment validity: A unifying concept for reconceptualizing the identification of learning disabilities. *Learning Disabilities Research & Practice, 13,* 204–219.

Fuchs, L.S., & Fuchs, D. (2005, Sept./Oct.). Responsiveness-to-intervention: A blueprint for practitioners, policy makers, and parents. *Teaching Exceptional Children,* 57–61.

Fuchs, L. S., & Vaughn, S. (2006, March). Response-to-intervention as a framework for the identification of learning disabilities. *NASP Communiqué, 34*(6), 1–6.

Good, R. H. III, & Kaminski, R. A. (2002). *Dynamic indicator of basic early literacy skills (DIBELS)* (6th ed.). Eugene, OR: Institute for the Development of Educational Achievement.

Gorsuch, R. L. (1983, August). *The theory of continuous norming.* Paper presented at the meetings of the American Psychological Association, Anaheim, CA.

Gorsuch, R. L. (2005). Continuous parameter estimation model: Expanding the standard statistical paradigm. *Chiang Mai Journal of Science, 32*(1), 11–21. (Journal of the Science Faculty of Chiang Mai University, Thailand); available at www.science.cmu.ac.th/journal-science/josci.html.

Gregory, R. J. (2007). *Psychological testing* (5th ed.). Boston: Pearson/Allyn & Bacon.

Gresham, F. M. (2002). Responsiveness to intervention: An alternative approach to the identification of learning disabilities. In R. Bradley, L. Danielson, & D. Hallahan (Eds.), *Identification of learning disabilities: Research to practice* (pp. 467–519). Mahwah, NJ: Lawrence Erlbaum.

Guilford, J. P. & Fruchter, B. (1978). *Fundamental statistics in psychology and education.* New York: McGraw Hill.

Hale, J. B., Flanagan, D. P., & Naglieri, J. A. (2008). Alternative research-based methods for IDEA 2004 identification of children with specific learning disabilities. *NASP Communiqué, 36*(8), 14–15.

Hale, J. B., Kaufman, A. S., Naglieri, J. A., & Kavale, K. A. (2006). Implementation of IDEA: Integrating response to intervention and cognitive assessment methods. *Psychology in the Schools, 43*(7), 723–770.

Hambleton, R. K., Swaminathan, H., & Rogers, H. J. (1991). *Fundamentals of item response theory.* Newbury Park, CA: Sage Publications.

Hill, I. D. (1976). Algorithm ASI00: Normal-Johnson and Johnson-Normal transformations. *Applied Statistics, 25,* 190–192.

Hill, I. D., Hill, R., & Holder, R. L. (1976). Algorithm AS99: Fitting Johnson curves by moments. *Applied Statistics, 25,* 180–189.

Hillerich, R. L. (1978). *A writing vocabulary of elementary children.* Springfield: Charles Thomas.

Holland, P. W., & Wainer, H. (Eds.). (1993). *Differential item functioning.* Mahwah, NJ: Erlbaum.

Horn, J. L. (1965). *Fluid and crystallized intelligence.* Unpublished doctoral dissertation. Urbana–Champaign: University of Illinois.

Horn, J. L. (1985). Remodeling old models of intelligence. In B. B. Wolman (Ed.), *Handbook of intelligence* (pp. 267–300). New York: Wiley.

Horn, J. L. (1994). Theory of fluid and crystallized intelligence. In R. J. Sternberg (Ed.), *Encyclopedia of human intelligence* (pp. 443–451). New York: Macmillan.

Horn, J. L., & Cattell, R. B. (1966). Refinement and test of the theory of fluid and crystallized general intelligences. *Journal of Educational Psychology, 57,* 253–270.

IDEA: Individuals with Disabilities Education Act (1997). 20 U.S.C. 1400 *et seq*; U.S. Statutes at Large, 104, 1103-1151, Public Law 105-17, reauthorization and amendment to Public Law 101-476, 1990.

IDEIA: Individuals with Disabilities Education Improvement Act (2004). Public Law No. 108-446, § 632, 118 Stat. 2744.

Jastak, J. F. (1946). *Wide Range Achievement Test*. Wilmington, DE: C. L. Story Co.

Johnson, N. L. (1949). Systems of frequency curves generated by methods of translation. *Biometrika, 36,* 149–176.

Kamphaus, R. W. (2001). *Clinical assessment of child and adolescent intelligence* (2nd ed.). Boston: Allyn & Bacon.

Kaufman, A. S., & Kaufman, N. L. (2004a). *Kaufman Brief Intelligence Test—Second Edition*. Circle Pines, MN: American Guidance Service.

Kaufman, A. S., & Kaufman, N. L. (2004b). *Kaufman Test of Educational Achievement—Second Edition—Comprehensive Form*. Circle Pines, MN: American Guidance Service.

Kaufman, A. S. & Kaufman, N. L. (2005). *Kaufman Test of Educational Achievement—Second Edition—Brief Form*. Circle Pines, MN: American Guidance Service.

Lezak, M. D., Howieson, D. B., & Loring, D. W. (2004). *Neuropsychological assessment* (4th ed.). New York: Oxford University Press.

Mather, N., & Woodcock, R. W. (2001a). *WJ III Tests of Achievement Examiner's Manual*. Rolling Meadows, IL: Riverside.

Mather, N., & Woodcock, R. W. (2001b). *WJ III Tests of Cognitive Abilities Examiner's Manual*. Rolling Meadows, IL: Riverside.

McGrew, K. S., & Woodcock, R. W. (2001). *Woodcock-Johnson III: Technical Manual*. Rolling Meadows, IL: Riverside.

Messick, S. (1980). Test validity and the ethics of assessment. *American Psychologist, 35,* 1012–1027.

Minshew, N. J., & Golstein, G. (1998). Autism and a disorder of complex information processing. *Mental Retardation and Developmental Disabilities, 4,* 129–136.

Minshew, N. J., & Williams, D. L. (2007). The new neurobiology of autism: Cortex, connectivity, and neuronal organization. *Neurological Review, 64,* 945–950.

Naglieri, J. A. (2007). RTI alone is not sufficient for SLD identification: Convention presentation by OSEP director Alexa Posny. *NASP Communiqué, 35*(8), 53.

Naglieri, J. A., & Crockett, D. P. (2005). Response to intervention (RTI): Is it a scientifically proven method? *SCOPE Newsletter of the Washington State Association of School Psychologists, 28*(1), 4–5.

National Association of School Psychologists (2007). NASP IDEA information webpage, Part B: IDEA 2004 regulations. Available at http://www.nasponline.org/advocacy/IDEAinformation.aspx.

National Association of State Directors of Special Education (2006). *Response to intervention: Policy considerations and implementation*. Alexandria, VA: NASDSE.

National Center for Education Statistics (2002, March). Children 3 to 21 years old served in federally funded programs for the disabled, by type of disability: 1976–2000. *Digest of Education Statistics*, United States Department of Education. Retrieved from http://nces.ed.gov/programs/digest/d03/tables dt052.asp.

No Child Left Behind Act (2002). Reauthorization of the Elementary and Secondary Education Act 2001, Public Law 107-110, *U.S. Statutes at Large*.

Nunnally, J. C. (1967). *Psychometric theory*. New York: McGraw-Hill.

O'Bryant, S. E., Schrimsher, G. W., & Jile, J. R. (2005). Discrepancies between self-reported years of education and estimated reading level. *Applied Neuropsychology, 12,* 5–11.

O'Callaghan, F. V., O'Callaghan, M., Najman, J. M., Williams, G. M., & Bor, W. (2007). Prenatal alcohol exposure and attention, learning, and intellectual ability at 14 years. *Early Human Development, 83,* 115–123.

Paniagua, F. A. (2005). *Assessing and treating culturally diverse clients: A practical guide* (3rd ed.). Thousand Oaks, CA: Sage.

Posny, A. (2007, March). IDEA 2004: Top ten issues that affect school psychologists. Featured session at the annual meeting of the *National Association of School Psychologists*, New York.

Psychological Corporation (1999). *Wechsler Abbreviated Scale of Intelligence*. San Antonio, TX: Author.

Psychological Corporation (2002). *Wechsler Individual Achievement Test: Second Edition*. San Antonio, TX: Author.

Rasch, G. (1980). *Probabilistic models for some intelligence and attainment tests*. Chicago: University of Chicago Press.

Reynolds, C. R., & Kamphaus, R. W. (2003). *Reynolds Intellectual Assessment Scales*. Lutz, FL: Psychological Assessment Resources.

Reynolds, C. R., Livingston, R. B., & Willson, V. (2006). *Measurement and assessment in education*. Boston: Pearson/Allyn-Bacon.

Robertson, G. J. (2001). *Wide Range Achievement Test—Expanded Edition*. Wilmington, DE: Wide Range.

Roid, G. H. (1983, August). *Generalization of continuous norming: Cross-validation of test-score mean estimates*. Paper presented at the meetings of the American Psychological Association, Anaheim, CA.

Roid, G. H. (1986). Computer technology in testing. In B. S. Plake & J. C. Witt (Eds.), *The future of testing: Buros-Nebraska symposium on measurement and testing* (vol. 2, pp. 29–69). Hillsdale, NJ: Erlbaum.

Roid, G. H. (1989). *Continuous norming by the method of moments: The JSKEW program*. [Computer software documentation]. Vancouver, WA: Assessment Research.

Roid, G. H. (1992, April). *Smoothing score distributions using moments: Applications in the norming of tests*. Paper presented at the meetings of the National Council on Measurement in Education, San Francisco.

Roid, G. H. (2003). *Stanford-Binet Intelligence Scales—Fifth Edition—Technical Manual*. Austin, TX: Pro-Ed.

Roid, G. H. (2006). Developing ability tests. In S. Downing & T. Haladyna (Eds.), *Handbook of test development*. Mahwah, NJ: Erlbaum.

Roid, G. H. (2008). Complex information processing in an adolescent with autism spectrum disorder: A single-case study. Unpublished study, School of Education, Southern Methodist University, Dallas, TX.

Roid, G. H., & Barram, R. A. (2004). *Essentials of Stanford-Binet Intelligence Scales*. New York: Wiley.

Roid, G. H., Gorsuch, R. L., Pomplun, M., & Reynolds, C. R. (2003, August). *Twenty years of research on continuous norming*. Symposium presented at the meeting of the American Psychological Association, Chicago.

Roid, G. H., & Ledbetter, M. (2006). *WRAT4 Wide Range Achievement Test—Fourth Edition—Progress Monitoring Version Professional Manual*. Lutz, FL: Psychological Assessment Resources.

Roid, G. H., & Miller, L. J. (1997). *Leiter International Performance Scale—Revised*. Wood Dale, IL: Stoelting.

Saint-Aubin, J., & Klein, R. M. (2008). The influence of reading skills on the missing-letter effect among elementary school students. *Reading Research Quarterly*, *43*, 132–146.

Salvia, J., & Ysseldyke, J. E. (2007). *Assessment in special and inclusive education*. Boston: Houghton-Mifflin.

Sattler, J. M. (2008). *Assessment of children: Cognitive applications* (5th ed.). La Mesa, CA: Author.

Shinn, M. R. (Ed.) (1998). *Advanced applications of curriculum-based measurement*. New York: Guilford.

Stuebing, K. K., Fletcher, J. M., LeDoux, J. M., Lyon, G. R., Shaywitz, S. E., & Shaywitz, B. A. (2002). Validity of IQ-discrepancy classifications of reading disabilities: A meta-analysis. *American Educational Research Journal*, *39*, 469–518.

Taylor, S. E., Frackenpohl, H., White, C. E., Nieroroda, B. W., Browning, C. L., & Birsner, E. P. (1989). *EDL core vocabularies in reading, mathematics, science, and social studies: A revised core vocabulary*. Austin, TX: Steck-Vaughn.

Tellegen, A., & Briggs, P. F. (1967). Old wine in new skins: Grouping Wechsler subtests into new scales. *Journal of Consulting Psychology*, *31*, 499–506.

Tsatsanis, K. D., Dartnall, N., Cicchetti, D., Sparrow, S. S., Klin, A., & Volkmar, F. R. (2003). *Journal of Autism and Developmental Disorders*, *33*(1), 23–30.

U.S. Bureau of the Census. (2001). Current population survey, March 2001. [Data file]. Washington, DC: U.S. Department of Commerce.

U.S. Department of Education. (2004). *Building the legacy, IDEA 2004 website*. Washington, DC: Office of Special Education Programs (OSEP). Available at http://idea.ed.gov.

Vaughn, S., & Fuchs, L. S. (2003). Redefining learning disabilities as inadequate response to instruction:

The promise and potential problems. *Learning Disabilities Research & Practice, 18*, 137–146.

Vaughn, S., Linan-Thompson, S., & Hickman, P. (2003). Response to instruction as a means of identifying students with reading/learning disabilities. *Exceptional Children, 69*(4), 391–409.

Wechsler, D. (1939). *Wechsler-Bellevue Scales*. New York: Psychological Corporation.

Wechsler, D. (1997). *Wechsler Adult Intelligence Scale—Third Edition*. San Antonio, TX: Psychological Corporation.

Wechsler, D. (2003). *Wechsler Intelligence Scale for Children—Fourth Edition*. San Antonio, TX: Psychological Corporation.

Wilkinson, G. S. (1993). *Wide Range Achievement Test—Third Edition*. Lutz, FL: Psychological Assessment Resources.

Wilkinson, G. S., & Robertson, G. J. (2006). *WRAT4 Wide Range Achievement Test professional manual* (4th ed.). Lutz, FL: Psychological Assessment Resources.

Woodcock, R. W. (1999). What can Rasch-based scores convey about a person's test performance? In S. E. Embretson & S. L. Hershberger (Eds.), *The new rules of measurement: What every psychologist and educator should know* (pp. 105–128). Mahwah, NJ: Erlbaum.

Woodcock, R. W., & Dahl, M. N. (1971). *A common scale for the measurement of person ability and test item difficulty*. (AGS Paper No. 10). Circle Pines, MN: American Guidance Service.

Wright, B. D., & Linacre, J. M. (1999). *WINSTEPS: Rasch analysis for all two-facet models*. Chicago: MESA Press.

Wright, B. D., & Stone, M. (1979). *Best test design*. Chicago: MESA Press.

Zachary, R. A., & Gorsuch, R. L. (1985). Continuous norming: Implications for the WAIS-R. *Journal of Clinical Psychology, 41*(1), 86–94.

Author Index

SUBJECT INDEX